MW00826592

MEDICAL LIABILITY AND TREATMENT RELATIONSHIPS

EDITORIAL ADVISORS

Vicki Been
Elihu Root Professor of Law
New York University School of Law

Erwin Chemerinsky
Alston & Bird Professor of Law
Duke University School of Law

Richard A. Epstein
James Parker Hall Distinguished Service Professor of Law
University of Chicago Law School
Peter and Kirsten Bedford Senior Fellow
The Hoover Institution
Stanford University

Ronald J. Gilson
Charles J. Meyers Professor of Law and Business
Stanford University
Marc and Eva Stern Professor of Law and Business
Columbia Law School

James E. Krier
Earl Warren DeLano Professor of Law
The University of Michigan Law School

Richard K. Neumann, Jr.
Professor of Law
Hofstra University School of Law

David Alan Sklansky
Professor of Law
University of California at Berkeley School of Law

Kent D. Syverud
Dean and Ethan A. H. Shepley University Professor
Washington University School of Law

Elizabeth Warren
Leo Gottlieb Professor of Law
Harvard Law School

ASPEN PUBLISHERS

MEDICAL LIABILITY AND TREATMENT RELATIONSHIPS

Second Edition

Mark A. Hall
Fred D. and Elizabeth L. Turnage Professor of Law and Public Health
Wake Forest University

Mary Anne Bobinski
Dean and Professor
University of British Columbia Faculty of Law

David Orentlicher
Samuel R. Rosen Professor of Law
Indiana University School of Law, Indianapolis

™ Wolters Kluwer
Law & Business

AUSTIN   BOSTON   CHICAGO   NEW YORK   THE NETHERLANDS

© 2008 Aspen Publishers. All Rights Reserved.
http://lawschool.aspenpublishers.com

No part of this publication may be reproduced or transmitted in any form or by any means, electronic or mechanical, including photocopy, recording, or any information storage and retrieval system, without permission in writing from the publisher. Requests for permission to make copies of any part of this publication should be mailed to:

Aspen Publishers
Attn: Permissions Department
76 Ninth Avenue, 7th Floor
New York, NY 10011-5201

To contact Customer Care, e-mail customer.care@aspenpublishers.com, call 1-800-234-1660, fax 1-800-901-9075, or mail correspondence to:

Aspen Publishers
Attn: Order Department
PO Box 990
Frederick, MD 21705

Printed in the United States of America.

1 2 3 4 5 6 7 8 9 0

ISBN 978-0-7355-7005-4

Library of Congress Cataloging-in-Publication Data

Hall, Mark A., 1955-
    Medical liability and treatment relationships / Mark A. Hall, Mary Anne Bobinski, David Orentlicher. – 2nd ed.
        p. cm.
    Includes bibliographical references and index.
    ISBN 978-0-7355-7005-4 (alk. paper)
    1. Medical laws and legislation–United States–Cases. 2. Physicians–Malpractice–United States–Cases. 3. Physician and patient–United States–Cases. I. Bobinski, Mary Anne. II. Orentlicher, David, 1955- III. Title.

KF3821.A7H35 2008
344.7304'1–dc22

                                                                    2007049154

About Wolters Kluwer Law & Business

Wolters Kluwer Law & Business is a leading provider of research information and workflow solutions in key specialty areas. The strengths of the individual brands of Aspen Publishers, CCH, Kluwer Law International and Loislaw are aligned within Wolters Kluwer Law & Business to provide comprehensive, in-depth solutions and expert-authored content for the legal, professional, and education markets.

CCH was founded in 1913 and has served more than four generations of business professionals and their clients. The CCH products in the Wolters Kluwer Law & Business group are highly regarded electronic and print resources for legal, securities, antitrust and trade regulation, government contracting, banking, pension, payroll, employment and labor, and healthcare reimbursement, and compliance professionals.

Aspen Publishers is a leading information provider for attorneys, business professionals, and law students. Written by preeminent authorities, Aspen products offer analytical and practical information in a range of specialty practice areas from securities law and intellectual property to mergers and acquisitions and pension/benefits. Aspen's trusted legal education resources provide professors and students with high-quality, up-to-date, and effective resources for successful instruction and study in all areas of the law.

Kluwer Law International supplies the global business community with comprehensive English-language international legal information. Legal practitioners, corporate counsel, and business executives around the world rely on the Kluwer Law International journals, loose-leafs, books, and electronic products for authoritative information in many areas of international legal practice.

Loislaw is a premier provider of digitized legal content to small law firm practitioners of various specializations. Loislaw provides attorneys with the ability to quickly and efficiently find the necessary legal information they need, when and where they need it, by facilitating access to primary law as well as state-specific law, records, forms, and treatises.

Wolters Kluwer Law & Business, a unit of Wolters Kluwer, is headquartered in New York and Riverwoods, Illinois. Wolters Kluwer is a leading multinational publisher and information services company.

To Larry C. Hall, Ph.D., for showing me the joys of an academic life.
—*M.A.H.*

To my partner Holly and our daughter Anna, and to my parents, for their encouragement.
—*M.A.B.*

To the memory of Prof. Herman I. Orentlicher, for his commitment to "neutral skepticism," rigorous standards, and, above all, decency.
—*D.O.*

To Bill Curran, for his guiding light.

Summary of Contents

Contents

2

The Treatment Relationship: Formation, Termination, and Regulation

3

■

The Treatment Relationship: Confidentiality, Consent, and Conflicts of Interest

Preface

The Content and Organization of This Book

This book contains the materials from *Health Care Law and Ethics* (7th ed., 2007) that are focused on medical liability and treatment relationships, with updates through August 2007. As the larger casebook nears its half-century anniversary, we pause to reflect on the remarkable metamorphosis of health care law from a subspecialty of tort law, to a mushrooming academic and practice field whose tentacles reach into myriad scholarly disciplines and areas of substantive law. Each of this book's six prior editions reflects an important stage in this evolutionary growth. Health care law originated as a separate field of professional practice and academic inquiry during the 1960s, when the first edition of the casebook was first published. Under the somewhat grandiose label of "medical jurisprudence," the primary focus at first was on medical proof in all kinds of criminal and civil litigation, on medical malpractice actions against physicians, and on public health regulation. The principal concern was how traditional bodies of legal doctrine and practice — such as criminal, tort, and evidence law — should apply in medical settings.

During the 1970s, bioethics became a major additional area of concern as a consequence of the right to die movement spawned by the *Quinlan* case, and the focus on individual autonomy contained in the informed consent doctrine and the landmark decision on reproductive decision-making in Roe v. Wade. Law courses during this and earlier periods were taught under the heading of "law and medicine."

In the 1980s economic and regulatory topics formed the third component of health care law, as exemplified by the increasing application of antitrust laws to the health care industry, and the growing body of legal disputes under Medicare and Medicaid. This newer dimension accelerated its growth into the 1990s with the spread of HMOs and other managed care organizations, which propelled various corporate and contractual restructurings. These newer topics found their way into courses described as "health law." New developments present continuing challenges to each of these areas of health care law and ethics. In the new millennium, biotechnology, consumer-driven health care, medical confidentiality, and bioterrorism are examples of emerging issues that receive increased attention in this new edition.

This path of development has resulted in an academic discipline defined more by an accretion of topics drawn from historical events than by a systematic conceptual organization of issues. Each of the four major branches — malpractice, bioethics, public health, and financing/regulation — stands apart from the others and is thought to be dominated by a distinct theme. The principal concern of malpractice law is quality of care; bioethics is concerned with individual autonomy; public health poses the rights of patients against the state; and the primary focus of financing and regulatory law is access to care and the cost of care. As a consequence, health care law has yet to become a truly integrated and cohesive discipline.[1] It is too much the creature of history and not of systematic and conceptual organization.

Our major ambition in the casebook is to remedy this state of disarray. This field has reached a stage of maturity that calls for stepping back and rethinking how all of its parts best fit together as a conceptual whole. In our view that conceptual whole is best organized according to the fundamental structural relationships that give rise to health care law. These relationships are:

1. The patient/physician relationship, which encompasses the duty to treat, confidentiality, informed consent, and malpractice
2. State oversight of doctors and patients, which encompasses the right to die, reproductive rights, physician licensure, and public health
3. The institutions that surround the treatment relationship, encompassing public and private insurance, hospitals and HMOs, and more complex transactions and organizational forms

We develop the traditional themes of quality, ethics, access, and cost throughout each of these three divisions. We also address cutting edge and controversial topics such as AIDS, genetics, managed care, and rationing, but not as discrete topics; instead, we integrate these developments within a more permanent, overarching organizational structure, which is capable of absorbing unanticipated new developments as they occur.

In deciding which topics to present in each section and in what depth, our basic guide has been to focus on the essential attributes of the medical enterprise

---

[1] This disarray is reflected by the ongoing confusion over competing names for the field. Although "law and medicine" and "health care law" appear to signify the same topic, the first term is understood to mean older style malpractice subject matter, and the second term is used to refer to newer economic and regulatory issues. Paradoxically, whereas "health care law" and "health law" might be thought to signify somewhat different fields — the latter not restricted to medical treatment and therefore encompassing public health issues — in fact they are taken to mean the same thing.

that make it uniquely important or difficult in the legal domain. Health care law is about the delivery of an extremely important, very expensive, and highly specialized professional service. If it were otherwise, this book would likely not exist. Some lawyers and scholars maintain that there is no unifying concept or set of ideas for health care law; instead, it is merely a disparate collection of legal doctrines and public policy responses, connected only by the happenstance that they involve doctors and hospitals in some way — much as if one had a course on the law of green things or the law of Tuesdays.[2] It would be far more satisfying to find one or more organizing principles that explain not only what makes the disparate parts of health care law cohere, but also why that coherence distinguishes health care law from other bodies of integrated legal thought and professional practice.

We believe those organizing principles can, in part, be found in the phenomenology of what it is to be ill and to be a healer of illness. These two human realities are permanent and essential features that distinguish this field from all other commercial and social arenas. They permeate all parts of health care law, giving it its distinctive quality and altering how generic legal doctrine and conventional theories of government respond to its problems and issues. Health care law might still be worth studying even without these unique attributes of medical encounters, but it is much more engaging and coherent because of them. It is these attributes that give rise to an interrelated set of principles that justify classifying health care law as a coherent and integrated academic and professional discipline. For additional discussion, see The History and Future of Health Care Law: An Essentialist View, 41 Wake Forest L. Rev. 347 (2006).

Accordingly, we stress the essential attributes of medical encounters throughout these materials by incorporating insights from other academic disciplines and theoretical perspectives. Behavioral disciplines such as psychology, sociology, and anthropology help to illuminate the nature of medical knowledge and the lived experience of illness, dependency, and trust as they occur in real-life medical encounters. Findings from health services research published in the health policy literature create a stronger empirical and theoretical base for exploring health care law, one that better exposes its broad social impact. Analytical disciplines, such as economics and moral and political theory, create the foundation for understanding developments in financing, regulation, and bioethics. And, the perspectives of feminist, communitarian, and critical race theory demonstrate the limitations of conventional analytical models and help us understand how health care law must evolve to accommodate viewpoints and concerns that have been excluded in the past.[3]

---

[2] For a similar claim relating to cyberlaw, see Frank H. Easterbrook, Cyberspace and the Law of the Horse, 1996 U. Chi. Legal F. 207, 207–208 (1996).

[3] For additional discussion of the overall content of health care law and approaches to teaching it, see Symposium, Rethinking Health Law, 41 Wake Forest L. Rev. 341 (2006); Symposium, The Field of Health Law: Its Past and Future, 14 Health Matrix 1 (2004); American Society of Law and Medicine Task Force on Health Law Curricula, Health Law and Professional Education, 63 U. Det. L. Rev. 245 (1985); William J. Curran, Titles in the Medicolegal Field: A Proposal for Reform, 1 Am. J.L. & Med. 1 (1975); Symposium, Teaching Health Law, 38 J. Leg. Educ. 485 (1988); Symposium, 6 J. Health Admin. Educ. 221 (1988); Clark Havighurst, American Health Care and the Law: We Need to Talk!, 19(4) Health Aff. 84 (July 2000).

In the first chapter, we have collected background and introductory readings that are relevant in a number of places throughout the book, as well as to several different approaches to teaching the course. These are intended for teachers and students to draw on selectively when and where they see fit.

The death of Bill Curran, the original author of the casebook, left us with a considerable burden to shoulder. Although Prof. Curran was involved in the conceptual reorganization of these materials, he was unable to contribute to their selection and editing. Still, his presence is felt in every part of these materials through the inspiration of his mentoring, his friendship, and his vast body of work.

We intend that this book will continue to serve as more than a teaching tool, and will prove useful as an ongoing resource for conducting research in health care law. To that end we provide substantial bibliographic notes in each section. Also, we have created a dedicated World Wide Web site to serve this book: www. health-law.org. It contains interesting background materials, updates of important events since publication, additional relevant topics that were excluded due to space constraints, and links to other resources on the internet.

The following is a bibliography of resources and readings that relate to research in health care law generally. Additional bibliographic references that relate to particular parts of health care law can be found at pages 28 and 274.

Treatises and Texts: Barry Furrow et al., Health Law (2d ed. 2001); Mark A. Hall, Ira Mark Ellman, and Daniel S. Strouse, Health Care Law and Ethics in a Nutshell (2d ed. 1999); Michael MacDonald et al., Treatise on Health Care Law; John H. Robinson, Roberta M. Berry & Kevin McDonnell, eds., A Health Law Reader: An Interdisciplinary Approach (1999); World Health Organization, International Digest of Health Legislation.

Health Care Law Journals and Recurring Symposia: American Journal of Law and Medicine (Boston Univ.); Annals of Health Law (Loyola-Chicago); DePaul Journal of Health Care Law; Food, Drug and Cosmetic Law Journal; Health Law & Policy Abstracts and Public Health Law Abstracts (SSRN on-line journals); Health Matrix (Case Western Univ.); Houston Journal of Health Law & Policy; Indiana Health Law Review (Indiana Univ.-Indianapolis); Journal of Contemporary Health Law and Policy (Catholic Univ.); Journal of Health & Biomedical Law (Suffolk), Journal of Health and Hospital Law (St. Louis Univ., AHLA); Journal of Health Care Law & Policy (Univ. of Maryland); Journal of Law and Health (Cleveland-Marshall); Journal of Law, Medicine and Ethics (ASLME); Journal of Legal Medicine (So. Illinois Univ.); Medical Trial Technique Quarterly; Journal of Medicine and Law; St. Louis Univ. Law Journal; Seton Hall Law Review; Quinnipiac Health Law Journal; Whittier Law Review; Yale Journal of Health Policy, Law and Ethics.

Leading Medical, Industry, and Health Policy Journals: American Journal of Public Health; American Medical News (AMA); Health Affairs (published by Project Hope); Health Care Financing and Delivery (SSRN on-line journal), Health Care Financing Review (DHHS); Health Economics, Policy and Law (Cambridge Press), Health Services Research; Inquiry (published by Excellus, a Blue Cross plan in Rochester, New York); Hospitals and Health Networks (AHA); Journal of the American Medical Association; Journal of Health Politics,

Policy and Law; Medical Care; Milbank Memorial Fund Quarterly; Modern Healthcare; New England Journal of Medicine.

Health Law Societies, Digests, and Newsletters: ABA Forum on Health Law (newsletter); American College of Legal Medicine (Milwaukee; journal); American Society of Law, Medicine, and Ethics (Boston; two journals); BNA Health Law Reporter (Washingon, D.C.; weekly); American Health Lawyers Association (Washington, D.C.; monthly digest and newsletter, bimonthly journal); Specialty Law Digest: Health Care Law (monthly).

Acknowledgments

This manuscript could not have been prepared without the thoughtful advice of our colleagues who commented on drafts and gave us suggestions for revision (especially Bill Brewbaker, Seth Chandler, Judy Failer, Hank Greely, David Hyman, Eleanor Kinney, Jack Nelson, Mark Pescovitz, Phil Peters, and Dan Strouse), without the diligent help of those students and staff who assisted us over the past few years (Sarah Batut, Chet Chea, Nathan Childs, Tyler Hall, Sarah Harbottle, Laura Hermer, David Higgins, Faith Long Knotts, James Martin, Michael Schrader, and Betsy Segal), and without the superhuman patience of our families (who, curiously, wish to remain anonymous). Finally, we thank the authors and publishers who granted permission to use each of the excerpts of copyrighted material in these readings.

Mark A. Hall
Mary Anne Bobinski
David Orentlicher

December 2007

1

Introduction

The following two overview cases and the accompanying notes are intended to introduce issues and themes that are pursued in different parts of this book. You are not expected to retain their analyses and holdings at this point; you only need to get a sense of the range of topics that are covered in different courses that might be taught from this book.

The readings that follow these cases introduce background information and overarching perspectives that are important for understanding the legal issues developed throughout this book. Although lifted out of their respective contexts, we present them at the outset because they raise cross-cutting themes that cannot be cabined within a single chapter. Therefore, it will be necessary to revisit these readings from time to time throughout the course.

A. OVERVIEW CASES

■ In re Baby K
16 F.3d 590 (4th Cir. 1994)

Wilkins, Circuit Judge.

The Hospital instituted this action against Ms. H, Mr. K, and Baby K, seeking a declaratory judgment that it is not required under the Emergency Medical Treatment and Active Labor Act (EMTALA), 42 U.S.C.A. §1395dd (West

1992),[2] to provide treatment other than warmth, nutrition, and hydration to Baby K, an anencephalic infant. Because we agree with the district court that EMTALA gives rise to a duty on the part of the Hospital to provide respiratory support to Baby K when she is presented at the Hospital in respiratory distress and treatment is requested for her, we affirm.

I

Baby K was born at the Hospital in October of 1992 with anencephaly, a congenital malformation in which a major portion of the brain, skull, and scalp are missing. While the presence of a brain stem does support her autonomic functions and reflex actions, because Baby K lacks a cerebrum, she is permanently unconscious. Thus, she has no cognitive abilities or awareness. She cannot see, hear, or otherwise interact with her environment.

When Baby K had difficulty breathing on her own at birth, Hospital physicians placed her on a mechanical ventilator. This respiratory support allowed the doctors to confirm the diagnosis and gave Ms. H, the mother, an opportunity to fully understand the diagnosis and prognosis of Baby K's condition. The physicians explained to Ms. H that most anencephalic infants die within a few days of birth due to breathing difficulties and other complications. Because aggressive treatment would serve no therapeutic or palliative purpose, they recommended that Baby K only be provided with supportive care in the form of nutrition, hydration, and warmth. Physicians at the Hospital also discussed with Ms. H the possibility of a "Do Not Resuscitate Order" that would provide for the withholding of lifesaving measures in the future.

The treating physicians and Ms. H failed to reach an agreement as to the appropriate care. Ms. H insisted that Baby K be provided with mechanical breathing assistance whenever the infant developed difficulty breathing on her own, while the physicians maintained that such care was inappropriate. As a result of this impasse, the Hospital sought to transfer Baby K to another hospital. This attempt failed when all of the hospitals in the area with pediatric intensive care units declined to accept the infant. In November of 1992, when Baby K no longer needed the services of an acute-care hospital, she was transferred to a nearby nursing home.

Since being transferred to the nursing home, Baby K has been readmitted to the Hospital three times due to breathing difficulties. Each time she has been provided with breathing assistance and, after stabilization, has been discharged to the nursing home. Following Baby K's second admission, the Hospital filed this action to resolve the issue of whether it is obligated to provide emergency medical treatment to Baby K that it deems medically and ethically inappropriate. Baby K's

---

[2] The Hospital also sought declaratory relief under §504 of the Rehabilitation Act of 1973 (Rehabilitation Act), 29 U.S.C.A. §794 (West Supp. 1993); the Americans with Disabilities Act of 1990 (ADA), 42 U.S.C.A. §§12101 et seq. (West 1993); the Child Abuse Prevention and Treatment Act (Child Abuse Act), 42 U.S.C.A. §§5101-5106h (West Supp. 1993); and the statutes and common law of Virginia. In addressing these provisions, the district court concluded that a failure to provide respiratory support to Baby K because of her condition of anencephaly would constitute discrimination in violation of the ADA and the Rehabilitation Act but declined to rule on the application of the Child Abuse Act or Virginia law. Because we conclude that the Hospital has a duty to render stabilizing treatment under EMTALA, we need not address its obligations under the remaining federal statutes or the laws of Virginia.

guardian ad litem and her father, Mr. K, joined in the Hospital's request for a declaration that the Hospital is not required to provide respiratory support or other aggressive treatments. . . .

II

Congress enacted EMTALA in response to its "concern that hospitals were 'dumping' patients [who were] unable to pay, by either refusing to provide emergency medical treatment or transferring patients before their emergency conditions were stabilized." Brooks v. Maryland General Hospital Inc., 996 F.2d 708, 710 (4th Cir. 1993). Through EMTALA, Congress sought "to provide an 'adequate first response to a medical crisis' for all patients," Baber v. Hospital Corp. of America, 977 F.2d 872, 880 (4th Cir. 1992), by imposing two duties on hospitals that have entered into Medicare provider agreements.

First, those hospitals with an emergency medical department must provide an appropriate medical screening to determine whether an emergency medical condition exists for any individual who comes to the emergency medical department requesting treatment. A hospital fulfills this duty if it utilizes identical screening procedures for all patients complaining of the same condition or exhibiting the same symptoms.

An additional duty arises if an emergency medical condition is discovered during the screening process. EMTALA defines an "emergency medical condition" as including:

> a medical condition manifesting itself by acute symptoms of sufficient severity (including severe pain) such that the absence of immediate medical attention could reasonably be expected to result in—
> (i) placing the health of the individual . . . in serious jeopardy,
> (ii) serious impairment to bodily functions, or
> (iii) serious dysfunction of any bodily organ or part. [42 U.S.C.A. §1395dd(e) (1)(A).]

When an individual is diagnosed as presenting an emergency medical condition:

> the hospital must provide either—
> (A) within the staff and facilities available at the hospital, for such further medical examination and such treatment as may be required to stabilize the medical condition, or
> (B) for the transfer of the individual to another medical facility in accordance with subsection (c) of this section. [42 U.S.C.A. §1395dd(b)(1).]

The treatment required "to stabilize" an individual is that treatment "necessary to assure, within reasonable medical probability, that no material deterioration of the condition is likely to result from or occur during the transfer of the individual from a facility." 42 U.S.C.A. §1395dd(e)(3)(A). Therefore, once an individual has been diagnosed as presenting an emergency medical condition, the hospital must provide that treatment necessary to prevent the material deterioration of the individual's condition or provide for an appropriate transfer to another facility.

In the application of these provisions to Baby K, the Hospital concedes that when Baby K is presented in respiratory distress a failure to provide "immediate medical attention" would reasonably be expected to cause serious impairment of her bodily functions. Thus, her breathing difficulty qualifies as an emergency medical condition, and the diagnosis of this emergency medical condition triggers the duty of the hospital to provide Baby K with stabilizing treatment or to transfer her in accordance with the provisions of EMTALA. Since transfer is not an option available to the Hospital at this juncture,[5] the Hospital must stabilize Baby K's condition. . . .

III

. . . As the Hospital acknowledged during oral argument, Baby K resides at the nursing home for months at a time without requiring emergency medical attention. Only when she has experienced episodes of bradypnea or apnea[9] has Baby K required respiratory support to prevent serious impairment of her bodily functions. It is bradypnea or apnea, not anencephaly, that is the emergency medical condition that brings Baby K to the Hospital for treatment. . . . The Hospital does not allege that it would refuse to provide respiratory support to infants experiencing bradypnea or apnea who do not have anencephaly. Indeed, a refusal to provide such treatment would likely be considered as providing no emergency medical treatment. . . .

[The Hospital argues] that, in redressing the problem of disparate emergency medical treatment, Congress did not intend to require physicians to provide medical treatment outside the prevailing standard of medical care. The Hospital asserts that, because of their extremely limited life expectancy and because any treatment of their condition is futile, the prevailing standard of medical care for infants with anencephaly is to provide only warmth, nutrition, and hydration. Thus, it maintains that a requirement to provide respiratory assistance would exceed the prevailing standard of medical care. However, the plain language of EMTALA requires stabilizing treatment for any individual who comes to a participating hospital, is diagnosed as having an emergency medical condition, and cannot be transferred. . . . The Hospital has been unable to identify, nor has our research revealed, any statutory language or legislative

---

[5] In order for a hospital to transfer a patient prior to stabilization, EMTALA requires: (1) the patient or a person acting on the patient's behalf to request a transfer in writing after being informed of the risks involved and the obligations of the hospital under EMTALA; or (2) a proper certification that the medical benefits expected from the transfer outweigh the risks involved. 42 U.S.C.A. §1395dd(c)(1). In addition, the transfer must meet the criteria for an appropriate transfer which include the requirement that a qualified receiving facility agree to accept that the patient and to provide appropriate medical treatment. 42 U.S.C.A. §1395dd(c)(1)(B), (c)(2). Since Ms. H objects to the transfer of Baby K, since the Hospital has not obtained a certificate that the benefits of a transfer would outweigh the medical risks involved, and since no qualified medical facility has agreed to accept Baby K, the requirements for transfer prior to stabilization have not been met. If Ms. H requests a transfer or the Hospital obtains a certification that the benefits of a transfer would outweigh the risks involved, and all of the requirements for an appropriate transfer are met, then the Hospital could, of course, transfer Baby K to another qualified medical facility prior to stabilization.

[9] Bradypnea is an "abnormal slowness of breathing." Dorland's Illustrated Medical Dictionary 230 (27th ed. 1988). In an infant who has established and sustained spontaneous breathing, apnea describes the cessation of respiration for more than sixty seconds. Id. at 112.

history evincing a congressional intent to create an exception to the duty to provide stabilizing treatment when the required treatment would exceed the prevailing standard of medical care. We recognize the dilemma facing physicians who are requested to provide treatment they consider morally and ethically inappropriate, but we cannot ignore the plain language of the statute because "to do so would 'transcend our judicial function.'" *Baber*, 977 F.2d at 884. The appropriate branch to redress the policy concerns of the Hospital is Congress. . . .

IV

It is beyond the limits of our judicial function to address the moral or ethical propriety of providing emergency stabilizing medical treatment to anencephalic infants. We are bound to interpret federal statutes in accordance with their plain language and any expressed congressional intent. Congress rejected a case-by-case approach to determining what emergency medical treatment hospitals and physicians must provide and to whom they must provide it; instead, it required hospitals and physicians to provide stabilizing care to any individual presenting an emergency medical condition. EMTALA does not carve out an exception for anencephalic infants in respiratory distress any more than it carves out an exception for comatose patients, those with lung cancer, or those with muscular dystrophy—all of whom may repeatedly seek emergency stabilizing treatment for respiratory distress and also possess an underlying medical condition that severely affects their quality of life and ultimately may result in their death. Because EMTALA does not provide for such an exception, the judgment of the district court is affirmed.

Notes: Rationing, Justice, and the Doctor-Patient Relationship

1. *Introduction to Complexity.* How many different issues can you identify in the *Baby K* case? There are many problems raised by the case, most of which are not overtly addressed in the opinion. The complexity of health care issues is one of the major themes of this book. A wide range of philosophical debates and legal rules can be implicated by the facts (and frailties) of human biology. This creates a variety of lenses through which to view any case.

One method of studying the health care system is purely *descriptive*, looking at how health care providers and patients *actually* interact. How does the legal system respond to the problems created by biological frailty and the development of medical knowledge? Another focus is normative: How *should* providers and patients interact, and how *should* the legal system regulate health care relationships?

Under either the descriptive or the normative approach, health care interactions implicate one or more of four different sets of legal or ethical analysis. (1) We can look at the doctor-patient relationship in terms of legal duties and liabilities, focusing on whether the health care provider met her professional obligations to her patient under malpractice or fiduciary law. (2) We can also consider broader philosophical issues such as what is the proper realm of patient autonomy, and what is a provider's *moral* duty to act for the benefit of the patient ("beneficence"). (3) A medical case can also implicate broader societal issues, such as whether third-parties or the state in general has a stake in the treatment decision. This focus falls in the realm known as public health law, and implicates constitutional issues. (4) Finally, the medical encounter can be viewed through an organizational or economic lens, which focuses on who pays for the treatment and what institutional constraints are created by the setting in which treatment is provided. Can you identify how each of these four perspectives might be pertinent to *Baby K*?

Despite the variety of issues encountered in this book and the diversity of perspectives, there is a fundamental coherence to health care law. It lies in the fundamental nature of illness and the healing encounter. To use a common metaphor, imagine we are in a dark room with a mysterious object. We can use all of our other senses to determine the nature of the object: smell, taste, touch, etc. Although each person's sensory experiences might be very different, the fundamental nature of the object remains the same.

2. *What Really Happened in* Baby K? Baby K, whose name was Stephanie Keene, ultimately lived for two and a half years in a pediatric nursing facility. She died in the emergency room of Fairfax Hospital in Fairfax, Virginia — the same hospital in the *Baby K* case — after being taken there by ambulance for the sixth time. Her anencephaly had been diagnosed by ultrasound during the sixteenth week of her gestation, and her mother, Contrenia Harrell, decided to carry her to term, believing (according to press accounts) that "'all life is precious'" and that God would guide Stephanie's life. Other local hospitals reportedly refused to accept a transfer of Baby K shortly after her birth.

Baby K's medical bills ultimately reached almost $1 million. They were covered in part by her mother's insurance with an HMO and in part by Medicaid. These financing systems are described in sections C.1 and C.3. They often do not pay the full costs of treatment. Nevertheless, hospital officials stated that the costs of Baby K's care were not a factor in the hospital's lawsuit. Even so, the hospital may have been thinking about the implications of the case for future patients, and the cost of caring for patients like Baby K are likely to be an issue for other hospitals as health insurers increasingly employ capitation rates for reimbursement, and as Medicare and Medicaid continue to limit their reimbursement rates.

The readings in section C.2 discuss the growing crisis over health care spending, and section D.2 discusses the importance of having an accurate understanding of how these cases arise in the real world. Do any of these additional facts and speculations alter your instincts about who should make the treatment decision for a patient like Baby K? Do you think the insurers should have a stake in the decision? Would it be reasonable to tell Baby K's mother she can insist on treatment but not on payment, thereby remaining liable for the bills? If she still insisted on treatment, but the hospital knew she could never pay, should it still have to treat?

3. *A Medical Miracle?* Some might scoff at Ms. Harrell's reported belief in a medical miracle, but one may in fact have occurred here. As the court noted, anencephalic children generally do not live very long; fewer than 10 percent of such children survive more than a week. Baby K may be the longest lived child with anencephaly. Rather than a miracle, however, her length of life may indicate

that the general lack of aggressive treatment for anencephalic children results in their actual lifespans being considerably shorter than their potential lifespans. The readings in section B.3 give more insight into why patients look to physicians for miracles, and how doctors decide what care is most beneficial.

4. *Unusual or Typical?* The *Baby K* case involves a fact situation that is the converse of the typical court case involving life-sustaining treatment. Such cases usually involve physicians who insist on treatment over the objections of the patient or the patient's family. Yet, the *Baby K* situation may become more typical as the result of greater pressures on physicians to limit medical costs. The care of dying patients is an obvious place to look for cost savings. Does this suggestion contravene our deeply-treasured value of individual autonomy? Does this value hold the same force when society's resources are at stake? If care were terminated for Baby K, would the result be to force sacrifices by society's most vulnerable to benefit the comfortable or well-to-do? These perspectives are developed further in section D.3.

5. *The Court's Decision.* Do you agree with the majority's or the dissent's analysis of EMTALA? Note that, as the majority opinion indicates, EMTALA was passed in response to hospitals' refusing to provide care to patients who had neither insurance nor personal resources with which to pay for emergency care. Despite this legislative history, EMTALA has been interpreted to preclude refusals of emergency care on grounds other than the patient's inability to pay. Do you think Congress intended for EMTALA to require treatment of anencephalic children with ventilators? If Ms. Keene also had a cardiac defect that required open heart surgery to repair, and she were brought to the emergency room because of distress related to the heart condition, do you think the court would have required the hospital to perform the surgery? If not, then how can the court require the hospital to provide a ventilator for anencephalic children? Compare Bryan v. Rectors and Visitors of the University of Virginia, 95 F.3d 349 (4th Cir. 1996) (rejecting an EMTALA claim against hospital after physicians withheld resuscitative treatment from a hopelessly ill patient who suffered a heart attack and died).

Concerns about principle go both ways in this case. It is accepted practice to give anencephalic infants artificial nutrition and hydration through feeding tubes, as was done for Baby K. Is there any principled or practical distinction that justifies giving artificial feeding but refusing artificial breathing? If you can see such a distinction, should it be the sole province of physicians to apply, or is it a distinction that only patients and family can draw? See Chapter 2 for further discussion of this and other aspects of EMTALA and of patients' rights to decide.

As n.2 of the *Baby K* opinion indicates, the lower court found that withholding a ventilator would also violate the Rehabilitation Act of 1973 and the Americans with Disabilities Act of 1990. Both of these Acts prohibit discrimination against persons on account of their disabilities. As the court suggested, one could argue that Baby K was being denied treatment of her respiratory problems on account of her having the disability of anencephaly. Is this an appropriate way to characterize what was going on in the *Baby K* case? Why do you think the appellate court preferred to decide this case on the basis of an unlawful denial of emergency care rather than on the basis of unlawful disability discrimination?

6. *The Hospital's and the Physicians' Decision.* Inasmuch as the costs of Ms. Keene's care were fully reimbursed by the insurers, why do you suppose the hospital and the physicians were unwilling to provide emergency ventilatory treatment to Ms. Keene? After all, the treatment was life-sustaining, and it was clearly desired by Ms. Keene's mother. Do you think it was appropriate for the physicians to try to override the wishes of Ms. Keene's mother?

■ WICKLINE v. STATE
239 Cal. Rptr. 810 (Cal. Ct. App. 1986)

[Read the excerpt at page 483.]

Notes: Liability and Managed Care

1. *Holding Doctors Responsible for Their Mistakes.* Why do you suppose Mrs. Wickline chose not to sue her doctors? Did they deserve to be sued, in your opinion? If they had been, would they have been found liable? What standard of care did the court use to determine liability? What source of evidence was used to establish this standard and whether it was breached?

In addition to being sued in tort, several other legal and social mechanisms punish those who make medical mistakes or encourage them to do better. Consider briefly the structural differences among: licensing regulations, ethical sanctions, and market forces.

2. *Managed Care.* The process of utilization review used by Medi-Cal is widespread, both in government programs and under conventional private insurance. As described in section C.3, this is one of several techniques for saving money that are known more generally as "managed care." Other managed care techniques include restricting a patient's choice of physician and paying physicians in a manner that rewards them for economizing. Presently over half of privately insured people in the United States are covered under "alternative delivery systems" such as HMOs that employ some or all of these techniques.

3. *Medical Judgment.* Why did opinions vary so widely on the proper treatment of Mrs. Wickline (four vs. eight days postsurgery)? Is there supposed to be general agreement about medical questions of this nature? What nonmedical factors (other than money) might influence the decision when to send Mrs. Wickline home? Section B.4 offers additional explanation and discussion of medical decisionmaking.

4. *Medical Mistakes.* Why did things go so wrong, even prior to Mrs. Wickline's discharge from the hospital? Could anything have been done to avoid the bad course of events in the hospital? What systems should be in place to encourage doctors to do their best, and how much professional (not necessarily legal) accountability should there be when they fail to live up to perfection? Section B.5 explains that physicians are subjected to much greater monitoring of the outcomes of their treatment than ever before.

5. *The Duty to Treat.* Is it realistic for the court to tell Mrs. Wickline's physicians that they have to continue treating her even if Medicaid reimbursement runs out? If she had no insurance to begin with, would they be required to accept her initially? If they are free to turn her away, would they be deterred from accepting her, knowing her insurance might not cover all the care that tort law might require? Should tort law demand less of doctors who treat patients with insufficient or no insurance?

B. THE NATURE OF MEDICAL PRACTICE

The remainder of this chapter contains introductory and background materials that relate broadly to several or all portions of the book. The readings are diverse and introduce a wide range of challenging ideas and important information. You should read through the assigned parts at the outset, and then come back to individual excerpts as they become relevant to the discussion of particular legal topics in your course.

We begin with a description of the human condition of illness and the professional practice of medicine, since these are what distinguish health care law from other fields of legal study. It is essential throughout this book to have some appreciation of the impact that illness has on how people function, the intricacies of medical decisionmaking, and how doctors and patients interact. To focus your thoughts on these issues, reflect on your own experiences with medical care, and consider the following list of popular "misconceptions" (developed by Alain Enthoven). What observations and evidence emerge from these readings to rebut or qualify each of these commonly held notions?

1. The doctor should be able to know what conditions the patient has, to answer the patient's questions precisely, and to prescribe the right treatment. If the doctor isn't, that is incompetence or even malpractice.
2. For each medical condition, there is a "best" treatment. It is up to the doctor to know about that treatment and to use it. Anything else is unnecessary surgery, waste, fraud, or underservice.
3. Medicine is an exact science. Unlike 50 or 100 years ago, there is now a firm scientific base for what the doctor does. Standard treatments are supported by scientific proof of efficiency.
4. Medical care consists of standard products that can be described precisely and measured meaningfully in standard units such as "inpatient days," "outpatient visits," or "doctor office visits."
5. Much of medical care is a matter of life and death or serious pain or disability.
6. More medical care is better than less care.
7. People have no control over the timing of their need for medical care. Whatever care is needed is needed right away.

1. Doctors and Hospitals

∎ HEALTH CARE PAST AND PRESENT
Robert Rhodes
Health Care Politics, Policy, and Distributive Justice:
The Ironic Triumph (1992)*

Death before the nineteenth century was an ever-looming presence in our ancestors' thoughts and a frequent visitor to their families. They feared it and had little control over it. Sudden death was as central to attitudes prior to the twentieth century as the cemetery was to every village and town. . . .

Resignation and fatalism toward natural occurrences characterize preindustrial societies, just as a sense of self-direction and control characterize modern society. . . . Modern societies have faith that they can control the future. A futurist orientation allows for savings, capital formation, long periods of education, and lifestyles that deny instant gratification for future health. Preindustrial conditions do not reward such faith. . . . Uncontrollable natural or supernatural forces took away life, and one needed to reconcile one's fate to the four horsemen of the apocalypse: disease, famine, pestilence, and drought.

The twentieth century represents perhaps the clearest triumph of science over fatalism. . . . The modern hospital, the professionalism of physicians and nurses, and effective pharmaceuticals, have dramatically altered mortality rates and improved the quality of life in postindustrial states.

For those entering a hospital prior to 1900, the probability of treatment helping, rather than harming, would be less than fifty-fifty, and the odds would be considerably poorer prior to 1870. Today, we identify hospitals as technologic citadels of sophisticated medical practice. But their preindustrial origins were as religious and charitable institutions for the hopelessly sick and poor. They were places to comfort the indigent dying.

For the first three quarters of the nineteenth century, medical personnel were not in charge of hospitals. . . . In the main, hospitals at that time were places for the homeless poor and insane to die. The affluent classes were treated at home. For a variety of reasons, however, hospitals became central to medical practice and education between 1870 and 1910.[6] . . .

[T]he development of the medical profession parallels particular developments of the hospital. This is especially true of surgery, which enjoyed a dramatic increase of prestige and precision during this time. Technological advances played a major role in changing surgery. Before painkilling drugs, surgical methods in the first half of the nineteenth century depended upon powerful and swift physicians whose craft and tools were closer to the corner butcher. Mortality rates of about 40 percent followed amputation.

Three developments altered the brutality and mortality rates and allowed abdominal surgery, which was rarely performed prior to 1890. Dentist William Morton's demonstration of ether at Massachusetts General Hospital in 1846 ushered in a means of eliminating pain and allowed more careful and delicate

---

* Copyright © 1992, State University of New York Press. Reprinted by permission.
[6] Paul Starr, The Social Transformation of American Medicine 151 (1982).

surgery. Joseph Lister's discovery of antisepsis in 1867 gradually led to new procedures during surgery to prevent infection. However, antisepsis was poorly understood. Lister's technique was based on the use of carbolic acid spray, but his methods were adopted only over a long period of time. Fatal infections continued even after using the spray because antiseptic procedures were not followed carefully until after 1880. Soon, sterile procedures were properly followed and surgery rapidly expanded. Finally, the development of the X-ray in 1895, along with other diagnostic tools, opened the way for abdominal surgery for appendicitis, gallbladder, and stomach ulcers. Thoracic surgery and surgery of the nervous and cardiovascular systems developed in the early 1900s.

TRIUMPH AND TRAGEDY

By 1950, the cliché a "medical miracle" had rich meaning. Infant mortality rates in the United States were fewer than 15 per 100,000 births, down from 300 or so per 100,000 at the turn of the century. Pneumonia, once whispered by medical staff who witnessed the suffering of the dying to be the "old man's relief," now was easily controlled with penicillin. Infectious diseases in particular dramatically declined in the first half of the twentieth century. Improvement in health was a triumph of modernity, and part of that triumph was a consequence of modern medicine. There is, however, much debate about the weight of medicine's contribution, compared to other modern factors. . . .

Our dramatic advances in health are also related to improved nutrition, lifestyle, and education, as well as to medical advancements. The literature of health care points, in particular, to . . . proper diet, minimal tension, absence of smoking or heavy drinking, daily exercise, and a lifestyle that provides low-risk factors for accidents. Advances in health and longevity are more closely tied to higher income, better diets, and especially greater education than to advances in medicine. . . .

Yet, American perception of well-being is closely identified with medicine. Paradoxically, much of the public's present disenchantment with medicine is the consequence of this identification. Modern medicine has advanced to the frontiers of preserving life, but only by increasingly more expensive therapies and diagnoses to preserve life "on its margins." That is, additional expenditures and efforts to treat disease produce diminishing results in proportion to the effort. We are just beginning to learn that our scientific capacity to triumph over illness, physical anomalies, and death, on many occasions with medical miracles, brings with it a special brand of tragedy.

We have become totally modern. No more can we explain death and suffering as a consequence of fate. It is our medicine, or lack of it, that denies death and suffering. We know we must choose who receives scarce resources and who does not. No longer can we attribute to fate or to God the responsibility for making life-and-death decisions. Yet, these life-and-death decisions involve very expensive procedures and technologies and often contribute only marginally to extending life. Examples are well known and regularly make front-page newspaper drama: organ transplants, aggressive treatment of terminal patients, neonates under 750 grams, or long-term comatose patients.

These new choices challenge our basic values and frequently produce conflict. . . . Conflict is father to politics and law, and politics determines who gets what, when, and how. Conflict also forces moral reassessment of traditional attitudes and postures, including the justice question: "Who *should* get what, when and how."

How do we distribute health care? How should we? How does political power within the present economic system determine the distribution of health care? These questions obviously spill over the boundaries of economics, politics, sociology, law, medicine, history, and philosophy. In particular, looming over the politics of health care is a sense of the tragic, as well as the majestic. Tragedy points to human endeavors that are virtuous and honorable, yet carry the seeds of their own downfall. Our efforts to lessen the suffering and lengthen the lives of Americans through accessible, affordable, quality health care represent the best of our traditions and have been, on balance, an American success story. Sometimes we fall short in that effort because some group is unreasonably left behind in the political shuffle. The [45] million Americans who [have] no health coverage represent[] such a group. At other times, our very success leads to exasperating dilemmas of bioethics and distributive justice that would cross the eyes of a Solomon. Our dilemma over public financing for costly organ transplants at the expense of other badly needed programs or continued aggressive treatment of comatose or terminally ill loved ones are poignant, modern examples. It is here where triumph merges with tragedy.

■ DOCTORS, PATIENTS, AND HEALTH INSURANCE: THE ORGANIZATION AND FINANCING OF MEDICAL CARE
Herman Miles Somers & Anne Ramsay Somers
1961

. . . The popular conception of the doctor-patient relationship is a mixture of fact and fancy. Until World War II the general practitioner family doctor was still in the majority. The one-to-one relationship of a personally chosen physician—where economic and other factors permitted any choice—with his patient was the most common form of medical practice. In big cities the doctor had an office, usually mahogany and leather, sparsely equipped with simple diagnostic aids, a few surgical tools, and some antiseptic drugs. But, especially in rural areas and suburbs, he was more often found in the homes of his patients doing his rounds, working at the bedside of the sick and injured. His black bag held almost all his equipment. His records were kept partly in a small notebook, mostly in his mind and heart. He appeared indefatigable, compassionate, and available wherever and whenever needed. . . .

This doctor of the past has been idealized in story, picture, and legend. . . . Despite its apparent anachronisms, the picture still appeals to people's sentiments—even to those fully aware of its use as a public relations device. It has the warmth and intimate concern that no hypodermic needle—no complex of steel and tubing—can replace, however effective they may be. Although medical miracles are now performed successfully between strangers, doctors and patients both believe that the absence of continuity, personal concern, and individual attention are detrimental to the best medical care. This is not without foundation.

The origin of the "traditional" doctor-patient relationship reaches deep into the past. From the beginning of medical history, the practicing physician has been part priest, part technician, part personal or family counselor. In early days, when medicine had very little in the way of scientific knowledge to rely on, it was inevitable that the subjective priestly element should be dominant. . . .

In modern times medicine has become more scientific. But the traditional reliance on mystical forces and a highly authoritarian doctor-patient relationship persists to a degree unknown in other contemporary human relations. . . . The relationship of citizen and state, of employer and employee, of teacher and pupil, parent and child, even of husband and wife, have undergone profound and acknowledged changes as a result of the technological and socio-economic trends of the past few centuries. But there is no general acknowledgment or acceptance of the significant change that has, in fact, been taking place in the doctor-patient relationship. Of the manifold and complex reasons, only a few of the more important can be noted here.

First and basic is the persistence — in spite of scientific progress — of large elements of uncertainty and fear regarding illness and medical care which are conducive to continued reliance on hope, faith, confidence and other subjective factors on the part of both doctor and patient. "Honor thy physician because of the need thou hast of him." So said apocryphal Ecclesiastes to the Hebrews thousands of years ago. And still, today, patients yearn to have confidence in their doctors, to idealize them, to endow them with superhuman powers. Talcott Parsons, the Harvard sociologist, reconciles the use of such subjective factors — the use of "modern magic" — with the scientific basis of modern medicine by calling it a "functional bias."

> The basic function of magic is to bolster the self-confidence of actors in situations where energy and skill *do* make a difference but where, because of uncertainty factors, outcomes cannot be guaranteed. This fits the situation of the doctor, but in addition on the side of the patient it may be argued the *belief* in the possibility of recovery is an important factor in it. If from purely a technical point of view both the individual doctor and the general tradition are optimistically biased it ought to help. . . . Of course this argument must not be pressed too far.

As the boundaries of medical ignorance and uncertainty are pushed back, one would expect this resort to supra-scientific factors to decline, and, indeed, it has in the case of bacterial and other diseases where the cause and cure are clearly established. But the reduced role of subjective factors in the treatment of specific cases has been more than offset by an increasing interest in the role of the emotions in illness. A widespread increase in psychotherapy and psychosomatic medicine has renewed the emphasis on a personal doctor and a personal doctor-patient relationship of a type that permits knowledge of the "whole [person]." . . .

Moreover it is now widely believed that illness, *per se*, tends to create — even in the most intellectual of patients — an attitude of dependence, of "regression" to helplessness, and perhaps to childlike behavior. . . . In this state, confidence in the authority and benevolence of the doctor, as well as in his scientific knowledge and technical skill — the now-familiar "father-image" — is generally desired and often desirable.

Finally, there is the impenetrable mystery of death. The physician's relation to this event — however helpless he in fact may be — has endowed him, in the eyes of centuries of patients, with an aura of the mystery. To the extent that the physician identifies himself with this priestly role and takes on himself the burden associated therewith, or at least appears to do so through the gravity of his personal demeanor and behavior, his supra-scientific role continues to be respected and perpetuated, reinforcing in the eyes of individual patients and society at large his status as a dispenser of increasingly scientific medicine.

■ COMPETING SOLUTIONS: AMERICAN HEALTH CARE PROPOSALS AND INTERNATIONAL EXPERIENCE
Joseph White
1995

America's systems for delivering and paying for medical care are notably more complex than those of most other countries. Many doctors work in more than one hospital, making governance of medical staffs difficult; specialists are harder to coordinate because there are more of them; and the proliferation of forms of managed care means rapid change in patterns of gatekeeping and referral.

PHYSICIANS

American doctors go through extensive training to work long hours for high pay. The typical medical school program requires, after four years of college, four more years of "undergraduate" medical education. During the final two years, students receive some clinical training. Virtually all graduates then must complete some graduate medical education in order to be licensed to practice medicine. This education is obtained in residency programs, mainly in hospitals affiliated with medical schools. Normally only one year of residency (as an intern) is needed for licensure, but up to eight years (for neurosurgeons) may be required for certification as a specialist.

    ... Given the length of their training and the size of their debts, it is understandable that most physicians feel entitled to incomes that are much higher than those of most other Americans. ... [The median physician salary is about $200,000, roughly five times that of the average American worker. The range across specialties is broad. Pediatricians and general practitioners typically earn around $150,000, common medical specialists (cardiology, dermatology, anes-thesiology) are in the $225,000-$300,000 range, while heart surgeons and brain surgeons can earn well over $500,000. Some doctors earn substantially more from entrepreneurial activities such as medical patents and investments in various health care organizations.]

An unusually high proportion of American doctors are trained to specialize. Fewer than 10 percent of American doctors [call] themselves general practitioners (GPs), the standard term for primary care physicians. But because a specialist such as a family practitioner, internist, pediatrician, or obstetrician-gynecologist may be a person's regular physician, between 33 and 40 percent of physicians (depending on who is counting) are mainly primary care providers. [Specialists who receive several years of extra training and pass additional exams are designated as "Board Certified," meaning that they comply with voluntary, private standards set by the American Specialty Boards, which operate under the auspices of the AMA. At one time, board certification was relatively rare, but now the vast majority of new doctors obtain certification. About two dozen boards now exist, covering not only standard specialties but also areas of general practice such as family medicine and internal medicine.] . . .

Two-thirds of physicians practice in offices, the vast majority with admitting privileges to a hospital. Many practice in more [than one hospital] (for example, a nice suburban hospital for simple cases, and a high-tech academic medical center for difficult ones). Hospitals therefore must compete for admissions by making those physicians happy, such as by having the fanciest equipment. . . .

INSTITUTIONAL CARE

Long-term or chronic care, especially for the aged, is a complicated system on its own, and the potential expenses of long-term care are so great that it is highly unlikely that any reform will do much about it. [Therefore, the focus here is] on the costs of the current American health care system, of which one major component is hospital services for acute care.

The American supply of hospitals is dominated by private nonprofit hospitals — many owned by religious organizations. [About two-thirds] of hospital beds [are] provided by the nonprofits, 10 percent by the for-profit sector. The rest, just over a quarter of the beds, [are] in federal, state, or local facilities. It is hard to identify much difference between the behavior and efficiency of the for-profit and private nonprofits. If private institutions are more efficient, the savings go largely or entirely to investors.

Americans spend a great deal of money on hospitals: [about 40 percent] of all spending on patient care. But . . . the hospital is not as dominant a provider as it once was or still is in other countries. Hospitals and doctors tried to avoid regulation by moving care to ostensibly freestanding ambulatory care facilities. Examples include kidney dialysis units, and radiology group practices with close relations with hospitals. Some payers encouraged the shift, believing those facilities would be cheaper. . . .

Back in the traditional hospitals, the nature of care depends greatly on hospitals' relationships with doctors and medical schools, and on hospitals' catchment areas — the areas from which they get most of their patients. . . .

A suburban hospital can generally provide sophisticated care, such as cardiac bypass surgery, but it is not as likely to have clinical professors who are able to provide extremely specialized care for "interesting" cases. All hospitals want the most advanced equipment, but the academic medical centers must have it for research and training. These centers rely heavily on residents and interns for delivery of care and, most important, are likely to have a much lower-class population of patients.

Many of the [academic medical centers] are in inner cities. They are likely to have large outpatient departments to train the students (residents) and serve the local population, which feeds into the inpatient wards; the emergency room not only gets emergencies but also serves as an outpatient clinic for some for the population. All of this is the good news: If a major teaching hospital is in the inner city, then either a large and endowed institution or a state government pays for some care for the inner-city poor.

When local hospitals receive little funding for education, poor populations must frequently rely on a hospital financed by a strapped city or county budget. Such hospitals — for example, Cook County in Chicago, Boston City, and Charity in New Orleans — have interns and residents to do the work because of their relationship with a training program, but nowhere near the resources of a freestanding university hospital. All hospitals in the inner city try to convince Medicare that they deserve an extra subsidy for treating a poorer, less-insured, and often sicker population. The federal government calls these disproportionate share payments. One of the huge issues for American health care reform is what will happen to the academic medical centers and the remaining urban public hospitals if payment systems allow competing insurers to favor hospitals that are less expensive because they have lesser teaching and subsidy burdens.

Another major issue is how a bias toward specialized, high-technology medicine, created in part by how medical education is financed and how physicians are paid, is reinforced by arrangements for capital investment in American medicine. There are hardly any measures in place to prevent a "medical arms race" among hospitals that seek the most advanced technology in order to attract physicians and generate revenue. . . .

Because for years insurers would pay whatever physicians and hospitals billed, and hospitals relied on physicians to provide patients, hospitals competed for patients by having the best equipment, and insurers ended up paying for excess treatments and higher charges per treatment. At one time also physicians could refer patients to any specialist they wished, and patients could go directly to a specialist without referral.

The rise of managed care and of more aggressive bargaining by insurers has begun to change this basic pattern. Insurers have become more likely to refuse to approve a given service or to insist on a lower price. Hospitals still need to attract physicians by offering the best equipment, however, so they are caught between the demands of doctors and payers. Meanwhile insurers are limiting choice of and access to specialists by building closed panels, in which a person covered by a plan either cannot use or must pay a surcharge to use any provider who is not on special contract to the plan. A patient might find that her doctor of 20 years' standing is no longer part of her insurance plan; a physician might find that many of his patients can afford referral only to three nephrologists whom he does not know. One of the key issues in reform is whether these new restrictions on choice of physician are necessary.

■ DOCTORS, PATIENTS, AND HEALTH INSURANCE: THE ORGANIZATION AND FINANCING OF MEDICAL CARE
Herman Miles Somers & Anne Ramsay Somers
1961

[T]he conflict between [hospital] medical staff and [hospital] management has become both sharper and more open in recent years. The roots of this conflict — the basic dichotomy in hospital organization — go back to eighteenth century Britain and the establishment of the Anglo-American tradition of voluntary hospitals. There was no such dichotomy in medieval days when hospitals were operated, with little medical assistance, by monastic orders for the sick poor. There is generally no such duality in the major Continental hospitals which are usually run, with unquestioned authority, by full-time chiefs of medical services. The distinguishing feature of the Anglo-American voluntary hospital, however, has been its use by private physicians for private patients with little or no accompanying administrative or financial responsibility. . . .

Recent developments — the hospital's changing role, its increase in size, complexity, utilization, cost, and its greatly altered financial base — have intensified the inherent instability of this administrative structure. . . . Lay influences on hospital administration and policy are clearly increasing. Ultimate policy responsibility has always rested with lay trustees. Traditionally, they limited their oversight to balancing the books. With the tremendous increase in hospital costs, however, this single concern has led to increasing surveillance over the hospital's total functioning, including the organization of the medical staff. The hospital administrator, traditionally an untrained individual content to play a fairly subservient role and socially outranked by doctor and trustee alike, is being transformed into a professional with increasing self-confidence and authority. . . .

At the same time the hospital has become an indispensable workshop for the modern physician, who finds it virtually impossible to practice good medicine without hospital affiliation. The hospital is the center of his professional world, and he is acknowledged to be its key figure. Fully 40 percent of private physician income is now earned in the hospital. Naturally he wants "his" institution equipped with the latest scientific and technological facilities. But the doctor's relationship to the hospital is peculiarly ambiguous. As a rule he assumes neither administrative nor financial responsibility. Yet, in practice, his is the most powerful voice in the organization. He alone admits and discharges patients; he alone can diagnose, prescribe, and treat patients — still the chief purpose for which the hospital exists. With his high professional status, he may, in most hospitals, countermand administrative orders and defy lay authority with relative impunity. The result is the confusing duality that prevails today throughout the hospital system, public and private. . . .

It is sometimes proposed that hiring the medical staff on a salary or contract basis would increase the doctors' sense of responsibility for hospital administration and help clarify lines of accountability. It could integrate the administrative structure without restricting professional integrity. This is the general pattern in a few of the nation's best hospitals, such as the Henry Ford in Detroit and the Cleveland Clinic Hospital. Most of the profession is, however, vigorously opposed to such practice, alleging "hospital domination," "lay control," or the "corporate practice of medicine." Some hospitals have taken a middle road — employing full-time medical directors (this is frequently the practice in government hospitals) and in a few instances, full-time chiefs of medical services. This too is generally frowned on by physicians in private practice. . . .

Many hospital spokesmen, however, content themselves with pleading for physician cooperation in assuring some responsibility for hospital operations and costs. . . . But such recommendations are usually set in a purely hortatory context. It is not clear how such preachments are to influence the individual doctor. The "medical staff" of which he is a member is in most instances simply a term for the collectivity of physicians authorized to practice in a particular hospital. The staff can be as disciplinary an instrument as it chooses to be, but in most places it has chosen minimal responsibility. . . . By and large the staff still prefers not to interfere with the practices of the individual physician.

■ CLINICAL DECISION MAKING FROM THEORY TO PRACTICE
David M. Eddy
1996

Medical practice is in the middle of a profound transition. Most physicians can remember the day when, armed with a degree, a mission, and confidence, they could set forth to heal the sick. Like Solomon, physicians could receive patients, hear their complaints, and determine the best course of action. While not every patient could be cured, everyone could be confident that whatever was done was the best possible. Most important, each physician was free, trusted, and left alone to determine what was in the best interest of each patient.

All of that is changing. . . . Now physicians must deal with second opinions, precertification, skeptical medical directors, variable coverage, outright denials, utilization review, threats of cookbook medicine, and letters out of the blue chiding that Mrs. Smith is on two incompatible drugs. Solomon did not have to call anyone to get permission for his decisions. What is going on?

What is going on is that one of the basic assumptions underlying the practice of medicine is being challenged. This assumption is not just a theory about cholesterol, antiarrhythmia, or estrogens. This assumption concerns the intellectual foundation of medical care. Simply put, the assumption is that whatever a physician decides is, by definition, correct. The challenge says that while many decisions no doubt *are* correct, many are not, and elaborate mechanisms are needed to determine which are which. Physicians are slowly being stripped of their decisionmaking power.

Notes: Doctors and Hospitals

1. *History and Description.* For general histories and descriptions of the health care delivery system, see David Smith & Arnold Kaluzny, The White Labyrinth: A Guide to the Health Care System (2d ed. 1986); Harry A. Sultz & Kristina M. Young, Health Care USA: Understanding Its Organization and Delivery (2d ed. 1999). For more extensive historical accounts of the transformation of hospitals and their role in modern medicine, see Guenter B. Risse, Mending Bodies, Saving Souls: A History of Hospitals (1999); Charles Rosenberg, The Care of Strangers (1987); David Rosner, A Once Charitable Enterprise (1982); Rosemary Stevens, In Sickness and in Wealth: American Hospitals in the Twentieth Century (1989).

2. *The Two-Headed Monster.* The unique structure of American hospitals, in which doctors are independent but essential to their financial well-being, has been described as "attractive as a two-headed monster" and as "stable as a three-legged

stool." See H. L. Smith, Two Lines of Authority are One Too Many, 84 Modern Hosp. 59 (March 1955). This division of authority is mirrored throughout the organizational structure of the health-care system. For instance, hospitals, unlike any other business organization, are required by state licensure laws and private accreditation standards to have *two* sets of corporate bylaws, one for the hospital administration and a second for the medical staff. Similarly, health insurance traditionally pays hospitals separately from doctors, as reflected in the distinctions between Blue Cross (hospital insurance) and Blue Shield (physician insurance) and between Medicare Part A and Part B.

3. *Power Relationships in Medicine.* Medical sociologists and organizational theorists have produced a rich literature discussing the role of physicians within medical institutions. Leading examples are Eliot Freidson, Doctoring Together (1975); Eliot Freidson, Profession of Medicine (1970); Paul Starr, The Social Transformation of American Medicine (1982); Jeffrey Harris, The Internal Organization of Hospitals: Some Economic Implications, 8 Bell J. Econ. 467 (1977). For an exploration of how these insights illuminate a variety of legal doctrines and public policy debates, see Mark A. Hall, Institutional Control of Physician Behavior: Legal Barriers to Health Care Cost Containment, 137 U. Pa. L. Rev. 431 (1988) ("Because the law absorbs and reflects the values and relationships of traditional medicine, it has codified the ethic of professional dominance, effectively shielding physicians from the institutional influence contemplated by revolutionary changes in health care policy."); Sara Rosenbaum, The Impact of United States Law on Medicine as a Profession, 289 JAMA 1546 (2003).

2. The Culture of Medicine

■ MAGIC OR MEDICINE? AN INVESTIGATION OF HEALING AND HEALERS*
Robert Buckman & Karl Sabbagh
1995

Despite the enormous variety of their forms and formats and their lack of any apparent common ingredient, every interaction between a patient and a healer shares a common structure. In each consultation, (1) the patient comes to the healer with an idea that something is wrong. (2) The healer then tries to find out what the cause of the problem is and (3) makes some intervention—a drug, a spell, a recommendation or something else. After the consultation, (4) the patient (or society on the patient's behalf) rewards the healer for his or her time and trouble. Finally, (5) there is some measure of the outcome of the consultation, something that wouldn't have happened if the consultation hadn't taken place. This might be a measurable improvement (or deterioration) in some physical parameter of the illness or a subjective sense of feeling better (or worse).

---

* Copyright © 1995, Prometheus Books. Reprinted by permission.

And that is all there is to it. In all its guises, in all cultures and in all languages, those are the basic steps in what appears to be a complex and varied first dance between patient and healer which forms the basis of the relationship between them. As a means of analyzing the patient-doctor/healer relationship in greater detail, we propose to start by examining . . . [the first] component of the consultation. . . . This leads to a . . . conclusion that some may find surprising, namely that the exact definition of what constitutes a disease or an illness is determined not by biology but by society. Certainly, there is a class of health problems that are seen in a similar way in all societies. For instance, if a previously fit man suddenly clutches his chest, looks white and sweaty and is acutely short of breath even at rest, then in Western society we would say that this man has probably had a heart attack, and we would prove it with ECGs and blood tests. It might be that in another society that episode is regarded as a visitation from a malevolent spirit, but even so it would be recognized as a serious, acute and unheralded problem — albeit a visitation, not a myocardial infarct.

However, not all diseases are as clear-cut as a heart attack. Some are far more difficult to define and pigeon-hole and are classified differently in different societies. In Germany, for example, doctors prescribe six times the amount of heart drugs per person than in England or France. This is not because of a greater incidence of coronary artery disease in Germany — in fact, there is less of it than in France — and it clearly has no effect on death rates since the mortality from all forms of heart disease is the same in all countries. One of the major reasons is that the German language doesn't have a way of distinguishing heart problems from any other kind of chest pain. . . .

[T]he English and the Americans don't attribute vague chest pains to the heart unless there's some solid evidence for genuine heart disease. Thus *Herzinsuffizienz* is an illness-label that is almost exclusive to Germany — hence, perhaps, the excessive prescription of heart drugs. In the same way, in France, a large number of nonspecific symptoms are attributed to a *crise de foie* — a "crisis of the liver." In fact, approximately 80 percent of problems attributed to a crisis of the liver are actually migraine. And most of the rest are minor gastrointestinal conditions. . . . Similarly, in the American medical view, minor illnesses are much more likely to be ascribed to (unspecified) viral illnesses. This is in line with the prevailing mood of the times in America in which disease is seen as an external invasive threat and there is a predilection for diagnosing infections since they can often be dealt with actively and quickly. . . .

Now consider a common event (in many lives) — a hangover. We all expect a hangover if we drink excessively; so is a hangover an expected consequence of ordinary life or is it a disease? Whether or not it is a disease, is it an illness? What about bereavement? We expect to be sad after the death of someone we love — if the bereaved person cries continuously for a week, is that an illness? If he or she cries for six months, is that an illness? And what about adolescence? In Montana, a change in financing of private hospitals led to many general hospitals quickly changing themselves into psychiatric hospitals. Unfortunately, there were not enough patients to fill them, so there was a sudden epidemic of new diagnoses. Teenagers who had falling grades at school were now diagnosed as psychiatrically disturbed (with a major advertising campaign to get the point across to the parents) and were admitted to a hospital — at four times the rate that occurred in neighboring Utah. . . .

These [examples] again emphasize the partly arbitrary—and rather parochial—definitions of disease and illness. Each society decides for itself at the time what are legitimately regarded as diseases or illnesses. Those definitions vary from culture to culture. Furthermore, those conditions that we regard as normal today may be diagnosed as illnesses tomorrow.

■ THE TYRANNY OF HEALTH*
Faith T. Fitzgerald
331 New Eng. J. Med. 196 (1994)

There has recently been much in both lay and medical literature on the promotion of healthy lifestyles. Once upon a time people did not have lifestyles; they had lives. Those lives were filled with work and play, battle and respite, excitement and boredom, but principally with the day-to-day struggle for existence, centered largely around the family, birth, death, disease, and health. What is the difference between a lifestyle and a life? Central to it, I believe, is the concept that lifestyle is something one chooses, and life is something that happens to one. This distinction will affect the future of medicine, and certainly health care reform, in this country. The emphasis on healthy lifestyles, although salutary in many ways, has a very dark side to it and has led to the increasing peril of a tyranny of health in the United States. To explain the potential dangers of the emphasis on healthy lifestyles, I here review the concept of health and its role in the fabric of our society.

A healthy lifestyle is said to be essential to the promotion of wellness. What is wellness? In 1946, the World Health Organization, largely in revulsion against the activities of Nazi physicians and the creatures who worked with them, redefined health as "a state of complete physical, mental, and social well being, and not merely the absence of disease or infirmity." This has become known as "wellness," a highly desirable state. A well or healthy person is one who is not only physically whole and vigorous, but also happy and socially content. What a good idea! . . .

Concurrently, and perhaps naively, both the lay public and the medical profession began to confuse the ideal of health with the norm for health. That is, we went from "Wouldn't it be great to have this be the definition of health" to "This *is* the definition of health." Having accepted the view that health should be a perfect state of wellness, we went on to declare that it was. But if one accepts the idea that physical vigor and emotional and social contentment are not only desirable, but also expected, there is a problem. If health is normal, then sickness and accidents are faults. Who or what is at fault varies: environmental pollution, for example, or government plots, doctors themselves, diet, radon, or political bias. We now act as if we really believe that disease, aging, and death are unnatural acts and all things are remediable. All we have to do, we think, is know enough (or spend enough), and disease and death can be prevented or fixed. . . .

---

* Excerpted with permission of the publisher. Copyright © 1994, Massachusetts Medical Society.

In his paper "Medical Nemesis," Illich[2] wrote in 1974 that classifying all the troubles of humanity as medical problems is actually antithetical to true health, in that it limits the ability of people to learn to cope with pain, sickness, and death as integral parts of life. Health, he maintained, is not freedom from the inevitability of death, disease, unhappiness and stress, but rather the ability to cope with them in a competent way. If this is true, then the more medicine and society direct individual behavior, the less autonomous, and therefore the less healthy, the individual may become.

We must beware of developing a zealotry about health, in which we take ourselves too seriously and believe that we know enough to dictate human behavior, penalize people for disagreeing with us, and even deny people charity, empathy, and understanding because they act in a way of which we disapprove. Perhaps the health care crisis could be resolved, in part, if we [health care professionals realized that] . . . we cannot fix everything (though we do some things marvelously well), nor can our patients — no matter how intelligent or attentive — prevent all disease and death. We may be trying to do too much and thus diluting an awareness and application of what we can do well.

■ THE MACHINE AT THE BEDSIDE*
Stanley Joel Reiser & Michael Anbar
1984

Technology has altered significantly the form and meaning of the medical relationship. It allows us to direct our vision and attention to variables singled out by it as significant. Thus, stethoscopes increase the significance of chest sounds, X-rays of anatomic shadows, electrocardiograms of waves on a graph, computers of printouts, dialysis machines of chemical balances, and so forth. Such evidence is important for diagnosis and therapy, and the more precisely it can be stated, the more valuable it becomes. In comparison, evidence given by patients, and altered by its passage through the prism of their experience and personality, has seemed to the technological age of the past two centuries less substantive, accurate, and meaningful as a basis for clinical decisionmaking and actions. Increasingly, practioners encounter patients for relatively brief and intermittent periods — such as the consultant visiting a hospitalized patient whom he or she has never before met. In such visits the technical aspects often dominate, for there is no time or prior relationship to determine much about who the patient is, or what the patient thinks about the illness or the needs it engenders. And even in medical relationships that are not so discontinuous, technological measurements and measures tend to crowd out other dimensions of evaluation and therapeutics. To speak so of the attention focused on the technological features of practice does not diminish their great significance and benefit. Rather, it points out that they do not encompass all critical aspects of diagnosis or treatment. . . .

---

[2] Illich I. Medical nemesis. Lancet 1974;1:918-21.
* Copyright © 1984, Cambridge University Press. Reprinted with permission.

From the beginning of their introduction in the mid-nineteenth century, automated machines that generated results in objective formats such as graphs and numbers were thought capable of purging from health care the distortions of subjective human opinion. They were supposed to produce facts free of personal bias, and thus to reduce the uncertainty associated with human choice. This view, held by both practitioners and patients, stimulated the intense use of these devices, sometimes to excess. This excess has been characterized by overreliance on technologically depicted features of illness, inadequate understanding of the capabilities and limits of machines and the information they generate, and relative inattention to those aspects of medicine learned by inquiry into the patient's experiences and views. Machines can seem so accurate, so right. They can make us forget who made them, and who designed into them — with all the possibilities of human frailty and error — the programs that dictate their function. They can make us forget the hands and minds behind their creation; they can make us forget ourselves.

Notes: The Social Construction of Disease

1. *Is Anyone Healthy?* Students, especially younger ones, often fail to appreciate the extent to which health issues pervade society. According to one survey, in a typical *month* 80 percent of adults report some type of medical symptom, 20 percent visit a doctor, 6 percent visit an alternative (nontraditional) health care provider, and 4 percent go to a hospital. Larry Green et al., The Ecology of Medical Care Revisited, 344 New Eng. J. Med. 2021 (2001). See also Nortin M. Hadler, The Last Well Person (2004); Clifton Meador, The Last Well Person, 330 New Eng. J. Med. 440 (1994).

2. For additional views on the meaning of health and illness and the impact of medical technology, see Nancy King et al. (eds.), The Social Medicine Reader (2d ed. 2005); R.A. Deyo & D.L. Patrick, Hope or Hype: The Obsession with Medical Advances and the High Cost of False Promises (2005); Robert A. Aronowitz, Making Sense of Illness: Science, Society, and Disease (1998); Daniel Callahan, False Hopes: Why America's Quest for Perfect Health Is a Recipe for Failure (1998); Rene Dubos, Man, Medicine and Environment (1968); Michel Foucault, The Birth of the Clinic (1963); David Mechanic, Symptoms, Illness Behavior, and Help Seeking (1982); Roy Porter, The Greatest Benefit to Mankind (1998); David Rothman, Beginnings Count: The Technological Imperative in American Health Care (1997); Wm. B. Schwartz, Life Without Disease: The Pursuit of Medical Utopia (1998); Susan Sontag, Illness as Metaphor (1988); Richard A. Miller, Extending Life: Scientific Prospects and Political Obstacles, 80(2) Milbank Q. (2002); Lars Noah, Pigeonholing Illness: Medical Diagnosis as a Legal Construct, 50 Hastings L. Rev. 241 (1999); Talcott Parsons, The Sick Role and the Role of the Physician Reconsidered, 53 Health & Soc'y 257 (1975); Symposium, 21(2) Health Aff. (Mar. 2002); Symposium, 20(5) Health Aff. (Sept. 2001); Symposium, 25 J. Med. & Phil. 519 (2000); Developments, Medical Technology and the Law, 103 Harv. L. Rev. 1519 (1990).

3. The Phenomenology of Sickness and Healing

■ MAKING MEDICAL SPENDING DECISIONS*
Mark A. Hall
1997

THE ONTOLOGICAL ASSAULT OF ILLNESS

Illness is frequently described as an "ontological assault." It undermines one's personal identity by attacking the fundamental unity of mind and body. In a state of health, our body is part of an integrated sense of self that responds instinctively to our will and serves our inner purposes almost effortlessly. When illness strikes, our body becomes an enemy of self. It does not respond as we wish and its frailties dominate our conscious thoughts. Illness strikes at one of our most fundamental assumptions in everyday life — that we will continue to exist and function much as we have in the past. Serious illness shatters our "primordial sense of invulnerability."[3]

The profound incapacitating effect of this assault on our very being is much more debilitating than any of life's other major disruptions, whether they be divorce, incarceration or impoverishment. Physician and philosopher Edmund Pellegrino observes correctly that:

> In no other deprivation is the dissolution of the person so intimate that it impairs the capacity to deal with all other deprivations. The poor man can still hope for a change of fortune, the prisoner for a reprieve, the lonely for a friend. But the ill person remains impaired even when freed of these other constraints on the free exercise of his humanity.[4]

Consider also this account by a philosopher and patient who herself suffers from a severe chronic illness, multiple sclerosis:

> The most deeply held assumption of daily life is the assumption that I, personally, will continue to be alive and it is in light of this assumption that one engages in daily activities. The onset of illness, however, brings one concretely face-to-face with personal vulnerability. . . . Thus, the person who is ill . . . is unable readily to fit illness into the typified schema used to organize and interpret experience. . . . One finds oneself preoccupied with the demands of the here and now, confined to the present moment, unable effectively to project into the future.[5]

In addition to these profound internal effects, . . . when ill we are often immobilized and confined to bed in a prone position and subjected to mind-altering medications. This compromises our physical ability to act and deliberate and places us in a psychological state of dependency. Treatment also compromises physical integrity and exposes us to singular vulnerability by giving

---

* Copyright © 1997, Oxford University Press. Reprinted with permission.
[3] Silberman 1991. In addition to the sources cited in the following notes, see Pellegrino 1979; Pellegrino and Thomasma 1981; Cassell 1982; Cassell 1985; Kleinman 1988.
[4] Pellegrino 1982, at 159.
[5] Toombs 1992, at 21, 69.

physicians unprecedented access to our bodies and personal histories. Treatment requires us to expose every part of ourselves, down to our very blood and guts, while we remain prostrate or unconscious.

Typically, when ill, we do not resist what would otherwise be viewed as utterly repugnant invasions and vulnerabilities. Sickness returns us to an infantile state where our strongest desire is usually to be cared for and to be relieved of the responsibility and anxiety of deciding and acting.[6] "Such sick people . . . may plausibly prefer not to take on any kind of work, much less the fierce, foreign, and forbidding labor of medical decisions."[7] This is true even for the most knowledgeable of patients — physicians themselves. Franz Ingelfinger, M.D., long time editor of the eminently prestigious New England Journal of Medicine and an expert in diseases of the esophagus, found himself in a dilemma of how best to treat his own difficult case of cancer of the esophagus. His doctors, respecting their patient's world renowned expertise, were leaving this vexing decision to him:

> As a result, not only I but my wife, my son and daughter-in-law (both doctors), and other family members became increasingly confused and emotionally distraught. Finally, when the pangs of indecision had become nearly intolerable, one wise physician friend said, "What you need is a doctor." . . . When that excellent advice was followed, my family and I sensed immediate and immense relief.[8] . . .

[M]y description of the real experience of illness applies to simple and serious conditions alike. Sickness does not have to be life threatening for it to profoundly affect thinking and functioning. A bad flu bug, a relentless shooting pain, a case of food poisoning, an inconsolable child, or even an unexplained lump or a persistent bad cough can have these menacing and incapacitating effects at least to some degree. Even if this state of mind is the exception in medical treatment encounters, it nevertheless is the dominant explanation of why the medical system exists. . . . Medical ethics and health care policy should have its primary focus on the quintessential features of the treatment relationship even if those features account for only a fraction of [medical] decisions.

THE MYSTICAL POWER OF HEALING

[The condition of illness is only half of the story in a medical encounter. We must also understand something about the experience of healing. Modern medicine thinks of healing as occurring mainly through biochemical processes activated by medical interventions chosen based on diagnostic analysis and professional experience.] . . . Much of medicine is of this rational quality, but [this account ignores] an essential nonrational component of medicine. . . . This essential component is the mystical power of healing. By this, I mean the hidden elements of the treatment encounter that result in healing through what might be termed charismatic or self-healing means. The power of healing I refer to is the

---

[6] On this regression to infancy caused by sickness, see Burt 1979; Somers and Somers 1961, at 459-60.

[7] Schneider 1997.

[8] Ingelfinger 1980.

dimension of doctoring that enables physicians to confer relief through spiritual or emotional means akin to those used by parents or priests.[9]

Before alienating the skeptical reader entirely, let me illustrate with an everyday example from my own experience. Last year when my six-year-old daughter was suffering from a common earache, her distress brought her to inconsolable tears while waiting more than an hour to be seen by the doctor. I convinced a nurse to take her temperature, give her an aspirin, and say a few kind words of reassurance. Instantaneously, my daughter felt much better, far quicker than any possible pharmacological effect could have taken hold. I was puzzled by this abrupt improvement until I had my own excruciating earache a few weeks later and experienced exactly the same sort of instantaneous relief as soon as the doctor examined me and wrote a prescription. Knowing that I was in the good hands of a trained professional who offered the prospect of relief produced in me a sense of exhilaration and a release of anxiety accompanied by a pronounced improvement of my symptoms. This instantaneous recovery might be attributed simply to excessive nerves or to a more complex type of placebo effect but, however labeled or explained, it was effective. The pain was not just more bearable; it went away.

Researchers and physicians have documented countless similar examples of mundane and miraculous relief caused by a largely nonscientific or "nonspecific" process of healing.[10] This placebo effect is not limited to purely psychological states, bizarre conditions, especially susceptible patients, or to manipulative physicians. This effect has been documented in the treatment of diabetes, cancer, and heart disease, for instance, and without the physicians even intending to cause the effect. In one scientific study, two sets of patients were subjected to different surgical operations to treat angina (chest pain), one that performed the standard chest operation, and the other that only pretended to do so by cutting the skin under anesthesia. Both the sham and the real procedure produced equal relief of physical symptoms.[11] A review of other surgical and medical procedures once firmly believed to be effective but later discarded as entirely unfounded led one author to speculate that placebo healing effects may be present to a significant extent in 70 percent of clinical encounters.[12]

Those who have studied this nonspecific healing effect conclude that it pervades medicine, both in modern times and in prescientific and primitive cultures.[13] This is because the effect is connected more to the intervention of the healer than it is to the particular therapeutic agent used. Put another way, the doctor himself is a therapeutic agent, regardless of the actual effectiveness of the particular drug or procedure.[14] In each culture and each era, there has been a prevailing theory of medical treatment, many of which are pure fantasy if not dangerous, yet remarkably few have been proven to be wholly without benefit. Doctors and healers have been universally respected throughout the ages and across primitive and advanced societies; we can only assume that most of them

---

[9] On the prevalence of the image of physician as parent or priest, see May 1983.
[10] In addition to the sources in the following notes, see Spiro 1986; Brody 1980.
[11] Beecher 1961.
[12] Roberts 1993; Roberts 1995.
[13] Turner et al., 1994; Moerman 1983; Brody 1980.
[14] Suchman & Matthews 1988; Houston 1938.

have offered some form of relief despite the now apparent quackery they once practiced. Indeed, it has often been commented that the history of medicine until this century has been the history of the placebo effect. Now that medicine has a firm scientific foundation, this mystical or charismatic element has been surpassed by technological skill, but it will never be entirely displaced. One of the prominent trends in modern medicine is the revival of both popular and scientific interest in these poorly understood domains of caring for patients through alternative or holistic schools of medicine.[15]

The best scientific explanation for this charismatic healing effect is that the process of treatment, and not its specific content, has universal benefit for many or most illnesses, regardless of the specific physiological effects of the treatment. The treatment process has this universal healing power by virtue of the archetypal characteristics that activate the patient's own healing mechanisms — mechanisms that are still largely undiscovered and unexplained. This is best demonstrated by the fact that the basic structure of the treatment encounter is remarkably the same across all systems of medicine, including Western, Eastern, religious, herbal, and primitive. In each of these belief systems, society recognizes the healing powers of a professional elite (physicians or shamans), who administer personally to the patient with physical touching and healing agents (drugs or herbs), often in a dramatic and cathartic ritualistic setting (surgery or exorcism) specially designed for the purpose (hospital or bonfire). In the process, patients feel cared for (nurses or mystics), they are given an explanation for their condition (diagnosis or demonization) that is consistent with their prevailing belief system (scientific medicine or spirit worship), and they are assigned tasks of self care in which they take responsibility in part for their own improvement (dietary regimen or prayer).[16]

These many symbolic structural elements are thought to activate patients' internal healing powers through a variety of psychological channels. A patient who knows someone is devoted to caring for him is able to release the dread and anxiety that may be heightening discomfort and weakening the body's resistance. Believing in the power of the healer may enable the patient to regress to an earlier, more infantile state of mind that enhances this release and the resulting comfort. This confidence in the healer is elevated by the healer's status in society, his invocation of methods consistent with that society's belief system, and his offering an explanation of the otherwise troubling and disorienting disease that makes sense to the patient. And, this belief is further cemented by the ritualistic and dramatic elements of laying on of hands, taking of medication, climactic performance, and hallowed setting. . . .

Critical to this healing power is the patient's confidence and trust in the healer. "The image of omnipotence is an essential component of the healer."[17] The healer appears able to activate the patient's own healing mechanisms because the patient turns himself over both in mind and body to the healer. "A patient's hope and trust lead to a 'letting go' that counteracts stress and is often the key to

---

[15] Cohen 1995; Moyers 1993; Frohoch 1992; Siegel 1986; Cousins 1979; Siegel 1986.

[16] The leading work developing this explanation is Frank 1973. See also Brody 1992; Novack 1987; Spiro 1986.

[17] Cassell 1985, at 141. See also Cassell 1991.

getting well."[18] Psychiatrists, starting with Freud, have described this phenomenon as "transference," in which patients foist on their healers qualities they formerly attributed to their parents in infancy when parents were viewed as all powerful and all knowing. "Deep in patients' unconscious, physicians are viewed as miracle workers, patterned after the fantasied all-caring parents of infancy. Medicine, after all, was born in magic and religion, and the doctor-priest-magician-parent unity that persists in patients' unconscious cannot be broken."[19] . . .

I hasten to concede that none of these assertions are known with any degree of empirical confidence. We are forced into this highly speculative reading of anecdotal accounts from physicians, anthropologists, and enthnographic researchers since empirical testing of this nonspecific healing power is very difficult and has not been widely attempted.[20] Nevertheless, many informed observers and patients view the charismatic dimension of healing as fundamental to the treatment relationship.[21]

[PARTIAL BIBLIOGRAPHY]

Beecher, H. (1961). "Surgery as Placebo," 176 JAMA 1102.

Brody, H. (1992). The Healer's Power (New Haven, CT: Yale Univ. Press).

Brody, H. (1980). Placebos and the Philosophy of Medicine: Clinical, Conceptual, and Ethical Issues (Chicago: Univ. of Chicago Press).

Burt, R.A. (1979). Taking Care of Strangers: The Rule of Law in Doctor-Patient Relations (New York: The Free Press).

Cassell, E.J. (1991). The Nature of Suffering and the Goals of Medicine (Oxford Univ. Press).

Cassell, E.J. (1985). The Healer's Art (MIT Press).

Cassell, E.J. (1982). "The Nature of Suffering and the Goals of Medicine," 306 New Eng. J. Med. 639.

Cohen, M.H. (1995). "A Fixed Star in Health Care Reform: The Emerging Paradigm of Holistic Healing," 27 Ariz. St. Law J. 79.

Cousins, N. (1979). Anatomy of an Illness as Perceived by the Patient: Reflections on Healing and Regeneration (New York: W.W. Norton).

Frank, J.D. (1973). Persuasion and Healing: A Comparative Study of Psychotherapy (Baltimore: Johns Hopkins Univ. Press).

Frohoch, F.M. (1992). Healing Powers: Alternative Medicine, Spiritual Communities, and the State (Univ. Chicago Press).

Houston, R. (1938). "The Doctor Himself as a Therapeutic Agent," 11 Annals Int. Med. 1415.

Katz, J. (1984). The Silent World of Doctor and Patient (New York: The Free Press).

Kleinman, A. (1988). The Illness Narratives: Suffering, Healing, and the Human Condition (Basic Books).

Ingelfinger, F. (1980). "Arrogance," 303 New Eng. J. Med. 1507.

---

[18] Siegel 1986.

[19] Katz 1984, at 142-47, 192. See also Burt 1979.

[20] There are some scattered scientific studies demonstrating the placebo effect and the effect of certain of these healing rituals, but no scientific studies exploring what ingredients make this process work . . . [or are counterproductive].

[21] E.g., Brody 1992; Katz 1984; Burt 1979.

Moerman, D.E. (1983). "Physiology and Symbols: The Anthropological Implications of the Placebo Effect," in The Anthropology of Medicine, eds. L. Romanucci-Ross, et al. (Prager).

Moyers, B. (1993). Healing and the Mind (Doubleday).

Novack, D.H. (1987). "Therapeutic Aspects of the Clinical Encounter," 2 J. Gen. Intern. Med. 346.

Pellegrino, E.D. (1982). "Being Ill and Being Healed," in The Humanity of the Ill, ed. V. Kestenbaum (Univ. Tennessee Press).

Pellegrino, E.D. (1979). "Toward a Reconstruction of Medical Morality: The Primacy of the Act of Profession and the Fact of Illness," 4 J. Med. & Philo. 32.

Pellegrino, E.D. and Thomasma, D.C. (1981). A Philosophical Basis of Medical Practice (Oxford Univ. Press).

Roberts, A.H. (1995). "The Powerful Placebo Revisited: Magnitude of Nonspecific Effects," 1 Mind/Body Med. 35-43.

Roberts, A.H., et al. "The Power of Nonspecific Effects in Healing," 12 Clin. Psychol. Rev. 375.

Schneider, C.E. (1997). The Practice of Autonomy: Patients, Doctors, and Medical Decisions (forthcoming, Oxford Univ. Press).

Schneider, C.E. (1994). "Bioethics with a Human Face," 69 Ind. Law J. 1075-1104.

Siegel, B.S. (1986). Love, Medicine & Miracles (Harper & Row).

Silberman, C. (1991). "From the Patient's Bed," 13 Health Management Q. 12.

Somers, H.M. and Somers, A.R. (1961). Doctors, Patients and Health Insurance: The Organization and Financing of Medical Care (Washington, D.C.: Brookings Institution).

Spiro, H.M. (1986). Doctors, Patients, and Placebos (New Haven: Yale Univ. Press).

Suchman, A.L. and Matthews, D.A. (1988). "What Makes the Doctor-Patient Relationship Therapeutic? Exploring the Connexional Dimension of Medical Care," 108 Ann. Intern. Med. 125.

Toombs, S.K. (1992). The Meaning of Illness, A Phenomenological Account of the Different Perspectives of Physician and Patient (Boston: Kluwer Academic Publishers).

Turner, J.A., Deyo, R.A. and Loeser, J.D., et al. (1994). "The Importance of Placebo Effects in Pain Treatment and Research," 271 JAMA 1609-1614.

Notes: The Power of Medicine and the Vulnerability of Patients

1. *Illness.* Does your own experience with illness confirm or rebut the incapacitating and dehumanizing effects described by Mark Hall? Consider the additional accounts, both analytical and narrative, on the Web site for this book, www.health-law.org. For additional descriptions and analyses of the phenomenology of illness, see Howard Brody, Stories of Sickness (1987); Kathy Charmaz, Good Days, Bad Days: The Self in Chronic Illness and Time (1991); Norman Cousins, The Healing Heart (1983); David M. Frankford, Food Allergy and the Health Care Financing Administration: A Story of Rage, 1 Widener L. Symp. J. 159 (1996); Marsha Garrison & Carl Schneider, The Law of Bioethics 1-5 (2003); Michael C. Dohan, Reflections on a Bone Marrow Transplant, 132 Annals Internal Med. 587 (2000). Discussing how issues of trust and vulnerability affect a number of issues in health care law, see Mark A. Hall, Law, Medicine and Trust, 55 Stan. L. Rev. 463 (2002); Robert Gatter, Faith, Confidence, and Health Care: Fostering Trust in Medicine Through Law, 39 Wake Forest L. Rev. 395 (2004).

2. *Doctors, Patients, and Placebos.* These readings explain that the placebo effect is not isolated to a few psychologically susceptible individuals or conditions. It permeates medical encounters and typifies the doctor-patient relationship in ways that scientific medicine tends to ignore or deny. The mere encounter with a doctor appears to activate internal, self-healing mechanisms across a wide range of medical conditions, regardless of the actual treatments rendered. In short, doctors do not just administer placebos; they *are* placebos. Considering this, should the FDA deny approval for a drug because it acts "only" as a placebo? How does a doctor obtain informed consent from a patient when he knows the treatment is partially or totally intended to invoke a placebo effect? For additional discussion, see Kathleen M. Boozang, The Therapeutic Placebo: The Case for Patient Deception, 54 Fla. L. Rev. 687 (2002); Anne Harrington, The Placebo Effect: An Interdisciplinary Exploration (1997); The Science of the Placebo, Harry A. Guess et al. eds., (2002). See generally Amitai Aviram, The Placebo Effect of Law: Law's Role in Manipulating Perceptions, 75 Geo. Wash. L. Rev. 54 (2006) (discussing how, "like the placebo effect of medicine, a law may impact social welfare beyond its objective effects by manipulating the public's subjective perception of the law's effectiveness").

3. *Alternative and Conventional Healers.* There is now widespread social interest in alternative healing, both as a separate area of professional practice and as a component of conventional scientific practice. For further exploration, see Thomas A. Droege, The Faith Factor in Healing (1991); B. O'Connor, Healing Traditions: Alternative Medicine and the Health Professions (1995); Michael H. Cohen, Complementary and Alternative Medicine: Legal Boundaries and Regulatory Perspectives (1998); Barbara L. Atwell, Mainstreaming Complementary and Alternative Medicine in the Face of Uncertainty, 72 UMKC L Rev 593 (2004); Symposium, 31 J. L. Med. Ethics 183 (2003); Michael H. Cohen & Mary C. Ruggie, Integrating Complementary and Alternative Medical Therapies in Conventional Medical Settings, 72 U. Cin. L. Rev. 671-729 (2003); Joseph A. Barrette, The Alternative Medical Practice Act, 77 St. John's L. Rev. 75 (2003); Barbara L. Atwell, Mainstreaming Complementary and Alternative Medicine in the Face of Uncertainty, 72 UMKC L. Rev. 593 (2004); James A. Bulen, Complementary and Alternative Medicine: Ethical and Legal Aspects of Informed Consent to Treatment, 24 J. Leg. Med. 331 (2003); Kathleen M. Boozang, Is the Alternative Medicine? Managed Care Apparently Thinks So, 32 Conn. L. Rev. 567 (2000); notes on pages [141-144].

4. *Therapeutic Jurisprudence.* Consider the various implications these provocative readings have for law and public policy. Do they alter conventional legal notions about who should control decisionmaking in the treatment encounter? Do they suggest that health insurance should more freely cover untested or unorthodox therapies? When disputes arise over treatment decisions or insurance coverage, are patients capable of aggressively pursuing their legal rights? Are patients capable of acting as informed consumers in a medical marketplace in which they evaluate the costs and benefits of different treatment options? Questions like these are addressed by a branch of legal thought known as "therapeutic jurisprudence," which views law as a therapeutic agent. This perspective asks whether normal social and behavioral assumptions realistically fit the medical arena, and whether legal rules do a good job of fostering the

therapeutic goals of medicine. For leading examples, focused mainly on mental health and criminal law, see David B. Wexler, Therapeutic Jurisprudence: The Law as a Therapeutic Agent (1990); David Wexler & Bruce Winnick, Essays in Therapeutic Jurisprudence (1991); Law in a Therapeutic Key, David B. Wexler & Bruce J. Winnick eds., (1996); Marshall B. Kapp, The Law and Older Persons: Is Geriatric Jurisprudence Therapeutic (2003). For an attempt to further develop this perspective in health care law, see Hall, supra, 55 Stan. L. Rev. 463 (2002).

4. The Nature of Medical Judgment

■ VARIATIONS IN PHYSICIAN PRACTICE:
THE ROLE OF UNCERTAINTY*
David M. Eddy**
3 Health Affairs 74, No. 2 (Summer 1984)

...An analysis of procedure rates for Medicare patients in 13 large metropolitan areas in the United States showed that for more than half the procedures studied, the rates varied more than 300 percent between the areas with high and low rates. Another study that compared utilization rates in 16 large communities in four states found more than threefold differences between the highest and lowest rates for heart bypass, thyroid, and prostate surgery; fivefold differences for specific back and abdominal surgeries; sevenfold differences for knee replacements; and almost 20-fold differences for carotid endarterectomies. . . . In Vermont, the chance of having one's tonsils removed as a child are 8 percent in one community and 70 percent in another. In Iowa, 15 percent of the men younger than 85 years in one region have had prostatectomies compared with more than 60 percent in another. In Maine, the chance of hysterectomy by the age of 70 years varies across communities from less than 20 percent to more than 70 percent.[11] While some of the variations might be explained by differences in disease incidence, available resources, and patient preferences, it is impossible to explain all of them. . . .

Why do physicians vary so much in the way they practice medicine? At first view, there should be no problem. There are diseases — neatly named and categorized by textbooks, journal articles, and medical specialty societies. There are various procedures physicians can use to diagnose and treat these diseases. It should be possible to determine the value of any particular procedure by applying it to patients who have a disease and observing the outcome. And the rest should be easy — if the outcome is good, the procedure should be used for patients with that disease; if the outcome is bad, it should not. Some variation in practice patterns can be expected due to differences in the incidence of various diseases,

---

* Copyright © 1984, The People-to-People Health Foundation, Inc., Project Hope. Reprinted with permission.

** Dr. Eddy is a physician researcher, formerly on the faculty of Duke University, and now a consultant in Jackson Hole, Wyoming. The first paragraph is taken from a later work, Clinical Decision Making: From Theory to Practice (1996).

[11] Wennberg J. Dealing with medical practice variation: a proposal for action, Health Aff. 1984; 3:6.

patients' preferences, and the available resources, but these variations should be small and explainable.

The problem of course is that nothing is this simple. Uncertainty, biases, errors, and differences of opinions, motives, and values weaken every link in the chain that connects a patient's actual condition to the selection of a diagnostic test or treatment. This [reading] describes some of the factors that cause decisions about the use of medical procedures to be so difficult, and that contribute to the alarming variations we observe in actual practice. It examines the components of the decision problem a physician faces, and the psychology of medical reasoning, focusing in particular on the role of uncertainty. Finally, it suggests some actions to reduce uncertainty and encourage consistency of good medical practice.

Uncertainty creeps into medical practice through every pore. Whether a physician is defining a disease, making a diagnosis, selecting a procedure, observing outcomes, assessing probabilities, assigning preference, or putting it all together, he is walking on very slippery terrain. It is difficult for nonphysicians, and for many physicians, to appreciate how complex these tasks are, how poorly we understand them, and how easy it is for honest people to come to different conclusions.

DEFINING A DISEASE

If one looks at patients who are obviously ill, it is fairly easy to identify the physical and chemical disorders that characterize that illness. On the other hand, a large part of medicine is practiced on people who do not have obvious illnesses, but rather have signs, symptoms, or findings that may or may not represent an illness that should be treated. Three closely related problems make it difficult to determine whether or not a patient actually has a disease that needs to be diagnosed or treated.

One problem is that the dividing line between "normal" and "abnormal" is not nearly as sharp as a cursory reading of a textbook would suggest. . . .

A second problem is that many "diseases," at least at the time they are diagnosed, do not by themselves cause pain, suffering, disability, or threat to life. They are considered diseases only because they increase the probability that something else that is truly bad will happen in the future. . . .

The difficulty of defining a disease is compounded by the fact that many of the signs, symptoms, findings, and conditions that might suggest a disease are extremely common. If a breast biopsy were performed on a random sample of senior citizens, fully 90 percent of them could have fibrocystic disease. If obesity is a disease, the average American is diseased. By the time they reach seventy, about two-thirds of women have had their uteruses removed. . . .

Given these uncertainties about what constitutes a disease, it should not be surprising that there are debates about the definitions of many diseases, and when there is agreement about a definition, it is often blatantly and admittedly arbitrary. A quick review of the literature reveals multiple definitions of glaucoma, diabetes, fibrocystic disease of the breast, coronary artery disease, myocardial infarction, stroke, and dozens of other conditions. Morbid obesity is defined as 100 percent above the ideal weight. But what is "ideal," and why 100 percent? The lesson is that for many conditions a clinician faces, there is no clear definition of disease that provides an unequivocal guide to action, and there is wide room for differences of opinion and variations in practice. . . .

[E]ven when sharp criteria are created, physicians vary widely in their application of these criteria—in their ability to ask about symptoms, observe signs, interpret test results, and record the answers. The literature on "observer variation" has been growing for a long time. . . . A group of experts compiled 100 electrocardiogram tracings, 50 of which showed myocardial infarctions, 25 of which were normal, and 25 of which showed some other abnormality (according to the experts). These EKGs were then given to ten other cardiologists to test their diagnostic abilities. The proportion of EKGs judged by the ten cardiologists to show infarcts varied by a factor of two. If you had an infarct and went to physician A, there would be a 28 percent chance the physician would have missed it. If you did not have an infarct and went to physician B, there would be a 26 percent chance that physician would have said you had one. . . .

Thirteen pathologists were asked to read 1,001 specimens obtained from biopsies of the cervix, and then to repeat the readings at a later time. On average, each pathologist agreed with himself only 89 percent of the time (intraobserver agreement), and with a panel of "senior" pathologists only 87 percent of the time (interobserver agreement). Looking only at the patients who actually had cervical pathology, the intraobserver agreement was only 68 percent and the interobserver agreement was only 51 percent. The pathologists were best at reading more advanced disease and normal tissue, but were labeled "unsatisfactory" in their ability to read the precancerous and preinvasive stages.

Similar studies have been reported for the presence of clubbing of the fingers, anemia, psychiatric disease, and many other signs, symptoms, and procedures. Even if there were no uncertainty about what constitutes a disease and how to define it, there would still be considerable uncertainty about whether or not a patient has the signs, symptoms, and findings needed to fit the definition.

SELECTING A PROCEDURE

The task of selecting a procedure is no less difficult. There are two main issues. First, for any patient condition there are dozens of procedures that can be ordered, in any combination, at any time. The list of procedures that might be included in a workup of chest pain or hypertension would take more than a page, spanning the spectrum from simply asking questions, to blood studies, to X-rays. Even for highly specific diagnostic problems, there can be a large choice of procedures. For example, if a woman presents with a breast mass and her physician wants to know its approximate size and architecture, the physician might contemplate an imaging procedure. The choice could include mammography, ultrasonography, thermography, diaphanography, computed tomography, lymphography, Mammoscan, and magnetic resonance imaging. A physician who chose mammography would still have to decide between xeromammography and film mammography, with several brands being available for the latter. There are about a dozen procedures that apply the principles of thermography. And why should a diagnostic workup be limited to one test? Why not follow a negative mammogram with a computed tomogram (or vice versa)? For the detection of colorectal cancer, a physician can choose any combination of fecal occult blood tests (and there are more than a dozen brands), digital examination, rigid sigmoidoscopy, flexible 30 cm sigmoidoscopy, flexible 60 cm sigmoidoscopy, barium enema (either plain or air contrast), and colonoscopy. These choices are not trivial. Most procedures have different mechanisms of action and a long list of pros and cons. Different brands of fecal occult blood tests have very different sensitivities and specificities, and film mammography and xeromammography differ in their radiation exposure by a factor of about four. These procedures are for relatively well-defined diseases; imagine the problems of selecting procedures to evaluate symptoms like fatigue, headache, or fever that can have about a dozen causes. . . .

In theory, much of the uncertainty just described could be managed if it were possible to conduct enough experiments under enough conditions, and observe the outcomes. Unfortunately, measuring the outcomes of medical procedures is one of the most difficult problems we face. The goal is to predict how the use of a procedure in a particular case will affect that patient's health and welfare. Standing in the way are at least a half dozen major obstacles. The central problem is that there is a natural variation in the way people respond to a medical procedure. Take two people who, to the best of our ability to define such things, are identical in all important respects, submit them to the same operative procedure, and one will die on the operating table while the other will not. Because of this natural variation, we can only talk about the probabilities of various outcomes — the probability that a diagnostic test will be positive if the disease is present (sensitivity), the probability that a test will be negative if the disease is absent (specificity), the probability that a treatment will yield a certain result, and so forth.

One consequence of this natural variation is that to study the outcomes of any procedure it is necessary to conduct the procedure on many different people, who are thought to represent the particular patients we want to know about, and then average the results. . . . Some diseases are so rare that, in order to conduct the ideal clinical trials, it would be necessary to collect tens of thousands, if not hundreds of thousands, of participants. A good example concerns the frequency of the Pap smear. One might wonder why the merits of a three-year versus one-year frequency cannot be settled by a randomized controlled trial. Because of the low frequency of cervical cancer, and the small difference in outcomes expected for the two frequencies, almost one million women would be required for such a study. . . .

Finally, even when the best trials are conducted, we still might not get an answer. Consider the value of mammography in women under fifty, and consider just one outcome — the effect on breast cancer mortality. Ignore for the time being the radiation hazard, false-positive test results, inconvenience, financial costs, and other issues. This is one of the best-studied problems in cancer prevention, benefiting from the largest (60,000 women) and longest (more than 15 years) completed randomized controlled trial, and an even larger uncontrolled study involving 270,000 women screened for five years in 29 centers around the country. Yet we still do not know the value of mammography in women under 50. The first study showed a slight reduction in mortality, but it was not statistically significant. The larger study suggested that mammography has improved since the first study, and that it is now almost as good in younger women as in older women, but the study was not controlled and we do not know if "almost" is good enough. Even for women over 50, where the first study showed a statistically significant reduction in breast cancer mortality (of about 40 percent at ten years), there is enough uncertainty about the results that no fewer than four additional trials have been initiated to confirm the results. These trials are still in progress.

Unable to turn to a definitive body of clinical and epidemiological research, a clinician or research scientist who wants to know the value of a procedure is left with a mixture of randomized controlled trials, nonrandomized trials, uncontrolled trials, and clinical observations. The evidence from different sources can easily go in different directions, and it is virtually impossible for anyone to sort things out in his or her head. Unfortunately, the individual physician may be most impressed by observations made in his or her individual practice. This source of evidence is notoriously vulnerable to bias and error. What a physician sees and remembers is biased by the types of patients who come in; by the decisions of the patients to accept a treatment and return for follow-up; by a natural desire to see good things; and by a whole series of emotions that charge one's memory. On top of these biases, the observations are vulnerable to large statistical errors because of the small number of patients a physician sees in a personal practice. . . .

Now assume that a physician can know the outcomes of recommending a particular procedure for a particular patient. Is it possible to declare whether those outcomes are good or bad? Unfortunately, no. The basic problem is that any procedure has multiple outcomes, some good and some bad. The expected reduction in chest pain that some people will get from coronary artery bypass surgery is accompanied by a splitting of the chest, a chance of an operative mortality, days in the hospital, pain, anxiety, and financial expense. Because the outcomes are multiple and move in different directions, tradeoffs have to be made. And making tradeoffs involves values.

Just as there is a natural variation in how each of us responds to a medical procedure, there is a variation in how we value different outcomes. The fact that General Motors alone produces more than 50 distinct models of automobiles, not to mention dozens of options for each model, demonstrates how tastes about even a single item can vary. Imagine the variation in how different people value pain, disability, operative mortality, life expectancy, a day in a hospital, and who is going to feed the dogs. . . .

[B]ecause decisions about procedures are typically made by physicians on behalf of their patients, the physicians must infer their patients' values, and keep them distinct from their own personal preferences. This raises the second problem, communication. It is difficult enough to assess one's own values about the outcomes of a complicated decision (think about switching jobs); consider having someone else try to learn your thoughts and do it for you. The room for error in communications can be appreciated by returning to the experiment in which four physicians asked 993 coal miners about cough, shortness of breath, pain, and sputum. The variation in their reports of responses to a simple question like, "Do you have a cough?" was large [from 150 to 300 percent variation in reporting the symptom present]; imagine a question like, "How do you feel about operative morality?"

PUTTING IT ALL TOGETHER

The final decision about how to manage a patient requires synthesizing all the information about a disease, the patient, signs and symptoms, the effectiveness of dozens of tests and treatments, outcomes and values. All of this must be done without knowing precisely what the patient has, with uncertainty about signs and symptoms, with imperfect knowledge of the sensitivity and specificity of tests, with no training in manipulating probabilities, with incomplete and biased information about outcomes, and with no language for communicating or assessing values. If each piece of this puzzle is difficult, it is even more difficult for anyone to synthesize all the information and be certain of the answer. It would be an extremely hard task for a research team; there is no hope that it could occur with any precision in the head of a busy clinician. Hence the wide variability in the estimates physicians place on the values of procedures.

[A] final example document[s] how difficult it is to combine information from many sources to estimate the value of a particular procedure. . . . A survey of 1,000 11-year-old schoolchildren in New York City found that 65 percent had undergone tonsillectomy. The remaining children were sent for examinations to a group of physicians and 45 percent were selected for tonsillectomy. Those rejected were examined by another group of physicians and 46 percent were selected for surgery. When the remaining children were examined again by another group of physicians, a similar percent were recommended for tonsillectomy, leaving only 65 students. At that point, the study was halted for lack of physicians.

CONSEQUENCES

The view of anyone who wants a close look at the consequences of different medical procedures is, at best, smoky. Some procedures may present a clear picture, and their value, or lack of it, may be obvious; putting a finger on a bleeding carotid artery is an extreme example. But for many, if not most medical procedures, we can only see shadows and gross movements. We usually know the direction in which various outcome measures can move when a medical activity is undertaken, but we typically do not know the probabilities they will move in those directions, or how far they will move. We certainly do not know how a particular individual will respond. Words like "rare," "common," and "a lot" must be used instead of "one out of 1,000," or "seven on a scale of one to ten."

There is also a strong tendency to oversimplify. One of the easiest ways to fit a large problem in our minds is to lop off huge parts of it. In medical decisions, one option is to focus on length of life and discount inconvenience, pain, disability, short-term risks, and financial costs. A physician can also draw on a number of simplifying heuristics. Anyone uncomfortable dealing with probabilities can use the heuristic, "If there is any chance of (the disease), the (procedure) should be performed." If one cannot estimate the number of people to be saved, one can use the heuristic, "If but one patient is saved, the effort is worthwhile." If one cannot contemplate alternative uses of resources that might deliver a greater benefit to a population, there is the heuristic, "Costs should not be considered in decisions about individual patients." There is a general purpose heuristic, "When in doubt, do it." Or as one investigator wrote, "An error of commission is to be preferred to an error of omission." Unfortunately, a large number of incentives encourage simplifications that lead to overutilization. It is time-consuming, mentally taxing, and often threatening to colleagues for a physician to undertake a deep analysis of a confusing clinical problem. A physician is less likely to be sued for doing too much than too little. Most physicians' incomes go up if they do more, and go down if they do less. Hospitals get to fill more beds and bill for more procedures, laboratories collect more money for services, and companies sell more drugs, devices, and instruments. The more that is done, the more the providers win. The losers are patients, consumers, and taxpayers—anyone who has to undergo a valueless procedure or pay the bill.

In the end, given all the uncertainties, incentives, and heuristics, a physician will have to do what is comfortable. If it is admitted that the uncertainty surrounding the use of a procedure is great, and that there is no way to identify for certain what is best, or to prove that any particular action is right or wrong, the safest and most comfortable position is to do what others are doing. The applicable maxim is "safety in numbers." A physician who follows the practices of his or her colleagues is safe from criticism, free from having to explain his or her actions, and defended by the concurrence of colleagues.

Notes: Medical Decisionmaking

1. *The Nature of Medical Judgment.* An even better sense of medical decisionmaking can be had from examining a range of particular medical cases. To some extent, this is possible by reading the cases in this book, but for the most part the intricacies of the medical decisions are described in only an abbreviated fashion. A good example of one, full-length case discussion, which illustrates many of the dimensions of uncertainty of judgment described by David Eddy, is provided on the Web site for this book, www.health-law.org. For additional readings on the nature of medical judgment, see Kathryn Montgomery, How Doctors Think (2006); Jerome Grupman, How Doctors Think (2007); Atul Gawande, Complications: A Surgeon's Notes on an Imperfect Science (2002); Kathryn Hunter, Doctors' Stories: The Narrative Structure of Medical Knowledge (1991).

2. *Medical Terminology.* Prior editions of this book contained information about medical terminology, medical science, and anatomy. Lawyers who practice in this field must eventually acquire a fair amount of medical knowledge, and many law students enjoy learning something about a different profession's specialized vocabulary. Others see medical terminology as an obstacle to understanding what's really happening in these cases. We have chosen to cater to the latter group; our feeling is that if you end up working in this field, you will have plenty of opportunity to learn the terminology later. Here, when cases contain uncommon medical terms, we will define them for you. If we fail to do so, most terms used in this book are contained in better-quality general dictionaries. For those who want more specialized information, here is a sampling of medical dictionaries, some written especially for lawyers and others for medical professionals or for the lay public: Dorland's Illustrated Medical Dictionary; Slee's Health Care Terms; Taber's Cyclopedic Medical Dictionary.

■ LAW AND MEDICINE
William J. Curran
1st ed. 1960

There may have been a time when doctors and lawyers had much in common, but today their environments are radically divergent and the problem of mutual understanding is a real one. The doctor is trained in a dynamic and experimental science, he is seeking truth in a physical world. He is steeped in the practical judgment, though he avoids generalization. The lawyer, on the other hand, lives within the generalities of the law. The courts apply justice through the advocacy system and seek truth through the burden of proof. When the doctor or other medical person comes into contact with the courts and lawyers, he is often mystified and is generally impatient with the conservatism of the courts in accepting the advances of science. The lawyer often does not seem to the doctor to be seeking truth, but only to place blame.

Most lawyers are Aristotelian in method, if not in philosophy. So are law students by the time they are seniors. That is to say, they work from settled principles on stated fact situations. While they are seeking the results of their deductive logic, their facts remain unchanged. This is not the case in science and in medicine. The scientist seeks truth within the scientific method. The physician is also an experimentalist, an empiricist. At times, however, he does not like being called a scientist, particularly when he is treating a patient. Then he may prefer the title of artisan—but still an empirical artisan.

The failure to understand the basic difference in method between doctors and lawyers is often a stumbling block to greater cooperation between the two professions. It often leads the lawyer into error in presenting the medical issues in a legal action. It may seem obvious that a lawyer should understand the physician's methods as well as his conclusions. Yet, when the attorney accepts a case and prepares it for trial, he tends not to do this. If his client has a back injury, he is interested only in the doctor's conclusions in regard to that injury. He may study the basis for the physician's conclusions in regard to this case, but he rarely does anything more until the next case comes along when again he is interested only in *that* injury. . . .

■ PHYSICIANS VERSUS LAWYERS: A CONFLICT OF CULTURES
Daniel M. Fox*
AIDS and the Law (H. Dalton & S. Burris eds., 1987)

If we are to move in the direction of cooperation rather than conflict, we must understand the roots of the antagonism between the professions and the contemporary forces that threaten to deepen it.

I emphasize physicians' antagonism to lawyers, because I suspect that most lawyers are not normally antagonistic toward physicians. Physicians, on the other

---

* Daniel Fox is widely known and published in the health care public policy field. He is the president of the Milbank Memorial Fund, and he previously held various positions in academics and government.

hand, believe they are being taken advantage of by lawyers who do not understand medicine or value it properly. They are, moreover, mortified because the conflict is usually displayed in public settings controlled by lawyers — court proceedings and legislative hearings.

The conflict between physicians and lawyers, though it is rooted in the modern history of the two professions, has become more intense in recent years as the authority most people accord to physicians has diminished. Some physicians accuse lawyers of helping to undermine public confidence in them by mindlessly pursuing malpractice litigation. Many attribute their rising premiums for malpractice insurance to the work of greedy and unscrupulous lawyers. Physicians often blame lawyers for the mass of regulations that burden them. In an astonishing display of professional bigotry, the new president of the Association of American Medical Colleges told a medical school graduating class in June 1986, "We're swimming in shark-infested waters where the sharks are lawyers."

To most physicians, adversarial proceedings are an ineffective and irrational method for resolving conflict. Where Anglo-American lawyers presume that a person accused of a crime is innocent until proven guilty in a court of law, physicians believe it is dangerous to make any presumption before examining evidence. Similarly, most physicians do not understand the history or the logic of lawyers' claim that formalized conflict between plaintiffs and defendants in a courtroom or around a table resolves disagreements with reasonable equity and preserves social peace.

Physicians are trained to rely on two methods of addressing conflicts about data and their interpretation. The first method is the assertion of authority from the top of a hierarchy in which power is derived from knowledge. The second method is peer review discussion to consensus among experts of roughly equal standing and attainment. Both methods, the hierarchical and the consensual, rest on the assumption that truth is best determined by experts. . . .

Note: Law vs. Medicine: A Culture Clash

Here are some additional perspectives on the differences and commonalities between doctors and lawyers:

> Doctors and lawyers are not alike, either by disposition, or by education, or in practice. Even though the basic objectives of our two professions are the same, namely, to serve society, the education and practice of each are worlds apart. . . . The adversary system squeezes the doctor into roles and settings with which he is unfamiliar and in which he is ineffective. . . . The adversary system, as effective as it may be in achieving justice, is clearly ineffective in establishing truth in medicine. Charles G. Guild, III, M.D., Lawyers Doctors and Medical Malpractice: A Surgeon Reacts, *in* E. D. Shapiro et al., Medical Malpractice (2d ed. 1966).

> If a doctor were called on to treat typhoid fever he would probably try to find out what kind of water the patient drank, and clean out the well so that no one else could get typhoid from the same source. But if a lawyer were called on to treat a typhoid patient he would give him thirty days in jail, and then he would think that nobody else would ever dare to drink the impure water. If the patient got well

in fifteen days, he would be kept until his time was up; if the disease was worse at the end of thirty days, the patient would be released because his time was out. As a rule, lawyers are not scientists. They think that there is only one way to make men good, and that is to put them in such terror that they do not dare to do bad. Meyer Levin, Compulsion (1956) (taken from the defense attorney's closing argument to the jury).

For additional books and articles that illustrate differences of professional approach, ethical principles, and cultural values between lawyers and physicians (not necessarily with that intention in mind), see J. Katz, The Silent World of Doctor and Patient (1984); Peter Jacobson & Gregg Bloche, Improving Relations Between Attorneys and Physicians, 294 JAMA 2083 (2005); William M. Sage, The Lawyerization of Medicine, 26 J. Health Pol. Pol'y & L. 1179 (2001); Alan A. Stone, Law's Influence on Medicine and Medical Ethics, 312 New Eng. J. Med. 310 (1985).

5. Evidence-Based Medicine

■ OVERSIGHT OF THE QUALITY OF MEDICAL CARE: REGULATION, MANAGEMENT, OR THE MARKET?*
Timothy Jost**
3 Ariz. L. Rev. 825 (1995)

The most important factor driving change has been an ever quickening reorganization of the health care industry, a reorganization that is becoming revolutionary rather than simply evolutionary in nature. The prevalence of the sole practitioner mode that dominated medical practice until the last two decades continues to decline as group practices and physicians employed by health care institutions or managed care organizations or allied with hospitals in integrated delivery systems become ever more common. The large health care corporation, whose power was long resisted by the medical profession, seems now to have carried the day.[83] Both institutions that provide health care, such as hospitals or nursing homes, and entities that pay for health care, including insurers or self-insured employers, have become much more interested in overseeing the work of the professionals who practice within them or whose care they purchase. The emergence of managed care organizations that both pay for and provide care, moreover, gives lay managers even greater control over medical practice.

---

* Copyright © 1995 by the Arizona Board of Regents. Reprinted by permission.

** Newton D. Baker, Professor of Law, Washington and Lee University School of Law.

[83] This transformation was noted early on by Paul Starr, The Social Transformation of American Medicine 40-44 (1982), at 420-49 and Arnold S. Relman, The New Medical-Industrial Complex, 303 New Eng. J. Med. 963 (1980), and has continued at an accelerating pace. . . . It has also been noted in the legal literature, where some welcome it, Mark Hall, Institutional Control of Physician Behavior: Legal Barriers to Health Care Cost Containment, 137 U. Pa. L. Rev. 431 (1988), and others decry it, David Frankford, Creating and Dividing the Fruits of Collective Economic Activity: Referrals Among Health Care Providers, 89 Colum. L. Rev. 1861 (1989).

In tandem with this change, and perhaps driven by it, has come a revolution in information processing. Developments in information processing technology in the second half of the twentieth century have dramatically enhanced the ability of the health care industry to collect, process, and analyze data. These advances create the possibility of engaging in analysis of the outcomes of health care processes.[87] Data describing large numbers of patients can be studied to determine the efficacy of alternative diagnostic and treatment modalities. This information in turn contributes to the construction of practice guidelines, which describe best practices. These practice guidelines can in some instances be reduced to algorithms that can be used to enable computer review of the quality of the practices of individual practitioners or institutions.[90] Outcome data can also be used to support pattern analysis, comparing the outcome of the care provided by individual practitioners or institutions with average or optimal practice as revealed by outcome analysis. . . .

[I]nformation processing technology and industry reorganization permit much greater oversight of health care by lay managers. Once it is possible to describe the quality of physician practices in terms that lay managers can apply or in algorithms that computers can manipulate, the genie is out of the bottle and physician dominance of quality oversight has been broken. In the last half-decade, health care institutions have begun to move from traditional physician-led quality assurance to a new management-led and data-driven philosophy of quality oversight: continuous quality improvement or total quality management.

The continuous quality improvement or total quality management movement is based on quality improvement strategies developed in the industrial setting. The ideas of Demming, Juran, Schewhart and others had a significant impact on Japanese, and then American industrial production. Within the past few years these ideas have begun to be applied widely in health care as well.[99] . . .

The quality improvement philosophy is based on several principles: . . . Energy is better directed toward improving the system through which care is delivered than toward looking for "bad apples." Most quality deficiencies are caused by faulty systems, not by incompetents working within those systems. One can accomplish more, therefore, by raising the mean of the performance curve than by chopping off the tail. This emphasis on improving the average performance rather than punishing the bad actor is perhaps the clearest distinction between quality improvement and traditional quality assurance, which has tended to be preoccupied with looking for "bad apples." This orientation gives quality improvement a more positive tone than quality assurance, thus making it more palatable to hospital employees and medical staff. It also results in a heavy emphasis on process and on systems. . . .

---

[87] See, e.g., Paul M. Ellwood, Shattuck Lecture — Outcomes Management: A Technology of Patient Experience, 318 New Eng. J. Med. 1549 (1988); Arnold Relman, Assessment and Accountability: The Third Revolution in Medical Care, 319 New Eng. J. Med. 1220 (1988).

[90] See William L. Roper et al., Effectiveness in Health Care: An Initiative to Evaluate and Improve Medical Practice, 319 New Eng. J. Med. 1197 (1988) (describing HCFA's interest in outcomes research).

[99] See, e.g., Donald M. Berwick et al., Curing Health Care: New Strategies for Quality Improvement (1991); Ellen J. Gaucher & Richard J. Coffey, Total Quality in Healthcare: From Theory to Practice (1993). . . .

Any program directed at improving or assuring quality—be it private, public, or some combination of the two—will have to find a means to affect the behavior of individuals or institutions. A key question that must be answered, therefore, before turning to a consideration of the comparative strengths of various institutions that might address quality problems, is what levers are available to improve the quality of professional judgment and of health care production processes.

The first such lever is the generation and dissemination of information. . . . [H]owever, expectations as to what can be accomplished through data collection and dissemination for influencing medical judgment should be modest. In the final analysis, medical practice cannot be reduced to statistics.

Second, . . . the culture of professionalism has played an important role in stimulating quality. The professional was a gentleman who rose above the crass concerns of merchants to dedicate himself to serving the needs of his patients with clear and undivided judgment. The concern that licensure boards have traditionally shown for professional ethics and for unprofessional conduct can be understood in part as an attempt to suppress normative error, and thus to sustain a culture in which quality was valued and promoted.

[Third,] . . . sanctions have a legitimate role, however marginal, in encouraging quality. Sanctions can be used to exclude from the market practitioners or institutions that totally lack the capacity to make appropriate professional judgments or to carry out effective production processes. Corrective or educative sanctions can improve the performance of those who have the basic capacity to do well but need information or direction. Punitive and deterrent sanctions may be appropriate for normative deficiencies that result in technical or judgment errors or for careless production processes. . . .

Fourth, incentives have an obvious role to play in encouraging quality. The market stimulates quality in other sectors of the economy by directing business toward those merchants who can deliver value for money. Incentives such as money, recognition, power, independence, or anything else of value can be used to encourage professionals or institutions to improve production processes or to be more attentive in making professional judgments and applying professional skills. . . .

Some commentators believe that the information processing revolution, aided by market restructuring, offers the promise of overcoming the traditional deficiencies of health care markets. If consumers have information about the comparative outcomes of professional care—it is contended—they can evaluate the quality of that care without needing to understand the professional judgments that produced those outcomes. If consumers possess comparative information about patient satisfaction with health care institutions, they need not understand the production processes that produced patient satisfaction in one institution or dissatisfaction in another. In the final analysis, we are told that if consumers can be given "report cards," the market will produce quality. But has the information revolution solved the market failures that originally justified regulation?

There are reasons to believe that it has not, or at least not totally. . . . The idea of comparison shopping for health care raises a host of methodological questions with respect to data collection and presentation. . . . [A] host of "noise" problems must be overcome. Outcomes data are meaningless or misleading unless they are adjusted for severity of illness, the presence of do not resuscitate orders or comorbidities, and other factors not under the control of providers. The history of the Health Care Financing Administration (HCFA) mortality surveys shows how devilishly difficult it can be both to adjust adequately for the host of exogenous factors that can affect mortality and to quell suspicions that attempted adjustments are not adequate. HCFA [now known as CMS] ultimately dropped its reporting because it determined that a high percentage of the lowest performing hospitals were institutions that served the poorest and most needy patients and because it could not solve intractable problems with its measurement methodology.[212] Similarly, California's outcome assessment program found that some of the state's most sophisticated hospitals rated poorly on outcome indices because they had been most aggressive in reporting complications of surgery to maximize Medicare Diagnosis Related Group reimbursement. Adjusting for risk, on the other hand, permits providers to play games with outcome reporting systems by inflating risk data about their patients, thus improving risk adjusted performance. . . . Adjusting for age, for example, may mask problems in treatment of the elderly. Finally, even if perfect risk adjustment could be achieved, some providers are still likely to appear as outliers simply because of random variation, a factor unlikely to be appreciated by consumers. . . .

How consumers will use the report card is also problematic. . . . If a report card covers a dozen plans or institutions, each with 50 quality measures, consumers would be dealing with 600 discrete bits of information — many of which might be continuous rather than binary variables — and a nearly infinite variety of combinations of variables. One potential result in this information-rich environment would be "information overload." Consumers might simply be overwhelmed by the quantity of information, and make choices randomly related to their actual optimal choice. . . .

The deficiencies of the market . . . ensure the existence of a continuing legitimate role for quality regulation. . . . The costs of government intervention point, however, to a limited rather than an expansive government role. . . . The task of professional regulation needs to be refocused on assuring initial and ongoing competency and the professionalism that supports it. Prevention of error should by and large be left to management, and accountability to consumers be assured through the market and through an independent ombudspersons' office responsible for investigating consumer complaints. All the resources of modern technology must then be brought to bear on the residual tasks of regulation.

Note: Outcomes and Effectiveness Assessment

The Information Revolution. Various aspects of the movement toward "evidence-based medicine" have generated a voluminous literature, some descriptive, some analytical, and some critical. For a sampling, in addition to the sources Timothy Jost cites, see Symposium, 24(1) Health Affairs (Jan. 2005); Symposium, 23 Health Affairs (Oct. 2004) (special supp.); Troyen A. Brennan &

---

[212] Jesse Green et al., Analyzing Hospital Mortality: The Consequences of Diversity in Patient Mix, 265 JAMA 1849, 1849-1853 (1991); Rolla Edward Park et al., Explaining Variations in Hospital Death Rates, 264 JAMA 484 (1990).

Donald M. Berwick, New Rules: Regulation, Markets and the Quality of American Health Care (1996); Michael L. Millenson, Demanding Medical Excellence (1997); David Frankford, Scientism and Economism in the Regulation of Health Care, 19 J. Health Pol. Pol'y & L. 773 (1994); Mark A. Hall et al., Measuring Medical Practice Patterns: Sources of Evidence from Health Services Research, 37 Wake Forest L. Rev. 779 (2002); John V. Jacobi, Patients at a Loss: Protecting Health Care Consumers Through Data Driven Quality Assurance, 45 Kan. L. Rev. 705 (1997); Wendy Mariner, Outcomes Assessment in Health Care Reform: Promise and Limitations, 20 Am. J.L. & Med. 37 (1994); Lars Noah, Medicine's Epistemology: Mapping the Haphazard Diffusion of Knowledge in the Biomedical Community, 44 Ariz. L. Rev. 373 (2002); Sandra Tanenbaum, Knowing and Acting in Medical Practice: The Epistemological Politics of Outcomes Research, 19 J. Health Pol. Pol'y & L. 27 (1994); Sandra Tanenbaum, What Physicians Know, 329 New Eng. J. Med. 1268 (1993); Symposium, 17(4) Health Aff. (July-Aug. 1998); Symposium, 76 Milbank Q. 515 (1998).

Medicare now requires hospitals, in order to obtain full reimbursement, to participate in public reporting of ten comparative quality measures (focused on heart failure and pneumonia). See http://www.cms.hhs.gov/HospitalQualityInits/. For studies that examine the impact of comparative outcomes measures such as report cards on actual consumer and provider behavior, see D. Mukamel & A. Mushlin, Quality of Care Information Makes a Difference, 36 Med. Care 945 (1998) (finding some impact); Mark Chassin, Achieving and Sustaining Improved Quality, 21(4) Health Aff. 40 (July 2002) (same); S. Mennemeyer et al., Death and Reputation: How Consumers Acted Upon HCFA Mortality Information, 34 Inquiry 117 (1997) (finding no impact); Ashish K. Jha & Arnold M. Epstein, The Predictive Accuracy of the New York State Coronary Artery Bypass Surgery Report-Card System, 25(3) Health Aff. 844 (June 2006) (same); David Dranove, Daniel Kessler, Mark McClellan, & Mark Satterthwaite, Is More Information Better? The Effects of "Report Cards" on Health Care Providers, 111 J. Pol. Econ. 555 (2003) (finding negative impact by prompting physicians and hospitals to avoid sicker or more severe cases). For a critique of the reliability and usefulness of physician report cards, see Timothy Hofer et al., The Unreliability of Individual Physician "Report Cards" for Assessing the Costs and Quality of Care of a Chronic Disease, 281 JAMA 2098 (1999) (finding that report cards "were unable to detect reliably true practice differences" and that their use "may foster an environment in which physicians can most easily avoid being penalized by avoiding . . . [more difficult patients who have not responded well to treatment]"); Comment, 29 Pepp. L. Rev. 585 (2002).

C. THE HEALTH CARE FINANCING AND DELIVERY SYSTEM

The readings in this section describe the economic and regulatory forces that shape how health care is delivered in the United States. All of us have some exposure to the world of medicine but few law students have reason to understand the intricacies of this financing and delivery system and how it has developed.

This understanding is essential in a course that focuses on the full range of legal and public policy issues pertaining to the delivery and payment for medical care. Those issues have naturally taken shape according to the structural components and historical growth of the health care sector and its various institutions.

We begin with a rudimentary overview of the history of health insurance and of the principal events that have shaped its development. Included in this is a discussion of whether there is a "crisis" in American medicine. We finish with an introduction to more recent innovations such as HMOs. As you read through this alphabet soup of actors, institutions, and acronyms, rather than memorizing all the details, try to construct a coherent story line of how the health care sector took shape over time and how its various pieces interconnect at present. You don't need to master all the details now, for they will reemerge throughout the course, but it will be easier to remember them at the end if you have an initial framework to attach them to.

1. Insurance and Regulation

■ U.S. HEALTH CARE COVERAGE AND COSTS: HISTORICAL DEVELOPMENT AND CHOICES FOR THE [FUTURE]*
Randall R. Bovbjerg, Charles C. Griffin, & Caitlin Carroll**
21 J.L. Med. & Ethics 141 (1993)

American health policy today faces dual problems of too little coverage at too high a cost. Our combined system of private and public financing leaves about one seventh of the population without insurance coverage from any source. At the same time, the coverage Americans do have costs ever-larger shares of our country's productive capacity, well above what other countries pay and what many people, health plans, businesses, and governments want to pay. This "paradox of excess and deprivation"[2] results from the incremental approach the U.S. has taken to solving incompatible policy goals of widening health insurance coverage while trying to control costs and maintain a high level of quality. This essay examines the American record over the past 60 years in pursuing this incremental approach and draws from it lessons for the current effort to reform the system.

PRE-1929: ERECTING MEDICAL INFRASTRUCTURE AND ESCHEWING NATIONAL HEALTH INSURANCE

Neither medicine nor health coverage was very advanced prior to the Great Depression.[3] Accustomed to the medical miracles of the late twentieth century,

---

* Reprinted with the permission of the American Society of Law, Medicine & Ethics. Updated by the editors of this book to reflect recent developments.

** The authors are, respectively, Senior Research Associate, Health Policy Center, The Urban Institute: Economist, The World Bank; and Research Assistant, The Urban Institute. Bovbjerg's name is pronounced "Boh-berg."

[2] Alain Enthoven and Richard Kronick, A Consumer-Choice Health Plan for the 1980s, 320 New Eng. J. Med. 29 (1989).

[3] Joseph A. Califano, Jr., America's Health Care Revolution: Who Lives? Who Dies? Who Pays? (New York: Random House, 1986); Paul Starr, The Social Transformation of American Medicine (New York: Basic Books, 1982); Edward Shorter, The Health Century (New York: Doubleday, 1987);

one tends to forget that nineteenth century doctors could do little for patients, and hospitals were mainly charity wards where the poor went to die. Medical practice was totally unregulated, and competing theories of disease and treatment flourished. Antiseptic surgery developed only in the latter part of the century. At that same time, local, state, and national medical associations began to promote professional standards (of their own design) as well as the enactment of state licensure requirements. By 1912, it could be said that "for the first time in human history, a random patient with a random disease consulting a doctor chosen at random stands a better than 50/50 chance of benefiting from the encounter."[4]

By the 1920s, today's familiar patterns of accreditation and licensure were set for medical education, medical practice, and hospitals. Doctors practiced almost exclusively as solo, office-based practitioners on a fee-for-service basis. Physicians treated their own patients in hospitals, rather than referring them to hospital-based specialists, often salaried, as in much of Europe. Community-based, voluntary hospitals were well established in most of the country, with not-for-profits dominant, basically serving as workshops for community physicians. Still, for most Americans, illness, injury, and early death were more to be suffered than helped by a doctor, much less insured against.

A good thing, too, for insurance coverage was virtually nonexistent, whether private or public. True, some private insurers were willing to write a kind of "health insurance," but only covering loss of income from disability, not physician or hospital bills. Historically, insurance theory — and commercial insurers — thought the term *health insurance* an oxymoron. The reason was that sickness, or more precisely, the use of medical services, was not believed to be an "insurable risk." . . .

Insurance may also have seemed less important because expenses for available care were not large relative to typical incomes. The average day in a hospital cost only a few dollars, and physicians did not charge — or earn — large amounts. . . . In short, in the era before health insurance, when patients themselves paid for almost all health care, the medical economy behaved much like the rest of the economy and was small relative to the whole. All together, the nation spent only about 3.5 percent of gross [domestic] product (GDP) on health care (Table 1).

1929-1940: ENTER HEALTH INSURANCE

Then came the birth of the "Blues," the true beginnings of health insurance as we now know it. . . . Blue Cross plans were organized by hospital associations, typically at the state level. The first Blues-style hospital plan started in 1934 with special New York enabling legislation. Very quickly, physicians followed suit, organizing their own Blue Shield plans, first for in-hospital surgical care, then for medical services as well. Blues plans had unique service areas, not competing with one another, and had strong ties to hospital associations and medical

---

Rosemary Stevens, In Sickness and in Wealth: American Hospitals in the Twentieth Century (New York: Basic Books 1989).

[4] This contemporaneous pronouncement came from Harvard Professor L. Henderson, calling the year 1912 "a Great Divide." Quoted in Richard Harris, A Sacred Trust (New York: New American Library, 1966), 5.

societies. . . .[8] By 1938, 1.4 million Americans were enrolled in 38 Blue Cross plans. Only after the hospitals and the Blues proved the market viable did ordinary insurers begin to write coverage for medical bills. . . .

Table 1
The Rising Tide of Medical Costs: 1929-[2005]

Time period	Health care share of GDP at end of period (percent)	Annual growth in real health care dollars, per capita (percent)
1929	3.5	—
1929-1940	4.0	1.4
1940-1950	4.5	4.0
1950-1960	5.3	3.6
1960-1970	7.3	6.5
1970-1980	9.1	3.8
1980-1990	12.2	4.4
1990-2000	14.1	~4.5
2001-2005	16.0	~4

These early Blues, followed by commercial plans, set the pattern for health coverage that still dominates U.S. health financing. Patients were given "free choice of provider" (able to use almost any provider, not limited to contracted doctors or hospitals), with relatively low out-of-pocket cost at the time of service. Providers received retroactive fee-for-service payment (not an advance salary, capitation, or contracted amount) for all services they deemed "medically necessary." Risk pooling and financing came from insurers acting as "third parties," at a remove both from patients (first parties) and from providers (second). . . .

At first, there was no cost problem, for when coverage reached few people, benefit and payment levels were low, and medical technology did not exist to provide very sophisticated care. There appears to have been virtually no appreciation for how expensive this mode of operation would ultimately prove to be.

Blues plans were publicly perceived to have a more social role than "ordinary" insurance. Their not-for-profit status, chartered as "hospital (and medical) service corporations," rather than as insurance companies, reflect this perception. . . . In hindsight, the Blues also reflected the economic and professional self-interest of medical providers, seeking to strengthen private practice, institutionalize fee-for-service billing, and promote fiscal and clinical independence from outside control. They helped strengthen providers as private entrepreneurs. . . .

---

[8] Odin W. Anderson, Blue Cross Since 1929 (Cambridge, MA: Ballinger Publishing Co., 1975); Sylvia Law, Blue Cross: What Went Wrong? (2d ed.) (New Haven: Yale University Press, 1976); Paul Starr, The Social Transformation of American Medicine (New York: Basic Books, 1982).

THE 1940s [AND 1950s]: WORKPLACE GROUPS:
GREAT LEAP FORWARD

Private health insurance took a great leap forward in the 1940s. The economy moved back to full employment, manufacturing surged, and urbanization accelerated. It became rather common for manufacturing workers, especially through unions, to seek group health coverage as a fringe benefit of employment. . . . The tax treatment of fringe benefits encouraged employment group coverage. IRS administrative decisions, later codified in the Internal Revenue Code of 1954, deemed such benefits taxable neither to employer nor employee. Hence, through workplace insurance, health services could be prepaid with pre-tax dollars, reducing the cost of private coverage by savings on tax otherwise due. As tax levels rose, this tax subsidy became a more valuable benefit. . . .

The federal government supplied some health services, but only to identifiably "federal" populations. For example, the armed services, veterans, and the merchant marine all had dedicated hospitals; and the Indian Health Service operated on reservations. Interestingly, federal coverage of these populations was achieved predominantly through direct service delivery operations rather than through the financing of purchases from private providers. At the local level, states and municipalities also ran some hospitals and medical clinics. Local institutions often specialized in tuberculosis or mental health care, but some also provided general acute care, notably cities' public general hospitals. Most hospital care, however, remained the province of not-for-profit community hospitals.

This era also brought heavier public subsidy to the mainly private suppliers of care. Immediately after the war, the federal Hill-Burton Act made available grants to expand and modernize hospital capacity, which had suffered during the war. Soon thereafter, federal grants were also made available for medical education. In addition, with the post-war enlargement of the National Institutes of Health, federal policy greatly expanded support for basic research. . . .

The 1950s brought health coverage to much of the middle class through a combination of private action and the tax subsidy. By 1960, over two thirds of Americans had private coverage, but over 55 percent of personal health spending still came from patients' own pockets rather than from insurance coverage. . . .

The beginnings of price increases were becoming visible, though without being considered a major problem. . . . As one example, the average hospital expense/day was only $7.98 in 1950, but rose to $16.46 in 1960. . . .

THE 1960s [AND 1970s]: ENTER BIG GOVERNMENT,
INCREMENTALLY

The sixties were marked by further incremental expansion of coverage, with most attention paid to expansion of government-subsidized care for those omitted by private coverage (the poor, the frail, the aged) through the intervention of federal medical entitlement programs. The theory was that beneficiaries would be entitled to medical service. An emerging reality was that providers were entitled to collect what they wanted from government. The decade began with John F. Kennedy's newly activist leadership seeking a "New Frontier" that included federal medical coverage, at least for the elderly. Strong opposition came from fiscal conservatives and from medical interest groups, spearheaded by the AMA [American Medical Association], which supported voluntary private insurance. Opponents objected on the ground that "socialized medicine" would ultimately allow federal bureaucrats to control clinical decisions in medicine (as well as medical incomes). . . .

After President Lyndon B. Johnson's landslide victory in 1964, federally funded *Medicare* was enacted to provide conventional third-party coverage for the aged (those within the Social Security system and past retirement age) and the disabled (those unable to work). The program was patterned on the Blues, with automatic entitlement to Part A hospital coverage (parallel to Blue Cross) and voluntary enrollment in Part B physician and other coverage (Blue Shield). The state-federal *Medicaid* program was created, almost as an afterthought, to cover what one might call the "deserving" poor (basically those unable to work by virtue of age, blindness, or disability). Medicaid built on the Kerr-Mills precedent of state discretion operating within a federal set of rules. . . .

By virtue of the vastly increased public role in financing coverage as well as continued growth in private coverage, the pattern of U.S. health spending shifted markedly. Whereas in 1960 over half of total health spending was still met by patients' direct out-of-pocket payments, by 1970 the patient's share had dropped to only 35 percent, while the federal share doubled to over 20 percent. . . .

Medicare essentially adapted Blues' reimbursement principles to public payment; the prime objective was to give beneficiaries access to private providers. The program was created as a third party outside medical transactions, responsible for reimbursing hospitals for their "reasonable costs" retrospectively and physicians for their actual submitted bills. . . . Superimposing this public largesse on top of existing payment mechanisms favorable to providers understandably failed to promote cost-conscious tradeoffs between value and cost of services.

This decade of greatly subsidized demand and provider-driven payment spurred further hospital expansion and upgrading, as well as the entry of many new physicians, as manpower policy simultaneously responded to a perceived "physician shortage." Medical price rises became much larger than the general rate of inflation. Average hospital expense per day, for example, rose from $16.46 in 1960 to $53.95 in 1970. As one early-seventies commentator noted, the price of a hospital room in the early 1950s was about that of a good hotel, but by end of the 1960s, hospital prices had left hotels well behind. Usage of services also increased. . . .

Much of the 1960s growth was intentional, especially for serving the elderly and others previously without coverage. Such expansion continues to seem desirable from today's perspective. In hindsight, however, a key problem was not mere price increases and new benefits to encourage new services, but rather the "blank check" fashion in which expanded coverage was removed entirely from disciplined evaluation of the benefit obtained from new services. Neither public nor private payers made any attempt to signal *how much* new care was enough, either through payment rules and incentives or through explicit provisions about benefits or utilization of care. Medical "need" was once thought to set a natural limit on services; in fact, "need" is an expansive, not a limiting concept. All signals were for more of everything: scientific research and technological innovation, insurance benefits, and clinical services. Given free rein, medical care can expand enormously as we have since learned. Additional care can almost always offer some level of legitimate benefit to some patients. . . .

By the end of the 1960s, the basic patterns of U.S. health care delivery and financing were set: Private hospitals and physicians delivered most health care. Employers voluntarily provided private insurance to workers. Governments provided public insurance to those too old or unable to work (through public plans modelled on the private ones). All plans retrospectively reimbursed provider-set charges or costs. Each plan paid separately for its own financing, based on its own experience. Generous fee-for-service reimbursement encouraged even more services, with no built-in controls on price or utilization. . . .

[T]he 1970s became the first decade of "cost containment." Health prices were frozen (along with all others), then regulated by federal wage and price controls under President Nixon's "Economic Stabilization Program." Health controls were kept on for some months after others were lifted, and costs were effectively held down. Thereafter, inflation returned with a vengeance. There were so many manifestations of increased cost consciousness in the public sector that only the highlights can be mentioned. For example, a single 1972 omnibus bill strengthened federal health planning regulation, required utilization/quality review of Medicare hospitalizations, and limited the allowed annual growth of prevailing Medicare physician fees. Two years later, the National Health Planning Act required states, under threat of losing all federal health monies, to regulate hospital growth through certificates of need. Also in 1974, the HMO Act, sought reform reflecting a mix of regulation and market-oriented approaches. Many state governments also experimented with "prospective reimbursement" or hospital "rate setting" to control hospital costs, which were (and are) the largest share of health spending. In sharp contrast, the private sector response to rising costs was more muted. . . .

Costs continued to grow rapidly. The medical care CPI again outpaced the CPI for all items. Real medical spending outgrew real GDP by a factor of two, down slightly from the 1960s' two and a half. By 1980, health's share of GDP reached 9.1 percent (Table 1). . . .

THE 1980s: EVERY PLAN FOR ITSELF, AS COSTS RISE AND COVERAGE DROPS

The 1980s began with the self-consciously conservative administration of Ronald W. Reagan, who was philosophically committed to a limited federal role in health care. Still, there were expectations of an actively "pro-competitive" federal reform that would promote private coverage and private economizing. Academic and other theorists had developed such ideas, which were encouraged by the "privatizing" rhetoric of the new administration. . . . Probably the decade's most significant federal action came in 1983, when the administration and Congress collaborated in creating a Prospective Payment System (PPS) for inpatient hospital services under Medicare. In place of retrospective cost-based reimbursement, hospitals were to be paid fixed amounts per case, with rates set in advance for each of nearly 500 types of case, called "DRGs." Under this scheme, each institution is at financial risk for each case; a hospital earns no more for spending more and is able to keep the balance if it spends less. . . .

Some states experimented further with prospective payment for hospitals, either regulating only Medicaid rates or also covering most or all other payers. . . . Other states took market-oriented approaches: Arizona solicited competitive bids for HMO-like plans to cover its first-ever Medicaid program enrollees and California negotiated special hospital discounts for its Medicaid recipients' care through "selective contracting."

The private sector also showed new aggressiveness in attempting to contain costs during the 1980s. . . . Most significantly but with more difficulty, firms increasingly sought to move toward "managed care" and away from open-ended coverage of whatever services doctors and patients choose. Managed care includes not merely HMOs but also new entities called "PPOs" or other plans with limitations on what physicians and what services could be used. . . .

The U.S. has thus tried a mélange of different strategies for cost containment, both regulatory and market-oriented in nature. But all have been incremental (e.g., "managed care" for particular plans, administered prospective pricing for Medicare hospital payments) rather than system-wide (e.g., budgetary limits, restructured rules on insurance choice and pricing). And all have their weaknesses . . . and powerful opponents.

With regard to health care coverage, the 1980s saw the first-ever drop in percentage of the population with coverage, driven by a drop in private health insurance coverage. For 1990, the total share of the population with private coverage dropped 5-10 percentage points. . . .

Many factors helped cause the decline in private coverage, but two were paramount: rising costs and declining insurance pooling. First, the continuing rise in health care costs has made insurance premiums too high to continue to attract new purchasers. . . . Second, risk pools have continued to disaggregate, as more and more firms self-insure and experience rating spreads to ever-smaller groups. This continuing trend means that firms with high-risk employees or a bad year of experience can no longer count on insurance to spread these costs. These problems are worst in the "small group" insurance market (often defined as under 50 or 25 employees). . . . Even those with large-group coverage fear for their coverage. Not only has corporate "downsizing" cost many employees their jobs, but cost-containment has led to sudden medical cutbacks as well. . . .

Some cost-containment efforts did help moderate the rate of growth in health spending, especially for hospital care. . . . Nonetheless, medical spending continued to grow rapidly. During the 1980s, real health care spending grew at 4.4 percent a year, over two and a half times as fast as real GDP, just as in the fast-growth 1960s. Health therefore consumed fully 12.2 percent of GDP in 1990, a total of $666 billion or about $2,566 per capita. . . .

[I]n the 1960s, U.S. health care spending was not far out of line with that of other developed countries, given the higher level of U.S. national income. Since then, especially in the 1980s, U.S. spending as a share of GDP has increased rapidly, whereas other countries' growth has been more controlled. Other developed countries all faced what they considered unacceptable cost increases in the 1970s and 1980s, but almost all implemented social limits on further growth, with significant success. The result is that the U.S. spends far more on health care than any other developed nation. . . .

ENTERING THE [NEW CENTURY]: OMINOUS TRENDS IN COST AND COVERAGE

Health spending is about to grow right off the charts, thanks to the magic of compound interest. The projections are truly staggering for policymakers worried about the federal deficit, workers' earnings, or international competitiveness — and these are not the worst-case scenarios, just extrapolations of current trends. For the year [2005, health spending reached 16 percent of GDP (Table 1), some $2 trillion or about $6,700 per capita], according to federal statisticians. . . . As disquieting as these statistics are, [this] century's "out years" (as budgeters call them) will be even worse: Health's share of GDP is projected to climb to some [20 percent in 2015], mostly paid by government. Such projections assume continuation of today's trends in price inflation, growth in utilization and intensity of services, growth and aging of the population, and other factors. Such numbers greatly inspire reformers. . . .

Where are we headed next? That is the subject of much discussion . . . on Capitol Hill. . . . The political and practical backing for some change seems strong. But we end on a rather pessimistic note. This situation has existed before. Very high expectations attended earlier debates [on national health insurance], yet earlier reform plans all ended as incremental changes to the same basic system. Recent experience shows, however, that a failure to fundamentally reform the system will only put off the day of reckoning, and not for long, as the tide of rising costs continues to erode the gains made over the last four decades. The underlying question is whether the current crisis will conquer the historic inertia of the payment system, which now nurtures a huge economic sector of politically active people. . . .

Health Coverage by Source, 2005

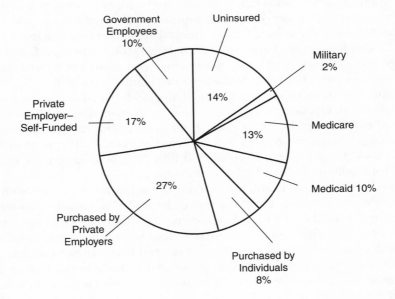

■ THE SAD HISTORY OF HEALTH CARE COST CONTAINMENT AS TOLD IN ONE CHART
Drew E. Altman and Larry Levitt
21(2) Health Affairs 9 (March 2002)*

What [this] Exhibit shows is that no approach our nation has tried, over the past thirty-five years, to control health costs has had a lasting impact. When Medicare and Medicaid passed in the mid-1960s, the new public programs took some of the burden of health spending off of the private sector, but only temporarily. By the late 1960s the rate of increase in private health spending per capita shot up. In the early 1970s wage and price controls had a dramatic impact on health care costs. But again, the impact was short-lived, and the rate of increase in private health spending rose dramatically after a few years. When President Jimmy Carter threatened tough cost containment regulation in the late 1970s, the health care industry organized what it called the "Voluntary Effort." The rate of increase in per capita private-sector health spending fell rapidly but then bounced back within a few years. Managed care and the threat of the Clinton health care reform plan appeared to have had a dramatic impact on the rate of increase in private health spending in the mid-1990s, but by the late 1990s it was on the rise again, reaching double-digit rates of increase by 2001. . . .

**Annual Change in Private Health Spending Per Capita
(Adjusted for Inflation), 1961-2001**

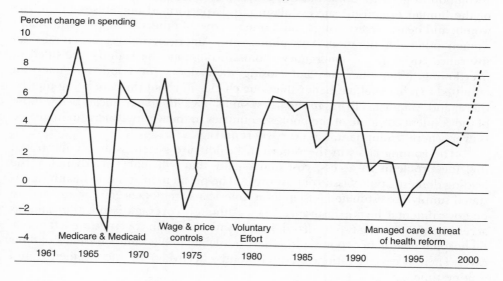

Some believe that we will not get a handle on health care costs as a nation until we are ready to make tough decisions about rationing medical care. An equally plausible scenario is that the apparent failure of all approaches reflects the

---

* Reprinted with the permission of Project Hope.

American people's uncontainable desire for the latest and best health care, and that what we will do in the future is try small things that will work at the margin, complain a lot, but ultimately pay the bill.

2. The Crisis in Coverage and Spending

■ THE FUTURE OF THE AMERICAN HEALTH CARE SYSTEM
Henry T. Greely*
3 Stan. L. & Pol'y Rev. 16 (1991)

It was the best of times, it was the worst of times, it was the age of wisdom, it was the age of foolishness, it was the epoch of belief, it was the epoch of incredulity, it was the season of Light, it was the season of Darkness, it was the spring of hope, it was the winter of despair, we had everything before us, we had nothing before us, we were all going direct to Heaven, we were all going direct the other way — in short, the period was so far like the present period, that some of its noisiest authorities insisted on its being received, for good or for evil, in the superlative degree of comparison only.

Like Dickens's *ancien régime,* today's American medicine is a study in vivid contrasts. Infant mortality in the United States has just reached a record low; the revolution in genetics holds out the promise of unbelievably detailed knowledge of the human organism; successful surgery is performed on fetuses still in the womb; and hearts, livers, lungs, and bone marrow of others recall to life men and women otherwise doomed. Yet [almost one American in six] has no health insurance coverage; . . . emergency rooms throughout the country are filled to overflowing, when they are not closing their doors for good; an American admitted to a hospital has better than one chance in about thirty of being injured there; and Americans living in the worst slums have life expectancies below those of the residents of some of the poorest countries in the world. American medicine is everywhere triumphant, but everywhere in rags. . . .

The coming crisis in the American health care system is amply illustrated [by] the problems in access, cost and quality that will make health policy the leading domestic policy issue of [our time]. The problem of access to health care is stated simply: An estimated [48] million Americans are not covered by any private or governmental health insurance plan. Although coverage is not the same as access, neither are the two divorced. People without health coverage are left to rely on hospital emergency rooms and, where available, public clinics for most of their care. Their access is rationed largely (and effectively) by inconvenience and waiting time. . . .

Cost of a service cannot be considered without also considering the quality of the service received. Measuring quality in health care is difficult, but two general problems, one actual and one perceived, are apparent in American medicine.

---

* Professor of Law, Stanford University.

The actual problem is that health care is an uncertain science and the hospital a dangerous place. This commonplace truth recently took on renewed importance as the Harvard Medical Practice Study published its powerful review of the quality of medical care in New York hospitals. . . . Projecting the percentages across the country leads to the conclusion that about 1.5 million people are injured in hospitals by their medical care each year; about 400,000 of these people are injured by negligence. . . .

The perceived problem with quality is more subtle. Americans have longer — and healthier — life spans than ever before, but we do not *feel* healthy or well cared for. In the midst of unprecedented health, we perceive ourselves in unprecedented danger. Some of this may result from expectations that have outstripped reality; some may be from the frequent and frequently conflicting stories of new health threats — threats in food, water, air, and even in the imperceptible fluctuating electromagnetic fields of modern life. Each new study produces news stories, anxiety, and confusion.

Access, costs, and quality are all meaningless without some grounds for comparison, but medical comparisons are very difficult. Different countries deliver health care in different ways. What is satisfactory to one country's citizens and what is feasible in one country's political system may prove worthless in another's. Nonetheless, for whatever their value, we can make some comparisons. . . . [The United States spends 75 to 100 percent more per capita on health care than does Canada, France, Germany, and many northern European and Scandinavian countries, and 150 to 300 percent more per capita than England, Japan, Spain, and several other European countries.]

It is hard to know what those funds buy in terms of health because health is a product of so much more than medical care. Nevertheless, the casual observer can see no reason to believe that Americans are healthier than citizens of other rich countries; our life expectancy and infant mortality statistics show that, at least in some respects, we are less healthy.

In its technical brilliance, American health care is unsurpassed. Its best care would have seemed miraculous just a few years ago. But the bad side of American health care is very bad, and there is reason to think that it will get worse before it gets better. For one thing, the coming years will see a further increase in both the number of the elderly in the population and their percentage of the population. The growth will be particularly great among those over 85, the people most likely to make heavy use of the medical system. New technology, for which one can almost always read "expensive" new technology, continues to invade medicine. . . .

An outside observer might conclude that America's greatest domestic problem over the next decade will be something other than health care — education, poverty, racism, crime, and the decaying infrastructure are some of the many possibilities. But, unlike those issues, the problems of the health system will soon reach a condition where the middle class will demand that something *must* be done. The nature and timing of the collapse cannot be predicted, but like the *ancien régime* a little more than 200 years ago, it is increasingly clear that the system cannot continue indefinitely.

■ WHY CONSERVATIVES DON'T TALK ABOUT AMERICA'S HEALTH SYSTEM
Democratic Study Group, U.S. House of Representatives
1991

Even though the United States devotes a far larger share of its GDP to health care than any other of the 23 industrialized countries, it does not rank similarly high in terms of the basic indicators of health status. Rather, the standing of the United States ranges from somewhere below the middle (life expectancy for women) to close to the bottom (infant mortality).

Despite our high level of health care spending, the United States ranks 21st out of the 23 industrialized countries in terms of infant mortality — ahead of only Portugal and Greece. . . . The United States ranks *18th* among the 23 industrialized countries in terms of life expectancy for males — again despite the high level of health care spending in the United States. . . .

Like infant mortality, life expectancy is also clearly linked to socioeconomic status, and there is a much lower male life expectancy among the disproportionately poor black population in the United States. However, even the life expectancy for white males in the United States is lower than the male life expectancy in 13 of the 23 industrialized countries (including such diverse countries as France, Greece, Australia, and Canada). . . . For women, life expectancy in the United States ranks 15 out of 23. Countries with a higher female life expectancy than the United States include Spain, Greece, Canada, France, West Germany, and Sweden. . . .

While Americans are spending considerably more for health care than citizens of other industrialized countries — and may well be getting less for what we spend — it is nevertheless possible that Americans simply prefer the particular style of medicine and health care delivery that has developed in the United States. That is, we might be paying more than West Europeans, but getting in return a system with which we are satisfied.

A good indication of whether the level of satisfaction with the health care system is, in fact, higher in the United States than abroad is provided by . . . comparisons between attitudes in the United States and Canada. . . . [These] two nations have generally similar cultures and lifestyles but rather different health care systems (the Canadian system being a publicly funded program of universal health insurance [that spends about 45 percent less per capita]). . . .

[T]he level of satisfaction with health care services received was significantly higher in Canada than in the United States: 67 percent of Canadians stated they were *very* satisfied with the health care services they had received during the last year, compared to only 35 percent in the United States. Further, 18 percent of Americans surveyed were actually *dis*satisfied with the health care services they had received, while only 5 percent of Canadians were similarly dissatisfied. . . .

The data presented in this section suggest that the health care crisis in the United States is *not* the inevitable result of modern medicine. Rather, West European nations, Canada, and Japan all manage to spend significantly smaller fractions of their GDP on health care than the United States, while simultaneously providing broader access to health care than is available in this country.

Further, citizens of these other industrialized nations seem to receive at least as much (and generally more) health care services in the form of doctor visits and hospital stays as received by Americans. Overall health status in these other nations seems no worse (and generally better) than in the United States, and Western Europe appears to be ahead of the United States in addressing major health problems such as heart attacks and breast cancer.

■ DANGEROUS MEDICINE: A CRITICAL ANALYSIS OF CLINTON'S HEALTH PLAN
Doug Bandow*
1993

In his [1993] State of the Union speech the president stated that "our government will never again be fully solvent until we tackle the health-care crisis." . . . If one took his rhetoric seriously one would think that people were dying in droves due to inadequate medical care. . . . The theme of "crisis" has been repeated endlessly by [political] aides, legislators, journalists, and analysts. Yet there is, demonstrably, no *crisis*. Problems, yes. Serious problems, yes. But a "crisis," no.

Indeed, if you become seriously ill, there is no better nation in which to become sick than the United States. America's death rate, perhaps the best measure of access to and quality of care, is among the lowest, and often *the* lowest, for most major illnesses. In some cases the differences are quite dramatic: You are twice as likely to die from a hernia or intestinal obstruction in Sweden than in the U.S., three times as likely to die from an ulcer in Great Britain than in America, and seven times as likely to die from prostate disease in Sweden than in the U.S.

This is not to say that American *health* is equal to that elsewhere. Infant mortality and life expectancy lag behind those of many other industrialized states, but that reflects serious social pathologies absent from many other nations. For example, the U.S. has many problems characteristic of Third World states in its inner cities. . . . [O]verall health figures are dramatically affected by America's high rates of homicide, drug use, and AIDS. . . . In short, if Americans survive to enter a nursing home, their life expectancy rises to the longest in the world. The fact that many do not survive is not a fault of the present health care system — nor will it be affected by health care "reform."

American medicine is particularly good at treating the injured and sick because it rewards research and innovation, and utilizes the latest medical techniques and technologies. The pharmaceutical industry, for instance, is one of America's most competitive businesses internationally. American companies have developed a larger share of significant new drugs than any other nation. These products actually reduce total health care costs by cutting the need for surgery and other expensive alternative procedures. Naturally, these products also save lives and ameliorate suffering for millions of people.

Compared to other nations the U.S. also makes available more high-tech devices and procedures. . . . America has four times as many open-heart surgeries as Germany and six times as much radiation therapy and eight times as many magnetic resonance imaging [machines] as Canada. . . . American physicians, with

---

* The author was a senior fellow at the Cato Institute, which is known for its libertarian and free market public policy positions.

a universe of modern technology at their fingertips, are the envy of the world's physicians. . . .

[S]pending/GDP ratios alone do not demonstrate the existence of a problem, let alone a crisis. There is no "right" amount of money to spend on health care and comparisons with other nations help little. Based on purchasing-power parities (rather than misleading exchange-rate measurements), America has the highest standard of living in the world: the U.S. gross domestic product per capita is more than 55 percent higher than that of Western Europe, 35 percent more than in Australia, 28 percent greater than in Japan, and 11 percent higher than in Canada. There is nothing strange, then, about Americans devoting an increasing share of their incomes on medical attention as they grow more prosperous. Surely there is at least as much justification for spending a marginal dollar on health as on a nicer car, more recreation, or another beer.

Notes: The Crisis in American Medicine

1. *The Perpetual Crisis.* American medicine has been declared to be in a "crisis" since at least the early 1960s. See Marion Sanders, The Crisis in American Medicine (1961). Can things really be all that bad if they've been like this so long? Another self-proclaimed iconoclast who doesn't think we are necessarily spending too much on health care is the highly-respected health economist Joseph P. Newhouse, An Iconoclastic View of Health Cost Containment, Health Aff., Supp. 1993, at 152. Harvard economist David Cutler claims that increased medical spending over the past several decades has produced increases in average health that are worth several times more than their aggregate costs. David M. Cutler, Your Money or Your Life: Strong Medicine for America's Health Care System (Oxford Univ. Press, 2004). For a counter argument and evidence, see Elliott S. Fisher, Medical Care: Is More Always Better?, 349 New Eng. J. Med. 1665 (2003); Nortin M. Hadler, The Last Well Person (2004). See generally Symposium, 22 (1) Health Aff. 1 (Jan. 2003).

Even if there is not a "crisis," there is still clearly a serious problem in American medicine. In case you're still not convinced, consider the following additional facts, opinions, and anecdotes.

> Medicine, like many other American institutions, suffered a stunning loss of confidence in the 1970s. Previously, two premises had guided government health policy: first, that Americans needed more medical care — more than the market alone would provide; and second, that medical professionals and private voluntary institutions were best equipped to decide how to organize those services. . . . In the 1970s this mandate ran out. The economic and moral problems of medicine displaced scientific progress at the center of public attention. Enormous increases in cost seemed ever more certain; corresponding improvements in health ever more doubtful. The prevailing assumptions about the need to expand medical care were reversed: The need now was to curb its apparently insatiable appetite for resources. In a short time, American medicine seemed to pass from stubborn shortages to irrepressible excess, without ever having passed through happy sufficiency. [Paul Starr, The Social Transformation of American Medicine 379 (1982).]

Studies indicate that at least 25 percent of the money we spend on health care is wasted. . . . Millions of unnecessary procedures and tests are performed each year. Almost half the coronary bypasses, the majority of cesarean sections, and a significant proportion of many other procedures, such as pacemaker implants and carotid endarterectomies, are unnecessary or of questionable value. A former editor of the Journal of the American Medical Association is convinced that more than half of the forty million medical tests performed each day "do not really contribute to a patient's diagnosis or therapy." Doctors order many procedures and tests to protect themselves from potential medical malpractice liability. Some procedures are performed because doctors simply do not know the precise circumstances under which many procedures work. [Joseph A. Califano, Rationing Health Care: The Unnecessary Solution, 140 U. Pa. L. Rev. 1525 (1992).]

How much does an overnight stay at a Virginia hospital cost? . . . A year ago, Mr. Shipman, a 43-year-old former furniture salesman from Herndon, Va., experienced severe chest pains during the night. . . . Suspecting a heart attack, doctors first performed a cardiac catheterization to examine and unblock the coronary arteries. Then, they inserted a stent, a small metal device that props open a blocked artery so the blood flows better to the heart. Lacking health insurance, Mr. Shipman . . . checked himself out of the hospital against medical advice. Since then, Mr. Shipman and his wife, Alina, have received hospital bills totaling $29,500. . . . In addition, there were other bills: some $1,000 for the ambulance trip, $6,800 from the cardiologist who performed the stent procedure, and several thousand dollars for the local emergency-room visit. In all, the two-day health crisis left the Shipmans saddled with medical bills totaling nearly $40,000. Once solidly middle class, the couple says the debt triggered a gradual unraveling of their lives. "Middle class or not, when you have a bill of $37,000 hanging over your head, that's all you think about," says Ms. Shipman. . . . "You eat, sleep and breathe that bill." [Lucette Lagnado, Anatomy of a Hospital Bill, Wall St. J., Sept. 21, 2004, at B1.]

In May of 2002, a panel of experts . . . released a report documenting . . . [that] the long-term uninsured face a twenty-five percent greater likelihood of premature death than do insured Americans. Institute of Medicine, Care Without Coverage (National Academy Press, Washington, D.C., 2002). . . . In sum, an estimated 18,000 Americans, six times the number killed in the attacks of September 11, die annually because they are uninsured. . . . The uninsured [also] . . . face, day by day, the risk of imminent financial disaster. Medical expenses are one of the leading causes of bankruptcy in the United States. Melissa B. Jacoby, Teresa A. Sullivan, and Elizabeth Warren, Rethinking the Debates Over Health Care Financing: Evidence from the Bankruptcy Courts, 76 New York University Law Rev 387 (2001). . . . Lack of health insurance is among the greatest threats to financial security that Americans currently face. [Timothy Jost, Disentitlement: Health Care Entitlements and the Threats That They Face (2003).]

There is no U.S. health care system. What we call our health care system is, in daily practice, a hodgepodge of historic legacies, philosophical conflicts, and competing economic schemes. Health care in America combines the tortured, politicized complexity of the U.S. tax code with a cacophony of intractable political, cultural, and religious debates about personal rights and responsibilities. Every time policymakers, corporate health benefits purchasers, or entrepreneurs try to fix something in our health care system, they run smack into its central reality: the primary producers and consumers of medical care are uniquely, stubbornly self-serving as they chew through vast sums of other people's money. Doctors and hospitals stumble their way through irresolvable conflicts between personal gain and ethical responsibilities; patients struggle with the acrimony and anguish that accompany life-and-death medical decisions; consumers, paying for the most part with everybody's money but their own, demand that the system serve them with the immediacy and flexibility of other industries; and health insurers are trapped in the middle, trying to keep everybody happy. A group of highly imaginative, energetic people armed with the world's largest Mark-n-Wipe board could not purposefully design a more complex, dysfunctional system if they tried. It is a $1.3 trillion per year fiasco narrated with moral shrillness and played out one competing anecdote after another. [J.D. Kleinke, Oxymorons: The Myth of a U.S. Health Care System 1 (2001).]

2. *More Facts and Figures.* One way to put health care spending in context is to realize that it accounts for a larger portion of our gross domestic product than any other sector of the economy—more than housing, food, or transportation. Another way to capture the economic impact is to realize that the annual cost for private health insurance in 2006 averaged more than $11,000 for a family or $4000 for an individual. The following graph provides additional detail about historical spending levels for the health care sector.

National Health Spending, Selected Years

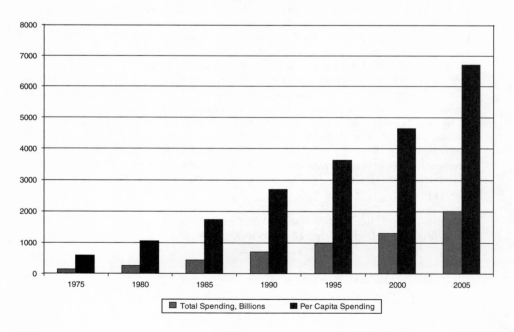

For more readings that describe the evolution of the health care financing and delivery system and the various public policy problems it currently faces, see the series of articles in the New England Journal of Medicine starting with John K. Iglehart, The American Health Care System: Expenditures, 340 New Eng. J. Med. 70 (1999); David Mechanic, The Truth About Health Care: Why Reform is Not Working in America (2006); Julius B. Richmond & Rashi Fein, The Health Care Mess: How We Got into It and What It Will Take to Get Out (2005); Paul Krugman & Robin Wells, The Health Care Crisis and What to Do About It, 53 N.Y. Review of Books No. 5 (March 23, 2006). A fascinating account of the early history of health insurance is Herman Somers & Anne Somers, Private Health Insurance, 46 Cal. L. Rev. 376, 508 (1958).

There is seemingly an endless appetite for facts and figures about the U.S. health care delivery system. Those who wish more, or more recent, numbers can find them in the annual editions of the American Hospital Association's *Hospital Statistics*, in the annual reports of the Medicare Payment Advisory Commission (MedPac), in periodic issues of *Health Affairs* and on the Web pages for the U.S. Census Bureau and the Centers for Medicare and Medicaid Services (CMS), which are linked to the Web page for this book, www.health-law.org.

3. *International Comparisons.* According to one analysis, the poor U.S. performance on aggregate health statistics is not due to major differences in health habits or lifestyles, since the United States ranks in the middle or toward the top in fat, alcohol, and cigarette consumption, and its health rankings remain low even when comparing only the white population and when excluding automobile deaths. Instead, this author argues that the lower U.S. rankings are due in large part to the relatively inadequate system of primary care physicians and the overuse of high-risk procedures. Barbara Starfield, Is U.S. Health Really the Best in the World?, 284 JAMA 483 (2000). Another prominent study found that the British are much healthier than Americans in all major disease areas, such as diabetes, heart disease, stroke, lung disease, and cancer, even after controlling for all relevant sociodemographic factors. J. Banks, M. Marmot, et al., Disease and Disadvantage in the United States and England, 295 JAMA 2037 (2006). Considering a broad range of indicators of health status and health care access, the World Health Organization ranked the U.S. health care system thirty-seventh in the world. See also Cathy Schoen et al., U.S. Health System Performance: A National Scorecard, 25 Health Aff. w457 (Sept. 2006).

3. Changes in Financing and Delivery Systems

■ MEDICARE AND THE AMERICAN HEALTH CARE SYSTEM: 1996 REPORT TO CONGRESS
Prospective Payment Assessment Commission

National health care expenditures . . . increased at more than twice the economywide rate of inflation since 1975. . . . Recently, however, the increase in health care spending has slowed. . . . The recent changes in health care expenditure trends are due partly to pressure exerted by private payers. Employers that purchase coverage for employees and their dependents increasingly are demanding health insurance products that control their outlays yet preserve quality. This pressure has resulted in a shift toward managed care plans, which often have benefit packages that are similar to or more generous than traditional indemnity insurance, but at lower prices. Like indemnity offerings, managed care plans receive a premium for assuming the financial risk of providing a defined set of benefits for each person. Unlike traditional indemnity insurers, though, these plans attempt to constrain expenditures by playing an active role in the delivery of services. . . .

The most common managed care models are health maintenance organizations (HMOs), preferred provider organizations (PPOs), and point-of-service (POS) plans. In a traditional HMO plan, subscribers must receive their care from a limited group of providers. PPO and POS subscribers may not be subject to the same level of plan oversight as in HMOs: Generally they may go to any provider, but their out-of-pocket payments are lower if they choose participating providers that give the insurer discounted rates. . . .

Managed care plans use a variety of techniques to control their costs. First, they actively seek providers with lower-cost practice patterns and offer them a defined patient base in exchange for favorable payment rates. By limiting the number of providers or by creating strong financial incentives to choose certain ones, managed care plans influence which providers subscribers will use. Through this selective contracting, managed care plans can substantially affect providers' revenues. Plans' bargaining positions are strongest in areas with excess provider capacity. Providers that choose not to participate or that are not selected by the managed care plan may experience a decline in their patient volume.

In addition, managed care plans often use discounted fee-for-service rates to control their costs. They also use per case, per day, or per person payments to shift some of the financial risk of treating patients to providers. Per case or per day payments are generally made to hospitals, whereas per person payments are more often made to physicians, predominately primary care practitioners. These payment methods reward providers for delivering care efficiently, discouraging unnecessary service use.

A per person, or capitation, payment system is the most comprehensive way to shift financial risk to providers. Under capitation, providers receive a prepaid sum to furnish a defined set of services to a plan's enrollees. This creates a monetary incentive for physicians to limit patients' use of services (or encourage preventive services) because the physician receives the same payment regardless of the volume or intensity of care, or even if no care is provided at all. Many managed care plans also require primary care physicians to act as "gatekeepers" to specialty care or hospital services. Under these arrangements, the primary care physician must preauthorize any services a patient receives. While these physicians usually do not bear the full financial risk for the additional services, delegating the gatekeeping function enables managed care plans to use financial incentives to limit referrals. . . .

Hospitals are seeking alternative revenue streams by broadening the scope of services they offer and competing for patients with other types of providers, [such as outpatient departments. By 1995], . . . outpatient services represented 28.8 percent of total hospital revenue. Similarly, a growing number of hospitals are venturing into the post-acute care market, where payments are still dominated by fee-for-service methods. Hospitals are developing skilled nursing facilities (SNFs) or are using acute care beds as swing beds to provide skilled nursing services. In addition, they are establishing their own rehabilitation units and home health agencies. . . .

Along with controlling their costs and seeking alternative revenue sources, hospitals are attempting to broaden (or maintain) their market share by securing a patient base through arrangements with other providers or managed care plans. Such arrangements have the potential to make overall service delivery more efficient and provide patients with a continuum of care. In 1994, for instance, 21 percent of community hospitals participated in health networks — groups of hospitals, physicians, other providers, insurers, or community agencies that coordinate and deliver a broad spectrum of services. Anecdotal evidence suggests that most hospitals have some type of arrangement, such as joint ventures or informal alliances, with other providers. Entering into arrangements with physicians is an increasingly popular strategy for hospitals. Such relationships can bolster a hospital's ability to secure managed care contracts. . . .

The long-term effects of the changing environment on hospitals are still unclear. . . . Hospitals traditionally have been viewed as the hub of the health care system and often have the capital reserves necessary to finance collaborations with other providers. Those that aggressively pursue such arrangements not only can improve their chances of being the hospital of choice for inpatient services, but also can exert more influence over medical practice decisions. In areas where managed care systems exert more control, however, hospitals may be viewed as cost centers with little input into delivery decisions.

PHYSICIANS

Historically, physicians determined not only which services would be provided, but where those services would be delivered. These decisions generally were made with little accountability for costs. Managed care is changing this. . . . One indication of the level of financial pressure physicians are facing is the [reduced growth] in physician income. . . . Some physicians are responding to the intensified pressures by selling their practices to hospitals or managed care organizations, and becoming employees of those entities. In 1990, nearly 70 percent of physicians reported they were self-employed. By 1995, this share had dropped to 55 percent. . . .

Because physicians generate the demand for hospital services, they have leverage to assume a leadership role in arrangements with other providers. As health care funds become more and more limited, physicians — especially those who deliver primary care services — have an opportunity to play a larger part in deciding how those dollars will be distributed. . . .

■ THE HEALTH CARE REVOLUTION: REMAKING MEDICINE IN CALIFORNIA*
Barbara Marsh
L.A. Times, Aug. 31, 1995

To find out where the nation's health care system may be headed, ask anybody in San Diego. San Diegans know more than most Americans about managed care, which controls costs by limiting consumer choice. About two-thirds of insured San Diego residents were enrolled in health maintenance organizations last year—one of the highest levels in the country. "Every other major city and county in the country will be facing within five years the situation we are facing today," predicts Dr. Robert Ross, the county's health director. . . .

The system apparently pleases the healthy majority of consumers with access to doctors and hospitals at affordable prices. But those with unusual, chronic or serious illnesses often fail to benefit. Many San Diegans can't switch health plans because their employers offer only one. And consumers find it extremely difficult to fight a system that gives doctors financial incentives to minimize treatment. . . .

Surveys suggest that San Diegans generally are satisfied with their health care. . . . San Diegans were especially pleased with the quality of their care and the minimal paperwork involved. Eighty-five percent said they would recommend their doctor to a friend. . . .

Of course, managed care in San Diego—like elsewhere—isn't the result of a consumer revolt. It arose because employers threw up their hands at the rising costs of employee health care. In the late 1970s, an unusually active group of large employers—including defense and aerospace contractors, retailers, banks and local schools—got together to brainstorm ways to rein in double-digit increases in health benefits. The group even launched its own network of hospitals and physicians offering services at rates below traditional insurance plans. So employers couldn't have been more receptive when HMOs rushed into the market in the early 1980s. . . .

And many local hospitals, clinics, physicians and other providers have merged to form or align themselves with four vast systems that deliver managed care: HealthCare System, Scripps Health Corp., UCSD Healthcare and Kaiser. Experts predict more consolidation. . . .

Here as elsewhere, managed care has created an excess of specialist physicians. Many are fleeing San Diego for places still unpenetrated by HMOs. One day late in June, with a moving van parked outside his office, Dr. Steven Kotner fought back tears as he told how HMOs had lured away his patients with cheap insurance prices. "The majority would have stayed with me if they could," he says. His wife Andy, who managed his practice, defiantly lifts her chin to add, "They want us in Tennessee!"

Meanwhile, primary physicians, the workhorses of managed care, shoulder the patient burden. Dr. Laura Nathanson, a family practitioner in Encinitas, says it's tough to keep track of the terms of her patients' 18 different health plans. Her practice employs two staffers to keep up with the plans' ever-changing lists of

---

* Copyright © 1995, Los Angeles Times. Reprinted with permission.

approved providers, so patients won't get charged for services that aren't covered. When she's on call at night, Nathanson keeps three separate lists of approved test centers, hospitals and emergency rooms so she can direct patients to the right place. "I routinely tell patients, 'Don't go anywhere—even to Nordstrom's—unless you've had your visit authorized,'" she jokes. . . .

Consumer advocates say people here generally understand little about what they're buying when they join an HMO. Jeanne Ertle, executive director of San Diego Neighbor to Neighbor, a local activist group, says consumers don't carefully compare benefits, co-payments, or deductibles. "Ultimately, it's the bottom line," says Ertle. "Which one can they afford?" . . . So HMOs and managed care get mixed reviews from today's San Diegans. As the nation continues to wrestle with health care reform, the ambiguities will only deepen.

Managed care, for instance, has yet to tackle the problem of San Diego's growing population of uninsured residents. . . . Five years ago, Celia Martinez, who cares for a paralyzed invalid, says she applied for insurance through Kaiser's plan for individuals. The 63-year-old woman, who stands 5 foot 4 and weighs 200 pounds, says Kaiser refused to allow her to join because she weighs too much. Earlier this summer, Martinez broke her arm, couldn't work for six weeks—and found herself having to arrange a payment plan for the care she received through UCSD Medical Center. "When it comes to California, they don't help you," she says. "You don't get no help. Everything is pay, pay, pay." . . .

■ TRANSCRIPT OF INTERVIEW WITH JAIME ROBINSON, Ph.D.*
Lehman Brothers Industry Expert Conference Call Series
May 17, 2002

As we go into the new decade, the insurance industry is reevaluating whether it wants to be America's method of health care cost control. It's found that this is a very difficult and very unappreciated job. It appears to the public that there is a tradeoff between corporate profits and individual health care, which is a very, very bad image for the industry. The insurers now want to have a completely different image, which is helping the consumer make health care choices. . . .

I think the battle is over and the providers won. The health plans don't really want to get in there and second-guess doctor decision making. That just proved to be a turf where the providers were very strong, and had the support of the patients and the regulators. . . . There is a lot of lousy medicine being practiced out there that the insurance companies could detect, and could clean up, but they could never convince anybody that they're doing it for the right reasons rather than simply for their own profits.

They've essentially abandoned that role. Increasingly they want to see themselves as a financial services company, like a Fidelity, [which manages investment funds for retirement accounts.] . . . Fidelity offer[s] a stock fund and a bond fund and a mixed fund and employees can allocate their savings across these

---

* Prof. Robinson is a health economist at the University of California at Berkeley. Reprinted with the permission of Prof. Robinson and Lehman Brothers.

however they want [with the help of] some decision support tools. . . . The health plans want to do that on the health plan side. "We have our PPO product and our HMO product and our Medical Savings Account product and we're not going to try to force people to pick one or the other. We're going to give them choices. We're going to give them information about the different products, about their prices, about access and about quality. We're going to give them Internet based decision support and tools, and we're going to let them choose. After that, what happens is between the patient and their doctor and their hospital. We, the insurance company, are not going to be responsible for that." . . .

One of the reasons that the insurance industry wants to get out of managed care and go back to being like the financial services industry is that it wants to stop being continually compared to the tobacco industry. It doesn't want to be the second most hated industry in America. The industry needs to re-brand itself as a consumer friendly decision support and information industry rather than something that's trying to save money for corporations.

Notes: Managed Care vs. Consumer-Driven Care

1. *Managed Care Is Here to Stay.* Despite fierce resistance by many doctors and some patients, managed care is here to stay, and, indeed, has become the dominant form of insurance. However, enrollment has shifted rather dramatically in recent years from tightly managed HMO plans to PPO and POS plans that give patients more options. Regardless of the form managed care takes, it raises a host of legal, ethical, and regulatory issues that are explored throughout this book. For now, consider these broad inquiries: Are you concerned that insurers are interfering with medical judgment by deciding what treatments to pay for? Would you be more comfortable with a regime that let physicians and patients decide for themselves, but rewarded physicians for saving money or punished them for being excessive? Or, is the answer to make patients pay much more out of pocket so that they regulate their own spending decisions?

2. *Consumer-Driven Care.* For a fuller account of Prof. Robinson's views, see The End of Managed Care, 285 JAMA 2622 (2001), where he observes:

> [The following] problems will plague a consumer-driven health care system. First, despite the widespread dissemination of information, . . . even the most sophisticated and Internet-enabled consumer . . . will face significant obstacles in understanding the quality and even the true price of health insurance and health care services. . . . [C]onsumers vary enormously in their financial, cognitive, and cultural preparedness to navigate the complex health care system. The new paradigm fits most comfortably the educated, assertive, and prosperous and least comfortably the impoverished, meek, and poorly educated. . . . Finally, the emerging era will make transparent and render difficult the redistribution of income from rich to poor that otherwise results from the collective purchasing and administration of health insurance.

The consumer-driven movement is occurring in several different ways. One is simply to *increase co-payments and deductibles* significantly, even for HMOs, which traditionally have imposed only minimal cost-sharing obligations on patients. The second is for employers to contribute only a fixed amount toward the cost of health insurance (*'defined contribution'*) and let employees shop for whatever coverage they want, rather than pay for all or most of the cost of a group policy that the employer selects. A complementary approach is for the government to subsidize insurance through a *tax credit* that operates like a voucher. Third, insurers are adopting an approach to provider contracting known as *'tiered networks'*:

> Health plans, employers and hospitals are returning to notions of preferred providers and health plans. . . . The basic notion involves dividing hospitals and groups of physicians so that even though all of them may be listed in that thick provider directory, not all are created equal. For example, a hospital may say that 10 of 12 hospitals in an area are on a preferred list. If an enrollee is admitted to one of those hospitals no co-payment or deductible is required. But if the same enrollee goes to one of the two local hospitals that are not on the preferred list ("affiliated hospitals"), they are required to pay a deductible or co-payment of anywhere from $100 to $400 per day. These arrangements are referred to as "tiering" of providers. . . . Under certain systems, [providers] may set their own price and decide for themselves whether they want to be in the low, medium or high tier. . . .
>
> The move to tiering is partly a response to a change in the economic balance of power between health plans and providers. . . . In the early days of managed care, health plans did not contract with all hospitals and clinics. Instead, they offered a limited panel of providers the promise of more patients in exchange for discounted prices. Soon the sales people took over and decided that very broad provider networks were needed in order to match the competition, resulting in the extensive network overlap that now exists. . . . Many hospitals [then] used their newly found leverage to exit from [managed care] contracts. . . . By establishing tiers of providers, some health plans have returned to the old notion of identifying certain hospitals as preferred. At this point, that preference is based on pricing, although health plans say that they want to reach a point where tiering of hospitals and clinics would be based on measures of quality. Allan Baumgarten, Tiering Approaches for Health Plans: Incentives and Information for Consumers (June 17, 2002).

See also Symposium, W3 Health Aff. 135 (March 2003). Other examples of increased consumerism are prescription drug manufacturers' much more aggressively advertising directly to consumers rather than only to physicians, and the wealth of medical and health insurance information now available on the Internet. Consumer-driven ideas are being applied even to the Medicaid program for the poor. Jeb Bush, Market Principles: The Right Prescription for Medicaid, 17 Stan. L. & Pol'y Rev. 33 (2006).

The pros, cons, and legal implications of consumer-driven health care are being extensively debated and analyzed. For a sampling of the literature, see Regina Herzlinger, ed., Consumer-Driven Health Care: Implications for Providers, Payers, and Policymakers (2004); Timothy S. Jost, Health Care at Risk: A Critique of the Consumer-Driven Movement (2007); Malcom Gladwell, The Moral-Hazard Myth, The New Yorker, Sept. 8, 2005; James C. Robinson, Reinvention of Health Insurance in the Consumer Era, 291 JAMA 1880 (2004);

John V. Jacobi, Consumer-Driven Health Care and the Chronically Ill, 38 U. Mich. J. L. Ref, 531 (2005); Amy B. Monahan, The Promise and Peril of Ownership Society Health Care Policy, 80 Tul. L. Rev. 777 (2006); Marshall B. Kapp, Patient Autonomy in the Age of Consumer-Driven Health Care, 2 J. Health & Biomed. L. 1 (2006); Haavi Morreim, High-Deductible Health Plans: New Twists on Old Challenges from Tort and Contract, 59 Vand. L. Rev. 1207 (2006); Mark A. Hall, Paying for What You Get, and Getting What You Pay For, 69 Law & Contemp. Prob. 159 (Autumn 2006); Peter D. Jacobson & Micahel R. Tunick, Consumer-Directed Health Care and the Courts: Let the Buyer (And Seller) Beware, 26(3) Health Aff. 704 (June 2007); Symposium, 39 Health Serv. Res. 1049 (2004); Symposium, 24(6) Health Aff. (Dec. 2005); Symposium, 25(6) Health Aff. w516 (2006); Symposium, 28 J. Leg. Med. 1 (2007).

For a good overview of managed care generally, see Peter Kongstvedt, Managed Care: What It Is and How It Works (2d ed. 2002); Jacob S. Hacker & Theodore R. Marmor, How Not to Think About "Managed Care," 32 U. Mich. J. L. Ref. 661 (1999). For additional discussion of broad changes in the health care system, see Understanding Health System Change: Local Markets, National Trends (Paul B. Ginsburg & Cara S. Lesser eds., 2001); John K. Iglehart, Changing Health Insurance Trends, 347 New Eng. J. Med. 956 (347).

3. *The Onslaught of Acronyms.* Regrettably, the health care field is overrun with acronyms. Since 1970 or so, no new institution or phenomenon seemingly can exist in medicine without being known primarily by its three-to-five-letter abbreviation. Most of the specialized organizational terms and acronyms you will encounter in these readings are collected and defined in the glossary at page 525 for convenient reference throughout the semester.

2

■

The Treatment Relationship: Formation, Termination, and Regulation

This book explores the legal issues that lie at the core of the provider-patient relationship. By provider, we mean doctors, hospitals, and other people and institutions that deliver health care services. Chapter 2 examines the basic structure of the treatment relationship, including topics such as the duty to treat and the formation and termination of the treatment relationship. Chapter 3 considers the fiduciary nature of the treatment relationship, with coverage including confidentiality, informed consent, and conflicts of interest. Chapter 4 is devoted to medical malpractice liability. These patient care issues all spring directly from how providers and patients interact at the point of treatment. Although these interactions are certainly influenced by institutional, financial, and regulatory forces, this external environment is not explored in depth in this book.

The provider-patient relationship is governed primarily by contract, tort, and fiduciary law—all aspects of private rather than public law. The treatment relationship starts and ends in contract law. Contract principles determine whether there is a duty to accept a patient and whether treatment can be terminated. But, between these defining points, the *content* of the treatment relationship is determined primarily by tort and fiduciary law, not by contract. That is because the treatment encounter creates what is known as a "relational contract," one that governs a complex relationship by incorporating external social norms rather than by specifying detailed performance requirements and standards. Cf. Maureen Armour, A Nursing Home's Good Faith Duty "To" Care: Redefining a Fragile Relationship Using the Law of Contract, 39 St. Louis U. L.J. 217 (1994). Tort and fiduciary law are richer sources for social and professional norms relating to medicine than the law generated by commercial sales. Ultimately, however, medical relationships are constrained by government regulations that determine who is allowed to practice one of the healing arts and whether any particular treatments are unsafe or ineffective.

To better understand this interconnected web of legal doctrine, we begin with a chapter on the basic structure and regulation of the treatment relationship: how it is formed, how it is terminated, and the extent to which it can be altered and defined by private agreement or constrained by government regulation. In the following two chapters, we look more at the content of treatment relationships, starting first with the fiduciary duties of confidentiality, candor, and loyalty, and then in the next chapter considering the full extent of malpractice liability.

While the focus of the following three chapters is, respectively, contract, fiduciary, and tort law, the divisions among these bodies of law are not so neatly confined. Each set of private law concepts can be felt throughout this book. Thus, there is a broad inquiry that connects all of these chapters: To what extent should the structure and content of medical relationships be defined by the parties themselves, by legal norms based in conventional common law doctrine, or by explicit legislative oversight tailored specifically to the medical context?

Ordinarily, the patient-provider relationship is a consensual one to which both parties must agree. Therefore, an individual physician may, generally speaking, refuse to accept patients for any reason or for no reason. The same is true to a lesser extent for hospitals and other institutions. But this general freedom of contract is limited in several important ways. Hospitals may not turn patients away in emergencies until they have at least stabilized the patient's condition. Neither may doctors or hospitals refuse patients for certain discriminatory reasons, such as the patient's race, sex, or HIV-status. Once treatment has begun, it may not be ceased without proper arrangements being made. And providers may not impose unreasonable conditions on their agreement to treat. While historically a physician's freedom to turn away patients found its limitations primarily in the law, the growth of formal arrangements between managed care health plans and physicians means that a provider's obligation to treat is being increasingly defined by the private agreements among the patient, insurance plan, and provider. The following materials explore the origins of, and limits on, this freedom of contract between providers and patients.

A. THE DUTY TO TREAT

1. The Duty to Accept Patients

■ HURLEY v. EDDINGFIELD
59 N.E. 1058 (Ind. 1901)

BAKER, Justice.

The appellant sued appellee for $10,000 damages for wrongfully causing the death of his intestate. The court sustained appellee's demurrer to the complaint, and this ruling is assigned as error.

The material facts may be summarized thus: At and for years before decedent's death appellee was a practicing physician at Mace, in Montgomery county, duly licensed under the laws of the state. He held himself out to the public as a general practitioner of medicine. He had been decedent's family physician. Decedent became dangerously ill, and sent for appellee. The messenger informed appellee of decedent's violent sickness, tendered him his fee for his services, and stated to him that no other physician was procurable in time, and that decedent relied on him for attention. No other physician was procurable in time to be of any use, and decedent did rely on appellee for medical assistance. Without any reasons whatever, appellee refused to render aid to decedent. No other patients were requiring appellee's immediate service, and he could have gone to the relief of decedent if he had been willing to do so. Death ensued, without decedent's fault, and wholly from appellee's wrongful act. The alleged wrongful act was appellee's refusal to enter into a contract of employment. Counsel do not contend that, before the enactment of the law regulating the practice of medicine, physicians were bound to render professional service to every one who applied. The act regulating the practice of medicine provides for a board of examiners, standards of qualification, examinations, licenses to those found qualified, and penalties for practicing without license. The act is a preventive, not a compulsive, measure. In obtaining the state's license (permission) to practice medicine, the state does not require, and the licensee does not engage, that he will practice at all or on other terms than he may choose to accept. Counsel's analogies, drawn from the obligations to the public on the part of innkeepers, common carriers, and the like, are beside the mark. Judgment affirmed.

■ WILMINGTON GENERAL HOSPITAL v. MANLOVE
174 A.2d 135 (Del. 1961)

SOUTHERLAND, Chief Justice.

This case concerns the liability of a private hospital for the death of an infant who was refused treatment at the emergency ward of the hospital. The facts are these:

On January 4, 1959, Darien E. Manlove, the deceased infant, then four months old, developed diarrhea. The next morning his parents consulted Dr. Hershon. They asked whether the medicine they had for him was all right and the doctor said that it was. In the evening of the same day Mrs. Manlove took the baby's temperature. It was higher than normal. They called Dr. Hershon, and he prescribed additional medication (streptomycin), which he ordered delivered by a pharmacy.

Mrs. Manlove stayed up with the child that night. He did not sleep. On the morning of January 6th the parents took the infant to Dr. Hershon's office. Dr. Thomas examined the child and treated him for sore throat and diarrhea. He prescribed a liquid diet and some medicine. . . .

On the morning of January 7th (a Wednesday) [the infant's] temperature was still above normal — 102. Mr. and Mrs. Manlove determined to seek additional medical assistance. They knew that Dr. Hershon and Dr. Thomas were not in their offices on Wednesdays, and they took their infant to the emergency ward of the Wilmington General Hospital.

There is no real conflict of fact as to what occurred at the hospital. The parents took the infant into the reception room of the Emergency Ward. A nurse was on duty. They explained to the nurse what was wrong with the child, that is, that he had not slept for two nights, had a continuously high temperature, and that he had diarrhea. Mr. Manlove told the nurse that the child was under the care of Dr. Hershon and Dr. Thomas, and showed the nurse the medicines prescribed. The nurse explained to the parents that the hospital could not give treatment because the child was under the care of a physician and there would be danger that the medication of the hospital might conflict with that of the attending physician. The nurse did not examine the child, take his temperature, feel his forehead, or look down his throat. The child was not in convulsions, and was not coughing or crying. There was no particular area of body tenderness.

The nurse tried to get in touch with Dr. Hershon or Dr. Thomas in the hospital and at their offices, but was unable to do so. She suggested that the parents bring the baby Thursday morning to the pediatric clinic.

Mr. and Mrs. Manlove returned home. Mrs. Manlove made an appointment by telephone to see Dr. Hershon or Dr. Thomas that night at eight o'clock. At eight minutes past three o'clock in the afternoon the baby died of bronchial pneumonia. . . .

It was assumed by both parties below that the hospital was a private hospital and not a public one — that is, an institution founded and controlled by private persons and not by public authority. The trial court disagreed, finding a quasi-public status in the receipt of grants of public money and tax exemptions. . . . Hence, the court concluded, liability may be imposed on the defendant in an emergency case.

We are compelled to disagree with the view that the defendant has become a public (or quasi-public) hospital. It is admitted (although the record does not show it) that it is privately owned and operated. We find no dissent from the rule that such a hospital is a private hospital, and may, at least in the absence of control by the legislature, conduct its business largely as it sees fit. . . .

Moreover, the holding that the receipt of grants of public money requires the hospital to care for emergency cases, as distinguished from others, is not logical. Why emergency cases? If the holding is sound it must apply to all the hospital services, and that conclusion, as we shall see, is clearly unsound. . . .

We are of opinion that the defendant is a private and not a public hospital, in so far as concerns the right of a member of the public to demand admission or treatment. What, then, is the liability of a private hospital in this respect?

Since such an institution as the defendant is privately owned and operated, it would follow logically that its trustees or governing board alone have the right to determine who shall be admitted to it as patients. No other rule would be sensible or workable. Such authority as we have found supports this rule. "A private hospital owes the public no duty to accept any patient not desired by it, and it is not necessary to assign any reason for its refusal to accept a patient for hospital service." 41 C. J. S. Hospitals §8, p.345. . . .

. . . Does that rule apply to the fullest extent to patients applying for treatment at an emergency ward? . . .

It may be conceded that a private hospital is under no legal obligation to the public to maintain an emergency ward, or, for that matter, a public clinic. But the maintenance of such a ward to render first-aid to injured persons has become a well-established adjunct to the main business of a hospital. If a person, seriously hurt, applies for such aid at an emergency ward, relying on the established custom to render it, is it still the right of the hospital to turn him away without any reason? In such a case, it seems to us, such a refusal might well result in worsening the condition of the injured person, because of the time lost in a useless attempt to obtain medical aid. Such a set of circumstances is analogous to the case of the negligent termination of gratuitous services, which creates a tort liability. Restatement, Law of Torts, "Negligence," §323. . . .

As above indicated, we are of opinion that liability on the part of a hospital may be predicated on the refusal of service to a patient in case of an unmistakable emergency, if the patient has relied upon a well-established custom of the hospital to render aid in such a case. . . .

Applying this rule here, we inquire, was there an unmistakable emergency? Certainly the record does not support the view that the infant's condition was so desperate that a layman could reasonably say that he was in immediate danger. The learned judge indicated that the fact that death followed in a few hours showed an emergency; but with this we cannot agree. It is hindsight. And it is to be noted that the attending physician, after prescribing for the child one morning before, did not think another examination that night or the next morning was required. If this case had gone to the jury on the record here made, we would have been required to hold that it was insufficient to establish liability. We cannot agree that the mere recitation of the infant's symptoms was, in itself, evidence of an emergency sufficient to present a question for the jury. Before such an issue could arise there would have to be evidence that an experienced nurse should have known that such symptoms constituted unmistakable evidence of an emergency. . . .

The possibility that the case might turn on additional evidence respecting the matters we have touched upon was not considered either by the court or counsel. In the circumstances we think the case should go back for further proceedings. We should add, however, that if plaintiff cannot adduce evidence showing some incompetency of the nurse, or some breach of duty or some negligence, his case must fail. Like the learned judge below, we sympathize with the parents in their loss of a child; but this natural feeling does not permit us to find liability in the absence of satisfactory evidence.

For the reasons above set forth the order denying summary judgment is affirmed, without approving the reasons therefor set forth in the court's opinion.

■ SOPHIE'S CHOICES: MEDICAL AND LEGAL RESPONSES TO SUFFERING
Lois Shepherd*
72 Notre Dame L. Rev. 103 (1996)

[U]nprecedented claims to rights based on the avoidance of suffering are being made and recognized in courts and legislatures. The basis of such appeals is a belief that the suffering imposed by nature need not be tolerated and that such

* Law professor at Florida State University. Reprinted with permission. Copyright © 1996, Notre Dame Law Review, University of Notre Dame. The editors and Aspen Law Books are required to state that they bear any responsibility for any errors that may have occurred in reprinting or editing this excerpt.

suffering instills in the suffering individual a right to relief. Suffering thus becomes a sufficient condition for a right. There need be no tortfeasor nor any societally caused harm, nor any inequality for a suffering individual (or such individual's advocate) to claim relief. . . . In such instances the basis of the rights espoused is the principle that people should not be required to suffer when the means are available to end or altogether avoid such suffering. . . .

I think we can look at a number of possible reasons why there is pressure to talk about and recognize rights based in suffering. . . . [W]e appear to be developing a collective conscience, a shared empathy, and a feeling of responsibility for the welfare of others, especially in matters of health. As this collective conscience develops in a country whose jurisprudence gives great deference to individual rights, there is a developing sense that in matters of social welfare we have certain rights. These certain "positive" rights are rights *to* certain goods or services, rather than simply rights to non-interference with respect to obtaining such goods or services. This plays out in the health care arena in an incrementally emerging right to health care. This right emerges in those situations when our collective conscience cannot turn away — when the suffering is acute and visible — such as when a patient arrives at the emergency room in need of immediate attention. . . .

[C]hanges in the legal culture reflect a heightened public awareness and appreciation of others' suffering. This may be due, in part, to the fact that historical distinctions between public and private have blurred, so that, according to Hannah Arendt, the two realms "constantly flow into each other like waves in the never-resting stream of the life process itself."[155] Concerns that were originally and exclusively the province of the family, where the necessary tasks for the survival of life took place, have become a "collective" concern. We are now a "collective of families economically organized into the facsimile of one super-human family." . . .

In the collective conscience, we share not only a growing awareness of the suffering, and especially the visible suffering, of others, but a growing sense of responsibility to help others avoid avoidable suffering. We find conceptual support for this heightened social responsibility in such theories as the feminist ethic of care. The ethic of care requires attending to responsibilities and relationships, rather than attending to rights and fairness (the ethic of justice). Rather than learning and then applying abstract principles, such as equality, reciprocity, and property rights that have universal applicability (since all are grounded in an ethic of justice), an individual or society acting under the ethic of care would seek responses that are appropriate to the particular case.

Much of the recent work on the ethic of care is an outgrowth of Carol Gilligan's 1982 work, *In a Different Voice*, in which she presents her empirical findings that women and men tend to reason about moral problems from different approaches. . . . Gilligan writes:

> The moral imperative that emerges repeatedly in interviews with women is an injunction to care, a responsibility to discern and alleviate the "real and recognizable trouble" of this world. For men the moral imperative appears as an injunction to respect the rights of others and thus to protect from interference the rights to life and self-fulfillment.

---

[155] Hannah Arendt, The Human Condition 33 (1958).

Whether there are gender differences in moral reasoning or not, . . . we continue to move along the path of a collective conscience in matters of health. [T]he responsibility we feel for the care of others becomes duty, and in the language of advocacy for recognition and adherence to that duty, we see constant recourse to the familiar language of rights. To give proper weight to a concern within our rights-based constitutional framework, there is pressure to . . . create new, unprecedented expectations of rescue-like behavior.

■ WIDEMAN v. SHALLOWFORD COMMUNITY HOSPITAL
826 F.2d 1030 (11th Cir. 1987)

HILL, Circuit Judge.

This case presents the novel question of whether a county government's alleged practice of using its emergency medical vehicles only to transport patients to certain county hospitals which guarantee the payment of the county's medical bills violates a right protected by the federal constitution. We hold that such a practice, even if proved, would not violate any established constitutional right. . . .

I. BACKGROUND

The facts underlying this case are undeniably tragic. On April 12, 1984, Toni Wideman, who at the time was four months pregnant, began experiencing abdominal pain. She called her obstetrician, Dr. John Ramsey, who instructed her to come immediately to Piedmont Hospital. Ms. Wideman called the 911 emergency telephone number in DeKalb County and requested an ambulance to take her to Piedmont. Three employees of the DeKalb County Emergency Medical Service (EMS) responded to this call. Ms. Wideman claims that she again informed the EMS employees to take her to Piedmont where her doctor was waiting, but they refused and, instead, took her against her wishes to Shallowford Community Hospital. After a substantial delay, during which the attending physician at Shallowford spoke by phone with Dr. Ramsey, Ms. Wideman was transferred to Piedmont. At that point, however, Dr. Ramsey was unable to stop her labor, and Ms. Wideman gave birth to a premature baby, named Ebony Laslun Wideman, who survived for only four hours. . . .

. . . It seems that both parties, as well as the district court, have assumed that the alleged policy violates a cognizable constitutional right, which the plaintiffs characterize as their right to the provision of essential medical treatment and services by the county.[3] However, . . . the proper resolution of this case requires us first to determine whether the Constitution grants a right to medical care and treatment in these circumstances. . . .

---

[3] The constitutional right alleged by the plaintiffs arguably may be characterized as the much more specific right to the medical care and services of their choice. Ms. Wideman was provided with medical care in this case; indeed, she was rushed to a hospital in an ambulance provided by the county. Her claim appears to be that she should have been able to direct the ambulance wherever she wanted to go. For purposes of our analysis, however, we shall consider the plaintiffs' alleged constitutional right as they have characterized it.

III.A. EXISTENCE OF A CONSTITUTIONAL RIGHT TO ESSENTIAL MEDICAL CARE

Beginning from the broadest prospective, we can discern no general right, based upon either the Constitution or federal statutes, to the provision of medical treatment and services by a state or municipality. If such a right exists at all, it must derive from the Fourteenth Amendment's due process clause, which forbids a state to deprive anyone of life, liberty or property without due process of law. The due process clause, however, has traditionally been interpreted as protecting certain "negative liberties," i.e., an individual's right to be free from arbitrary or discriminatory action taken by a state or municipality. This circuit has recognized the "well established notion that the Constitution limits the actions the states can take rather than mandating specific obligations." Bradberry v. Pinellas County, 789 F.2d 1513, 1517 (11th Cir. 1986). . . .

Two Supreme Court decisions dealing with access to abortions also support our conclusion that there is no general right to medical care or treatment provided by the state. In Maher v. Roe, 432 U.S. 464 (1977), two indigent women brought suit challenging a Connecticut regulation prohibiting the funding of abortions that were not medically necessary. The plaintiffs argued under the Fourteenth Amendment that the state regulation impinged on their constitutional right to an abortion, as recognized in Roe v. Wade, 410 U.S. 113 (1973). The Court upheld the state regulation, concluding that *Roe* did not declare an unqualified constitutional right to an abortion; rather, that case declared a woman's right to be protected from unduly burdensome interference with her freedom to decide whether to terminate her pregnancy. Significantly, in reaching this result, the Court noted that "the Constitution imposes no obligation on the states to pay the pregnancy-related medical expenses of indigent women, or indeed to pay any of the medical expenses of indigents." *Maher*, 432 U.S. at 469 (footnote omitted).

The Court's subsequent decision in Harris v. McRae, 448 U.S. 297 (1980), reinforced the constitutional distinction between requiring the state to provide medical services and prohibiting the state from impeding access to such services. The plaintiffs in *Harris* challenged the constitutionality of the Hyde amendment, which denied public funding for certain medically necessary abortions, as violating their due process liberty interest in deciding whether to terminate a pregnancy. The Supreme Court held that although the liberty protected by the due process clause prohibits unwarranted government interference with freedom of choice in the context of certain personal decisions, "it does not confer an entitlement to such funds as may be necessary to realize all the advantages of that freedom." . . . More recently, the Court has interpreted *Maher* and *Harris* as standing for the proposition that, "as a general matter, the state is under no constitutional duty to provide substantive services for those within its border." Youngberg v. Romeo, 457 U.S. 307, 317 (1982).

Several court of appeals decisions have addressed the issue of whether a state or municipality has a duty under the Fourteenth Amendment to provide various protective services to its citizens. Almost without exception, these courts have concluded that governments are under no constitutional duty to provide police, fire, or other public safety services. . . .

B

That there exists no such general right to the provision of medical care and services by the state, however, does not end our inquiry. Both the Supreme Court and various circuit courts have indicated that the existence of a "special custodial or other relationship" between an individual and the state may trigger a constitutional duty on the part of the state to provide certain medical or other services. In these special circumstances, the state's failure to provide such services might implicate constitutionally protected rights.

For example, the Supreme Court has held that the Eighth Amendment prohibition against cruel and unusual punishments, applicable to the states via the Fourteenth Amendment, requires states to provide medical care for those whom it is punishing by incarceration.... Similarly, the Court has held that an involuntarily committed mental patient retains ... a clear Fourteenth Amendment right "to adequate food, shelter, clothing, and medical care." *Youngberg*, 457 U.S. at 315 . . .

Following this rationale, a constitutional duty can arise only when a state or municipality, by exercising a significant degree of custody or control over an individual, places that person in a worse situation than he would have been had the government not acted at all. Such a situation could arise by virtue of the state affirmatively placing an individual in a position of danger, effectively stripping a person of her ability to defend herself, or cutting off potential sources of private aid. The key concept is the exercise of coercion, dominion, or restraint by the state. . . .

In the present case, we conclude that DeKalb County did not exercise a degree of coercion, dominion, or restraint over Ms. Wideman sufficient to create a "special relationship," . . . The county did not force or otherwise coerce her into its ambulance; it merely made the ambulance available to her, and she entered it voluntarily. Ms. Wideman's physical condition at the time might have required her to seek immediate medical help, and that need might have induced her to make use of the service provided by the county, hoping that she could convince the EMS employees to take her where she wanted to go. Her physical condition, however, cannot be attributed to the county. . . . Therefore, the county was under no affirmative constitutional duty to provide any particular type of emergency medical service for her. . . .

. . . Because the Constitution does not require municipalities to provide any emergency medical services at all, it would be anomalous indeed to hold them liable for providing limited services which happen to be less extensive than a particular citizen may desire. . . .

Notes: The Differing Obligations of Physicians and Hospitals; Hospitals as Quasi-Public Facilities

1. *The "No Duty" Rule.* As the *Hurley* court suggests, physicians are not obligated to provide care to a particular patient unless they have agreed to do so. A standard characterization of this principle appears in Oliver v. Brock, 342 So. 2d 1, 3 (Ala. 1976):

A physician is under no obligation to engage in practice or to accept professional employment, but when the professional services of a physician are accepted by another person for the purposes of medical or surgical treatment, the relation of physician and patient is created. The relation is a consensual one wherein the patient knowingly seeks the assistance of a physician and the physician knowingly accepts him as patient. The relationship between a physician and patient may result from an express or implied contract, either general or special, and the rights and liabilities of the parties thereto are governed by the general law of contract. . . . 61 Am. Jur. 2d, Physicians, Surgeons, and Other Healers, §96.

This "no duty" rule is consistent with tort law's normal "Good Samaritan" doctrine, which does not require individuals, even professionals, to come to the aid of strangers in distress. A physician's *ethical,* as opposed to legal, duty is somewhat more demanding, however. The American Medical Association's Principles of Medical Ethics state that a "physician shall, in the provision of appropriate patient care, except in emergencies, be free to choose whom to serve. . . ." Council on Ethical and Judicial Affairs, Code of Medical Ethics: Current Opinions with Annotations xv (2006-2007). Why couldn't this ethical pledge be converted into an implied promise that physicians make to the public at large? See William E. May, Medical Ethics: Code and Covenant or Philanthropy and Contract?, 5(6) Hastings Ctr. Rep. 29 (1975). Doesn't the public rely on physicians as much as they do on hospital emergency rooms? Consider especially Dr. Eddingfield's status as the plaintiff's family physician. Despite these qualms, *Hurley* is still thought to state the prevailing law for physicians.

2. *Triggering a Treatment Relationship.* A physician's complete freedom to refuse treatment exists only if a treatment relationship has not been initiated. We discuss below what actions constitute the initiation of treatment; but here, the fact that Dr. Eddingfield may have treated Mr. Hurley in the past did not suffice, because the law considers treatment relationships to coincide with "spells of illness." Thus, once a patient recovers from an illness or stops seeking treatment, a new treatment relationship must be formed in order to invoke a duty of continuing treatment. See, e.g., Castillo v. Emergency Medicine Associates, 372 F.3d 643, 648-652 (4th Cir. 2004).

Consider how this issue might come out differently when the patient receives medical care from a health maintenance organization (HMO). In this regard, see Hand v. Tavera, 864 S.W.2d 678 (Tex. Ct. App. 1993) (holding that "when the health-care plan's insured shows up at a participating hospital emergency room, and the plan's doctor on call is consulted about treatment or admission, there is a physician-patient relationship between the doctor and the insured").

3. *The Hospital's Duty.* Despite the reluctance of the *Manlove* court to find a duty to treat, it is considered a groundbreaking case in that it paved the way for other courts to make more definitive findings of hospital liability for the refusal of emergency care. See, e.g., Stanturf v. Sipes, 447 S.W.2d 558 (Mo. 1969) (hospital may be liable for refusing to treat frostbite victim who could not post $25 deposit); Mercy Medical Center v. Winnebago County, 206 N.W.2d 198 (Wis. 1973) ("It would shock the public conscience if a person in need of medical emergency aid would be turned down at the door of a hospital"); but see Campbell v. Mincey, 413 F. Supp. 16 (N.D. Miss. 1975) (no obligation of hospital emergency room to care

for pregnant woman in labor). Many states impose a requirement of open emergency rooms by statute or regulation. See Waxman & Dorn, States Take the Lead in Preventing Patient Dumping, 22 Clearinghouse Rev. 136 (1988). See generally Karen Rothenberg, Who Cares? The Evolution of the Legal Duty to Provide Emergency Care, 26 Hous. L. Rev. 21 (1989); Judith L. Dobbertin, Note, Eliminating Patient Dumping: A Proposal for Model Legislation, 28 Val. U.L. Rev. 291, 321-331 (1993); Annot., 11 A.L.R. Fed. 683 (1972).

How do you explain the fact that hospitals have a duty to provide emergency care to all who seek it while physicians are under no such obligation? Arguably, it does not make sense to expect physicians to be available at all times, while hospitals can reasonably be expected to always have someone staffing their emergency rooms. But what about just expecting physicians to be available during their regular office hours for emergencies? Can't doctors factor into their scheduling the possibility of emergencies? Don't they in fact already do that? Is part of the issue that physicians may not necessarily have the expertise for any emergency patient that comes though the door? Suppose the physician is a dermatologist and is confronted with a cardiac emergency. Is there anything the doctor reasonably could do besides call 911?

Hospitals, too, may be able to limit their obligation according to their capacity or expertise. Suppose a hospital has no emergency room because it specializes in elective surgeries. Or suppose the emergency room is full? When this happens, hospital emergency departments often place themselves on "drive-by" status, which means they alert ambulances not to stop there. One court held this was permissible in the case of a child who consequently suffered brain damage, even though the hospital had treated the child many times in the past and had encouraged his parents to pass up other closer hospitals and come there if he had serious problems. Davis v. Johns Hopkins Hospital, 622 A.2d 128 (Md. 1993).

4. *The Meaning of Reliance.* Why is the *Manlove* reliance theory limited to just emergency care? Observe the court's reasoning that "such a refusal [of treatment] might well result in worsening the condition of the injured person, because of the time lost in a useless attempt to obtain medical aid." Presumably, this is true only in a very serious or "unmistakable" emergency. It might be possible, however, to argue for other types of reliance. Suppose, for instance, that a prospective patient chose to live in the community because of the presence of a hospital, and it would thereby frustrate his or her reliance if the hospital could deny care in nonemergencies as well as emergencies. Such patients may have a psychological reliance but no *detrimental* reliance in the sense of a material change in one's position for the worse.

Where reliance is detrimental, should the patient have to demonstrate actual reliance in the particular case, rather than reliance being assumed? The *Manlove* court appeared to treat only the detriment part as requiring proof, not the psychological expectation. Should we presume that patients always legitimately expect emergency rooms to be open to them? Consider, for instance, Guerrero v. Copper Queen Hospital, 537 P.2d 1329 (Ariz. 1975), which found that a hospital in a border town owned by a local mining company had a duty to render emergency aid to two severely burned Mexican children who were injured in their home across the border.

5. *Physicians "On Call." Hurley* and *Manlove* appear consistent because one is about doctors and the other is about hospitals. But does it make sense for hospitals to have a duty to accept emergency patients if the doctors who work there are free to refuse treatment? Courts have resolved this problem by holding that a doctor who is "on call" for a hospital emergency room voluntarily undertakes the hospital's greater duty of care. The leading decision is Hiser v. Randolph, 617 P.2d 774 (Ariz. 1980). At 11:45 P.M. one night, Bonita Hiser came to the emergency room at Mojave County General Hospital in a semi-comatose condition arising out of an exacerbation of her juvenile onset diabetes. Along with the seven other doctors in the area, Dr. Randolph took turns as the on-call physician for the emergency room, a duty for which he was paid $100 per 12-hour shift, and he was on call when Mrs. Hiser came to the hospital. When the emergency room nurse called Dr. Randolph, he refused to come in. He claimed this was because he lacked the expertise to treat diabetes, but there was also evidence that his refusal was based on personal animosity toward Mrs. Hiser or the fact that Mrs. Hiser's husband was a lawyer. Mrs. Hiser died because of the delay in treatment. The court found that Dr. Randolph breached his duty of care arising from his status as an on-call physician. According to the court,

> the obviously intended effect of the [hospital's] bylaws and rules and regulations was to obligate the emergency room doctor "on call" to provide emergency treatment to the best of the doctor's ability to any emergency patient of the hospital. Under these circumstances, the lack of a consensual physician-patient relationship before a duty to treat can arise has been waived by the signatory doctors.

But see Childs v. Weis, 440 S.W.2d 104 (Tex. Ct. App. 1969) (physicians on emergency call were under no specific duty to see all patients who presented themselves to the emergency room).

A similar analysis is possible for HMO physicians. See St. Charles v. Kender, 646 N.E.2d 411 (Mass. Ct. App. 1995) (HMO subscriber is a third-party beneficiary of an HMO's contracts with its physicians; contract was breached when physician failed to return patient's calls for an appointment). In Hand v. Tavera, 864 S.W.2d 678 (Tex. Ct. App. 1993), Lewis Hand went to the Humana Hospital (Village Oaks) emergency room because of a three-day headache. He also had high blood pressure, and his medical history revealed that his father had died of an aneurysm. The emergency room physician was able to control Mr. Hand's blood pressure and headache temporarily with medication but ultimately concluded that Mr. Hand should be admitted to the hospital. Hospital admissions required the approval of another physician under the Humana Health Care Plan, so the emergency room physician called Dr. Robert Tavera, the physician responsible that evening for authorizing admissions of Humana patients. Dr. Tavera decided that Mr. Hand should be treated as an outpatient. A few hours after returning home, Mr. Hand suffered a stroke. The trial court granted Dr. Tavera summary judgment on the ground that no patient-physician relationship had been formed, but the appellate court held that a patient-physician relationship existed by virtue of Mr. Hand's membership in the Humana Health Care Plan and Dr. Tavera's designation "as the doctor acting for the Humana plan that night." As the court observed, "Hand paid premiums to Humana to purchase medical care in advance of need . . . and Tavera's medical group agreed to treat Humana enrollees in exchange for the fees received from Humana. In effect, Hand had paid in advance for the services of the Humana plan doctor on duty that night, who happened to be Tavera, and the physician-patient relationship existed." Which actions constitute the formation of a doctor-patient relationship is discussed further at pages 118-122. As discussed there, when physicians serve as on-call *consultants* to the emergency room, courts generally require some involvement in the patient's care before finding a duty to treat.

6. *The Quasi-Public Status of Hospitals.* Another basis for imposing a duty to treat, distinct from the reliance theory, is the assertion that physicians or hospitals owe duties to the public at large simply by virtue of their having chosen to become licensed health care providers. It is a version of this argument that the *Hurley* court rejects with the cryptic comment that "analogies, drawn from the obligations to the public on the part of innkeepers, common carriers, and the like, are beside the mark." In ancient common law, certain occupations and businesses were considered to be "common callings," meaning that they could not turn away customers without a good reason. Innkeepers and public transport ("common carriers") were the classic examples. The reasons for these heightened public service duties were the importance of the service, the monopoly status of the business, and the support it received from the government. See Charles Burdick, The Origin of the Peculiar Duties of Public Service Companies, 11 Colum. L. Rev. 514, 616, 742 (1911); O. W. Holmes, Jr., Common Carriers and the Common Law, 13 Am. L. Rev. 40 (1879). In modern times, these "businesses affected with a public interest" are the public utilities (electric, phone, trains, etc.), and common law duties of public service have been supplanted by overt government regulation. This body of common law has therefore become somewhat archaic, but it is still sometimes invoked against trade associations or labor unions that refuse membership. See generally, Comment, Judicial Intervention in Admission Decisions of Private Professional Associations, 49 U. Chi. L. Rev. 840 (1982); Developments, Judicial Control of Actions of Private Associations, 76 Harv. L. Rev. 983 (1963).

This body of law has been used to characterize hospitals as "quasi-public" facilities for purposes of giving *physicians* rights of access to their medical staffs. Considering that patients are the ultimate customers for whom public benefit is intended, shouldn't this analogy have even more application to them? It would be ironic indeed to insist on physician access but deny patient access. Nevertheless, the *Manlove* court rejected this view. In other states, more recent decisions have been more receptive to the quasi-public characterization. For instance, in Thompson v. Sun City Community Hospital, 688 P.2d 605 (Ariz. 1984), the court found that a cause of action exists against a hospital that stabilized a patient with a severed artery and then transferred him for financial reasons. The court based the duty to treat on the general public policy embodied in hospital licensing regulations and private accreditation standards. Also, in Payton v. Weaver, considered at page 129, the court suggested in dictum that this public service theory could be used to impose a community-wide obligation on kidney dialysis centers to share the burden of treating an unwanted disruptive patient. Cf. A.J.G. Priest, Possible Adaptation of Public Utility Concepts in the Health Care Field, 35 L. & Contemp. Probs. 839 (1970).

7. *The Private Status of Physicians.* Reconsider the situation of physicians. Why shouldn't medical practice by physicians be considered a "common calling" or a quasi-public service? Indeed, it turns out that, in fifteenth-century English law, physicians were included on the list of common callings along with blacksmiths and other important professions. Perhaps today the missing ingredient is that a physician rarely has a local monopoly; usually there are several in town. But not always. One court found a common law duty to treat where the sole physician practice group in town refused to accept a patient who had filed a complaint against one of the doctors in the group. Leach v. Drummond Medical Group, 192 Cal. Rptr. 650 (Cal. Ct. App. 1983).

In a few state statutes, regulatory law imposes some limited duties on physicians to provide care for patients. In Massachusetts, for instance, physicians, as a condition of being licensed, must agree to charge Medicare patients no more than Medicare's "reasonable charge." This has been held not to violate the constitutional rights of physicians. Dukakis v. Massachusetts Medical Society, 815 F.2d 790 (1st Cir. 1987).

8. *Paying vs. Indigent Patients.* Perhaps this body of law is not more developed because doctors and hospitals rarely turn away patients who can pay. For patients who cannot pay, the public service theory is usually no help, since the common law never required common callings to serve people for free. Only the reliance theory reaches this result, but it is restricted to severe emergencies, those in which the patient is worse off for having made a futile attempt to secure service. Only in Arizona have courts used a public service theory to impose a duty to treat patients who cannot pay, and there too the duty is limited to emergency care. (Should it be?)

9. *Enforcement of Public Rights.* For patients who cannot pay, regulatory law places hospitals under somewhat greater duties than the common law to treat both emergency and nonemergency patients, but these public law duties are limited and are not enforceable by individual patients. The federal Hill-Burton Act (42 U.S.C. §291) requires hospitals who have received construction grants under the Act to provide 3 percent of their care to indigent patients for 20 years. See James Blumstein, Court Action, Agency Reaction: The Hill-Burton Act as a Case Study, 69 Iowa L. Rev. 1227 (1984); Kenneth Wing, The Community Service Obligation of Hill-Burton Health Facilities, 23 B.C. L. Rev. 577 (1982). Construction funding under the Act ceased a number of years ago, however, so few hospitals are still under this obligation, and even when the law was in effect individual patients could not easily enforce it. See generally AHA v. Schweiker, 721 F.2d 170 (7th Cir. 1983); Rand E. Rosenblatt, Health Care Reform and Administrative Law: A Structural Approach, 88 Yale L.J. 243 (1978).

Another source of relevant law is charitable tax exemption. Nonprofit hospitals are considered to be "charities" that are exempt from property and income tax. Part of this charitable status includes an obligation to treat some patients for free. Federal law restricts this free-care obligation to emergency patients, as do most states, but a few states are beginning to require hospitals to devote a certain percentage of their overall services to patients who cannot pay. Once again, however, this is a community service obligation owed to the public at large, not to individual patients, and so it cannot be enforced very easily by private action. Finally, the Joint Commission on Accreditation of Healthcare Organizations

(JCAHO) private accreditation standards require hospitals to accept patients without regard to "source of payment," but this is interpreted to mean accepting all patients with some source of payment (e.g., not turning away Medicaid patients) rather than a duty to accept patients who cannot pay.

This leaves us with the following patchwork of laws: for physicians, no common law duty to treat, even in emergencies. For hospitals: (1) a common law duty to treat emergency patients regardless of payment, but only in severe emergencies; (2) common law and regulatory duties to treat all patients who can pay; but (3) no enforceable duty to treat nonemergency or mild emergency patients who cannot pay. This set the stage for enactment of a new federal statute, the Emergency Medical Treatment and Active Labor Act (EMTALA), discussed in the *Burditt* case at page 85.

Notes: Moral and Constitutional Rights to Health Care

1. *Moral Rights to Treatment.* The discussion of legal rights to treatment surely must be informed by how our society views moral rights to health care. While Lois Shepherd argues that we are evolving toward a more caring community (page 73), what message does society send when the law limits the right to treatment so narrowly as to encompass only serious emergencies? Does the emergency care limitation suggest that we are trying to limit care to the most compelling needs and to avoid people demanding too much care (emergencies being thought of as unpredictable). This might be seen as a partial embodiment of the "rescue principle," which declares that the strongest ethical demand in medicine is to help those in greatest need. In this regard, the moral dimension of medicine is stronger than in any other commercial arena, because there is no equivalent requirement that grocers, restaurants, or hotels provide their services for free to people in dire straits. What justifies this distinction? Is it that if food and housing were available on demand, it would be too easy to abuse the privilege? But what kinds of incentives for patients does a right only to emergency care generate? Is the reluctance of the courts to find even broader rights to health care a reflection of the difficulty in deciding who to hold responsible for vindicating these rights? Or perhaps it reflects the difficulty in defining what a right to health care would include. Consider in this regard the difference between defining a right to housing and a right to health care.

The moral issue can also be debated from a broader, social perspective. So far, we have thought only about whether patients have a right to demand treatment from particular doctors and hospitals. Even where they do not have these private rights, perhaps they have a claim to a more public right, one that society as a whole owes to provide minimally decent health care to all. We currently recognize this claim to basic social support for education and to a more limited extent for food and housing. But for health care, there is no national safety net. Medicaid coverage provides health insurance for the poor, but less than half of those living in poverty are eligible. Almost 47 million Americans have no health insurance of any kind. Perhaps this social inequity is politically and morally sustainable only because private hospital emergency rooms exist as a last resort for those without insurance. Could it be, then, that the heightened private law duties of hospitals have weakened our nation's public law commitment to health care access? See Mark A. Hall, The Unlikely Case in Favor of Patient Dumping, 28 Jurimetrics 389 (1988). For an argument that private law duties tend to undermine voluntary charity, see Richard Epstein, Mortal Peril: Our Inalienable Right to Health Care? (1997). For responses to Epstein, see *Symposium: Is America's Health Care System in Mortal Peril?*, 1998 U. Ill. L. Rev. 683.

2. *Positive vs. Negative Liberty.* If there is a moral right to health care generally, it is clearly not vindicated as a substantive due process right by the U.S. Constitution. *Wideman* is a classic statement of the principle that the Bill of Rights embodies primarily negative, not positive, liberties, that is, it is concerned mainly with freedoms from government imposition, not rights to government assistance. Thus, the Constitution becomes relevant to health care when the government bans treatment choices or forces treatment, but not when it simply declines to assist in obtaining treatment. In this regard, the U.S. Constitution differs markedly from constitutional models in Europe.

Wideman was followed by an important Supreme Court opinion confirming its general analysis in this regard. In DeShaney v. Winnebago County Department of Social Services, 489 U.S. 189 (1989), the Court held that no constitutional violation occurred in a case where a child was left with permanent brain damage when a state social services agency failed to intervene aggressively enough to prevent child abuse. The state had received several reports of severe beatings by the father. The Court reaffirmed "that the due process clauses generally confer no affirmative right to governmental aid," and it reasoned that the state agency had not assumed a "special relationship" with the child by virtue of having made some ineffectual efforts to protect him since the agency did nothing to make him more vulnerable to the danger. See also Archie v. Racine, 847 F.2d 1211 (7th Cir. 1988) (en banc) (§1983 action not maintainable for city rescue service's negligent failure to dispatch ambulance; no constitutional right to treatment exists).

3. *Institutional Responsibilities of Mental Hospitals.* An exception to this negative liberty principle exists for individuals over whom the state has control, and it has generated significant litigation with respect to mental hospitals. An early, highly influential decision addressing the constitutional right to treatment in the context of state institutionalization is Judge Frank Johnson's remarkable order taking direct charge over the administration of Alabama's state mental hospital because of its persistent failure to provide any meaningful form of treatment. Wyatt v. Stickney, 325 F. Supp. 781 (M.D. Ala. 1971), 344 F. Supp. 373 (M.D. Ala. 1972). See also O'Connor v. Donaldson, 422 U.S. 563 (1975) (civil commitment to psychiatric hospital invalid without treatment); Comment, Wyatt v. Stickney and the Right of Civilly Committed Mental Patients to Adequate Treatment, 86 Harv. L. Rev. 1282 (1973). In Thomas S. v. Morrow, 781 F.2d 367 (4th Cir. 1986), the court found a constitutional duty to provide community-based mental health services in order to ensure the availability of a least restrictive means of treatment for patients that would otherwise have to be involuntarily committed. In Olmstead v. L.C., the U.S. Supreme Court found a duty under the Americans with Disabilities Act for states to place individuals with mental disabilities in less restrictive community settings rather than in institutions. 527 U.S. 581 (1999).

Prisoners are another class of persons who gain certain rights to health care by virtue of their confinement. There, the rights rest also in the Eighth Amendment's prohibition against cruel and unusual punishment.

4. *Equal Protection.* In Maher v. Roe, 432 U.S. 464, 469-470 (1977), discussed in *Wideman*, the Court identified another possible source of a constitutional duty to treat: "The Constitution imposes no obligation on the states to pay . . . any of the medical expenses of indigents. But when a state decides to alleviate some of the hardships of poverty by providing medical care, the manner in which it dispenses benefits is subject to constitutional limitations." For example, in Memorial Hospital v. Maricopa County, 415 U.S. 250 (1974), the Court struck down Arizona's requirement of a year's residence in a county as a condition of receiving nonemergency medical care at county expense as infringing on the right to travel. Might a state be subject to an equal protection attack for funding some procedures but not others? See Doe v. Colautti, 592 F.2d 704 (3d Cir. 1978) (finding no violation of the equal protection clause when Pennsylvania's medical assistance program provided less generous benefits for psychiatric care than for general medical care).

5. *Legislative Mandates.* In Harris v. McRae, 448 U.S. 297 (1980), another abortion funding case discussed in *Wideman*, the Court addressed a nonconstitutional theory for compelling government funding of health care. States that participate in Medicaid are, generally speaking, required to fund most medically necessary forms of treatment. Beal v. Doe, 432 U.S. 438, 444 (1977). Although *McRae* found this statutory requirement to be inapplicable to abortions, in other cases the medical necessity mandate has proved to be an effective tool for obtaining Medicaid coverage. Ellis v. Patterson, 859 F.2d 52 (8th Cir. 1988) (requiring reasonable funding once a state decides to provide coverage for liver transplants); Rush v. Parham, 625 F.2d 1150 (5th Cir. 1980) (requiring funding for sex change operations in certain circumstances). However, there is no statutory requirement that Medicaid be funded at a level sufficient to cover all people who need it.

■ BURDITT v. U.S. DEPARTMENT OF HEALTH AND HUMAN SERVICES
934 F.2d 1362 (5th Cir. 1991)

REAVLEY, Circuit Judge.

Hospitals that execute Medicare provider agreements with the federal government pursuant to 42 U.S.C. §1395cc must treat all human beings who enter their emergency departments in accordance with the Emergency Medical Treatment and Active Labor Act (EMTALA), 42 U.S.C. §1395dd. Hospitals and responsible physicians found to have violated EMTALA's requirements are subject to civil money penalties. [This case is an appeal by Dr. Burditt of a $20,000 fine assessed against him by the Department of Health and Human Services. EMTALA also provides for a private cause of action, with prevailing plaintiffs entitled to monetary damages from the offending hospital and appropriate equitable relief. Damages may not be recovered from physicians in a private cause of action, however.] . . .

I.A. FACTS

Mrs. Rosa Rivera arrived in the emergency room of DeTar Hospital in Victoria, Texas at approximately 4:00 p.m. on December 5, 1986. At or near term with her sixth child, she was experiencing one-minute, moderate contractions every three minutes and her membranes had ruptured. Two obstetrical nurses, Tammy Kotsur and Donna Keining, examined her and found indicia of labor and dangerously high blood pressure. Because Rivera had received no prenatal care, and had neither a regular doctor nor means of payment, Kotsur telephoned Burditt, who was next on DeTar's rotating call-list of physicians responsible for such "unaligned" obstetrics patients. Upon hearing Rivera's history and condition, Burditt told Kotsur that he "didn't want to take care of this lady" and asked her to prepare Rivera for transfer to John Sealy Hospital in Galveston, Texas, 170 miles away. Burditt agreed to call back in five to ten minutes.

Kotsur and Keining told the nursing supervisor, Jean Herman, and DeTar's administrator, Charles Sexton, of their belief that it would be unsafe to transfer Rivera. When Burditt called back, Keining told him that, according to Sexton's understanding of hospital regulations and federal law, Burditt would have to examine Rivera and personally arrange for John Sealy to receive her before he could legally transfer her. Keining asked Burditt for permission to start an intravenous push of magnesium sulfate as a precaution against convulsive seizures. Burditt told Keining to begin administering this medication only if Rivera could be transported by ambulance. . . .

Burditt arrived at approximately 4:50 to examine Rivera. He confirmed her blood pressure to be the highest he had ever seen, 210/130, and he assumed that she had been hypertensive throughout her pregnancy. As the experienced head of DeTar's obstetrics and gynecology department, Burditt knew that there was a strong possibility that Rivera's hypertension would precipitate complications which might kill both Rivera and her baby. He also knew that the infants of hypertensive mothers are at higher-than-normal risk of intrauterine growth retardation. He estimated that Rivera's baby was six pounds — less than normal weight — and arranged her transfer to John Sealy, a perinatal facility better equipped than DeTar to care for underweight infants. . . .

At approximately 5:00, Herman showed Burditt DeTar's guidelines regarding EMTALA, but he refused to read them. Burditt told Herman that Rivera represented more risk than he was willing to accept from a malpractice standpoint. Herman explained that Rivera could not be transferred unless Burditt signed a DeTar form entitled "Physician's Certificate Authorizing Transfer." Burditt asked for "that dang piece of paper" and signed his name under the following:

> I have examined the patient, _____, and have determined that, based upon the information available to me at this time, the medical benefits reasonably expected from the provision of appropriate medical treatment at another medical facility outweigh the increased risks to the patient's medical condition from effecting [the] transfer. The basis for my conclusion is as follows: _____

Burditt listed no basis for his conclusion and remarked to Herman that "until DeTar Hospital pays my malpractice insurance, I will pick and choose those patients that I want to treat."

Burditt then went to care for another unaligned patient, Sylvia Ramirez, while the nurses arranged Rivera's transfer. They found another obstetrical nurse, Anita Nichols, to accompany Rivera to John Sealy. Burditt returned to the nurses' station and stayed there from 5:30 to 6:18. He never again examined Rivera or asked about her medical condition, though he inquired several times about the status of her transfer. Burditt delivered the Ramirez baby at 6:22. Afterward, Nichols told him the results of her examination of Rivera and informed him that the ambulance had arrived. Based exclusively on Nichols' statements, Burditt concluded that Rivera's condition had not changed since his examination two hours before. Burditt did not reexamine Rivera though he saw her being wheeled to the ambulance. He did not order any medication or life support equipment for Rivera during her transfer.

Nichols delivered Rivera's healthy baby in the ambulance approximately 40 miles into the 170-mile trip to John Sealy. She directed the driver to nearby Ganado Hospital to get a drug called pitocin to staunch Rivera's bleeding. While there, Nichols telephoned Burditt, who ordered her to continue to John Sealy despite the birth. Instead, per Rivera's wishes, Nichols returned Rivera to DeTar, where Burditt refused to see her because she failed to proceed to John Sealy in accordance with his instructions. Burditt directed that Rivera be discharged if she was stable and not bleeding excessively. A DeTar official pressed Burditt to allow Dr. Shirley Pigott to examine Rivera. Rivera stayed at DeTar under Pigott's care for three days and left in good health. . . .

II.A.1. Screening

Because Rivera presented herself to DeTar's emergency department and a request was made on her behalf for care, EMTALA required DeTar to

> provide for an *appropriate* medical screening examination *within the capability of the hospital's emergency department* to determine whether or not an emergency medical condition . . . exists or to determine if the individual is in active labor. . . . 42 U.S.C. §1395dd(a) (emphasis added).

The parties agree that DeTar appropriately screened Rivera and discovered that she had an "emergency medical condition" — severe hypertension — within the meaning of 42 U.S.C. §1395dd(e)(1).[3]

II.A.2. Emergency Medical Condition and Active Labor

Patients diagnosed with an "emergency medical condition" or "active labor" must either be treated or be transferred in accordance with EMTALA. Burditt claims that Rivera received all of the care that she was due under EMTALA because he stabilized her hypertension sufficiently for transfer and she was not in active labor when she left DeTar for John Sealy.

---

[3] EMTALA defines "emergency medical condition"

> as a medical condition manifesting itself by acute symptoms of sufficient severity (including severe pain) such that the absence of immediate medical attention could reasonably be expected to result in —
> (A) placing the patient's health in serious jeopardy,
> (B) serious impairment to bodily functions, or
> (C) serious dysfunction of any bodily organ or part.

42 U.S.C. §1395dd(e)(1) (Supp. IV 1987).

II.a.2.a. Unstable Emergency Medical Condition

Rivera's blood pressure was 210/130 at 4:00 and 5:00. This was the last reading known to Burditt before he facilitated her transfer. Nurses also measured her blood pressure as 173/105 at 5:30, 178/103 at 5:45, 186/107 at 6:00, and 190/110 at 6:50. Experts testified that Rivera's hypertension put her at high risk of suffering serious complications, including seizures, heart failure, kidney dysfunction, tubular necrosis, stroke, intracranial bleeding, placental abruption, and fetal hypoxia. This is substantial, if not conclusive evidence that Rivera entered and exited DeTar with an emergency medical condition.

Burditt argues that he fulfilled EMTALA's requirements with respect to Rivera's hypertension by "stabilizing" it, or

> provid[ing] such medical treatment of the condition as may be necessary to assure, within reasonable medical probability, that no material deterioration of the condition is likely to result from [a] transfer. . . . 42 U.S.C. §1395dd(e)(4)(A).

He claims that the magnesium sulfate that he ordered for Rivera has an antihypertensive effect that complements its primary anticonvulsive purpose.

Development of any of the possible complications could have killed or seriously injured Rivera, her baby, or both, and thus would constitute a "material deterioration" under 42 U.S.C. §1395dd(e)(4)(A). Any deterioration would "result" from transfer in that Rivera would have received better care for any complication at DeTar than in the ambulance. Thus, Burditt could not have stabilized Rivera unless he provided treatment that medical experts agree would prevent the threatening and severe consequences of Rivera's hypertension while she was in transit. [The HHS appeals board] could properly disregard Burditt's testimony and accept that of all other testifying experts in holding that Burditt provided no such treatment, and thus did not stabilize Rivera's emergency medical condition. . . .

II.a.2.b. Active Labor

EMTALA defines "active labor" as labor at a time when

> (B) there is inadequate time to effect safe transfer to another hospital prior to delivery, or
> (C) a transfer may pose a threat [to] the health and safety of the patient or the unborn child. 42 U.S.C. §1395dd(e)(2)(B)-(C).

This statutory definition renders irrelevant any medical definition of active labor. . . .

Burditt challenges the ALJ's finding that, at approximately 5:00, there was inadequate time to safely transfer Rivera to John Sealy before she delivered her baby. Dr. Warren Crosby testified that, based on Burditt's own examination results, Rivera would, more likely than not, deliver within three hours after Burditt [made the decision to transfer her to] John Sealy. . . . Burditt does not challenge [the] conclusion that the ambulance trip from DeTar to John Sealy takes approximately three hours. We therefore hold that [the HHS appeals board] properly concluded that Rivera was in active labor under 42 U.S.C. §1395dd(e)(2)(B).

The ALJ also found that Rivera was in active labor under clause C at the time Burditt examined her. There is always some risk of a vehicular accident in transit, so transfer always "may" pose a threat to the health and safety of the patient or fetus. . . . We believe that Congress intended clause C to extend EMTALA's . . . protection to women in labor who have any complication with their pregnancies regardless of delivery immanency. Because better medical care is available in a hospital than in an ambulance, whether a transfer "may pose a threat" under 42 U.S.C. §1395dd(e)(2)(C) depends on whether the woman in labor has any medical condition that could interfere with the normal, natural delivery of her healthy child. Under the statutory language, a woman in labor is entitled to EMTALA's . . . protections upon a showing of possible threat; it does not require proof of a reasonable medical probability that any threat will come to fruition. . . .

The record overwhelmingly confirms that Rivera's hypertension could have interfered with a normal delivery, and she was thus in active labor under 42 U.S.C. §1395dd(e)(2)(C). . . .

II.A.3. Treat or Transfer

Upon discovery of active labor or an emergency medical condition, EMTALA usually requires hospitals to treat the discovered condition. Under certain circumstances, however, EMTALA allows hospitals to transfer patients instead of treating them. 42 U.S.C. §1395dd(b)(1)(B). . . . [The court went on to find that Burditt had not satisfied the requirements under EMTALA for a transfer before stabilization. Under EMTALA, transfer is permitted if the patient requests transfer *or* the physician has certified in writing that the medical benefits of transfer outweigh the increased risks to the patient. In addition, the receiving hospital must be capable of providing the needed treatment and must have agreed to accept the transfer. Finally, the transfer must occur with appropriate personnel and transportation, including appropriate life support measures. While Burditt had obtained consent from John Sealy before the transfer, he had not reasonably concluded that the benefits of transfer outweighed the risks nor had he arranged for the transfer with appropriate personnel and transportation.]

II.C. EMTALA's CONSTITUTIONALITY

As his final attempt to escape [liability], Burditt claims that EMTALA effects a public taking of his services without just compensation in contravention of the Constitution's Fifth Amendment.

Assuming *arguendo* that professional services constitute property protected by the takings clause, Burditt has not shown that EMTALA effects a taking. EMTALA imposes no responsibilities directly on physicians; it unambiguously requires hospitals to examine and stabilize, treat, or appropriately transfer all who arrive requesting treatment. Its provision for sanctions against physicians who knowingly violate its requirements is merely an enforcement mechanism that does not alter its explicit assignment of duties.

Governmental regulation that affects a group's property interests "does not constitute a taking of property where the regulated group is not required to participate in the regulated industry." Whitney v. Heckler, 780 F.2d 963, 972 (11th Cir.), *cert. denied*, 479 U.S. 813 (1986).

Two levels of voluntariness undermine Burditt's taking assertion. Only hospitals that voluntarily participate in the federal government's Medicare program must comply with EMTALA. Hospitals must consider the cost of complying with EMTALA's requirements in deciding whether to continue to participate in the Medicare program.

Second, Burditt is free to negotiate with DeTar or another hospital regarding his responsibility to facilitate a hospital's compliance with EMTALA. Thus, physicians only voluntarily accept responsibilities under EMTALA if they consider it in their best interest to do so. Accordingly, Burditt's claim under the takings clause is without merit. . . .

Notes: The Federal Patient Dumping Statute

1. *Historical Background.* Congress passed the Emergency Medical Treatment and Active Labor Act (EMTALA) as part of the Consolidated Omnibus Reconciliation Act of 1986 (COBRA), in response to the perception that state law was too weak to prevent widespread patient dumping. While EMTALA, or COBRA, has worked better than previous legal efforts, in part because of the private right of action, there are still concerns that patient dumping persists at unacceptable levels. One scholar argues, however, that

> EMTALA is a virtual catalogue of how to get a statute wrong. First, generalize from unrepresentative anecdotal evidence in identifying the problem. Draft the statute sloppily, and leave the most important words undefined or defined too broadly. Finance the resulting open-ended entitlement with an unfunded mandate imposed on private parties. . . . [Design the enforcement system] to reward the wrong people. Finally, apply the statute even after the world on which it depended has vanished. Any one of these problems would be bad enough in isolation, but their combined effect is devastating to the interests EMTALA was intended to protect.

David A. Hyman, Dumping EMTALA: When Bad Laws Happen to Good People (1998) (not yet published). As you read the following notes, see if you can determine why someone might reach such a conclusion. Nevertheless, Prof. Hyman acknowledges that

> the statute is wildly popular across the entirety of the political spectrum and among such disparate interest groups as physicians, advocates for the poor, [academics,] and consumer groups. Unlike many reforms, EMTALA does not create a new administrative bureaucracy; it does not favor the interests of the well-connected against the less fortunate; its on-budget costs are modest; and it seems to be no more intrusive than is absolutely necessary to accomplish its objectives. David A. Hyman, Patient Dumping and EMTALA: Past Imperfect/Future Shock, 8 Health Matrix 29 (1998).

For further discussion of these and other aspects of EMTALA, see Russell Korobkin, Determining Health Care Rights from Behind a Veil of Ignorance, 1998 U. Ill. L. Rev. 801; Sara Rosenbaum, Bruce Siegel, & Marsha Regenstein,

EMTALA and Hospital "Community Engagement": The Search for a Rational Policy, 53 Buffalo L. Rev. 499 (2005); Karen Rothenberg, Who Cares? The Evolution of the Legal Duty to Provide Emergency Care, 26 Houston L. Rev. 21 (1989); Dana E. Schaffner, Note, EMTALA: All Bark and No Bite, 2005 U. Ill. L. Rev. 1021; Lawrence E. Singer, Look What They've Done to My Law, Ma: COBRA's Implosion, 33 Hous. L. Rev. 113 (1996); Annot., 104 A.L.R. Fed. 166 (1991).

Dr. Michael Burditt was the first physician fined for an EMTALA violation, and his actions were vigorously defended by the Texas Medical Association. For a critical view of the Fifth Circuit's decision in the Burditt case, see David Hyman, Lies, Damned Lies, and Narrative, 73 Ind. L.J. 797, 824-832 (1998).

2. *Screening and Stabilizing.* EMTALA creates two distinct duties. First, the duty to screen patients is triggered by their arrival at the hospital, and it ceases if it is determined they are not in what the statute defines as an "emergency" condition. Second, if they are in an emergency condition, then the hospital must stabilize them. (The statutory requirements are similar for patients in active labor.) Most litigation has arisen at the first stage, in cases where patients claim the hospital failed entirely to evaluate or recognize their emergency condition. But that is not our main concern here. Our concern is, if there clearly is an emergency, how far does the duty to treat extend? Do hospitals have to perform bypass surgery after they halt a heart attack? Although *Burditt* found that "stabilizing" care was not rendered in that case, what about other typical situations? Consider whether the outcome would be any different under EMTALA than it was under this state law decision: Joyner v. Alton Ochsner Medical Foundation, 230 So. 2d 913 (La. Ct. App. 1970) (auto accident victim did not "require immediate admission" after stabilizing care was rendered, despite "multiple deep facial lacerations, a possible head injury, traumatic damage to the teeth and multiple bruises and contusions of the body, resulting in considerable loss of blood"). Consider whether the duty to treat under EMTALA is as strong as it is under this state law decision: Thompson v. Sun City Community Hospital, 688 P.2d 605 (Ariz. 1984) (a cause of action exists against a hospital that stabilized a patient with a severed artery and then transferred him for financial reasons). Is the federal statute any more demanding than the *Manlove* reliance theory? See generally M. Hall, The Unlikely Case in Favor of Patient Dumping, 28 Jurimetrics J. 389 (1990) ("In the great majority of cases, the federal standard will do nothing to prevent patient dumping. . . . Even for those patients who do require stabilization prior to transfer, the federal law will result only in a delay in the transfer."); Kenneth R. Wing & John R. Campbell, The Emergency Room Admission: How Far Does the "Open Door" Go?, 63 U. Det. L. Rev. 119 (1985).

According to the Eleventh Circuit, the stabilization requirement of EMTALA applies only when a hospital discharges a patient or transfers the patient to another hospital. Harry v. Marchant, 291 F.3d 767 (11th Cir. 2002) (en banc). See also Bryan V. Rectors and Visitors of the University of Virginia, 95 F.3d 349, 352 (4th Cir. 1996) (also observing that the stabilization requirement of EMTALA is defined in terms of transfer or discharge).

In its requirement to stabilize emergency patients, EMTALA does not require the impossible. If a hospital does not have the facilities or personnel necessary to fully stabilize a patient, and the patient must be transferred to a more sophisticated hospital to receive needed care, the first hospital can transfer the patient to the more sophisticated hospital without violating EMTALA. The transferring hospital must do all it can to stabilize the patient's condition, but it need not do what it cannot do. Cherukuri v. Shalala, 175 F.3d 446 (6th Cir. 1999) (absolving physician at small rural hospital after the physician transferred two patients who needed surgery to stop internal bleeding from an automobile accident).

3. *The Patient's Indigency.* While the passage of EMTALA was motivated by concerns about private hospitals "dumping" indigent or uninsured patients on public hospitals, the statutory language imposes no requirement that patients show that they were denied emergency services because of indigency or lack of insurance. See 42 U.S.C. §1395dd(a) ("if any individual . . . comes to the emergency department . . . , the hospital must provide for an appropriate medical screening examination within the capability of the hospital's emergency department"). Accordingly, courts have generally held that it is irrelevant why a person did not receive an appropriate screening exam or, if an emergency was identified, why a person did not receive stabilizing care before discharge or transfer. As one court observed, "[EMTALA] applies to any and all patients, not just to patients with insufficient resources." Brooker v. Desert Hosp. Corp., 947 F.2d 412, 415 (9th Cir. 1991). *Accord* Summers v. Baptist Medical Center, 91 F.3d 1132 (8th Cir. 1996); Gatewood v. Washington Healthcare Corp., 933 F.2d 1037, 1040 (D.C. Cir. 1991).

The Supreme Court addressed the motive question in the context of EMTALA's stabilization requirement and rejected any need to show an improper motive. Roberts v. Galen of Virginia, Inc., 525 U.S. 249 (1999). The Court "express[ed] no opinion" on the need to show an improper motive for a claim of inappropriate medical screening.

Perhaps the most controversial extension of EMTALA beyond economic discrimination occurred in the *Baby K* case. In In re Baby K, 16 F.3d 590 (4th Cir. 1994), parents of an anencephalic child sought ventilatory treatment of their child during periodic bouts of respiratory distress. After the second of three such episodes, the hospital sought judicial permission to withhold the ventilator when the child next came to the emergency room. In the view of the hospital, it was medically and ethically inappropriate to ventilate the child given her limited life expectancy, her total absence of consciousness, and the futility of treatment at improving her condition. According to the hospital, the only appropriate treatment for the child was the treatment "it would provide other anencephalic infants — supportive care in the form of warmth, nutrition, and hydration." The court rejected the hospital's argument. It observed that EMTALA requires stabilizing treatment in the event of a medical emergency, and the child's respiratory distress met EMTALA's definition of a medical emergency. If there was to be an exception for "futile" care under EMTALA, Congress would have to write that exception into the statute. The court's opinion in *Baby K* is presented in Chapter 1.

The *Baby K* decision raises serious questions about the ability of society to contain health care costs. If the hospital in the case could not deny a ventilator to an anencephalic child, how could any emergency medical care be withheld on the ground that its high costs were not justified by its minimal benefit? Is there a distinction between the economic or other discrimination prohibited by EMTALA and the denial of care that results when a hospital is concerned about the limits of society's resources?

Perhaps in recognition of these concerns, the Fourth Circuit limited the impact of *Baby K* two years later. In Bryan v. Rectors and Visitors of the University of Virginia, 95 F.3d 349 (4th Cir. 1996), an EMTALA claim was brought on behalf of a patient who died of a heart attack after her physicians decided that "no further efforts to prevent her death should be made." Twenty days before the heart attack, the patient had been admitted to the hospital in respiratory distress. Eight days before the heart attack, apparently because of the hopelessness of the patient's condition, her physicians decided to withhold further life-sustaining treatment, including cardiopulmonary resuscitation, in the event of a cardiac arrest. When she suffered her heart attack, no efforts were made to prevent her death. According to the court, there was no EMTALA violation because EMTALA "was intended to regulate the hospital's care of the patient only in the immediate aftermath of the act of admitting her for emergency treatment and while it considered whether it would undertake longer-term full treatment or instead transfer the patient to a hospital that could and would undertake that treatment." Id. at 352.

4. *Preventive Dumping.* There has been concern that hospitals would try to evade their EMTALA obligations by dumping patients before they reach the emergency room. For example, when called by a paramedic or emergency medical technician who is transporting a patient by ambulance, the emergency room staff might direct the ambulance to another hospital. Early cases suggested that hospitals would have considerable freedom to prevent patients from reaching the emergency room. See Miller v. Medical Center of Southwest Louisiana, 22 F.3d 626 (5th Cir. 1994) (hospital not liable under EMTALA for refusing to accept the transfer of a patient who needed specialized emergency care beyond the capabilities of the transferring hospital); Johnson v. University of Chicago Hospitals, 982 F.2d 230 (7th Cir. 1992) (hospital not liable for diverting an ambulance to another hospital).

Subsequent amendment of the EMTALA regulations and case law interpreting the amendment have limited the ability of hospitals to engage in preventive dumping. Under one regulation, patients have come to the hospital's emergency room for purposes of EMTALA once they have reached any part of the hospital's property, including a hospital-owned ambulance service. 42 C.F.R. §489.24(b) (2007) (applied in Hernandez v. Starr County Hospital District, 30 F. Supp. 2d 970 (S.D. Tex. 1999); Preston v. Meriter Hosp., Inc., 700 N.W.2d 158 (Wis. 2005)). The same regulation permits hospitals to divert non-hospital-owned ambulance services if the emergency department "does not have the staff or facilities to accept any additional emergency patients." 42 C.F.R. §489.24(b)(4). The Ninth Circuit has interpreted this provision to mean that a hospital violates EMTALA when it diverts a non-hospital-owned ambulance in the absence of an inability to provide treatment for the patient. Arrington v. Wong, 237 F.3d 1066 (9th Cir. 2001). See Caroline J. Stalker, Comment, How Far Is Too Far?: EMTALA Moves from the Emergency Room to Off-Campus Entities, 36 Wake Forest L. Rev. 823 (2001).

Note that there is some ambiguity to §489.24(b). Although the regulation seems to limit the ability of hospitals to divert non-hospital-owned ambulances, it also states that "[a]n individual in a non-hospital-owned ambulance off hospital property is not considered to have come to the hospital's emergency department even if a member of the ambulance staff contacts the hospital by telephone or telemetry communications and informs the hospital that they want to transport the individual to the hospital for examination and treatment."

A related question is whether patients must come to the emergency department, as opposed to other parts of the hospital, to trigger EMTALA. As indicated, under 42 C.F.R. §489.24(b), EMTALA is triggered when a patient is anywhere on the hospital's property. Thus, a First Circuit decision emphasizes the point that a hospital's duty to stabilize before transfer applies to any patient in the hospital, "regardless of how that person enters the institution or where within the walls he may be when the hospital identifies the problem." Lopez-Soto v. Hawayek, 175 F.3d 170, 173 (1st Cir. 1999) (observing that the stabilization requirement of EMTALA applies to an individual who "comes to a hospital" and holding that EMTALA applies when a pregnant woman is admitted to the maternity ward and taken to the operating room for a cesarean section, and her infant is born with respiratory distress and needs emergency care).

5. *Dumping After Admission to the Hospital.* Courts disagree as to whether EMTALA's stabilization requirement continues to apply once the patient has been admitted to the hospital. Cases have arisen in which patients were admitted to the hospital for treatment and, after a few or more days of treatment, were transferred to another hospital or discharged before their illness was fully treated. Some courts have concluded that the obligation to stabilize persists throughout the patient's hospitalization. See Thornton v. Southwest Detroit Hospital, 895 F.2d 1131 (6th Cir. 1990); Lee v. Alleghany Regional Hospital Corporation, 778 F. Supp. 900 (W.D. Va. 1991); Smith v. Richmond Memorial Hospital, 416 S.E.2d 689 (Va. 1992).

Other courts have concluded that the stabilization requirement ceases upon the patient's admission to the hospital. Bryan v. Rectors and Visitors of the University of Virginia, 95 F.3d 349, 352 (4th Cir. 1996); James v. Sunrise Hospital, 86 F.3d 885 (9th Cir. 1996); Bryant v. Adventist Health Systems/West, 289 F.3d 1162 (9th Cir. 2002). Note that in *Bryan* and *Bryant*, the courts were deciding about the stabilization requirement for care rendered during the patient's hospital stay and not in the context of a transfer or discharge. Hence, it is not surprising that the courts were especially concerned about converting state malpractice claims into federal EMTALA claims. See note 6, infra, this page.

In *Bryant,* the Court observed that the stabilization requirement would not cease upon the patient's admission to the hospital "if a patient demonstrates in a particular case that inpatient admission was a ruse to avoid EMTALA's requirements." 289 F.3d at 1169. A federal district court invoked that point in a case in which a patient was sent home after admission but before his injuries had been stabilized. Morgan v. North Mississippi Medical Center, Inc., 403 F. Supp. 2d 1115, 1130 (S.D. Ala. 2005). Although the court denied the hospital's motion to dismiss the EMTALA claim, it ultimately concluded on summary judgment that the hospital had not engaged in a ruse to avoid EMTALA's requirements when it admitted the patient. Morgan v. North Mississippi Medical Center, Inc., 458 F. Supp. 2d 1341 (S.D. Ala. 2006).

In a final rule that took effect in 2003, the Centers for Medicare and Medicaid Services took the position that a hospital's obligations cease once the patient has been admitted to the hospital as an inpatient. 42 C.F.R. §489.24(d)(2).

6. *Appropriate Medical Screening*. In interpreting EMTALA's requirement of an "appropriate medical screening examination," courts have recognized an important tension between ensuring access to emergency care for all persons and creating a federal cause of action for charges of malpractice in the emergency room. If a person is sent home from the emergency room after a physician wrongly concludes that there is no serious health problem, the mistaken diagnosis may reflect either the negligent provision of care or the purposeful denial of care. A hospital trying to evade its EMTALA obligations might do so by giving undesired patients short shrift when screening them. At the same time, patients who have been injured by malpractice may try to bring their claim under both state tort law and federal EMTALA law, thereby increasing their potential recovery, gaining access to a federal forum and its quicker judgments, and increasing its bargaining power with the hospitals by virtue of the latter's possible loss of its participation in Medicare. EMTALA claims are often appended to state tort claims when people sue for injuries allegedly caused by inadequate emergency care. Singer, supra, 33 Hous. L. Rev. at 118 & n.22.

Courts have consistently stated that EMTALA cannot be used to bring claims for medical malpractice, and they have tried to distinguish between a denial of care and the negligent provision of care by looking at whether the hospital screened the patient in the same way it screens similarly situated patients. As the D.C. Circuit explained, the issue is whether the hospital "conform[ed] its treatment of a particular patient to its standard screening procedures. . . . [A]ny departure from standard screening procedures constitutes inappropriate screening." Gatewood v. Washington Healthcare Corporation, 933 F.2d 1037, 1041 (D.C. Cir. 1991). Similarly, the Fourth Circuit has stated that EMTALA's screening requirement is designed to prevent "disparate treatment." Vickers v. Nash General Hospital, Inc., 78 F.3d 139, 143 (4th Cir. 1996). Hospitals are obligated only to "apply uniform screening procedures to all individuals coming to the emergency room." In re Baby K, 16 F.3d 590, 595 (4th Cir. 1994). *Accord* Correa v. Hosp. San Francisco, 69 F.3d 1184 (1st Cir. 1995); Summers v. Baptist Medical Center, 91 F.3d 1132, 1138 (8th Cir. 1996); Repp v. Anadarko Municipal Hospital, 43 F.3d 519, 522 (10th Cir. 1994); Holcomb v. Monahan, 30 F.3d 116, 117 (11th Cir. 1994).

The Sixth Circuit has adopted a similar standard, although it has indicated that the departure from the hospital's standard screening procedures must have resulted from some invidious motive like bias against the patient on the basis of "race, sex, politics, occupation, education, personal prejudice, drunkenness, spite . . . distaste for the patient's condition (e.g., AIDS patients). . . . " Cleland v. Bronson Health Care Group, Inc., 917 F.2d 266, 271-272 (6th Cir. 1990); Roberts v. Galen of Virginia, 111 F.3d 405, 408-409 (6th Cir. 1997), *rev'd in part*, 525 U.S. 249 (1999). Even if the Sixth Circuit requires some invidious motive, would it ever be difficult to find a bias lurking that would be unacceptable under the *Cleland* standard? Perhaps not often, but see Garrett v. Detroit Med. Ctr., 2007 U.S. Dist. LEXIS 17584 (E.D. Mich. Mar. 14, 2007) (dismissing patient's EMTALA claim on grounds that the defendant hospital transferred the patient to a hospital so he could be treated at a hospital that was "in-network" for his insurance).

Despite the courts' admonition that EMTALA does not create a federal malpractice cause of action, there inevitably will be some overlap between

EMTALA claims and malpractice claims. Do you see how a requirement that hospitals provide all patients with their standard screening procedures amounts to requiring that the hospitals provide nonnegligent care? See Demetrios G. Metropoulos, Note, Son of COBRA: The Evolution of a Federal Malpractice Law, 45 Stan. L. Rev. 263 (1992).

As the preceding discussion indicates, courts have interpreted the requirement of an appropriate screening examination as an equal treatment right rather than an entitlement right. But isn't EMTALA a statute that grants an entitlement rather than a right of equal treatment? Is there a way to define appropriate screening examination as an entitlement without turning it even more clearly into the equivalent of nonnegligent care?

2. Wrongful Reasons to Reject Patients

While physicians or hospitals may, for most patients, refuse to treat for "good" reasons (such as inability to pay), or even for no particular reason, they may not deny care for the wrong reasons. For example, the federal civil rights acts make it unlawful for physicians and hospitals that receive federal money (such as Medicare and Medicaid) to discriminate on the basis of a patient's race, sex, religion, disability or other enumerated characteristics. On the other hand, without a statute that specifically prohibits the particular reason for discrimination, morally problematic denials of care are generally permissible, as the *Walker* case at page 105 demonstrates. When a patient is protected from discrimination by a civil rights statute, may a physician nevertheless refuse to treat on grounds of religious belief? The California Supreme Court has granted certiorari to answer that question for a patient denied fertility services, allegedly on the basis of her sexual orientation. North Coast Women's Care Medical Group, Inc. v Superior Court, 2006 Cal. LEXIS 8074 (2006).

The following materials focus on disability discrimination as the most recent and controversial form of statutory prohibition. In so doing, we do not mean to neglect the obvious importance of race and gender discrimination laws. At one time in our country's history, it was commonplace, especially in the South, for hospitals to refuse admission to blacks. These and other forms of overt discrimination have now largely disappeared as the result of various prohibitions contained in federal and state regulatory law, as well as in the hospital industry's own private accreditation code. See generally Sara Rosenbaum et al., U.S. Civil Rights Policy and Access to Health Care by Minority Americans, 57 Med. Care Res. & Rev. 226 (2000).

Serious concerns remain, however, over more subtle forms of racial and gender bias in the delivery of health care services. One form occurs in the location of health care facilities, which in inner cities are sometimes older, less accessible, or not as well equipped. See Daniel K. Hampton, Note, Title VI Challenges by Private Parties to the Location of Health Care Facilities: Toward a Just and Effective Action, 37 B.C. L. Rev. 517 (1996). Discrimination can also arise in individual treatment decisions. Numerous studies have documented that physicians treat blacks, and sometimes women, differently for the same medical conditions. For instance, blacks are less likely than whites to receive a kidney transplant, coronary artery bypass surgery or other major surgical procedures. Others respond that these studies are not as conclusive as they may appear because of real or possible differences in income, medical considerations, biological factors, and patient preferences.

No cases have yet arisen that attack differential treatment patterns as forms of racial or gender discrimination, but when they do, they will confront the problems of which medical justifications are permissible and the extent to which courts will inquire into the complexities of medical judgment. The outcome of these questions undoubtedly will be influenced by how the courts have resolved similar disputes over disability discrimination.

The analysis of discrimination under disability statutes is inherently complicated. Often a person's disability is relevant in deciding whether the person is a candidate for treatment. For example, it would not make much sense to transplant a kidney or liver into a patient dying of cancer. As we will see, unlawful denials of care can occur both from a refusal to treat at all or a refusal to provide certain kinds of care after the patient-physician relationship is formed.

■ UNITED STATES v. UNIVERSITY HOSPITAL
729 F.2d 144 (2d Cir. 1984)

PRATT, Circuit Judge.

. . . Baby Jane Doe was born on October 11, 1983 at St. Charles Hospital in Port Jefferson, New York. She was suffering from multiple birth defects, the most serious of which were myelomeningocele, commonly known as spina bifida, a condition in which the spinal cord and membranes that envelop it are exposed; microcephaly, an abnormally small head; and hydrocephalus, a condition characterized by an accumulation of fluid in the cranial vault. In addition, she exhibited a "weak face," which prevents the infant from closing her eyes or making a full suck with her tongue; a malformed brain stem; upper extremity spasticity; and a thumb entirely within her fist.

As a result of the spina bifida, the baby's rectal, bladder, leg, and sensory functions were impaired. Due to the combination of microcephaly and hydrocephalus, there was an extremely high risk that the child would be so severely retarded that she could never interact with her environment or with other people.

At the direction of the first pediatric neurosurgeon to examine her, the baby was immediately transferred to University Hospital for dual surgery to correct her spina bifida and hydrocephalus. Essentially, this would entail excising a sac of fluid and nerve endings on the spine and closing the opening, and implanting a shunt to relieve pressure caused by fluid build-up in the cranial cavity. The record indicates that these dual, corrective surgical procedures were likely to prolong the infant's life, but would not improve many of her handicapping conditions, including her anticipated mental retardation.

After consulting with several physicians, nurses, religious advisors, a social worker, and members of their family, the parents of the baby decided to forego the corrective surgery. Instead, they opted for a "conservative" medical treatment consisting of good nutrition, the administration of antibiotics, and the dressing of the baby's exposed spinal sac.

Litigation surrounding Baby Jane Doe began on October 16, when A. Lawrence Washburn, Jr., a Vermont attorney unrelated to the child and her family, commenced a proceeding in New York State Supreme Court seeking appointment of a guardian ad litem for the child and an order directing University Hospital to perform the corrective surgery, [contending that failure to do so would violate Section 504 of the Rehabilitation Act of 1973, 29 U.S.C. §794.] . . .

. . . The Appellate Division found that the "concededly concerned and loving parents have made an informed, intelligent, and reasonable determination based upon and supported by responsible medical authority." As the court elaborated:

> The record confirms that the failure to perform the surgery will not place the infant in imminent danger of death, although surgery might significantly reduce the risk of infection. On the other hand, successful results could also be achieved with antibiotic therapy. Further, while the mortality rate is higher where conservative medical treatment is used, in this particular case the surgical procedures also involved a great risk of depriving the infant of what little function remains in her legs, and would also result in recurring urinary tract and possibly kidney infections, skin infections and edemas of the limbs.

Thus, the Appellate Division determined that the parents' decision was in the best interest of the infant and that there was, therefore, no basis for judicial intervention. . . . [The Appellate Division's decision was affirmed by the New York Court of Appeals, but on the ground that the trial court had abused its discretion in permitting the case to go forward. The Court of Appeals observed that (a) Mr. Washburn (the petitioner) had no direct interest in the case (b) Mr. Washburn had not contacted the State Department of Social Services, which had primary responsibility under state law for initiating child abuse proceedings and (c) the trial court had failed to seek the Department of Social Service's assistance.

Meanwhile, as the state court proceedings were unfolding, HHS received a complaint that Baby Jane Doe was being denied medical treatment because of her handicap. In response to the complaint, HHS obtained the record of the state court proceedings and, after personal review by the Surgeon General, requested the infant's medical records from the hospital. When the hospital refused to provide the records, HHS brought its case in federal court, alleging that the hospital was violating Section 504 of the Rehabilitation Act. The federal district court granted summary judgment for the hospital on two grounds: first, the hospital refused to operate on Baby Jane Doe, not because of her handicap, but because her parents did not consent to the procedures; and second, the parents' refusal of treatment was reasonable given the medical options. The federal government appealed, resulting in this opinion.]

To focus more sharply on this central issue, it is first necessary to examine the theory upon which the government predicates its [claim]. The theory rests on two premises. First, the government draws a distinction between decisionmaking based on a "bona fide medical judgment," which without definition it concedes to be beyond the reach of §504, and decisionmaking based solely on an individual's handicap, which it argues is covered by §504. Second, the government identifies Baby Jane Doe's microcephaly, which the record indicates will result in severe mental retardation, as the handicapping condition. From these premises, the government reasons that if a newborn infant suffering from spina bifida and hydrocephalus, but not microcephaly, would receive treatment or services that differ from those provided to an infant suffering from all three defects, or alternatively, if the hospital would seek a state court order compelling surgery in the former case, but not in the latter, then a violation of §504 would have been established. . . .

With this unsettled regulatory background in mind, we turn to the statutory language, which is fundamental to any issue of statutory construction. Section 504 provides in pertinent part as follows:

> No otherwise qualified handicapped individual in the United States, as defined in section 706(7) of this title, shall, solely by reason of his handicap, be excluded from the participation in, be denied the benefits of, or be subjected to discrimination under any program or activity receiving federal financial assistance.

Under 29 U.S.C. §706(7)(B), "the term 'handicapped individual' means . . . any person who (i) has a physical or mental impairment which substantially limits one or more of such person's major life activities, (ii) has a record of such an impairment, or (iii) is regarded as having such an impairment." . . .

[We] next consider whether [Baby Jane Doe] possibly can be considered an "otherwise qualified" handicapped individual or to have been "subjected to discrimination" under §504. These two issues are intertwined.

The leading cases construing the "otherwise qualified" criterion of §504 have involved allegedly discriminatory denials of admission to certain educational programs. Southeastern Community College v. Davis, 442 U.S. 397 (1979); Doe v. New York University, 666 F.2d 761 (2d Cir. 1981). In that context, this court in Doe v. New York University recognized that

> it is now clear that [the phrase "otherwise qualified handicapped individual"] refers to a person who is qualified *in spite of* her handicap and that an institution is not required to disregard the disabilities of a handicapped applicant, provided the handicap is relevant to reasonable qualifications for acceptance, or to make substantial modifications in its reasonable standards or program to accommodate handicapped individuals but may take an applicant's handicap into consideration, along with all other relevant factors, in determining whether she is qualified for admission. [Id. at 775 (emphasis in original).]

Doe establishes that §504 prohibits discrimination against a handicapped individual only where the individual's handicap is unrelated to, and thus improper to consideration of, the services in question. As defendants here point out, however, where medical treatment is at issue, it is typically the handicap itself that gives rise to, or at least contributes to, the need for services. Defendants thus argue, and with some force, that the "otherwise qualified" criterion of §504 cannot be meaningfully applied to a medical treatment decision. Similarly, defendants argue that it would be pointless to inquire whether a patient who was affected by a medical treatment decision was, "solely by reason of his handicap, . . . subjected to discrimination."

The government's answer to both these arguments is that Baby Jane Doe can be viewed as suffering from not one, but multiple handicaps. Indeed, the crux of the government's case is that her microcephaly is the operative handicap, and that the requested records are necessary to determine whether she has been discriminated against solely for that reason.

Despite its superficial logic, the government's theory is flawed in at least two respects. First, the government's view of "otherwise qualified" is divorced from the statutory language. As the mainstream of cases under §504 exemplifies, the phrase "otherwise qualified" is geared toward relatively static programs or activities such as education, employment, and transportation systems. As a result, the phrase cannot be applied in the comparatively fluid context of medical treatment decisions without distorting its plain meaning. In common parlance, one would not ordinarily think of a newborn infant suffering from multiple birth defects as being "otherwise qualified" to have corrective surgery performed or to have a hospital initiate litigation seeking to override a decision against surgery by the infant's parents. If Congress intended §504 to apply in this manner, it chose strange language indeed.

Second, in arguing that Baby Jane may have been "subjected to discrimination" the government has taken an oversimplified view of the medical decisionmaking process. Where the handicapping condition is related to the (conditions) to be treated, it will rarely, if ever, be possible to say with certainty that a particular decision was "discriminatory." It is at this point that the analogy to race, relied on so heavily by the dissent, breaks down. Beyond the fact that no two cases are likely to be the same, it would invariably require lengthy litigation primarily involving conflicting expert testimony to determine whether a decision to treat, or not to treat, or to litigate or not to litigate, was based on a "bona fide medical judgment," however that phrase might be defined. Before ruling that congress intended to spawn this type of litigation under §504, we would want more proof than is apparent from the face of the statute.

The legislative history, moreover, indicates that congress never contemplated that §504 would apply to treatment decisions of this nature. . . . [According to t]he Senate Report accompanying the 1974 amendments:

> . . . Section 504 was enacted to prevent discrimination against all handicapped individuals . . . in relation to federal assistance in employment, housing, transportation, education, health services, or any other federally-aided programs. Examples of handicapped individuals who may suffer discrimination in receipt of federally-assisted services . . . are as follows: physically or mentally handicapped children who may be denied admission to federally-supported school systems on the basis of their handicap; handicapped persons who may be denied admission to federally-assisted nursing homes on the basis of their handicap; those persons whose handicap is so severe that employment is not feasible but who may be denied the benefits of a wide range of federal programs. . . . S. Rep. No. 1297, supra at 6388-6389.

This passage provides the best clue to congressional intent regarding §504's coverage of "health services." As Judge Gesell noted in American Academy of Pediatrics v. Heckler, 561 F. Supp. at 401:

> The legislative history . . . [on this subject] focuses on discrimination against adults and older children and denial of access to federal programs. As far as can be determined, no congressional committee or member of the House or Senate ever even suggested that section 504 would be used to monitor medical treatment of defective newborn infants or establish standards for preserving a particular quality of life. No medical group appeared alert to the intrusion into medical practice which some doctors apprehend from such an undertaking, nor were representatives of parents or spokesmen for religious beliefs that would be affected heard. . . .

We are aware, of course, that "where the words and purpose of a statute plainly apply to a particular situation, . . . the fact that the specific application of the statute never occurred to Congress does not bar us from holding that the situation falls within the statute's coverage." United States v. Jones, 607 F.2d 269, 273 (9th Cir. 1979), *cert. denied*, 444 U.S. 1085 (1980). Here, however, the government's theory not only strains the statutory language but also goes well beyond congress's overriding concern with guaranteeing handicapped individuals access to programs or activities receiving federal financial assistance. Further, the situation in question is dramatically different in kind, not just in degree, from the applications of §504 discussed in the legislative history. . . .

This void in the legislative history is conspicuous for another reason. Prior to the enactment of the Rehabilitation Act, congress had passed a number of measures limiting federal involvement in medical treatment decisions. For example, the very first section of the medicare law, . . . codified at 42 U.S.C. §1395, . . . provides that "nothing in this subchapter shall be construed to authorize any federal officer or employee to exercise any supervision or control over the practice of medicine or the manner in which medical services are provided." . . .

In view of this consistent congressional policy against the involvement of federal personnel in medical treatment decisions, we cannot presume that congress intended to repeal its earlier announcements in the absence of clear evidence of congressional intent to do so. . . .

In the present case, Baby Jane Doe has been treated in an evenhanded manner at least to the extent that the hospital has always been and remains willing to perform the dual, corrective surgeries if her parents would consent. Requiring the hospital either to undertake surgery notwithstanding the parents' decision or alternatively, to petition the state court to override the parents' decision, would impose a particularly onerous affirmative action burden upon the hospital. . . .

WINTER, Circuit Judge, dissenting.

Since I believe that §504 applies to the provision of medical services to handicapped infants, I respectfully dissent. . . . Section 504 . . . states with as much clarity as is reasonably possible that in some circumstances recipients of federal financial assistance may not differentiate between individuals on grounds that one or more is handicapped. . . . Although modern courts frequently rely upon legislative history to reach results at odds with the seemingly plain language of a statute, only the most compelling reasons should induce a court to override statutory language because the legislative history is silent on a particular point. Such compelling circumstances might exist in the present case if Congress had no reason to address the questions at hand when it enacted §504. It hardly needs stating that the underlying issues brim with political and moral controversy and portend to extend the hand of the federal government into matters traditionally governed by an interaction of parental judgment and state authority. Were I able to conclude that Congress had no reason to address these issues in its consideration of §504, I would concur with the majority on the grounds that specific consideration by the Congress of this political and moral minefield would be appropriate before applying the statute as written.

However, such a conclusion is untenable since §504 is no first step into a hitherto uncharted legal wilderness. As the Senate Report stated:

> Section 504 was patterned after, and is almost identical to, the antidiscrimination language of section 601 of the Civil Rights Act of 1964, 42 U.S.C. 2000d-1 (relating to race, color, or national origin), and section 901 of the Education Amendments of 1972, 42 U.S.C. 1683 (relating to sex). The section therefore constitutes the establishment of a broad government policy that programs receiving federal financial assistance shall be operated without discrimination on the basis of handicap. S. Rep. No. 1297, 93d Cong., 2d Sess., *reprinted* in 1974 U.S. Code Cong. & Ad. News 6373, 6390.

Section 504 was thus enacted against a background of well understood law which was explicitly designated as a guide to interpretation. Congress was persuaded that a handicapped condition is analogous to race and that, so far as the administration of federal financial assistance is concerned, discrimination on the basis of a handicap should be on statutory par with discrimination on the basis of race.

Once §504's legislative heritage is acknowledged, the "void" in the legislative history is eliminated and the many issues raised by defendants with regard to medical decisions, parental judgments and state authority simply evaporate. The government has never taken the position that it is entitled to override a medical judgment. Its position rather is that it is entitled under §504 to inquire whether a judgment in question is a bona fide medical judgment. While the majority professes uncertainty as to what that means, application of the analogy to race eliminates all doubt. A judgment not to perform certain surgery because a person is black is not a bona fide medical judgment. So too, a decision not to correct a life threatening digestive problem because an infant has Down's Syndrome is not a bona fide medical judgment. The issue of parental authority is also quickly disposed of. A denial of medical treatment to an infant because the infant is black is not legitimated by parental consent. Finally, once the legislative analogy to race is acknowledged, the intrusion on state authority becomes insignificant. . . .

Bragdon v. Abbott, 524 U.S. 624 (1998). Invoking the Americans with Disabilities Act's (ADA's) protection from discrimination based on disability, a woman with HIV infection challenged her dentist's refusal to fill her cavity unless he performed the procedure in a hospital. (The woman, Sidney Abbott, would have been responsible for the cost of using the hospital's facilities.) Important issues in the case were whether HIV infection constitutes a disability for purposes of the ADA and whether the dentist could nevertheless justify denying treatment in his office to protect himself from becoming infected with HIV during the procedure. (The ADA generally tracks the framework of the Rehabilitation Act's protection against discrimination based on disability but expands to more people the protection of the Rehabilitation Act.)

The Court concluded that Ms. Abbott's HIV infection constituted a disability under the ADA on the ground that HIV infection is a "physical . . . impairment that substantially limits one or more . . . major life activities." 42 U.S.C. §12102(2)(A). According to the Court, HIV infection is a physical impairment from the moment of infection because the virus immediately begins to damage an infected person's white blood cells and because of the severity of the disease. As to whether HIV infection substantially limits a major life activity, the Court observed that it might have identified many major life activities substantially limited by HIV infection. Since Ms. Abbott claimed that HIV infection substantially limited her ability to have children, the Court restricted its inquiry to that life activity. As an activity "central to the life process itself," reproduction constitutes a major life activity, wrote the Court. Moreover, HIV infection substantially limits reproduction in two ways: "First, a woman infected with HIV who tries to conceive a child imposes on the man a significant risk of becoming infected. . . . Second, an infected woman risks infecting her child during gestation and childbirth. . . ." The Court also noted that, even though the risk of transmission of HIV from mother to infant could be reduced by treatment to 8 percent, such a risk of transmitting a fatal disease rose to the level of a substantial limitation.

As to whether the dentist could defend his insistence on treatment at a hospital, he would have to show that Ms. Abbott "pose[d] a direct threat to [his] health or safety. . . ." 42 U.S.C. §12182(b)(3), with direct threat defined as "a significant risk to the health or safety of others that cannot be eliminated by a modification of policies, practices, or procedures or by the provision of auxiliary aids or services." Id. In assessing whether the dentist's fear of HIV transmission was objectively reasonable, "the views of public health authorities, such as the U.S. Public Health Service, CDC, and the National Institutes of Health, are of special weight and authority. The views of these organizations are not conclusive, however. A health care professional who disagrees with the prevailing medical consensus may refute it by citing a credible scientific basis for deviating from the accepted norm." The Court remanded the case for consideration of the dentist's defense of a direct threat to his health if he were to fill Ms. Abbott's cavity in his office instead of a hospital.

On remand, the First Circuit found in favor of Ms. Abbott. The court concluded that, because of the availability of universal precautions to prevent transmission of HIV infection from patient to dentist, the dentist could not justify his denial of treatment in terms of the need to protect himself from becoming infected with HIV. Abbott v. Bragdon, 163 F.3d 87 (1st Cir. 1998), cert. denied, 526 U.S. 1131 (1999). (Universal precautions are measures that health care providers are supposed to take with every patient to prevent the spread of infectious diseases like HIV and hepatitis. Examples of universal precautions are the wearing of gloves and other protective attire by health care providers, the use of special wastebaskets to dispose of used needles, and sterilization of medical instruments after each use.) The First Circuit decided that once physicians take universal precautions, no significant risk of HIV transmission remains.

■ GLANZ v. VERNICK
756 F. Supp. 632 (D. Mass. 1991)

MAZZONE, Judge.

In April, 1989, plaintiff's decedent, Raymond Vadnais, brought this suit alleging discrimination in violation of §504 of the Rehabilitation Act of 1973 (the "Act"), 29 U.S.C. §794. . . . The allegations in the complaint can be briefly summarized as follows. In December, 1986, defendant Dr. Vernick saw Mr. Vadnais at the Ear, Nose, and Throat Clinic (the "ENT Clinic") at Beth Israel Hospital and treated him for severe pain in the right ear, at first by prescribing antibiotics and ear drops. In January, 1987, Dr. Vernick diagnosed a perforation in Mr. Vadnais's right ear and, at Mr. Vadnais's third visit, recommended surgery to repair the perforation. After Mr. Vadnais agreed to undergo surgery, Dr. Vernick learned that Mr. Vadnais was infected with HIV and in March, 1987, informed Mr. Vadnais that he would not perform the operation. The ear condition persisted, causing severe pain and discomfort, while Mr. Vadnais continued the ineffective use of antibiotics and ear drops.

In August, 1988, Dr. Yale Berry, unaware of Mr. Vadnais's HIV status, performed the surgery, curing Mr. Vadnais's ear problem. Subsequently, Mr. Vadnais brought this lawsuit seeking . . . compensatory damages for the pain and suffering and emotional distress caused by the delay in receiving corrective surgery, along with punitive damages and attorney's fees. . . .

Count I of the complaint charges that Dr. Vernick, . . . by refusing to perform surgery, unlawfully discriminated against Mr. Vadnais because of his handicap, HIV seropositivity, in violation of §504 of the Rehabilitation Act. . . .

Section 504 states in pertinent part that "no otherwise qualified handicapped individual in the United States . . . shall, solely by reason of his handicap, be excluded from the participation in, be denied the benefits of, or be subjected to discrimination under any program or activity receiving federal financial assistance. . . ." 29 U.S.C. §794.

The defendants argue that summary judgment is appropriate for several . . . reasons. . . . [including] the ground that Mr. Vadnais was not "otherwise qualified" for elective ear surgery. They argue that it is proper for a doctor to consider a patient's handicap in determining whether a patient is qualified for surgery. On the basis of this argument, they conclude that Mr. Vadnais was not "otherwise qualified" for surgery because his HIV disease increased his risk of infection, and, furthermore, that the court should defer to the doctor's determination that it was in his patient's best interest to postpone surgery.

The defendants cannot be faulted for considering Mr. Vadnais's handicap in determining whether he was "otherwise qualified" for surgery. In School Bd. v. Arline, 480 U.S. 273, 287-289 (1987), the Supreme Court held that the defendant school board could consider the risks posed by the plaintiff's contagious disease (tuberculosis) in determining whether she was otherwise qualified to teach school. It follows that, in the present case, the defendants can take into account the risks imposed — both on the patient and on themselves — by the prospect of surgery on an HIV-positive patient. Of course, if they properly conclude that there are risks, they must also consider whether it is possible to make reasonable accommodations to enable the patient to undergo surgery despite those risks.

As the Court made clear in *Arline*, the "otherwise qualified" determination requires an individualized inquiry and appropriate findings of fact. With respect to the defendants' assertions about the risks of surgery, the facts are in dispute. The defendants contend that surgery was postponed because Dr. Vernick thought that Mr. Vadnais was "AIDS positive," because the proposed ear surgery was elective, and because it would pose significant risks to the patient. In addition, they offer Dr. Berry's statement in his deposition that he would not have performed the surgery had he known that Mr. Vadnais had AIDS. The plaintiff offers the contradicting evidence that Mr. Vadnais was HIV-positive and had not yet been diagnosed as having AIDS when surgery was refused. Moreover, Dr. Vernick in answers to interrogatories and Dr. Berry in his deposition stated that they do not consider HIV seropositivity alone as a disqualifying factor for surgery. Based on the evidence that the plaintiff has produced, facts are certainly available to warrant the conclusion that Mr. Vadnais was "otherwise qualified" for surgery. Moreover, the defendants have not produced any evidence that reasonable accommodations could not have been made.

There is some merit to the argument that the court should defer to a doctor's medical judgment. Cf. *Arline*, 480 U.S. at 288 ("courts normally should defer to the reasonable medical judgments of public health officials" when conducting "otherwise qualified" inquiry). Accepting this argument at face value, however, would completely eviscerate §504's function of preventing discrimination against the disabled in the healthcare context. A strict rule of deference would enable doctors to offer merely pretextual medical opinions to cover up discriminatory decisions. The evidentiary approach to §504 cases discussed in Pushkin v. Regents of the Univ. of Colo., 658 F.2d 1372 (10th Cir. 1981), properly balances deference to sound medical opinions with the need to detect discriminatory motives. The plaintiff must first make out a prima facie case that he was otherwise qualified for surgery, and only then does the burden shift to the defendant to show that the plaintiff's handicap made him unqualified. The plaintiff, however, must still be given an opportunity "to prove either that the reason given by defendants is a pretext or that the reason . . . 'encompasses *unjustified* consideration of the handicap itself.'" *Leckelt*, 714 F. Supp. at 1385 (citing *Pushkin*, 658 F.2d at 1387) (emphasis added). . . .

■ WALKER v. PIERCE
560 F.2d 609 (4th Cir. 1977)

BRYAN, Senior Circuit Judge.

Violation of their civil rights was laid in this action for damages and declaratory and injunctive relief by Virgil Walker and Shirley Brown, black females, to Clovis H. Pierce, the attending obstetrician at the Aiken County Hospital in South Carolina for sterilizing them, or threatening to do so, solely on account of their race and number of their children, while they were receiving medical assistance under the Medicaid program. . . .

Centering the controversy is the policy previously announced and constantly pursued in practice by the doctor, testified to by him as follows:

> My policy was with people who were unable to financially support themselves, whether they be on Medicaid or just unable to pay their own bills, if they were having a third child, to request they voluntarily submit to sterilization following the delivery of the third child. If they did not wish this as a condition for my care, then I requested that they seek another physician other than myself.

There is no question of his professional qualifications or experience.

As drawn by the plaintiffs, he is the arch-offender. The accusation is incursion upon their constitutional rights of privacy, due process of law and equal protection of the law as well as of their statutory privileges against discrimination on account of their race and color, all by subjecting or threatening the plaintiffs as citizens of the United States with involuntary sterilization. . . .

Virgil Walker had completed the seventh grade, was separated from her husband and was receiving Aid to Families with Dependent Children and Medicaid benefits. Expecting her fourth child, she first went to Pierce on January 7, 1972. During this consultation, he discussed family planning and his sterilization policy. Walker refused to consent. The issue again came up at the second visit and she again declined. Walker testified that Pierce threatened to have her state assistance terminated unless she cooperated. She called another doctor, but he was not taking new patients.

On February 4, 1972, Spears, a Department of Social Services caseworker assigned to Walker, received a note from Pierce's office asking that he talk with Walker about sterilization. Thereupon, Spears, according to his testimony, spoke with her on February 17th, offering to get her a second doctor. On the other hand, Walker stated that Spears had said there was nothing he could do. Then she returned to Pierce and subsequently signed a consent form for sterilization.

Her fourth child was delivered at the Aiken County Hospital April 16, 1972 by Dr. Billy Burke, an obstetrician who substituted for Pierce on occasion. Burke discussed tubal ligation with Walker. Her response was that she did not want additional children and understood that it would be a permanent sterilization. Two more consent forms were then signed. Pierce performed the operation April 17, 1972. She protested no further because, she said, it would have been futile.

Walker's hospital bills and doctor's fees were paid by Medicaid. Under the South Carolina plan operated by the Department of Social Services, the patient-physician relationship is one of free choice for both parties. The physician, under no contract with the state, simply submits his bill when treatment is concluded to the Medicaid insurance carrier instead of the patient. . . .

We perceive no reason why Dr. Pierce could not establish and pursue the policy he has publicly and freely announced. Nor are we cited to judicial precedent or statute inhibiting this personal economic philosophy. Particularly is this so when all persons coming to him as patients are seasonably made fully aware of his professional attitude toward the increase in offspring and his determination to see it prevail. At no time is he shown to have forced his view upon any mother. Indeed, quite the opposite appears. In the single occasion in this case of a sterilization by this doctor, not just one but three formal written consents were obtained — the first before delivery of the fourth child and two afterwards. . . .

[The court also held that Dr. Pierce was not a state actor and therefore could not be found to have violated his patients' constitutional rights.]

Notes: Discriminatory Denials of Care

1. *Subsequent Developments.* In the end, the parents in *University Hospital* agreed to have a shunt implanted to drain the fluid in their daughter's brain, although the surgery was delayed because of an infection that was likely related to the opening in her spine. The child, Keri-Lynn, has done much better than predicted. Although she is confined to a wheelchair, she can talk, and she attends a school for developmentally disabled children. At age 20, she had attained a first or second grade level of scholastic achievement. Experts continued to disagree as to whether surgery to close Keri-Lynn's spine would have improved her outcome. Jamie Talan, A Fighter's Spirit; 20-year-old Keri-Lynn — Baby Jane Doe — Beat Steep Odds, Newsday, October 13, 2003, at A3; B. D. Colen, What Ever Happened to Baby Jane Doe?, 24(3) Hastings Center Rep. 2, 2 (1994).

2. *The Americans with Disabilities Act. University Hospital* and *Glanz* were decided under the Rehabilitation Act, which applies only to federally funded programs or services and federal executive agencies. Since those cases, the Americans with Disabilities Act (ADA) has gone into effect, and its provisions apply to all nonfederal providers of health care services, public or private. The statutory language of the ADA was designed to track the Rehabilitation Act and court decisions interpreting that Act.

For further discussion of the ADA and denials of health care, see Carl H. Coleman, Conceiving Harm: Disability Discrimination in Assisted Reproductive Technologies, 50 UCLA L. Rev. 17 (2002); Mary A. Crossley, Of Diagnoses and Discrimination: Discriminatory Nontreatment of Infants with HIV Infection, 93 Colum. L. Rev. 1581 (1993); E. Haavi Morreim, Futilitarianism, Exoticare, and Coerced Altruism: The ADA Meets Its Limits, 25 Seton Hall L. Rev. 883 (1995); David Orentlicher, Destructuring Disability: Rationing of Health Care and Unfair Discrimination Against the Sick, 31 Harv. C.R.-C.L. L. Rev. 49 (1996); Philip G. Peters, Jr., When Physicians Balk at Futile Care: Implications of the Disability Rights Laws, 91 Nw. U. L. Rev. 798 (1997); and Philip G. Peters, Jr., Health Care Rationing and Disability Rights, 70 Ind. L. J. 491 (1995).

3. *Definition of Disability.* As indicated by the Supreme Court in *Bragdon*, one has to determine whether a person is in fact disabled under the ADA or Rehabilitation Act before deciding whether there has been unlawful discrimination on account of disability. Until recently, it did not seem to be very difficult for plaintiffs to prove that they were disabled under the ADA. Disability can be shown not only by the presence of a disabling condition but also by a history of a disabling condition or by showing that one is regarded by others as having a disabling condition. 42 U.S.C. §12102(2). Moreover, the legislative history

indicated that the judgment whether a patient is disabled should be made assuming that no treatment is provided. Thus, even if a patient's disabling symptoms could be alleviated with medication, the patient would still be considered disabled under the ADA. H.R. Rep. No. 485(II), 101st Cong., 2d Sess., at 52 (1990).

In 1999, the Supreme Court raised the bar on the definition of disability by holding that a person is not actually disabled if medications or medical devices can alleviate the disabling symptoms. Moreover, the Court established a relatively high threshold for showing that one is disabled because of being "regarded as having" a disabling condition. Sutton v. United Air Lines, 527 U.S. 471 (1999).

In *Sutton*, the plaintiffs had been denied jobs as commercial airline pilots because of poor eyesight even though glasses or contact lenses would give them 20/20 vision or better. Because the plaintiffs were not visually impaired with corrective lenses, they could not claim to be actually disabled. As to the "regarded as being disabled" inquiry, the Court observed that the airline only declined to hire them as commercial airline pilots. Because many other jobs were still open to the plaintiffs, including regional pilot or pilot instructor jobs, they were not regarded as being substantially limited in their employment opportunities.

As *Bragdon* suggests, satisfying the definition of disability in the health care context will likely not be as demanding as in the employment context.

For a very helpful discussion about defining disability, see Mary Crossley, The Disability Kaleidoscope, 74 Notre Dame L. Rev. 621 (1999).

4. *When Denial of Treatment Is Discriminatory*. What standard does the *Glanz* court suggest for deciding whether a denial of care constitutes unlawful discrimination on the basis of disability? What theories does the *University Hospital* court use to find no unlawful discrimination when medical care is withheld from a severely disabled newborn? Which of the different approaches do you think makes the most sense?

Note that, while the court's decision in *University Hospital* rested in part on the fact that Baby Jane Doe's parents agreed to the withholding of care, there is much more to the opinion. In addition, another court reached the same result as *University Hospital* in a case in which the parents charged that the physicians' treatment recommendations were biased by the presence of the child's severe disability and that the physicians failed to disclose their bias when obtaining the parents' consent to withhold care. Johnson v. Thompson, 971 F.2d 1487, 1493-1494 (10th Cir. 1992) (citing *University Hospital* for the proposition that, "[w]here the handicapping condition is related to the condition(s) to be treated, it will rarely, if ever, be possible to say . . . that a particular decision was 'discriminatory.'"). There are other reasons to discount parental agreement. As Judge Winter observed in his *University Hospital* dissent, parental agreement does not necessarily vitiate a discrimination claim. The parents may not be adequately representing the child's interests.

Both *Glanz* and *University Hospital* take the view that a person's disability can be a relevant consideration in the person's access to health care. If a disability affects the benefit that the patient can receive from health care, then the disability can be a factor in deciding how to treat the patient. But that leaves most disabled persons subject to denials of health care. The immune system compromise of an HIV-infected person, for example, will have wide-ranging effects on that person's response to medical or surgical therapy. Crossley, supra, at 160. Indeed, the argument in *Glanz* that Mr. Glanz's HIV infection would predispose him to infection would apply to any HIV-infected patient undergoing surgery. How do we consider the effects of a person's disability without discriminating unfairly against that person? What if it is true that a disabled person would not gain as much benefit from treatment as a nondisabled person? Is an appropriate analogy the educational services that states are required to provide in the primary public schools for children with disabilities? See New Mexico Association for Retarded Citizens v. New Mexico, 678 F.2d 847, 854-855 (10th Cir. 1982) (requiring special education to ensure that children with disabilities receive an education appropriate to their needs).

Rather than avoiding the care of certain patients by claiming that the patient is not a candidate for care (as in *University Hospital* or *Glanz*), physicians might claim that the patient needs to be referred for more specialized care. In Lesley v. Chie, 250 F.3d 47 (1st Cir. 2001), the U.S. Court of Appeals for the First Circuit addressed a disability discrimination claim in the context of a physician's referral of the patient to a more specialized colleague. In *Leslie,* the court considered "the extent to which a court should defer to a physician's claim that he lacks the experience, knowledge, or other prerequisites necessary to address the medical conditions that allegedly prompted his referral of a patient to another physician." The case arose after an obstetrician referred an HIV-infected, pregnant woman to another hospital for drug therapy designed to prevent transmission of HIV to the woman's child. The other hospital had a special Women and Infants HIV Program. The court found no Rehabilitation Act violation, writing,

> Under the Rehabilitation Act, a patient may challenge her doctor's decision to refer her elsewhere by showing the decision to be devoid of any reasonable medical support. This is not to say, however, that the Rehabilitation Act prohibits unreasonable medical decisions as such. Rather, the point of considering a medical decision's reasonableness in this context is to determine whether the decision was unreasonable in a way that reveals it to be discriminatory. In other words, a plaintiff's showing of medical unreasonableness must be framed within some larger theory of disability discrimination. For example, a plaintiff may argue that her physician's decision was so unreasonable — in the sense of being arbitrary and capricious — as to imply that it was pretext for some discriminatory motive, such as animus, fear, or "apathetic attitudes." See, e.g., Howe v. Hull, 874 F. Supp. 779, 788-89 (N.D. Ohio 1994) (under ADA, jury could find doctor's diagnosis that plaintiff had extremely rare disorder requiring transfer was pretextual, where patient only had an allergic drug reaction, and doctor did not mention the rare disorder in requesting the transfer but only mentioned plaintiff's HIV-status). Or, instead of arguing pretext, a plaintiff may argue that her physician's decision was discriminatory on its face, because it rested on stereotypes of the disabled rather than an individualized inquiry into the patient's condition — and hence was "unreasonable" in that sense. [Id. at 55.]

To what extent are the costs of care relevant to the analysis? If Baby Jane Doe's care cost thousands instead of hundreds of thousands of dollars, should that make a difference in deciding whether disability discrimination occurred? If you think social costs are relevant, then why does the denial of care by Dr. Pierce seem more troubling than the withholding of care from Baby Jane Doe? Wasn't he also concerned primarily about social costs? Is his decision worse because it was directed toward only the poor, or because welfare status is correlated with race? Or is it that sterilization is reminiscent of discredited eugenic social policies of the past?

5. *Infectious Patients.* As *Bragdon* indicates, an outright denial of care on account of the person's HIV status is unlawful disability discrimination. However, *Bragdon* and *Glanz* also indicate that the freedom of a physician to deny care on the basis of a patient's infected status depends not only on whether the infection affects the patient's ability to benefit from treatment but also on the risk to the physician of becoming infected from the patient. How should the risk be taken into account? What if an orthopedic surgeon refuses to operate on an HIV-infected (or hepatitis-infected) patient on the grounds that orthopedic surgery is "bloody" and involves exposure to sharp edges of bone as well as to sharp surgical instruments? What if the surgeon already provides care to a significant number of HIV-infected patients and the surgeon is trying to have a child? Should it matter whether the denial of care is for elective rather than essential surgical procedures? Consider a dermatologist who refuses to perform a hair transplant on an HIV-infected person on the ground that the procedure invariably causes significant bleeding from the patient's scalp. It is important to note that the circuit courts disagree on exactly when a risk is serious enough to be "significant." For a discussion of the different standards, see Onishea v. Hopper, 171 F.3d 1289, 1296-1299 (11th Cir. 1999) (interpreting "significant risk" in the context of a Rehabilitation Act case).

Concerns about discrimination against HIV-infected physicians are discussed at page 242.

B. THE STRUCTURE OF THE TREATMENT RELATIONSHIP

1. Forming a Patient-Physician Relationship

In general, it is clear when a patient-physician relationship has been created. A patient seeks care, and the physician provides the care. In many situations, however, it is not so clear whether a relationship was formed. There may have been some interaction between the patient and the physician, for example, a telephone call or conversation, but not enough interaction to create a professional relationship. Or the patient's physician may have consulted another physician, and the question is whether the second physician's participation creates a professional relationship between that physician and the patient. In some cases, as we saw in *Hiser*, when physicians refuse to see patients, the patients will claim that the physicians had previously bound themselves to provide care. There will also be cases when the physician actually examines the patient, but the examination is arranged on behalf of an employer or insurer. Then the issue arises whether the physicians' primary obligation is to the patient or to the company that retains him. Finally, when a physician clearly has obligations to a patient, issues arise over whether those obligations extend to third parties who might also be harmed by the physicians' professional decisions. The following materials explore each of these issues in varying depth.

■ADAMS v. VIA CHRISTI REGIONAL MEDICAL CENTER
19 P.3d 132 (Kan. 2001)

ALLEGRUCCI, Justice.

This is a personal injury and wrongful death action filed by Albert and Forestean Adams, the parents of Nichelle Adams, who died as a result of a ruptured ectopic pregnancy. . . .

In July 1992, Nichelle Adams was 22 years old and was living with her parents and her younger sister. On July 22, Mrs. Adams got home from work at approximately 8:40 p.m. to find that Nichelle had been complaining about her stomach and had gone to bed. Mrs. Adams was concerned because Nichelle generally was a very active person.

Dr. Ohaebosim, an osteopath, who had been a family practitioner for 22 years, had been the family physician for Mr. and Mrs. Adams and their three children for several years. He had a patient file on Nichelle, but he had not seen her in his office since 1988. On July 6, Nichelle completed a form for Planned Parenthood in which she answered "no" to the question "Do you have a family physician?" Dr. Ohaebosim continued to provide medical care to other members of the family. Mrs. Adams had gotten medical advice from Dr. Ohaebosim over the telephone on a number of occasions.

Until 1990, Dr. Ohaebosim included as part of his family practice the treatment of women through pregnancy, labor, and delivery. He delivered over a thousand babies. After 1990, he continued to treat pregnant women for nonpregnancy-related conditions and to make the determination for women that they were pregnant, but he referred women to other practitioners for prenatal care, labor, and delivery. Dr. Ohaebosim testified about sending a letter to his patients to advise them that he would no longer be providing obstetrical care. He also testified that he advised all the hospitals, "I don't deliver babies any more." He further stated, "This is my notice written. I'm writing to inform you that I would cease delivering babies on January, 1990, on the 1st of January, 1990." Mrs. Adams testified that she did not receive a letter from the doctor advising that he no longer offered obstetrical care. She was unaware that Dr. Ohaebosim had eliminated obstetrical care from his practice.

At approximately 9 p.m. on July 22, Mrs. Adams called Dr. Ohaebosim. She got his answering service, and then the doctor called Mrs. Adams right back. She told Dr. Ohaebosim that Nichelle was 5 to 8 weeks pregnant and was experiencing abdominal pain. Mrs. Adams later told a doctor at the hospital that she mentioned shortness of breath to Dr. Ohaebosim in the telephone conversation, but Dr. Ohaebosim later denied it, and at the time of trial Mrs. Adams could not remember telling him anything other than Nichelle was pregnant and had abdominal pain.

Dr. Ohaebosim testified that 8 weeks is the typical time when an ectopic pregnancy becomes symptomatic because the fetus becomes too large for the fallopian tube. When Mrs. Adams told Dr. Ohaebosim of Nichelle's condition, he did not suspect that Nichelle might have an ectopic pregnancy. . . .

Dr. Ohaebosim testified that he told Mrs. Adams that abdominal pain is not abnormal during pregnancy but to take Nichelle to the emergency room if she got any worse. He also told her to have Nichelle see a doctor the next day. Mrs. Adams testified that Dr. Ohaebosim did not mention taking Nichelle to the emergency room, but that he did say to bring her into his office the next day. Dr. Ohaebosim and Mrs. Adams agreed that he did not ask her any questions about Nichelle's condition.

At approximately midnight, Mrs. Adams drove Nichelle to the hospital, where she was admitted into the emergency room at 12:25 a.m. on July 23. By the time Nichelle was taken into an examining room, she was agitated and thrashing around. While Mrs. Adams was alone with Nichelle in the examination room, Nichelle vomited. Mrs. Adams called for help, and, when hospital personnel took over Nichelle's care, Mrs. Adams was taken to a nursing station to call her husband. . . . Before her husband arrived at the hospital, Mrs. Adams was told that Nichelle had gone into cardiac arrest. Later she was told that Nichelle was being taken to surgery.

Dr. Ohaebosim was not contacted with regard to Nichelle until approximately 4 p.m. on July 23. He immediately went to the hospital. Nichelle was on life support systems and nonreactive to the light Dr. Ohaebosim shined in her eyes. He discussed Nichelle's condition with her family, and at approximately 6:30 p.m. she died after being removed from the support systems pursuant to her family's decision. There was evidence that Nichelle might have lived if she had received medical care at 9 or 9:30 p.m. on July 22, instead of after midnight.

Mr. and Mrs. Adams, individually and as administrators of the estate of Nichelle Adams, sued St. Francis Regional Medical Center and Dr. Ohaebosim. . . .

Dr. Ohaebosim contends that there was no physician-patient relationship between him and Nichelle Adams on July 22, 1992, and that in the absence of a physician-patient relationship, no duty arose. . . .

The factors Dr. Ohaebosim advances in support of his position that no physician-patient relationship existed on July 22, 1992, between him and Nichelle Adams are the following:

1. A physician-patient relationship did exist on that date between him and Mrs. Adams.
2. He had not seen, talked to, or treated Nichelle for approximately four years prior to July 22.
3. He did not speak to Nichelle on July 22.
4. His only knowledge of Nichelle's obstetric history was the information provided by Mrs. Adams during the telephone conversation.
5. He no longer provided obstetrical care.
6. He "took no action other than discussing, in very general terms," Nichelle's condition with Mrs. Adams.
7. He did not consider Nichelle to be his patient, and Nichelle did not consider him to be her doctor.

Of these factors, the key to resolving this issue is Dr. Ohaebosim's own statement that he discussed Nichelle's condition with Mrs. Adams. In doing so, he consented to give medical advice about Nichelle's condition and he gave it. It is immaterial that he had not seen Nichelle for several years. It is immaterial that he did not speak directly to Nichelle on July 22. It is not significant in the circumstances that he states that he did not consider Nichelle to be his patient and that Nichelle did not consider him to be her doctor. He did consider Mrs. Adams to be his patient. He was a family physician, and in years past he had treated her daughter, Nichelle. When Mrs. Adams spoke to him by telephone on July 22 and told him that Nichelle was 5-8 weeks pregnant and experiencing abdominal pain, Dr. Ohaebosim did not say that he did not consider Nichelle to be his patient. He did not say that he no longer provided obstetrical care. Rather than suggesting to Mrs. Adams that she contact another doctor at that time, he listened to what Mrs. Adams told him about Nichelle and gave her his medical opinion in response. Dr. Ohaebosim's undertaking to render medical advice as to Nichelle's condition gave rise to a physician-patient relationship. Thus, even if the earlier physician-patient relationship between Dr. Ohaebosim and Nichelle had lapsed or been extinguished, it was renewed.

The essential difference between the facts of this case and those cited by Dr. Ohaebosim is his taking some action to give medical assistance. Typical of the cases he cites is Ortiz v. Shah, 905 S.W.2d 609 (Tex. App. 1995). Ortiz was taken to the emergency room with a gunshot wound. The emergency room nurse paged Dr. Shah, who was the "on call" surgeon. Before Dr. Shah reached the hospital, Ortiz had been treated in the emergency room and taken to surgery, where he died. Dr. Shah had no prior relationship with Ortiz. Dr. Shah never saw the patient Ortiz. He never talked to him, and he never gave any advice to anyone about Ortiz's care. He simply told the nurse who contacted him that he was on his way to the hospital. Dr. Shah had taken no action that affected the medical treatment received by Ortiz. Dr. Ohaebosim, in contrast, gave his medical opinion about Nichelle Adams' condition. His opinion was that she was experiencing nothing unusual, which served to reassure Mrs. Adams about her daughter's condition and dissuade her from promptly seeking medical attention for Nichelle.

Dr. Ohaebosim contends that he declined to treat Nichelle. He did not decline to express his medical opinion about her condition. Thus, he cannot be said to have declined to treat her. A physician-patient relationship existed between Dr. Ohaebosim and Nichelle, and a duty of care was owed by Dr. Ohaebosim to Nichelle. . . .

■ CLANTON v. VON HAAM

340 S.E.2d 627 (Ga. Ct. App. 1986)

CARLEY, Judge.

. . . Mrs. Clanton went to a hospital emergency room complaining of pain in her back. While there, she developed numbness in her legs and experienced difficulty walking. She was examined by a doctor who was on duty in the emergency room and who then released her with a prescription for pain medicine. When she returned home, the pain worsened and the numbness increased. Mrs. Clanton telephoned the emergency room and was told that the doctor who had seen her had gone home. Mrs. Clanton then called the answering service of appellee and his partner, both of whom had previously treated her for a totally unrelated condition. Appellee returned her call within a few minutes and listened to a recital of her symptoms. However, according to the allegations of the complaint, appellee "refused to make a house call and refused to agree to meet Mrs. Clanton at the hospital, but rather told her that it was too late in the evening and she would have to wait to see him in the morning." After the telephone conversation with appellee, Mrs. Clanton's condition continued to deteriorate. Several hours later, she was admitted to the hospital for treatment by another physician. She is now paralyzed. Appellants' complaint alleged that appellee "knew or should have known that Mrs. Clanton's condition was critical and in the absence of action would result in paraplegia. As a direct and proximate result of [appellee's] negligent failure to recognize the need for immediate treatment and of his negligent failure to advise Mrs. Clanton to return to the hospital for immediate additional care, Mrs. Clanton has sustained painful personal injuries and is now a paraplegic."

Appellee moved for summary judgment and supported the motion by his own affidavit. In that affidavit, he stated that, insofar as Mrs. Clanton's current physical condition is concerned, no physician-patient relationship contemplating treatment thereof had existed prior to or was created by the phone call. According to appellee's affidavit, in that conversation he had "recommended that [Mrs.] Clanton take the medication prescribed for her by another physician earlier that evening [in the emergency room] and contact him later the same morning at [appellee's] office." However, Mrs. Clanton's own version of appellee's conversation was significantly different. According to her deposition, appellee "just said, you know, there wasn't nothing he could do for me." Mrs. Clanton also testified that appellee had not asked her "to come see him in the morning or [said] that he would see [her] in the morning or anything like that." . . .

The trial court granted appellee's motion. Appellants appeal, contending that it was error to grant summary judgment as there remained two genuine issues of material fact. The two issues that appellants perceive to remain for jury resolution are whether a physician-patient relationship existed between appellee and Mrs. Clanton and whether appellee was negligent in treating her. Appellee's focus is on the first issue. . . . The evidence is that, notwithstanding the late hour, appellee, who had treated Mrs. Clanton previously but for a totally unrelated condition, elected to return her telephone call. He then listened to a full recital of her symptoms. However, this alone does not create a patient-physician relationship.

> Merely that the defendant was a physician and knew of the condition of the plaintiff would not devolve upon him the duty of rendering to her medical care, even though he was applied to for services by the plaintiff herself and through others; for there is no rule of law that requires a physician to undertake the treatment of every patient who applies to him. . . . "[O]ne who has secured a [medical] license according to statute is not liable for damages alleged to result from the refusal to take a case." Buttersworth v. Swint, [186 S.E. 770, 772 (Ga. 1936)].

The crucial issue is whether the evidence regarding the telephone conversation would authorize a finding of a "consensual transaction" whereby Mrs. Clanton became appellee's patient for treatment of her then existing condition. Appellee testified that, in his late night conversation, he "recommended" that Mrs. Clanton continue the immediate course of treatment prescribed by another physician and that she should call him back in the morning. An individual, hearing only such a recommendation in response to a late night solicitation for medical assistance might well assume that he or she had been accepted as a patient by the physician rendering it and, to his or her ultimate detriment, follow that advice and suspend further efforts to secure medical treatment from another source. However, it is undisputed that that did not happen in the instant case. Notwithstanding what appellee states he may have "recommended" to Mrs. Clanton, she herself interpreted the conversation as a total refusal of her efforts to secure appellee's medical services. It is undisputed that she never considered that, as the result of the telephone call, appellee had undertaken to render his medical expertise available to her then or at any time in the future. There is no dispute that Mrs. Clanton never relied upon any medical advice whatsoever from appellee and that she was in no way dissuaded from seeking medical attention elsewhere as the result of the conversation. She ultimately seeks to recover, not on the basis that appellee actually afforded her negligent treatment which she then followed to her injury, but solely on the basis that appellee refused to initiate non-negligent treatment by which she might have avoided injury. The evidence thus shows without contradiction that there was never a "consensual transaction" between appellee as treating physician and Mrs. Clanton as patient regarding her current physical condition. The evidence showing that no relationship was created which gave rise to any professional duty, the breach of which duty proximately caused Mrs. Clanton's existing condition, the trial court did not err in granting summary judgment. . . .

■ REYNOLDS v. DECATUR MEMORIAL HOSPITAL
660 N.E.2d 235 (Ill. App. 1996)

McCULLOUGH, Judge.

. . . The only issue is whether, as a matter of law, a telephone conference between treating pediatrician Dr. Sharon Bonds and [Dr. Thomas] Fulbright concerning Kevin [Reynolds]'s condition created a physician-patient relationship between Kevin and Fulbright. . . . The trial court found there was no physician-patient relationship and, therefore, no duty was owed by Fulbright to plaintiffs. We affirm. . . .

At about 10:45 P.M. on November 29, 1990, Kevin was seen in the emergency room of Decatur Memorial Hospital by Dr. Terry Balagna. The history given indicated he was injured at 8:30 or 9 P.M. by falling while jumping on the couch in the family living room. Upon examination, an abnormal breathing pattern was observed. Tests were conducted to discover the possibility of an infection or an electrolyte or metabolic problem. Cervical spine X-rays were taken at about 1:05 A.M. which appeared normal. Nevertheless, Kevin was admitted to the hospital. Balagna called Bonds, a pediatrician, to examine him.

Bonds arrived at the hospital at about 1:45 A.M. on November 30, 1990. At that time, Kevin's temperature was 102 degrees Fahrenheit. Bonds made a quick assessment of plaintiff and took a history from Barbara [Reynolds, Kevin's mother], which indicated Kevin had jumped off the couch, landed on his arm, walked to his mother, and gradually become limp after that. Bond noticed the child's breathing difficulties and that he was flaccid. She reviewed the emergency room records and X-ray reports, conducted reflex tests, and noticed he was moving his head. His neck was not tender. Among the possible reasons for his condition which Bonds considered were neurologic, traumatic, metabolic, infectious, or post-infectious problem. Because of the fever, she was leaning toward the infectious process diagnosis, and she did not consider a spinal cord injury. A history of a two-foot fall with a normal 2 1/2-year-old child did not indicate to her the existence of a cervical cord injury from trauma.

At 2:05 A.M., Bonds telephoned Fulbright[, a neurologist,] at his home. She advised Fulbright that Kevin walked following the fall, he had an elevated temperature and was flaccid and responsive, and the cervical spine X-rays were negative. She probably told him the child was flaccid from the neck down, including all four extremities. Fulbright inquired if the child had a stiff neck. Bonds said she did not know, went to check Kevin's neck, and returned to inform Fulbright that his neck was stiff. At the end of the conversation, Fulbright suggested a spinal tap to determine whether meningitis, encephalitis, or something similar was involved. Bonds did not ask Fulbright to treat Kevin, nor did Fulbright commit himself to further involvement with Kevin. Bonds was under the impression that Fulbright would see Kevin if she contacted him and requested that he treat Kevin.

Fulbright's recollection of his telephone conversation was as follows:

> Dr. Bonds called me regarding Kevin Reynolds. She related to me that the patient had presented with a history of a fall, I believe from a couch. The height estimated to be less than two feet. She related that the child was listless, and that the child was febrile with a fever of — on the order of 102 degrees Fahrenheit. I questioned Dr. Bonds regarding the history. My first concern was the veracity of the history. My major concern here was the question of child abuse. There was some report on her part that the history had been somewhat inconsistent. That in itself is a hallmark of abuse. I questioned her specifically as to whether or not she felt abuse was operative in this case. She stated relatively emphatically that she did not think that it was. She did not think that the fall was overly significant because of its apparently benign nature, that is, a fall from a low height of a young child as happens to every young child. The question of the cause of the fever and the possible neurological causes of the fever was raised. The question of meningitis was discussed. The question of an ascending neuritis was discussed. The performance of a lumbar puncture was discussed. The conclusion was that Dr. Bonds would perform the lumbar puncture and let me know if she wanted me to see the child thereafter. I offered to make myself physically available if she wished. We elected to proceed with the plan of her performing the lumbar puncture and letting me know if she needed me there.

Fulbright often received informal inquiries from other doctors asking questions and seeking suggestions. These inquiries do not include a request to see a patient, review a patient, or render an opinion, but only to discuss the case. He considered this a courtesy service for which he did not bill. He offered to make himself available because the other physician may be inhibited about asking him to see the patient due to the late hour or the marginal neurosurgical nature of the case.

. . . Fulbright stated he did not receive another call from Bonds or anyone else at the hospital with regard to Kevin's condition or treatment. Kevin's family never asked Fulbright to treat Kevin, and he never saw, examined, or came to a diagnosis as to Kevin's condition. Fulbright did not bill for any services to Kevin. . . .

[Bonds concluded that Kevin had an infectious cause for his symptoms. In fact, he had suffered a spinal cord injury that left him with quadriplegia.]

In a negligence action for medical malpractice, there must be a duty owed by defendant to the plaintiff, a breach of duty, an injury proximately caused by the breach, and resultant damages. The determination of whether the parties stood in such a relationship to one another that the law would impose on defendant a duty of reasonable conduct for the benefit of the plaintiff is a question of law. That policy determination is based on consideration of the likelihood of injury, the magnitude of the burden of guarding against it, and the consequences of placing that burden on the defendant. . . .

The relationship of physician and patient is . . . a consensual relationship in which the patient knowingly seeks the physician's assistance and the physician knowingly accepts the person as a patient. A consensual relationship can exist where other persons contact the physician on behalf of the patient, but this is not a case in which Fulbright was asked to provide a service for Kevin, conduct laboratory tests, or review test results. Fulbright did nothing more than answer an inquiry from a colleague. He was not contacted again and he charged no fee. A doctor who gives an informal opinion at the request of a treating physician does not owe a duty of care to the patient whose case was discussed. . . .

Plaintiffs suggest that what needs to be done is to find a physician-patient relationship to result from every such conversation. The consequence of such a rule would be significant. It would have a chilling effect upon practice of medicine. It would stifle communication, education and professional association, all to the detriment of the patient. The likely effect in adopting plaintiffs' argument also would be that such informal conferences would no longer occur. . . .

■ LYONS v. GRETHER
239 S.E.2d 103 (Va. 1977)

POFF, Justice.

. . . Plaintiff, a blind person, accompanied by her four-year-old son and her guide dog, arrived at defendant's "medical office" on the morning of October 18, 1975, a Saturday, to keep an appointment "for treatment of a vaginal infection." She was told that defendant would not treat her unless the dog was removed from the waiting room. She insisted that the dog remain because she "was not informed of any steps which would be taken to assure the safety of the guide dog, its care, or availability to her after treatment." Defendant "evicted" plaintiff, her son, and her dog, refused to treat her condition, and failed to assist her in finding other medical attention. By reason of defendant's "wrongful conduct," plaintiff was "humiliated" in the presence of other patients and her young son, and "for another two days while she sought medical assistance from other sources," her infection became "aggravated" and she endured "great pain and suffering." . . . [P]laintiff demanded damages resulting from "breach of his duty to treat." [The trial court dismissed the case.] . . .

Although there is some conflict of authority, the courts are in substantial accord upon the rules concerning the creation of a physician-patient relationship and the rights and obligations arising therefrom. In the absence of a statute, a physician has no legal obligation to accept as a patient everyone who seeks his services. A physician's duty arises only upon the creation of a physician-patient relationship; that relationship springs from a consensual transaction, a contract, express or implied, general or special, and a patient is entitled to damages resulting from a breach of a physician's duty. Whether a physician-patient relationship is created is a question of fact, turning upon a determination whether the patient entrusted his treatment to the physician and the physician accepted the case.

We consider first whether the facts stated in the motion for judgment, and the reasonable inferences deducible therefrom, were sufficient to allege the creation of a physician-patient relationship and a duty to treat. Standing alone, plaintiff's allegation that she "had an appointment with defendant" would be insufficient, for it connotes nothing more than that defendant had agreed to see her. But plaintiff alleged further that the appointment she had been given was "for treatment of a vaginal infection." The unmistakable implication is that plaintiff had sought and defendant had granted an appointment at a designated time and place for the performance of a specific medical service, one within defendant's professional competence, viz., *treatment* of a particular ailment. It is immaterial that this factual allegation might have been contradicted by evidence at trial. Upon demurrer, the test of the sufficiency of a motion for judgment is whether it states the essential elements of a cause of action, not whether evidence might be adduced to defeat it. . . . [The court went on to observe that, on remand, there was also a factual question as to whether Dr. Grether's refusal to treat Ms. Lyons amounted to a lawful termination of their professional relationship.]

Notes: Creating the Patient-Physician Relationship

1. *Telephone Calls by a Prospective Patient.* Was it appropriate for the court to grant summary judgment against Ms. Clanton? What if a jury believed Dr. Von Haam's version of their conversation? Would his version have provided sufficient evidence of a patient-physician relationship? Is it appropriate to read *Lyons* as holding that scheduling a specific appointment creates a professional relationship, or was this case driven by the physician's reason for cancelling the appointment? Compare Weaver v. University of Michigan Board of Regents, 506 N.W.2d 264, 266 (Mich. Ct. App. 1993) (merely scheduling an appointment does not by itself establish a patient-physician relationship).

The ease with which a treatment relationship can be formed perhaps explains why hospital emergency room staff have been accused of engaging in what is known as a "wallet biopsy" — asking the patient or family more detailed questions about insurance and financial responsibility when they first come in than they do about the patient's condition, in order to be sure they can refuse treatment if the patient cannot pay and is not in a serious condition. For additional examples and discussion from the case law, see Annot., What Constitutes Physician-Patient Relationship for Malpractice Purposes, 17 A.L.R. 4th 132 (1982).

2. *Consultations by a Patient's Physician.* As the *Reynolds* court concluded, when a colleague of a patient's physician is informally consulted for advice rather than being asked to see the patient, conduct laboratory tests, or render a formal opinion, the "curbside" consultation does not create a patient-physician relationship between the patient and the colleague. In one case, which is probably at the extreme, the court so held even though the treating physician consulted a colleague in response to concerns expressed by the patient's mother about the appropriateness of care being provided her daughter. In that case, the treating physician reassured the mother on the basis of the consultation and also mentioned the consultation on his discharge summary. Oliver v. Brock, 342 So. 2d 1 (Ala. 1976). See also Irvin v. Smith, 31 P.3d 934 (Kan. 2001); Stutes v. Samuelson, 180 S.W.3d 750 (Tex. Ct. App. 2005). However, if a physician assumes some responsibility for diagnostic or treatment decisions, then a patient-physician relationship may be created. See Crisp Regional Hospital v. Oliver, 621 S.E.2d 554, 560-561 (Ga. Ct. App. 2005) (jury could conclude that a patient-physician relationship was formed when the physician wrote an order for an MRI scan before patient's first appointment with the physician). For a sense of the distinction between informal, curbside consultations and more formal consultations, see Farrin A. Manian & David A. Janssen, Curbside Consultations: A Closer Look at a Common Practice, 275 JAMA 145 (1996).

Do you agree with the policy reasons given by the *Reynolds* court for its holding? Given the principle that a patient-physician relationship is not created by a consultation, does this effectively mean that patients receive the benefit of free consultations but they "pay" for the consultations by "waiving" their right to sue the consulted physician? If that is what is going on here, does it follow that patients should be able to waive their right to sue their treating physician in exchange for a lower fee for their care? See discussion of Tunkl v. Regents of the University of California and related cases at page 123.

Phone consultations with a medical specialist are much more likely to lead to the formation of a patient-physician relationship when the physician is serving as an "on-call" physician to the hospital's emergency room, as illustrated by two Missouri cases. In Corbet v. McKinney, 980 S.W.2d 166 (Mo. Ct. App. 1998), a patient sued an emergency room physician for misdiagnosis of an ear problem and also sued an ear, nose, and throat specialist who had been telephoned by the emergency room physician. Since the specialist had not seen or billed the patient and was not under any contractual obligation to participate in the patient's care, the court held that no patient-physician relationship had been created. In contrast, in Millard v. Corrado, 14 S.W.3d 42 (Mo. Ct. App. 1999), the court found a patient-physician relationship between a patient and an on-call physician who never saw the patient and who allegedly failed to respond quickly enough to his pages, on the ground that the hospital bylaws required on-call physicians to respond to calls within a reasonable amount of time.

While the Missouri court in *Millard* found a duty to treat for the on-call consultant based solely on the physician's preexisting contractual obligation, courts in Georgia and Michigan have followed an Ohio decision, McKinney v. Schlatter, 692 N.E.2d 1045 (Ohio Ct. App. 1997), in requiring some involvement by the physician in the patient's care. See Anderson v. Houser, 523 S.E.2d 342 (Ga. Ct. App. 1999); Oja v. Kin, 581 N.W.2d 739 (Mich. Ct. App. 1998). (Note that the Ohio Supreme Court rejected the *McKinney* test in a later case, *Lownsbury*, mentioned below.)

Some courts avoid the entire debate over whether a full-scale doctor-patient relationship has been triggered and hold simply that the physician owes a duty of care to the extent of his or her involvement, whatever that is. Diggs v. Arizona Cardiologists, 8 P.3d 386 (Ariz. Ct. App. 2000). For instance, in Mozingo v. Pitt County Memorial Hospital, 415 S.E.2d 341 (N.C. 1992), the court allowed suit against a physician who merely supervised the obstetrical residents who made an error. The supervising physician was at home "on call" when the difficulty arose and responded immediately when asked to come to the hospital. By the time he arrived, the delivery had been completed. The court accepted the plaintiff's allegations that supervising physicians have a duty to check in periodically when they know that a difficult case is in the hospital. Thus, duty was imposed by virtue of the physician's supervising status even though he never saw the patient until it was too late. *Accord* Lownsbury v. Van Buren, 762 N.E.2d 354 (Ohio 2001). But see Prosise v. Foster 544 S.E.2d 331 (Va. 2001) (no patient-physician relationship solely on account of on-call physician's obligation to supervise medical residents in the emergency room).

3. *Employment or Insurance Physicals.* Patients are often examined by physicians in situations in which the physician is retained by a third party. For example, a company may require a preemployment examination, or an insurer may require an examination before issuing a policy or paying benefits. In general, no patient-physician relationship is created when the physician examines a patient at the request and for the benefit of a third party, and the patient therefore has no cause of action if the physician fails to diagnose a disease or disclose abnormal findings. Payne v. Sherrer, 458 S.E.2d 916 (Ga. Ct. App. 1995) (no cause of action for breach of confidentiality against a physician who examined employee on behalf of employer); Saari v. Litman, 486 N.W.2d 813 (Minn. Ct. App. 1992) (no professional relationship when patient was examined for insurer after claiming coverage for treatment of injuries suffered in an automobile accident); Murphy v. Blum, 554 N.Y.S.2d 640 (App. Div. 1990) (no cause of action for basketball referee who was not told of abnormal EKG findings by physician who performed yearly physical examinations for the NBA).

However, there are important exceptions to this general principle. For example, the physician may have a duty "to take reasonable steps to make information available timely to the examinee of any findings that pose an imminent danger to the examinee's physical or mental well-being." Green v. Walker, 910 F.2d 291, 296 (5th Cir. 1991) (interpreting Louisiana law in a case in which a physician allegedly failed to diagnose lung cancer during an annual employment examination). *Accord* Stanley v. McCarver, 92 P.3d 849 (Ariz. 2004); Reed v. Bojarski, 764 A.2d 433 (N.J. 2001) (both imposing a duty of care on physicians who find evidence of serious illness). A patient-physician relationship may also be found if the physician "affirmatively" advises the patient on "how to be treated." Hickey v. Travelers Insurance Co., 558 N.Y.S.2d 554 (App. Div. 1990) (workers' compensation physician mistakenly advised employee that surgery was not necessary to treat work-related injuries). See also Webb v. T.D., 951 P.2d 1008 (Mont. 1997) (liability when physician negligently diagnoses a patient's condition and communicates the misdiagnosis directly to the patient).

While the physician may not have an affirmative duty to the patient, the physician does have a duty not to harm the patient. Armstrong v. Morgan, 545 S.W.2d 45 (Tex. Ct. App. 1977) (employee lost job because physician allegedly misreported his health condition after an examination related to a promotion); Greenberg v. Perkins, 845 P.2d 530 (Colo. 1993) (physician referred patient for an evaluation that aggravated an old back injury). Dyer v. Trachtman, 679 N.W.2d 311 (Mich. 2004) (physician allegedly tore shoulder cartilage that had been recently repaired surgically by another physician).

A few states permit malpractice claims to be brought in the absence of a patient-physician relationship. Daly v. United States, 946 F.2d 1467 (9th Cir. 1991) (job applicant had undergone a preemployment examination, and the radiologist failed to diagnose a potentially serious lung disease or inform the applicant of the abnormal X-ray). Finally, even where the examining physician has no duty to the patient, the third party that requires the exam and chooses the physician may have a duty of care. Dornak v. Lafayette General Hospital, 399 So. 2d 168 (La. 1981) (employer liable for failing to disclose tuberculosis diagnosed during preemployment examination).

For further discussion, see Patrick D. Blake, Note, Redefining Physicians' Duties: An Argument for Eliminating the Physician-Patient Relationship Requirement in Actions for Medical Malpractice, 40 Ga. L. Rev. 573 (2006).

4. *Duties to Third Parties.* Similar issues arise when physicians have a clear treatment relationship with a patient but their treatment decisions affect third parties. The question then is whether the physician owes a duty of care to someone who is not their patient and who may be a complete stranger. For example, if a physician negligently stops prescribing a drug to control a patient's seizures, and the patient injures a third party because of a seizure while driving an automobile, does the third party have a malpractice cause of action against the physician?

The issue here is similar to the question of a physician's duty to warn third parties who might be injured by the physician's patient (because the patient may act on a psychotic delusion, for example), or who share a health risk with the patient (either because the patient carries an infectious disease, or because the patient and third party share a genetic risk of disease). That issue is taken up in Chapter 3. In both kinds of cases, there is a common issue as to whether the physician owes a duty of care to the third party. The two kinds of cases differ in that here the issue is whether a physician owes a duty of nonnegligence to third parties, while in the other cases the issue is whether the physician has a duty to warn third parties of their risk.

While courts generally recognize some duty of nonnegligence to third parties, they differ on the extent of that duty. In Welke v. Kuzilla, 375 N.W.2d 403 (Mich. Ct. App. 1985), the court found liability simply because the injury to the third party was reasonably foreseeable. In that case, a woman driving her car was killed in an automobile collision that was allegedly precipitated by medication given by the physician to the driver of the other car. *Accord* Cram v. Howell, 680 N.E.2d 1096 (Ind. 1997); Joy v. Eastern Maine Medical Center, 529 A.2d 1364 (Me. 1987); Hardee v. Biomedical Applications of South Carolina, 636 S.E.2d 629 (S.C. 2006) (all three cases imposing duties to warn patient of risks of driving and/or to ensure that patient was able to drive safely before leaving the doctor's office).

Other states find a duty only when there is a "special relationship" between the third party and either the patient or the physician. Thus, in Renslow v. Mennonite Hospital, 367 N.E.2d 1250 (Ill. 1977), the court held a hospital and physician liable for prenatal injuries to a child from blood transfusions that nine years earlier had caused Rh-sensitization in the child's mother. However, the same court rejected liability when a passenger was injured in an automobile accident allegedly caused because the car's driver was impaired by medications that the physician negligently prescribed, observing that the relationship between driver and passenger does not have the intimacy of mother and fetus. Kirk v. Michael Reese Hospital, 513 N.E.2d 387, 399 (Ill. 1987).

A New York court has required the additional showing that the physician had "sufficient ability and authority to control the conduct" of the patient before finding a duty of care to third parties. The court found no duty of care to the children of a driver who crashed into a bridge abutment after losing consciousness, allegedly because of negligently prescribed medication, on the ground that the driver "was free to accept or reject defendant's diagnosis and advice and she was at liberty to seek a second opinion. . . . [S]he had the right to decide what treatment and advice she would accept or reject." Conboy v. Mogeloff, 567 N.Y.S.2d 960, 961-962 (App. Div. 1991). Is this a fair characterization of the way patients respond when physicians prescribe medication for them?

Other relevant cases include Calwell v. Hassan, 925 P.2d 422 (Kan. 1996) (no duty to third party injured by patient when the patient already knew of the risk to others from her sleeping disorder and the physician's treatment did not increase the risk); Wilschinsky v. Medina, 775 P.2d 713 (N.M. 1989) (finding a duty to a third party injured by the patient in an automobile accident when the patient had just come from the physician's office where she was injected with a drug known to affect judgment and driving ability); Lester ex rel. Mavrogenis v. Hall, 970 P.2d 590 (N.M. 1998) (declining to apply *Wilschinsky* when five days elapsed between the prescription of a drug and the automobile accident).

In an interesting twist on the third-party question, courts have considered whether a kidney donor can sue a physician on the ground that the physician's negligence caused the recipient's need for the kidney transplant. The courts have rejected such claims on the ground that no patient-physician relationship existed between the donor and the recipient's physician. See, e.g., Dabdoub v. Ochsner Clinic, 802 So. 2d 651 (La. Ct. App. 2000); Moore v. Shah, 458 N.Y.S.2d 33 (N.Y. App. Div. 1982). When a physician's negligence causes kidney transplant surgery to be unsuccessful, there also is no patient-physician relationship between the donor and the recipient's physician. See Ornelas v. Fry, 727 P.2d 819 (Ariz. Ct. App. 1986); Malik v. William Beaumont Hospital, 423 N.W.2d 920 (Mich. Ct. App. 1988).

Third-party questions also arise in the context of reproductive medicine. If a physician fails to diagnose a genetic disorder in a couple's child (who is the actual patient), the couple may not be aware of the risk that future children will inherit the same disorder. Courts have found a duty of care to the parents in such situations. See Molloy v. Meier, 679 N.W.2d 711 (Minn. 2004) (finding a duty to parents when physicians failed to test child with Fragile X syndrome and second child was also born with the syndrome); Schroeder v. Perkel, 432 A.2d 834 (N.J. 1981) (finding a duty to parents on grounds of negligent diagnosis when physicians failed to identify cystic fibrosis in a child, and the parents became pregnant with a second child with cystic fibrosis).

2. Limiting the Scope of the Treatment Relationship

In contrast with finding that a provider has no obligation to a third party or ostensible patient, it might be conceded that a treatment relationship exists but that the provider's obligation is limited in some important respects. The section considers both limitations on the standard of care that determines liability and limitations on other obligations such as the scope of practice.

■ TUNKL v. REGENTS OF THE UNIVERSITY OF CALIFORNIA
383 P.2d 441 (Cal. 1963)

TOBRINER, Justice.

. . . Hugo Tunkl brought this action to recover damages for personal injuries alleged to have resulted from the negligence of two physicians in the employ of the University of California Los Angeles Medical Center, a hospital operated and maintained by the Regents of the University of California as a nonprofit charitable institution . . . for the primary purpose of aiding and developing a program of research and education in the field of medicine. . . . Upon his entry to the hospital, Tunkl signed a document setting forth certain "Conditions of Admission." The crucial condition number six reads as follows:

> RELEASE: The hospital is a nonprofit, charitable institution. In consideration of the hospital and allied services to be rendered and the rates charged therefor, the patient or his legal representative agrees to and hereby releases The Regents of the University of California, and the hospital from any and all liability for the negligent or wrongful acts or omissions of its employees, if the hospital has used due care in selecting its employees. . . .

Plaintiff at the time of signing the release was in great pain, under sedation, and probably unable to read. At trial plaintiff contended that the release was invalid, asserting that a release does not bind the releasor if at the time of its execution he suffered from so weak a mental condition that he was unable to comprehend the effect of his act. The jury, however, found against plaintiff on this issue. Since the verdict of the jury established that plaintiff either knew or should have known the significance of the release, this appeal raises the sole question of whether the release can stand as a matter of law. . . .

We begin with the dictate of the relevant Civil Code §1668. The section states: "All contracts which have for their object, directly or indirectly, to exempt anyone from responsibility for his own fraud, or willful injury to the person or property of another, or violation of law, whether willful or negligent, are against the policy of the law."

The course of §1668, however, has been a troubled one. . . . Some of the cases have applied the statute strictly, invalidating any contract for exemption from liability for negligence. . . . Other cases hold that the statute prohibits the exculpation of gross negligence only; still another case states that the section forbids exemption from active as contrasted with passive negligence. In one respect, as we have said, the decisions are uniform. The cases have consistently held that the exculpatory provision may stand only if it does not involve "the public interest."[6] . . . [C]ourts [have] struck down exculpatory clauses as contrary to public policy in the case of a contract to transmit a telegraph message and in the instance of a contract of bailment. . . .

If, then, the exculpatory clause which affects the public interest cannot stand, we must ascertain those factors or characteristics which constitute the public interest. The social forces that have led to such characterization are volatile and dynamic. No definition of the concept of public interest can be contained within the four corners of a formula. The concept, always the subject of great debate, has ranged over the whole course of the common law. . . .

In placing particular contracts within or without the category of those affected with a public interest, the courts have revealed a rough outline of that type of transaction in which exculpatory provisions will be held invalid. Thus the attempted but invalid exemption involves a transaction which exhibits some or all of the following characteristics. It concerns a business of a type generally thought suitable for public regulation. The party seeking exculpation is engaged in performing a service of great importance to the public, which is often a matter of practical necessity for some members of the public. The party holds himself out as willing to perform this service for any member of the public who seeks it, or at least for any member coming within certain established standards.[12] As a result of the essential nature of the service, in the economic setting of the transaction, the party invoking exculpation possesses a decisive advantage of bargaining strength against any member of the public who seeks his services. In exercising a superior bargaining power the party confronts the public with a standardized adhesion contract of exculpation, and makes no provision whereby a purchaser may pay additional reasonable fees and obtain protection against negligence. Finally, as a result of the transaction, the person or property of the purchaser is placed under the control of the seller, subject to the risk of carelessness by the seller or his agents. . . .

In the light of the decisions, we think that the hospital-patient contract clearly falls within the category of agreements affecting the public interest. To meet that test, the agreement need only fulfill some of the characteristics above outlined; here, the relationship fulfills all of them. . . . The would-be patient is in

---

[6] The view that the exculpatory contract is valid only if the public interest is not involved represents the majority holding in the United States. . . .

[12] . . . There is a close historical relationship between the duty of common carriers, public warehousemen, innkeepers, etc. to give reasonable service to all persons who apply, and the refusal of courts to permit such businesses to obtain exemption from liability for negligence. . . .

no position to reject the proffered agreement, to bargain with the hospital, or in lieu of agreement to find another hospital. The admission room of a hospital contains no bargaining table where, as in a private business transaction, the parties can debate the terms of their contract. As a result, we cannot but conclude that the instant agreement manifested the characteristics of the so-called adhesion contract. . . .

Defendant [next] contends that while the public interest may possibly invalidate the exculpatory provision as to the paying patient, it certainly cannot do so as to the charitable one. . . . [W]e see no distinction in the hospital's duty of due care between the paying and nonpaying patient. The duty, emanating not merely from contract but also tort, imports no discrimination based upon economic status. . . . To immunize the hospital from negligence as to the charitable patient because he does not pay would be as abhorrent to medical ethics as it is to legal principle. . . .

In substance defendant here asks us to modify our decision in Malloy v. Fong, 37 Cal. 2d 356, 232 P.2d 241 (1951), which removed the charitable immunity; defendant urges that otherwise the funds of the research hospital may be deflected from the real objective of the extension of medical knowledge to the payment of claims for alleged negligence. Since a research hospital necessarily entails surgery and treatment in which fixed standards of care may not yet be evolved, defendant says the hospital should in this situation be excused from such care. But the answer lies in the fact that possible plaintiffs must prove negligence; the standards of care will themselves reflect the research nature of the treatment; the hospital will not become an insurer or guarantor of the patient's recovery. To exempt the hospital completely from any standard of due care is to grant it immunity by the side-door method of a contractual clause exacted of the patient. We cannot reconcile that technique with the teaching of *Malloy*. . . .

The judgment is reversed.

Notes: Limiting the Standard of Care and Scope of Practice

1. *Limiting Liability.* Other courts that have disallowed contractual provisions that would relieve doctors of malpractice liability include Emory University v. Porubiansky, 282 S.E.2d 903 (Ga. 1981) (university dental clinic's liability release was void as against public policy even though the clinic was used for training purposes as part of the dental school); Meiman v. Rehabilitation Center, Inc., 444 S.W.2d 78 (Ky. 1969) (rehabilitation facility's liability release was invalid as being against public policy). Olson v. Molzen, 558 S.W.2d 429 (Tenn. 1977) (physician's liability release for an abortion patient was invalid as contrary to public policy).

Nevertheless, partial waivers may be allowed in some situations. The leading example is Madden v. Kaiser Foundation Hospitals, 552 P.2d 1178 (Cal. 1976), excerpted and discussed at page 428, which upheld a provision in an HMO contract that required malpractice claims to be decided by arbitration. Unlike in *Tunkl*, arbitration does not alter the standard of care, only the process of dispute resolution; the limitation was imposed on healthy employees as part of their health insurance, not on a sick patient coming to the hospital; and the limitation was part of a contract negotiated by a very large employer on behalf of its workers, in a situation where the employees had a choice of other health insurance that did not contain this limitation.

Waivers or limitations of liability are also commonly enforced when, for good reason, physicians depart from standard medical practice. This might occur, for instance, if a patient insists on leaving the hospital "against medical advice" (a so-called discharge A.M.A.). Such patients are asked to sign a waiver or release from liability for harm resulting from refusing recommended treatment. Consider also a patient, who for religious or other reasons, insists on a type of treatment that is not medically recommended, or one who agrees to participate in a medical experiment. See, e.g., Colton v. New York Hospital, 414 N.Y.S.2d 866 (Sup. Ct. 1979) (permitting release from liability for injury resulting from nonnegligent care when the treatment—a kidney transplant—was experimental); Shorter v. Drury, 695 P.2d 116 (Wash. 1985) (permitting a hospital to require a Jehovah's Witness patient who refused blood transfusions to release the hospital, its personnel, and the patient's physician from liability for any injury resulting from the refusal); See generally 6 A.L.R.3d 704.

2. *Scope of Practice; Futility.* The remainder of these notes explore other types of limitations on a physician's or hospital's treatment obligation. One such limitation concerns the scope of practice. Physicians are entitled to limit their practice to a particular specialty and geographic area. See, e.g., McNamara v. Emmons, 97 P.2d 503 (Cal. 1939) (physician absolved of responsibility for follow-up care when patient had gone to stay 20 miles out-of-town, and the physician arranged for care with another physician where the patient was staying).

Also, physicians are not obligated to provide care that offers no medical benefit. However, there is considerable disagreement as to when medical treatment becomes futile.

3. *Conscientious Objection.* In some situations, physicians or other medical workers may have a conscientious objection to providing care. For example, obstetrician-gynecologists often are unwilling to perform abortions. Congress and many state legislatures have enacted so-called conscience clause statutes that protect medical personnel from retaliatory measures for refusing to participate in abortions. See 42 U.S.C. §300a-7 (2007) (known as the "Church Amendment"). Because only a minority of obstetrician-gynecologists perform abortions, abortions are not available in many parts of the country. Should a state respond to the poor access of its residents to abortion by requiring that, as a condition of licensure, obstetrician-gynecologists must be willing to perform abortions?

A physician who is morally opposed to abortion may be not only unwilling to perform abortions but also unwilling to facilitate abortions by referring patients to an abortion provider or informing them of the option to have an abortion. Would a refusal to discuss abortion violate the patient's right to informed consent? See Rust v. Sullivan, 500 U.S. 173, 195 (1991) (permitting the federal government to refuse family planning funds to organizations that counsel or refer for abortions where there is no medical need).

Issues about conscientious objection also arise when patients request that life-sustaining treatment be withdrawn, and may arise in other circumstances as well. For a thorough analysis of different contexts and legal implications, see Anne Dellinger & Anne Vickery, When Staff Object to Participating in Care, 28 J. Health & Hosp. L. 269 (1995).

3. Terminating the Treatment Relationship

■ RICKS v. BUDGE
64 P.2d 208 (Utah 1937)

HANSON, Justice.

This is an action for malpractice against the defendants who are physicians and surgeons at Logan, Utah, and are copartners doing business under the name and style of the "Budge Clinic." . . . [P]laintiff alleges that he was suffering from an infected right hand and was in immediate need of medical and surgical care and treatment, and there was danger of his dying unless he received such treatment; that defendants for the purpose of treating plaintiff sent him to the Budge Memorial Hospital at Logan, Utah; that while at the hospital and while he was in need of medical and surgical treatment, defendants refused to treat or care for plaintiff and abandoned his case. . . .

The evidence shows that on or about March 8, 1935, plaintiff caught the middle finger of his right hand on a barbed wire. Soon thereafter the finger and hand began to swell and became reddened. In the early morning of March 11th, plaintiff went to the Budge Memorial Hospital to seek treatment from the defendants. Dr. S. M. Budge . . . made two lateral incisions in the finger, waited a few hours to see the result, and then later the same morning deepened the incisions in order to reach the pus, which he believed had developed. A gauze wick was then put in each incision for the purpose of drainage.

The plaintiff remained in the hospital from March 11th until March 15th, during which time he was under the care of Dr. S. M. Budge. . . . On the morning of March 15th, plaintiff told the nurse and Dr. Budge that he intended leaving the hospital that morning. Dr. Budge advised plaintiff against leaving, but notwithstanding the protests of Dr. Budge, plaintiff left the hospital after paying the amount that was due at that time. . . .

[T]he evidence shows that when plaintiff left the hospital on March 15th, Dr. Budge advised him to continue the same treatment that had been given him at the hospital, and that if the finger showed any signs of getting worse at any time, plaintiff was to return at once to Dr. Budge for further treatment; that on the morning of March 17th, plaintiff telephoned Dr. Budge, and explained the condition of his hand; that he was told by the doctor to come to his office, and in pursuance of the doctor's request, plaintiff reported at the doctor's office at 2 P.M. on that day. Dr. Budge again examined the hand[,] told plaintiff the hand was worse and . . . said to plaintiff: "You have got to go back to the hospital." . . . Plaintiff left immediately for the hospital. . . . Within a short time after the arrival of plaintiff, Dr. [Budge] arrived at the hospital. Plaintiff testified: "He [meaning Dr. S. M. Budge] came into my room and said, 'You are owing us. I am not going to touch you until that account is taken care of.'" (The account referred to was, according to plaintiff, of some years' standing and did not relate to any charge for services being then rendered.) Plaintiff testified that he did not know what to say to the doctor, but that he finally asked the doctor if he was going to take care of him, and the doctor replied: "No, I am not going to take care of you. I would not take you to the operating table and operate on you and keep you here 30 days, and then there is another $30.00 at the office, until your account is taken care of."

Plaintiff replied: "If that is the idea, if you will furnish me a little help, I will try to move."

Plaintiff testified that this help was furnished, and that after being dressed, he left the Budge Memorial Hospital to seek other treatment. . . . He walked to the Cache Valley Hospital, a few blocks away, and there met Dr. Randall, who examined the hand. Dr. Randall testified that when the plaintiff arrived at the Cache Valley Hospital, the hand was swollen with considerable fluid oozing from it; that the lower two-thirds of the forearm was red and swollen from the infection which extended up in the arm, and that there was some fluid also oozing from the back of the hand, and that plaintiff required immediate surgical attention; that immediately after the arrival of plaintiff at the hospital he made an incision through the fingers and through the palm of the hand along the tendons that led from the palm and followed those tendons as far as there was any bulging, and opened it up thoroughly all the way to the base of the hand and put drain tubes in. Plaintiff remained under the care of Dr. Randall for approximately a month. About two weeks after the plaintiff entered the Cache Valley Hospital, it became necessary to amputate the middle finger and removed about an inch of the metacarpal bone.

Dr. S. M. Budge testified that at the time he sent the plaintiff to the Budge Memorial Hospital on March 17th, plaintiff was in a dangerous condition and needed immediate surgical and medical attention; that the reason for sending him to that hospital was in order to give him the necessary immediate surgical and medical attention. . . . The plaintiff testified that at the time he was sent to the hospital by the defendants on March 17th, his hand was badly swollen; that he was unable to move any of his fingers on that hand; that the hand was full of blisters which had broken and were oozing. . . . Dr. S. M. Budge arrived at the hospital a short time after the arrival of plaintiff for the purpose of giving plaintiff such medical and surgical attention as he deemed necessary. There can be no question from the evidence that it was the intention of Dr. S. M. Budge to operate at once on plaintiff's hand.

Defendants contend: (1) That there was no contract of employment between plaintiff and defendants and that defendants in the absence of a valid contract were not obligated to proceed with any treatment. . . . We cannot agree. . . . The evidence shows that plaintiff had been under the care and treatment of the defendants at the Budge Memorial Hospital from March 11th to March 15th; that when he left that hospital on March 15th, Dr. S. M. Budge said to him: "If you are going home, you had better follow out the treatment at home just as near as you can the same as you were doing here. Here is another thing I want to tell you, if you see any signs of that finger getting worse at any time, you come in and see me immediately." On March 17th, plaintiff, realizing that his condition was getting worse, telephoned Dr. S. M. Budge and was told by that doctor to come to the doctor's office, which plaintiff did; that there both Dr. S. M. Budge and Dr. D. C. Budge examined the hand; that Dr. D. C. Budge indicated on it where it should be opened; and that under the instructions of these doctors plaintiff was returned to the hospital for no other purpose than having his hand operated upon at once.

Under this evidence, it cannot be said that the relation of physician and patient did not exist on March 17th. It had not been terminated after its commencement on March 11th. When the plaintiff left the hospital on March 15th, he understood that he was to report to Dr. S. M. Budge if the occasion required and was so requested by the doctor. Plaintiff's return to the doctor's office was on the advice of the doctor. While at the doctor's office, both Dr. S. M. Budge and Dr. D. C. Budge examined plaintiff's hand and they ordered that he go at once to the hospital for further medical attention. That plaintiff was told by the doctor to come to the doctor's office and was there examined by him and directed to go to the hospital for further treatment would create the relationship of physician and patient. That the relationship existed at the time the plaintiff was sent to the hospital on March 17th cannot be seriously questioned.

We believe the law is well settled that a physician or surgeon, upon undertaking an operation or other case, is under the duty, in the absence of an agreement limiting the service, of continuing his attention, after the first operation or first treatment, so long as the case requires attention. The obligation of continuing attention can be terminated only by the cessation of the necessity which gave rise to the relationship, or by the discharge of the physician by the patient, or by the withdrawal from the case by the physician after giving the patient reasonable notice so as to enable the patient to secure other medical attention. A physician has the right to withdraw from a case, but if the case is such as to still require further medical or surgical attention, he must, before withdrawing from the case, give the patient sufficient notice so the patient can procure other medical attention if he desires. . . .

[The court remanded the case for consideration of whether Mr. Ricks suffered any physical and mental suffering by virtue of having to go to Cache Valley Hospital for care.]

■ PAYTON v. WEAVER
182 Cal. Rptr. 225 (Cal. Ct. App. 1982)

GRODIN, Judge.

Occasionally a case will challenge the ability of the law, and society, to cope effectively and sensitively with fundamental problems of human existence. This is such a case. Appellant, Brenda Payton, is a 35-year-old black woman who suffers from a permanent and irreversible loss of kidney function, a condition known as chronic end stage renal disease. To stay alive, she must subject herself two or three times a week to hemodialysis (dialysis), a process in which the patient's circulatory system is connected to a machine through which the blood is passed. Using salts and osmotic membranes, artificial kidneys in the machine drain the blood of excess liquids and accumulated impurities. Without such treatment, the volume of liquids in the patient's system will increase dangerously; liquid will begin to fill the lungs, making breathing difficult and possibly leading to heart failure. The resulting toxic waste buildup and chemical imbalances can also threaten the function of the heart and other organs.

Brenda has other difficulties. Unable to care for her children, she lives alone in a low-income housing project in West Oakland, subsisting on a $356 per month Social Security check. She has no family support; one brother is in prison and another is a mental patient. She confesses that she is a drug addict, having been addicted to heroin and barbiturates for over 15 years. She has alcohol problems, weight problems and, not surprisingly, emotional problems as well.

Despite these difficulties Brenda appears from the record to be a marvelously sympathetic and articulate individual who in her lucid moments possesses a great sense of dignity and is intent upon preserving her independence and her integrity as a human being. At times, however, her behavior is such as to make extremely difficult the provision of medical care which she so desperately requires.

The other principal figure in this case is respondent John C. Weaver, Jr., a physician specializing in kidney problems. He conducts his practice through respondent Biomedical Application of Oakland, Inc. (BMA), which operates an outpatient dialysis treatment unit on the premises of respondent Providence Hospital.

Dr. Weaver began treating Brenda in 1975 when, after the birth of Brenda's twin daughters, her system rejected a transplanted kidney. . . . On December 12, 1978, Dr. Weaver sent Brenda a letter stating he would no longer permit her to be treated at BMA because of her "persistent uncooperative and antisocial behavior over . . . more than . . . three years . . . her persistent refusal to adhere to reasonable constraints of hemodialysis, the dietary schedules and medical prescriptions . . . the use of barbiturates and other illicit drugs and because all this resulted in disruption of our program at BMA."

In the latter part of 1978, Brenda applied for admission to the regular dialysis treatment programs operated by respondents Alta Bates and Herrick Hospitals, and was refused.

For several months Dr. Weaver continued to provide Brenda with necessary dialysis on an emergency basis, through Providence. On April 23, 1979, he again notified her by letter that he would no longer treat her on an outpatient basis. This letter led to Brenda's filing of a petition for mandate to compel Dr. Weaver, BMA, and Providence to continue to provide her with outpatient dialysis services. That litigation was settled by a stipulated order which called for continued treatment provided Brenda met certain conditions: that she keep all appointments at their scheduled time; that she refrain from use of alcohol and drugs; that she maintain prescribed dietary habits; and that she "in all respects cooperate with those providing her care and abide by her physician's prescribed medical regimen." Later, a sixth stipulation was added: that Brenda would "enter into and participate in good faith in a program of regular psychotherapy and/or counselling."

Dr. Weaver and BMA continued treatment of Brenda as an outpatient pursuant to the stipulation, but on March 3, 1980, Dr. Weaver, contending that Brenda had failed to fulfill any part of the bargain, again notified her that treatment would be terminated. He provided her with a list of dialysis providers in San Francisco and the East Bay, and volunteered to work with her counsel to find alternative care.

Brenda then instituted a second proceeding, again in the form of a petition for writ of mandate, this time naming Herrick and Alta Bates Hospitals as respondents, along with Dr. Weaver, BMA and Providence. . . .

The trial court, after a lengthy evidentiary hearing, found that Brenda had violated each and every condition which she had accepted as part of the stipulated order providing for continued treatment, and that finding is basically undisputed.

There was evidence that Brenda continued, after the stipulated order, to buy barbiturates from pushers on the street at least twice a week; that she failed to restrict her diet, gaining as much as 15 kilograms between dialysis treatments; that she continued to be late and/or miss appointments; that due primarily to missed appointments she had 30 emergencies requiring hospitalization in the 11 months preceding trial; that she would appear for treatment in an intoxicated condition; that she discontinued her program of counseling after a brief period; and, as the trial court found, she displayed in general "gross non-cooperation with her treating physician, BMA of Oakland and Providence Hospital." The trial court found that her behavior in these respects was "knowing and intentional."

Brenda's behavior was found to affect not only Dr. Weaver but the other patients and the treating staff as well. Dialysis treatment is typically provided to several patients at a time, all of them connected to a single dialysis machine. There was evidence that Brenda would frequently appear for treatment late or at unscheduled times in a drugged or alcoholic condition, that she used profane and vulgar language, and that she had on occasion engaged in disruptive behavior, such as bothering other patients, cursing staff members with obscenities, screaming and demanding that the dialysis be turned off and that she be disconnected before her treatment was finished, pulling the dialysis needle from the connecting shunt in her leg causing blood to spew, and exposing her genitals in a lewd manner. The trial court found that during the times she has sought treatment "her conduct has been disruptive, abusive, and unreasonable such as to trespass upon the rights of other patients and to endanger their rights to full and adequate treatment," and that her conduct "has been an imposition on the nursing staff." The court determined that, on balance, the rights and privileges of other patients endangered by Brenda's conduct were superior to the rights or equities which Brenda claimed.

DISCUSSION

We begin our analysis by considering the trial court's conclusion that Dr. Weaver and the clinic with which he is associated have no present legal obligation to continue providing Brenda with dialysis treatment. . . .

. . . Brenda relies upon the general proposition that a physician who abandons a patient may do so "only . . . after due notice, and an ample opportunity afforded to secure the presence of other medical attendance." Lathrope v. Flood, 63 P. 1007, 1008 (1901).

The trial court found, however, that Dr. Weaver gave sufficient notice to Brenda, and discharged all his obligations in that regard, and that finding, also, is amply supported. Dr. Weaver supplied Brenda with a list of the names and telephone numbers of all dialysis providers in San Francisco and the East Bay, and it is apparent from the record that nothing would have pleased him more than to find an alternative facility for her, but there is no evidence that there is anything further he could have done to achieve that goal under the circumstances.

During the proceedings, the trial court observed that Dr. Weaver "is one of the most sensitive and honest physicians that I have been exposed to either in a courtroom or out of a courtroom," that he was "in fact sensitive to [Brenda's] needs, that he has attempted to assist her to the best of his medical abilities, that he continues to have concern for her as a person and has continued to serve her medical needs," and that "[the] man has the patience of Job." It appears that Dr. Weaver has behaved according to the highest standards of the medical profession, and that there exists no basis in law or in equity to saddle him with a continuing sole obligation for Brenda's welfare. The same is true of the clinic, the BMA.

We turn now to Brenda's contention that Herrick and Alta Bates Hospitals violated their obligations under Health and Safety Code §1317 [to provide emergency care] by denying her admission to their regular outpatient dialysis programs in late 1978. The trial court found that at the time Brenda applied for admission to these programs she was not in an "emergency condition," by which the court obviously meant that she was in no imminent physical danger on the day she applied. Brenda contends, however, that her illness is itself "a chronic/acute emergency which requires that she receive medical treatment every third day to avoid death," and that such a condition qualifies for mandated service under §1317. . . .

. . . While end stage renal disease is an extremely serious and dangerous disease, which can create imminent danger of loss of life if not properly treated, the need for continuous treatment as such cannot reasonably be said to fall within the scope of §1317. There are any number of diseases or conditions which could be fatal to the patient if not treated on a continuing basis. If a patient suffering from such a disease or condition were to appear in the emergency room of a hospital in need of immediate life-saving treatment, §1317 would presumably require that such treatment be provided. But it is unlikely that the legislature intended to impose upon whatever health care facility such a patient chooses the unqualified obligation to provide continuing preventive care for the patient's lifetime.

It does not necessarily follow that a hospital, or other health care facility, is without obligation to patients in need of continuing medical services for their survival. While it has been said that "[a] private hospital owes the public no duty to accept any patient not desired by it, and it is not necessary to assign any reason for its refusal to accept a patient for hospital service" (41 C.J.S. Hospitals, §8, p.345), it is questionable whether a hospital which receives public funding under the Hill-Burton Act (42 U.S.C. §291), and perhaps from other sources, can reasonably be said to be "private" in that sense. Rather, where such a hospital contains a unique, or scarce, medical resource needed to preserve life, it is arguably in the nature of a "public service enterprise," and should not be permitted to withhold its services arbitrarily, or without reasonable cause. And, while disruptive conduct on the part of a patient may constitute good cause for an individual hospital to refuse continued treatment, since it would be unfair to impose serious inconvenience upon a hospital simply because such a patient selected it, it may be that there exists a *collective* responsibility on the part of the providers of scarce health resources in a community, enforceable through equity, to *share* the burden of difficult patients over time, through an appropriately devised contingency plan.

This argument was not presented to the trial court, however, and the record is not adequate to support relief on that ground as a matter of law. . . . Whatever collective responsibility may exist, it is clearly not absolute, or independent of the patient's own responsibility.

Notes: Abandonment Liability

1. *The* Payton *Case.* After the court decided the *Payton* case, dialysis providers in the area did arrange to share the responsibility for treating Ms. Payton. The court's suggestion of a public service obligation is mentioned at the end of its opinion. For additional discussion, see Stella Smetanka, Who Will Protect the "Disruptive" Dialysis Patient? 32 Am. J. L. & Med. 53 (2006).

How might Ms. Payton have challenged Dr. Weaver's decision to discontinue care under the Americans with Disabilities Act? See David Orentlicher, Denying Treatment to the Noncompliant Patient, 265 JAMA 1579 (1991). Is it so clear that noncompliance is a legitimate basis for a physician to stop treating a patient? Why might a patient not follow the physician's recommendations? If noncompliance is an accepted justification for terminating the patient-physician relationship, what implications does that have for the patient's right to refuse medical treatment?

What do you think about the fact that the court decided to mention the plaintiff's race? Is her race relevant to a full assessment of the case? For a case similar to *Payton* with the opposite result, see Brown v. Bower, No. 586-0759(B) (S.D. Miss. Dec. 21, 1987).

For a discussion of termination of care on grounds of conscience, see John K. Davis, Conscientious Refusal and a Doctor's Right to Quit, 29 J. Med. Philosophy 75 (2004) (arguing that a physician can terminate care only if "the doctor's refusal does not make the patient worse off than she would have been had she gone to another doctor in the first place").

2. *Ricks v. Budge.* What are the critical factors that resulted in the courts coming to different conclusions in *Ricks* and *Payton* as to the physician's liability? Was it fair to hold the Drs. Budge responsible for Mr. Ricks' difficulties when he originally left the hospital against their advice? Why not conclude that the patient-physician relationship ended when Mr. Ricks left the hospital and that the Drs. Budge refused to renew the relationship when they found that Mr. Ricks had an unpaid bill?

3. *Abandonment Liability.* Once a patient-physician relationship is formed, it is implicit that the relationship continues as long as the patient needs treatment for the condition that brought the patient to the physician. Once the need is satisfied, the relationship ends. The professional relationship can also be ended explicitly if the patient unilaterally chooses to dispense with the physician's services or if both parties agree to the termination of the relationship. Finally, as the *Payton* case demonstrates, physicians can terminate the patient-physician relationship as long as they give notice to the patient such that the patient has sufficient opportunity to secure care from another physician. Failure to adhere to the required notice can result in abandonment liability if the patient is injured as a result.

Strictly speaking, abandonment liability results from purposefully ceasing treatment for primarily nonmedical reasons, not from mistakenly ceasing treatment due to medical error. In other words, it is more akin to breach of contract than to medical malpractice. Nevertheless, courts and lawyers often confuse the two theories when patients are injured by failure to treat. See generally Comment, The Action of Abandonment in Medical Malpractice Litigation, 36 Tulane L. Rev. 834 (1962); Annot., Liability of Physician Who Abandons Care, 57 A.L.R.2d 432 (1958).

4. *Lack of Payment*. As the *Ricks* case indicates, failure of a patient to pay does not permit the physician to discontinue care before satisfying the usual requirements for terminating the patient-physician relationship. This principle contrasts with the physician's freedom to take a patient's ability to pay into account when deciding whether to commence a professional relationship. As one court observed in a case in which a physician treated a patient for a miscarriage but suspended his care before the end of her need for treatment,

> Whether the patient be a pauper or a millionaire, whether he be treated gratuitously or for reward, the physician owes him precisely the same measure of duty, and the same degree of skill and care. He may decline to respond to the call of a patient unable to compensate him; but if he undertake the treatment of such a patient, he cannot defeat a suit for malpractice, nor mitigate a recovery against him, upon the principle that the skill and care required of a physician are proportioned to his expectation of pecuniary recompense. Becker v. Janinski, 15 N.Y.S. 675, 677 (Civ. Ct. 1891).

For further discussion of the effects of cost containment on the standard of care, see pages 329-331.

While a physician may not simply discontinue care because of nonpayment, nonpayment is an acceptable basis for a physician to terminate the patient-physician relationship so long as the termination is accomplished properly. See, e.g., Surgical Consultants, P.C. v. Ball, 447 N.W.2d 676, 682 (Iowa App. 1989) (terminating care for nonpayment is permissible because there is no "evidence that the physician has terminated the relationship at a critical stage of the patient's treatment [or] that the termination was done without reason or sufficient notice to enable the patient to procure another physician"). The critical issue is whether proper termination entails only notice or also requires that the patient actually secure another physician. The usual practice is for physicians to find a substitute and arrange the transfer themselves if, for instance, they are retiring from practice or going on vacation. This avoids any question of liability. There is little legal guidance where another willing physician cannot be located but a patient who cannot pay still receives ample notice. What does *Payton* suggest as the answer? See Mark Hall, A Theory of Economic Informed Consent, 31 U. Ga. L. Rev. 511 (1997).

C. REGULATING THE TREATMENT RELATIONSHIP

1. Professional Licensure

■ THE ABUSE OF OCCUPATIONAL LICENSING
Walter Gellhorn
44 U. Chi. L. Rev. 6 (1976)

[L]iterally hundreds of occupations are subject to licensing laws in one or more states. . . . [I]n many parts of this country today aspiring bee keepers, embalmers, lightening rod salesmen, septic tank cleaners, taxidermists, and tree surgeons must obtain official approval before seeking the public's patronage. After examining the roster of those who must receive official permission to function, a cynic might conclude that virtually the only people who remain unlicensed in at least one of the United States are clergymen and university professors, presumably because they are nowhere taken seriously. . . .

If occupational licensing resulted simply in downgrading the word *profession* or in enlarging the ranks of the "learned," one would have small cause for alarm. After all the complexities of modern life have created new demands for special training and perceptions. . . .

Licensing has done far more than simply gratify the understandable status-longing of semiskilled or specialized workers. . . . It has also badly eroded the right to work, one of man's most precious liberties.

Licensing has only infrequently been imposed upon an occupation against its wishes. . . . [L]icensing has been eagerly sought — always on the purported ground that licensure protects the uninformed public against incompetence or dishonesty, but invariably with the consequence that members of the licensed group become protected against competition from newcomers. That restricting access is the real purpose, and not merely a side effect, of many if not most successful campaigns to institute licensing schemes can scarcely be doubted. Licensing, imposed ostensibly to protect the public, almost always impedes only those who desire to enter the occupation or "profession"; those already in practice remain entrenched without a demonstration of fitness or probity. . . .

The restrictive consequence of licensure is achieved in large part by making entry into the regulated occupation expensive in time or money or both. . . .

[M]any special interests perceive themselves as nurturers of the public interest rather than as self-seekers. . . . But occupational licensing has typically brought higher status for the producer of services at the price of higher costs to the consumer; it has reduced competition; it has narrowed opportunity for aspiring youth by increasing the costs of entry into a desired occupational career; it has artificially segmented skills so that needed services, like health care, are increasingly difficult to supply economically; it has fostered the view that unethical practices will prevail unless those entrenched in a profession are assured of high incomes; and it has caused a proliferation of official administrative bodies, most of them staffed by persons drawn from and devoted to furthering the interests of the licensed occupations themselves. . . .

Notes: Professional Licensure

1. *Historical Roots.* During the nineteenth century, snake oil salesmen and other quacks roamed the countryside preying on the gullible public with unfounded promises of miracle cures. To eliminate such practices, around the turn of the twentieth century every state began to license medical practitioners. The typical Medical Practice Act makes it a criminal offense to practice medicine without a physician's license and establishes the grounds for revocation or suspension of a license. The job of medical licensure and discipline is entrusted to a Board of Medical Examiners, which usually consists predominantly of physicians.

Some alternative practitioners, such as osteopaths, chiropractors, and podiatrists, have likewise been successful in petitioning the legislature for recognition and protection through professional licensure and self-regulation. As these materials demonstrate, however, this patchwork of licensing provisions does not include a number of other alternative healing arts that consumers evidently desire.

2. *Physician Supply.* Most states require M.D.s to graduate from an AMA-accredited medical school (or, for foreign medical graduates, certification by the Educational Commission for Foreign Medical Graduates (ECFMG) and an internship in an AMA-approved residency program). As a result, medical licensure essentially cedes to the medical profession control of how many doctors can enter practice, since the AMA can control the size of medical school classes through the accreditation process and the ECFMG can control the certification process. Mark A. Peterson, From Trust to Political Power: Interest Groups, Public Choice, and Health Care, 26 J. Health Pol. Pol'y & L. 1145 (2001).

Allowing the medical profession to control entry into its own market creates the anticompetitive risk that the AMA will act out of economic self-interest to maintain artificial shortages. Barriers to entry into service professions tend automatically to drive up prices by creating a supply shortage. Reuben Kessel, Price Discrimination in Medicine, 1 J.L. & Econ. 20 (1959); Reuben Kessel, The A. M.A. and the Supply of Physicians, 35 Law & Contemp. Probs. 267 (1970).

Concern about physician shortages seems misplaced these days, when we are much more apt to hear about the "glut" of physicians, particularly of specialists. The ratio of physicians to citizens in the United States has been steadily increasing, rising from 146 physicians/100,000 in 1950 to 233/100,000 in 1990, to 276/100,000 in the year 2000. Some experts argue that the ideal ratio lies somewhere between 160 and 200 physicians per 100,000. In the mid-1990s policymakers were particularly concerned with reducing the number of specialists, who were thought to drive up the cost of care by providing services that could be more cheaply provided by family practitioners or others. The geographic distribution of physicians clearly remains problematic. Many rural areas have found it difficult to attract physicians. A similar problem can be found in some urban centers, where physicians have not been willing to establish practices that serve low-income populations. Edward S. Salsberg & Gaetano J. Forte, Trends in the Physician Workforce, 1980-2000, 21(5) Health Aff. 165 (2002).

3. *Licensure vs. Credentialing.* While his criticisms may be overstated, Walter Gellhorn suggests that the protection of public health is only one, possibly minor, motivation behind occupational licensure schemes. Do his criticisms seem applicable to the current system of licensure in health care? What benefits does a system of licensing health care professionals have over a system of accreditation or certification? Licensure statutes theoretically provide an absolute barrier to the provision of some services by unlicensed persons. Under an accreditation or certification scheme, consumers would be able to choose whether to seek care from an unaccredited or uncertified person. Health care payers, such as insurance companies, might be empowered to reject payment claims made by those lacking certification. Licensure schemes are preferred where there is a risk that consumers might not be able to exercise reasoned judgment about the qualifications of their health care providers, perhaps because of lack of knowledge, the decisionmaking

deficits created by disease, or financial distress. See Timothy Stoltzfus Jost, Oversight of the Quality of Medical Care: Regulation, Management, or the Market, 37 Ariz. L. Rev. 825 (1995); Randall G. Holcombe, Eliminating Scope of Practice and Licensing Laws to Improve Health Care, 31 J. L. Med. & Ethics 236 (2003).

How would you assess whether the licensure system is an effective mechanism for protecting public health? As a preliminary matter, you might want to analyze the fit between licensure requirements and the public health. That is, do the licensing requirements bear some rational relationship to the protection of health? Are they sufficiently stringent? Do they injure the public by excluding some potential providers who are capable of performing valuable services? The degree of continuing protection is also important. Does the licensure statute provide adequate mechanisms to identify practitioners who present a risk to their patients? Does the licensure authority have the interest, ability, and resources to police those who have been admitted to the profession?

4. *Assessing the Effectiveness of Disciplinary Actions.* For many years, the professional disciplinary process was characterized by lax enforcement, giving rise to criticisms that professions were incapable of self-regulation. See S. Gross, Of Foxes and Hen Houses: Licensing and the Health Profession (1984). Historically, medical boards tended to rely on local medical or professional societies to report and document disciplinary cases. Carl F. Ameringer, State Medical Boards and the Politics of Public Protection (1999). In recent years, boards have had other valuable sources of information about physician conduct. The Health Care Quality Improvement Act establishes a centralized data bank that collects information about (1) disciplinary actions from all states, (2) malpractice settlements, and (3) negative hospital privileges determinations. State licensure authorities report information to the centralized data bank and in turn collect information that can be used to identify physicians likely to be delivering poor quality care. 42 U.S.C. §§11131-11137 (2000). See page 453. Patients may also complain to the boards directly.

The growth in quality-related information has not always been followed by aggressive pursuit of physicians delivering substandard care. Most boards do not have adequate staff to respond to the volume of complaints and to conduct extensive investigations of unprofessional conduct. Consumer groups regularly complain about the continuing failure of self-regulation. According to the Federation of State Medical Boards, there were 4,015 "prejudicial or punitive" actions taken against physicians in 2001. Assume that this means that boards took prejudicial action against about .62 percent of physicians in 2001. Does this seem adequate?

Consumers now have much greater access to information about physicians. For a small fee, you can now find out from a variety of Web sites about physicians who have been disciplined by state or federal governments. In some states, consumers can also get information about malpractice judgments and settlements. See Chapter 4.E. Will this information help or confuse consumers? See Mark J. Greenwood, The Physician Profile Database, 21 J. Leg. Med. 477 (2000); Deborah Haas-Wilson, Arrow and the Information Market Failure in Health Care: The Changing Content and Sources of Health Care Information, 26 J. Health Pol. Pol'y & L. 1031 (2001).

5. *Overview.* The next two sets of cases and notes focus on the state's efforts to protect public health through the licensure process. The first set explores licensure as statutory fencing that keeps some persons from providing health care services altogether and that separates providers into different categories of professionals with at least somewhat distinct areas of permissible practice. The second set analyzes licensure as a policing technique in which licensing authorities investigate and discipline allegedly errant providers.

■ STATE v. MILLER
542 N.W.2d 241 (Iowa 1995)

ANDREASEN, Justice.

Albert C. Miller appeals from his convictions for practicing medicine without a license. He urges . . . that the record contains insufficient evidence to support his convictions. We affirm the judgment of the district court.

Miller was charged by a trial information with seven counts of practicing medicine without a license. [Most of the offenses were Class D felonies.] . . .

Several persons testified at trial describing treatments they received from Miller in his home for various ailments. His usual method of treatment was to put a lock of the person's hair or a photograph of the person into a machine called a radionics device. After recording numerous readings from the device on a chart, he would treat the person by administering mild electric shocks from a "function generator," massaging the person's feet or neck, or placing large magnets next to the person. In addition, he often sold or recommended natural vitamins or nutrients to the people who visited him. Although Miller did not charge for the treatments, he consistently accepted donations of $10 for each treatment. He did not have any license to practice medicine, osteopathy, or surgery.

Dr. John Renner, M.D., Director of the Consumer Health Information Research Institute, testified as an expert witness for the state. He found the various treatments and vitamins given by Miller to his patients, while not necessarily harmful, were generally not medically useful. In his opinion the primary danger was not from the medicine itself, but from the fact it delayed appropriate, potentially beneficial, medical treatment.

On July 14, 1994, the jury returned verdicts finding Miller guilty on all seven counts. He was sentenced to a term of incarceration not to exceed five years on six counts. On the seventh count, he was sentenced to four months in the county jail. All the sentences were suspended and Miller was placed on probation for five years. . . .

We must uphold the jury's verdict unless the record lacks substantial evidence to support the charges. Substantial evidence is evidence which could convince a rational jury the defendant is guilty of the crimes charged beyond a reasonable doubt. . . .

Miller was charged with practicing medicine and osteopathic medicine in violation of Iowa Code §147.2. Two separate instructions were given to the jury defining the practice of medicine and osteopathic medicine. One instruction . . . provided the following definition:

The practice of medicine and osteopathic medicine means holding one's self out as being able to diagnose, treat, or prescribe for any human disease, pain, injury, deformity, or physical or mental condition and who shall either offer or undertake, by any means or methods, to diagnose, treat, or prescribe for any human disease, pain, injury, deformity or physical or mental condition.

The other instruction provided that the following "persons shall be deemed to be engaged in the practice of medicine and osteopathic medicine":

1. Persons who publicly profess to be physicians or who publicly profess to assume the duties incident to the practice of medicine and osteopathic medicine.
2. Persons who prescribe, or prescribe and furnish medicine for human ailments. . . .

Miller argues that he did not publicly profess to be a physician or publicly profess to assume the duties incident to the practice of medicine and osteopathic medicine. He emphasizes that he never advertised nor described himself as a doctor; he would sometimes recommend that his customers consult a licensed physician or chiropractor; and he only met people in his home, not in an office.

We conclude there is sufficient evidence to conclude that Miller publicly professed to assume the duties incident to the practice of medicine and osteopathic medicine. We have defined the "duties incident to the practice of medicine" to include diagnosing patients' ailments and prescribing the proper treatment. Witnesses testified that they were treated by Miller for various ailments including arthritis, rash, infection, headaches, constipation, and neck, shoulder, and back pain. Although he may not have referred to himself as a doctor, he led his customers to believe that he could diagnose and treat their ailments. Even though Miller did not formally advertise his treatments, he gained a large local customer base by means of referral from one customer to another. The fact that Miller would sometimes recommend that his customers consult a licensed physician or chiropractor does not detract from the fact that he would diagnose and treat their physical conditions, at least up to a certain point.

We also conclude there was sufficient evidence that Miller routinely prescribed and furnished medicine. Miller argues that he sold or recommended only natural vitamins or nutrients. His defense, through the testimony of a witness, was that vitamins and nutrients were not medicines, but food.

We have broadly construed the statutory words "prescribe and furnish medicine" to include administering any substance or remedy in the treatment of an ailment or disease. The fact that a substance may also have value as a food "will not deprive of its character as a medicine if it be administered and employed for that purpose." State v. Bresee, 114 N.W. 45, 47 (1907).

It is evident [the defendant] was catering to patronage of the sick who were asking relief from their ills, and, if [he] listened to their statements, assured them of [his] ability to help them out, and supplied them with [his] alleged appropriate remedies giving instructions for their application or use, this would seem to come . . . within the ordinary and usual signification attached to the words "prescribing" or "prescribing and furnishing medicines," as they are commonly used and understood. Id.

We believe Miller's actions of selling or recommending natural vitamins to his customers constitutes furnishing a substance or remedy for treating their ailments.

We conclude there is sufficient evidence to convince a rational jury beyond a reasonable doubt that Miller was guilty of practicing medicine and osteopathic medicine without a license.

[On an ironic note, the court also rejected Miller's appellate lawyers' claim that the district court had erred in permitting him to represent himself at trial. Miller had initially sought to appoint "unlicensed" counsel to represent him at trial and chose to represent himself when his request was rejected. The court held that Miller knowingly and intelligently waived his right to licensed representation.]

Notes: Unlicensed Practice of Medicine

1. *Criminal Prosecution.* Note that the unlicensed practice of medicine is a criminal offense; persons convicted of the offense can be fined and imprisoned. Suppose that the patient of an unlicensed provider is injured in the course of receiving care. Is the provider liable in tort under a negligence per se theory? See Chapter 4.C.1. Jurisdictions may also criminalize "assisting" in the unlicensed practice of medicine. This criminal offense can have civil law implications as well. Physicians and other licensed health care professionals are subject to professional disciplinary action, such as license revocation or suspension, for assisting in the unlicensed practice of medicine. Annot., 99 A.L.R.2d 654 (1965).

2. *Defining Medical Practice.* The legislative definition of the "practice of medicine" typically is quite broad, as can be seen by examining the jury instructions in *Miller.* The breadth of the definition is important because persons who engage in the specified activities without an appropriate license are subject to criminal penalties. How far can the definition of medical practice be stretched?

The various exotic and peripheral ministrations successfully attacked under the medical licensure statutes range from the sublime to the ridiculous. Magnetism, mental suggestion, faith healing, color wave therapy, reflexology, massage, hypnotism, tattooing, and electrical hair removal all have been held to constitute the practice of medicine. See State v. White, 560 S.E.2d 420 (S.C. 2002) (state statute restricting tattooing to licensed physicians for cosmetic or reconstructive purposes does not violate free speech and is valid exercise of police power); Mark Hall, Institutional Control of Physician Behavior, 137 U. Penn. L. Rev. 431, 453 (1988) (collecting cases). Even the commonplace practice of offering nutritional advice might subject the advisor to criminal prosecution, as in *Miller.* Courts have found that some activities, such as ear piercing and cosmetic hair removal, lie outside the sometimes seemingly unlimited scope of medical practice.

3. *Vagueness and Overbreadth.* The very breadth of the typical medical practice act definition suggests a trap for the unwary, who might unexpectedly confront criminal liability for engaging in seemingly innocuous activities. Do the

instructions given to the jury in *Miller* provide appropriate guidance for their decision? Defendants have challenged these statutes on vagueness grounds; however, courts have been understandably reluctant to agree and have upheld the statutes by artfully using a number of different techniques of statutory construction. See People v. Rogers, 641 N.W.2d 595 (2001) (statutory definition not facially overbroad or unconstitutionally vague).

4. *A Right to Provide Care?* Defendants have been equally unsuccessful in their attempts to claim a constitutional right to provide care. Courts uniformly have upheld state licensing regulations so long as they are rationally related to serving some legitimate state interest. In Williamson v. Lee Optical of Oklahoma, Inc., the plaintiff challenged the constitutional validity of Oklahoma's licensure provisions that made it "unlawful for any person not a licensed optometrist or ophthalmologist to fit lenses to a face or to duplicate or replace into frames lenses or other optical appliances, except upon written prescriptive authority of an Oklahoma licensed ophthalmologist or optometrist." 348 U.S. 483, 485 (1955). The district court had held a portion of the statute unconstitutional, finding in part that it unreasonably prohibited opticians from making duplicate lenses for persons whose glasses were lost or broken. The Court upheld the statute, using classic rational basis review:

> The Oklahoma law may exact a needless, wasteful requirement in many cases. But it is for the legislature, not the courts, to balance the advantages and disadvantages of the new requirement. It appears that in many cases the optician can easily supply the new frames or new lenses without reference to the old written prescription. . . . But the law need not be in every respect logically consistent with its aims to be constitutional. It is enough that there is an evil at hand for correction, and that it might be thought that the particular legislative measure was a rational way to correct it.
>
> The day is gone when this Court uses the due process clause of the Fourteenth Amendment to strike down state laws, regulatory of business and industrial conditions, because they may be unwise, improvident, or out of harmony with a particular school of thought. . . . Id. at 487-488.

The Court also rejected an equal protection claim, again stating the applicable rational basis test in classic terms:

> The problem of legislative classification is a perennial one, admitting of no doctrinaire definition. Evils in the same field may be of different dimensions and proportions, requiring different remedies. Or so the legislature may think. Or the reform may take one step at a time, addressing itself to the phase of the problem which seems most acute to the legislative mind. The legislature may select one phase of one field and apply a remedy there, neglecting the others. The prohibition of the equal protection clause goes no further than the invidious discrimination. We cannot say that that point has been reached here. . . . Id. at 489.

The rational-basis approach adopted in *Lee* has been applied in nearly every case since. See, e.g., National Ass'n for the Advancement of Psychoanalysis v. California Board of Psychology, 228 F.3d 1043 (9th Cir. 2000) (upholding state's mental health licensing scheme under rational basis test); Lange-Kessler v. Department of Education of New York, 109 F.3d 137 (2d Cir. 1997) (state midwifery licensing statute is rationally related to a legitimate state interest); Sherman v. Cryns, 786 N.E.2d 139 (Ill. 2003) (same).

States often provide an exception to the normal rules governing the practice of medicine for religious practitioners. See, e.g., Cal. Bus. & Prof. Code §2063 ("Nothing in this chapter shall be construed . . . [to] regulate, prohibit, or apply to any kind of treatment by prayer, nor interfere in any way with the practice of religion"); Board of Medical Quality Assurance v. Andrews, 260 Cal. Rptr. 113 (Cal. Ct. App. 1989) (statute limited to use of prayer). Is this religious exemption required by the First Amendment? Does an exemption for religious practitioners violate the First Amendment's prohibition of state establishment of religion? Does the exemption for religious practitioners undercut the rationale for general licensure requirements — if the public health is at risk from "unscientific" practitioners, then shouldn't the public be protected from religious practitioners? See, e.g., Lauren A. Greenberg, Comment, In God We Trust: Faith Healing Subject to Liability, 14 J. Contemp. Health L. & Pol'y 451 (1998). Most academic attention focuses on the liability of parents for child neglect for the use of religious or spiritual healers. See, e.g., Symposium, 76 Notre Dame L. Rev. 109-208 (2000).

5. *A Right to Receive Treatment?* What of patients' rights to make their own decisions about health care? Do patients have any constitutionally protected interest in being able to choose to receive health care services of one type or another, from one type of provider or another? The issue was not raised in *Miller* but has been litigated elsewhere. Most courts have found that there is no fundamental right of access to treatment by unlicensed providers. See, e.g., Mitchell v. Clayton, 995 F.2d 772, 775-776 (7th Cir. 1993). The Supreme Court's ruling in the physician-assisted suicide cases suggests that the Constitution does not give patients a protected interest in obtaining particular types of medical treatment. What if, however, a case could be made that the particular treatment is the only one that might work? See Chapter 2.C.3 for discussion of related constitutional issues.

6. *Midwifery.* In the 1970s, the "rebirth" of natural childbirth and midwifery led to a wave of prosecutions for the unlicensed practice of medicine or nursing by midwives. Courts routinely rejected claims that a woman's "right to privacy" protected her decision to use unlicensed midwives in childbirth. In Lange-Kessler v. Department of Education of New York, 109 F.3d 137 (2d Cir. 1997), for example, a midwife and some women of childbearing age challenged a New York statute that required that midwives meet certain educational requirements and that they have a back-up agreement with a licensed physician or hospital. The court rejected the privacy claims, noting that Roe v. Wade did not give women the right to choose a particular type of health care provider. See also Annot., 59 A.L. R.4th 929 (1988). In a rare victory for midwives, the Kansas Supreme Court ruled that the practice of midwifery does not constitute the unlicensed practice of medicine or nursing. State Board of Nursing v. Ruebke, 913 P.2d 142 (Kan. 1996). See generally Stacey A Tovino, American Midwifery Litigation and State Legislative Preferences for Physician-Controlled Childbirth, 11 Cardozo Women's

L.J. 61 (2004); Laura D. Hermer, Midwifery: Strategies on the Road to Universal Legislation, 13 Health Matrix 325 (2003).

7. *Alternative Healing Techniques.* Interest in alternative therapies is not limited to midwifery and acupuncture. There are a wide variety of alternatives, some of which are being integrated into conventional medical practice and research. The National Institutes of Health (NIH) created the Office of Alternative Medicine (OAM) in 1992 to fund research designed to test the efficacy of a wide range of alternative therapies. See also Chapter 1.B.3. For discussion of licensure issues, see John Lunstroth, Voluntary Self-Regulation of Complementary and Alternative Medicine Practitioners, 70 Alb. L. Rev. 209 (2006).

What factors explain the apparent successes of these alternative therapies? Why did Miller's patients seek his assistance? First, of course, critics of the medical system note that the appeal of alternative therapies can be directly related to the "ills" of traditional medicine. Medical practice is expensive, impersonal, and bureaucratic. Second, alternative therapies apparently work, at least some therapies for some people. Even if the alternative therapy is scientifically worthless, a significant percentage of people given a placebo will experience relief from their symptoms and even an improvement in their condition. See Chapter 1. B.3. Given these data, perhaps licensure requirements keep people from seeking out potentially effective care. On the other hand, perhaps a licensure code strengthens the effectiveness of traditional medical practice by adding the state's imprimatur to the provider's care.

8. *Interprofessional Disputes.* Rules prohibiting the unlicensed practice of various professions also serve to establish boundaries between particular classes of health care providers. Persons providing health care services pursuant to statutory authorization are not guilty of the unlicensed practice of medicine. Thus a nurse is not engaging in the unlicensed practice of medicine when she or he makes a nursing diagnosis or provides nursing services to a patient. Sermchief v. Gonzales, 660 S.W.2d 683 (Mo. 1983).

Still, interprofessional turf battles are waged, particularly where nonphysician health care providers have attempted to expand their scope of practice. See, e.g., Brown v. Belinfante, 557 S.E.2d 399 (Ga. Ct. App. 2001) (oral surgeon violates dental practice act by performing face-lift); Connecticut State Medical Society v. Connecticut Board of Examiners of Podiatry, 546 A.2d 830 (Conn. 1988) (litigation to determine whether podiatrists can treat ankles). See also Barbara J. Safriet, Closing the Gap Between Can and May in Health-Care Providers' Scopes of Practice: A Primer for Policy Makers, 19 Yale J. on Reg. 301 (2002); Lori B. Andrews, The Shadow Health Care System: Regulation of Alternative Health Care Providers, 32 Hous. L. Rev. 1273, 1275 (1996); Mary Beck, Improving America's Health Care: Authorizing Independent Prescriptive Privileges for Advanced Practice Nurses, 29 U.S.F. L. Rev. 951 (1995).

9. *Physician Extenders.* Physicians often delegate functions to other types of health care practitioners, such as nurses or physicians assistants. The educational training of these other health care providers can vary widely. Traditionally, nurses have performed a wide range of functions within the health care system, sometimes under the control of physicians and sometimes exercising independent, nursing judgment. Physician assistants, in contrast, have traditionally been characterized as "dependent" practitioners, who perform only tasks delegated by

physicians. Many states now certify or otherwise regulate physician assistants to ensure that they are appropriately supervised.

Can physicians delegate tasks to assistants who are not independently licensed, without assisting in the unlicensed practice of medicine? Some legislatures have been extremely active in attempting to mark the bounds of appropriate delegation. Others provide physicians broad discretion to delegate tasks however they want as long as they do so consistent with proper medical standards, they supervise and retain responsibility, and the person doing the tasks does not purport to be practicing medicine. See, e.g., Tex. Occ. Code Ann. §157.001.

Nurse practitioners and physician assistants play a particularly important role in providing medical services in rural and central urban areas, where physicians are rare. Residents of these areas will often not have access to any health care unless they can be treated by "physician extenders." As a consequence, many states permit physicians to delegate more tasks, such as signing certain prescriptions, in "medically underserved" areas of the state. See generally Laura Hermer & William Winslade, Access to Health Care in Texas: A Patient Centered Perspective, 35 Tex Tech L Rev 33 (2004); Joy L. Delman, The Use and Misuse of Physician Extenders, 24 J. Leg. Med. 249 (2003).

Physicians assistants or nurses performing delegated tasks generally do so pursuant to physician's orders, standing medical orders, standing delegation orders, or written protocols. Courts, administrative agencies, and legislatures have struggled to define when a physician's degree of supervision is inadequate. Some jurisdictions have at least partially defined the degree of required supervision by establishing periodic physician reviews (e.g., daily status reports, once a week on site direction, etc.) and limiting the number of persons who the physician can supervise. Should surgeons be permitted to delegate some tasks during surgery to persons not licensed to practice medicine?

10. *Telemedicine and Interstate Practice of Medicine.* Health care provider licensure is a matter of state law. How should this state-level system respond to the growing nationalization of health care practice, in which physicians in other states may use telemedicine technology to diagnose and recommend treatment for patients? Many states have amended their licensing statutes or regulations in recent years to respond to this issue, for example, by tightening rules that prohibit out-of-state physicians from providing regular and ongoing direct care to patients. See, e.g., Ronald L. Scott, Cybermedicine and Virtual Pharmacies, 103 W. Va. L. Rev. 407 (2001); Alison M. Sulentic, Crossing Borders: The Licensure of Interstate Telemedicine Practitioners, 25 J. Legis. 1 (1999); Linda Fentiman, Internet Pharmacies and the Need for a New Federalism: Protecting Consumers While Increasing Access to Prescription Drugs, 56 Rutgers Law Review 119 (2003); John Blum, Internet Medicine and the Evolving Legal Status of the Physician-Patient Relationship, 24 J. Leg. Med. 413 (2003); Arnold J. Rosoff, On Being a Physician in the Electronic Age, 46 St. Louis U. L. J. 111 (2002); Note, 23 Cardozo L. Rev. 1107 (2002); Symposium, 46 St. Louis U. L.J. 1-110 (2002).

Do physicians performing utilization review services for insurance companies need to be licensed in the states where the patients are receiving care?

■ MODI v. WEST VIRGINIA BOARD OF MEDICINE
465 S.E.2d 230 (W. Va. 1995)

ALBRIGHT, Justice.

This case is a contested administrative proceeding initiated by the West Virginia Board of Medicine (the Board) . . . against Shakuntala Modi, M.D., a psychiatrist . . . engaged in a solo practice in Wheeling. The disciplinary proceeding grows out of Dr. Modi's care and treatment of William Abbott by use of a technique known as depossession therapy. The Notice of Hearing prepared by the Board and served on Dr. Modi charged [her with various violations of the state medical practice act and the Board's regulations.] . . .

From the hearing examiner's report it may be ascertained that on June 1, 1990, the appellee here, Dr. Shakuntala Modi, undertook to treat Mr. William Abbott in her office by use of depossession therapy, . . . [which] involves the use of hypnosis or hypnotherapy to relieve individuals of fears arising from such individuals' beliefs or feelings that they are or may be possessed by spirits. . . . Dr. Modi did not thoroughly discuss the intended therapy with Mr. Abbott or obtain a written consent for the therapy from him. After commencing the depossession therapy session with Mr. Abbott, it appears that Dr. Modi worked with the patient for about four hours, utilizing what Dr. Modi described as hypnotherapy. According to Mr. Abbott, Dr. Modi engaged in various incantations and called upon angels to lift dead souls out of his body in the course of the extended therapy session.

Mr. Abbott filed a complaint against Dr. Modi with the West Virginia Board of Medicine . . . [and] the Board then instituted the present proceeding, setting forth [various] charges, including the charge that Dr. Modi had improperly billed an insurance company $480.00 for psychotherapy when, in fact, she had engaged in depossession therapy. . . . The hearing examiner's report described five ultimate issues . . . :

1. Did the Board establish that . . . a reasonable, prudent physician in the same specialty would not recognize depossession therapy as being acceptable under similar conditions and circumstances?
2. Did Dr. Modi . . . [use] an experimental therapy without first obtaining a full, informed and written consent from Mr. Abbott?
3. Did Dr. Modi . . . [file] a false report with the patient's insurance carrier when she described her use of depossession therapy as psychotherapy . . . ?
4. Did Dr. Modi engage in unprofessional [practice] . . . by using depossession therapy and billing the patient's insurer for the service?
5. [What is the appropriate sanction for any violation?] . . .

In his report, the hearing examiner concluded that the Board of Medicine had the burden of proof to establish its charges by "full, preponderating and clear evidence." He further concluded that Dr. Modi was entitled to adduce evidence from experts who were not licensed to practice medicine in any of the United States. . . .

[Based on the hearing examiner's recommendations], the Board found that Dr. Modi is unqualified to practice medicine without certain limitations. With respect to sanctions, the Board order adopted the hearing examiner's recommendation for a public reprimand and a fine of $1,000. It also adopted and expanded upon the education recommendation. Finally, the Board order required that Dr. Modi develop and obtain Board approval of a particular form of "informed" written consent for the use of depossession therapy and that a copy of the approved form, signed by any patient undergoing depossession therapy, be submitted by Dr. Modi with any bill sent an insurance company for such therapy. . . .

After reviewing the record, this court concludes that . . . the Board made inadequate findings of fact and incorrect conclusions of law. . . . [Also], the billing requirement imposed upon Dr. Modi was arbitrary and capricious and was done without legal authority. . . . However, given the finding by the hearing examiner and the Board that Dr. Modi used an experimental therapy without obtaining a signed, written and informed consent, . . . this cause [must be] remanded for further proceedings consistent with this opinion. . . .

ERRORS OF LAW BELOW

[The court notes that judicial review of contested medical board disciplinary actions is governed by the state's Administrative Procedure Act. Under the Act, circuit courts are permitted to reverse, vacate, or modify Board findings, inferences, conclusions, decisions, or orders only where they (1) violate constitutional or statutory provisions; (2) exceed the statutory or judicial authority of the agency; (3) are made in violation of procedural rules; (4) are affected by other legal error; (5) are clearly wrong in view of the reliable, probative, and substantial evidence on the whole record; or (6) are arbitrary and capricious or characterized by an abuse of discretion or a clearly unwarranted exercise of discretion.]

[T]he Board order, cobbled together by the expedient of additions to and excisions from the hearing examiners report, is barely intelligible, if at all. . . . [Therefore], we are unable to discern from the Board order "a reasoned, articulate decision which sets forth the underlying evidentiary facts which lead the agency to its conclusion." . . . It appears that the lack of such a reasoned, articulate decision flows, at least in part, from the rejection by the Board of Medicine of the hearing examiner's recommended conclusion of law allowing the admission and consideration of the testimony of Dr. Modi's experts who were not physicians currently licensed to practice medicine in one of the United States. The Board argued below and argues here that [state law prohibits Dr. Modi's use of] . . . experts not licensed to practice medicine in one of the United States. . . . The hearing examiner disagreed, and so do we.

[The evidentiary statute in question] . . . relates to tort actions against health care providers, including physicians, not to disciplinary proceedings before the Board of Medicine. . . . [T]he Board of Medicine erroneously refused to consider, for whatever its probative value, the otherwise admissible testimony of experts supportive of Dr. Modi's assertion that depossession therapy is a recognized form of treatment and is not experimental. That error of law . . . requires that the conclusions of the Board based on those findings be set aside and that the sanctions imposed by reason of those conclusions be vacated.

We do not conclude that depossession therapy is or is not an acceptable form of care that would be employed by a reasonable, prudent physician in the same circumstances as those faced by Dr. Modi. We conclude only that the Board's findings in that regard are flawed by the mistake of law just described. We conclude also that we are confronted with the kind of agency ruling involving scientific data which the courts should not attempt to evaluate until such time as the agency presents a proper order making appropriate findings of fact and conclusions of law. . . .

On the present record, it appears that an adequate prima facie case that Dr. Modi experimented on a human subject without obtaining the written informed consent required by . . . [state law] was established by the evidence. However, the decision on that issue is also flawed by the failure of the Board to give any consideration to the evidence adduced from Dr. Modi's experts and the failure of the Board to make appropriate findings of fact and conclusions of law. . . .

[Also,] [i]t does appear that the Board of Medicine failed to consider fully the implications of a requirement that the written consent form contain the panoply of information that might be considered to be necessary to a full, informed consent and perhaps failed to consider fully how the wide variety of patients likely to undergo an "experimental" procedure in the future might best be brought to a suitable appreciation of the anticipated risks and benefits of a particular experimental procedure. Mindful that the resolution of such difficult questions involves complex issues of patient care and treatment which go far beyond the question of "depossession therapy," we leave the proper determination of the contents of the written consent form for consideration on remand, . . . defer[ring] to the administrative agency created to consider those issues on behalf of the medical profession. Given the wide ranging implications of such a determination, it may be appropriate for the Board of Medicine to address this matter by issuance of a regulation rather than by dealing with it in the confined circumstances of a contested administrative proceeding.

Next, we address the requirement of the Board that Dr. Modi submit to any insurance carrier for a patient undergoing depossession therapy a copy of the previously approved informed consent form signed by the subject patient. From the record, we glean that the Board of Medicine . . . wished to prevent practitioners of the therapy from being paid by insurance carriers for the therapy. . . . The court below found the Board's requirement that the consent form be submitted to an insurance carrier arbitrary. We agree. . . . [The state statute] sets forth the sanctions which may be imposed by the Board of Medicine upon a physician. After reviewing the statutory language, this court cannot conclude that the legislature has in any manner authorized the Board of Medicine to regulate or intervene in the manner directed by the Board order in the process by which physicians bill insurers for treatment. . . .

Affirmed in part; reversed in part; and remanded with directions.

Notes: Professional Disciplinary Actions

1. *Grounds for Disciplinary Action.* The statutes of each state establish a laundry list of activities that can lead to professional disciplinary action. The list represents

a legislative determination that the public's health or welfare is best protected by discouraging licensees from engaging in the proscribed conduct. Licensees who engage in these activities may have their licenses suspended or revoked, and may face other punishment. What types of conduct were at issue in *Modi*? Dr. Modi's use of "depossession therapy" gave rise to three major alleged violations of the disciplinary code: (1) providing treatment that would not be considered acceptable by a reasonable and prudent physician of the same specialty under similar circumstances; (2) providing experimental treatment without obtaining fully informed, written consent; and (3) filing a false claim for insurance reimbursement for unacceptable "treatment."

a. *Quality of Care.* The first charge in *Modi* clearly is related to what one might think of as the traditional domain of licensure: protecting patients from poor quality care. The claim is based on the failure to follow accepted medical practice. Does this disciplinary standard always protect patients? What if the "accepted" course of care is ineffective? How should this rule be applied where providers wish to employ alternative therapies, such as homeopathy? See In re Guess, 393 S.E.2d 833 (N.C. 1990) (state may prohibit use of homeopathy without specific showing of harm to patients).

Medical boards are also generally given the power to discipline physicians who have delivered substandard, incompetent, or negligent care. See, e.g., Annot., 28 A.L.R.3d 487 (1969); Annot., 22 A.L.R.4th 668 (1983); Halter v. State Department of Commerce & Economic Development, Medical Board, 990 P.2d 1035 (Alaska 1999) (repeated negligent conduct). The Board is not generally required to prove that any patients were actually harmed. Boards attempt to regulate the quality of care by disciplining providers whose competence may be affected by illness, age, or alcohol or drug dependence. See Annot., 93 A.L.R.2d 1398 (1964). Might the ADA restrict a board's ability to take disciplinary action against a physician who has a disability? See Kirbens v. Wyoming State Board of Medicine, 992 P.2d 1056 (Wyo. 1999) (under ADA, Board permitted to revoke license of physician who presented risk to health and safety of patients).

b. *Ethical Violations.* The second regulatory provision allegedly violated in *Modi* protects patient autonomy rights. Physicians are bound by ethical norms and, in *Modi*, by a specific regulation that required that written informed consent be obtained before providing experimental treatment. Legislatures and disciplinary boards have promulgated a number of different rules that attempt to define the appropriate relationship between provider and patient. Recently, for example, a number of jurisdictions have introduced or expanded bars on provider-patient sexual relationships. See, e.g., Heinmiller v. Department of Health, 903 P.2d 433 (Wash. 1995) (en banc) (social worker's sexual relationship with patient constituted act of moral turpitude); Annot., 59 A.L.R.4th 1104 (1988). Financial transactions with patients can also result in disciplinary action. Aronoff v. Board of Registration in Medicine, 652 N.E.2d 594 (Mass. 1995) (physician engaged in multiple transactions with patient being treated for borderline personality disorder).

c. *Other Professional Norms.* The third alleged violation in *Modi* concerned filing a false report. Boards often are charged with monitoring the physician's obligations to act within professional norms in his or her contacts with third parties ranging from governmental agencies to private insurance companies. See

Annot., 32 A.L.R.5th 57 (1995); Annot., 70 A.L.R.4th 132 (1989); Fisch v. Board of Registration in Medicine, 769 N.E.2d 1221 (Mass. 2002) (improper billing). Are these rules founded on the need to protect patients, society, or the integrity of the profession? How far should states be permitted to go in enacting regulations designed primarily for the protection of the profession as opposed to the protection of the patient?

d. *Restrictions on Advertising or Business Arrangements.* There are other disciplinary offenses that appear to have a more tangential relationship to the protection of patients and that might in fact be based primarily on the protection of the health care profession's economic interests. Professional disciplinary codes often attempt to restrict the range of permissible advertising or solicitation that may be employed by licensees. One rationale for these restrictions is that they prevent consumer fraud and abuse. Another is that they insulate the profession from the demands of competition, which might result in price wars and lost income. States generally may not restrict truthful, non-misleading professional advertisements without violating the First Amendment's protection of free speech. See, e.g., Thompson v. Western States Medical Center, 535 U.S. 357 (2002) (federal law prohibiting advertising and promotion of particular compounded drugs is unconstitutional restriction of commercial speech); Virginia State Board of Pharmacy v. Virginia Citizens Consumer Council, Inc., 425 U.S. 748, 762 (1976) (striking down ban on price advertising by pharmacists); Culpepper v. Arkansas Board of Chiropractic Examiners, 36 S.W.3d 335 (Ark. 2001) (ban on direct contact by chiropractors with potential patients unconstitutional); Lloyd v. Sutfin, 693 A.2d 73 (N.H. 1997) (unconstitutional to punish dentist for truthful advertising about inventing a new treatment for gum disease). More limited types of state advertising restrictions have been upheld. See, e.g., Desnick v. Department of Professional Regulation, 665 N.E.2d 1346 (Ill. 1996) (solicitation of professional patronage a permissible restriction on commercial speech); Texas State Board of Medical Examiners v. Burzynski, 917 S.W.2d 365 (Tex. Ct. App. 1996) (statute prohibiting advertisements about drugs affecting neoplasms is constitutional). See also Paula Berg, Toward a First Amendment Theory of Doctor-Patient Discourse and the Right to Receive Unbiased Medical Advice, 74 B.U. L. Rev. 201, 241-243 (1994); Ronald D. Rotunda, Professionalism, Legal Advertising, and Free Speech in the Wake of Florida Bar v. Went For It, Inc., 49 Ark. L. Rev. 703, 713-718 (1997).

What of professional disciplinary rules that forbid certain business arrangements, such as assisting in the corporate practice of medicine? Viewed in one light, these provisions indirectly protect patients by reducing the threat that economic motivations will override patient interests in the provider-patient relationship. Once again, however, it could readily be argued that these prohibitions serve to protect professional autonomy, regardless of the impact on patients.

2. *An Administrative Law Primer.* Each state legislature has established one or more administrative agencies charged with issuing implementing regulations, investigating potential violations, and conducting hearings to determine if the licensure statute and/or regulations have been violated. These administrative agencies, usually called the "Board of _____" (fill in the name of the licensed professional group), are staffed by persons with specialized expertise in

the subject of the licensure code. At least a majority of the board's membership, for example, will be composed of licensed members of the regulated profession. Board appointments typically are made by the governor, with some advice and consent input from the legislature. The board's staff may be involved in drafting regulations designed to implement statutory provisions. Some of the staff will investigate and prosecute potential violations of the licensing statute or board regulations. The agency also includes "hearing officers," individuals who will hear evidence, determine if a violation has occurred, and recommend an appropriate sanction. The agency typically has an internal appeals process with the final agency determination rendered by the board itself. The agency's procedures are likely to be established within its enabling legislation and within the state's Administrative Procedure Act.

The key point to this broad description of the agency process is that each agency can have three different roles: a quasi-legislative function (rulemaking), a quasi-executive function (e.g., investigating and prosecuting offenses), and a quasi-judicial function (holding hearings to determine whether violations have occurred and imposing sanctions). The combination of these functions into one entity raises a number of different constitutional and statutory issues that are studied at length in the typical course in Administrative Law. The *Modi* opinion contains a shorthand summary of the typical bases for challenging administrative determinations. For additional discussion, see materials on the website for this casebook, www.health-law.org; J. Bruce Bennet, The Rights of Licensed Professionals to Notice and Hearing in Agency Enforcement Actions, 7 Tex. Tech. Admin. L.J. 205 (2006); Annot., 10 A.L.R.5th 1 (1993); Annot., 74 A.L. R.4th 969 (1989).

Problem: Professional Licensure

Dr. Alicia Chuanski lives in an urban area in a state that has many underpopulated, rural areas. She has established a thriving family practice in the city. She is interested in expanding her practice into a rural area about 90 miles from her office. She hopes to set up a satellite office, staffed with a nurse and a physician's assistant. Dr. Chuanski plans to supervise the satellite office in several ways:

1. She will establish detailed protocols for the nurse and physician's assistant. They both will meet with patients, take patient histories and record patient symptoms, and establish baseline heart rates, blood pressures, and temperatures. The protocols will establish diagnostic or other procedures that should be followed for patients with particular symptoms. The protocols also will establish "opt-out" points: symptoms or complaints that indicate the need to refer patients to the nearest emergency room, which is about 20 miles away. Dr. Chuanski will leave a presigned prescription pad at the satellite for the use of the nurse and physician's assistant (pursuant to the protocols); prescriptions will be reviewed on a daily basis.

2. Dr. Chuanski will attempt to establish a back-up relationship with a nearby physician, perhaps one who maintains an office near the hospital mentioned above.
3. Dr. Chuanski will be available for phone consultations from 12-1:00 P.M. and from 4:30-5:30 P.M. every work day. Summary reports on the day's patients will be faxed to her each evening.
4. As the price of technology decreases, Dr. Chuanski will consider establishing a video link to the satellite so that she could "see" and "examine" patients from her office in the city.
5. Dr. Chuanski will visit the satellite once every ten days or so.

Evaluate Dr. Chuanski's plans. Will the nurse and/or physician's assistant be engaged in the unlicensed practice of medicine? Is Dr. Chuanski assisting in the unlicensed practice of medicine? Is Dr. Chuanski engaged in unprofessional conduct that could lead to disciplinary action? Where would you look to answer these questions? What additional information might you need to answer the questions? Can you suggest any improvements to Dr. Chuanski's plans?

2. Facility Licensure and Accreditation

■ PATIENT POWER: SOLVING AMERICA'S HEALTH CARE CRISIS
John C. Goodman & Gerald L. Musgrave
(1992)

In terms of rules, restrictions, and bureaucratic requirements, the health care sector is one of the most regulated industries in our economy. Consider Scripps Memorial Hospital, a medium-sized acute care facility in San Diego, California. As [the following] table shows, Scripps must answer to 39 governmental bodies and 7 nongovernmental bodies, and must periodically file 65 different reports, about one report for every four beds.[1] . . . Regulatory requirements intrude in a highly visible way on the activities of the medical staff and affect virtually every aspect of medical practice. Another California hospital, Sequoia Hospital in the San Francisco Bay area, has attempted to calculate how many additional employees are required as a result of government regulations.

---

[1] [The hospital association in New York once claimed that its members were subject to 174 regulatory bodies, and another survey found that hospitals have to submit themselves to over 50 different inspections and reports each year, often requiring into similar matters. B. Gray, The Profit Motive and Patient Care 112 (1991). The American Hospital Association claims that, for every hour of patient care, hospitals engage in 30 to 60 minutes of paperwork. Patients or Paperwork? The Regulatory Burden Facing America's Hospitals (2001). See also John Braithwaite & Valerie Braithwaite, The Politics of Legalism: Rules Versus Standards in Nursing-Home Regulation, 4 Soc. Leg. Stud. 307, 320 (1995) ("the poeople who inspect U.S. nursing homes are checking compliance with over a thousand regulations"); Christopher J. Conover, Health Care Regulation: A $169 Billion Hidden Tax (Cato Institute, 2004) (finding that health care regulation costs twice as much as its benefits are worth).

See generally Robert I. Field, Health Care Regulation in America: Complexity, Confrontation and Compromise (2007).]

Sequoia's [administrative and nursing] staff increased by 163.6 percent [from 450 to 736] between 1966 and 1990, even though the average number of patients per day (250) did not change. . . .

Regulatory Agencies Over Scripps Memorial Hospital, 1989

Agency
Government
Occupational Safety and Health Administration
San Diego County Health Department
State Board of Equalization (hazardous waste tax return)
Internal Revenue Service
Franchise Tax Board
Secretary of State
Medicare
State Board of Equalization (sales tax return)
California Hospital Facilities Commission
State Board of Health
Environmental Protection Agency
Department of Transportation
Department of Health Services
Air Resources Board
Office of Emergency Services
Health and Welfare Agency
Air Pollution Control/Air Quality Management District
Regional Water Quality Control Board
Local Sewering Agencies
San Diego Department of Health Services
State Licensing Board
Board of Registered Nursing
Licensed Vocational Nursing Board
U.S. Department of Labor
Industrial Welfare Commission
Fair Employment Practice Commission
National Labor Relations Board
Immigration and Naturalization Service
Employment Development Department
Social Security Administration
Employee Retirement Income Security Requirements
State Board of Pharmacy
Drug Enforcement Agency
Food and Drug Administration
Bureau of Narcotic Enforcement
California Department of Health, Radiologic Health Branch

Agency

Nongovernment
    Joint Commission on Accreditation of Hospitals
    American Hospital Association
    American Conference of Governmental Industrial Hygienists
    California Medical Association
    Radiation Safety Organization (Syncor, Inc.)
    National Association of Social Workers
    American College of Surgeons
    San Diego and Imperial Counties Organization for Cancer Control

Note: Facility Licensing, Accreditation, and Certification

Three terms are commonly used to describe the multi-level process for inspecting and approving health care facilities by state, federal, and private agencies: licensure, accreditation, and certification. Each of these terms has a specific meaning, and each represents a different level of significance for operation within the health care community. The requirements for licensure, accreditation, and certification exert a strong regulatory force on the organization and operation of health care facilities.

Licensure is the mandatory governmental process whereby a health care facility receives the right to operate. In the United States, licensure operates on a state-by-state basis. A health care facility (as that term is defined in the statute) cannot open its doors lawfully without a license from the appropriate state agency. Licensed health care facilities include hospitals, nursing homes, ambulatory surgery centers, freestanding emergency centers, pharmacies, and, in some instances, diagnostic centers. State licensing schemes also exist for various financing systems, both for ordinary health insurance and for innovative delivery systems such as HMOs, preferred provider organizations, and utilization review systems.

Accreditation is a private voluntary approval process through which a health care organization is evaluated and can receive a designation of competence and quality. Most private accreditation for health care organizations today is done under the auspices of the Joint Commission for the Accreditation of Healthcare Organizations (called "JCAHO," "Jayco," or "Joint Commission," formerly known as the Joint Commission for the Accreditation of Hospitals). The Joint Commission is governed by the major trade associations, primarily the American Medical Association, the American Hospital Association, the American College of Surgeons, and the American College of Physicians, and its accreditation programs serve all sorts of health care organizations, although its primary participants are hospitals. Although the Joint Commission is private and purely voluntary, historically it has wielded enormous power and influence because virtually no hospital of respectable size risks the business consequences of jeopardizing its accreditation status. However, the Joint Commission's dominance of facility accreditation is starting to wane somewhat in the face of increasing competition from other accrediting bodies for nonhospital facilities.

Certification is a voluntary procedure for health care organizations to meet the qualifications for participation in government funding programs, specifically Medicare and Medicaid. Although certification is voluntary, more often than not Medicare and Medicaid certification are necessary to the economic survival of a health care organization.

The three functions of licensure, accreditation, and certification are intertwined to a considerable extent. Joint Commission accreditation, for example, frequently satisfies the requirements for both state licensing and Medicare/Medicaid certification. Where this is not the case, Medicare/Medicaid certification surveys are often performed by the same agency and personnel that conduct state licensing surveys. Not only are the three functions intertwined, but there is also a high level of congruence among the various standards and processes employed in each function. Therefore, these materials will examine all three systems interchangeably.

■ ESTATE OF SMITH v. HECKLER
747 F.2d 583 (10th Cir. 1984)

McKay, Circuit Judge.

Plaintiffs . . . brought this class action on behalf of medicaid recipients residing in nursing homes in Colorado. They alleged that the Secretary of Health and Human Services (Secretary) has a statutory duty . . . to develop and implement a system of nursing home review and enforcement designed to ensure that medicaid recipients residing in medicaid certified nursing homes actually receive the optimal medical and psychosocial care that they are entitled to under the Act. The plaintiffs contended that the enforcement system developed by the Secretary is "facility oriented," not "patient oriented" and thereby fails to meet the statutory mandate. . . .

[P]laintiffs instituted the lawsuit in an effort to improve the deplorable conditions at many nursing homes. They presented evidence of the lack of adequate medical care and of the widespread knowledge that care is inadequate. Indeed, the district court concluded that care and life in some nursing homes is so bad that the homes "could be characterized as orphanages for the aged." . . . [Nevertheless] [t]he trial court denied relief. This appeal is from that judgment. . . .

An understanding of the Medicaid Act (the Act) is essential to understand plaintiffs' contentions. The purpose of the Act is to enable the federal government to assist states in providing medical assistance to "aged, blind or disabled individuals, whose income and resources are insufficient to meet the costs of necessary medical services, and . . . rehabilitation and other services to help such . . . individuals to attain or retain capabilities for independence or self care." To receive funding, a state must submit to the Secretary and have approved by the Secretary a plan for medical assistance which meets the requirements of 42 U.S.C. §1396a(a). . . . The plan must include descriptions of the standards and methods the state will use to assure that medical or remedial care services provided to the recipients "are of high quality." . . . The appropriate state agency must determine on an ongoing basis whether participating institutions meet the requirements for continued participation in the Medicaid program. . . . In conducting the review, however, the states must use federal standards, forms, methods and procedures. . . .

Among other things, the regulations provide for the frequency and general content of patients' attending physician evaluations, nursing services with policies "designed to ensure that each patient receives treatments, medications, . . . diet as prescribed . . . rehabilitative nursing care as needed, . . . is kept comfortable, clean, well-groomed, [is] protected from accident, injury, an infection, and [is] encouraged, assisted, and trained in self-care and group activities." The rehabilitative nursing care is to be directed toward each patient achieving an optimal level of self-care and independence. The regulations require a written patient care plan to be developed and maintained for each patient. . . . Finally, the regulations provide for treatment of the social and emotional needs of recipients.

The Secretary has established a procedure for determining whether state plans comply with the standards set out in the regulations. This enforcement mechanism is known as the "survey/certification" inspection system. Under this system, the states conduct reviews of nursing homes. . . . The Secretary then determines, on the basis of the survey results, whether the nursing home surveyed is eligible for certification and, thus, eligible for Medicaid funds. . . .

The plaintiffs do not challenge the substantive medical standards, or "conditions of participation," which have been adopted by the Secretary and which states must satisfy to have their plans approved. Rather, plaintiffs challenge the enforcement mechanism the Secretary has established. The plaintiffs contend that the federal forms . . . which states are required to use, evaluate only the physical facilities and theoretical capability to render quality care. They claim that . . . out of the 541 questions contained in the Secretary's form which must be answered by state survey and certification inspection teams, only 30 are "even marginally related to patient care or might require any patient observation. . . ." Plaintiffs contend that the enforcement mechanism's focus on the facility, rather than on the care actually provided in the facility, results only in "paper compliance" with the substantive standards of the Act. Thus, plaintiffs contend, the Secretary has violated her statutory duty to assure that federal Medicaid monies are paid only to facilities which meet the substantive standards of the Act — facilities which actually provide high quality medical, rehabilitative and psychosocial care to resident Medicaid recipients. . . .

Congress intended the Secretary to be responsible for assuring that federal Medicaid money is given only to those institutions that actually comply with Medicaid requirements. The Act's requirements include providing high quality medical care. . . . Being charged with this function, we must conclude that a failure to promulgate regulations that allow the Secretary to remain informed, on a continuing basis, as to whether facilities receiving federal money are meeting the requirements of the Act, is an abdication of the Secretary's duty. . . .

■ COSPITO v. HECKLER

742 F.2d 72 (3d Cir. 1984)

GARTH, Circuit Judge.

Appellants Douglas Cospito, et al., ("the Patients") are or have been patients at the Trenton Psychiatric Hospital (TPH). In 1975, TPH lost its accreditation from codefendant Joint Commission on Accreditation of Hospitals (JCAH) [now known as JCAHO, for Healthcare Organizations]. As a result, codefendant Secretary of the Department of Health, Education, and Welfare (now the Department of Health and Human Services) terminated various federal benefits which were conditioned upon the beneficiaries being treated at a qualified psychiatric hospital. . . . The Patients brought this action in district court challenging the loss of their federal benefits on several constitutional grounds. . . .

Beginning in 1973, TPH was surveyed under the standards for "psychiatric facilities" recently promulgated under the auspices of JCAH. Following the 1973 survey, major deficiencies were disclosed in several areas, including patient treatment, staffing, environment, and fire safety. TPH was accredited for only one year, and was notified that these deficiencies must be corrected to maintain accreditation. In 1974, however, many of the same deficiencies were found again. A preliminary decision was made by JCAH not to accredit. At TPH's request, a resurvey was conducted in May, 1975, which again resulted in a preliminary decision not to accredit. TPH did not appeal from that decision, and the deaccreditation became final. . . .

JCAH is an Illinois not-for-profit corporation formed in 1951 for the purpose of creating and maintaining professional standards for evaluating hospital performance. The body is governed by a 22-member Board of Commissioners. Its constituent members consist of the American College of Physicians, the American College of Surgeons, the American Dental Association, the American Hospital Association, and the American Medical Association. . . .

The survey itself consists of an on-site visit conducted by a team of surveyors designated by JCAH. The surveyors evaluate the quality of the facility's environment and review its administrative records to determine whether they conform to applicable standards. . . .

JCAH accreditation, however, must be distinguished from certification by the Secretary for eligibility in federal assistance programs. While JCAH accreditation may, depending on the circumstances, be a component of certification, the two are not necessarily coextensive, and at least as a matter of terminology, we will refer to the two separately. . . .

The Patients at TPH had, before decertification by the Secretary, been the beneficiaries of three types of federally funded benefits: (1) Medicare, (2) Medicaid, and (3) Supplemental Social Security Income. . . . When TPH was decertified in 1975, all of the benefits described above were terminated, since TPH was no longer an institution eligible under Medicare and Medicaid. . . . The Patients brought suit in district court alleging that deprivation of their Medicare, Medicaid, and Social Security benefits was unconstitutional. They alleged lack of procedural due process, lack of substantive due process, lack of equal protection, and unconstitutional delegation of authority to JCAH. . . .

Our analysis of the procedural due process aspects of this case is guided by the Supreme Court's decision in O'Bannon v. Town Court Nursing Center, 447 U.S. 773 (1980), which involved facts comparable to those presented here. In *Town Court*, residents of a nursing home claimed a violation of due process when they lost federal benefits as a result of the decertification of their facility. Like the Patients here, they claimed a right to a pretermination hearing.

The Supreme Court found as a threshold matter, however, that the residents of the nursing home had not been deprived of any protectable property interest, and thus, absent this foundation, no due process right was triggered. Writing for the Court, Justice Stevens found that patients did not have a settled interest in receiving benefits at any [particular] facility, including a decertified one, and therefore there had been no deprivation of "property." . . .

[T]he only factor which even arguably distinguishes this case from *Town Court* is the fact that the Patients are unable to transfer out of TPH [because they were involuntarily committed under state mental health law]; [therefore], they are barred from receiving federal benefits at another qualified institution. Thus, they contend that there has been an actual "deprivation" of a protectable interest. Even accepting that contention, however, . . . [b]ecause any loss of benefits to the Patients was only "indirectly" caused by the Secretary's decision to decertify TPH, whatever deprivation which was suffered [by virtue of the state-law psychiatric commitment] was not the result of any [federal] governmental action. The Patients are therefore not in a position to claim any Fifth Amendment due process protection, even if they alleged a "deprivation."[17] . . .

Finally, we turn to the Patients' argument that the Medicare (and thus Medicaid) provisions improperly delegate authority to JCAH, in derogation of Congress' ultimate responsibility to establish federal policy. . . . We need not reach the question of whether delegation of such authority to a private entity breaches the constitutional barrier, since our reading of the Medicare statute, which in turn is applicable to the Medic[aid] and Social Security programs, convinces us that the Secretary retains ultimate authority over decertification decisions, through the ability to engage in a "distinct part" survey. . . .

While JCAH accreditation may, under certain circumstances, independently satisfy the statutory requirements for participation in Medicare, the Secretary is free to prescribe standards which are higher than those of the Commission, in which case JCAH accreditation would not be effective. Moreover, if the Secretary determines that, despite JCAH accreditation, a particular hospital nevertheless has serious deficiencies, he may, after appropriate notice, decertify the institution. On the other hand, if the Secretary chose to promulgate a standard lower than that of JCAH, a general hospital could presumably be certified by meeting only that lesser standard, even if it did not meet the requirements imposed by the Commission.

The Patients argue, however, that in the case of psychiatric hospitals, the statute places JCAH accreditation in a position of ascendancy over approval by the

---

[17] The district court granted summary judgment on the procedural due process claim for the reason that, in its opinion, the procedures used adequately safeguarded the Patients' interests, [a]pplying the tests of Mathews v. Eldridge, 424 U.S. 319 (1976). . . . Without disagreeing with the district court's reasoning, we note that our analysis makes it unnecessary to reach the issues addressed by the court below. . . .

Secretary, thus leading to the question of unconstitutional delegation to a private group. Our reading of the statute leads us to disagree. While Congress did choose to give special attention to JCAH accreditation in the context of psychiatric hospitals,[27] it still provided the "distinct part" survey as a mechanism whereby the Secretary could independently determine whether a particular institution was qualified for participation. Through consecutive or simultaneous distinct part surveys, therefore, it is possible to obtain a de novo evaluation by the Secretary on the adequacy of a hospital's facilities. . . .

Since, in effect, all actions of JCAH are subject to full review by a public official who is responsible and responsive to the political process, we find that there has been no real delegation of authority to JCAH.[29] . . .

BECKER, Circuit Judge, dissented.

Notes: Facility Regulation and Accreditation

1. *Which Facilities Are Covered?* The first question under any licensing scheme is its jurisdiction. Jurisdictional issues arise with increasing frequency as the result of innovative service delivery and ownership arrangements in the medical industry. One common issue is whether a license for a central facility such as a hospital covers satellite facilities such as urgent care centers, or whether they must be separately licensed. Another issue is whether a speciality clinic, say for abortions or for expensive diagnostic scans, can be treated as simply a physician's office, which does not require a facility license. See RIH Medical Foundation v. Nolan, 723 A.2d 1123 (R.I. 1999) (physician-owned corporation that operates physician offices is exempt from health facility licensing). A third issue is whether an existing license covers the buyer or lessor of a health facility, and whether turning the facility's operation over to a management company requires applying for a formal transfer of the license. Often, the same questions apply generally to accreditation and certification. Usually, the only way to know the answer is to simply ask the governing authorities, since statutes and regulations frequently fail to flesh out these details. The consequences for wrongly interpreting licensing jurisdiction can be severe. In one case, the court refused to enforce any of the contracts entered into by an unlicensed nursing agency. U.S. Nursing Corp. v. St. Joseph Medical Center, 39 F.3d 790 (7th Cir. 1994).

2. *"Doc-in-a-Box."* Sometimes, these jurisdictional issues are resolved by statute. One contemporary instance relates to ambulatory care centers, colloquially known as "Doc-in-a-Box." These store-front medical clinics cater to no-wait, no-appointment medical needs of an urgent nature, short of life-or-limb-threatening conditions. They provide a more convenient and sometimes less expensive alternative to hospital emergency rooms for conditions such as broken

---

[27] The legislative history reveals that Congress intended "to support the efforts of the various professional accrediting organizations sponsored by the medical and hospital associations. . . ."

[29] Our resolution of this issue renders somewhat academic the Patients' contention that it was improper for JCAH to "subdelegate" the responsibility for evaluating psychiatric hospitals to the various accreditation councils. Since we have found that no real authority was actually vested in JCAH, it follows that there could be no improper "subdelegation" of authority to divisions of the Commission. . . .

legs, bad cuts, and sudden illnesses. There is an argument that ambulatory centers are nothing more than glorified doctors' offices and therefore require no facility license apart from the physicians' medical licenses. However, many states have amended their statutes to cover these facilities, especially when they specialize in surgery. Note, 11 Health L. 1 (1999).

3. *Measuring Quality Through Structure or Outcomes.* The next question under any of these regulatory or quasi-regulatory schemes is their content. A detailed understanding is beyond the scope of this book. However, it is possible to convey the gist of this content in terms of Donabedian's famous distinction among structural, process, and outcomes measures of quality, summarized at page 293. State licensing authorities, like the Medicaid nursing home requirements in *Estate of Smith*, do not inquire into the actual outcomes of patient treatment. Instead, facility licensure provisions typically read like a gigantic building code for the industry, specifying a host of architectural, safety, and sanitation minutiae. Similarly, the Joint Commission accreditation standards traditionally have addressed only the organizational and structural aspects of each hospital department — issues such as whether bylaws are properly drafted, whether proper committees are established, and whether administrative structures contain proper monitoring and documentation — rather than attempting any direct assessment of the actual outcomes of medical care in the hospital. This point was articulated in an Internet discussion group by someone who worked as a hospital therapist and department manager for 13 years:

> We never worried about JCAHO until the three months prior and the two days of the inspection. In the three months prior we backdated all the documentation that we needed to get through the inspection, and in the two days they were there we spent telling them how focused we were on quality, etc. As long as the paperwork is in order, people can be dying in the halls and there could be guppies in the IV fluids; the JCAHO wouldn't notice.

For an extensive critique of the traditional structural and process measures of institutional quality and an argument for adopting outcomes measures, see Troyen Brennan & Donald Berwick, New Rules: Regulation, Markets and the Quality of American Health Care (1996), which also contains an excellent overview and historical account of licensure and accreditation.

4. *Process and Outcomes Measures.* The *Smith* case presaged a move away from purely structural measures of quality. That decision resulted in a statutory amendment (known as OBRA '87) and an extensive set of regulations that govern in considerable detail the treatment plans, living environment, legal rights, and human dignity of nursing home patients. 42 C.F.R. §§483 et seq. These regulations are focused primarily on the process of care. See generally David Bohm, Striving for Quality Care in America's Nursing Homes, 4 DePaul J. Health Care L. 317 (2001); Jennifer Brady, Long-Term Care under Fire: A Case for Rational Enforcement, 18 J. Contemp. Health L. & Pol'y 1 (2001); Comment, 73 U. Colo. L. Rev. 1013 (2002); Symposium, 26 J. Leg. Med. 1 (2005).

Recently, there has been a considerable push to move even further toward evaluating institutions based on the outcomes of treatment. For instance, CMS has proposed fundamentally revising the standards for hospital participation in

Medicare and Medicaid to focus much more extensively on outcomes of care and systems for continuous quality improvement. The proposed standards would require each patient to receive a comprehensive assessment of care needs and a coordinated plan of care within 24 hours of admission, and would require hospitals to have systems that continuously monitor and improve care through data-driven methods of quality assessment that focus on patient outcomes and satisfaction. 62 Fed. Reg. 66,726 (1997). So far, however, the only provisions that have been adopted are those resembling the nursing home standards that focus on informing patients of their rights and protecting them from excessive use of restraints. 42 C.F.R. §482 (2006).

Another prominent initiative has been taken by the Joint Commission, which intends to streamline accreditation standards and focus more on patient safety issues. One key feature is a self-assessment and a "sentinel event" policy that requires hospitals to take the following actions whenever there is an unexpected death or serious injury resulting from treatment: inform the patient or family, conduct a "root cause" analysis, and institute a corrective action plan. However, hospitals do not have to report these events to the Joint Commission, since doing so might compromise the hospital's ability to protect the information from discovery in lawsuits. Symposium, 35 J. Health L. 179 (2002). As a result, this outcomes initiative has become simply another process measure, one that requires institutions to assess internally their bad outcomes rather than enforcing mandatory outcomes standards.

Outcomes measures of quality may find their purest expression in the accreditation of HMOs and other types of integrated delivery systems. The National Committee for Quality Assurance (NCQA) is the leading accreditation organization for these new comprehensive financing and delivery systems. From the start, it has spearheaded a focus on outcomes measures in the form of the quality report cards discussed at pages 43 and 298. These report cards adopt a standard reporting format about matters such as patient satisfaction, childhood immunization rates, and other broad indicators of health status (not just medical treatment) in the covered population. The aim is to provide this information as a basis on which subscribers and employers can comparison shop based on both price and quality, thereby substituting more market-based forces for regulatory oversight.

5. *Challenging Adverse Decisions.* The third major area of concern under licensure, accreditation, and certification programs are the processes for determining compliance and challenging adverse decisions. Space limitations preclude us from covering these important aspects of public oversight and legal practice. In brief summary, substantial procedural protections are usually built into these regulatory schemes, so challenges for denial of due process usually fail. The most intense disputes arise when licensing inspectors find such glaring safety concerns that the facility is shut down immediately without a chance for correction or rebuttal. These shutdowns have been challenged as unconstitutional, but usually without success considering the patient protection concerns at stake and the ample procedural rights following a temporary shutdown.

Constitutional challenges depend on the presence of state action, which usually does not exist for private accreditation. McKeesport v. Accreditation Council for Graduate Medical Education, 24 F.3d 519 (3d Cir. 1994). Contra

St. Agnes Hospital v. Riddick, 668 F. Supp. 478 (D. Md. 1987) (state action exists where private accreditation affects state licensure). Therefore, suit against accreditation organizations depends on somewhat obscure common law theories of fairness in business dealings. There are only a few such cases, the leading ones arising in connection with physician accreditation and membership in professional societies. They reason that when membership organizations control important economic and public interests, they must provide rational reasons and a fair process for their exclusion decisions. See Pinsker v. Pacific Coast Society of Orthodontists, 526 P.2d 253 (Cal. 1974); Falcone v. Middlesex County Medical Society, 170 A.2d 791 (N.J. 1961). See generally Robert Trefney, Judicial Intervention in Admissions Decisions of Private Professional Associations, 49 U. Chi. L. Rev. 840 (1992).

6. *The Public Role of Private Accreditation. Cospito* raises the important public policy question of whether public regulatory authorities cede too much control to private accreditation organizations that are controlled by the regulated industry. State licensure of health care facilities, like federal certification, sometimes defers to the Joint Commission, either by using its accreditation as a proxy for licensure or by incorporating many of its standards. Even if this passes constitutional muster, it still deserves critique for whether this essentially self-regulatory approach is good public policy. See generally Symposium, Private Accreditation in the Regulatory State, 57 Law & Contemp. Probs. No. 4 (1994) (exploring this and a number of other important legal and public policy issues concerning accreditation). It is worth observing that, although the Joint Commission arose from the hospital industry, it is now sufficiently independent that it is receiving harsh criticism from hospitals for the expense and intrusiveness of its inspections. At the same time, consumer groups such as Public Citizen are lashing out against the Joint Commission for its "dangerously cozy relationship" with the hospital industry and its "clear conflict of interest" as both industry regulator and industry advocate. Modern Healthcare, July 15, 1996, at 6.

3. Regulating Access to Drugs

■ UNITED STATES v. RUTHERFORD
442 U.S. 544 (1979)

MARSHALL, J., delivered the opinion for a unanimous Court.

The question presented in this case is whether the Federal Food, Drug, and Cosmetic Act precludes terminally ill cancer patients from obtaining Laetrile, a drug not recognized as "safe and effective" within the meaning of . . . 21 U.S.C. §321(p)(1) ["the statute"].

I

[T]he Federal Food, Drug, and Cosmetic Act . . . prohibits interstate distribution of any "new drug" unless the Secretary of Health, Education, and Welfare approves an application supported by substantial evidence of the drug's safety and effectiveness.[11] As defined . . . [by the statute], the term "new drug" includes

> [a]ny drug . . . not generally recognized, among experts qualified by scientific training and experience to evaluate the safety and effectiveness of drugs, as safe and effective for use under the conditions prescribed, recommended, or suggested in the labeling. . . .

In 1975, terminally ill cancer patients and their spouses brought this action to enjoin the government from interfering with the interstate shipment and sale of Laetrile, a drug not approved for distribution under the Act. Finding that Laetrile, in proper dosages, was nontoxic and effective, the district court ordered the government to permit limited purchases of the drug by one of the named plaintiffs. [T]he court of appeals for the Tenth Circuit . . . instructed the district court to remand the case to the Food and Drug Administration for determination whether Laetrile was a "new drug" under [the statute]. . . . After completion of administrative hearings, the Commissioner . . . determined first that no uniform definition of Laetrile exists; rather, the term has been used generically for chemical compounds similar to, or consisting at least in part of, amygdalin, a glucoside present in the kernels or seeds of most fruits. The Commissioner further found that Laetrile in its various forms constituted a "new drug" . . .

---

[11] Section 505, as set forth in 21 U.S.C. §355, provides in part:

> (a) . . . No person shall introduce or deliver for introduction into interstate commerce any new drug, unless an approval of an application filed pursuant to subsection (b) of this section is effective with respect to such drug.
>
> (b) . . . Any person may file with the Secretary an application with respect to any drug subject to the provisions of subsection (a) of this section. Such person shall submit to the Secretary as a part of the application (1) full reports of investigations which have been made to show whether or not such drug is safe for use and whether such drug is effective in use. . . .
>
> (d) . . . If the Secretary finds . . . that (1) the investigations . . . required to be submitted to the Secretary . . . do not include adequate tests by all methods reasonably applicable to show whether or not such drug is safe for use under the conditions prescribed, recommended, or suggested in the proposed labeling thereof; (2) the results of such tests show that such drug is unsafe for use under such conditions or do not show that such drug is safe for use under such conditions; . . . (4) . . . he has insufficient information to determine whether such drug is safe for use under such conditions; or (5) . . . there is a lack of substantial evidence that the drug will have the effect it purports or is represented to have under the conditions of use prescribed, recommended, or suggested in the proposed labeling thereof; or (6) based on a fair evaluation of all material facts, such labeling is false or misleading in any particular; he shall issue an order refusing to approve the application. . . . As used in this subsection . . . , the term "substantial evidence" means evidence consisting of adequate and well-controlled investigations, including clinical investigations, by experts qualified by scientific training and experience to evaluate the effectiveness of the drug involved, on the basis of which it could fairly and responsibly be concluded by such experts that the drug will have the effect it purports or is represented to have under the conditions of use prescribed, recommended, or suggested in the labeling or proposed labeling thereof.
>
> (i) . . . The Secretary shall promulgate regulations for exempting from the operation of the foregoing subsections of this section drugs intended solely for investigational use by experts qualified by scientific training and experience to investigate the safety and effectiveness of drugs. . . .

The Secretary has delegated his approval authority to the Commissioner of the Food and Drug Administration. See 21 CFR §5.10(a)(1) (1978).

because it was not generally recognized among experts as safe and effective for its prescribed use. . . .

On review of the Commissioner's decision, the district court sustained his determination that Laetrile, because not generally regarded as safe or effective, constituted a new drug. . . . [T]he court held that, by denying cancer patients the right to use a nontoxic substance in connection with their personal health, the Commissioner had infringed constitutionally protected privacy interests.

The court of appeals addressed neither the statutory nor the constitutional rulings of the district court. Rather, the Tenth Circuit held that "the 'safety' and 'effectiveness' terms used in the statute have no reasonable application to terminally ill cancer patients." Since those patients, by definition, would "die of cancer regardless of what may be done," the court concluded that there were no realistic standards against which to measure the safety and effectiveness of a drug for that class of individuals. The court of appeals therefore approved the district court's injunction permitting use of Laetrile by cancer patients certified as terminally ill. . . .

II

The Federal Food, Drug, and Cosmetic Act makes no special provision for drugs used to treat terminally ill patients. By its terms, . . . the Act requires premarketing approval for "any new drug" unless it is intended solely for investigative use or is exempt under one of the Act's grandfather provisions. And . . . [the statute] defines "new drug" to encompass "[a]ny drug . . . not generally recognized . . . as safe and effective for use under the conditions prescribed, recommended, or suggested in the labeling." . . .

In the instant case, we are persuaded by the legislative history and consistent administrative interpretation of the Act that no implicit exemption for drugs used by the terminally ill is necessary to attain congressional objectives or to avert an unreasonable reading of the terms *safe* and *effective*. . . .

Nothing in the history of the 1938 Food, Drug, and Cosmetic Act, which first established procedures for review of drug safety, or of the 1962 Amendments, which added the current safety and effectiveness standards in . . . [the statute],[12] suggests that Congress intended protection only for persons suffering from curable diseases. To the contrary, in deliberations preceding the 1938 Act, Congress expressed concern that individuals with fatal illnesses, such as cancer, should be shielded from fraudulent cures. See, e.g., 79 Cong. Rec. 5023 (1935). . . .

In implementing the statutory scheme, the FDA has never made exception for drugs used by the terminally ill. As this Court has often recognized, the construction of a statute by those charged with its administration is entitled to substantial deference. . . .

---

[12] Under the 1938 Act, a "new drug" was one not generally recognized by qualified experts as safe for its recommended use. §201(p)(1), 52 Stat. 1041. The Drug Amendments of 1962, Pub. L. 87-781, 76 Stat. 789, redefined the term to include drugs not generally recognized as effective or safe for their intended use. §201(p)(1), 21 U.S.C. §321(p)(1). . . . In addition, the Amendments provided that no new drug application may be approved absent substantial evidence that the drug is effective as well as safe under prescribed conditions. §505(d), 21 U.S.C. §355(d). See n.11, supra.

In the court of appeals' view, an implied exemption from the Act was justified because the safety and effectiveness standards set forth in . . . [the statute] could have "no reasonable application" to terminally ill patients. 582 F.2d, at 1236. We disagree. . . . Only when a literal construction of a statute yields results so manifestly unreasonable that they could not fairly be attributed to congressional design will an exception to statutory language be judicially implied. Here, however, we have no license to depart from the plain language of the Act, for Congress could reasonably have intended to shield terminal patients from ineffectual or unsafe drugs.

A drug is effective within the meaning of . . . [the statute] if there is general recognition among experts, founded on substantial evidence, that the drug in fact produces the results claimed for it under prescribed conditions. Contrary to the court of appeals' apparent assumption, effectiveness does not necessarily denote capacity to cure. In the treatment of any illness, terminal or otherwise, a drug is effective if it fulfills, by objective indices, its sponsor's claims of prolonged life, improved physical condition, or reduced pain. . . .

Thus, the Commissioner generally considers a drug safe when the expected therapeutic gain justifies the risk entailed by its use. For the terminally ill, as for anyone else, a drug is unsafe if its potential for inflicting death or physical injury is not offset by the possibility of therapeutic benefit. . . .

[Further,] if an individual suffering from a potentially fatal disease rejects conventional therapy in favor of a drug with no demonstrable curative properties, the consequences can be irreversible. . . . The FDA's practice also reflects the recognition, amply supported by expert medical testimony in this case, that with diseases such as cancer it is often impossible to identify a patient as terminally ill except in retrospect. Cancers vary considerably in behavior and in responsiveness to different forms of therapy.[13] Even critically ill individuals may have unexpected remissions and may respond to conventional treatment. Thus, as the Commissioner concluded, to exempt from the Act drugs with no proved effectiveness in the treatment of cancer "would lead to needless deaths and suffering among . . . patients characterized as 'terminal' who could actually be helped by legitimate therapy."

It bears emphasis that although the court of appeals' ruling was limited to Laetrile, its reasoning cannot be so readily confined. To accept the proposition that the safety and efficacy standards of the Act have no relevance for terminal patients is to deny the Commissioner's authority over all drugs, however toxic or ineffectual, for such individuals. If history is any guide, this new market would not be long overlooked. Since the turn of the century, resourceful entrepreneurs have advertised a wide variety of purportedly simple and painless cures for cancer, including liniments of turpentine, mustard, oil, eggs, and ammonia; peat moss; arrangements of colored floodlamps; pastes made from glycerin and limburger

---

[13] The Commissioner noted that these unexpected behavior patterns may account for anecdotal claims of Laetrile's effectiveness. Users of Laetrile who experience spontaneous remissions or delayed responses to conventional therapy after its abandonment may ascribe their improvement to Laetrile without any objective basis for that attribution. . . . Particularly since accepted cancer treatments such as chemotherapy and radiation often have painful side effects, the Commissioner concluded that patients who subjectively perceive improvement after substituting Laetrile for these modes of therapy may erroneously believe that their condition has been arrested or ameliorated.

cheese; mineral tablets; and "Fountain of Youth" mixtures of spices, oil, and suet. In citing these examples, we do not, of course, intend to deprecate the sincerity of Laetrile's current proponents, or to imply any opinion on whether that drug may ultimately prove safe and effective for cancer treatment. But this historical experience does suggest why Congress could reasonably have determined to protect the terminally ill, no less than other patients, from the vast range of self-styled panaceas that inventive minds can devise.

We note finally that construing . . . [the statute] to encompass treatments for terminal diseases does not foreclose all resort to experimental cancer drugs by patients for whom conventional therapy is unavailing. . . . [Another section of the Act] exempts from premarketing approval drugs intended solely for investigative use if they satisfy certain preclinical testing and other criteria. An application for clinical testing of Laetrile by the National Cancer Institute is now pending before the Commissioner. That the Act makes explicit provision for carefully regulated use of certain drugs not yet demonstrated safe and effective reinforces our conclusion that no exception for terminal patients may be judicially implied. Whether, as a policy matter, an exemption should be created is a question for legislative judgment, not judicial inference. The judgment of the court of appeals is reversed. . . .

Notes: The Scope and Constitutionality of Pharmaceutical Regulation

1. *Federal and State Regulation of Pharmaceuticals.* The federal government has enacted a complex web of food, drug, and medical device regulations under the federal authority to regulate interstate commerce. The power to regulate interstate commerce includes the power to regulate commerce to protect public health. For a thorough overview of regulation, see Kenneth R. Piña & Wayne L. Pines (eds.), A Practical Guide to Food and Drug Law and Regulation (2d ed. 2002); Richard Merrill, The Architecture of Government Regulation of Medical Products, 82 Va. L. Rev. 1753 (1996). See also Philip J. Hilts, Protecting America's Health: The FDA, Business, and One Hundred Years of Regulation (2003).

2. *The Drug Approval Process.* As noted in *Rutherford*, new drugs must be proven to be "safe" and "effective" in treating a particular condition. 21 U.S.C. §355. The approval process typically requires the completion of three phases of drug trials:

(a) Phase 1.

(1) Phase 1 studies are typically closely monitored and may be conducted in patients or normal volunteer subjects. These studies are designed to determine the metabolism and pharmacologic actions of the drug in humans, the side effects associated with increasing doses, and, if possible, to gain early evidence on effectiveness. . . .

(b) Phase 2. Phase 2 includes the controlled clinical studies conducted to evaluate the effectiveness of the drug for a particular indication or indications in patients with the disease or condition under study and to determine the common short-term side effects and risks associated with the drug. Phase 2 studies are typically well controlled, closely monitored, and conducted in a relatively small number of patients, usually involving no more than several hundred subjects.

(c) Phase 3. Phase 3 studies are expanded controlled and uncontrolled trials. They are performed after preliminary evidence suggesting effectiveness of the drug has been obtained, and are intended to gather the additional information about effectiveness and safety that is needed to evaluate the overall benefit-risk relationship of the drug and to provide an adequate basis for physician labeling. Phase 3 studies usually include from several hundred to several thousand subjects. [21 C.F.R. §312.21.]

3. *FDA Regulation of Drugs Used to Treat Terminal Illness.* Note that the *Rutherford* opinion is almost solely concerned with the issue whether the FDA's statutorily granted power to regulate the safety and effectiveness of drugs could be applied to drugs used to treat terminal conditions. Phrased in this way, this question of statutory interpretation almost answers itself. The language of the Act appears broad enough to cover these drugs; Congress had been concerned about fraudulent exploitation of the seriously ill; the drugs had always been regulated under FDA policy; and no implied exemption was required by history or logic. The Court therefore held that Congress intended for these drugs to be regulated under the Food, Drug, and Cosmetic Act and that the FDA's policy did not exceed its statutory mandate.

Under current federal regulations, patients with serious or life-threatening illnesses may be given access to certain types of investigational new drugs under some circumstances. 21 C.F.R. §312.34. Patients with serious illnesses typically will only obtain access after the drug has cleared Phase 3 or after all clinical trials have been completed. Patients who have immediately life-threatening diseases may obtain access before Phase 3 trials have been completed, "but ordinarily not earlier than Phase 2." Id. Despite this compassionate use regulation, the FDA has generally refused to allow terminally ill patients access to new drugs that have tested only through Phase I trials.

4. *Pharmaceutical Choice as a Constitutional Right?* Why did the *Rutherford* Court not consider whether the FDA's regulation of laetrile violates the constitutional rights of terminally ill cancer patients? Shouldn't a terminally ill patient — for whom traditional, accepted treatments have failed — have the right to choose unapproved treatments? The district court had found a constitutional violation, but the Tenth Circuit Court of Appeals had decided the case on other grounds. On remand from the Supreme Court decision, the Tenth Circuit confronted and rejected this claim, holding that "the decision by the patient whether to have a treatment or not is a protected right, but his selection of a particular treatment, or at least a medication, is within the area of governmental interest in protecting public health." Rutherford v. United States, 616 F.2d 455, 457 (10th Cir. 1980).

The issue dramatically reemerged with the D.C. Circuit's initial decision in Abigail Alliance for Better Access to Developmental Drugs and Washington Legal Foundation v. von Eschenbach, 445 F.3d 470 (2006), reversed en banc 495 F.3d 695 (D.C. Cir. 2007). The plaintiffs sought "to enjoin the FDA from enforcing the policy barring the sale of post-Phase I investigational new drugs to terminally ill patients not in Phase II trials." Id. at 473-74; and 21 C.F.R. §312.34, supra.

A panel of the D.C. Circuit initially held that the trial court had erred in dismissing the complaint, finding that:

> where there are no alternative government-approved treatment options, a terminally ill, mentally competent adult patient's informed access to potentially life-saving investigational new drugs determined by the FDA after Phase I trials to be sufficiently safe for expanded human trials warrants protection under the Due Process Clause. The prerogative asserted by the FDA—to prevent a terminally ill patient from using potentially life-saving medication to which those in Phase II clinical trials have access—thus impinges upon an individual liberty deeply rooted in our Nation's history and tradition of self-preservation. . . . [W]e remand the case . . . to determine whether the FDA's policy . . . is narrowly tailored to serve a compelling governmental interest.

Id. at 486. On rehearing, the en banc court reversed, ruling that the plaintiffs' claim did not involve any fundamental constitutionally protected right and that the FDA's approach would easily survive rational basis review:

> Although terminally ill patients desperately need curative treatments, . . . their deaths can certainly be hastened by the use of a potentially toxic drug with no proven therapeutic benefit. . . . [P]rior to the distribution of a drug outside of controlled studies, the Government has a rational basis for ensuring that there is a scientifically and medically acceptable level of knowledge about the risks and benefits of the drug. We therefore hold that the FDA's policy of limiting access to investigational drugs is rationally related to the legitimate state interest. . . . Id. at 713. Compare Seeley v. Washington State, 940 P.2d 604 (Wash. 1997)

(terminally ill cancer patient has no constitutional right to use marijuana to control nausea).

Is restricting access to potential treatments for terminally ill patients consistent with the jurisprudence governing the termination of life-sustaining treatment? With case law on a woman's right to choose abortion?

5. *The FDA and Drug Development Efforts.* The FDA has been criticized for unnecessary delays in the approval of important drugs. The laetrile dispute in the 1970s paved the way for vigorous protests by AIDS activists in the 1980s and 1990s. Congress sought to speed up the development of new drugs by providing additional incentives to pharmaceutical firms. Under the Orphan Drug Act, Pub. L. No. 97-414, 96 Stat. 2049 (1983), as amended, those companies are encouraged to develop and market drugs for rare illnesses, where the relatively small number of persons affected might otherwise not constitute a sufficient market to sustain the research and development costs of providing treatment. In 1997, Congress also enacted the Food and Drug Administration Modernization Act, Pub. L. No. 105-115, 111 Stat. 2296 (1997) (reforms included codification of fast-track and other measures designed to improve access to drugs). See Thomas Roberts, Jr. & Bruce Chabner, Beyond Fast Track for Drug Approvals, 351 N. Eng. J. Med. 501 (2004); Eve Slater, Today's FDA, 352 N. Eng. J. Med. 293 (2005).

Any effort to speed up the approval of new drugs inevitably creates the risk that truncated studies and review will result in the release of drugs with unknown hazards and effectiveness; the current debate focuses on whether the reform of the drug approval process has gone too far or not far enough. See Steven R. Salbu, The FDA and Public Access to New Drugs: Appropriate Levels of Scrutiny in the Wake of HIV, AIDS, and the Diet Drug Debacle, 79 B.U. L. Rev. 93 (1999). See also David Healy, Did Regulators Fail over Selective Serotonin Reuptake Inhibitors?, 333 BMJ 92 (2006); Karen E. Lasser et al., Timing of New Black Box Warnings and Withdrawals for Prescription Medications, 287 JAMA 2215 (2002) (research reveals that serious adverse drug reactions emerged in 10 percent of new drugs approved by FDA between 1975 and 1999; drug must be on the market for many years before true level of safety is known); Susan Okiel, What Ails the FDA? 352 New Eng. J. Med. 1063 (2005); Eric J. Topol, Failing the Public Health — Rofecoxib, Merck, and the FDA, 351 New Eng. J. Med. 1707 (2004).

6. *Women and Minorities in Drug Research.* As noted in the discussion of human experimentation at page 270, medical research has at least sometimes been advanced at the expense of minorities and other disadvantaged groups. Ironically, in recent years medical researchers have also been subjected to criticism for excluding women and minorities from participation in important research efforts. Researchers sometimes kept women from participating in drug research trials because of fears that women could expose fetuses to potentially unsafe drugs during pregnancy. See Seminar on Women in Clinical Trials of FDA-Regulated Products: Who Participates and Who Decides?, 48 Food & Drug L.J. 161 et seq. (1993). The exclusion of minorities often stemmed from the methodology used to attract research subjects. See C. Bartlett et al., The Causes and Effects of Socio-Demographic Exclusions from Clinical Trials, 9(38) Health Tech. Assess. iii (2005) (comparing U.S. and U.K. data)

The exclusion of women and minorities from drug research has had two results: (1) excluded groups did not have access to potentially effective (though possibly risky and ineffective) experimental treatments, and (2) researchers failed to gather data on whether there were group-related variations in the effectiveness of the experimental drugs. Congress responded to these concerns with the NIH Revitalization Act of 1993. The statute requires researchers to include women and minorities in NIH-funded research and, where practicable, to include sufficient numbers to determine whether the studied drug is as effective in these groups. 42 U.S.C. §289a-2; http://grants1.nih.gov/grants/funding/women_min/women_min. htm. See also Karen L. Baird, The New NIH and FDA Medical Research Policies, 24 J. Health Pol. Pol'y & L. 531 (1999); Allen L. Gifford et al., Participation in Research and Access to Experimental Treatments by HIV-Infected Patients, 346 New Eng. J. Med. 1373 (2002); Asefeh Heiat, Cary P. Gross, & Harlan M. Krumholz, Representation of the Elderly, Women, and Minorities in Heart Failure Clinical Trials, 162 Arch. Int. Med. 1682 (2002); Lisa C. Ikemoto, In the Shadow of Race: Women of Color in Health Disparities Policy, 39 U.C. Davis L. Rev. 1023 (2006); T.E. King, Jr., Racial Disparities in Clinical Trials, 346 New Eng. J. Med. 1400 (2002); and Symposium, The Responsible Use of Racial and Ethnic Categories in Biomedical Research: Where Do We Go from Here?, J. L. Med. & Ethics 483-558 (2006).

7. *Drug Labeling, "Off-Label Use" and the Learned Intermediary Doctrine.* Under the regulatory policy of the FDA, each prescription drug carries a package-insert label with quite elaborate information on the methods of administering the drug,

conditions for which the drug is recommended, as well as warnings about contraindications for use and about known dangers and side effects. The package inserts have considerable, although not totally controlling, influence over the proper standard of accepted patient care related to the drug. Physicians may, and often do, prescribe drugs for "off-label" uses, although there has been controversy in recent years about insurance reimbursement for such use. The FDA has also been concerned about whether manufacturers should be permitted to disseminate information about off-label uses to physicians. The agency initially took the view that these communications should be severely restricted to prevent circumvention of the labeling process. The Food and Drug Administration Modernization Act of 1997 authorizes manufacturers to inform physicians about off-label scientific research studies in some cases. See Lars Noah, Medicine's Epistemology: Mapping the Haphazard Diffusion of Knowledge in the Biomedical Community, 44 Ariz. L. Rev. 373, 443-447 (2002) (summarizing history and noting argument that restrictions violate First Amendment). See also Madlen Gazarian, Off-Label Use of Medicines: Consensus Recommendations for Evaluating Appropriateness, 185 Med. J. Aust. 544 (2006); David C. Radley, Stan N. Finkelstein, & Randall S. Stafford, Off-Label Prescribing Among Office-Based Physicians, 166 Arch. Intern. Med. 1021 (2006).

In the prescription drug field, the courts have quite uniformly accepted the package-insert warnings to physicians as meeting the drug manufacturers' legal obligation. The physician is expected to be a "learned intermediary" between the company and the patient in protecting the patient and in providing direct information about the drug to the patient. The retail pharmacist is also a source of advice for drug consumers. These assumptions have been shaken somewhat by the expansion of direct-to-consumer (DTC) advertising by pharmaceutical companies. See, e.g., Prescription-Drug Advertisements, 21 C.F.R. §202.1 (2006); Meredith Rosenthal et al., Promotion of Prescription Drugs to Consumers, 346 New Eng. J. Med. 498 (2002) (DTC advertising tripled from 1996 to 2000, though still merely 15 percent of total sum spent on drug promotion); Sidney M. Wolfe, Direct-to-Consumer Advertising — Education or Emotion Promotion, 346 New Eng. J. Med. 524 (2002). For a discussion about direct-to-consumer advertising in the context of the Vioxx controversy, see Ernst Bernt, To Inform or Persuade? Direct-to-Consumer Advertising of Prescription Drugs, 352 New Eng. J. Med. 325 (2005); Henry Waxman, The Lessons of Vioxx — Drug Safety and Sales, 352 New Eng. J. Med. 2576. (2005); Susan Okie, Raising the Safety Bar — The FDA's Coxib Meeting, 352 N. Eng. J. Med. 1283. (2005).

8. *The FDA and New Regulatory Challenges: Dietary Supplements and Genetic Tests.* The regulation of dietary supplements has been controversial, in part because of industry claims that the supplements are more like food than they are like classic pharmaceuticals. The FDA's suggestion that it might regulate supplements as though they were drugs drew Congressional action in the form of the Dietary Supplement Health and Education Act of 1994, Pub. L. No. 103-417, 108 Stat. 4325 (1994) ("DSHEA"). The DSHEA gives the FDA the authority to "regulate[] vitamins, minerals, herbs, amino acids, and other dietary substances. Dietary supplements are generally regulated in a manner similar to food and the FDA is authorized to prevent adulterated products from entering the market." Nutraceutical v. von Eschenbach, 459 F.3d 1033, 1035 (2006)

(interpreting DSHEA; upholding FDA ban on ephedrine-alkaloid dietary supplements). A dietary supplement is adulterated if it "presents a significant or unreasonable risk of illness or injury" under suggested or ordinary use. 21 U.S.C. §342(f)(1). See Symposium, The Dietary Supplement Health and Education Act: Regulation at the Crossroads, 31 Amer. J. L. & Med. 147-363 (2005); Lars Noah & Barbara Noah, A Drug by Any Other Name . . . ? Paradoxes in Dietary Supplement Risk Regulation, 17 Stan. L. & Pol'y Rev. 165 (2006); Institute of Medicine, Dietary Supplements: A Framework for Evaluating Safety (2005).

The regulation of genetic tests is also controversial. Are genetic tests best regulated as medical devices? Laboratory procedures and standards? Clinical practice? See David C. Bonnin, The Need for Increased Oversight of Genetic Testing: A Detailed Look at the Genetic Testing Process, 4 Hou. J. Health L. & Pol'y 149 (2003); Douglas A. Grimm, FDA, CLIA, or a "Reasonable Combination of Both": Toward Increased Regulatory Oversight of Genetic Testing, 41 U. S.F. L. Rev. 107 (2006); Anny Huang, FDA Regulation of Genetic Testing: Institutional Reluctance and Public Guardianship, 53 Food Drug L. J. 555 (1998); Neil A. Holtzman, FDA and the Regulation of Genetic Tests, 41 Jurimetrics J. 53 (2000); Richard A. Merrill, Genetic Testing: A Role for the FDA?, 41 Jurimetrics J. 63 (2000).

(b) Federal-State Conflicts: State Regulation and Medicinal Marijuana

The Food and Drug Administration (FDA) does not have jurisdiction over wholly intrastate manufacture and distribution of drugs, which may be regulated by the state. The intrastate exception to federal regulation is rarely applicable. See Texas State Board of Medical Examiners v. Burzynski, 917 S.W.2d 365 (Tex. Ct. App. 1996). States criminalize the sale of unapproved drugs and subject licensed health care professionals who prescribe or administer unapproved drugs to disciplinary action. See, e.g., People v. Privitera, 591 P.2d 919 (Cal. 1979) (defendants convicted of felony conspiracy to sell and prescribe laetrile).

Several states enacted "medicinal marijuana" laws in the early 2000s, for the most part through voter referenda. These state laws purported to shield from prosecution persons involved in prescribing, using, or possessing marijuana for specified medical purposes. The California initiative is typical:

§11362.5. Medical use. . . .

(b)(1) The people of the State of California hereby find and declare that the purposes of the Compassionate Use Act of 1996 are as follows:

(A) To ensure that seriously ill Californians have the right to obtain and use marijuana for medical purposes where that medical use is deemed appropriate and has been recommended by a physician who has determined that the person's health would benefit from the use of marijuana in the treatment of cancer, anorexia, AIDS, chronic pain, spasticity, glaucoma, arthritis, migraine, or any other illness for which marijuana provides relief.

(B) To ensure that patients and their primary caregivers who obtain and use marijuana for medical purposes upon the recommendation of a physician are not subject to criminal prosecution or sanction.

(C) To encourage the federal and state governments to implement a plan to provide for the safe and affordable distribution of marijuana to all patients in medical need of marijuana.

(2) Nothing in this section shall be construed to supersede legislation prohibiting persons from engaging in conduct that endangers others, nor to condone the diversion of marijuana for nonmedical purposes.

(c) Notwithstanding any other provision of law, no physician in this state shall be punished, or denied any right or privilege, for having recommended marijuana to a patient for medical purposes.

(d) . . . . [State criminal laws], relating to the possession of marijuana, and . . . relating to the cultivation of marijuana, shall not apply to a patient, or to a patient's primary caregiver, who possesses or cultivates marijuana for the personal medical purposes of the patient upon the written or oral recommendation or approval of a physician.

(e) For the purposes of this section, "primary caregiver" means the individual designated by the person exempted under this section who has consistently assumed responsibility for the housing, health, or safety of that person. Cal. Health & Safety Code Ann. §11362.5. See also People v. Mower, 49 P.3d 1067 (Cal. 2002) (interpreting key elements).

Proponents argued that the drug could be used to treat glaucoma and to reduce nausea and weight loss for persons undergoing chemotherapy. Opponents noted that marijuana is regulated by the federal Controlled Substances Act (CSA) and that federal law trumps state law. Controlled Substances Act, 21 U.S.C. §§801-971 (2006); U.S. Const. art. VI cl. 2. In Gonzales, Attorney General, et al. v. Raich et al. 545 U.S. 1 (2005), the Supreme Court ruled that Congressional authority to regulate interstate commerce includes the power to prohibit the local cultivation and use of marijuana for medical purposes even in the eleven states that permit it. See Susan Okie, Medical Marijuana and the Supreme Court, 353 New Eng. J. Med. 648 (2005); George J. Annas, Jumping Frogs, Endangered Toads, and California's Medical Marijuana Law, 353 New Eng. J. Med. 2291 (2005); Lawrence Gostin, Medical Marijuana, American Federalism, and the Supreme Court, 294 JAMA 842 (2005); Note, 118 Harv. L. Rev. 1985 (2005).

Problem: Drug Importation

Drugs approved for sale in the United States are often available at lower prices in other countries. Should senior citizens and the chronically ill be able to organize drug shopping trips to Canada and Mexico and to bring drugs back into the United States? What if the bargain hunters can demonstrate that they hold a valid prescription for the drugs and that the drugs have been approved for sale in the U.S.? Would state legislation authorizing or facilitating the importation be invalid?

The FDA Web site includes a page devoted to the topic; see http://www.fda. gov/importeddrugs/. See also United States v. Rx Depot, Inc., 438 F.3d 1052 (10th

Cir.), cert. denied 127 S.Ct. 80 (2006) (disgorgement order related to reimportation profits upheld); and 21 U.S.C §381(d)(1). For commentary on the reimportation issue see generally, Abigail Zuger, Rx: Canadian Drugs, 349 New Eng. J. Med. 2188 (2003); Richard Frank. Prescription Drug Prices 351 New Eng. J. Med. 1375 (2004); and Kevin Outersson, Pharmaceutical Arbitrage: Balancing Access and Innovation in International Prescription Drug Markets, 5 Yale J. Health Pol'y, L & Ethics 193 (2005).

3

██

The Treatment Relationship: Confidentiality, Consent, and Conflicts of Interest

A. THE FIDUCIARY NATURE OF THE TREATMENT RELATIONSHIP

The interactions between healers and those hoping to be healed are complex. Science, sociology, and psychology all provide important perspectives on the rich character of these important relationships. As noted in Chapter 1.B.3 and the Buckman & Sabbagh excerpt at page 19, the experience of illness may include anxiety and physical distress that, combined with the patient's relative lack of knowledge, create a substantial power imbalance between the physician and patient. The potential vulnerability of the patient is the foundation of the topics explored in this chapter: confidentiality of medical information, informed consent, and conflicts of interest. Courts and legislatures have altered traditional contract or tort norms in these areas and have relied instead on the implied or expressed belief that the treatment relationship is a fiduciary one, in which the physician owes heightened duties to protect the vulnerable patient's interests. This chapter explores the extent to which physicians have fiduciary obligations to their patients as well as the implications of those obligations.

Fiduciary law can be thought of as a separate source of distinct legal duties or as a legal status that heightens or alters ordinary contract and tort law duties. Fiduciary principles impose a special measure of loyalty and devotion on several classes of professionals (lawyers, trustees, and general agents) by virtue of their control over an important subject matter, the vulnerability of their clients, and the resulting potential for abuse. The materials in Chapter 1.B.3 explain why some courts have found that "the relationship of patients and physicians is a fiduciary one of the highest degree. It involves every element of trust, confidence and good faith."[1] Doctors have a complex body of knowledge and skills that are critical to preserving the life and restoring the health of their patients. Doctors control their patients' welfare in the most vital aspects imaginable. Sick patients, by virtue of their debilitated and vulnerable state, are dependent on their physicians' judgments and actions. Accurate diagnosis requires patients to reveal the most personal details of their lives, and effective treatment often entails invasion of the most essential aspects of bodily intimacy, invading the very blood and guts of our integrated sense of self. Thus many legal decisions and commentators have recognized doctors' fiduciary status.[2] For a sampling of the literature, see Marc A. Rodwin, Medicine, Money and Morals: Physicians' Conflicts of Interest (1993); Peter D. Jacobson, Strangers in the Night: Law and Medicine in the Managed Care Era (2002); Maxwell J. Mehlman, Fiduciary Contracting: Limitations on Bargaining Between Patients and Health Care Providers, 51 U. Pitt. L. Rev. 365, 388-416 (1990); Frances H. Miller, Trusting Doctors: Tricky Business When It Comes to Clinical Research, 81 B.U. L. Rev. 423 (2001); Michelle Oberman, Mothers and Doctors' Orders: Unmasking the Doctor's Fiduciary Role in Maternal-Fetal Conflicts, 94 Nw. U. L. Rev. 451 (2000); Mark A. Hall et al., Trust in Physicians and Medical Institutions: What Is It, Can It Be Measured, and Does It Matter?, 79 Milbank Q. 613 (2001); Mark A. Hall, Law, Medicine, and Trust, 55 Stan. L. Rev. 463 (2002); Robert Gatter, Faith, Confidence and Health Care: Fostering Trust in Medicine Through Law, 39 Wake Forest L. Rev. 395, 396 (2004); and Mark A. Hall, Caring, Curing, and Trust: A Response to Gatter, 39 Wake Forest L. Rev. 447 (2004).

Classifying physicians as fiduciaries is a simple matter; it is much more difficult, however, to say precisely what obligations result. Fiduciary law is far from a seamless web. There is no integrated body of principles or precise doctrine that applies uniformly to all forms of fiduciary relationships.[3] Nonetheless, there are basic principles of fiduciary obligation that share a broad, familial resemblance across many categories of relationships. One of the common themes is a modification of the ordinary rules of contract. In a classic contractual relationship, neither party has a duty to maintain the secrecy of information provided by the other party and neither party has a duty to disclose information to the other about the qualities of the product or service sold or the particular needs of the purchaser. *Caveat emptor*, let the buyer beware, is the most common rule associated

---

[1] Lockett v. Goodill, 430 P.2d 589, 591 (Wash. 1967).

[2] Some authorities, however, distinguish confidential relations from fiduciary relations and declare that physicians are subject only to the former. See, e.g., **Restatement (Third) of Trusts §2** *cmt b(1)* **(2003)**; 1 Austin W. Scott & William F. Fratcher, The Law of Trusts §2.5, at 43 (4th ed. 1987). The primary thrust of the distinction, however, is one of burden of proof, not scope of obligation. The law does not assume that a position of trust exists in a confidential relation as quickly as it does in a fiduciary one, but where such trust exists, the duties are essentially the same.

[3] See L. S. Sealy, Fiduciary Relationships, 1962 Cambridge L.J. 69, 73 (observing that labelling a relationship fiduciary "does not warrant the inference that any particular fiduciary principle or remedy can be applied"). For other works that address fiduciary principles at this more general level, see Paul D. Finn, Fiduciary Obligations 15-76 (1977); M. Rodwin, Medicine, Money & Morals 179-211 (1993); J. C. Shephard, The Law of Fiduciaries 21-42 (1981); Tamar Frankel, Fiduciary Duties as Default Rules, 74 Or. L. Rev. 1209 (1995); Tamar Frankel, Fiduciary Law, 71 Cal. L. Rev. 795, 808-816 (1983); Austin W. Scott, The Fiduciary Principle, 37 Cal. L. Rev. 539, 541 (1949), Symposium, Trust Relationships, Part 1 of 2, B.U. L. Rev. 321-478 (2001); Deborah A. DeMott, Breach of Fiduciary Duty: On Justifiable Expectations of Loyalty and Their Consequences, 48 Ariz. L. Rev. 25 (2006).

with classic contract law. Parties to the contract can impose additional obligations on each other only by bargaining for specific contract terms.

As noted in Chapter 2, courts have modified the ordinary contract regime by limiting the ability to alter or waive the basic standard of care or by limiting the ability to terminate the relationship. This chapter explains that courts have modified these pure contract principles to provide additional special protections for patients. Courts have used ordinary tort law as well as fiduciary law to achieve these protections, holding, for example, that physicians can be sued for damages if they fail to maintain patient confidences or to disclose important information about any proposed treatment. State and federal regulators also have responded to fiduciary concerns by enacting a wide range of statutes and regulations designed to protect patient confidentiality and to control conflicts of interest.

As you read the following cases and statutes, consider how well courts and legislatures have responded to the unique attributes and requirements of the doctor-patient relationship. Are the protections sufficient? Are they excessive or dysfunctional? Notice that the focus of judicial and legislative concern is on individual health care providers, primarily physicians. When and how should similar obligations be imposed on other types of health care providers? Should similar rules be applied to facilities and institutions such as hospitals and HMOs?

B. CONFIDENTIALITY OF MEDICAL INFORMATION

Both patients and health care providers believe that the health care relationship creates a special duty on the part of the provider to protect the patient's interests. One example is the duty to protect the confidentiality of patient information. The common belief that there is such a duty obscures a significant number of important legal questions. What is the source of the obligation? On whom is the duty imposed? What are the limits of the duty? What remedies are available for breaches of confidentiality? Does the system of legal protections effectively balance patient rights, provider duties, and social interests? Courts once struggled to answer these questions using common law principles; however medical confidentiality (and the closely related subject of medical privacy) are increasingly governed by statutes and regulations.

1. The Duty to Maintain Confidentiality

■ DOE v. MARSELLE
675 A.2d 835 (Conn. 1996)

KATZ, Associate Judge.

The dispositive issue on appeal is whether in order to state a cause of action under General Statutes §19a-590[4] for a violation of General Statutes

---

[4] General Statutes §19a-590 provides: "Liability for violations. Any person, except as otherwise provided in this chapter, who wilfully violates any provision of this chapter shall be liable in a private cause of action for injuries suffered as a result of such violation. Upon a finding that an individual has

§19a-583 (AIDS),[5] the confidentiality provision of chapter 368x, entitled "AIDS Testing and Medical Information," a plaintiff must allege that the person who violated that provision intended to engage in the prohibited conduct and intended to produce the resulting injury. We conclude that a wilful violation of §19a-583 requires only a knowing disclosure of confidential human immunodeficiency virus (HIV) related information.

The following facts are undisputed. The plaintiff, Jane Doe, was a patient of the defendant Dionisio C. Flores, a surgeon, to whom, during the course of her treatment, she disclosed that she was infected with HIV. A surgical assistant employed by Flores, the named defendant Doris Marselle, after learning of the plaintiff's condition from her medical chart and from personal discussions with the plaintiff, consulted Flores regarding her intention to disclose the plaintiff's HIV status to Marselle's sons who were illegal drug users and who had friends in common with the plaintiff. Flores authorized Marselle to make the disclosures provided that she not identify the plaintiff by name.

When the plaintiff learned that Marselle had told at least three other individuals in the community that she was HIV positive, the plaintiff, who had never authorized the disclosures, brought a multicount complaint against Flores and Marselle alleging that they each had: . . . violated the confidentiality provisions of §19a-583 by intentionally disclosing her HIV status (first count). . . . Additionally, the plaintiff alleged that Flores had been negligent in failing to instruct his employees regarding their obligation to comply with General Statutes §19a-581(second count) et seq. . . .

Flores filed an "objection" to the complaint, challenging the sufficiency of the plaintiff's claims against him. Treating the objection as a motion to strike, the trial court ordered all counts against Flores stricken and rendered judgment in his favor. . . . As to the first count, the court stated that the plaintiff had failed to state a cause of action under §19a-590 because the allegations set forth in the pertinent four paragraphs of the first count did not contain the word *wilfully* and there were no allegations of an intent to injure that would allow the court to conclude that Flores' action had been wilful. Additionally, because §19a-590 authorizes an action only for wilful, as opposed to negligent, conduct and because the plaintiff had not alleged that Flores had intended to injure her when he authorized the disclosure, the trial court granted Flores' motion to strike the second . . . count.

In her appeal to the Appellate Court, the plaintiff argued that the term *wilful* in §19a-590 means "intentionally" as opposed to "accidentally" and that the trial court improperly had defined the term to mean intending to injure. The Appellate Court disagreed, concluding that in order to establish a violation of §19a-590, the plaintiff must allege that both the action and the resulting injury

---

been injured as a result of such violation, damages shall be assessed in the amount sufficient to compensate said individual for such injury." — Eds.

[5] General Statutes §19a-583 provides in relevant part: "Limitations on disclosure of HIV-related information. (a) No person who obtains confidential HIV-related information may disclose or be compelled to disclose such information. . . ." General Statutes §19a-581(8) defines "confidential HIV-related information" as "any information pertaining to the protected individual or obtained pursuant to a release of confidential HIV-related information, concerning whether a person has been counseled regarding HIV infection, has been the subject of an HIV-related test, or has HIV infection, HIV-related illness or AIDS, or information which identifies or reasonably could identify a person as having one or more of such conditions, including information pertaining to such individual's partners. . . ." — Eds.

had been intended. In the Appellate Court's view, because the plaintiff had failed to do so, the trial court properly rendered judgment for Flores. . . .

. . . "Wilful" has been defined many ways, and the applicable definition often turns on the specific facts of the case and the context in which it is used. . . . Consequently, in construing its meaning, we are guided by the language of §19a-590, both alone and in the context of the AIDS statute, as well as the underlying legislative purpose of the harm at which it is directed. We pay particular attention to "the societal [problem] which the legislature sought to address . . . in determining the true meaning of the statute." State v. Parmalee, 496 A.2d 186 (1985).

The AIDS statute was designed and intended to combat the AIDS epidemic, beginning with protecting confidentiality. The legislation imposes certain requirements on the testing and treatment of persons who may be HIV positive or who have AIDS. These requirements relate principally to the areas of informed consent for HIV testing and confidential treatment of HIV-related information, and are aimed at helping health care providers to identify those people with the disease, to treat them and to educate them in an attempt to put an end to the epidemic in our state. . . .

In order to accomplish the aforementioned goals, disclosure of confidential HIV-related information is prohibited except in very limited and discrete circumstances. General Statutes §19a-583(a)(1) through (12). . . .

A person who does not fall within these exceptions may petition the court for disclosure; however, a court order may be issued only when the moving party demonstrates a clear and imminent danger to the health of another or the public health and further demonstrates a compelling need for the test results that cannot be accommodated by other means. In assessing compelling need, the court must weigh, among other things, the need for disclosure against the privacy interest of the test subject and the public interest that may be disserved by disclosure that deters future testing or that may lead to discrimination. See General Statutes §19a-583(a)(10). Finally, even when disclosure is authorized, the AIDS statute strictly limits the terms of that disclosure. See General Statutes §19a-585. In short, the drafters of this legislation "crafted the bill very carefully to give protection while also enabling those who care for people with AIDS and HIV infection to have access to information needed for the patient's care." Conn. Joint Standing Committee Hearings, Public Health, Pt. 3, 1989 Sess., p.767.

Keeping this legislative history in mind, coupled with the elaborate statutory safeguards imposed against disclosure of HIV-related information, it is difficult to presume a definition of wilful that would make permissible the unauthorized disclosure of a person's HIV-related information except in the extreme situation where the person disclosing the information actually intends to injure the protected individual. We have noted that as part of its attempt to foster an increase in medical treatment for people with AIDS and HIV infection, the legislature created the AIDS statute to correct the problems, such as the lack of confidentiality, that have stood in the way of this goal. A definition of wilful that would require a plaintiff to prove that confidentiality was breached with the intent to cause injury would do nothing to advance the laudable goals of the legislation's sponsors. Indeed, were we to apply the definition of wilful proposed by Flores and adopted by the Appellate Court, a patient who is HIV positive, knowing that he or she could obtain redress for a violation of the confidentiality provisions in only the most egregious circumstances, would have no confidence that his or her status or test results would be zealously protected. This lack of confidence, in turn, would create a disincentive for that person to submit to testing. . . . It is not our practice to construe a statute in a way to thwart its purpose or lead to absurd results. . . . Consequently, we cannot endorse a definition of wilful that would allow virtually any disclosure of confidential HIV-related information.

Moreover, to limit the definition of wilful to the case of a medical provider who intended to cause the patient injury, as Flores argues, would be to provide a cure for which there is no disease. No one speaking on behalf of the legislation identified a problem with medical providers seeking to sabotage the ability of their AIDS patients to obtain good medical care. Nor has Flores argued that such a problem exists. Because we do not presume that the legislature enacted legislation that was devoid of purpose, we will not interpret wilful as Flores has proposed.

Rather, we interpret wilful to mean a knowing disclosure of confidential HIV-related information. Contrary to the Appellate Court's assertion, this interpretation does not render the term superfluous. Had the term *wilful* not been used, persons would be liable for inadvertent disclosures or nonvolitional acts. By establishing liability only for wilful violations, the legislature indicated that inadvertent violations would not be actionable. . . .

Finally, Flores argues that even if wilful means knowing, the allegations do not state a cause of action under §19a-590 against him. We disagree. The complaint alleges that Flores "affirmatively authorized" the disclosure with the sole proviso that Marselle not disclose the plaintiff's actual name. That disclosure clearly falls within the definition of "confidential HIV-related information" set forth in §19a-581(8). Moreover, Marselle was the "employee and agent" at all times relevant to the complaint. Flores' assertion that the plaintiff must specifically allege her reliance on the doctrine of respondeat superior ignores what we have often stated is our "responsibility to construe the complaint in the manner most favorable to sustaining its legal sufficiency."[16] (Internal quotation marks omitted.) Mahoney v. Lensink, 569 A.2d 518 (1990).

The judgment is reversed and the case is remanded for further proceedings according to law.

Notes: Common Law and Statutory Duties to Maintain Confidentiality

1. *A Constitutional Right of Confidentiality.* The issue of patient confidentiality is of special importance to state and federal health care providers or agencies. Several courts have found that individuals have a constitutionally protected interest in maintaining the privacy of their medical information. See, e.g., Doe v. City of New York, 15 F.3d 264 (2d Cir. 1994) (individuals have a constitutional

---

[16] Whether Marselle was indeed acting within the scope of her employment and whether Flores knew that Marselle's disclosure "reasonably could" allow those in receipt of the information to identify the plaintiff are questions that must be determined by a factfinder.

right of privacy in their medical information; court employs a balancing test to determine whether the government entity's interest in disclosure is "substantial" enough to outweigh the individual's privacy interest). This "informational privacy" interest has its roots in the Supreme Court's decision in Whalen v. Roe, 429 U.S. 589 (1977). In that case, the Court upheld a state program that created a centralized data bank with the names of all persons in the state who had been prescribed certain controlled substances. In dicta, however, the Court noted that the state might have some constitutional obligation to maintain the confidentiality of the information it collected.

2. *The Doctrinal Basis for a Common Law Duty to Maintain Confidentiality.* Most states provide a private cause of action against licensed health care providers who impermissibly disclose confidential information obtained in the course of the treatment relationship to third parties. See Annot., 48 A.L.R.4th 668 (1986). Generally, a physician-patient relationship must be formed before the duty to maintain confidences arises. See Howes v. United States, 887 F.2d 729 (6th Cir. 1989) (psychologist and psychiatrist not liable for disclosing information about husband's drug and alcohol use that had been provided by nonpatient wife). Depending on the jurisdiction, the claim may be phrased as a breach of contract, as an act of malpractice, as a breach of fiduciary duty, as an act of fraud/ misrepresentation, or as a breach of a specific civil statute permitting the award of damages. See Biddle v. Warren General Hospital, 715 N.E.2d 518 (Ohio 1999) (finding breach of confidentiality to be an independent tort); Givens v. Mullikin ex rel. Estate of McElwaney, 75 S.W.3d 383 (Tenn. 2002) (implied covenant of confidentiality found in contract for treatment). In addition, licensed health care providers who breach the confidentiality of their patients run the risk of professional disciplinary action. See, e.g., Seider v. Board of Examiners of Psychologists, 762 A.2d 551 (Me. 2000). State privacy rules may also be applied outside the treatment relationship. See Washburn v. Rite Aid Corp., 695 A.2d 495 (R.I. 1997).

The doctrinal basis of the common law claim can be important to prospective plaintiffs. If the claim arises in contract, plaintiffs will have the benefit of the (generally longer) contract statute of limitations. Plaintiffs alleging breaches of contract will also avoid some of the procedural barriers to malpractice suits established as part of tort reform efforts in many states. See, e.g., Pierce v. Caday, 422 S.E.2d 371 (Va. 1992) (breach of confidentiality claim is subject to notice requirements imposed by malpractice reform statutes). See also Chapter 4. C.3. Finally, plaintiffs in contract suits need prove only that the physician failed to honor the degree of confidentiality that was promised. They need not find and present expert medical testimony on the question of whether the health care provider defendant violated the applicable standard of care. Cf. Berger v. Sonneland, 26 P.3d 257 (Wash. 2001) (expert medical testimony required in malpractice claim). A few courts have considered whether breach of confidentiality claims should be subject to the ordinary negligence statute of limitations or the special statute of limitations imposed for malpractice claims. See, e.g., Tighe v. Ginsberg, 540 N.Y.S.2d 99 (App. Div. 1989) (disclosure of medical records is a breach of fiduciary duty subject to the longer negligence statute of limitations). For a review of the trends in health care privacy that concentrates on the U.S. but also looks at the UK and Australia see: Roger S. Magnusson, The Changing Legal and Conceptual Shape of Health Care Privacy, 32 J.L. Med. & Ethics 680 (2004).

3. *Statutory Protection.* The *Marselle* case provides an example of an increasingly important source of liability for health care providers who impermissibly disclose patient information. Many states have passed statutes governing the confidentiality of information provided in the health care provider-patient relationship. Some of these state statutes were enacted to build upon recent federal medical privacy initiatives, discussed in note 4. See Symposium, 2 Yale J. Health Pol'y L. & Ethics 325 (2002). The state statutes must be examined to determine (1) what types of information are protected from disclosure; (2) who has the duty to maintain confidentiality; (3) the standard of care applied to determine a breach of the duty; (4) the circumstances under which confidentiality may be breached; (5) the circumstances under which the duty terminates; and (6) the relationship between the statutory duty and other state or federal laws. As a patient, would you prefer that the confidentiality of patient information be protected under a common law or a statutory standard? As a health care provider?

The statute at issue in *Marselle* imposed liability for "wilful[] violat[ions]" of its confidentiality requirements. The defendant physician argued that this required proof that he had intended to violate the statute and had intended to injure the plaintiff. The court rejected this claim, holding that a "knowing disclosure" was sufficient. To reach this result, the court pursued a relatively elaborate process of statutory interpretation, determining at the outset that its analysis should not be limited "solely to the words of the statute" but should also consider the underlying policies and objectives of the state legislature. Are you convinced by the court's analysis?

Note that the court also holds that physicians may be held liable for disclosures made by other persons who are (presumed at least) to be under their control and direction. What did Flores do to "wilfully" violate the statute? The duty to maintain confidentiality generally includes the obligation to have in place policies and procedures designed to reduce the risk of accidental or intentional disclosures. Compare Behringer v. The Medical Center at Princeton, 592 A.2d 1251 (N.J. Super. Ct. Law Div. 1991) (hospital liable for failing to have in place policies to protect the confidentiality of the HIV status of a patient-surgeon), with Rosen v. Montgomery Surgical Center, 825 So.2d 735 (Ala. 2001) (court rejects invasion of privacy claim based on actions of nonphysician employee of hospital).

Connecticut is not alone in providing additional protection for specific types of information believed to be particularly sensitive or prone to misuse. See, e.g., Annot. 12 A.L.R.5th 149 (1993). Do state rules providing additional protection for certain types of health care information, such as information regarding HIV status, represent good public policy?

Advances in genetics may create additional privacy concerns. Scientists are increasingly able to link human genes with the risk of developing various human maladies. Individuals have a definite interest in maintaining the confidentiality of their genetic predisposition for a variety of ills. At the same time, other affected family members, insurers, and others have an interest in gaining access to this information. Should legislatures grant special statutory protections for genetic privacy? Commentators have observed that a person's genetic makeup is uniquely private and personal. It may be thought of as a "future diary" that reveals much about what is likely to happen to them. People might also be thought to have a greater privacy interest simply because genetic technology is so new and the possible uses are frightening to many. Accordingly, the issue of genetic privacy has occupied the attention of several commentators. Patricia Roche et al., The Genetic Privacy Act, 37 Jurimetrics J. 1 (1997). Lawrence O. Gostin & James G. Hodge, Jr., Genetic Privacy and the Law: An End to Genetics Exceptionalism, 40 Jurimetrics J. 21 (1999); Mark A. Hall, Legal Rules and Industry Norms: The Impact of Laws Restricting Health Insurers' Use of Genetic Information, 40 Jurimetrics J. 93 (1999).

4. *Overview of Federal Privacy Regulations (HIPAA).* Until relatively recently, few federal laws specifically focused on medical privacy. See 42 U.S.C. §290dd-2 (protecting the confidentiality of records relating to substance abuse treatment). The federal government has become much more involved in the protection of the confidentiality of health information. The Health Insurance Portability and Accountability Act of 1996, Pub. L. No. 104-191, §264, 110 Stat. 1936 (1996), gave the Secretary of Health and Human Services authority to regulate some aspects of medical privacy if Congress failed to enact privacy regulations. Congress indeed failed to act, and the Clinton administration released the initial federal privacy regulations in December 2000. 65 Fed. Reg. 82,462-82,829 (Dec. 28, 2000). The Bush administration adopted significant revisions to the privacy regulations in 2002. 67 Fed. Reg. 53,182 (Aug. 14, 2002) (affecting 45 C.F.R. §§160, 164).

In general, the federal privacy regulations impose an obligation to maintain the confidentiality of individually identifiable health information on certain "covered entities," which include health plans, health care clearinghouses, and health care providers who transmit health information in electronic form during certain transactions. 45 C.F.R. §160.102(a). These entities must (1) adopt internal procedures to protect the privacy of protected health information; (2) train employees regarding privacy procedures; (3) designate a privacy officer; (4) secure patient records that contain protected information; and (5) ensure that agreements with other entities (called "business associates") include terms requiring the protection of privacy.

Most disclosures of personally identifiable health information related to "treatment, payment, or health care operations" (called "TPO" in the increasingly common HIPAA lingo of health lawyers and consultants) do not require specific written consent. 45 C.F.R. §164.502, §164.506. Patients must be given an opportunity to agree or object to or to authorize other types of disclosures. Id. and §164.508. Covered entities are required to notify patients of the entities' privacy policies and must make a good-faith effort to secure a written acknowledgment from the patient. 45 C.F.R. §164.520. The complex regulatory framework addresses a host of other issues, ranging from the de-identification of health information, to the use of health information in research, to the responsibility of the covered entities to ensure that business associates comply with privacy requirements. A violation of the regulations may result in a significant civil penalty or criminal liability or both. The regulations do not provide a private cause of action or remedy. Acara v. Banks, 470 F.3d 569 (5th Cir. 2006).

Information about the current version of the federal rules can be found at www.hhs.gov/ocr/hipaa and Georgetown's Health Privacy Project, available at www.healthprivacy.org. For discussion and critique, see Richard A. Epstein, HIPAA on Privacy: Its Unintended and Intended Consequences, 22 Cato J. 13 (2002); Symposium, Modern Studies in Privacy Law, 86 Minn. L. Rev. 1097-1540 (2002); Lawrence O. Gostin, James G. Hodge, Jr., Mira S. Burghardt, Balancing Communal Goods and Personal Privacy Under a National Health Informational Privacy Rule, 46 St. Louis U. L.J. 5 (2002); Diane Kutzko et al., HIPAA in Real Time: Practical Implications of the Federal Privacy Rule, 51 Drake L. Rev. 403 (2003); Marie C. Pollio, The Inadequacy of HIPAA's Privacy Rule: the Plain Language Notice of Privacy Practices and Patient Understanding, 50 N.Y.U. Ann. Surv. Am. L. 579 (2004); David R. Morantz, HIPAA's Headaches: A Call for a First Amendment Exception to the Newly Enacted Health Care Privacy Rules, 53 U. Kan. L. Rev. 479 (2005); June Mary Zekan Makdisi, Commercial Use of Protected Health Information under HIPAA's Privacy Rule: Reasonable Disclosure or Disguised Marketing, 82 Neb. L. Rev. 741 (2004); Meredith Kapushion, Hungry, Hungry HIPAA: When Privacy Regulations Go Too Far, 31 Fordham Urb. L. J. 1483 (2004); Carl E. Schneider, HIPAA-cracy, 36(1) Hastings Center Rep. 10 (Jan.-Feb. 2006).

5. *The Significance of HIPAA.* The federalization of health information privacy is significant in several respects. First, federal rules may establish a floor that "evens out" the basic level of protection across states. Second, federal rules impose obligations on specified health care entities rather than focusing solely on physicians or other licensed health care providers. Third, the federal rules explicitly permit states to enact more protective rules so long as they do not conflict with federal law. See 45 C.F.R. §160.203 (state preemption rules). Many states are considering additional legislation; some have already enacted special medical privacy bills incorporating and/or expanding HIPAA's protections. See, e.g., Tex. Health & Safety Code §181.001 et seq. See generally Symposium, 2 Yale J. Health Pol'y L. & Ethics 325 (2002). The federal Gramm-Leach-Bliley Act, which focuses on financial records privacy, has also sparked state reform efforts targeting health insurers, banks, and other financial services entities. See 15 U.S.C. §§6801-6810. Courts are beginning to explore the interaction of HIPAA with other types of rules governing the confidentiality of medical information. See Smith v. American Home Products Corp. Wyeth-Ayerst Pharmaceutical, 855 A.2d 608 (N.J. Super. L. 2003) (HIPAA and state discovery rules).

6. *HIPAA in the Courts.* Initial efforts to challenge HIPAA on constitutional or statutory grounds have failed. In South Carolina Med. Ass'n v. Thompson, 327 F.3d 346 (4th Cir. 2003), the court rejected the plaintiffs' claims that the HIPAA regulations constituted an unconstitutionally vague and improper, standardless delegation of legislative authority. See also Citizens for Health v. Leavitt, Sec'y U.S. Dep't Health and Human Services, 428 F.3d 167 (3d Cir. 2005) (rejecting constitutional and statutory challenges to the regulations allowing use of health information for TPO without specific informed consent). For a summary of litigation under HIPAA, see Annot., 194 A.L.R. Fed. 133 (2004).

7. *Confidentiality as a Rule of Evidence.* The confidentiality of patient-physician communications is often also protected under rules of evidence. This evidentiary "privilege" prohibits the discovery of protected information. State rules of evidence almost always provide for a physician-patient privilege. The rule may be invoked by the physician or by the patient, but only the patient generally has the

power to waive the privilege. See 81 Am. Jur. 2d *Witnesses* §§436, 490. The privilege may be limited to communications with physicians. In Buchanan v. Mayfield, 925 S.W.2d 135 (Tex. App. 1996), for example, the court held that the statutory privilege accorded to "confidential communications between a physician and a patient" did not apply to the communications between a dentist and a patient.

The Federal Rules of Evidence do not include a physician-patient privilege, see Charles Alan Wright & Kenneth W. Graham, Jr., 25 Fed. Prac. & Proc. Evid. §5521 (RR 504) (discussing the rejection of a physician-patient privilege under the federal rules of evidence); Ralph Ruebner & Leslie Ann Reis, Hippocrates to HIPAA: a Foundation for a Federal Physician-Patient Privilege, 77 Temp. L. Rev. 505 (2004) (calls for a federal physician-patient privilege and discusses the foundation for that privilege). The Supreme Court recognized a "psychotherapist-patient" privilege under Rule 501 of the Federal Rules of Evidence in Jaffee v. Redmond, 116 S. Ct. 1923 (1996). Justice Stevens, writing for the majority, found that the privilege was "rooted in the imperative need for confidence and trust" and that it served important public and private interests. The majority applied the privilege to shield communications between a police officer and her social worker therapist, who provided counseling after the police officer shot an allegedly innocent person. Justice Scalia's dissent focused on the injustice created by the application of the privilege, including the loss of evidence of possible wrongdoing. There is no dangerous-patient exception to the federal psychotherapist-patient testimonial privilege even though the psychotherapist may have the statutory discretion to disclose confidential information about the patient to prevent harm to a third party or to the patient. U.S. v. Chase, 340 F.3d 978 (9th Cir. 2003).

Is the privilege necessary? Will people seek care from physicians or therapists without its protection? Empirical evidence suggests that perhaps they will. See Daniel W. Shuman, The Origins of the Physician-Patient Privilege and Professional Secret, 39 Sw. L.J. 661, 664-665 (1985) (noting the empirical evidence does not fully support utilitarian proponents of a privilege).

8. *Waiver and Other Exceptions.* The duty to maintain confidentiality is not ordinarily absolute under either common law or statute. Where the duty is derived from medical ethics and practice, for example, it will be limited by policies that permit disclosure for the protection of third parties. Statutes protecting the confidentiality of patient information often contain a general rule of confidentiality and then list situations under which that confidentiality can be breached. The "exceptions" to the duty to maintain confidentiality can be quite broad. Generally, patient information *may* be revealed when the patient consents, or when disclosure is necessary to protect the health and safety of either the patient or third parties. In some circumstances, health care providers may even have a *duty* to breach confidentiality imposed by common law or statute. This issue is discussed in more detail at pages 191.

Whether or not a patient has waived his or her right to confidentiality is a significant issue in litigation. See Annot., 21 A.L.R.3d 912 (1968); Reda v. Advocate Health Care, 765 N.E.2d 1002 (Ill. 2002) (plaintiff in neurological injury action had not placed mental condition at issue and had not waived privilege with respect to his mental health records); State ex rel. Crowden v. Dandurand, 970 S.W.2d 340 (Mo. 1998) (plaintiff waived confidentiality of those medical records connected to his claimed injuries, but "[a] medical provider that reveals privileged information by mailing records in lieu of attending a deposition may be sued in tort for breach of the fiduciary duty of confidentiality"); Suesbury v. Caceres, 840 A.2d 1285 (D.C. App. 2004) (physicians disclosure of information to a physician colleague in the same office "in the course of dealing with a matter related to the operation of that office" was not an "unconsented, unprivileged disclosure to a third party"). Should asserting one's fitness to be a parent in a child custody dispute constitute a waiver of the psychiatrist-patient privilege? See Laznovsky v. Laznovsky, 745 A.2d 1054 (Md. 2000) (no). See also Annot., 50 A.L.R.4th 714 (1986).

Should a patient be able to gain access to the identity and medical records of other patients? Baptist Memorial Hospital-Union County v. Johnson, 754 So. 2d 1165 (Miss. 2000) (hospital must disclose identity of patient who mistakenly breast-fed another patient's baby); Falco v. Institute of Living, 757 A.2d 571 (Conn. 2000) (psychiatrist-patient privilege prevented disclosure of identity of patient who attacked plaintiff in psychiatric hospital). See also Annot., 66 A.L.R.5th 591 (1999).

9. *Medical Records and Confidentiality.* Medical records are directly implicated in any effort to control the release of personally identifiable health information. The slow but steady creation, expansion, and sharing of electronic medical records creates a new set of disclosure risks. The federal government attempted to improve the security and privacy of electronic health care transactions in the HIPAA privacy and security regulations, discussed supra in notes 4-6. A report released by Congress's General Accounting Office in 2007 suggested that the federal push to create a nationally accessible medical records system has so far failed to address significant privacy concerns. Robert Pear, Warnings Over Privacy of U.S. Health Network, New York Times, February 18, 2007, at 16 col. 4.

10. *Patient Access to Medical Records.* Health care providers are generally deemed to "own" patient medical records. Patients are given a right of access to those records under federal and state law within certain limits.

The new HIPAA regulation gives patients a limited right of access to their own medical records. 45 C.F.R. §164.524 (some records, such as psychotherapy notes, are excluded). A patient may be denied access where a "licensed health care professional has determined, in the exercise of professional judgment, that the access requested is reasonably likely to endanger the life or physical safety of the individual or another person," but the determination is reviewable by a third party." Id. The regulation establishes guidelines for the time, form, and manner of access. Id. See also Paul V. Stearns, Commentary, Access to and Cost of Reproduction of Patient Medical Records: A Comparison of State Laws, 21 J. Legal Med. 79 (2000). Patients often have difficulty finding remedies for failures to provide access. Should a physician who refuses to release medical records be subjected to professional disciplinary action? See Balian v. Board of Licensure in Medicine, 722 A.2d 364 (Me. 1999) (striking down, on due process grounds, Board's attempt to discipline physician for failure to disclose).

11. *Adherence to Confidentiality.* Despite the legal rules, studies regularly demonstrate that patient confidentiality is often breached. See, e.g., P. A. Ubel et al., Elevator Talk: Observational Study of Inappropriate Comments in a Public Space, 99 Am. J. Med. 190 (1995) (investigators rode elevators and recorded comments of hospital employees; 13.9 percent of trips were marked by some form

of inappropriate commentary by employees, most frequently violations of patient confidentiality). See also Julia Slutsman, Nancy Kass, John McGready, & Matthew Wynia, Health Information, The HIPAA Privacy Rule, and Health Care: What Do Physicians Think?, 24(3) Health Aff. 832 (2005); E. J. Mlinek & J. Pierce, Confidentiality and Privacy Breaches in a University Hospital Emergency Department, 4 Acad. Emergency Med. 1142 (1997). What explains the gulf between legal standards and medical practice in this area?

12. *Disclosure of Information about Health Care Providers.* Patients might wish to have access to information about the health status of their health care providers. Should physicians be able to maintain the confidentiality of their own medical information? See infra at page 242 note 7.

2. The Duty to Breach Confidentiality

The duty to maintain confidentiality exists in an uneasy equilibrium with a potentially conflicting duty to breach confidentiality in some circumstances. Health care providers sometimes have not only a common law or statutory *authority* to breach confidentiality; they also have the *duty* to do so. Failure to meet this obligation can lead to criminal or civil liability. As you read the following materials, consider the perspective of health care providers. Are the rules governing confidentiality and disclosure in hopeless conflict, subjecting health care providers to "Catch-22" liability? Consider also the perspective of patients. Are the limits of confidentiality clear for patients? Is the protection afforded patient-provider communication sufficient to encourage necessary medical treatment? Finally, consider the costs to society created by duties to maintain confidentiality and duties to disclose. When should the interests of third parties be sufficient to outweigh the interests of patients in the confidentiality of medical information?

Florida provides a typical example of laws regarding the mandatory reporting of abuse, neglect, or exploitation of vulnerable adults:

> (1) Mandatory reporting. —
>   (a) Any person, including, but not limited to, any:
>   1. Physician, osteopathic physician, medical examiner, chiropractic physician, nurse, paramedic, emergency medical technician, or hospital personnel engaged in the admission, examination, care, or treatment of vulnerable adults;
>   2. Health professional or mental health professional other than one listed in subparagraph 1;
>   3. Practitioner who relies solely on spiritual means for healing;
>   4. Nursing home staff; assisted living facility staff; adult day care center staff; adult family-care home staff; social worker; or other professional adult care, residential, or institutional staff; . . . who knows, or has reasonable cause to suspect, that a vulnerable adult has been or is being abused, neglected, or exploited shall immediately report such knowledge or suspicion to the central abuse hotline. Fla. Stat. Ann. §415.1034 (2006).

Section 415.1034(b) describes specific types of information about the alleged victim, perpetrator, and types of injuries. Persons who knowingly and willfully fail to make reports or who prevent others from doing so are subject to misdemeanor criminal liability. Id. §415.111. Persons who report matters in good faith are immune from statutory liability.

Notes: Statutory Disclosure Obligations

1. *Structure of Statutory Obligations.* Each state imposes disclosure obligations on health care professionals by statute. The statute typically will establish (1) who has the duty to disclose information; (2) the events or information that must be disclosed; (3) to whom the information must be disclosed; and (4) the immunities or liabilities associated with the disclosure obligation. State disclosure obligations generally apply to a wide range of licensed health professions, such as physicians, nurses, nursing home staff members, social workers, and others. The HIPAA privacy rules permit providers to make these disclosures. 45 C.F.R. §164.512.

2. *Types of Disclosure Duties.* Most disclosure obligations are associated with the risk of harm to others through criminal activity or the transmission of disease. The Florida statute focuses on the danger of elder abuse, a matter of particular concern in retirement communities. The disclosure duty stems from concerns that members of this group may not be able to communicate their abuse to others. Like other states, Florida imposes a similar disclosure obligation for instances of suspected child abuse. Fla. Stat. Ann. §39.201 (2007).

States also require physicians and others to report gunshot or knife wounds to police authorities. See, e.g., N.Y. Penal Law §265.25 (McKinney 2007). See generally Mark A. Hall, Hospital and Physician Disclosure of Information Concerning a Patient's Crime, 63 U. Det. L. Rev. 145 (1985). The disclosure will alert appropriate authorities to the probability that a crime has occurred, but it is not especially helpful in preventing imminent harm. Citizens do not have a general obligation to disclose possible criminal activity; what justifies the existence of a disclosure obligation here? Arguably, the health care provider who gives medical treatment to a gunshot victim is more than a passive bystander, insofar as he or she may help perpetrators to elude law enforcement officers. In addition, the ordinary rules favoring confidentiality may not apply; individuals who have been shot or knifed may be highly motivated to seek health care whether or not their treatment will be confidential.

What about wounds not serious enough to fall within the scope of a reporting statute but which might nonetheless reveal evidence of criminal activity? Suppose that a district attorney serves grand jury subpoenas duces tecum on nearly two dozen hospitals, seeking "[a]ny and all records pertaining to any male Caucasian patient between the ages of 30 to 45 years, . . . [treated during a two-day period] for a laceration, puncture wound or slash, or other injury caused by or possibly caused by a cutting instrument and/or sharp object, said injury being plainly observable to a lay person without expert or professional knowledge. . . ." The subpoenas expressly exclude from discovery information obtained by licensed health care professionals obtained while attending the patient and necessary to provide care for the patient. Should the hospitals comply? See In re Grand Jury Investigation in New York County, 779 N.E.2d 173 (N.Y. 2002) (upholding appellate decision quashing the subpoenas).

Finally, states also require health care providers to report information about individuals who have been diagnosed with certain contagious or transmissible diseases. See pages 192-194. See also In re Grand Jury Subpoena for Medical Records of Payne, 839 A.2d 837 (N.H. 2004) (statute requiring physicians to report bodily injuries arising from criminal acts insufficient to provide unilateral authority for government subpoena of medical records).

3. *Disclose to Whom?* States require disclosures to different types of state authorities. Some disclosures are made directly to law enforcement personnel. See, e.g., N.Y. Penal Law §265.25 (McKinney 2006) (gunshot wounds disclosed to police). States have also established special "hotlines" for certain types of disclosures, such as those regarding child or elder abuse. See, e.g., Fla. Stat. Ann. §39.201 (2007). Contagious or transmissible disease reports are most often directed to state public health authorities. See, e.g., Fla. Stat. Ann. 384.25 (2007) (sexually transmitted diseases reported to health department). The statutes generally provide that the confidentiality of some types of reported information will be protected from further disclosure. See, e.g., id. These confidentiality protections may be constitutionally required. See pages 178-179.

4. *Immunities and Liabilities.* Providers who file mandatory reports about diseases or abuse are usually immune from damages for any mistake and resulting harm. See Zamstein v. Marvasti, 692 A.2d 781 (Conn. 1997). But see Runyon v. Smith, 749 A.2d 852 (N.J. 2000). Less clear is the legal exposure for a professional who is in a position to file a report, but who fails to do so. Under some statutes, a failure to comply with statutory reporting requirements can lead to criminal or civil liability. New York's child abuse reporting statute provides one example of a typical statutory scheme:

> 1. Any person, official or institution required by this title to report a case of suspected child abuse or maltreatment who willfully fails to do so shall be guilty of a class A misdemeanor.
>
> 2. Any person, official or institution required by this title to report a case of suspected child abuse or maltreatment who knowingly and willfully fails to do so shall be civilly liable for the damages proximately caused by such failure. N.Y. Social Services Law §420 (McKinney 2006).

Should children injured by a provider's failure to report child abuse be permitted to bring suit in jurisdictions where the reporting statute does not include a specific civil remedy? Courts are divided. See Annot., 73 A.L.R.4th 782 (1989). Should a subsequent child abuse victim be permitted to sue the provider on the theory that if the provider had reported the first victim the second victim would not have been at risk? Marcelletti v. Bathani, 500 N.W.2d 124 (Mich. Ct. App. 1993) (no). A provider's failure to follow reporting rules can also spark professional disciplinary action. In the Matter of Schroeder, 415 N.W.2d 436 (Minn. Ct. App. 1988). Should a health care provider have a duty to disclose the limits of confidentiality before providing services to her patients? See Marks v. Tenbrunsel, 910 So.2d 1255 (Alabama 2005) (patient not permitted to pursue claim against psychologist who reported alleged child abuse even though patient claims he was assured of confidentiality); Hayes v. State, 667 N.E.2d 222 (Ind. Ct. App. 1996) (holding that therapist had no duty to warn client that disclosures of child sexual abuse would be reported to state authorities).

5. *Common Law Disclosure Requirements.* As the next case reveals, disclosure obligations also arise under common law.

■ BRADSHAW v. DANIEL
854 S.W.2d 865 (Tenn. 1993)

ANDERSON, Justice.

We granted this appeal to determine whether a physician has a legal duty to warn a nonpatient of the risk of exposure to the source of his patient's noncontagious disease — Rocky Mountain Spotted Fever. . . .

On July 19, 1986, Elmer Johns went to the emergency room at Methodist Hospital South in Memphis, Tennessee, complaining of headaches, muscle aches, fever, and chills. He was admitted to the hospital under the care and treatment of the defendant, Dr. Chalmers B. Daniel, Jr. Dr. Daniel first saw Johns on July 22, 1986, at which time he ordered the drug Chloramphenicol, which is the drug of choice for a person in the latter stages of Rocky Mountain Spotted Fever. Johns' condition rapidly deteriorated, and he died the next day, July 23, 1986. An autopsy was performed, and the Center for Disease Control in Atlanta conclusively confirmed, in late September 1986, that the cause of death was Rocky Mountain Spotted Fever. Although Dr. Daniel communicated with Elmer Johns' wife, Genevieve, during Johns' treatment, he never advised her of the risks of exposure to Rocky Mountain Spotted Fever, or that the disease could have been the cause of Johns' death.

A week after her husband's death, on August 1, 1986, Genevieve Johns came to the emergency room of Baptist Memorial Hospital in Memphis, Tennessee, with similar symptoms of chills, fever, mental disorientation, nausea, lung congestion, myalgia, and swelling of the hands. She was admitted to the hospital and treated for Rocky Mountain Spotted Fever, but she died three days later, on August 4, 1986, of that disease. It is undisputed that no patient-physician relationship existed between Genevieve Johns and Dr. Daniel.

The plaintiff, William Jerome Bradshaw, is Genevieve Johns' son. He filed this suit alleging that the defendant's negligence in failing to advise Genevieve Johns that her husband died of Rocky Mountain Spotted Fever, and in failing to warn her of the risk of exposure, proximately caused her death. . . . Dr. Gelfand [an expert witness for the defense] testified that the medical standard of care did not require a physician treating a patient infected with, or suspected of being infected with, Rocky Mountain Spotted Fever to treat the family of the patient in contact with him, or to warn them of the risk of exposure to the disease or the risk of exposure to ticks or tick bites. The plaintiff responded with the affidavit of Dr. Burt Prater. Dr. Prater testified that because of the clustering effect of the disease, the medical standard of care required that a physician treating a patient with symptoms of Rocky Mountain Spotted Fever advise the family of the patient as to the incubation period, the symptoms of the disease, and the need for immediate medical attention upon manifestation of the symptoms. Dr. Prater further testified that the defendant, Dr. Daniel, negligently failed to diagnose Elmer Johns' fatal disease of Rocky Mountain Spotted Fever and failed to warn his wife, Genevieve Johns, of the incubation period of the disease, the symptoms, and the need to seek medical treatment upon manifestation of the symptoms. He also testified that the disease, if untreated, has a 40 percent mortality rate, but if treated promptly, has a 4 percent mortality rate. Based on the affidavits, the defendant's motion for summary judgment was denied. The case was . . . tried before a jury, which returned a verdict of $50,000 against the defendant. . . .

LEGAL DUTY

The defendant physician argues that he owed his patient's wife no legal duty because first, there was no physician-patient relationship, and second, Rocky Mountain Spotted Fever is not a contagious disease and, therefore, there is no duty to warn of the risk of exposure.

We begin our analysis by examining how we determine when a legal duty may be imposed upon one for the benefit of another. While duty was not part of the early English common law jurisprudence of tort liability, it has since become an essential element in negligence cases. . . . [T]he imposition of a legal duty reflects society's contemporary policies and social requirements concerning the right of individuals and the general public to be protected from another's act or conduct. Indeed, it has been stated that " 'duty' is not sacrosanct in itself, but is only an expression of the sum total of those considerations of policy which lead the law to say that the plaintiff is entitled to protection." W. Keeton, Prosser and Keeton on the Law of Torts §53 at 358. . . .

The defendant contends that the absence of a physician-patient relationship negates the existence of a duty in this case. While it is true that a physician-patient relationship is necessary to the maintenance of a medical malpractice action, it is not necessary for the maintenance of an action based on negligence, and this Court has specifically recognized that a physician may owe a duty to a nonpatient third party for injuries caused by the physician's negligence, if the injuries suffered and the manner in which they occurred were reasonably foreseeable. Wharton Transport Corp. v. Bridges, 606 S.W.2d 521, 526 (Tenn. 1980) (physician owed duty to third party injured by disabled truck driver's negligence, where the physician was negligent both in his physical examination and certification of the truck driver for the employer).

Here, we are asked to determine whether a physician has an affirmative duty to warn a patient's family member about the symptoms and risks of exposure to Rocky Mountain Spotted Fever, a noncontagious disease. Insofar as we are able to determine, there is no reported decision from this or any other jurisdiction involving circumstances exactly similar to those presented in this case.

We begin by observing that all persons have a duty to use reasonable care to refrain from conduct that will foreseeably cause injury to others. In determining the existence of a duty, courts have distinguished between action and inaction. Professor Prosser has commented that "the reason for the distinction may be said to lie in the fact that by 'misfeasance' the defendant has created a new risk of harm to the plaintiff, while by 'nonfeasance' he has at least made his situation no worse, and has merely failed to benefit him by interfering in his affairs." Prosser, §56 at 373.

Because of this reluctance to countenance nonfeasance as a basis of liability, as a general rule, under the common law, one person owed no affirmative duty to warn those endangered by the conduct of another. Prosser, §56 at 374; Tarasoff v.

Regents of University of California, 17 Cal. 3d 425 (1976). To mitigate the harshness of this rule, courts have carved out exceptions for cases in which the defendant stands in some special relationship to either the person who is the source of the danger, or to the person who is foreseeably at risk from the danger. Accordingly,

> while an actor is always bound to prevent his acts from creating an unreasonable risk to others, he is under the affirmative duty to act to prevent another from sustaining harm only when certain socially recognized relations exist which constitute the basis for such legal duty. Harper & Kime, The Duty to Control the Conduct of Another, 43 Yale L.J. 886, 887 (1934).

One of the most widely known cases applying that principle is *Tarasoff*, supra, in which the California Supreme Court held that when a psychotherapist determines or, pursuant to the standards of his profession, should determine that his patient presents a serious danger of violence to another, the therapist has an affirmative duty to use reasonable care to protect the intended victim against such danger, and the duty may require the physician to warn the intended victim of the danger. The special relationship of the patient to his psychotherapist supported imposition of the affirmative duty to act for the benefit of third persons. . . .

Decisions of other jurisdictions have employed the same analysis and held that the relationship of a physician to his patient is sufficient to support the duty to exercise reasonable care to protect third persons against foreseeable risks emanating from a patient's physical illness. Specifically, other courts have recognized that physicians may be liable to persons infected by a patient, if the physician negligently fails to diagnose a contagious disease, or having diagnosed the illness, fails to warn family members or others who are foreseeably at risk of exposure to the disease. . . . [S]ee generally Annot., 3 A.L.R.5th 370 (1992). . . .

Returning to the facts of this case, first, it is undisputed that there was a physician-patient relationship between Dr. Daniel and Elmer Johns. Second, here, as in the contagious disease context, it is also undisputed that Elmer Johns' wife, who was residing with him, was at risk of contracting the disease. This is so even though the disease is not contagious in the narrow sense that it can be transmitted from one person to another. Both Dr. Daniel and Dr. Prater, the plaintiff's expert, testified that family members of patients suffering from Rocky Mountain Spotted Fever are at risk of contracting the disease due to a phenomenon called clustering, which is related to the activity of infected ticks who transmit the disease to humans. Dr. Prater also testified that Dr. Daniel negligently failed to diagnose the disease and negligently failed to warn his patient's wife, Genevieve Johns, of her risk of exposure to the source of disease. Dr. Daniel's expert disputed these conclusions, but Dr. Daniel conceded there is a medical duty to inform the family when there is a diagnosis of the disease. Thus, this case is analogous to the *Tarasoff* line of cases adopting a duty to warn of danger and the contagious disease cases adopting a comparable duty to warn. Here, as in those cases, there was a foreseeable risk of harm to an identifiable third party, and the reasons supporting the recognition of the duty to warn are equally compelling here.

We, therefore, conclude that the existence of the physician-patient relationship is sufficient to impose upon a physician an affirmative duty to warn identifiable third persons in the patient's immediate family against foreseeable risks emanating from a patient's illness. Accordingly, we hold that under the factual circumstances of this case, viewing the evidence in a light most favorable to the plaintiff, the defendant physician had a duty to warn his patient's wife of the risk to her of contracting Rocky Mountain Spotted Fever, when he knew, or in the exercise of reasonable care, should have known, that his patient was suffering from the disease. Our holding here is necessarily limited to the conclusion that the defendant physician owed Genevieve Johns a legal duty. We express no opinion on the other elements which would be required to establish a cause of action for common-law negligence in this case.

Accordingly . . . this cause is remanded to the trial court for proceedings consistent with this opinion. . . .

Notes: Common Law Duty to Warn

1. *Overview.* Was Dr. Daniel negligent in his treatment of his patient, Elmer Johns? Daniel appropriately identified the cause of Johns' illness and provided treatment. On what basis can he be held liable for injuries to someone who was not his patient? The court notes that the existence of a physician-patient relationship generally is a prerequisite to the maintenance of a malpractice action. It finds, however, that the absence of a relationship is no barrier to an ordinary negligence action. See Chapter 2.B.1, discussing a physician's duty to third parties. However, the court still must confront whether there is a "special relationship," due to the oft-described distinction between "misfeasance" and "nonfeasance" (creating a risk of harm versus failing to protect others from a risk of harm created by another). As a general rule, nonfeasance does not constitute actionable negligence. Restatement (Third) Torts §37 (Tentative Draft 4, 2004). The "special relationship" rule is an exception to this principle. Restatement (Third) Torts §41, 42 (Tentative Draft 4, 2004). The key in many third party liability cases therefore is whether there is a "special relationship" that justifies the imposition of liability for nonfeasance. Note that some jurisdictions are hostile toward the expansion of physicians' duties to third parties. See, e.g., Thapar v. Zezulka, 994 S.W.2d 635 (Tex. 1999).

Once the existence of a duty is established, the court must determine its scope. The scope of the duty is determined in large part by the nature of the risk and the physician's ability to reduce the risk reasonably. Note that, in duty to warn situations, some risks can be reduced simply by warning the patient. As an example, suppose that a physician treats a patient for epilepsy and fails to tell the patient to refrain from driving. The patient has a seizure and runs into an oncoming car. Although the physician may have a duty to the driver of the other car, the accident and injury could easily have been avoided by warning the patient not to drive. If the patient had been warned, and had refrained from driving, no breach of confidentiality would have been required and there would have been no conflict between the duty to maintain confidentiality and the duty to protect others from harm. The discussion in this section focuses on the more difficult cases where physicians might have to breach patient confidentiality in order to protect third parties.

2. *Categorizing Cases: A General Theory of Liability or a Laundry List?* The first problem in these common law liability cases lies in determining the existence of a "special relationship." The *Bradshaw* court notes that the physician-patient relationship has been used to support the imposition of liability in cases involving dangerous psychiatric patients and patients with contagious illnesses. Courts have also noted the importance of the physician-patient relationship in some automobile and child abuse cases. Does this indicate that physicians will always be held liable for injuries caused by or to their patients? Or, are courts developing a list of situations in which physicians may be held liable? If so, what principles or factors determine whether the physician owes a duty to the third party? Are disclosure obligations limited to physicians, or do other types of health care professionals face the same threat of liability?

a. *Contagious Diseases.* One well-developed line of cases holds physicians liable for injuries to non-patients caused by communicable diseases. Physicians have been held liable for failing to diagnose the contagious condition. See, e.g., Jones v. Stanko, 160 N.E. 456 (Ohio 1928) (physician fails to diagnose smallpox and puts neighbors at risk for infection). But see Ellis v. Peter, 627 N.Y.S.2d 707 (App. Div. 1995) (failure to diagnose TB; no duty to warn). Liability has also been imposed for failure to warn others about the risk of transmission. See, e.g., Skillings v. Allen, 173 N.W. 663 (Minn. 1919) (negligent failure to disclose risk of transmission of scarlet fever); Gammill v. United States, 727 F.2d 950, 954 (10th Cir. 1984) (physician may be found liable for failing to warn persons at risk for exposure of the danger). But see McNulty v. City of New York, 792 N.E.2d 162 (N.Y. 2003) (defendant physicians did not owe friend of person infected with meningitis a duty to warn her of the risk of infection); Santa Rosa Health Care Corp. v. Garcia, 964 S.W.2d 940 (Tex. 1998) (no duty to warn wife of hemophiliac of risk of HIV). See generally Annot., 3 A.L.R.5th 370 (1992). Note that *Bradshaw* is an extension of this principle — Rocky Mountain Spotted Fever is not contagious but it is likely that others in the patient's household may have come into contact with infected ticks.

Courts also have drawn an analogy between contagious conditions and genetic conditions. What are a physician's obligations when she discovers that a patient has serious heritable genetic condition? *Compare* Safer v. Estate of Pack, 677 A.2d 1188 (N.J. Super. 1996) (physicians have a duty to warn those known to be at risk of avoidable harm from genetically transmissible conditions; duty extends to the physician's patient and to members of the immediate family of the patient who may be adversely affected by a failure to warn; physician may have a duty to warn family members), *with* Pate v. Threlkel, 661 So. 2d 278 (Fla. 1995) (applying contagious disease concepts in context of a genetically transmittable condition but holding that duty met by notifying patient of character of condition). See also Kenneth Offit et al., The "Duty to Warn" a Patient's Family Members about Hereditary Disease Risks, 292 JAMA 1469 (2004); Roberta Berry, The Genetic Revolution and the Physician's Duty of Confidentiality, 18 J. Leg. Med. 401 (1997); Ellen Wright Clayton, What Should the Law Say about Disclosure of Genetic Information to Relatives?, 1 J. Health Care L. & Pol'y 373 (1998); Sonia M. Suter, Whose Genes Are These Anyway? Familial Conflicts over

Access to Genetic Information, 91 Mich. L. Rev. 1854 (1993); K. Wolff et al., Confidentiality versus Duty to Inform—An Empirical Study on Attitudes Toward the Handling of Genetic Information, 143 Am. J. Med. Genet. A. 142 (2007) (most respondents wished to be informed about a hereditary disease in their family; study included consideration of conditions under which breach of confidentiality would be deemed acceptable).

The duty to protect third parties from harm in contagious disease cases has become highly controversial because of the risk of HIV transmission. Do physicians have an obligation to warn third parties when their patients continue to engage in activities that present the risk of HIV transmission? The answer is complicated somewhat by the existence of special statutes protecting the confidentiality of HIV-related information, which may restrict the ability to disclose information even when others may be at risk. See generally Bernard Friedland, HIV Confidentiality and the Right to Warn—The Health Care Provider's Dilemma, 80 Mass. L. Rev. 3 (1995); Sheila Taub, Doctors, AIDS, and Confidentiality in the 1990s, 27 J. Marshall L. Rev. 331 (1994).

b. *Mental Illness*. Another set of cases involve a mental health professional's duty to protect third parties from his or her patient. The leading case is Tarasoff v. Regents of University of California, 551 P.2d 334 (Cal. 1976), discussed briefly in *Bradshaw*. In *Tarasoff*, a therapist knew that a patient had made threats of violence toward a young woman. The therapist unsuccessfully attempted to commit the patient for treatment. The patient murdered the young woman, whose parents then sued the patient's mental health care providers. The California Supreme Court, relying in part on Restatement (Second) of Torts §315, supra, held that psychotherapists could be held liable for failing to exercise reasonable care to protect a third party where the therapists know or should know that their patient presents a serious danger of violence to another. The court held that therapists might have an obligation to warn those at risk and specifically rejected the defendants' contention that such a warning would impermissibly breach client confidentiality. *Tarasoff* was much discussed by commentators through the late 1970s and 1980s. For more current discussion of *Tarasoff* and its progeny, see Fillmore Buckner & Marvin Firestone, Where the Public Peril Begins: 25 Years after *Tarasoff*, 21 J. Legal Med. 187 (2000). See also Annot. 83 A.L.R.3d 1201 (1978).

Tarasoff has been an important opinion, almost always cited by courts and legislative bodies whether it is followed or rejected. See, e.g., Munstermann v. Alegent Health-Immanuel Medical Center, 716 N.W.2d 73 (Neb. 2006) (establishing scope of psychiatrist's liability to third parties); Powell v. Catholic Medical Center, 749 A.2d 301 (N.H. 2000) (discussing implications of state codification of *Tarasoff*-type rule); Estates of Morgan v. Fairfield Family Counseling Center, 673 N.E.2d 1311 (Ohio 1997) (psychiatrist-outpatient relationship is a "special relationship" justifying imposition of duty to protect third parties).

Many jurisdictions have adopted only a narrow reading of *Tarasoff* or have rejected it completely. In Nasser v. Parker, 455 S.E.2d 502 (Va. 1995), for example, the court considered whether the defendant physician and hospital had a duty to warn a victim about the impending release of a former boyfriend who had threatened to kill her. The court noted the special relationship rule found in

§315, but held that no special relationship existed without an additional showing of an ability to control the patient's conduct:

> Accordingly, we disagree with the holding of *Tarasoff* that a doctor-patient relationship or a hospital-patient relationship alone is sufficient, as a matter of law, to establish a "special relation" under Restatement §315(a). Within the context of the Restatement, there is nothing special about the ordinary doctor-patient relationship or hospital-patient relationship. We think there must be added to those ordinary relationships the factor, required by [Restatement] §319, of taking charge of the patient, meaning that the doctor or hospital must be vested with a higher degree of control over the patient than exists in the ordinary doctor-patient or hospital-patient relationship before a duty arises concerning the patient's conduct. Id. at 506. See also Boulanger v. Pol, 900 P.2d 823 (Kan. 1995) (no special relationship between psychiatrist and voluntary mental patient); Thapar v. Zezulka, 994 S.W.2d 635 (Tex. 1999) (no duty to warn). See also Cal. Civ. Code §43.92 (2006) (limiting *Tarasoff*-type liability).

c. *Driving Impairments*. Most driving impairment cases involve the physician's obligation to warn the patient about the risks of driving. See, e.g., Burroughs v. Magee, 118 S.W.3d 323 (Tenn. 2003) (physician owed a duty of care to third parties to inform his patient of the possible adverse impact of medications on driving ability); Weigold v. Patel, 840 A.2d 19 (Conn. App. 2004) (no liability where patient aware of tendency to fall asleep while driving). See generally Annot., 43 A.L.R. 4th 153 (1986). Where a state statute requires physicians to report certain driving impairments, physicians can be held liable for injuries to third parties. See, e.g., Harden by Harden v. Allstate Ins. Co., 883 F. Supp. 963 (D. Del. 1995). But see Praesel v. Johnson, 967 S.W.2d 391 (Tex. 1998) (no negligence per se or common law duty).

3. *A Risk of Harm*. The risk of harm is clear in some cases, particularly those involving serious contagious diseases. The issue is more problematic in the case of psychiatric patients. Can mental health professionals accurately predict which patients will present a risk of harm to others? The *Tarasoff* court used a professional standard of care to measure the scope of the physicians' obligation to third parties: If the defendant knew or should have known of the risk, using professional judgment, then liability may follow. Tarasoff v. Regents of University of California, 551 P.2d 334 (Cal. 1976). See also Estates of Morgan v. Fairfield Family Counseling Center, 673 N.E.2d 1311, 1325 (Ohio 1997) (psychotherapists need not have perfect predictive power).

4. *Foreseeable and Identifiable Third Parties*. Many contagious disease and psychiatric dangerousness cases suggest that a health care provider's duty to disclose is established by a specific risk to foreseeable and identifiable third parties. See, e.g., *Bradshaw* and *Tarasoff*, supra. This requirement serves at least two purposes: It bolsters the sense that the risk of harm is imminent, and it suggests that a disclosure requirement is reasonable. Where a health care provider knows the identity of the person at risk of harm, it seems reasonable to require that that person be warned about the risk. A few courts have also been willing to impose a duty to breach confidentiality even where the risk is more generalized, however. In Schuster v. Altenberg, 424 N.W.2d 159 (Wis. 1988), the court held

that a duty to breach confidentiality existed even in cases where there was no "readily identifiable target" of the patient's violent tendencies. Id. at 172-174. In such cases, the therapist has the duty to inform police so that emergency commitment proceedings can be initiated.

In cases where the claim is based on the physician's failure to disclose information to the *patient* rather than to the injured third parties, courts have not limited liability to situations in which the third party is known or identifiable. See, e.g., Reisner v. Regents of the University of California, 37 Cal. Rptr. 2d 518 (Cal. Ct. App. 1995) (physicians owed a duty to HIV-infected boyfriend to disclose to patient or her parents her HIV status; failure to disclose occurred long before sexual relationship between young people began).

5. *Disclose to Whom?* As noted above, in most cases a physician's duty to third parties is discharged by disclosing the risk to his or her patient. See, e.g., Emerich v. Philadelphia Center for Human Development, Inc., 720 A.2d 1032 (Pa. 1999) (duty satisfied by statement to victim that she should not go to patient's apartment); Pate v. Threlkel, 661 So. 2d 278 (Fla. 1995). Where the patient presents a risk of harm to an identifiable third party, many jurisdictions also will impose a duty to disclose the risk to that person. See, e.g., *Tarasoff*, supra. Sometimes the provider's disclosure obligation can be met through an institutional disclosure mechanism. In Casarez v. NME Hospital, 883 S.W.2d 360 (Tex. App. 1994), for example, a nurse who allegedly contracted HIV from a patient sued the patient's physician for failing to warn him of the patient's condition. The court held that the physician complied with his obligations by notifying the hospital's infection control and quality assurance committees of his patient's condition.

In the absence of a statute, should a court require a physician who knows that a patient presents a risk of harm through driving to disclose this information to state authorities? What if the patient is informed of the risk and states that she will continue to drive despite the danger?

6. *Zone of Reasonable Judgment.* Given the conflicting nature of the duties to disclose and to protect confidentiality, and the ambiguities associated with each duty, do physicians have enough guidance to allow them to avoid liability? Even if the duties were precisely defined, it would be tricky at best to walk the narrow line between them. But where the extent of each duty is uncertain, it may be impossible to avoid liability. Disclosing may give rise to damages or ethical sanctions for breach of confidentiality, whereas keeping quiet may result in damages for injuries caused to others. What's a doctor to do? Should the law provide for a neutral zone between these two duties, in which disclosure is discretionary, but not mandatory? In other words, doctors would have a qualified privilege to disclose if they do so in the good faith belief that disclosure is necessary to prevent harm, but could not be sued for failing to disclose unless_____. The issue then becomes: How would you fill in the blank? See Mark A. Hall, Hospital and Physician Disclosure of Information Concerning a Patient's Crime, 63 U. Det. L. Rev. 145 (1985) (advocating a qualified privilege with respect to the duty to report serious crimes committed by patients).

7. *HIPAA Privacy and the Duty to Disclose.* Note that the federal privacy rules permit covered entities to disclose personally identifiable health information without the patient's authorization or consent in some circumstances:

A covered entity may, consistent with applicable law and standards of ethical conduct, use or disclose protected health information, if the covered entity, in good faith, believes that the use or disclosure: [] [i]s necessary to prevent or lessen a serious and imminent threat to the health or safety of a person or the public; and [] [is] to a person or persons reasonably able to prevent or lessen the threat, including the target of the threat. . . . [45 C.F.R. §164.512.]

Discussion Problems

Consider how you would analyze the following problems. What law(s) or regulations would apply in your state? Will the health care provider have a duty to maintain confidentiality, the authority to breach confidentiality, or a duty to disclose the information?

- A 30-year-old woman meets with a physician who had also treated her mother. The woman asks the physician for specific information about her mother's medical history. The woman argues that she needs the information to determine whether she is at a significantly higher risk for (a) cancer, (b) high blood pressure, or (c) glaucoma. Should it matter whether the woman's mother is deceased? On this last point, see also Jessica Berg, Grave Secrets: Legal and Ethical Analysis of Postmortem Confidentiality, 34 Conn. L. Rev. 81 (2001).
- A drug treatment center's admission form includes the following notice:

  We understand that persons who have problems with drugs and alcohol may fear that treatment information will be disclosed to others, including family members or employers. Rest assured that your medical treatment information will be protected from disclosure as provided by law.

  A patient undergoes voluntary HIV testing and receives a positive test result. May or must the treatment center disclose the patient's HIV status to other patients? What if it appears that the HIV-infected patient has begun a sexual relationship with another patient?
- Law enforcement officials are concerned about another possible Anthrax bioterrorism event. Local authorities approach pharmacies in a particular town, seeking information about recent prescriptions for antibiotics. May the pharmacies release the information to law enforcement officials? Suppose that a physician in the town recently received a call from a patient, inquiring about a prescription for an antibiotic thought to be effective against Anthrax. May or must the physician disclose this information to anyone?

C. INFORMED CONSENT

1. Goals, Aspirations, Policies

In Chapter 1.B.3 and in the introduction to this chapter we explained the obvious fact that the physician-patient relationship is characterized by a huge imbalance of power, owing to the vulnerability of illness and treatment and physicians' vastly superior knowledge and skills. This power imbalance may be further accentuated by economic and cultural factors. What should the medical and legal response be to these inequalities in the physician-patient relationship? Historically, or perhaps apocryphally, a patient's reverence for her physician was a source of comfort and an important underpinning to the psychology of a cure. A wide range of factors — perhaps among them the anti-establishment views of the 1960s, the consumer movement of the 1970s, the startling advances and lingering failures of medical progress, and the expansion of specialties such as "bioethics" and "health law" — have combined to challenge the authority and supremacy of the physician. The most prominent legal tool used by those seeking to reform the physician-patient relationship is the doctrine of informed consent. It is believed that requiring physicians to provide more information to their patients will help to redress the power imbalance problems created by the inequality of knowledge. As you read the materials on informed consent, consider how effective the law has been, or conceivably could be, in accomplishing this reformist mission. Consider also what model the reformists envision for the ideal patient-physician interaction, and whether all (or many) patients actually subscribe to that model.

■ PATIENT-CENTERED MEDICINE:
A PROFESSIONAL EVOLUTION
Christine Laine & Frank Davidoff*
275 JAMA 152, 152-153 (1996)

In the past, physicians commonly withheld diagnostic information from patients with patients' tacit consent. Hippocrates advocated "concealing most things from the patient while you are attending to him . . . revealing nothing of the patient's future or present condition." . . . The attitude[] of Hippocrates . . . would undoubtedly get [him] into trouble today. Patients increasingly expect to know not only their diagnoses, but also details of pathophysiology, treatment options, and prognosis. . . . Patients expect and often demand information that used to be only within physicians' reach, and physicians increasingly expect to share such information with patients.

The transformation in attitudes surrounding disclosure of diagnoses is particularly striking when one considers cancer. . . . A 1961 study . . . revealed that . . . 90 percent of physicians surveyed preferred not to tell cancer patients their diagnoses. . . . [B]y 1979 . . . 97 percent of physicians surveyed preferred to disclose a diagnosis of cancer. . . .

Beyond "honesty is the best policy," the argument for informing patients is that information enables patients to participate in medical decisions. In more physician-centered days, physicians would decide what was best for their patients, and patient participation was limited to compliance with physicians' orders. As medicine becomes more patient centered, participation begins with the patient

---

*Dr. Laine is Senior Deputy Editor, and Dr. Davidoff is now an Editor Emeritus, at the Annals of Internal Medicine, published by the American College of Physicians. Dr. Lane is also affiliated with the Division of Internal Medicine at Jefferson Medical College, Thomas Jefferson University.

helping to decide what the physician will order, and the emphasis shifts from compliance to participation.

■ RETHINKING INFORMED CONSENT
Peter H. Schuck*
103 Yale L.J. 899, 900-905 (1994)

The doctrine requiring physicians to obtain a patient's informed consent before undertaking treatment is relatively young, having first appeared in a recognizable, relatively robust form only in 1957.[1] Yet the values that underlie the doctrine have an ancient pedigree. The consent norm had occupied a prominent and honored place in our legal thought for many centuries before the courts began to develop a jurisprudence of informed consent in health care.[2] Also well established was the cognate notion that consent must be informed or knowledgeable in some meaningful sense if we are to accord it legal or moral significance. . . .

The doctrine of informed consent in health care shared in the more general expansion of American tort liability that proceeded well into the 1980s and that now appears to have stabilized. Everyone, it seems, favors the principle of informed consent; it is "only" the specific details and applications of the doctrine that arouse serious debate. In order to map and enlarge this debate, it is useful to distinguish three different versions of informed consent doctrine. The first is the letter and spirit of the doctrine as developed primarily by courts—the law "in books." The second is the doctrine as imagined, feared, and often caricatured by some physicians—the law "in the mind." The third version, a consequence both of the gap between the first two and of other situational constraints, is the doctrine as actually practiced by clinicians—the law "in action." (Of course, there are almost as many laws-in-action as there are distinct physician-patient relationships.)

Most commentators on informed consent deploy one or more of these versions of the law. Generally (and crudely) speaking, these commentators fall into two camps: idealists and realists. Informed consent idealists—primarily some judges and medical ethicists—advocate a relatively expansive conception of the physician's obligation to disclose and elicit information about risks and alternatives.[18] More specifically, the idealists tend to define informed consent law's pivotal concepts—materiality of risk, disclosure, alternatives, and causation—broadly and subjectively from the perspective of the individual patient rather than that of the professional, while defining the law's exceptions to the duty narrowly. Perhaps most important, idealists emphasize the qualitative dimension

---

* Reprinted by permission of The Yale Law Journal Company and Fred B. Rothman & Company. The author is the Simeon E. Baldwin Professor of Law at Yale Law School.

[1] See Jay Katz, The Silent World of Doctor and Patient 48-84 (1984); see also Ruth R. Faden & Tom L. Beauchamp, A History and Theory of Informed Consent 235-273 (1986).

[2] See, e.g., Ford v. Ford, 10 N.E. 474, 475 (Mass. 1887) [assault defined in part by absence of consent].

[18] See, e.g., Canterbury v. Spence, 464 F.2d 772, 787 (D.C. Cir. 1972) (principle of informed consent requires that physician disclose information that reasonable patient would wish to know in making treatment decisions); Truman v. Thomas, 611 P.2d 902, 906-907 (Cal. 1980) (patient must be apprised of risks of not undergoing treatment, even if she has refused treatment); see also Katz, supra note 1, at 48-84.

of physician-patient interactions concerning treatment decisions. They insist that these interactions be dialogic rather than authoritative, tailored to the individual patient's emotional needs and cognitive capacities rather than formulaic, aimed at maximizing patient autonomy and comprehension rather than mere information flow, and sensitive to the distortions that can be created by power differentials between physician and patient.

The idealists employ a distinctive rhetorical strategy. Capitalizing on the universal support for the principles and goals of informed consent, they point to the often striking difference between the law in books and the law in action — a difference that I call the "informed consent gap." The existence of this gap, they argue, shows that the law in action falls far short of the law in books. Since the law that they think should be in the books is often even more demanding, the true gap is wider still. The problem, then, is not so much the law in books, which tends to demand too little of physicians; rather, it is the laws in action and in the mind. For the idealist, therefore, the goal of reform must be to close the informed consent gap by conforming the law in action, at the very least, to the law now in books.

The realists — primarily practicing physicians — harbor a different vision of informed consent.[20] Although they emphatically do not contest the principle and goals of informed consent, they do question whether most patients really desire the kind of dialogue that the idealists propose. They also question whether, whatever patients desire, the gains in patient autonomy and improved outcomes produced by the dialogue are worth the additional time, money, and needless patient anxiety and confusion that informed consent may entail. Like the idealists, many realists employ a characteristic rhetoric. Rather than master the doctrinal details of the informed consent law in books, they point instead to the law in their minds, which they can easily caricature in order to demonstrate the law's folly. Although some realists do not concede that the law in action actually deviates from the law in their minds, many others readily admit that a gap does in fact exist. To them, however, this gap simply demonstrates how impractical the idealists' vision is and why it cannot be implemented in the demanding world of contemporary clinical practice.

In a real sense, then, informed consent idealists and realists argue past one another, producing a debate that is oblique and inconclusive rather than pointed and fruitful. For several related reasons, it is time to revisit this debate. These reasons include the intense public concern about rising health care costs, the bureaucratization of the physician-patient relationship, and the organization of health care delivery into units with some degree of market power over providers. Is the informed consent gap to be deplored or tolerated? Should physicians' legal obligations to disclose be further expanded, retained in their present form, or reduced? . . .

---

[20] Perhaps the most articulate of the realists is Dr. Thomas P. Duffy. See Thomas P. Duffy, Agamemnon's Fate and the Medical Profession, 9 W. New Eng. L. Rev. 21 (1987) (reviewing and criticizing Jay Katz's approach). Dr. Sherwin Nuland advances a more moderate realist position in his . . . book. See Sherwin B. Nuland, How We Die: Reflections on Life's Final Chapter 258-261, 265-267 (1994) (distinguishing inter alia, between family physicians, who can and should engage in meaningful informed consent dialogue with patients, and specialists, who cannot realistically be expected to do so).

Notes: The Theory and Practice of Informed Consent

1. *Using Legal Rules to Foster Autonomy.* Peter Schuck suggests that informed consent idealists seek to promote individual autonomy while informed consent realists argue that the goals of complete individual autonomy cannot be met, at least not without great cost. As you read the following materials, identify the interests protected by the informed consent doctrine. A number of commentators have concluded that the doctrine fails to protect individual interests or to promote individual autonomy. See, e.g., Jay Katz, Informed Consent—Must It Remain a Fairy Tale?, 10 J. Contemp. Health L. & Pol'y 69 (1993).

Should we blame the law for this shortcoming, or is it inherently incapable of regulating the subtle and minute interactions between doctors and patients? Dr. Jay Katz, one of the law's most visionary and respected advocates of heightened informed consent, believes that "the radically different climate of physician-patient decisionmaking . . . cannot be implemented by judicial, legislative, or administrative orders." Jay Katz, The Silent World of Doctor and Patient 228 (1984). Similarly, a prestigious blue-ribbon ethics commission recognized that

> further evolution of legal standards toward a firmer protection of individual self-determination in medical decisions must be tempered by a recognition of the law's limits as an instrument of social control. . . . [T]he Commission is concerned that efforts to draw the law further into regulating the subtler aspects of relations between patients and health care professionals may prove ineffective, burdensome and ultimately counterproductive.

President's Commission for the Study of Ethical Problems in Medicine and Biomedical and Behavioral Research, Making Health Care Decisions: A Report on the Ethical and Legal Implications of Informed Consent in the Patient-Practitioner Relationship 30, 204, 252 (1982).

For a critique of the current system of patient autonomy and the physician-patient fiduciary relationship see: Roger B. Dworkin, Getting What We Should from Doctors: Rethinking Patient Autonomy and the Doctor-Patient Relationship, 13 Health Matrix 235 (2003); M. Greg Bloche, The Invention of Health Law, 91 Cal. L. Rev. 247 (2003). For a discussion and critique of new models of "shared decisionmaking" in health care, see Carl E. Schneider, Void for Vagueness, Hastings Center Report 10 (January-February 2007).

2. *Informed Consent in Practice.* Also consider the problems raised by the implementation of the doctrine. The process of health care decisionmaking described in narratives by physicians often suggests the irrelevance of the legal framework. See, e.g., Atul Gawande, Complications: A Surgeon's Notes on an Imperfect Science (2002). Has the process of providing informed consent through signed consent forms become as ritualized and meaningless as the exchange of a peppercorn in land transactions? Empirical studies often cast doubt on the efficacy of the practice of informed consent. In one pathbreaking article, Alan Meisel & Loren H. Roth reviewed the empirical data on informed consent. Alan Meisel and Loren H. Roth, Toward an Informed Discussion of Informed Consent: A Review of the Empirical Studies, 25 Ariz. L. Rev. 265 (1983). They found that few patients understood or remembered what they had been told about their

medical condition and treatment options. Other research confirms these findings. In one typical study, patients facing either anterior cervical fusion or lumbar laminectomy were given a training session on the procedures by a neurosurgeon and a clinical nurse specialist with a master's degree in neurosurgery. D. A. Herz, J. E. Looman, & S. K. Lewis, Informed Consent: Is It a Myth?, 30 Neurosurgery 453 (1992). Patients were given a "simple" written test immediately after the training session; the mean patient score was only 43.5 percent. Six weeks later, the mean test score dropped to 38.4 percent. The authors concluded that health care providers "cannot necessarily expect accurate patient or family recall or comprehension. Fulfillment of the doctrine of informed consent by neurosurgeons may very well be mythical." See also A. M. Adams & A. F. Smith, Risk Perception and Communication: Recent Developments and Implications for Anaesthesia, 56 Anaesthesia 745 (2001).

There are a number of explanations for the gap between disclosure and comprehension/retention. Patients are often sick or emotionally vulnerable at the time of the disclosure; information may be presented in a highly technical and incomprehensible fashion; patients may not have the intelligence or educational background necessary to understand medical information; and patients may not feel able to ask important follow-up questions. See, e.g., S. J. Philipson, M. A. Doyle, S. G. Gabram, C. Nightingale & E. H. Philipson, Informed Consent for Research: A Study to Evaluate Readability and Processibility to Effect Change, 43 J. Investig. Med. 459 (1995) (96 percent of consent forms studied found to have readability levels higher than the target level of an eighth grade reading ability). Despite these problems, patients often report that they are satisfied with the informed consent process. See, e.g., F. W. Verheggen, R. Jonkers & G. Kok, Patients' Perceptions on Informed Consent and the Quality of Information Disclosure in Clinical Trials, 29 Patient Educ. Couns. 137 (1996). Informed consent issues are particularly salient in developing countries. See Michael T. Krosin et al., Problems in Comprehension of Informed Consent in Rural and Peri-Urban Mali, West Africa, Clinical Trials 306 (2006).

3. *Information That Is Harmful: Genetics and HIV.* Information is not always welcome. Some types of information may increase anxiety and decrease enjoyment of life without appreciably adding to decisionmaking ability. See Karen Rothenberg, Breast Cancer, the Genetic "Quick Fix," and the Jewish Community, 7 Health Matrix 97 (1997). Imagine a genetic condition associated with the early onset of severe dementia and death for which there is no effective preventive treatment. How many people would want to know how and when they are going to die? But how do you ask whether someone wants to know this without tipping them off to the truth? One solution to this dilemma is to have a more elaborate informed consent process before giving the test, in which patients are told that the information obtained might be upsetting or might affect their ability to obtain life or health insurance or threaten their job security. Then patients could choose not to be tested at all. See Consensus Statement, Genetic Testing for Susceptibility to Adult-Onset Cancer: The Process and Content of Informed Consent, 277 JAMA 1467 (1997); American Society of Clinical Oncology, Policy Statement Update: Genetic Testing for Cancer Susceptibility, 21 J. Clin. Onc. 2397 (2003). This expansive approach to pretest counseling obviously would put a crimp in the approach that many clinicians take toward routine testing, in which

screening tests are done without any notice at all, much less with elaborate informed consent.

Advances in genetics raise an additional dilemma. If one patient wants the information and consents to testing, does this invade the privacy of family members who may not want to know the information or even to have the information created? Again, they might suffer either psychological effects or adverse financial effects from insurance or employment. Dworkin argues that genetic medicine requires us to adapt our individual autonomy model of informed consent so that it becomes more family-centered. How would one obtain consent from an extended family? Is agreement by every competent adult required, or only a critical mass, or only a single family matriarch or patriarch?

4. *Do Patients Want Decisional Autonomy?* Several commentators have argued that patients want to be informed but do not actually want to make their own health care decisions. Carl Schneider, a law professor at the University of Michigan, after reviewing empirical studies of patient interest in medical decisionmaking, concluded:

> Taken as a whole, these studies surveyed a considerable variety of populations — from the perfectly well to the dangerously sick. They asked patients about their own conditions and about hypothetical illnesses. They framed their respondent's choices in a variety of ways. And their virtually universal conclusion was that, while patients commonly wish to be informed about their medical circumstances, at least a quite substantial number of them did not want to make their own medical decisions, or perhaps even to participate in those decisions in any very significant way. . . .
>
> One might suppose that if patients were ever to assert their decisional authority it would be after hearing the alarming recitation of risks that characterizes the process of informed consent. Yet a number of studies of that process "strongly suggest that refusals attributable to disclosures are rarely, if ever, seen." Similarly, a study of why patients refuse treatment found an average of 4.6 refusals per 100 patient days. The reasons for refusal were complex, and generally there was more than one "cause" per patient. But two kinds of reasons stood out: first, a failure to tell the patient about the purpose of what was proposed; second, psychological factors, prominently including "characterological factors" (for example, using a refusal to accept treatment as a way of expressing a wish to be cared for) and "other psychoses." While the first of these causes reconfirms the wish for information we have so frequently encountered, neither of them is inconsistent with a reluctance to take control of medical decisions. And the dog that did not bark in the night is the absence of any significant number of patients who heard a doctor's recommendation and reached a different conclusion on the merits. Carl E. Schneider, Bioethics with a Human Face, 69 Ind. L.J. 1075, 1097, 1099 (1994). Professor Schneider also noted significant evidence that "the more severe a patient's illness, the less likely the patient is to want to make medical decisions." Id. at 1101.

5. *Individual Autonomy as a Cultural Norm.* Some have argued that the law in this area represents an obsession with Western values and norms that seem less relevant to those from other cultures. For cultural and comparative perspectives on the doctrine, see Leslie J. Blackhall et al., Ethnicity and Attitudes Toward Patient Autonomy, 274 JAMA 820 (1995); Joseph A. Carrese & Lorna A. Rhodes, Western Bioethics on the Navajo Reservation: Benefit or Harm?, 274 JAMA 826

(1995); Lawrence O. Gostin, Informed Consent, Cultural Sensitivity, and Respect for Persons, 274 JAMA 844 (1995); Frances H. Miller, Denial of Health Care and Informed Consent in English and American Law, 18 Am. J.L. & Med. 37 (1992); Kristina Orfali & Elisa J. Gordon, Autonomy Gone Awry: A Cross-Cultural Study of Parents' Experiences in Neonatal Intensive Care Units, 25 Theoretical Med. 329 (2004).

6. *Individual Autonomy and Medical Research.* Commentators have been particularly concerned with the role of informed consent in medical research. See, e.g., George J. Annas, Questing for Grails: Duplicity, Betrayal and Self-Deception in Postmodern Medical Research, 12 J. Contemp. Health L. & Pol'y 297 (1996); Ruth R. Faden & Tom L. Beauchamp, A History and Theory of Informed Consent 151-232 (1986). The issue is explored in greater depth at pages 245-247.

7. *Informed Consent v. Traditional Malpractice.* Despite academic interest, informed consent theories play a role in a relatively small percentage of claims against physicians, at least as measured by opinions published in computerized databases such as Westlaw. As you read these materials, consider the role that informed consent theories appear to play in traditional malpractice litigation. Of what relevance is it that informed consent claims are rarely brought alone but are most often seen in cases where plaintiffs also are asserting traditional negligence claims?

8. *The Spectrum of Informed Consent Standards.* Both courts and legislatures have participated in the redefinition of the roles in the physician-patient relationship. They have responded to the inequality in knowledge between providers and patients in at least four distinct ways. Some jurisdictions, about half in fact, use some version of a "professional malpractice" standard, under which physicians are required to disclose to patients that information which would have been disclosed by the reasonable, minimally competent physician. (See Chapter 4 for a detailed discussion of the theory of malpractice claims.) A substantial number of states use the "material risk" or "reasonable patient" standard, which requires disclosure of risks that a reasonable patient would consider to be material in making a medical treatment decision. A small number of jurisdictions take an even more protective approach, requiring disclosure of information that a particular patient (as contrasted with a "rational" patient) would have wanted to make his or her decision. Finally, courts seeking tools to regulate the nature of the physician-patient relationship have recently turned to fiduciary law as a source of additional disclosure obligations for physicians.

9. *Additional Commentaries.* The literature in this area is voluminous. Some particularly useful law review commentaries (in addition to those cited in Schuck's article) include Jamie Staples King & Benjamin W. Moulton, Rethinking Informed Consent: The Case for Shared Medical Decision-Making, 32 Amer. J. L. & Med. 429 (2006); Sheldon F. Kurtz, The Law of Informed Consent: From "Doctor Is Right" to "Patient Has Rights," 50 Syracuse L. Rev. 1243 (2000); Grant H. Morris, Dissing Disclosure: Just What the Doctor Ordered, 44 Ariz. L. Rev. 313 (2002); William M. Sage, Regulating Through Information: Disclosure Laws and American Health Care, 99 Colum. L. Rev. 1701 (1999); Marjorie Maguire Schultz, From Informed Consent to Patient Choice: A New Protected Interest, 95 Yale L.J. 219 (1985). For a classic attack on the fundamental theory of informed consent liability,

see Richard Epstein, Medical Malpractice: The Case for Contract, 1976 Am. Bar. Found. Res. J. 87. The major treatise is Fay A. Rozovsky, Consent to Treatment: A Practical Guide (2000). There are several important books on the subject, including Carl E. Schneider, The Practice of Autonomy: Patients, Doctors, and Medical Decisions (1998); Ruth R. Faden & Tom L. Beauchamp, A History and Theory of Informed Consent (1986); Jessica W. Berg et al., Informed Consent: Legal Theory and Practice (2001). For general discussions of informed consent, see George P. Smith, II, The Vagaries of Informed Consent, 1 Ind. Health L. Rev. 109 (2004); and Annot., 88 A.L.R. 3d 1008 (1978).

2. The Competing Disclosure Standards

■ CANTERBURY v. SPENCE
464 F.2d 772 (D.C. Cir.), cert. denied, 409 U.S. 1064 (1972)

[Appellant Canterbury, a 19-year-old clerk-typist who had experienced persistent back pain, sought care from Dr. Spence. Dr. Spence conducted a number of tests to determine the cause of the back pain and eventually recommended that Canterbury undergo a laminectomy. According to the court, Canterbury "did not raise any objection to the proposed operation nor did he probe into its exact nature." Dr. Spence spoke with Canterbury's mother by telephone. She asked "if the recommended operation was serious and Dr. Spence replied 'not any more than any other operation.'" It is unclear whether Mrs. Canterbury consented to the operation before it took place; she did sign a consent form afterward. The laminectomy was performed without any apparent difficulties. During the recovery period, however, hospital personnel failed to assist Canterbury during the process of voiding, and Canterbury fell out of his bed while attempting to void. Canterbury developed signs of partial paralysis a few hours after the fall, which were only partially improved by another operation.]

At the time of the trial . . . [he] required crutches to walk, still suffered from urinal incontinence and paralysis of the bowels, and wore a penile clamp. . . . [H]e [had] held a number of jobs, but had constant trouble finding work because he needed to remain seated and close to a bathroom. The damages appellant claims include extensive pain and suffering, medical expenses, and loss of earnings.

Appellant filed suit in the district court on March 7, 1963, four years after the laminectomy and approximately two years after he attained his majority. The complaint stated several causes of action against each defendant. Against Dr. Spence it alleged, among other things, negligence in the performance of the laminectomy and failure to inform him beforehand of the risk involved. Against the hospital the complaint charged negligent postoperative care in permitting appellant to remain unattended after the laminectomy, in failing to provide a nurse or orderly to assist him at the time of his fall, and in failing to maintain a side rail on his bed. . . .

At the close of appellant's case in chief, each defendant moved for a directed verdict and the trial judge granted both motions. . . . The judge did not allude specifically to the alleged breach of duty by Dr. Spence to divulge the possible consequences of the laminectomy.

We reverse. The testimony of appellant and his mother that Dr. Spence did not reveal the risk of paralysis from the laminectomy made out a prima facie case of violation of the physician's duty to disclose which Dr. Spence's explanation did not negate as a matter of law. . . .

Suits charging failure by a physician[6] adequately to disclose the risks and alternatives of proposed treatment are not innovations in American law. They date back a good half-century, and in the last decade they have multiplied rapidly. There is, nonetheless, disagreement among the courts and the commentators on many major questions, and there is no precedent of our own directly in point. For the tools enabling resolution of the issues on this appeal, we are forced to begin at first principles.

The root premise is the concept, fundamental in American jurisprudence, that "[e]very human being of adult years and sound mind has a right to determine what shall be done with his own body. . . ."[12] True consent to what happens to one's self is the informed exercise of a choice, and that entails an opportunity to evaluate knowledgeably the options available and the risks attendant upon each. The average patient has little or no understanding of the medical arts, and ordinarily has only his physician to whom he can look for enlightenment with which to reach an intelligent decision. From these almost axiomatic considerations springs the need, and in turn the requirement, of a reasonable divulgence by physician to patient to make such a decision possible.[15]

A physician is under a duty to treat his patient skillfully but proficiency in diagnosis and therapy is not the full measure of his responsibility. The cases demonstrate that the physician is under an obligation to communicate specific information to the patient when the exigencies of reasonable care call for it. . . .

A reasonable revelation in these respects is not only a necessity but, as we see it, is as much a matter of the physician's duty. It is a duty to warn of the dangers lurking in the proposed treatment, and that is surely a facet of due care. It is, too, a duty to impart information which the patient has every right to expect. The patient's reliance upon the physician is a trust of the kind which traditionally has exacted obligations beyond those associated with arms length transactions. His dependence upon the physician for information affecting his well-being, in terms of contemplated treatment, is well-nigh abject. As earlier noted, long before the instant litigation arose, courts had recognized that the physician had the responsibility of satisfying the vital informational needs of the patient. More recently, we ourselves have found "in the fiducial qualities of [the physician-patient] relationship the physician's duty to reveal to the patient that which in his

---

[6] Since, there was neither allegation nor proof that the appellee hospital failed in any duty to disclose, we have no occasion to inquire as to whether or under what circumstances such a duty might arise.

[12] Schloendorff v. Society of New York Hospital, 211 N.Y. 125, 105 N.E. 92, 93 (1914). . . .

[15] In duty-to-disclose cases, the focus of attention is more properly upon the nature and content of the physician's divulgence than the patient's understanding or consent. Adequate disclosure and informed consent are, of course, two sides of the same coin — the former a sine qua non of the latter. But the vital inquiry on duty to disclose relates to the physician's performance of an obligation, while one of the difficulties with analysis in terms of "informed consent" is its tendency to imply that what is decisive is the degree of the patient's comprehension. As we later emphasize, physician discharges the duty when he makes a reasonable effort to convey sufficient information although the patient, without fault of the physician, may not fully grasp it. . . .

best interests it is important that he should know." We now find, as a part of the physician's overall obligation to the patient, a similar duty of reasonable disclosure of the choices with respect to proposed therapy and the dangers inherently and potentially involved.

This disclosure requirement, on analysis, reflects much more of a change in doctrinal emphasis than a substantive addition to malpractice law. It is well established that the physician must seek and secure his patient's consent before commencing an operation or other course of treatment. It is also clear that the consent, to be efficacious, must be free from imposition upon the patient. It is the settled rule that therapy not authorized by the patient may amount to a tort—a common law battery—by the physician. And it is evident that it is normally impossible to obtain a consent worthy of the name unless the physician first elucidates the options and the perils for the patient's edification. Thus the physician has long borne a duty, on pain of liability for unauthorized treatment, to make adequate disclosure to the patient.[36] . . .

Duty to disclose has gained recognition in a large number of American jurisdictions, but more largely on a different rationale. The majority of courts dealing with the problem have made the duty depend on whether it was the custom of physicians practicing in the community to make the particular disclosure to the patient. . . . We agree that the physician's noncompliance with a professional custom to reveal, like any other departure from prevailing medical practice, may give rise to liability to the patient. We do not agree that the patient's cause of action is dependent upon the existence and nonperformance of a relevant professional tradition.

There are, in our view, formidable obstacles to acceptance of the notion that the physician's obligation to disclose is either germinated or limited by medical practice. To begin with, the reality of any discernible custom reflecting a professional consensus on communication of option and risk information to patients is open to serious doubt. We sense the danger that what in fact is no custom at all may be taken as an affirmative custom to maintain silence, and that physician-witnesses to the so-called custom may state merely their personal opinions as to what they or others would do under given conditions. . . . Respect for the patient's right of self-determination on particular therapy demands a standard set by law for physicians rather than one which physicians may or may not impose upon themselves.

More fundamentally, the majority rule overlooks the graduation of reasonable-care demands in Anglo-American jurisprudence and the position of professional custom in the hierarchy. . . .

There is . . . no basis for operation of the special medical standard where the physician's activity does not bring his medical knowledge and skills peculiarly into play. . . .

---

[36] We discard the thought that the patient should ask for information before the physician is required to disclose. Caveat emptor is not the norm for the consumer of medical services. Duty to disclose is more than a call to speak merely on the patient's request, or merely to answer the patient's questions; it is a duty to volunteer, if necessary, the information the patient needs for intelligent decision. The patient may be ignorant, confused, over-awed by the physician or frightened by the hospital, or even ashamed to inquire. See generally Note, Restructuring Informed Consent: Legal Therapy for the Doctor-Patient Relationship, 79 Yale L.J. 1533, 1545-1551 (1970). . . .

[T]he physician's duty to disclose is governed by the same legal principles applicable to others in comparable situations, with modifications only to the extent that medical judgment enters the picture. We hold that the standard measuring performance of that duty by physicians, as by others, is conduct which is reasonable under the circumstances.

Once the circumstances give rise to a duty on the physician's part to inform his patient, the next inquiry is the scope of the disclosure the physician is legally obliged to make. The courts have frequently confronted this problem but no uniform standard defining the adequacy of the divulgence emerges from the decisions. . . .

The larger number of courts, as might be expected, have applied tests framed with reference to prevailing fashion within the medical profession. . . .

In our view, the patient's right of self-decision shapes the boundaries of the duty to reveal. That right can be effectively exercised only if the patient possesses enough information to enable an intelligent choice. The scope of the physician's communications to the patient, then, must be measured by the patient's need, and that need is the information material to the decision. Thus the test for determining whether a particular peril must be divulged is its materiality to the patient's decision: All risks potentially affecting the decision must be unmasked. And to safeguard the patient's interest in achieving his own determination on treatment, the law must itself set the standard for adequate disclosure.

Optimally for the patient, exposure of a risk would be mandatory whenever the patient would deem it significant to his decision, either singly or in combination with other risks. Such a requirement, however, would summon the physician to second-guess the patient, whose ideas on materiality could hardly be known to the physician. That would make an undue demand upon medical practitioners, whose conduct, like that of others, is to be measured in terms of reasonableness. Consonantly with orthodox negligence doctrine, the physician's liability for nondisclosure is to be determined on the basis of foresight, not hindsight; no less than any other aspect of negligence, the issue on nondisclosure must be approached from the viewpoint of the reasonableness of the physician's divulgence in terms of what he knows or should know to be the patient's informational needs. . . .

From these considerations we derive the breadth of the disclosure of risks legally to be required. The scope of the standard is not subjective as to either the physician or the patient; it remains objective with due regard for the patient's informational needs and with suitable leeway for the physician's situation. In broad outline, we agree that "[a] risk is thus material when a reasonable person, in what the physician knows or should know to be the patient's position, would be likely to attach significance to the risk or cluster of risks in deciding whether or not to forego the proposed therapy."

The topics importantly demanding a communication of information are the inherent and potential hazards of the proposed treatment, the alternatives to that treatment, if any, and the results likely if the patient remains untreated. The factors contributing significance to the dangerousness of a medical technique are, of course, the incidence of injury and the degree of the harm threatened. A very small chance of death or serious disablement may well be significant; a potential disability which dramatically outweighs the potential benefit of the therapy or the detriments of the existing malady may summons discussion with the patient.

There is no bright line separating the significant from the insignificant; the answer in any case must abide a rule of reason. Some dangers — infection, for example — are inherent in any operation; there is no obligation to communicate those of which persons of average sophistication are aware. Even more clearly, the physician bears no responsibility for discussion of hazards the patient has already discovered, or those having no apparent materiality to patients' decision on therapy. . . .

No more than breach of any other legal duty does nonfulfillment of the physician's obligation to disclose alone establish liability to the patient. An unrevealed risk that should have been made known must materialize, for otherwise the omission, however unpardonable, is legally without consequence. Occurrence of the risk must be harmful to the patient, for negligence unrelated to injury is nonactionable. And, as in malpractice actions generally, there must be a causal relationship between the physician's failure to adequately divulge and damage to the patient.

A causal connection exists when, but only when, disclosure of significant risks incidental to treatment would have resulted in a decision against it. The patient obviously has no complaint if he would have submitted to the therapy notwithstanding awareness that the risk was one of its perils. On the other hand, the very purpose of the disclosure rule is to protect the patient against consequences which, if known, he would have avoided by forgoing the treatment. The more difficult question is whether the factual issue on causality calls for an objective or a subjective determination. . . .

It has been assumed that the issue is to be resolved according to whether the factfinder believes the patient's testimony that he would not have agreed to the treatment if he had known of the danger which later ripened into injury. . . .

In our view, this method of dealing with the issue on causation comes in second-best. It places the physician in jeopardy of the patient's hindsight and bitterness. It places the factfinder in the position of deciding whether a speculative answer to a hypothetical question is to be credited. It calls for a subjective determination solely on testimony of a patient-witness shadowed by the occurrence of the undisclosed risk.

Better it is, we believe, to resolve the causality issue on an objective basis: in terms of what a prudent person in the patient's position would have decided if suitably informed of all perils bearing significance. If adequate disclosure could reasonably be expected to have caused that person to decline the treatment because of the revelation of the kind of risk or danger that resulted in harm, causation is shown, but otherwise not. The patient's testimony is relevant on that score of course but it would not threaten to dominate the findings. . . .

In the context of trial of a suit claiming inadequate disclosure of risk information by a physician, the patient has the burden of going forward with evidence tending to establish prima facie the essential elements of the cause of action, and ultimately the burden of proof — the risk of nonpersuasion — on those elements. . . . The burden of going forward with evidence pertaining to a privilege not to disclose, however, rests properly upon the physician. . . .

We now delineate our view on the need for expert testimony in nondisclosure cases. . . .

The guiding consideration our decisions distill, however, is that medical facts are for medical experts and other facts are for any witnesses — expert or not — having sufficient knowledge and capacity to testify to them. It is evident that many of the issues typically involved in nondisclosure cases do not reside peculiarly within the medical domain. Lay witness testimony can competently establish a physician's failure to disclose particular risk information, the patient's lack of knowledge of the risk, and the adverse consequences following the treatment. Experts are unnecessary to a showing of the materiality of a risk to a patient's decision on treatment, or to the reasonably expectable effect of risk disclosure on the decision. These conspicuous examples of permissible uses of nonexpert testimony illustrate the relative freedom of broad areas of the legal problem of risk nondisclosure from the demands for expert testimony that shackle plaintiffs' other types of medical malpractice litigation. . . .

This brings us to the remaining question . . . whether appellant's evidence was of such caliber as to require a submission to the jury. [T]he evidence was clearly sufficient to raise an issue as to whether Dr. Spence's obligation to disclose information on risks was reasonably met or was excused by the surrounding circumstances. Appellant testified that Dr. Spence revealed to him nothing suggesting a hazard associated with the laminectomy. His mother testified that, in response to her specific inquiry, Dr. Spence informed her that the laminectomy was no more serious than any other operation. When, at trial, it developed from Dr. Spence's testimony that paralysis can be expected in 1 percent of laminectomies, it became the jury's responsibility to decide whether that peril was of sufficient magnitude to bring the disclosure duty into play. There was no emergency to frustrate an opportunity to disclose, and Dr. Spence's expressed opinion that disclosure would have been unwise did not foreclose a contrary conclusion by the jury. There was no evidence that appellant's emotional makeup was such that concealment of the risk of paralysis was medically sound. Even if disclosure to appellant himself might have bred ill consequences, no reason appears for the omission to communicate the information to his mother, particularly in view of his minority. The jury, not Dr. Spence, was the final arbiter of whether nondisclosure was reasonable under the circumstances. . . .

Reversed and remanded for new trial.

■ CULBERTSON v. MERNITZ
602 N.E.2d 98 (Ind. 1992)

KRAHULIK, Justice.

Roland B. Mernitz, M.D., (Appellee-Defendant) seeks transfer from the Court of Appeals' reversal of a summary judgment entered in his favor. Culbertson v. Mernitz (1992), Ind. App., 591 N.E.2d 1040. The issue squarely presented in this petition is whether expert medical testimony is required to establish the standard of care of health care providers on the issue of informed consent. . . .

The facts of the case are as follows. Dr. Mernitz first saw Patty Jo Culbertson on March 28, 1988. Her chief complaint was that of uncontrollable leakage of urine and discharge from the vagina. After performing a physical examination, Dr. Mernitz . . . recommend[ed] . . . that she . . . undergo a surgical procedure known as a MMK [Marshall Marchetti Krantz] procedure in order to suspend the bladder and either a hysterectomy or cryosurgery to freeze the infected tip of the cervix. Dr. Mernitz contends that he advised her of the general risks of any surgery, viz. infection, bleeding, and death, and that, with respect to the bladder suspension, he explained to her the risk that the procedure could fail and the possibility that she would be unable to void. . . . Both parties . . . agree that Dr. Mernitz did not advise her of a risk that the cervix could become adhered to the wall of the vagina.

Following this office visit, Mrs. Culbertson decided to proceed with the bladder suspension and cryosurgery. She was admitted to the hospital and underwent these procedures. Post-surgically, Mrs. Culbertson's cervix adhered to the wall of her vagina. Dr. Mernitz prescribed medication for this condition, but Mrs. Culbertson became dissatisfied with his care and saw another surgeon who eventually performed a total abdominal hysterectomy, bilateral salpingo-oophorectomy which involves the removal of both ovaries, and another bladder suspension.

Following this surgery, Mr. and Mrs. Culbertson filed a proposed complaint against Dr. Mernitz with the Indiana Department of Insurance in four counts. . . . Count II alleged that Dr. Mernitz failed to inform Mrs. Culbertson of the alternatives to surgery and the inherent risks and complications of surgery. . . .

A medical review panel was convened and, after submission of evidence to it, issued its written opinion. . . . With respect to the informed consent issue alleged in Count II, the panel ruled:

> The Panel determines that [Dr. Mernitz] did not advise [Mrs. Culbertson] of the complication of cervical adhesion to the vagina; the Panel further determines that such non-disclosure does not constitute a failure to comply with the appropriate standard of care, as such complication is not considered a risk of such surgery requiring disclosure to the patient.

The Culbertsons filed their civil action in a complaint that mirrored the allegations of the proposed complaint. After answering this complaint, Dr. Mernitz moved for summary judgment relying on the expert opinion issued by the medical review panel. The Culbertsons did not file an affidavit or other evidence in opposition to the motion for summary judgment, but argued to the trial court that the "prudent patient" standard should be utilized in evaluating informed consent claims. The trial court entered summary judgment [for the defendants]. . . . [W]e must determine the role, if any, played by expert medical opinion in resolving claims of medical malpractice premised upon a failure to obtain an informed consent.

The courts, historically, have established the standard of care required of physicians when treating patients. The law requires that a physician treating a patient possess and exercise that degree of skill and care ordinarily possessed and exercised by a physician treating such maladies.

. . . In order for a lay jury to know whether a physician complied with the legally prescribed standard of care, expert testimony has generally been held to be required. This requirement was premised on the logical belief that a non-physician could not know what a reasonably prudent physician would or would not have done under the circumstances of any given case. Therefore, an expert familiar with the practice of medicine needed to establish what a reasonably prudent physician would or would not have done in treating a patient in order to set before the jury a depiction of the reasonably prudent physician against which to judge the actions of the defendant physician. An exception was created in cases of res ipsa loquitur on the premise that in such cases a lay jury did not need guidance from a physician familiar with medical practice as to what was required of a reasonably prudent physician because the deficiency of practice "spoke for itself." Kranda v. Houser-Norborg Med. Corp., 419 N.E.2d 1024, 1042 (Ind. App. 1981). This was the settled law of most American jurisdictions, including Indiana, prior to the early 1970s when two cases on the opposite coasts carved out an additional exception to the requirement of expert medical testimony in the area of "informed consent." [The court summarized Cobbs v. Grant, 8 Cal. 3d 229 (1972), and Canterbury v. Spence, 464 F.2d 772 (D.C. Cir.), cert. denied, 409 U.S. 1064 (1972).]

INFORMED CONSENT IN INDIANA JURISPRUDENCE

[The court reviewed Indiana case law and concluded that Indiana followed the medical malpractice standard in informed consent cases. Under this standard, physicians are required to disclose that which the reasonably careful, skillful, and prudent physician would disclose under the same or similar circumstances. In general, medical expert testimony will be required to determine whether a physician has violated her duty, "unless the situation is clearly within the realm of laymen's comprehension."]

Resolution of the issue of the necessity of expert medical testimony in informed consent cases depends on whether the issue is viewed through the eyes of the physician or the patient. When viewed through the eyes of the physician, it is easy to see that a physician should not be required to guess or speculate as to what a hypothetical "reasonably prudent patient" would "need to know" in order to make a determination. A physician should only be required to do that which he is trained to do, namely, conduct himself as a reasonably prudent physician in taking a history, performing a physical examination, ordering appropriate tests, reaching a diagnosis, prescribing a course of treatment, and in discussing with the patient the medical facts of the proposed procedure, including the risks inherent in either accepting or rejecting the proposed course of treatment. From a physician's viewpoint, he should not be called upon to be a "mind reader" with the ability to peer into the brain of a prudent patient to determine what such patient "needs to know," but should simply be called upon to discuss medical facts and recommendations with the patient as a reasonably prudent physician would.

On the other hand, from the patient's viewpoint, the physician should be required to give the patient sufficient information to enable the patient to reasonably exercise the patient's right of self-decision in a knowledgeable manner. Viewed from this vantage point, the patient does not want the medical profession to determine in a paternalistic manner what the patient should or should not be told concerning the course of treatment. Thus, such a patient would view the reasonably prudent physician standard as destroying the patient's right of self-decision and, impliedly, placing such decision under the exclusive domain of the medical profession. While this viewpoint may or may not have been justified in 1972 when *Canterbury* and *Cobbs* were decided, a review of medical ethics standards of care in 1992 should assuage this fear.

The 1992 Code of Medical Ethics, as prepared by the Council on Ethical and Judicial Affairs of the American Medical Association, sets forth the medical profession's standard on informed consent. It reads as follows:

> The patient's right of self-decision can be effectively exercised only if the patient possesses enough information to enable an intelligent choice. The patient should make his own determination on treatment. The physician's obligation is to present the medical facts accurately to the patient or to the individual responsible for his care and to make recommendations for management in accordance with good medical practice. The physician has an ethical obligation to help the patient make choices from among the therapeutic alternatives consistent with good medical practice. Informed consent is a basic social policy for which exceptions are permitted (1) where the patient is unconscious or otherwise incapable of consenting and harm from failure to treat is imminent; or (2) when risk-disclosure poses such a serious psychological threat of detriment to the patient as to be medically contraindicated. Social policy does not accept the paternalistic view that the physician may remain silent because divulgence might prompt the patient to forego needed therapy. Rational, informed patients should not be expected to act uniformly, even under similar circumstances, in agreeing to or refusing treatment.

We recognize this statement as a reasonable statement on the issue of informed consent. There is no need to change Indiana law on this issue. We therefore hold that, except in those cases where deviation from the standard of care is a matter commonly known by lay persons, expert medical testimony is necessary to establish whether a physician has or has not complied with the standard of a reasonably prudent physician.

In the present case we cannot say that the risk of the adherence of the cervix to the vaginal wall is a matter commonly known to lay persons. Therefore, the Culbertsons needed to provide expert medical testimony to refute the unanimous opinion issued by the medical review panel in order to present a material issue of fact as to what a reasonably prudent physician would have discussed concerning this proposed surgery. Without the presentation of such expert medical opinion, the trial court could only conclude that there was no genuine issue of material fact and that summary judgment should be entered for Dr. Mernitz.

[Justice Dickson's dissenting opinion is omitted.]

Notes: Competing Disclosure Standards

1. *The Objective Patient-Centered Standard vs. the Professional Standard.* Why did the *Canterbury* court reject the professional standard of disclosure? One criticism of the malpractice standard is that it measures the scope of required disclosures by

customary practice rather than by the patient's need to know. The *Culbertson* court considered and rejected this argument, noting that the 1992 Code of Medical Ethics promulgated by the American Medical Association recognizes a physician's duty to provide information to patients. Does *Canterbury*'s material risk standard provide any significant additional protections given current norms of medical practice? A recent empirical study suggests that informed consent claims are more likely to succeed in jurisdictions that have adopted the "patient-centered" standard of disclosure. David M. Studdert, et al., Geographic Variation in Informed Consent Law: Two Standards for Disclosure of Treatment Risks, 4 J. Empirical Studies 103 (2007).

2. *The Implications of* Canterbury's *Patient-Centered or Material Risk Standard.* How are providers to know whether a risk should be deemed material? Is there any way for a physician to make this determination before providing care for the patient or before litigating the issue? What factors does the court suggest are relevant to the determination of materiality? How would you advise a physician who is considering whether to inform patients about the following risks associated with a particular type of cosmetic surgery: (1) a .01 percent risk of death from anesthesia; (2) a 1 percent risk of severe bleeding that would require a blood transfusion (which carries additional risks, ranging from fever to heart failure to transmission of HIV); (3) a 3 percent risk of postoperative infection (which would require treatment by antibiotics, which carry a small risk of adverse reactions); (4) a 5 percent risk of nerve damage that could lead to localized paralysis and/or loss of sensation; and (5) a 10 percent risk that the cosmetic flaw will not be significantly improved.

Some legislatures have provided "safe harbors" for physicians. In Texas, for example, a Medical Disclosure Panel determines what disclosures should be made for certain types of procedures. Physicians disclosing risks pursuant to the Panel's guidelines enjoy a rebuttable presumption that their informed consent obligations have been met. Failure to follow the guidelines creates a rebuttable presumption of negligence. Tex. Civ. Prac. & Rem. Code §74.106 (2006).

3. *The Professional Disclosure Standard: The Dominant Rule.* About half of the states still follow the "professional" malpractice standard of disclosure rule in informed consent cases. In some states, the standard has been adopted by the courts; in others it has been imposed by the legislature. Jamie Staples King & Benjamin W. Moulton, Rethinking Informed Consent: The Case for Shared Decision-Making, 32 Amer. J. L. and Med. 429, 493-501 (2006) (state-by-state summary). In these jurisdictions, medical practice determines whether a particular type of information will be disclosed to patients. The standard protects physicians from liability so long as they disclose that which would be disclosed by the reasonably prudent physician under like or similar circumstances. In *Culbertson,* the court suggests that the professional malpractice standard will protect individual autonomy because it incorporates the view that individuals must be given enough information to make intelligent decisions. Was Mrs. Culbertson given enough information in this case?

4. *The Subjective Patient-Centered Disclosure Standard.* Note that the material risk standard requires the disclosure of information that a reasonable person would consider material in making a determination about treatment. In most circumstances, physicians are not required to provide information about risks that

might be considered significant by an individual patient. The *Canterbury* court recognizes this potential defect but finds that the imposition of a subjective disclosure standard would pose an "undue burden" on a physician—unless the physician knows of the patient's idiosyncratic views. See, e.g., Lugenbuhl v. Dowling, 676 So. 2d 602 (La. Ct. App. 1996); Robert Gatter, Informed Consent and the Forgotten Duty of Physician Inquiry, 31 Loy. U. Chi. L.J. 557 (2000). The overwhelming majority of those jurisdictions that use the "material risk" standard have followed the *Canterbury* approach by measuring the scope of disclosure by the objective patient. But cf. Macy v. Blatchford, 8 P.3d 204 (Or. 2000) (evidence of sexual relationship between physician and patient relevant to determine whether physician had met his statutory duty to "explain" proposed treatment because of the possible impact of the relationship on the patient's ability to understand).

5. *Expert Testimony under the Material Risk and Professional Disclosure Standards.* In jurisdictions following the professional disclosure standard, testimony by medical experts obviously will be required to determine whether the defendant met the standard of care. Will a plaintiff in a "material risk" jurisdiction be able to avoid this requirement? Testimony by medical experts will still be required to provide the fact finder with information about the nature and degree of risk associated with particular treatments. Experts may also be needed to help the fact finder determine whether the harm suffered by the plaintiff was caused by the procedure or by the plaintiff's underlying injury. See Annot., 52 A.L.R.3d 1084 (1973).

6. *Whose Duty? Disclosure as a "Professional" Rather Than "Institutional" Obligation.* Another important consequence of the doctrinal origins of the informed consent claim is that its application has been restricted to a limited range of health care professionals. See, e.g., Foster v. Traul, 120 P.3d 278 (Idaho 2005) (physician has duty to obtain informed consent; hospital merely assists in documentation). Should health care institutions have a duty to disclose some types of risks? Should there be an institutional duty to ensure that patients have given their informed consent to care? If so, what should be the doctrinal source of this obligation? The role of hospitals is further discussed infra at page 476 note 6.

7. *Informed Consent and Battery.* Why couldn't claims of this type be resolved using principles from battery cases? Plaintiffs pleading informed consent violations as battery actions have two key advantages: They do not have to prove a deviation from the standard of care and they have greater access to punitive damages awards. There are drawbacks, of course; a battery theory is difficult to apply where the medical treatment is noninvasive, and a defendant's insurance policy may exclude coverage for intentional torts.

In the typical informed consent claim, the patient has given technical consent to being "touched" by the defendant but argues that consent would not have been given if appropriate disclosures had been made. Courts generally reject battery claims because the patient has "consented" to the touching. In most jurisdictions, battery claims are reserved for those situations in which (1) the patient has not consented to any treatment at all, (2) the health care provider performs a completely different procedure than that for which consent was given, (3) the health care provider performs a procedure on the wrong area of the body, or (4) a different, unconsented-to provider performs the procedure. See, e.g, Gragg v. Calandra, 696 N.E.2d 1282 (Ill. App. Ct. 1998) (allegation that hospital conducted open heart surgery and then maintained patient on life support without patient's or family's consent addressed as medical battery); Coulter v. Thomas, 33 S.W.3d 522 (Ky. 2000) (physician's failure to remove blood pressure cuff as requested by patient addressed in battery claim, not under state informed consent statute); Annot., 39 A.L.R.4th 1034 (1985).

8. *Fraud and Misrepresentation.* Health care providers who misrepresent the risks associated with treatments could be held liable for fraud or misrepresentation. See, e.g., Annot., 42 A.L.R.4th 543 (1985).

9. *Free Speech and Informed Consent.* The First Amendment to the U.S. Constitution protects "freedom of speech." Do governmental efforts to regulate the content of physician-patient communication violate the First Amendment? The Supreme Court has upheld the constitutional validity of state laws that impose specific informed consent obligations on physicians performing abortions. Planned Parenthood of Southeastern Pennsylvania v. Casey, 505 U.S. 833, 884, (1992).

Notes: The Other Elements of a Nondisclosure Claim

1. *Elements of a Cause of Action.* Plaintiffs in informed consent claims generally will be required to prove that (1) the medical procedure carried a specific risk that was not disclosed, (2) that the physician violated the applicable standard of disclosure, (3) that the undisclosed risk materialized, and (4) that the failure to disclose the information caused the patient's injury.

2. *The Materialization of the Undisclosed Risk.* All jurisdictions require the plaintiff to show that the undisclosed risk actually materialized into harm. As a result, many failures to disclose information are never litigated. Does this make sense? Can you draw a parallel to the concept of proximate cause in traditional negligence actions? If the purpose of the informed consent doctrine is to protect individual autonomy and to encourage the transfer of information, doesn't a violation of the disclosure obligation cause a cognizable injury even without a physical harm? Several commentators have argued that individual autonomy would be better protected through the adoption of a "dignitary tort" doctrine, in which the failure to disclose information would be actionable even in the absence of any physical injury. See, e.g., Alan Meisel, A "Dignitary Tort" as a Bridge between the Idea of Informed Consent and the Law of Informed Consent, 16 L. Med. & Health Care 210, 211-214 (1988); Aaron D. Twerski & Neil B. Cohen, Informed Decision Making and the Law of Torts: The Myth of Justiciable Causation, 1988 U. Ill. L. Rev. 607, 655; Alan J. Weisbard, Informed Consent: The Law's Uneasy Compromise with Ethical Theory, 65 Neb. L. Rev. 749, 763-764 (1986).

How should damages be measured? "The damages analysis . . . involves a comparison between the condition a plaintiff would have been in had he or she been properly informed and not consented to the risk, with the plaintiff's impaired condition as a result of the risk's occurrence." Howard v. University of Medicine & Dentistry of N.J., 800 A.2d 73 (N.J. 2002). The damages calculations can be more difficult when the patient's initial condition is serious and there are no other alternative treatments.

3. *Objective Causation.* The causation issues associated with informed consent actions are somewhat complex. Most jurisdictions—including those applying the material risk standard—will require proof of objective causation. That is, a plaintiff will be required to show that a reasonable patient would not have undergone the treatment had the risk been disclosed. Does this version of the informed consent doctrine adequately protect the patient's right to the information necessary to participate in medical decisionmaking? Consider the range of circumstances in which the defendant will be found liable for failing to disclose information. The defendant will be held liable only where he or she suggests that a patient undergo a procedure that, had the true risks been disclosed, a reasonable patient would have refused to undergo. Why wouldn't this simply constitute ordinary malpractice?

How much of the "plaintiff's position" is the jury to consider within the limits of objective causation? See Bernard v. Char, 903 P.2d 667, 675-676 (Haw. 1995) (jury permitted to consider whether a reasonable person who was in great pain and who had no health insurance would have opted for tooth extraction or a more expensive root canal procedure); Ashe v. Radiation Oncology Associates, 9 S.W.3d 119, 123-24 (Tenn. 1999) (fact finder applying objective causation rules may take into account characteristics of plaintiff, including "idiosyncrasies, fears, age, medical condition, and religious beliefs"). At what point does the objective causation standard dissolve into a subjective standard?

4. *The Critique of Objective Causation.* Critics of the objective causation standard argue that it undercuts the goal of protecting individual autonomy. The standard is only a rough approximation or a surrogate device for the protection of individual autonomy because it works only so long as the individual is "reasonable." The Oklahoma Supreme Court has agreed:

> The *Canterbury* view certainly severely limits the protection granted an injured patient. To the extent the plaintiff, given an adequate disclosure, would have declined the proposed treatment, and a reasonable person in similar circumstances would have consented, a patient's right of self-determination is irrevocably lost. This basic right to know and decide is the reason for the full-disclosure rule. Accordingly, we decline to jeopardize this right by the imposition of the "reasonable man" standard. . . .
>
> If a plaintiff testifies he would have continued with the proposed treatment had he been adequately informed, the trial is over under either the subjective or objective approach. If he testifies he would not, then the causation problem must be resolved by examining the credibility of plaintiff's testimony. The jury must be instructed that it must find plaintiff would have refused the treatment if he is to prevail.
>
> Although it might be said this approach places a physician at the mercy of a patient's hindsight, a careful practitioner can always protect himself by insuring that he has adequately informed each patient he treats. If he does not breach this duty, a causation problem will not arise. Scott v. Bradford, 606 P.2d 554, 559 (Okla. 1979).

Oklahoma's "subjective causation" approach has not gained many adherents. But see Zalazar v. Vercimak, 633 N.E.2d 1223, 1227 (Ill. App. Ct. 1993) (severely limiting the use of objective causation and expert opinion in informed consent cases arising from cosmetic surgery). For a scholarly analysis of the causation issues in informed cases, see Aaron D. Twerski & Neil B. Cohen, Informed Decision Making and the Law of Torts: The Myth of Justiciable Causation, 1988 U. Ill. L. Rev. 607.

3. Limiting Liability for Failure to Disclose

▮ RIZZO v. SCHILLER
445 S.E.2d 153 (Va. 1994)

HASSELL, Justice.

In this appeal, we consider whether the plaintiffs presented sufficient evidence to establish a prima facie case of medical malpractice against a physician who allegedly failed to obtain the mother's informed consent to use obstetrical forceps to deliver her baby.

Michael Sean Rizzo, Jr., by Pamela Rizzo, his mother and next friend, Pamela Rizzo, individually, and Michael Sean Rizzo, Sr., filed this action against Maurice Schiller, M.D. The plaintiffs alleged that Dr. Schiller, an obstetrician and gynecologist, breached the standard of care owed to them when he assisted Ms. Rizzo with the delivery of Michael. Specifically, the plaintiffs alleged that Dr. Schiller was negligent in the use of obstetrical forceps during the delivery and that he failed to obtain Ms. Rizzo's informed consent to use the forceps.

The case was tried before a jury. The trial court granted Dr. Schiller's motion to strike the plaintiffs' informed consent claim. The case proceeded to the jury on the theory that Dr. Schiller was negligent in the use of the obstetrical forceps. The jury returned a verdict in favor of Dr. Schiller, and we awarded the plaintiffs an appeal on issues related to their informed consent claim.

Pamela Rizzo was admitted to Fairfax Hospital on November 7, 1989, about 9:00 A.M. She was in active labor, and Dr. Schiller was notified of her admission. Upon admission to the hospital, Ms. Rizzo signed the following form:

Authorization for Medical and Surgical Procedures

Patient History No. /P/9456

I hereby authorize Dr. Schiller, and/or other members of the Medical Staff of The Fairfax Hospital of his choice, to perform diagnostic or therapeutic medical and surgical procedures on and to administer anesthetics to Pamela Rizzo. I further authorize The Fairfax Hospital to dispose of any removed tissue or amputated parts.

11/07/89	[Signed] *Pamela S. Rizzo*
(Date)	(Signature)
[Signed] *Vera Thomas*	
(Witness)	(Relationship)

About 12 hours later, Ms. Rizzo's fetal membranes were artificially ruptured at 8:50 P.M., and about 10:00 P.M., she was "pushing with contractions." At 10:15 P.M., Dr. Schiller ordered that Ms. Rizzo be taken to the delivery room. While in the delivery room, Ms. Rizzo made a few, but unsuccessful, attempts to "push" the baby through the birth canal with her abdominal muscles. When Ms. Rizzo's attempts to "push" were unsuccessful, Dr. Schiller told her that he was going to use forceps to deliver the baby. Ms. Rizzo testified that "before I could even get my composure together, ask what they were for, why, [the forceps] were inside me. And my son's head was out, just the head."

[Michael Rizzo developed a subdural hematoma after his birth. Experts testified that the forceps injured his head, causing the hematoma and Michael's subsequently diagnosed cerebral palsy.]

Dr. Arner qualified as an expert witness on the subjects of obstetrics and gynecology and gave the following testimony. Even though Ms. Rizzo had been given certain medication, she was capable of making medical decisions. Ms. Rizzo would have been able to deliver Michael spontaneously, without the use of forceps, had Dr. Schiller simply waited. If forceps are used in "non-emergent situations," the patient should be informed about the use of the forceps and should be given the opportunity to participate in the decision regarding whether the forceps will be used. Dr. Arner opined that Dr. Schiller breached the standard of care owed to Ms. Rizzo because he failed to allow her to participate in the decision to use forceps.

The plaintiffs contend that the trial court erred by striking their evidence because they established a prima facie case that Dr. Schiller failed to obtain Ms. Rizzo's informed consent for the use of obstetrical forceps during Michael's delivery. Dr. Schiller, however, argues that the plaintiffs' evidence fails to establish a prima facie case and that the plaintiffs failed to present evidence of proximate causation. Furthermore, Dr. Schiller asserts that Ms. Rizzo was allowed to participate in the decision to use forceps because she signed the authorization form. We disagree with Dr. Schiller.

In Hunter v. Burroughs, 96 S.E. 360, 366-367 (1918), we held that "it is the duty of a physician in the exercise of ordinary care to warn a patient of the danger of possible bad consequences of using a remedy," but that the physician's failure to warn "is not per se an act of negligence." Rather, the physician owes a duty to make a reasonable disclosure to the patient of all significant facts under the circumstances. This duty is limited to those disclosures that a reasonable medical practitioner would provide under the same or similar circumstances. Bly v. Rhoads, 222 S.E.2d 783, 785-787 (1976). In most cases, expert testimony is necessary to establish those instances where the duty to disclose arises and what disclosures a reasonable medical practitioner would have made under the same or similar circumstances. Id.

We are of opinion that the plaintiffs presented sufficient evidence to establish a prima facie case that Dr. Schiller failed to obtain Ms. Rizzo's informed consent to use the obstetrical forceps. As we have already mentioned, Dr. Arner testified that the appropriate standard of care required that Dr. Schiller inform Ms. Rizzo about the use of the forceps and that she be given an opportunity to participate in the decision whether to use forceps. Ms. Rizzo testified that Dr. Schiller did not disclose any information to her about the use of the forceps and that he used the forceps without her consent.

It is true that Ms. Rizzo signed a document that purportedly is a consent form. However, this form did not inform her of any specific procedures that Dr. Schiller intended to perform; nor did it inform her of foreseeable risks associated with any procedures or risks in failing to perform any procedures. As Dr. Arner observed, the form is so general in nature that "you could also justify amputating her foot." We hold that the duty imposed upon a physician to obtain a patient's informed consent requires more than simply securing the patient's signature on a generalized consent form, similar to the form present here. The law requires informed consent, not mere consent, and the failure to obtain informed consent is tantamount to no consent.

We are also of opinion that the plaintiffs presented sufficient evidence of proximate causation as an element of their prima facie case. Here, the plaintiffs presented evidence from which the jury might have inferred that had Ms. Rizzo been informed of the possible consequences associated with the use of obstetrical forceps, she would have continued to assist in the birth process by "pushing" and that Michael would have been born spontaneously. The plaintiffs also presented evidence from which the jury could have found that but for the use of the forceps, Michael would not have suffered the brain injury.

Accordingly, we will remand this case for a trial of the plaintiffs' claims of lack of informed consent.

Notes: Limiting Liability for Failure to Disclose

1. *Informed Consent and Competence.* The patient's capacity is an important factor in informed consent cases. Physicians must secure consent from someone who has the legal capacity to give it. See generally Laura B. Dunn et al., Assessing Decisional Capacity for Clinical Research or Treatment: A Review of Instruments, 163 Am. J. Psychiatry 1323 (2006); Bruce J. Winick, Competency to Consent to Treatment: The Distinction between Assent and Objection, 28 Hous. L. Rev. 15 (1991); Annot., 25 A.L.R.3d 1439 (1969). Consent issues are particularly acute for in the treatment of minors. See generally, Jennifer L. Rosato, Let's Get Real: Quilting a Principled Approach to Adolescent Empowerment in Health Care Decision-Making, 51 DePaul L. Rev. 769 (2002); David Vukadinovich, Minors' Consent Rights to Treatment: Navigating the Complexity of State Laws, 37 J. Health L. 6667 (2004).

Where the patient is incapable of giving consent him- or herself, alternate decisionmaking methods have been adopted by courts and legislatures. Did Pamela Rizzo have the capacity to make intelligent health care decisions? Her medical expert testified affirmatively.

2. *The Limits of the Duty to Inform.* Courts and commentators have discussed five general limitations to the duty to disclose:

- *Common Knowledge.* There is no duty to disclose risks "of which persons of average sophistication are aware."
- *Patient Knowledge.* The patient cannot recover for the physician's failure to disclose a risk already known by the patient.

- *Emergencies.* There is no duty to disclose information in an emergency situation where the patient is not competent, immediate treatment is required to prevent more serious harm, and no substitute decisionmaker is available.
- *Therapeutic Privilege.* There is no duty to disclose information where the disclosure process would "foreclose rational decision" or "pose psychological damage" to the patient. The *Canterbury* court was particularly concerned about the need to circumscribe this exception lest it swallow the general rule. For academic commentary on the therapeutic exception, see, e.g., Kathleen M. Boozang, The Therapeutic Placebo: The Case for Patient Deception, 54 Fla. L. Rev. 687 (2002); Developments in the Law — Medical Technology and the Law, VI. The Right to Refuse Medical Treatment, 103 Harv. L. Rev. 1643, 1676 (1990). There are few reported applications of the rule. See, e.g., Barrai v. Betwee, 50 P.3d 946 (Haw. 2002) (psychiatrist fails to establish therapeutic privilege exception); and Marsingill v. O'Malley, 58 P.3d 495 (Alaska 2002) (plaintiffs essentially claim that physician should have applied the therapeutic privilege by withholding information about the likelihood that emergency room treatment would be painful or uncomfortable; patient allegedly suffered injuries from her decision to delay seeking emergency medical assistance after hearing about the nature of the likely treatment).
- *Waiver.* Although there are few court decisions on the issue, the disclosure doctrine's grounding in autonomy suggests that patients should be able to refuse information offered by the physician. See Stover v. Association of Thoracic & Cardiovascular Surgeons, 635 A.2d 1047, 1055-1056 (Pa. Super. Ct. 1993); & Mark A. Hall, A Theory of Economic Informed Consent, 31 Ga. L. Rev. 511 (1997).

These limitations on the duty to disclose may be announced by courts or, in professional disclosure standard jurisdictions, may be established by the testimony of medical experts. The defendant generally has the burden of proving that an exception to the duty to inform is present. For a general discussion of exceptions to the duty to disclose, see Alan Meisel, The "Exceptions" to the Informed Consent Doctrine: Striking a Balance between Competing Values in Medical Decisionmaking, 1979 Wis. L. Rev. 413.

3. *The "Consent" Process, or the Use of Forms.* Critics of the informed consent process argue that the ideal of a meaningful exchange of information between patient and physician has been replaced with the ritual of the informed consent form. How does the *Rizzo* court analyze the validity of the informed consent document signed by the plaintiff? Why shouldn't a physician be entitled to rely upon informed consent forms as a shield to liability? How was the document defective? Who should draft informed consent documents — health care providers or attorneys? Would a physician relying on the validity of an informed consent form have a malpractice claim against the drafter?

Physician defendants hope that a signed consent form will foreclose any informed consent claim. It is true that a properly completed form can establish at least a presumption that a patient has consented to treatment. Sometimes the presumption is established by statute. See, e.g., Ohio Rev. Code Ann. §2317.54. A form indicating only that a patient has received information and consents is probably not sufficient. See, e.g., Havens v. Hoffman, 902 P.2d 219, 223 (Wyo. 1995) (overturning physician's summary judgment; hospital form is an acknowledgment of the receipt of information but does not indicate the nature of the information disclosed). Should a signed consent form bar recovery where the patient did not read the disclosure before signing and where the physician failed to determine whether the form had been read? Roberts v. Cox, 669 So.2d 633, 640 (La. Ct. App. 1996) (jury determination that informed consent doctrine satisfied not "manifestly erroneous").

4. *Informed Consent Forms in Hospitals.* Hospital employees, such as nurses, often procure patients' signatures on informed consent forms prior to surgery. Does this mean that hospitals have a duty to obtain the informed consent of patients? Courts routinely find that the answer is "no." The duty to obtain informed consent is the physician's; the hospital's involvement in the process normally is considered to be merely facilitative. Annot., 88 A.L.R.3d 1008 (1978). For a cogent critique, see Robert Gatter, The Mysterious Survival of the Policy against Informed Consent Liability for Hospitals, 81 Notre Dame L. Rev. 1203 (2006).

5. *Forms and Assumption of Risk.* An informed consent form is essentially a written documentation of the patient's assumption of the disclosed risks, assumed in order to achieve a procedure's potential benefits. See Karp v. Cooley, 493 F.2d 408 (5th Cir. 1974) (directed verdict for the defendant affirmed; patient undergoing first attempted implantation of a mechanical heart had been given extensive information and counseling about the experimental nature of the treatment and its risks). Patients ordinarily are not permitted, however, to assume the risk that a procedure will be negligently recommended or performed; they assume only the risks that are non-negligently produced. In the typical case, then, a signed informed consent form signifies that the patient was informed of the required risks and agreed to accept those risks; a form is powerful evidence of a physician's compliance with the duty to disclose but is irrelevant to an ordinary malpractice action brought against a physician for delivering substandard care.

As is often true in legal matters, things are not quite this simple, however. As noted at page 435, informed consent and ordinary malpractice overlap and interact in several important respects. Where there are alternative standards of care or courses of treatment, obtaining informed consent may be important to the physician's malpractice defense that the physician complied with a "respectable minority" point of view. For instance, informed consent can justify departing from customary practice in order to participate in medical research or to try out an untested procedure. Similarly, informed consent might be used to bolster an affirmative defense that the patient assumed the risk or was contributorily negligent. See, e.g., Smith v. Hull, 659 N.E.2d 185 (Ind. Ct. App. 1995) (in a case involving injuries from treatment for baldness, a contributory negligence finding "was supported by evidence that patient sought out physician and hair injection procedure, received extensive literature and discussed risks with physician, and signed consent forms prior to undergoing procedures, . . . leav[ing] us with little doubt that Smith's desire to sport a full head of hair motivated him to pursue remedies that he knowingly undertook at his own peril"); Schneider v. Revici, which is excerpted and discussed at page 421.

6. *Contributory Negligence.* Should patients have an obligation to truthfully disclose information to their physicians? Should the obligation arise only in response to a physician's inquiries, or should patients have a duty to affirmatively disclose matters that a reasonable patient would think might be relevant to his or her medical treatment? In Brown v. Dibbell, 595 N.W.2d 358 (Wis. 1999), the court held that

> for patients to exercise ordinary care, they must tell the truth and give complete and accurate information about personal, family, and medical histories to a doctor to the extent possible in response to the doctor's requests for information when the requested information is material to a doctor's duty as prescribed by . . . [the informed consent statute] and that a patient's breach of that duty might, under certain circumstances, constitute contributory negligence. Id. at 368-369.

The court did not consider whether patients had a duty to disclose information sua sponte.

7. *Injury and Causation.* Note that Ms. Rizzo's claim would have failed if the undisclosed risk had not materialized, that is, if the use of forceps had not resulted in her son's injuries. How did Dr. Schiller's failure to disclose the risks associated with using forceps cause Michael Rizzo's injuries? The court holds that the plaintiffs presented sufficient evidence of proximate causation for a jury to decide in their favor. A jury could have decided that Ms. Rizzo, had she been appropriately informed, might have rejected the use of forceps and continued to "push" and that Michael's brain injuries would not have occurred. Assume that you represent the defendant. What types of counter-evidence might you want to present on this issue?

8. *Alternative Treatments.* Under the professional malpractice standard, a physician must disclose treatment alternatives if the reasonable, competent physician would have done so. The existence of alternative treatments would also be considered "material" under the patient-centered standard of disclosure. Annot., 38 A.L.R.4th 900 (1985). What should be the physician's disclosure obligation where a treatment alternative is not readily available, perhaps because of cost considerations or geographic location? See, e.g., Mark Hall, A Theory of Economic Informed Consent, 31 Ga. L. Rev. 511 (1997). Should the physician be required to disclose the option of "doing nothing"? See, e.g., Wecker v. Amend, 918 P.2d 658 (Kan. Ct. App. 1996) (yes).

9. *Informed Consent and the Therapeutic Placebo.* Physicians and medical researchers have long believed in the "placebo effect," under which some patients appear to improve after the administration of spurious "treatment," although some recent research results suggest that the effect may be overstated. See Franklin G. Miller & Donald L. Rosenstein, The Nature and Power of the Placebo Effect, 59 J. Clin. Epid. 331 (2006); John C. Bailar, The Powerful Placebo and the Wizard of Oz, 344 New Eng. J. Med. 1630 (2001); Asbjorn Hrobjarsson & Peter C. Gotzsche, Is the Placebo Powerless?, 344 New Eng. J. Med. 1594 (2001); The Placebo Effect: An Interdisciplinary Exploration (Anne Harrington, ed., 1997). Does the informed consent doctrine implicitly prohibit the use of placebos? Can you design a method of using placebos that would allow physicians (and patients) to gain the benefits of the placebo effect without violating the disclosure doctrine?

See Kathleen M. Boozang, The Therapeutic Placebo: The Case for Patient Deception, 54 U. Fla. L. Rev. 687 (2002).

10. *Diagnostic Tests vs. Treatments.* Should the duty to disclose alternatives depend on whether a treatment or a diagnostic test is at issue? Compare McGeshick v. Choucair, 9 F.3d 1229 (7th Cir. 1993) (Wisconsin informed consent statute does not impose duty to inform patient about diagnostic alternatives), with Martin v. Richards, 531 N.W.2d 70 (Wis. 1995) (statute covers diagnostic tests as well as treatments). Under the professional malpractice standard, the answer presumably would depend on whether the competent physician would disclose the information. *Martin* is a singularly interesting case, in which parents sued an emergency room physician for failing to disclose that a CT scan was available to examine their child and for failing to disclose that if the child had intracranial bleeding, she would have to be transferred to another facility. The child developed intracranial bleeding, which, though eventually treated, left her with partial spastic quadriplegia. The Wisconsin Supreme Court held that a physician's duty to discuss alternatives was broad enough to encompass a failure to disclose the existence of additional diagnostic techniques.

11. *Law in Books, Law in Action, and the "New" Model of Shared Decisionmaking.* Does the informed consent duty established under malpractice principles provide adequate protection for patient autonomy? Does it protect physicians from unwarranted intrusions into professional autonomy?

There have been flurries of reformist proposals over the past ten years exploiting the many weaknesses of the current legal approach to informed consent and advocating some form of "shared medical decisionmaking." Although the model has many variations, a recent description is typical:

> Shared medical decision-making is a process in which the physician shares with the patient all relevant risk and benefit information on all treatment alternatives and the patient shares with the physician all relevant personal information that might make one treatment or side effect more or less tolerable than others. Then, both parties use this information to come to a mutual medical decision. Jamie Staples King & Benjamin W. Moulton, Rethinking Informed Consent: The Case for Shared Medical Decision-Making, 32 Amer. J. L. & Med. 429, 431 (2006) (citations omitted).

Does this approach seem to address the problems with the current informed consent rules? Can you identify any practical or legal issues with the implementation of shared medical decisionmaking? For a recent critique of the model, see Carl E. Schneider, Void for Vagueness, Hastings Center Report 10 (January-February 2006)

Discussion Problem: Informed Refusals?

Dr. Claude R. Thomas was Mrs. Rena Truman's personal physician from 1963-1969. In 1969, another physician discovered that Mrs. Truman had advanced cervical cancer. Mrs. Truman died in 1970, at the age of 30. Rena Truman's children sued Dr. Thomas for failing to perform a Pap test on Mrs. Truman between 1964 and 1969. Trial testimony indicated that (1) if the Pap smear had been performed during this time period, Mrs. Truman's condition would have been discovered at an earlier stage and she probably would have lived; (2) medical practice required physicians to inform women of the purpose of a Pap test; and (3) Dr. Thomas repeatedly advised Mrs. Truman to undergo the test but did not specifically explain the possible consequences of her refusal. Consider this case under the professional and material risk standards of disclosure. What arguments can you make on behalf of Mrs. Truman's children? What arguments or defenses might you raise on behalf of Dr. Thomas? See Truman v. Thomas, 611 P.2d 902 (Cal. 1980).

4. Fiduciary Obligations, Conflicts of Interest, and Novel Disclosure Obligations

Depending on the jurisdiction, the informed consent doctrine has grown out of the rich soil of cases involving battery, malpractice, and fiduciary law. The doctrine has the potential for continued expansive growth, particularly in those jurisdictions emphasizing a physician's fiduciary obligations over the professional standard of care. In these states, the scope of informed consent is not limited by the current standard of professional conduct. As you read the following cases, consider whether the courts have gone too far or not far enough in regulating the scope of physician disclosure. Does the imposition of liability in these cases seem "just"? Do the courts' decisions seem consistent with the informed consent doctrine they purport to apply? What is the likely impact of these decisions on the nature of physician-patient communications? Are patients more likely to receive important information? What will physicians do to minimize liability?

■ AUTONOMY AND PRIVACY: PROTECTING PATIENTS FROM THEIR PHYSICIANS
Mary Anne Bobinski
55 U. Pitt. L. Rev. 291, 347-356 (1994)

. . . Jurisdictions with more generous disclosure requirements typically rely, at least in part, on fiduciary principles as a basis for the disclosure obligation. Fiduciary law thus presents a possible avenue for future growth of a more vibrant disclosure duty. Tort law and the law governing fiduciary relationships are similar in that they impose extra-contractual duties on individuals. The two regulatory schemes, however, differ in conception of those duties. Tort law most often imposes general duties irrespective of the status of the parties. The law of fiduciaries, in contrast, is based on the special character of the relationship between two parties. Courts struggling to define the scope of tort-based disclosure duties have often noted the fiducial characteristics of the doctor-patient relationship as a justification for disclosure. This linkage between ordinary tort and fiduciary principles creates the opportunity for both growth and confusion. Ordinary tort duties may be expanded or amplified because of the perceived relevance of fiduciary principles. To date, few courts have explicitly considered the implications of wholesale acceptance of the doctor-patient relationship as one subject to fiduciary law. There has been little judicial analysis of the appropriateness of applying fiduciary-based disclosure obligations to the physician-patient relationship, and virtually no judicial analysis of the special problems presented by provider-associated risk.

The first question is whether the relationship between physicians and patients is a fiduciary one. Fiduciary relationships are generally described as those in which some aspect of the relationship between the parties [such as an imbalance of power or knowledge] justifies the imposition of special obligations on one of them. Several treatises on fiduciary law name the physician-patient relationship as a fiduciary one and the courts have tended to concur. [See page 174.]

Next, the fiduciary duties that physicians owe to patients must be determined. Generally, a fiduciary must act for the benefit of another, but the specific duties imposed on a fiduciary will vary with the scope of the relationship between the parties. The fiduciary owes a duty of loyalty, "good faith, trust, special confidence and candor" to the other party. Obviously, it is not a breach of the fiduciary relationship for the fiduciary to receive compensation for her services. However, the fiduciary can breach her duty by engaging in self-dealing, by receiving bribes or kickbacks, or by misappropriating that knowledge or property which belongs to the entrustor. The role of disclosure in fiduciary law is somewhat complicated. The fiduciary's failure to disclose information to the entrustor can constitute an independent breach of fiduciary duty when the information was gathered in the course of the fiduciary's duties. Disclosure may also help determine whether an apparent breach of fiduciary duties has been "cured" by the consent of the entrustor. The validity of the entrustor's consent will be the important question because the fiduciary's influence over the entrustor may make any consent presumptively invalid. Disclosure in these cases is of evidentiary significance; it may bolster the fiduciary's claim that the entrustor's consent to the transaction was valid. As a substantive matter, disclosure may not be sufficient where the fiduciary's influence over the entrustor makes any — even informed — consent illusory. . . .

This analysis of fiduciary principles assumes that a breach will provide some effective remedy for patients. A fiduciary is liable to the entrustor for a breach of fiduciary duties. A breach of a fiduciary obligation can be remedied by voiding a transaction, by payment by the fiduciary to the trusting party of any impermissible benefits or profits, or by payment by the fiduciary to compensate the other party for actual damages, which may include compensation for personal injury. Courts are divided on whether the entrustor is required to show some specific injury flowed from the fiduciary's breach of her duties.

The significant number of courts that have applied fiduciary principles to the physician-patient relationship can be deceiving. Most courts have failed to consider the broader policy implications of classifying the physician-patient relationship as a fiduciary one; most have also failed to analyze the range of physicians' required fiduciary duties. Some courts have responded to these problems by hedging, noting that the relationship has fiducial "qualities" or "characteristics" or finding that it is a "confidential" relationship. . . .

The . . . [most important] judicial consideration of common law economic disclosure obligations occurred in Moore v. Regents of the University of California. . . .

■ MOORE v. THE REGENTS OF THE UNIVERSITY OF CALIFORNIA
793 P.2d 479 (Cal. 1990), cert. denied, 499 U.S. 936 (1991)

PANELLI, Justice.

We granted review in this case to determine whether plaintiff has stated a cause of action against his physician and other defendants for using his cells in potentially lucrative medical research without his permission. Plaintiff alleges that his physician failed to disclose preexisting research and economic interests in the cells before obtaining consent to the medical procedures by which they were extracted. . . . We hold that the complaint states a cause of action for breach of the physician's disclosure obligations, but not for conversion.

FACTS

. . . The plaintiff is John Moore (Moore), who underwent treatment for hairy-cell leukemia at the Medical Center of the University of California at Los Angeles (UCLA Medical Center). The five defendants are: (1) Dr. David W. Golde (Golde), a physician who attended Moore at UCLA Medical Center; (2) the Regents of the University of California (Regents), who own and operate the university; (3) Shirley G. Quan, a researcher employed by the Regents; (4) Genetics Institute, Inc. (Genetics Institute); and (5) Sandoz Pharmaceuticals Corporation and related entities (collectively Sandoz).

Moore first visited UCLA Medical Center on October 5, 1976, shortly after he learned that he had hairy-cell leukemia. After hospitalizing Moore and "withdrawing extensive amounts of blood, bone marrow aspirate, and other bodily substances," Golde confirmed that diagnosis. At this time all defendants, including Golde, were aware that "certain blood products and blood components were of great value in a number of commercial and scientific efforts" and that access to a patient whose blood contained these substances would provide "competitive, commercial, and scientific advantages."

On October 8, 1976, Golde recommended that Moore's spleen be removed. Golde informed Moore "that he had reason to fear for his life, and that the proposed splenectomy operation . . . was necessary to slow down the progress of his disease." Based upon Golde's representations, Moore signed a written consent form authorizing the splenectomy.

Before the operation, Golde and Quan "formed the intent and made arrangements to obtain portions of [Moore's] spleen following its removal" and to take them to a separate research unit. Golde gave written instructions to this effect on October 18 and 19, 1976. These research activities "were not intended to have . . . any relation to [Moore's] medical . . . care." However, neither Golde nor Quan informed Moore of their plans to conduct this research or requested his permission. Surgeons at UCLA Medical Center, whom the complaint does not name as defendants, removed Moore's spleen on October 20, 1976.

Moore returned to the UCLA Medical Center several times between November 1976 and September 1983. He did so at Golde's direction and based upon representations "that such visits were necessary and required for his health and well-being, and based upon the trust inherent in and by virtue of the physician-patient relationship. . . ." On each of these visits Golde withdrew additional samples of "blood, blood serum, skin, bone marrow aspirate, and sperm." On each occasion Moore travelled to the UCLA Medical Center from his home in Seattle because he had been told that the procedures were to be performed only there and only under Golde's direction.

"In fact, [however,] throughout the period of time that [Moore] was under [Golde's] care and treatment, . . . the defendants were actively involved in a number of activities which they concealed from [Moore]. . . ." Specifically, defendants were conducting research on Moore's cells and planned to "benefit financially and competitively . . . [by exploiting the cells] and [their] exclusive access to [the cells] by virtue of [Golde's] on-going physician-patient relationship. . . ."

Sometime before August 1979, Golde established a cell line from Moore's T-lymphocytes.[2] On January 30, 1981, the Regents applied for a patent on the cell line, listing Golde and Quan as inventors. "[B]y virtue of an established policy . . . , [the] Regents, Golde, and Quan would share in any royalties or profits . . . arising out of [the] patent." The patent issued on March 20, 1984, naming Golde and Quan as the inventors of the cell line and the Regents as the assignee of the patent. The Regent's patent also covers various methods for using the cell line to produce lymphokines. Moore admits in his complaint that "the true clinical potential of each of the lymphokines . . . [is] difficult to predict, [but] . . . competing commercial firms in these relevant fields have published reports in biotechnology industry periodicals predicting a potential market of approximately $3.01 Billion Dollars by the year 1990 for a whole range of [such lymphokines]. . . ." [Golde and his associates received several hundred thousand dollars over the next three years plus shares of stock, under agreements with Genetics Institute to develop the cell line products.]

Based upon these allegations, Moore attempted to state 13 causes of action.[4] . . . [T]he superior court sustained a general demurrer to the entire complaint. . . .

DISCUSSION

A. BREACH OF FIDUCIARY DUTY AND LACK OF INFORMED CONSENT

Moore repeatedly alleges that Golde failed to disclose the extent of his research and economic interests in Moore's cells[6] before obtaining consent to the medical procedures by which the cells were extracted. These allegations, in our

---

[2] A T-lymphocyte is a type of white blood cell. T-lymphocytes produce lymphokines, or proteins that regulate the immune system. Some lymphokines have potential therapeutic value. If the genetic material responsible for producing a particular lymphokine can be identified, it can sometimes be used to manufacture large quantities of the lymphokine through the techniques of recombinant DNA. . . . Moore's T-lymphocytes were interesting to the defendants because they overproduced certain lymphokines, thus making the corresponding genetic material easier to identify. . . .

[4] (1) "Conversion"; (2) "lack of informed consent"; (3) "breach of fiduciary duty"; (4) "fraud and deceit"; (5) "unjust enrichment"; (6) "quasi-contract"; (7) "bad faith breach of the implied covenant of good faith and fair dealing"; (8) "intentional infliction of emotional distress"; (9) "negligent misrepresentation"; (10) "intentional interference with prospective advantageous economic relationships"; (11) "slander of title"; (12) "accounting"; and (13) "declaratory relief."

[6] In this opinion we use the inclusive term *cells* to describe all of the cells taken from Moore's body, including blood cells, bone marrow, spleen, etc.

view, state a cause of action against Golde for invading a legally protected interest of his patient. This cause of action can properly be characterized either as the breach of a fiduciary duty to disclose facts material to the patient's consent or, alternatively, as the performance of medical procedures without first having obtained the patient's informed consent.

Our analysis begins with three well-established principles. First, "a person of adult years and in sound mind has the right, in the exercise of control over his own body, to determine whether or not to submit to lawful medical treatment." Cobbs v. Grant, 8 Cal. 3d 229, 242 (1972). Second, "the patient's consent to treatment, to be effective, must be an informed consent." *Cobbs*, 8 Cal. 3d at 242. Third, in soliciting the patient's consent, a physician has a fiduciary duty to disclose all information material to the patient's decision.

These principles lead to the following conclusions: (1) A physician must disclose personal interests unrelated to the patient's health, whether research or economic, that may affect the physician's professional judgment; and (2) a physician's failure to disclose such interests may give rise to a cause of action for performing medical procedures without informed consent or breach of fiduciary duty. . . .

Indeed, the law already recognizes that a reasonable patient would want to know whether a physician has an economic interest that might affect the physician's professional judgment. As the Court of Appeal has said, "[c]ertainly a sick patient deserves to be free of any reasonable suspicion that his doctor's judgment is influenced by a profit motive." Magan Medical Clinic v. Cal. State Bd. of Medical Examiners, 249 Cal. App. 2d 124, 132 (1967). The desire to protect patients from possible conflicts of interest has also motivated legislative enactments. Among these is Business and Professions Code §654.2. Under that section, a physician may not charge a patient on behalf of, or refer a patient to, any organization in which the physician has a "significant beneficial interest, unless [the physician] first discloses in writing to the patient, that there is such an interest and advises the patient that the patient may choose any organization for the purposes of obtaining the services ordered or requested by [the physician]." Similarly, under Health and Safety Code §24173, a physician who plans to conduct a medical experiment on a patient must, among other things, inform the patient of "[t]he name of the sponsor or funding source, if any, . . . and the organization, if any, under whose general aegis the experiment is being conducted."

It is important to note that no law prohibits a physician from conducting research in the same area in which he practices. Progress in medicine often depends upon physicians, such as those practicing at the university hospital where Moore received treatment, who conduct research while caring for their patients.

Yet a physician who treats a patient in whom he also has a research interest has potentially conflicting loyalties. This is because medical treatment decisions are made on the basis of proportionality—weighing the benefits to the patient against the risks to the patient. As another court has said, "the determination as to whether the burdens of treatment are worth enduring for any individual patient depends upon the facts unique in each case," and "the patient's interests and desires are the key ingredients of the decision-making process." A physician who adds his own research interests to this balance may be tempted to order a scientifically useful procedure or test that offers marginal, or no, benefits to the patient.[8] The possibility that an interest extraneous to the patient's health has affected the physician's judgment is something that a reasonable patient would want to know in deciding whether to consent to a proposed course of treatment. It is material to the patient's decision and, thus, a prerequisite to informed consent. . . .

We acknowledge that there is a competing consideration. To require disclosure of research and economic interests may corrupt the patient's own judgment by distracting him from the requirements of his health.[9] But California law does not grant physicians unlimited discretion to decide what to disclose. . . .

Accordingly, we hold that a physician who is seeking a patient's consent for a medical procedure must, in order to satisfy his fiduciary duty[10] and to obtain the patient's informed consent, disclose personal interests unrelated to the patient's health, whether research or economic, that may affect his medical judgment.

1. Dr. Golde

We turn now to the allegations of Moore's third amended complaint to determine whether he has stated such a cause of action. . . . Moore alleges that Golde actively concealed his economic interest in Moore's cells during this time period.

> [D]uring each of these visits . . . , and even when [Moore] inquired as to whether there was any possible or potential commercial or financial value or significance of his Blood and Bodily Substances, or whether the defendants had discovered anything . . . which was or might be . . . related to any scientific activity resulting in commercial or financial benefits . . . , the defendants repeatedly and affirmatively represented to [Moore] that there was no commercial or financial value to his Blood and Bodily Substances . . . and in fact actively discouraged such inquiries.

. . . In these allegations, Moore plainly asserts that Golde concealed an economic interest in the postoperative procedures. Therefore, applying the principles already discussed, the allegations state a cause of action for breach of fiduciary duty or lack of informed consent.

We thus disagree with the superior court's ruling that Moore had not stated a cause of action . . . [because he] failed to allege that the operation lacked a

---

[8] This is, in fact, precisely what Moore has alleged with respect to the postoperative withdrawals of blood and other substances.

[9] . . . [A] physician who orders a procedure partly to further a research interest unrelated to the patient's health should not be able to avoid disclosure with the argument that the patient might object to participation in research. In some cases, however, a physician's research interest might play such an insignificant role in the decision to recommend a medically indicated procedure that disclosure should not be required because the interest is not material. By analogy, we have not required disclosure of "remote" risks that "are not central to the decision to administer or reject [a] procedure." Truman v. Thomas, 27 Cal. 3d 285, 293 (1980).

[10] In some respects the term *fiduciary* is too broad. In this context the term *fiduciary* signifies only that a physician must disclose all facts material to the patient's decision. A physician is not the patient's financial adviser. As we have already discussed, the reason why a physician must disclose possible conflicts is not because he has a duty to protect his patient's financial interests, but because certain personal interests may affect professional judgment.

therapeutic purpose or that the procedure was totally unrelated to therapeutic purposes. In our view, neither allegation is essential. Even if the splenectomy had a therapeutic purpose, it does not follow that Golde had no duty to disclose his additional research and economic interests. As we have already discussed, the existence of a motivation for a medical procedure unrelated to the patient's health is a potential conflict of interest and a fact material to the patient's decision.

2. The Remaining Defendants

The Regents, Quan, Genetics Institute, and Sandoz are not physicians. In contrast to Golde, none of these defendants stood in a fiduciary relationship with Moore or had the duty to obtain Moore's informed consent to medical procedures. If any of these defendants is to be liable for breach of fiduciary duty or performing medical procedures without informed consent, it can only be on account of Golde's acts and on the basis of a recognized theory of secondary liability, such as respondeat superior. The procedural posture of this case, however, makes it unnecessary for us to address the sufficiency of Moore's secondary-liability allegations. . . .

B. CONVERSION

[In this portion of the opinion, the court rejected Moore's attempt to characterize the invasion of his rights as a conversion. The court reasoned that such an unprecedented extension of property law concepts is not warranted because strict liability would be too threatening to legitimate and socially useful scientific research.] For these reasons, we hold that the allegations of Moore's third amended complaint state a cause of action for breach of fiduciary duty or lack of informed consent, but not conversion.

MOSK, Justice, dissenting.
. . . I disagree with the majority's . . . conclusion that in the present context a nondisclosure cause of action is an adequate — in fact, a superior — substitute for a conversion cause of action. In my view the nondisclosure cause of action falls short on at least three grounds. First, . . . the majority's theory apparently is that the threat of [a damages action based on nondisclosure] . . . will have a prophylactic effect: It will give physician-researchers incentive to disclose any conflicts of interest before treatment, and will thereby protect their patients' right to make an informed decision about what may be done with their body parts.

The remedy is largely illusory. . . . There are two barriers to recovery. First, the patient must show that if he or she had been informed of all pertinent information, he or she would have declined to consent to the procedure in question. . . . The second barrier to recovery is still higher, and is erected on the first: It is not even enough for the plaintiff to prove that he personally would have refused consent to the proposed treatment if he had been fully informed; he must also prove that in the same circumstances no reasonably prudent person would have given such consent. . . . Few if any judges or juries are likely to believe that disclosure of . . . a possibility of research or development would dissuade a reasonably prudent person from consenting to the treatment. For example, in the case at bar no trier of fact is likely to believe that if defendants had disclosed their plans for using Moore's cells, no reasonably prudent person in Moore's position — i.e., a leukemia patient suffering from a grossly enlarged spleen — would have consented to the routine operation that saved or at least prolonged his life. Here . . . a motion for nonsuit for failure to prove proximate cause will end the matter. In this context, accordingly, the threat of suit on a nondisclosure cause of action is largely a paper tiger.

The second reason why the nondisclosure cause of action is inadequate for the task that the majority assign to it is that it fails to solve half the problem before us: It gives the patient only the right to refuse consent, i.e., the right to prohibit the commercialization of his tissue; it does not give him the right to grant consent to that commercialization on the condition that he share in its proceeds. . . . Third, the nondisclosure cause of action fails to reach a major class of potential defendants: all those who are outside the strict physician-patient relationship with the plaintiff. . . .

In sum, the nondisclosure cause of action (1) is unlikely to be successful in most cases, (2) fails to protect patients' rights to share in the proceeds of the commercial exploitation of their tissue, and (3) may allow the true exploiters to escape liability. It is thus not an adequate substitute, in my view, for the conversion cause of action. . . .

BROUSSARD, Justice, concurring and dissenting.
. . . I disagree with the suggestion in [Justice Mosk's] dissenting opinion that defendants will be able to avoid all liability under the breach-of-fiduciary-duty theory simply by showing that plaintiff would have proceeded with the surgical removal of his diseased spleen even if defendants had disclosed their research and commercial interest in his cells. . . . [I]n this context [of a breach of fiduciary duty] — unlike in the traditional "informed consent" context of *Cobbs* — a plaintiff should not be required to establish that he would not have proceeded with the medical treatment in question if his physician had made full disclosure, but only that the doctor's wrongful failure to disclose information proximately caused the plaintiff some type of compensable damage. . . . [I]n appropriate circumstances, punitive as well as compensatory damages would clearly be recoverable in such an action. Accordingly, [Justice Mosk] underestimates the potential efficacy of the breach-of-fiduciary-duty cause of action in dismissing the action as a "paper tiger."

■ HOWARD v. UNIVERSITY OF MEDICINE & DENTISTRY OF NEW JERSEY
800 A.2d 73 (N.J. 2002)

LAVECCHIA, J.
In this appeal we consider what causes of action will lie when a plaintiff contends that a physician misrepresented his credentials and experience at the time he obtained the plaintiff's consent to surgery. . . .

[The plaintiff suffered serious and progressive back injuries in an automobile accident but decided to forgo recommended surgery. The plaintiff was referred to Dr. Heary, a professor at the defendant University, after the plaintiff sustained additional back injuries in a second car accident.] Dr. Heary had two pre-operative consultations with plaintiff. In the first consultation,

Dr. Heary determined that plaintiff needed surgery to correct a cervical myelopathy secondary to cervical stenosis and a significantly large C3 C4 disc herniation. Because of the serious nature of the surgery, Dr. Heary recommended that plaintiff's wife attend a second consultation. The doctor wanted to explain again the risks, benefits, and alternatives to surgery, and to answer any questions concerning the procedure.

Plaintiff returned with his wife for a second consultation, but what transpired is disputed. An "Office Note" written by Dr. Heary detailing the contents of the consultation states that "[a]ll alternatives have been discussed and patient elects at this time to undergo the surgical procedure, which has been scheduled for March 5, 1997." Dr. Heary asserts that he informed plaintiff and his wife that the surgery entailed significant risks, including the possibility of paralysis. Plaintiffs dispute that they were informed of such risks. Further, they contend that during the consultation plaintiff's wife asked Dr. Heary whether he was Board Certified and that he said he was. Plaintiffs also claim that Dr. Heary told them that he had performed approximately sixty corpectomies in each of the eleven years he had been performing such surgical procedures. According to Mrs. Howard, she was opposed to the surgery and it was only after Dr. Heary's specific claims of skill and experience that she and her husband decided to go ahead with the procedure.

Dr. Heary denies that he represented that he was Board Certified in Neurosurgery.[1] He also denies that he ever claimed to have performed sixty corpectomies per year for the eleven years he had practiced neurosurgery.

Dr. Heary performed the surgical procedure on March 5, 1997, but it was unsuccessful. A malpractice action was filed alleging that Mr. Howard was rendered quadriplegic as a result of Dr. Heary's negligence. [The plaintiffs sought leave to add a fraud claim to their complaint. The trial court rejected the motion, the appellate division reversed, and the matter was appealed to the state supreme court.]

Presently, a patient has several avenues of relief against a doctor: (1) deviation from the standard of care (medical malpractice); (2) lack of informed consent; and (3) battery. . . . Plaintiffs' motion to amend the complaint to add a fraud claim raises the question whether a patient's consent to surgery obtained through alleged misrepresentations about the physician's professional experience and credentials is properly addressed in a claim of lack of informed consent, or battery, or whether it should constitute a separate and distinct claim based on fraud.

We focus first on the distinction between lack of informed consent and battery as they are recognized in New Jersey. The doctrine of informed consent was tied initially to the tort of battery, but its evolution has firmly established it as a negligence concept. . . . By the mid-twentieth century, as courts began to use a negligence theory to analyze consent causes of action, the case law evolved from the notion of consent to *informed* consent, balancing the patient's need for sufficient information with the doctor's perception of the appropriate amount of information to impart for an informed decision. . . . The doctrine of informed consent continued to be refined. See Natanson v. Kline, 350 P.2d 1093, 1106,

---

[1] Although he was Board Eligible at the time of Mr. Howard's surgery, Dr. Heary did not become Board Certified in Neurosurgery until November 1999. . . .

modified on other grounds, 354 P.2d 670 (1960) (holding that doctor's required disclosure was "limited to those disclosures which a reasonable medical practitioner would make under the same or similar circumstances," known as the "professional standard"). Eventually, the "prudent patient," or "materiality of risk" standard was introduced. Canterbury v. Spence, 464 F.2d 772, 786-88 (D.C. Cir.1972), cert. denied, 409 U.S. 1064 (1972). That patient-centered view of informed consent stresses the patient's right to self-determination, and the fiduciary relationship between a doctor and his or her patients. . . . [New Jersey originally followed the professional standard of disclosure but later adopted the patient-centered material risk standard discussed in *Canterbury*.]

Our common law also authorizes a medical battery cause of action where a doctor performs a surgery without consent, rendering the surgery an unauthorized touching. . . . In circumstances where the surgery that was performed was authorized with arguably inadequate information, however, an action for negligence is more appropriate. . . . Thus, although a claim for battery will lie where there has been "ghost surgery"[1] or where no consent has been given for the procedure undertaken, if consent has been given for the procedure only a claim based on lack of informed consent will lie. A claim based on lack of informed consent properly will focus then on the adequacy of the disclosure, its impact on the reasonable patient's assessment of the risks, alternatives, and consequences of the surgery, and the damages caused by the occurrence of the undisclosed risk. . . .

Few jurisdictions have confronted the question of what cause of action should lie when a doctor allegedly misrepresents his credentials or experience. Research has revealed only one jurisdiction that has allowed a claim based on lack of informed consent under similar circumstances. See Johnson v. Kokomoor, 545 N.W.2d 495 (Wis. 1996) (analyzing doctor's affirmative misrepresentation as claim for lack of informed consent and finding that reasonable person would have considered information regarding doctor's relative lack of experience in performing surgery to have been material in making intelligent and informed decision). Although some suggest that a claim based in fraud may be appropriate if a doctor actively misrepresents his or her background or credentials, we are aware of no court that has so held. . . .

The thoughtful decision of the Appellate Division notwithstanding, we are not convinced that our common law should be extended to allow a novel fraud or deceit-based cause of action in this doctor-patient context that regularly would admit of the possibility of punitive damages, and that would circumvent the requirements for proof of both causation and damages imposed in a traditional informed consent setting. We are especially reluctant to do so when plaintiff's damages from this alleged "fraud" arise exclusively from the doctor-patient relationship involving plaintiff's corpectomy procedure. . . . Accordingly, we hold that a fraud or deceit-based claim is unavailable to address the wrong alleged by plaintiff. We next consider whether a claim based on lack of informed consent is the more appropriate analytical basis for the amendment to the complaint permitted by the Appellate Division. . . .

---

[1] ["Ghost surgery" occurs if the patient consents to a surgical procedure to be performed by Physician A but the surgery actually is performed by Physician B. — EDS.]

Our case law never has held that a doctor has a duty to detail his background and experience as part of the required informed consent disclosure; nor are we called on to decide that question here. . . . Courts generally have held that claims of lack of informed consent based on a failure to disclose professional-background information are without merit. . . . Although personal credentials and experience may not be a required part of an informed consent disclosure under the current standard of care required of doctors, the question raised in this appeal is whether significant misrepresentations concerning a physician's qualifications can affect the validity of consent obtained. The answer obviously is that they can.

In certain circumstances, a serious misrepresentation concerning the quality or extent of a physician's professional experience, viewed from the perspective of the reasonably prudent patient assessing the risks attendant to a medical procedure, can be material to the grant of intelligent and informed consent to the procedure. See 1 Dan B. Dobbs, *The Law of Torts*, §251 at 660-61 (2001) (citing *Kokemoor, supra,* and discussing that some authority has begun to suggest that patient is entitled to information concerning doctor's experience in performing specific surgery). In *Kokemoor, supra,* the Supreme Court of Wisconsin reviewed a case in which the plaintiff alleged that her surgeon did not obtain her informed consent to perform a surgical procedure because he had misrepresented his experience in response to a direct question during a pre-operative consultation. 545 N.W.2d at 505. At trial, evidence was introduced suggesting that the type of surgery performed — basilar bifurcation aneurysm — was "among the most difficult in all of neurosurgery." Ibid. The court found that evidence of the defendant's lack of experience was relevant to an informed consent claim because "[a] reasonable person in the plaintiff's position would have considered such information material in making an intelligent and informed decision about the surgery." Ibid.

The allegation here is that defendant's misrepresentations concerning his credentials and experience were instrumental in overcoming plaintiff's reluctance to proceed with the surgery. The theory of the claim is not that the misrepresentation induced plaintiff to proceed with unnecessary surgery. . . . Rather, plaintiff essentially contends that he was misled about material information that he required in order to grant an intelligent and informed consent to the performance of the procedure because he did not receive accurate responses to questions concerning defendant's experience in performing corpectomies and whether he was "Board Certified." Plaintiff allegedly was warned of the risk of paralysis from the corpectomy procedure; however, he asserts that if he had known the truth about defendant's qualifications and experience, it would have affected his assessment of the risks of the procedure. Stated differently, defendant's misrepresentations induced plaintiff to consent to a surgical procedure, and its risk of paralysis, that he would not have undergone had he known the truth about defendant's qualifications. Stripped to its essentials, plaintiff's claim is founded on lack of informed consent.

As noted earlier, a patient-specific standard of what is material to a full disclosure does not apply in a claim based on lack of informed consent. Thus, plaintiff's subjective preference for a Board Certified physician, or one who had performed more corpectomies than defendant had performed, is not the actionable standard. Nonetheless, assuming the misrepresentations are proved, if an objectively reasonable person could find that physician experience was material in determining the medical risk of the corpectomy procedure to which plaintiff consented, and if a reasonably prudent person in plaintiff's position informed of the defendant's misrepresentations about his experience would not have consented, then a claim based on lack of informed consent may be maintained.

Modern advances in medicine coupled with the increased sophistication of medical consumers require an evolving notion of the reasonably prudent patient when assessing a claim based on lack of informed consent. . . . That said, most informed consent issues are unlikely to implicate a setting in which a physician's experience or credentials have been demonstrated to be a material element affecting the risk of undertaking a specific procedure. The standard requires proof on which an objectively reasonable person would base a finding that physician experience could have a causal connection to a substantial risk of the procedure. . . .

The alleged misrepresentations in this case about "physician experience" (credentials and surgical experience) provide a useful context for demonstrating the difficulty inherent in meeting the materiality standard required in order for physician experience to have a role in an informed consent case. We recognize that a misrepresentation about a physician's experience is not a perfect fit with the familiar construct of a claim based on lack of informed consent. The difficulty arises because physician experience is not information that directly relates to the procedure itself or one of the other areas of required medical disclosure concerning the procedure, its substantial risks, and alternatives that must be disclosed to avoid a claim based on lack of informed consent. But the possibility of materiality is present. If defendant's true level of experience had the capacity to enhance substantially the risk of paralysis from undergoing a corpectomy, a jury could find that a reasonably prudent patient would not have consented to that procedure had the misrepresentation been revealed. That presumes that plaintiff can prove that the actual level of experience possessed by defendant had a direct and demonstrable relationship to the harm of paralysis, a substantial risk of the procedure that was disclosed to plaintiff. Put differently, plaintiff must prove that the additional undisclosed risk posed by defendant's true level of qualifications and experience increased plaintiff's risk of paralysis from the corpectomy procedure.

The standard for causation that we envision in such an action will impose a significant gatekeeper function on the trial court to prevent insubstantial claims concerning alleged misrepresentations about a physician's experience from proceeding to a jury. We contemplate that misrepresented or exaggerated physician experience would have to significantly increase a risk of a procedure in order for it to affect the judgment of a reasonably prudent patient in an informed consent case. As this case demonstrates, the proximate cause analysis will involve a two-step inquiry.

The first inquiry should be, assuming a misrepresentation about experience, whether the more limited experience or credentials possessed by defendant could have substantially increased plaintiff's risk of paralysis from undergoing the corpectomy procedure. We envision that expert testimony would be required for such a showing. The second inquiry would be whether that substantially increased risk would cause a reasonably prudent person not to consent to undergo the procedure. If the true extent of defendant's experience could not affect materially the risk of paralysis from a corpectomy procedure, then the alleged misrepresentation could not cause a reasonably prudent patient in plaintiff's position to decline consent to the procedure. The court's gatekeeper function in respect of the first question will require a determination that a genuine issue of material fact exists requiring resolution by the factfinder in order to proceed to the second question involving an assessment by the reasonably prudent patient. Further, the trial court must conclude that there is a genuine issue of material fact concerning both questions in order to allow the claim to proceed to trial.

Finally, to satisfy the damages element in a claim based on lack of informed consent, a plaintiff typically has to show a causal connection between the inadequately disclosed risk of the procedure and the injury sustained. . . . If that risk materialized and harmed plaintiff, damages for those injuries are awarded. . . . Here, if successful in his claim based on lack of informed consent, plaintiff may receive damages for injuries caused by an inadequately disclosed risk of the corpectomy procedure. However, as noted, to be successful plaintiff must prove that defendant's allegedly misrepresented qualifications and experience can satisfy the stringent test for proximate causation that is required for physician experience to be material to the substantial risk of the procedure that occurred (paralysis) and injured plaintiff. If he can, then plaintiff may be compensated for that injury caused by the corpectomy irrespective of whether defendant deviated from the standard of care in performing the surgical procedure.

In conclusion, plaintiff's medical malpractice action will address any negligence in defendant's performance of the corpectomy procedure. We hold that in addition plaintiff may attempt to prove that defendant's alleged misrepresentation about his credentials and experience presents a claim based on lack of informed consent to the surgical procedure, consistent with the requirements and limitations that we have imposed on such a claim. . . .

Notes: Fiduciary Principles and the Disclosure of Provider-Associated Risks

1. *Do Fiduciary Principles Add Anything?* Why couldn't the *Moore* court analyze the facts solely using traditional informed consent analysis? Read the opinion to determine (1) the theory underlying the imposition of fiduciary obligations; (2) the scope of the fiduciary duty; (3) the actions that might constitute a breach of the duty; (4) the injury requirements, if any; and (5) the remedies for a breach of fiduciary duty. Do fiduciary duties expand or merely parallel the duties already created under the material risk standard in informed consent cases? What should Golde have done to avoid liability? Why doesn't the court impose disclosure duties on the other defendants? Would a conversion claim have been an easier basis of recovering damages from all of the defendants?

2. *Causation Problems in* Moore. Who has the better of the causation and damages arguments between Justice Mosk and Justice Broussard? On remand, Moore's claim was settled before going to trial, so the court never had to resolve these issues. The *Howard* court directly confronts the knotty causation questions

created by provider-associated risk disclosure claims. Will Mr. Howard be able to recover on his informed consent claim without expert proof that the surgeon violated the standard of care in the conduct of the surgery? Why or why not? See Starozytnyk v. Reich, 871 A.2d 733 (N.J. Super. 2005) (affirming dismissal of plaintiff's informed consent and fiduciary duty claims due to absence of proximate cause); Christine Grady et al., The Limits of Disclosure: What Research Subjects Want to Know About Investigator Financial Interests, 34 J. L. Med. & Ethics 592 (2006) (majority of respondents wanted to know about investigators' interest but "only a minority thought such financial information would influence their decisions about research participation in any way").

3. *The Theoretical Application of Fiduciary Theories to Remedy Economic Conflicts of Interest.* No one supposes that doctors must disclose the distorting effects of fee-for-service reimbursement, which might result in harms from unnecessary treatment. Cf. Wright v. Jeckle, 144 P.3d 301 (Wash. 2006) (rejecting claim that physician's direct sale of anti-obesity drug constituted a violation of fiduciary duty under state anti-kickback legislation merely because physician profited from sales). Should there nonetheless be a duty to disclose incentives related to managed care? Could you argue that incentives to reduce health care expenses in managed care are "common knowledge"?

If there is a financial disclosure obligation on the part of physicians participating in managed care arrangements, how great should the financial incentive be before it is considered "material"? Should the plaintiff be required to prove that the incentive was sufficient to affect physician decisionmaking in individual cases? Or can we presume that managed care companies would not use financial incentives unless they worked, by affecting physician decisions at least to some extent? Managed care physicians might argue that incentives are designed only to reduce unnecessary medical care and are not large enough to induce physicians to refrain from making necessary medical referrals. Even if incentives potentially affect necessary care, isn't the threat of a malpractice claim enough to ensure that physicians will still make appropriate referrals, or a sufficient remedy when they fail to do so?

And now, a final set of issues. If there is an obligation to disclose managed care financial incentives, should it be satisfied by a global disclosure when the patient first enrolls (and perhaps once a year thereafter), or must the incentives be repeated each time the patient seeks treatment? For an argument that disclosure at enrollment satisfies the fiduciary obligation, or perhaps acts as a waiver of subsequent disclosures, see Mark A. Hall, A Theory of Economic Informed Consent, 31 Ga. L. Rev. 511 (1997).

4. *Discussing the Costs of Care.* Curiously, there is virtually no legal or ethical guidance on whether physicians should tell patients how much treatment options cost. In the distant past, this may have been because physicians followed an ethic of treat first and bill later, letting patients pay what they were able. In the more recent past, this may be because insurance usually pays for the majority of costs. In the future, however, these cost-insulating features may soon recede, under the influence of "consumer-driven" health insurance plans that expose patients to much greater cost-sharing obligations. See pages 67–68. This will likely generate disputes by patients who feel they were not adequately informed about the costs of the treatments they agreed to. Under the informed consent and fiduciary

principles you have learned, should physicians have to volunteer information about costs, or only wait for patients to ask first? Does the answer differ for the costs of the physicians' own services versus costs charged by other providers, goods, or services the physician may recommend (such as lab tests, drugs, or specialist referrals)? For preliminary discussion, see Haavi Morreim, High-Deductible Health Plans: New Twists on Old Challenges from Tort and Contract, 59 Vand. L. Rev. 1207 (2006); G. Caleb Alexander et al., Rethinking Professional Ethics in the Cost-Sharing Era, 6(4) Am. J. Bioethics W17-W22 (2006); Marshall Kapp, Patient Autonomy in the Age of Consumer-Driven Health Care: Informed Consent and Informed Choice, 28 J. Leg. Med. 91 (2007).

5. *Financial Disclosure Claims in the Courts. Moore* appeared to open the door to using informed consent and/or fiduciary theories to protect patients from the risks created by a provider's financial arrangements with third parties, such as managed care organizations. Subsequent courts have tried to push the door shut, at least on some types of claims. In Neade v. Portes, 739 N.E.2d 496 (Ill. 2000), for example, the Illinois Supreme Court rejected the use of fiduciary theories in a case involving managed care incentives. Mr. Neade was only 37 but had a number of significant risk factors for heart disease. Mr. Neade began to experience radiating chest pain and shortness of breath. Mr. Neade's primary physician, Dr. Portes, authorized Mr. Neade's hospitalization. While hospitalized, Mr. Neade underwent a battery of tests that appeared to rule out heart disease. Thereafter, Dr. Portes failed to refer Mr. Neade for more specific tests for heart disease, despite recurring symptoms. Mr. Neade had a heart attack and died. Mr. Neade's estate brought claims for breach of fiduciary duty and medical negligence against Dr. Portes and others. Dr. Portes participated in a risk-sharing agreement with the patient's HMO that arguably gave the physician an incentive to deny referrals to his patients.

Relying in part on some of the language found in the United States Supreme Court's opinion in Pegram v. Herdrich, 530 U.S. 211 (2000) (exploring fiduciary duty under federal ERISA statute), discussed in Chapter 4 at page 500, the Illinois Supreme Court rejected the breach of fiduciary duty claim. The Illinois Supreme Court held that a cause of action for breach of fiduciary duty based on a physician's failure to reveal a financial interest in a medical incentive fund essentially duplicated the underlying medical negligence claim:

> [I]t is operative facts together with the injury that we look to in order to determine whether a cause of action is duplicative. In the case at bar, the operative fact in both [the malpractice and fiduciary duty] counts is Dr. Portes' failure to order an angiogram for Mr. Neade. Plaintiff alleges in both counts that Mr. Neade's failure to receive an angiogram is the ultimate reason for his subsequent death. Plaintiff also alleges the same injury in both her medical negligence claim and her breach of fiduciary duty claim, namely, Mr. Neade's death and its effect on plaintiff and her family. We determine that plaintiff's breach of fiduciary duty claim is a re-presentment of her medical negligence claim.
>
> An examination of the elements of a medical negligence claim and breach of fiduciary duty claim illustrates the way in which a breach of fiduciary duty claim would "boil down to a malpractice claim." *Herdrich*, 530 U.S. at—, 120 S.Ct. at 2157. To sustain an action for medical negligence, plaintiff must show: (1) the standard of care in the medical community by which the physician's treatment was measured; (2) that the physician deviated from the standard of care; and (3) that a

resulting injury was proximately caused by the deviation from the standard of care. . . . Thus, the standard of care is the relevant inquiry by which we judge a physician's actions in a medical negligence case. . . .

In contrast to an action for medical negligence, in order to state a claim for breach of fiduciary duty, it must be alleged that a fiduciary duty exists, that the fiduciary duty was breached, and that such breach proximately caused the injury of which the plaintiff complains. . . .

In order to sustain a breach of fiduciary duty claim against Dr. Portes, plaintiff would have to allege, inter alia, that: (1) had she known of the Medical Incentive Fund she would have sought an opinion from another physician; (2) that the other physician would have ordered an angiogram for Mr. Neade; (3) that the angiogram would have detected Mr. Neade's heart condition; and (4) that treatment could have prevented his eventual myocardial infarction and subsequent death. In order to prove the second element, plaintiff would have been required to present expert testimony that the expert, after examining Mr. Neade and considering his history, would have ordered an angiogram. This requirement relates to the standard of care consideration—the first prong in a traditional medical negligence claim—under which a physician is held to "the reasonable skill which a physician in good standing in the community would use." That is precisely what plaintiff must prove to support her breach of fiduciary duty claim. As the Supreme Court stated in *Herdrich*, the breach of fiduciary duty claim "would boil down to a malpractice claim, and the fiduciary standard would be nothing but the malpractice standard traditionally applied in actions against physicians." *Herdrich*, 530 U.S. at—, 120 S.Ct. at 2157. Thus, we need not recognize a new cause of action for breach of fiduciary duty when a traditional medical negligence claim sufficiently addresses the same alleged misconduct. The breach of fiduciary duty claim in the case at bar would be duplicative of the medical negligence claim.

Our decision to refrain from permitting the creation of this new cause of action finds additional support in statutory law. The Illinois legislature has placed the burden of disclosing HMO incentive schemes on HMOs themselves. . . .

Moreover, the outcome that would result if we were to allow the creation of a new cause of action for breach of fiduciary duty against a physician in these circumstances may be impractical. For example, physicians often provide services for numerous patients, many of whom may be covered by different HMOs. In order to effectively disclose HMO incentives, physicians would have to remain cognizant at all times of every patient's particular HMO and that HMO's policies and procedures. See, e.g., Mark Hall, A Theory of Economic Informed Consent, 31 Ga.L.Rev. 511, 525-26 (1997). . . . If we were to recognize a breach of fiduciary duty claim in the context of the case at bar, we fear the effects of such a holding may be unworkable. Neade v. Portes, 739 N.E.2d. at 502-506.

The court also held that evidence of the physician's financial incentives could be relevant on issues relating to interest and bias, in the event that physician testified in the medical negligence trial. Id. at 506.

Chief Justice Harrison dissented:

A complaint against a lawyer for professional malpractice may be couched in either contract or tort. . . . The same rule should apply here. Although this case involves medical rather than legal malpractice, that distinction is insignificant. . . . The right to assert claims for breach of fiduciary duty and negligence in the same professional malpractice action is not unfettered. When the same operative facts support a negligence count and a count for breach of fiduciary duty based on the same injury to the client, the counts are identical and the fiduciary duty count should be dismissed as duplicative. . . . In this case, however, the negligence and breach of fiduciary duty counts asserted by plaintiff are not identical. . . . As the appellate court correctly recognized,

> It is conceivable that a trier of fact could find both that Dr. Portes was within the standard of care and therefore not negligent in relying on the thallium stress test and the EKG in deciding that an angiogram was not necessary and also that Dr. Portes did breach his fiduciary duty in not disclosing his financial incentive arrangement and, as a proximate result thereof, Neade did not obtain a second opinion, suffered a massive coronary infarction, and died.

710 N.E.2d 418. . . .

Id. at 506. Other courts have reached similar results. See Weiss v. CIGNA Healthcare, Inc., 972 F. Supp. 748, 752 (S.D.N.Y. 1997); D.A.B. v. Brown, 570 N.W.2d 168 (Minn. Ct. App. 1997). But see Darke v. Estate of Isner, 20 Mass.L. Rptr. 419 (Mass. Superior Ct. 2005) (plaintiff's deceit claims survive summary judgment motion in case involving physician's failure to disclose financial interest in research). For an unsuccessful effort to use fiduciary theories in the context of obesity drug litigation, see Wright v. Jeckle, 90 P.3d 65 (Wash. App. 2004).

6. *Institutional Disclosure Obligations under Fiduciary Law.* Under common law principles, as *Moore* holds, institutions are generally free from the disclosure duties imposed on physicians. A federal statute, the Employee Retirement Income Security Act of 1974 (ERISA), regulates health plans provided as a benefit of employment. This statute has a number of important implications for the organization and delivery of health care in the United States. For present purposes, it is enough to note that the Supreme Court's decision in *Pegram* closed the door to efforts to use ERISA's fiduciary principles as a tool for imposing disclosure obligations on managed care employee benefit plans.

7. *Other Financial Conflicts.* As *Moore* briefly indicates, statutory law sometimes requires disclosure of certain kinds of financial conflicts of interest. A prime example is when physicians have investment or ownership interests in the facilities to which they refer their patients. State and federal laws prohibit or regulate these investment interests in many circumstances. Which approach strikes you as more appropriate: disclosure or prohibition/regulation?

Different types of financial and nonfinancial conflicts of interest permeate medical relationships, as they do most human affairs. (For example, the authors of this book receive modest royalties when their own students purchase it.) How assiduous should physicians be in avoiding or disclosing them? Consider, for instance, the many tactics that drug companies have used to encourage physicians to prescribe their products. Kickbacks and direct financial incentives are illegal; other types of arrangements have elicited increasing attention. See Troyen A. Brennan et al., Health Industry Practices That Create Conflicts of Interest: A Policy Proposal for Academic Medical Centers, 295 JAMA 429 (2006); Susan L. Coyle, Physician-Industry Relations. Part I: Individual Physicians, 136 Annals Internal Med. 396 (2002); The Council on Ethical and Judicial Affairs of the American Medical Association, Guidelines on Gifts to Physicians from Industry:

An Update, 56 Food & Drug L.J. 27 (2001). For an article that examines financial conflict of interest between physicians and medical device companies see Reed Abelson, Hospitals See Possible Conflict on Medical Devices for Doctors, N.Y. Times, Sept. 22, 2006 at A1.8. *Nonfinancial Provider-Associated Risks.* Should physicians have a duty to disclose risks to patients that arise from the identity of the provider rather than the type of procedure? *Howard* is part of a small new line of cases considering whether physicians have any duty to disclose provider risks, as distinguished from procedural risks.

(a) *Experience and Success Rates.* As discussed at pages 43 and 298, health care organizations and purchasers are developing and collecting information about health care outcomes for individual practitioners. Should health care providers have a duty to disclose their own "scorecards" to patients? How does the *Howard* court distinguish between informed consent and misrepresentation claims in this area?

For other cases involving physician experience, see Duffy v. Flagg, 905 A.2d 15 (2006) (informed consent does not require physician to give detailed account of her past experience with a procedure when answers would not have been relevant to key informed consent issues); DeGennaro v. Tandon, 873 A.2d 191 (Conn. App. 2005) (reasonable patient would consider lack of experience in using equipment, and lack of assistance, to be material information about provider-specific risk); Wlosinski v. Cohn, 713 N.W.2d 16 (Mich. App. 2005) ("raw success rates" need not be disclosed; interesting concurring and dissenting opinions); Duttry v. Patterson, 771 A.2d 1255 (Pa. 2001) (physician's personal characteristics and experience irrelevant in informed consent claim; misrepresentation claim possible); Johnson v. Kokemoor, 545 N.W.2d 495 (Wis. 1996) (applying informed consent principles to a case involving a physician's relative lack of experience).

For commentaries on the subject, see Heyward H. Bouknight, III, Note, Between the Scalpel and the Lie: Comparing Theories of Physician Accountability for Misrepresentations of Experience and Competence, 60 Wash. & Lee L. Rev. 1515 (2003); Janet L. Dolgin, The Evolution of the "Patient": Shifts in Attitudes About Consent, Genetic Information, and Commercialization in Health Care, 34 Hofstra L. Rev. 137 (2005) (critiquing expansion of disclosure obligation in *Howard*); Milt Freudenheim, To Find a Doctor, Mine the Data, N.Y. Times, Sept. 22, 2005, at C1; Aaron D. Twerski, The Second Revolution in Informed Consent: Comparing Physicians to Each Other, 94 Nw. U. L. Rev. 1 (1999); Aaron D. Twerski & Neil B. Cohen, Comparing Medical Providers: A First Look at the New Era of Medical Statistics, 58 Brook. L. Rev. 5 (1992); Robert Weinstein et al., Infection-Control Report Cards–Ensuring Patient Safety, 353 New Eng. J. Med. 225 (2005); J. Wilks et al., Surgeon with Worst Performance Figures Might Be the Best Option, 323 Brit. Med. J. 1071 (2001).

(b) *Abuse of Drug or Alcohol.* Would the reasonable patient consider a physician's cocaine addiction to be a material fact in deciding whether or not to undergo surgery? Would the professional standard of care require such a disclosure? Compare Albany Urology Clinic, P.C. v. Cleveland, 528 S.E.2d 777 (Ga. 2000) (no duty to disclose drug use under common law or state informed consent statute), with Hidding v. Williams, 578 So. 2d 1192 (La. Ct. App. 1991) (physician has duty to reveal his alcoholism; concurring opinion raises interesting causation problem).

(c) *Infection with HIV.* There has been a vigorous debate about whether a physician has or should have a duty to disclose his or her HIV status. See, e.g., Mary Anne Bobinski, Autonomy and Privacy: Protecting Patients from Their Physicians, 55 U. Pitt. L. Rev. 291 (1994). The application of the informed consent doctrine to the problem of HIV disclosure in health care is complicated by the fact that many patients are more fearful about the very low risk of HIV transmission from health care worker to patient than they are about other, larger risks. In addition, persons with HIV infection are protected from discrimination under a variety of statutes, including the Americans with Disabilities Act, unless they pose a "significant risk" to the health or safety of others. 42 U.S.C. §§12111-12113. From the perspective of the infected physician, disclosure ought not be required unless there is a significant risk of transmission. From the perspective of the patient, even a "less than significant" risk could be avoided by selecting an (apparently) uninfected health care provider. One court has resolved the conflict in favor of the patient's right to know:

[Dr. Behringer, a surgeon] argues: (1) the risk of transmission of HIV from surgeon to patient is too remote to require informed consent, and (2) the law of informed consent does not require disclosure of the condition of the surgeon. . . . [Dr. Behringer] argues that the use of the informed consent form is tantamount to a de facto termination of surgical privileges. [Dr. Behringer] further urges that patient reaction is likely to be based more on public hysteria than on a studied assessment of the actual risk involved.

The answer to these arguments is two-fold. First, it is the duty of the surgeon utilizing the informed consent procedure to explain to the patient the real risk involved. If the patient's fear is without basis, it is likewise the duty of the surgeon to allay that fear. This court recognizes that the burden imposed on the surgeon may not be surmountable absent further education of both the public and the medical community about the realities of HIV and AIDS. Second, the difficulties created by the public reaction to AIDS cannot deprive the patient of making the ultimate decision where the ultimate risk is so significant. The last word has not been spoken on the issue of transmission of HIV and AIDS. Facts accepted at one point in time are no longer accurate as more is learned about this disease and its transmission. . . .

[Dr. Behringer] further argues that there is no requirement under the doctrine of informed consent that a surgeon's physical condition be revealed as a risk of the surgery itself. The informed consent cases are not so narrow as to support that argument. In [a prior New Jersey Supreme Court case] . . . the court spoke of not only an evaluation of the nature of the treatment, but of "any attendant substantial risks.". . .

[Dr. Behringer] urges that these issues should be dealt with on a case-by-case basis, wherein the hospital or medical staff monitors an HIV-positive surgeon and makes a determination as to the surgeon's ability to perform a particular invasive procedure. . . . The position [Dr. Behringer] seeks to implement is replete with the "anachronistic paternalism" rejected in both Canterbury v. Spence, supra, and by the [New Jersey] Supreme Court. . . .

[The court summarized the views of several commentators, one of whom had noted the fiduciary character of the physician-patient relationship.] . . . The obligation of a surgeon performing invasive procedures, such as [Dr. Behringer], to reveal his AIDS condition, is one which requires a weighing of [Dr. Behringer's] rights against the patient's rights. New Jersey's strong policy supporting patient rights, weighed against [Dr. Behringer's] individual right to perform an invasive procedure as a part of the practice of his profession, requires the conclusion that the patient's rights must prevail. At a minimum, the physician must withdraw from performing any invasive procedure which would pose a risk to the patient. Where the ultimate harm is death, even the presence of a low risk of transmission justifies the adoption of a policy which precludes invasive procedures when there is "any" risk of transmission. In the present case, the debate raged as to whether there was "any" risk of transmission, and the informed-consent procedure was left in place. If there is to be an ultimate arbiter of whether the patient is to be treated invasively by an AIDS-positive surgeon, the arbiter will be the fully-informed patient. The ultimate risk to the patient is so absolute — so devastating — that it is untenable to argue against informed consent combined with a restriction on procedures which present "any risk" to the patient. Estate of Behringer v. Medical Center at Princeton, 592 A.2d 1251, 1279-1283 (N.J. Super. Ct. Div. 1991).

Problem: *Moore* Liability?

Consider the informed consent doctrine applicable in your state. What types of disclosures would be required in the following situations?

1. A physician recommending a surgical procedure necessary to save the patient's life will earn about $15,000 from the surgery and follow-up care. What if the surgery was for cosmetic purposes?

2. A physician recommends that a patient see a specialist for her condition. The physician is married to the specialist.

3. A physician providing care for an HMO patient earns a flat fee per month per patient. The physician is treating a patient's digestive complaints and suggests that the patient wait two months to see if the condition gets better on its own.

4. A physician providing care for an HMO patient with back pain suggests that the patient take a conservative approach to treatment, delaying expensive diagnostic tests and surgery for as long as possible. The physician's financial arrangements with the HMO include provisions that decrease the physician's income if the physician spends more than an allocated amount on diagnostic tests or hospitalization.

5. A physician describes herself as a social drinker. She only drinks during the evenings and on weekends. On average, she consumes about 21 mixed drinks per week.

6. A general internist learns that he has HIV infection.

7. A physician fails to inform a patient suffering from pancreatic cancer of the patient's low statistical life expectancy. The patient does not make the proper financial arrangements, causing substantial real estate and tax losses. See Arato v. Avedon, 858 P.2d 598 (Cal. 1993).

5. Human Experimentation and Research

The *Moore* litigation arose because of the alleged conflicts of interest created by the research interests of the defendants. Nightly news stories regularly focus on the results of medical research, touting the next great cures for long-feared diseases (as well as informing us about cures for diseases that we never knew existed). Society clearly has a strong interest in ensuring that medical research is not stymied by excessive regulation. Researchers and biotechnology companies may have significant economic interests in the research enterprise. Statistics are difficult to obtain because medical research is conducted in a range of public and private settings, funded by public and private sources, and regulated either by different federal regulatory entities or by much more diffuse common law rules. Medical research is commonly described as a multi-billion-dollar activity, with "an estimated 20 million Americans tak[ing] part in more than 41,000 clinical trials and uncounted more federally funded experiments." Tom Abate, Experiments on Humans: Business of Clinical Trials Soars, But Risk Unknown, S.F. Chron., Aug. 4, 2002, at A1.

There are two central concerns in the research context. The first is that experimental treatment is often not done for the patient's immediate benefit. Some patients may approach medical research thinking they will receive better care because it is "state of the art," but this is usually a false impression. Instead, the treatment that is being studied may be riskier; almost certainly its risks are less well known than standard treatment. Also, patients are often "randomized" "blindly" between an "experimental arm" and a "control arm." This means that, by luck of the draw, a significant percentage will receive ordinary treatment or even, in some cases, a placebo; participants generally will not know which type of care they will receive. Moreover, the innovation in treatment may have nothing at all to offer their condition, but may be intended solely to provide an improvement for other patients. The relevant distinction is between "therapeutic" and "nontherapeutic research." Only in the former is there something that a patient might benefit from immediately, but even then, patients are often asked to undergo risks that are greater than the potential rewards in order to further the aims of science.

Fully informed patients may be more than willing to accept these arrangements out of a sense of altruism and a desire to be a part of progress. But there is a second difficulty: How well informed are they, and how freely do they make their decision? Some patients may feel pressured in subtle ways without the knowledge of their physicians. Imagine a physician who eagerly pitches her pet research project, and a patient who fears (irrationally or not?) that disappointing his doctor will jeopardize his treatment. For other patients, coercion could be more overt. The reluctance of well-informed patients to participate in risky experiments might lead researchers either to conceal the experiment or to use patients from vulnerable or socially disadvantaged groups.

These concerns are not merely speculative. The history of medical research reveals both astounding advances and disquieting practices. Scientists have sought to expand the knowledge of human biology, illness, and treatment, often at the expense of the least fortunate in society: slaves, the poor, criminals, and other institutionalized persons. Several twentieth-century examples have left a legacy of fear and mistrust. Nazi scientists conducted a vigorous program of medical research on prisoners and internees during World War II. Their appalling lack of respect for human life and humane principles resulted in the Nuremberg Code. The Code's central tenet is a requirement that human research subjects give consent to participation in any research project. See Evelyn Shuster, Fifty Years Later: The Significance of the Nuremberg Code, 337 New Eng. J. Med. 1436 (1997).

Violations of human rights by researchers are not limited, however, to some distant time and distant place. Two examples of research abuses in the United States have had a profound impact. In the Tuskegee Study, which ran from the 1950s until the early 1970s, researchers studied the effects of untreated syphilis in a group of African-American men. The researchers purported to treat the men for their ailments but never disclosed to their subjects that they continued to suffer from a highly treatable, yet debilitating illness. The researchers' apparently cavalier disregard for their subjects has resulted in a legacy of distrust among minority and poor communities.

Recent revelations have been no more comforting. In the mid-1990s, the federal government revealed that hundreds of persons had been involuntarily, and in some cases unknowingly, subjected to research in which they were exposed to radiation and other harmful substances. President Clinton was forced to announce the adoption of newly strengthened protections for human subjects participating in classified research projects. Strengthened Protections for Human Subjects of Classified Research, 62 Fed. Reg. 26,367 (1997). See generally U.S. Advisory Comm. on Human Radiation Experiments, Final Report of the Advisory Committee on Human Radiation Experiments (Ruth Faden ed., 1996).

A special set of rules governs the disclosure and consent process in medical research. Federal regulations require an elaborate consent process in order for research to receive federal funding. U.S. Dep't Health & Human Servs., Protection of Human Subjects, 45 C.F.R. §§46.101-.409; U.S. Food & Drug Admin., Protection of Human Subjects, 21 C.F.R. §§50.1-.56. Entities that accept federally funded research projects also assure that they will protect human subjects in research projects funded by non-federal sources. 45 C.F.R. §46.103(b). Private foundations that fund research usually follow suit. The end result is that the federal regulations effectively govern most planned medical research in the United States. These federal rules, while influential, do not preempt state laws providing greater protection of human subjects. State regulation of research through the common law may become increasingly important.

■ **WHY INFORMED CONSENT? HUMAN EXPERIMENTATION AND THE ETHICS OF AUTONOMY**
Richard W. Garnett*
36 Cath. Law. 455 (1996)

. . . Why does consent have such moral power? Accept for now that our deference to consent is — perhaps mistakenly — rooted in a commitment to

---

*Law professor at Notre Dame Law School; B.A. Duke, 1990; J.D. Yale, 1995.

human dignity, expressed through respect for autonomy. Is consent's justifying role necessarily required by this commitment to human dignity? Why have we come to think that it is? Does our dignity as persons follow from, or does it instead create and condition, our autonomy? Do we respect consent because one feature of our dignity is that we always know what is best for us? Clearly we do not. . . .

III. REGULATING HUMAN EXPERIMENTATION THROUGH CONSENT

A. THE NUREMBERG CODE AND "INFORMED CONSENT"

The Nuremberg Code and the memory of the Nazi doctors' trial animate and permeate modern thinking about regulation of human experimentation. The Code was our most morally rigorous attempt to limit human experimentation. Its most memorable command was that, in medical research, "[t]he voluntary consent of the human subject is absolutely essential."[70] But while the Code has come to stand for "informed consent," it required more. It focused as much on the experiment itself, on the welfare of the subject, and on the conduct of the researcher as it did on the need for the subject's consent. Sadly, this broad focus has received relatively short shrift, and the consent principle has eclipsed the others.

The Code stands tall in memory but its influence has never lived up to its aims. Seen by many as a product of and reaction to Nazi terror, the Code is often dismissed as a context-bound relic, no longer useful for today's researchers. Pragmatists argue that the Code is simply too demanding, that its standards are too high for necessary research to meet, and that its absolutism cannot compete with the utilitarian and impersonal ethics of modern medicine. . . .

B. REGULATING EXPERIMENTATION AFTER NUREMBERG: THE STANDARD MODEL OF INFORMED CONSENT

. . . Today, human experimentation is regulated by a crazy-quilt of hortatory codes and maxims, scattered federal laws and regulations, and most importantly, by Institutional Review Boards,[85] which provide peer review of proposed experiments. "Informed consent" is still the touchstone, but modern regulations and procedures tolerate and expect deviations from this ideal. Thus, when addressing human experimentation — and they rarely do — courts occasionally mention the [Nuremberg] Code, but generally apply and enforce the more flexible informed consent requirements of later regulations.

The legal doctrine of informed consent as it has developed is quite different from the dignity-based commitment to self-determination animating the Nuremberg Code. The most important feature of today's regulatory regime is that it focuses on the subject's state of mind more than on the experiment itself. What is referred to here as the "Standard Model" of informed consent is this

---

[70] The Nazi Doctors and the Nuremberg Code: Human Rights in Human Experimentation 2 (George J. Annas & Michael A. Grodin eds., 1992).

[85] For a complete review of the structure and function of Institutional Review Boards, see, e.g., 45 C.F.R. §§46.107-111 (1994); 21 C.F.R. §§56.101-114 (1994). "IRB approval means the determination of the IRB that the research has been reviewed and may be conducted at an institution within the constraints set forth by the IRB and by other institutional and federal requirements." 45 C.F.R. §46.102(h).

subjectively oriented informed consent in the context of peer review. In practice, research peers have proven insufficiently critical when evaluating proposed experiments. In addition, the informed consent "requirement" is viewed as a chore and a ritual, an impersonal incantation, a hurried signing of papers. We know this is true, yet we cherish the myth of informed consent, skating over its lack of real content or impact. But because the Standard Model is a subterfuge aimed more at easing our consciences than at protecting research subjects, it fails both as a necessary condition for proposed experiments and as a justification for them.

IV. THE STANDARD MODEL IN ACTION: INFORMED CONSENT IN HARD CASES

. . . The Standard Model regulates experiments by requiring the subjects' informed consent. Comparatively little attention is given to the nature of the experiment itself—apart from its riskiness—or to the researcher's goals and intentions. Under the Standard Model, concern may be triggered by some characteristic of the subject (age, health, mental capabilities) or by the experiment's location (prison, hospital, university). These characteristics and locations, however, relate less to whether the researcher's plan is itself ethical, than whether the subject's consent was really given, or was truly informed. When experiments are prohibited, it is due to the quality, or lack thereof, of the consent given, not the propriety of the experiment itself. In these situations, whatever it is that gives the subject's consent its justificatory power—the mysterious indicia of autonomy worth respecting—is deemed lacking. To illustrate this dynamic at work, I review below the operation of the Standard Model in three paradigmatically hard cases.

A. PRISONERS

Prisoners have long been conveniently immobile, docile, and hence ideal subjects for research and experimentation. . . . Accordingly, experimentation on prisoners is carefully scrutinized under the Standard Model. The Department of Health and Human Services warns that "prisoners may be under constraints because of their incarceration which could affect their ability to make a truly voluntary and uncoerced decision whether or not to participate as subjects in research." . . .

B. THE TERMINALLY ILL

. . . As with prisoners, experimentation with terminally or grieviously ill patients distorts the Standard Model. Like children or the mentally handicapped, dying persons are often thought of as incapable of making informed decisions; and like prisoners, they are viewed as not "really" free, but instead, captive to the course of their disease and therefore under duress. Even when these patients are lucid, we fear their assessment of an experiment's benefits and risks may be skewed; we worry they might submit to quackery in a hopeless and desperate attempt to beat the inevitable. We also worry that the dying may, having abandoned all hope, submit to immoral experiments out of misplaced or entirely genuine altruism. Finally, we fear that we may be tempted to exploit these subjects' despair, incapacity, or altruism, and to railroad through experiments which might not otherwise pass ethical muster. . . .

C. CHILDREN

The use of children poses even thornier problems for research. We need to experiment on children; their problems and illnesses are often sui generis and can only be solved through experiments on them. However, the Standard Model assumes children cannot give adequate consent, and so it gives in to necessity, though the Nuremberg Code insisted that the subject's consent was essential. Because children cannot, by definition, give consent, we settle for less. In addition, because children are a necessary and unique research class, we are forced to face the steely utilitarian calculus that hides beneath the Standard Model's veneer of respect for persons.

The Standard Model requires someone's consent, and parents are the most obvious candidates. However, even parents might not be able to isolate and protect an individual child's safety and dignity, especially when another child is thrown into the equation. The same considerations that call into question whether a prisoner's consent was voluntary or informed might undermine a desperate parent's consent as well. . . .

■ GRIMES v. KENNEDY KRIEGER INSTITUTE, INC.
782 A.2d 807 (Md. 2001)

Opinion by CATHELL, J.

PROLOGUE

We initially note that these are cases of first impression for this Court. For that matter, precious few courts in the United States have addressed the issues presented in the cases at bar. . . .

In these present cases, a prestigious research institute, associated with Johns Hopkins University, based on this record, created a nontherapeutic research program whereby it required certain classes of homes to have only partial lead paint abatement modifications performed, and in at least some instances, including at least one of the cases at bar, arranged for the landlords to receive public funding by way of grants or loans to aid in the modifications. The research institute then encouraged, and in at least one of the cases at bar, required, the landlords to rent the premises to families with young children. In the event young children already resided in one of the study houses, it was contemplated that a child would remain in the premises, and the child was encouraged to remain, in order for his or her blood to be periodically analyzed. In other words, the continuing presence of the children that were the subjects of the study was required in order for the study to be complete. Apparently, the children and their parents involved in the[se] cases . . . were from a lower economic strata and were, at least in one case, minorities.

The purpose of the research was to determine how effective varying degrees of lead paint abatement procedures were. Success was to be determined by periodically, over a two-year period of time, measuring the extent to which lead dust remained in, or returned to, the premises after the varying levels of abatement modifications, and, as most important to our decision, by measuring the extent to which the theretofore healthy children's blood became contaminated with lead, and comparing that contamination with levels of lead dust in the houses over the same periods of time. [Some evidence suggests that families with young children were given priority in renting abated apartments.] . . . .

The same researchers had completed a prior study on abatement and partial abatement methods that indicated that lead dust remained and/or returned to abated houses over a period of time. . . . [The researchers also acknowledged that exposure to lead was "particularly hazardous for children"]. . . . After publishing this report, the researchers began the present research project in which children were encouraged to reside in households where the possibility of lead dust was known to the researcher to be likely, so that the lead dust content of their blood could be compared with the level of lead dust in the houses at periodic intervals over a two-year period.

Apparently, it was anticipated that the children, who were the human subjects in the program, would, or at least might, accumulate lead in their blood from the dust, thus helping the researchers to determine the extent to which the various partial abatement methods worked. There was no complete and clear explanation in the consent agreements signed by the parents of the children that the research to be conducted was designed, at least in significant part, to measure the success of the abatement procedures by measuring the extent to which the children's blood was being contaminated. It can be argued that the researchers intended that the children be the canaries in the mines but never clearly told the parents. . . .

The researchers and their Institutional Review Board apparently saw nothing wrong with the research protocols that anticipated the possible accumulation of lead in the blood of otherwise healthy children as a result of the experiment, or they believed that the consents of the parents of the children made the research appropriate. Institutional Review Boards (IRB) are oversight entities [that are within the organizational structure of the institution conducting the research]. In research experiments, an IRB can be required in some instances by either federal or state regulation, or sometimes by the conditions attached to governmental grants that are used to fund research projects. Generally, their primary functions are to assess the protocols of the project to determine whether the project itself is appropriate, whether the consent procedures are adequate, whether the methods to be employed meet proper standards, whether reporting requirements are sufficient, and the assessment of various other aspects of a research project. One of the most important objectives of such review is the review of the potential safety and the health hazard impact of a research project on the human subjects of the experiment, especially on vulnerable subjects such as children. Their function is not to help researchers seek funding for research projects.

In the instant case, as is suggested by some commentators as being endemic to the research community as a whole, infra, the IRB involved here, the Johns Hopkins University Joint Committee on Clinical Investigation, in part, abdicated that responsibility, instead suggesting to the researchers a way to miscast the characteristics of the study in order to avoid the responsibility inherent in nontherapeutic research involving children. . . .

While the suggestion of the IRB would not make this experiment any less nontherapeutic or, thus, less regulated, . . . [its action] shows two things: (1) that the IRB had a partial misperception of the difference between therapeutic and nontherapeutic research and the IRB's role in the process and (2) that the IRB was willing to aid researchers in getting around federal regulations designed to protect children used as subjects in nontherapeutic research. An IRB's primary role is to assure the safety of human research subjects — not help researchers avoid safety or health-related requirements. The IRB, in this case, misconceived, at least partially, its own role.

The provisions or conditions imposed by the federal funding entities, pursuant to federal regulations, are conditions attached to funding. As far as we are aware, or have been informed, there are no federal or state (Maryland) statutes that mandate that all research be subject to certain conditions. Certain international "codes" or "declarations" exist (one of which is supposedly binding but has never been so held) that, at least in theory, establish standards. We shall describe them, infra. Accordingly, we write on a clean slate in this case. We are guided, as we determine what is appropriate, by those international "codes" or "declarations," as well as by studies conducted by various governmental entities, by the treatises and other writings on the ethics of using children as research subjects, and by the duties, if any, arising out of the use of children as subjects of research.

Otherwise healthy children, in our view, should not be enticed into living in, or remaining in, potentially lead-tainted housing and intentionally subjected to a research program, which contemplates the probability, or even the possibility, of lead poisoning or even the accumulation of lower levels of lead in blood, in order for the extent of the contamination of the children's blood to be used by scientific researchers to assess the success of lead paint or lead dust abatement measures. Moreover, in our view, parents, whether improperly enticed by trinkets, food stamps, money or other items, have no more right to intentionally and unnecessarily place children in potentially hazardous nontherapeutic research surroundings, than do researchers. In such cases, parental consent, no matter how informed, is insufficient.

While the validity of the consent agreement and its nature as a contract, the existence or nonexistence of a special relationship, and whether the researchers performed their functions under that agreement pursuant to any special relationships are important issues in these cases that we will address, the very inappropriateness of the research itself cannot be overlooked. It is apparent that the protocols of research are even more important than the method of obtaining parental consent and the extent to which the parents were, or were not, informed. If the research methods, the protocols, are inappropriate then, especially when the IRB is willing to help researchers avoid compliance with applicable safety requirements for using children in nontherapeutic research, the consent of the parents, or of any consent surrogates, in our view, cannot make the research appropriate or the actions of the researchers and the Institutional Review Board proper.

The research relationship proffered to the parents of the children the researchers wanted to use as measuring tools, should never have been presented in a nontherapeutic context in the first instance. Nothing about the research was designed for treatment of the subject children. They were presumed to be healthy at the commencement of the project. As to them, the research was clearly nontherapeutic in nature. The experiment was simply a "for the greater good" project.[6] The specific children's health was put at risk, in order to develop low-cost abatement measures that would help all children, the landlords, and the general public as well. . . .

The research project at issue here, and its apparent protocols, differs in large degree from, but presents similar problems as those in the Tuskegee Syphilis Study conducted from 1932 until 1972 . . . the intentional exposure of soldiers to radiation in the 1940s and 50s . . . the tests involving the exposure of Navajo miners to radiation . . . and the secret administration of LSD to soldiers by the CIA and the Army in the 1950s and 60s. . . . [In] the Tuskegee Syphilis Study . . . patients infected with syphilis were not subsequently informed of the availability of penicillin for treatment of the illness, in order for the scientists and researchers to be able to continue research on the effects of the illness. . . . [P]erhaps [the] most notorious . . . [nontherapeutic research project was] the deliberate use of infection . . . in order to study the degree of infection and the rapidity of the course of the disease in the . . . typhus experiments at Buchenwald concentration camp during World War II. These programs were somewhat alike in the vulnerability of the subjects; uneducated African American men, debilitated patients in a charity hospital, prisoners of war, inmates of concentration camps and others falling within the custody and control of the agencies conducting or approving the experiments. In the present case, children, especially young children, living in lower economic circumstances, albeit not as vulnerable as the other examples, are nonetheless, vulnerable as well.

It is clear to this Court that the scientific and medical communities cannot be permitted to assume sole authority to determine ultimately what is right and appropriate in respect to research projects involving young children free of the limitations and consequences of the application of Maryland law. The Institutional Review Boards, IRBs, are, primarily, in-house organs. In our view, they are not designed, generally, to be sufficiently objective in the sense that they are as sufficiently concerned with the ethicality of the experiments they review as they are with the success of the experiments. . . . Here, the IRB, whose primary function was to insure safety and compliance with applicable regulations, encouraged the researchers to misrepresent the purpose of the research in order to bring the study under the label of "therapeutic" and thus under a lower safety

---

[6] The ultimate goal was to find the cost of the minimal level of effective lead paint or lead dust abatement costs so as to help landlords assess, hopefully positively, the commercial feasibility of attempting to abate lead dust in marginally profitable, lower rent-urban housing, in order to help preserve such housing in the Baltimore housing market. . . . The tenants involved, presumably, would be from a lower rent-urban class. . . . The children of middle class or rich parents apparently were not involved.

> Indeed, the literature on the law and ethics of human experimentation is replete with warnings that all subjects, but especially vulnerable subjects, are at risk of abuse by inclusion [as research subjects]. Those vulnerable subjects included prisoners, who are subject to coercion, . . . children and the elderly . . . and racial minorities, ethnic minorities, and women . . . whom history shows to be the most frequent victims of abuses in human experimentations. R. Alta Charo, Protecting Us to Death: Women, Pregnancy and Clinical Research Trials, 38 St. Louis U. L.J. 135, 135 (Fall, 1993). . . .

standard of regulation. The IRB's purpose was ethically wrong, and its understanding of the experiment's benefit incorrect.

The conflicts are inherent. This would be especially so when science and private industry collaborate in search of material gains. Moreover, the special relationship between research entities and human subjects used in the research will almost always impose duties.

In respect to examining that special relationship, we are obliged to further examine its nature and its ethical constraints. In that regard, when contested cases arise, the assessment of the legal effect of research on human subjects must always be subject to judicial evaluation. One method of making such evaluations is the initiation of appropriate actions bringing such matters to the attention of the courts, as has been done in the cases at bar. It may well be that in the end, the trial courts will determine that no damages have been incurred in the instant cases and thus the actions will fail for that reason. In that regard, we note that there are substantial factual differences in the . . . [separate cases under review]. But the actions, themselves, are not defective on the ground that no legal duty can, according to the trial courts, possibly exist. For the reasons discussed at length in the main body of the opinion, a legal duty normally exists between researcher and subject and in all probability exists in the cases at bar. Moreover, as we shall discuss, the consents of the parents in these cases under Maryland law constituted contracts creating duties. Additionally, under Maryland law, to the extent parental consent can ever be effective in research projects of this nature, the parents may not have been sufficiently informed and, therefore, the consents ineffective and, based on the information contained in the sparse records before this court, the research project . . . may have invaded the legal rights of the children subjected to it. . . .

II. FACTS & PROCEDURAL BACKGROUND . . .

The research study [giving rise to these cases] was sponsored jointly by the EPA and the Maryland Department of Housing and Community Development (DHCD). It was thus a joint federal and state project. The Baltimore City Health Department and Maryland Department of the Environment also collaborated in the study. It appears that, because the study was funded and sponsored in part by a federal entity, certain federal conditions were attached to the funding grants and approvals. There are certain uniform standards required in respect to federally funded or approved projects. We, however, are unaware of, and have not been directed to, any federal or state statute or regulation that imposes limits on this Court's powers to conduct its review of the issues presented. None of the parties have questioned this Court's jurisdiction in these cases. Moreover, 45 Code Federal Regulations (C.F.R.) 46.116(e) specifically provides: "The informed consent requirements in this policy are not intended to preempt any applicable federal, state, or local laws which require additional information to be disclosed in order for informed consent to be legally effective." Those various federal or state conditions, recommendations, etc., may well be relevant at a trial on the merits as to whether any breach of a contractual or other duty occurred, or whether negligence did, in fact, occur; but have no limiting effect on the issue of whether, at law, legal duties, via contract or "special relationships" are created in Maryland in experimental nontherapeutic research involving Maryland children. . . .

In summary, KKI conducted a study of five test groups of twenty-five houses each. The first three groups consisted of houses known to have lead present. The amount of repair and maintenance conducted increased from Group 1 to Group 2 to Group 3. The fourth group consisted of houses, which had at one time lead present but had since allegedly received a complete abatement of lead dust. The fifth group consisted of modern houses, which had never had the presence of lead dust. The twenty-five homes in each of the first three testing levels were then to be compared to the two control groups: the twenty-five homes in Group 4 that had previously been abated and the 25 modern homes in Group 5. The research study was specifically designed to do less than full lead dust abatement in some of the categories of houses in order to study the potential effectiveness, if any, of lesser levels of repair and maintenance.

If the children were to leave the houses upon the first manifestation of lead dust, it would be difficult, if not impossible, to test, over time, the rate of the level of lead accumulation in the blood of the children attributable to the manifestation. In other words, if the children were removed from the houses before the lead dust levels in their blood became elevated, the tests would probably fail, or at least the data that would establish the success of the test — or of the abatement results, would be of questionable use. Thus, it would benefit the accuracy of the test, and thus KKI, the compensated researcher, if children remained in the houses over the period of the study even after the presence of lead dust in the houses became evident. . . .

[The consent form for the study provided:]

PURPOSE OF STUDY:

As you may know, lead poisoning in children is a problem in Baltimore City and other communities across the country. Lead in paint, house dust and outside soil are major sources of lead exposure for children. Children can also be exposed to lead in drinking water and other sources. We understand that your house is going to have special repairs done in order to reduce exposure to lead in paint and dust. On a random basis, homes will receive one of two levels of repair. We are interested in finding out how well the two levels of repair work. The repairs are not intended, or expected, to completely remove exposure to lead.

We are now doing a study to learn about how well different practices work for reducing exposure to lead in paint and dust. We are asking you and over one hundred other families to allow us to test for lead in and around your homes up to 8 to 9 times over the next two years provided that your house qualifies for the full two years of study. Final eligibility will be determined after the initial testing of your home. We are also doing free blood lead testing of children aged 6 months to 7 years, up to 8 to 9 times over the next two years. We would also like you to respond to a short questionnaire every 6 months. This study is intended to monitor the effects of the repairs and is not intended to replace the regular medical care your family obtains. . . .

BENEFITS

To compensate you for your time answering questions and allowing us to sketch your home we will mail you a check in the amount of $5.00. In the future we would mail you a check in the amount of $15 each time the full questionnaire is completed. The dust, soil, water, and blood samples would be tested for lead at the Kennedy Krieger Institute at no charge to you. We would provide you with specific blood-lead results. We would contact you to discuss a summary of house test results and steps that you could take to reduce any risks of exposure. . . .

On appeal, appellant[s] seek[] review of the Circuit Court's decision granting KKI summary judgment. . . . [They] contend[] that KKI owed a duty of care . . . based on the nature of its relationship with [the children and parents participating in the study] . . . arising out of: (1) a contract between the parties; (2) a voluntary assumption by KKI; (3) a "special relationship" between the parties; and (4) a Federal regulation. . . . [The appellants argued that KKI was negligent in, for example, failing to notify a parent about elevated lead levels in a rental property for nine months, by which time her child had elevated blood levels of lead.]

III. DISCUSSION

A. STANDARD OF REVIEW

We resolve these disputes in the context of the trial court's granting of the appellee's motions for summary judgment in the two distinct cases. The threshold issues before this Court are whether, in the two cases presented, appellee, KKI, was entitled to summary judgment as a matter of law on the basis that no contract existed and that there is inherently no duty owed to a research subject by a researcher. Perhaps even more important is the ancillary issue of whether a parent in Maryland, under the law of this State, can legally consent to placing a child in a nontherapeutic research study that carries with it any risk of harm to the health of the child. We shall resolve all of these primary issues. . . .

B. GENERAL DISCUSSION

Initially, we note that we know of no law, nor have we been directed to any applicable in Maryland courts, that provides that the parties to a scientific study, because it is a scientific, health-related study, cannot be held to have entered into special relationships with the subjects of the study that can create duties, including duties, the breach of which may give rise to negligence claims. We also are not aware of any general legal precept that immunizes nongovernmental "institutional volunteers" or scientific researchers from the responsibility for the breaches of duties arising in "special relationships." Moreover, we, at the very least, hold that, under the particular circumstances testified to by the parties, there are genuine disputes of material fact concerning whether a special relationship existed between KKI and . . . [the appellants]. Concerning this issue, the granting of the summary judgment motions was clearly inappropriate. When a "special relationship" can exist as a matter of law, the issue of whether, given certain facts, a special relationship does exist, when there is a dispute of material fact in that respect, is a decision for the finder of fact, not the trial judge. We shall hold initially that the very nature of nontherapeutic scientific research on human subjects can, and normally will, create special relationships out of which duties arise. Since World War II the specialness or nature of such relationships has been frequently of concern in and outside of the research community.

As a result of the atrocities performed in the name of science during the Holocaust, and other happenings in the World War II era, what is now known as the

Nuremberg Code evolved. Of special interest to this Court, the Nuremberg Code, at least in significant part, was the result of legal thought and legal principles, as opposed to medical or scientific principles, and thus should be the preferred standard for assessing the legality of scientific research on human subjects. Under it, duties to research subjects arise. . . . [The court cited a work by distinguished Boston University Professor George Annas detailing the history of the Nuremberg Code and explaining the lack of U.S. case law regarding the regulation of research under the Nuremberg Code or any other source of regulation.] . . .

In arguing that a fuller disclosure should be made when consent is sought for nontherapeutic research, as opposed to therapeutic research, [ethicist Karine] Morin notes:

> Furthermore, as long as courts continue to interpret the doctrine of informed consent in experimentation as it applies in the context of treatment, the uniqueness of the protection needed for human research subjects will be overlooked. Failing to recognize that subjects who volunteer for the sake of the advancement of science are differently situated from patients who stand to benefit from treatment results in an analysis that misconceives the purpose of disclosure. Beyond informing the patient as to means available to treat him or her, a subject must become a voluntary and willing participant in an endeavor that may yield no direct benefit to him or her, or worse, that may cause harm. [Karine Morin, The Standard of Disclosure in Human Subject Experimentation, 19 J. Legal Med. 157, 220 (1998).] . . .

[T]here is no[t] [a] complete record of the specific compensation of the researchers involved. Although the project was funded by the EPA, at the request of KKI the EPA has declined to furnish such information to the attorney for one of the parties, who requested it under the federal Freedom of Information Act. Whether the research's character as a co-sponsored state project opens the records under the Maryland Public Information Act has apparently not been considered. Neither is there in the record any development of what pressures, if any, were exerted in respect to the researchers obtaining the consents of the parents and conducting the experiment. Nor, for the same reason, is there a sufficient indication as to the extent to which the Institute has joined with commercial interests, if it has, for the purposes of profit, that might potentially impact upon the researcher's motivations and potential conflicts of interest — motivations that generally are assumed, in the cases of prestigious entities such as John[s] Hopkins University, to be for the public good rather . . . [than] a search for profit.

We do note that the institution involved, the respondent here . . . is a highly respected entity, considered to be a leader in the development of treatments, and treatment itself, for children infected with lead poisoning. With reasonable assurance, we can note that its reputation alone might normally suggest that there was no realization or understanding on the Institute's part that the protocols of the experiment were questionable, except for the letter from the IRB requesting that the researchers mischaracterize the study.

We shall further address both the factual and legal bases for the findings of the trial courts, holding, ultimately, that the respective courts erred in both respects.

C. NEGLIGENCE

It is important for us to remember that appellants allege that KKI was negligent. Specifically, they allege that KKI, as a medical researcher, owed a duty of care to them, as subjects in the research study, based on the nature of the agreements between them and also based on the nature of the relationship between the parties. They contend specifically that KKI was negligent because KKI breached its duty to: (1) design a study that did not involve placing children at unnecessary risk; (2) inform participants in the study of results in a timely manner; and (3) to completely and accurately inform participants in the research study of all the hazards and risks involved in the study. . . .

Because this is a review of the granting of the two summary judgments based solely on the grounds that there was no legal duty to protect the children, we are primarily concerned with . . . whether KKI was under a duty to protect appellants from injury.[33] . . .

The relationship that existed between KKI and both sets of appellants in the case at bar was that of medical researcher and research study subject. Though not expressly recognized in the Maryland Code or in our prior cases as a type of relationship which creates a duty of care, evidence in the record suggests that such a relationship involving a duty or duties would ordinarily exist, and certainly could exist, based on the facts and circumstances of each of these individual cases. . . .

IV. THE SPECIAL RELATIONSHIPS

A. THE CONSENT AGREEMENT CONTRACT

Both sets of appellants signed a similar Consent Form prepared by KKI in which KKI expressly promised to: (1) financially compensate (however minimally) appellants for their participation in the study; . . . (2) collect lead dust samples from appellants' homes, analyze the samples, discuss the results with appellants, and discuss steps that could be taken, which could reduce exposure to lead; and (3) collect blood samples from children in the household and provide appellants with the results of the blood tests. In return, appellants agreed to participate in the study, by: (1) allowing KKI into appellants' homes to collect dust samples; (2) periodically filling out questionnaires; and (3) allowing the children's blood to be drawn, tested, and utilized in the study. If consent agreements contain such provisions, and the trial court did not find otherwise, and we hold from our own examination of the record that such provisions were so contained, mutual assent, offer, acceptance, and consideration existed, all of which created contractual relationships imposing duties by reason of the consent agreement . . . (as well, as we discuss elsewhere, by the very nature of such relationships).

By having appellants sign this Consent Form, both KKI and appellants expressly made representations, which, in our view, created a bilateral contract between the parties. At the very least, it suggests that appellants were agreeing with KKI to participate in the research study with the expectation that they would

---

[33] We note that there was little suggestion of actual permanent injury to the children involved with these two cases. Our opinion is not directed to the matter of whether damages can be proven in the present cases.

be compensated, albeit, more or less, minimally, be informed of all the information necessary for the subject to freely choose whether to participate, and continue to participate, and receive promptly any information that might bear on their willingness to continue to participate in the study. This includes full, detailed, prompt, and continuing warnings as to all the potential risks and hazards inherent in the research or that arise during the research. KKI, in return, was getting the children to move into the houses and/or to remain there over time, and was given the right to test the children's blood for lead. As consideration to KKI, it got access to the houses and to the blood of the children that had been encouraged to live in a "risk" environment. In other words, KKI received a measuring tool—the children's blood. Considerations existed, mainly money, food coupons, trinkets, bilateral promises, blood to be tested in order to measure success. "Informed consent" of the type used here, which imposes obligation and confers consideration on both researcher and subject (in these cases, the parents of the subjects) may differ from the more one-sided "informed consent" normally used in actual medical practice. Researcher/subject consent in nontherapeutic research can, and in this case did, create a contract.[35]

B. THE SUFFICIENCY OF THE CONSENT FORM

The consent form did not directly inform the parents of the fact that it was contemplated that some of the children might ingest lead dust particles, and that one of the reasons the blood of the children was to be tested was to evaluate how effective the various abatement measures were.

A reasonable parent would expect to be clearly informed that it was at least contemplated that her child would ingest lead dust particles, and that the degree to which lead dust contaminated the child's blood would be used as one of the ways in which the success of the experiment would be measured. The fact that if such information was furnished, it might be difficult to obtain human subjects for the research, does not affect the need to supply the information, or alter the ethics of failing to provide such information. A human subject is entitled to all material information. The respective parent should also have been clearly informed that in order for the measurements to be most helpful, the child needed to stay in the house until the conclusion of the study. Whether assessed by a subjective or an objective standard, the children, or their surrogates, should have been additionally informed that the researchers anticipated that, as a result of the experiment, it was possible that there might be some accumulation of lead in the blood of the children. The "informed" consent was not valid because full material information was not furnished to the subjects or their parents.

C. SPECIAL RELATIONSHIP

In Case Number 128, Ms. Hughes signed a Consent Form in which KKI agreed to provide her with "specific blood-lead results" and discuss with her "a summary of house test results and steps that [she] could take to reduce any risks of exposure." She contends that this agreement between the parties gave rise to a duty owed by KKI to provide her with that information in a timely manner. She

---

[35] We make no determination as to whether informed consent in a therapeutic medical context can generate contractual obligations.

signed the Consent Form on March 10, 1993. The project began almost simultaneously. KKI collected dust samples in the Monroe Street property on March 9, 1993, August 23, 1993, March 9, 1994, September 19, 1994, April 18, 1995, and November 13, 1995. The March 9, 1993 dust testing revealed what the researchers referred to as "hot spots," where the level of lead was "higher than might be found in a completely renovated house." . . . [T]his information was not furnished to Ms. Hughes until December 16, 1993, more than nine months after the samples had been collected and not until after Ericka Grimes's blood was found to contain elevated levels of lead. She contends that not only did KKI have a duty to report such information in a timely manner but that it breached this duty by delaying to such a time that her daughter was allowed to contract lead poisoning. Looking at the relevant facts of Case Number 128, they are susceptible to inferences supporting the position of appellant, Ericka Grimes, and, moreover, that, if true, would create a "special relationship" out of which duties would be created. Therefore, for this reason alone, the grant of summary judgment was improper. . . .

[T]he trial courts appear to have held that special relationships out of which duties arise cannot be created by the relationship between researchers and the subjects of the research. While in some rare cases that may be correct, it is not correct when researchers recruit people, especially children whose consent is furnished indirectly, to participate in nontherapeutic procedures that are potentially hazardous, dangerous, or deleterious to their health. As opposed to compilation of already extant statistics for purposes of studying human health matters, the creation of study conditions or protocols or participation in the recruitment of otherwise healthy subjects to interact with already existing, or potentially existing, hazardous conditions, or both, for the purpose of creating statistics from which scientific hypotheses can be supported, would normally warrant or create such special relationships as a matter of law.

It is of little moment that an entity is an institutional volunteer in a community. If otherwise, the legitimacy of the claim to noble purpose would always depend upon the particular institution and the particular community it is serving in a given case. As we have indicated, history is replete with claims of noble purpose for institutions and institutional volunteers in a wide variety of communities.

Institutional volunteers may intend to do good or, as history has proven, even to do evil and may do evil or good depending on the institution and the community they serve. Whether an institutional volunteer[36] in a particular community should be granted exceptions from the application of law is a matter that should be scrutinized closely by an appropriate public policy maker. Generally, but not always, the legislative branch is appropriately the best first forum to consider exceptions to the tort laws of this State — even then it should consider all ramifications of the policy — especially considering the general vulnerability of subjects of such studies — in this case, small children. In the

---

[36] Moreover, it is not clear that KKI was a mere volunteer in any event. It received funding for developing and conducting the research. Whether it recognized a profit is unknown from the record. The "for profit" nature of some research may well increase the duties of researchers to insure the safety of research subjects, and may well increase researchers' or an institution's susceptibility for damages in respect to any injuries incurred by research subjects.

absence of the exercise of legislative policymaking, we hold that special relationships, out of which duties arise, the breach of which can constitute negligence, can result from the relationships between researcher and research subjects.

D. THE FEDERAL REGULATIONS

A duty may be prescribed by a statute, or a special relationship creating duties may arise from the requirement for compliance with statutory provisions. Although there is no duty of which we are aware prescribed by the Maryland Code in respect to scientific research . . . , federal regulations have been enacted that impose standards of care that attach to federally funded or sponsored research projects that use human subjects. See 45 C.F.R. Part 46 (2000). 45 C.F.R. Part 46, Subpart A, is entitled "Basic HHS Policy for Protection of Human Research Subjects" and Subpart D of the regulation is entitled "Additional Protections for Children Involved as Subjects in Research." . . . [T]his study was funded, and co-sponsored, by the EPA and presumably was therefore subject to these federal conditions. These conditions, if appropriate administrative action has been taken, require fully informed consent in any research using human subjects conducted, supported, or otherwise subject to any level of control or funding by any federal department or agency. . . .

These federal regulations, especially the requirement for adherence to sound ethical principles, strike right at the heart of KKI's defense of the granting of the Motions for Summary Judgment. Fully informed consent is lacking in these cases. The research did not comply with the regulations. There clearly was more than a minimal risk involved. Under the regulations, children should not have been used for the purpose of measuring how much lead they would accumulate in their blood while living in partially abated houses to which they were recruited initially or encouraged to remain, because of the study. . . .

Clearly, KKI, as a research institution, is required to obtain a human participant's fully informed consent, using sound ethical principles. It is clear from the wording of the applicable federal regulations that this requirement of informed consent continues during the duration of the research study and applies to new or changing risks. In this case, a special relationship out of which duties might arise might be created by reason of the federally imposed regulations. The question becomes whether this duty of informed consent created by federal regulation, as a matter of state law, translates into a duty of care arising out of the unique relationship that is researcher-subject, as opposed to doctor-patient. We answer that question in the affirmative. In this State, it may, depending on the facts, create such a duty.

Additionally, the Nuremberg Code, intended to be applied internationally, and never expressly rejected in this country, inherently and implicitly, speaks strongly to the existence of special relationships imposing ethical duties on researchers who conduct nontherapeutic experiments on human subjects. The Nuremberg Code specifically requires researchers to make known to human subjects of research "all inconveniences and hazards reasonably to be expected; and the effects upon his health or person which may possibly come from his participation in the experiment." The breach of obligations imposed on researchers by the Nuremberg Code, might well support actions sounding in negligence in cases such as those at issue here. We reiterate as well that, given the facts and circumstances of both of these cases, there were, at the very least, genuine disputes of material facts concerning the relationship and duties of the parties, and compliance with the regulations.

V. THE ETHICAL APPROPRIATENESS OF THE RESEARCH

The World Medical Association in its Declaration of Helsinki . . . included a code of ethics for investigative researchers and was an attempt by the medical community to establish its own set of rules for conducting research on human subjects. . . .[39]

The determination of whether a duty exists under Maryland law is the ultimate function of various policy considerations as adopted by either the Legislature, or, if it has not spoken, as it has not in respect to this situation, by Maryland courts. In our view, otherwise healthy children should not be the subjects of nontherapeutic experimentation or research that has the potential to be harmful to the child. It is, first and foremost, the responsibility of the researcher and the research entity to see to the harmlessness of such nontherapeutic research. Consent of parents can never relieve the researcher of this duty. We do not feel that it serves proper public policy concerns to permit children to be placed in situations of potential harm, during nontherapeutic procedures, even if parents, or other surrogates, consent. Under these types of circumstances, even where consent is given, albeit inappropriately, policy considerations suggest that there remains a special relationship between researchers and participants to the research study, which imposes a duty of care. This is entirely consistent with the principles found in the Nuremberg Code.

Researchers cannot ever be permitted to completely immunize themselves by reliance on consents, especially when the information furnished to the subject, or the party consenting, is incomplete in a material respect. A researcher's duty is not created by, or extinguished by, the consent of a research subject or by IRB approval. The duty to a vulnerable research subject is independent of consent, although the obtaining of consent is one of the duties a researcher must perform. All of this is especially so when the subjects of research are children. Such legal duties, and legal protections, might additionally be warranted because of the likely conflict of interest between the goal of the research experimenter and the health of the human subject, especially, but not exclusively, when such research is commercialized. There is always a potential substantial conflict of interest on the part of researchers as between them and the human subjects used in their research. If participants in the study withdraw from the research study prior to its completion, then the results of the study could be rendered meaningless. There is thus an inherent reason for not conveying information to subjects as it arises, that might cause the subjects to leave the research project. That conflict dictates a stronger reason for full and continuous disclosure. . . .

---

[39] . . . Declaration of Helsinki, World Medical Assembly (WMA) 18th Assembly (June 1964), amended by 29th WMA Tokyo, Japan (October 1975), 35th WMA Venice, Italy (October 1983) and the 41st WMA Hong Kong (September 1989).

A special relationship giving rise to duties, the breach of which might constitute negligence, might also arise because, generally, the investigators are in a better position to anticipate, discover, and understand the potential risks to the health of their subjects. . . .

This duty requires the protection of the research subjects from unreasonable harm and requires the researcher to completely and promptly inform the subjects of potential hazards existing from time to time because of the profound trust that participants place in investigators, institutions, and the research enterprise as a whole to protect them from harm. . . .

While we acknowledge that foreseeability does not necessarily create a duty, we recognize that potential harm to the children participants of this study was both foreseeable and potentially extreme. A "special relationship" also exists in circumstances where such experiments are conducted.

VI. PARENTAL CONSENT FOR CHILDREN TO BE SUBJECTS OF POTENTIALLY HAZARDOUS NONTHERAPEUTIC RESEARCH

The issue of whether a parent can consent to the participation of her or his child in a nontherapeutic health-related study that is known to be potentially hazardous to the health of the child raises serious questions with profound moral and ethical implications. What right does a parent have to knowingly expose a child not in need of therapy to health risks or otherwise knowingly place a child in danger, even if it can be argued it is for the greater good? The issue in these specific contested cases does not relate primarily to the authority of the parent, but to the procedures of KKI and similar entities that may be involved in such health-related studies. The issue of the parents' right to consent on behalf of the children has not been fully presented in either of these cases, but should be of concern not only to lawyers and judges, but to moralists, ethicists, and others. The consenting parents in the contested cases at bar were not the subjects of the experiment; the children were. Additionally, this practice presents the potential problems of children initiating actions in their own names upon reaching majority, if indeed, they have been damaged as a result of being used as guinea pigs in nontherapeutic scientific research. Children, it should be noted, are not in our society the equivalent of rats, hamsters, monkeys, and the like. Because of the overriding importance of this matter and this Court's interest in the welfare of children—we shall address the issue.

Most of the relatively few cases in the area of the ethics of protocols of various research projects involving children have merely assumed that a parent can give informed consent for the participation of their children in nontherapeutic research. . . .

It is not in the best interest of a specific child, in a nontherapeutic research project, to be placed in a research environment, which might possibly be, or which proves to be, hazardous to the health of the child . . . in order to test methods that may ultimately benefit all children. . . .

One simply does not expose otherwise healthy children, incapable of personal assent (consent), to a nontherapeutic research environment that is known at the inception of the research, might cause the children to ingest lead dust. It is especially troublesome, when a measurement of the success of the research experiment is, in significant respect, to be determined by the extent to which the blood of the children absorbs, and is contaminated by, a substance that the researcher knows can, in sufficient amounts, whether solely from the research environment or cumulative from all sources, cause serious and long term adverse health effects. Such a practice is not legally acceptable. . . .

In the[se] case[s], no impartial judicial review or oversight was sought by the researchers or by the parents. . . . Science cannot be permitted to be the sole judge of the appropriateness of such research methods on human subjects, especially in respect to children. We hold that in these contested cases, the research study protocols [presented to the court] . . . were not appropriate. . . .

VII. CONCLUSION

We hold that in Maryland a parent, appropriate relative, or other applicable surrogate, cannot consent to the participation of a child or other person under legal disability in nontherapeutic research or studies in which there is any risk of injury or damage to the health of the subject.

We hold that informed consent agreements in nontherapeutic research projects, under certain circumstances can constitute contracts; and that, under certain circumstances, such research agreements can, as a matter of law, constitute "special relationships" giving rise to duties, out of the breach of which negligence actions may arise. We also hold that, normally, such special relationships are created between researchers and the human subjects used by the researchers. Additionally, we hold that governmental regulations can create duties on the part of researchers towards human subjects out of which "special relationships" can arise. Likewise, such duties and relationships are consistent with the provisions of the Nuremberg Code.

The determination as to whether a "special relationship" actually exists is to be done on a case by case basis. . . . The determination as to whether a special relationship exists, if properly pled, lies with the trier of fact. We hold that there was ample evidence in the cases at bar to support a fact finder's determination of the existence of duties arising out of contract, or out of a special relationship, or out of regulations and codes, or out of all of them, in each of the cases.

We hold that on the present record, the Circuit Courts erred in their assessment of the law and of the facts as pled in granting KKI's motions for summary judgment in both cases before this Court. Accordingly, we vacate the rulings of the Circuit Court for Baltimore City and remand these cases to that court for further proceedings consistent with this opinion. . . .

RAKER, J., concurring in result only:

These appeals present the narrow question of whether the Circuit Courts erred in granting summary judgments to appellee, the Kennedy Krieger Institute, a research entity, on the ground that, as a matter of law, it owed no duty to warn appellants, Ericka Grimes and Myron Higgins, et al., human subjects participating in its research study. I concur in the judgment of the Court only and join in the Court's judgment that the Circuit Courts erred in granting summary judgments to appellee. These cases should be remanded for further proceedings.

I concur in the Court's judgment because I find that appellants have alleged sufficient facts to establish that there existed a special relationship between the parties in these cases, which created a duty of care that, if breached, gives rise to an action in negligence. . . . I would hold that a special relationship giving rise to a duty of care, the breach of which would be the basis for an action in negligence, existed in these cases and would remand the cases at bar to the Circuit Courts for further proceedings. I agree with the majority that this duty includes the protection of research subjects from unreasonable harm and requires the researcher to inform research subjects completely and promptly of potential hazards resulting from participation in the study. . . . As a result of the existence of this tort duty, I find it unnecessary to reach the thorny question, not even raised by any of the parties, of whether the informed consent agreements in these cases constitute legally binding contracts. . . .

As I have indicated, this case presents a narrow question of whether a duty in tort exists between the plaintiffs and the defendants. . . . Nonetheless, the majority appears to have decided the issue of whether such duty of care was, in fact, breached as a matter of law, without a hearing or a trial on the merits.

I cannot join in the majority's sweeping factual determinations. . . .

On Motion for Reconsideration

Per Curiam.

The Court has considered the motion for reconsideration and the submissions by the various amici curiae. The motion is denied, with this explanation.

Some of the issues raised in this case, in the briefs and at oral argument, were important ones of first impression in this State, and the Court therefore attempted to address those issues in a full and exhaustive manner. The case reached us in the context of summary judgments entered by the Circuit Court, which entailed rulings that the evidence presented by the plaintiffs, for purposes of the motions, even when taken in a light most favorable to them, was insufficient as a matter of law to establish the prospect of liability. We disagreed with that determination. Although we discussed the various issues and arguments in considerable detail, the only conclusion that we reached as a matter of law was that, on the record currently before us, summary judgment was improperly granted — that sufficient evidence was presented in both cases which, if taken in a light most favorable to the plaintiffs and believed by a jury, would suffice to justify verdicts in favor of the plaintiffs. Thus, the cases were remanded for further proceedings in the Circuit Court. Every issue bearing on liability or damages remains open for further factual development, and any relevant evidence not otherwise precluded under our rules of evidence is admissible.

Much of the argument in support of and in opposition to the motion for reconsideration centered on the question of what limitations should govern a parent's authority to provide informed consent for the participation of his or her minor child in a medical study. In the Opinion, we said at one point that a parent "cannot consent to the participation of a child . . . in nontherapeutic research or studies in which there is any risk of injury or damage to the health of the subject." As we think is clear from Section VI of the Opinion, by "any risk," we meant any articulable risk beyond the minimal kind of risk that is inherent in any endeavor. The context of the statement was a non-therapeutic study that promises no medical benefit to the child whatever, so that any balance between risk and benefit is necessarily negative. As we indicated, the determination of whether the study in question offered some benefit, and therefore could be regarded as therapeutic in nature, or involved more than that minimal risk is open for further factual development on remand.

RAKER. Judge, dissenting.

I respectfully dissent from the order denying the motions for reconsideration. I adhere to the views previously expressed in my concurring opinion filed herein. . . . The majority's discussion of the ability of a parent or guardian to consent to the participation of a minor child in a nontherapeutic research study and the discussion regarding the ethics of the research conducted in these cases involve serious public policy considerations. The statements are a declaration of public policy that, in the posture of this case, are best left to the General Assembly. . . .

Notes: Conflicts of Interest and Human Subjects Research

1. *Federal Regulation.* Most of the field of clinical investigation is now very closely regulated by the federal Food and Drug Administration and by the Department of Health and Human Services' Office for Human Research Protections. U.S. Dep't of Health & Human Servs., Protection of Human Subjects, 45 C.F.R. §§46.101-.409; U.S. Food & Drug Admin., Protection of Human Subjects, 21 C.F.R. §§50.1-.58. The federal regulatory structure differs from informed consent law in that the penalty for violation is not damages but disqualification from federal funding. The regulatory focus, however, mirrors the informed consent themes already introduced in our discussion of fiduciary liability.

The regulations are designed to safeguard individual autonomy from overreaching by researchers. The mechanism used to provide protection is a combination of mandatory disclosure and individual assent. The researcher is charged with a special obligation to care for his or her research subject and to protect the subject from harm. The federal regulations require prior approval of informed consent process that typically includes written disclosures and consents. These documents are reviewed by interdisciplinary ethical review committees (called "institutional review boards" or "IRBs") located in hospitals, in other medical research centers, and in universities where research is conducted using human subjects. The federal regulations governing research involving human subjects explicitly preserve from preemption foreign, state, or local laws providing additional protections. 45 C.F.R. §46.101(f), (g). The relevant federal agency may also permit federal agencies to apply equivalent or more protective internationally recognized protections for human research subjects in research conducted in foreign countries. Id. §46.101(h). For a discussion of the importance of state regulation of pharmaceutical clinical trials, see Jeffrey Gibbs, State Regulation of Pharmaceutical Clinical Trials, 59 Food & Drug L.J. 265 (2004).

2. *Basic Definitions: What Is Research?* The federal regulations establish a broad definition of *research* as "a systemic investigation, including research development, testing, and evaluation, designed to develop or contribute to

generalizable knowledge." 45 C.F.R. §46.102(d). A "[h]uman subject" is "a living individual about whom the investigator (whether professional or student) conducting research obtains (1) data through intervention or interaction with the individual, or (2) identifiable private information." Id. 46.102(f). Should the collection of data about the side effects of drugs after they have been approved and sold in the marketplace be considered human subjects research? See Susan Okie, Safety in Numbers–Monitoring Risk in Approved Drugs, 352 N. Eng. J. Med. 1173 (2005). Is the line between medical treatment and medical research always clear? See Lars Noah, Informed Consent and the Elusive Dichotomy Between Standard and Experimental Therapy, 28 Am. J. L. and Med. 361 (2002).

Human subjects research is generally considered to be ethical so long as the participants consent, the risks to subjects are minimized, the selection of subjects is equitable, the anticipated benefits outweigh the risk to the subjects, data is monitored to protect patient safety, and subjects' privacy is protected. See, e.g., 45 C.F.R. §46.111. Therapeutic research provides the possibility of benefit to the research subject; some risk to the subject might therefore be tolerated so long as it is outweighed by the anticipated benefit and other criteria are met. Id. Nontherapeutic research does not offer a benefit to the subject; the research therefore cannot proceed unless the risks are minimal.

The *Grimes* court characterized the lead abatement research as involving more than minimal risk and suggested that parents might not be permitted to consent to nontherapeutic research involving children that poses more than a minimal risk. What is a minimal risk? Federal regulations provide that "minimal risk means that the probability and magnitude of harm or discomfort anticipated in the research are not greater in and of themselves than those ordinarily encountered in daily life. . . ." 45 C.F.R. §46.102(i). Is this the definition used by the *Grimes* court? Why didn't the *Grimes* court consider the risk to be minimal, given that children who live in older housing frequently are exposed to the risk of lead paint?

3. *The Role of IRBs.* Under federal law, the membership of an IRB is supposed to be diverse and professionally knowledgeable about research proposals and research ethics. 45 C.F.R. §46.107. The IRB must include at least one member who is unaffiliated with the institution. IRB members may not participate in the review of a research project in which they have a conflict of interest. Id.

The *Grimes* court was skeptical about the independence of IRBs. Commentators have raised many questions about the ability of potentially overworked and conflicted IRBs to safeguard research subjects. These criticisms and various reform proposals are well summarized in Carl Coleman, Rationalizing Risk Assessment in Human Subject Research, 46 Ariz. L. Rev. 1 (2004); Barbara Noah, Bioethical Malpractice: Risk and Responsibility in Human Research, 7 J. Health Care L. & Pol'y 175 (2004); Eve E. Slater, IRB Reform, 346 New Eng. J. Med. 1402 (2002); Robert Steinbrook, Improving Protection for Research Subjects, 346 New Eng. J. Med. 1425 (2002); Michael C. Christian et al., Central Institutional Review Board for Multi-Institutional Trials, 346 New Eng. J. Med. 1405 (2002).

4. *The Role of Informed Consent.* The federal regulations focus on the informed consent process as the major tool for protecting human subjects. The informed consent rules are much more detailed in some areas than common law rules but

do not preempt those laws. 45 C.F.R. §46.116. Note that federal law prohibits research sponsors from requiring waivers of liability for negligence. Id. Examine the informed consent form excerpted in the *Grimes* decision. In what way(s) was it deficient? For an overview of the current informed consent process globally and the continuing development of the informed consent doctrine see Jennifer Couture, The Changes in Informed Consent in Experimental Procedures: The Evolution of a Concept, 1 J. Health & Biomedical L. 125 (2004); Richard S. Saver, Medical Research and Intangible Harm, U. Cinc. L. Rev. 941 (2006).

5. *The Aftermath of* Grimes. There have been few lawsuits involving experimental medicine using either negligence or informed consent theories, despite the huge volume of activity involving research subjects. A few courts have considered whether clinical trial sponsors owe a fiduciary duty to participants. See, e.g., Suthers v. Amgen Inc. 441 F. Supp. 2d 478 (S.D.N.Y. 2006) (plaintiffs' complaint dismissed in case challenging drug company's decision to terminate clinical trial and deny access to experimental drug; no fiduciary duty owed); and Abney v. Amgen Inc., 443 F.3d 540 (6th Cir. 2006) (no fiduciary duty as the clinical trial sponsors were not acting primarily for the benefit of the participants). See also, Paul B. Miller & Charles Weijer, Fiduciary Obligation in Clinical Research, 34 J. L. Med. & Ethics 424 (2006) (advocating the view that physician-researchers have a fiduciary relationship with their patient-subjects); and E. Haavi Morreim, The Clinical Investigator as Fiduciary: Discarding a Misguided Idea, 33 J. L. Med. & Ethics 586 (2005) (critical of the application of fiduciary principles to the research context); E. Haavi Morreim, Litigation in Clinical Research: Malpractice Doctrines Versus Research Realities, 32 J. L. Med & Ethics 474 (2004) (advocating a specialized tort approach to cases involving research). See also Beth S. Rose & Vincent Lodato, Emerging Litigation Involving Human Subjects: A Future for Class Actions?, 35 The Brief 43 (Summer 2006); Carl H. Coleman, Duties to Subjects in Clinical Research, 58 Vand. L. Rev. 387 (2005).

The *Grimes* decision was understandably controversial. Imagine how medical researchers might feel about a decision that appears to compare a research study sponsored by the federal government and conducted by a leading research institution with Nazi war crimes. The *Grimes* decision sparked a number of commentaries, including Lainie Friedman Ross, In Defense of the Hopkins Lead Abatement Studies, 30 J. L. Med. & Ethics 50 (2002).

What did the court actually hold in *Grimes*? The lengthy opinion (more than seventy pages, heavily edited here) explores the broad terrain of human subjects research and appears to hold that (1) parents/surrogates cannot consent to the participation of their children/incompetents in nontherapeutic research where there is any risk of injury or damage to the health of the subject; (2) informed consent agreements in nontherapeutic research trials may create "special relationships," and violation of the agreements may be addressed in breach of contract and negligence; and (3) other sources of the "special relationship" include the researcher-subject relationship itself and governmental research regulations. How much does the court majority take back in the per curiam opinion rejecting reconsideration? The court suggests that the parties are free to present evidence on any of these issues. What evidence would you present for either side?

6. *Conflicts of Interest.* The *Grimes* court repeatedly expressed concerns about the conflicts of interest between human subjects and researchers. Researchers may

have a financial interest in the subject matter of their research that puts their research subjects at risk or affects the reliability of research results. See *Moore*, supra. See, e.g., Justin E. Beckelman, Yan Li, & Cary P. Gross, Scope and Impact of Financial Conflicts of Interest in Biomedical Research: A Systemic Review, 289 JAMA 454 (2003); Roy H. Perlis et al., Industry Sponsorship and Financial Conflict of Interest in the Reporting of Clinical Trials in Psychiatry, 162 Am. J. Psychiatry 1957 (2005).

A researcher's financial interests might also create broader risks, such as when a researcher signs a confidentiality agreement or "gag clause" limiting the public disclosure of research results or when a drug company seeks to hide negative information about the safety or efficacy of a new drug. For a discussion of the use of gag clauses in clinical trials, see Robert Steinbrook, Gag Clauses in Clinical-Trial Agreements, 352 N. Eng. J. Med. 2160 (May 2005). For discussion of initiatives designed to ensure access to both positive and negative information about the safety and efficacy of new drugs, see Robert Steinbrook, Public Registration of Clinical Trials, 351 N. Eng. J. Med. 315 (2004); Robert Steinbrook, Registration of Clinical Trials — Voluntary or Mandatory?, 351 N. Eng. J. Med. 1820 (2004); and Catherine D. De Angelis et al., Is This Clinical Trial Fully Registered? — A Statement from the International Committee of Medical Journal Editors, 352 N. Eng. J. Med. 2436 (2005).

A number of organizations have focused on methods of identifying and limiting conflicts of interest between researchers and research subjects. The Association of American Medical Colleges (AAMC) has issued guidelines on individual researcher conflicts and institutional conflicts. See www.aamc.org/research/coi/start.htm. See also DHHS's Office for Human Research Protections, Financial Relationships in Clinical Research (May 2004). See generally Robert Gatter, Walking the Talk of Trust in Human Subjects Research: The Challenge of Regulating Financial Conflicts of Interest, 52 Emory L.J. 327 (2003); Robert P. Kelch, Maintaining the Public Trust in Clinical Research, 346 New Eng. J. Med. 285 (2002); Karine Marin et al., Managing Conflicts of Interest in the Conduct of Clinical Trials, 287 JAMA 78 (2002); Michelle Mello, Brian Clarridge & David Studdert, Academic Medical Centers; Standards for Clinical-Trial Agreements with Industry, 352 N. Eng. J. Med. 2202 (2005); Kevin P. Weinfurt et al., Policies of Academic Medical Center for Disclosing Financial Conflicts of Interest to Potential Research Subjects, 81 Academic Med. 113 (2006); Kevin Williams, Managing Physician Financial Conflicts of Interest in Clinical Trials Conducted in the Private Practice Setting, 59 Food & Drug L.J. 45 (2004); Paul E. Kalb & Kristin Graham Koehler, Legal Issues in Scientific Research, 287 JAMA 85 (2002).

7. *The Economic Interests of Clinical Research Subjects.* Should clinical research subjects share in the economic value of discoveries? The ownership issue, famously raised in Moore v. Regents of the University of California, 793 P.2d 479 (Cal. 1990), supra, at page 226 has resurfaced. In Washington University v. Catalona, a federal district court found that fully informed tissue donors retained no ownership rights to their biological materials. 437 F. Supp. 2d 985 (2006). Universities were keenly interested in this outcome due to fears that research biobanks would be severely restricted if donor-patients could control the use of their donated tissues. See, Jocelyn Kaiser, Court Decides Tissue Samples Belong

to University, Not Patients, 312 Science 345 (2006); Rebecca Skloot, Taking the Least of You, N.Y. Times Magazine, April 16, 2006 at page 38.

The economic interests of research subjects have also been debated in the domain of intellectual property law. See, e.g., Greenberg v. Miami Children's Hospital Research Inst. Inc., 264 F. Supp. 2d 1064 (S.D.Fla. 2003) (dismissing all but unjust enrichment claims brought by families whose samples had been used to develop a genetic test for Canavan's Disease). See also Eliot Marshall, Genetic Testing: Families Sue Hospital, Scientist for Control of Canavan Gene, 290 Science 1062 (2000); Charlotte H. Harrison, Neither *Moore* Nor the Market: Alternative Models for Compensating Contributors of Human Tissue, 28 Am. J.L. & Med. 77 (2002).

8. *Research on Vulnerable Populations.* As Professor Richard Garnett notes, much of the controversy in human research has surrounded projects involving groups viewed as particularly vulnerable to coercion or abuse. Should it matter who or what the subject matter of the research is? Is it possible that some of the rules meant to prevent potential research subjects from feeling pressure to participate have gone too far? See David Orentlicher, Making Research a Requirement of Treatment: Why We Should Sometimes Let Doctors Pressure Patients to Participate in Research, 35 Hastings Center Report 20 (2005).

a. *Children.* The use of children in research presents special problems because the only "consent" available is parental consent, and parents do not always protect their children from harm. Federal regulations provide special protections for children serving as research subjects. See 45 C.F.R. §§46.401-.409 (HHS regulations); 21 C.F.R. §§50.50-.56 (FDA regulations). See also NIH Policy Guidance on the Inclusion of Children in Research (1998). Research can be particularly controversial if it involves pregnant women, fetuses, and neonates. 45 C.F.R. §§46.201-.20.

There are conflicting objectives of scientific research involving children: (1) ensuring that children benefit from the progress in medical care made possible by such research and (2) minimizing the risks to children from their participation in scientific research. See, e.g., Marilyn Field & Richard Behrman, Ethical Conduct of Clinical Research Involving Children (2004); Carrie Fisher & Thomas Keens, Participation of Children in Research, 26 Whittier L. Rev. 823 (2005); and Lainie Friedman Ross, Children in Medical Research: Access Versus Protection (2006).

Despite the controversy, public policy makers sometimes actually seek to encourage research involving children. One example involves pediatric drug testing. Many drugs have been tested only in adults, leaving physicians to choose between denying children access to potentially useful medications or guessing about the correct dosage for pediatric use. Congress has become very involved in the issue. See, e.g., Best Pharmaceuticals for Children Act, Pub. L. No. 107-109, 115 Stat. 1408 (2002) (incentives for pediatric research on certain drugs; expires due to sunset clause in 2007, absent congressional action); Pediatric Research Equality Act, Pub. L. No. 108-155 117 Stat. 1936 (2003) (permitting the FDA to require pediatric data in some circumstances). The FDA Web site includes a collection of material on pediatric issues, www.fda.gov/cder/pediatric/. See also, Holly Fernandez Lynch, Give Them What They Want? The Permissibility of Pediatric Placebo-Controlled Trials Under the Best Pharmaceuticals for Children Act, 16 Ann. Health L. 79 (2007).

b. *Patients with Life-Threatening Illnesses.* Research is an important issue for persons with terminal conditions. Where the current, tested treatments are ineffective, people are often tempted to view "research" as providing the best treatment. They may be particularly vulnerable to coercion and the implicit promises and hopes offered by researchers. On the other hand, of course, research in these areas is extremely important for current and future patients.

c. *Mentally Ill/Incompetent Patients.* Similar concerns exist about whether surrogates can give consent for research on mentally ill and other incompetent patients, with the additional concern about who is an appropriate surrogate. See generally Rebecca Dresser, Dementia Research: Ethics and Policy for the Twenty-First Century, 35 Ga. L. Rev. 661 (2001); Ethics in Psychiatric Research: A Resource Manual for Human Subjects Protection (Harold Alan Pincus et al., eds., 1999).

d. *Prisoners.* Should prisoners be permitted to participate in research, even when they "consent"? HHS regulations provide special protections for prisoners. See 45 C.F.R. §§46.301-.306; OHRP Guidance on the Involvement of Prisoners in Research (2003). The special rules require, for example, that a majority of the IRB members have no other association with the prison and that one member be a prisoner or prisoner representative. Another provision requires assurance that parole boards will not take the prisoner's participation into account; prisoners must also be informed of this policy. See also, Lawrence O. Gostin, Biomedical Research Involving Prisoners: Ethical Values and Legal Regulation, 297 JAMA 737 (2007) (proposals to modify rules governing research on prisoners); Barron H. Lerner, Subject or Objects? Prisoners and Human Experimentation, 356 N. Eng. J. Med. 1806 (2007).

9. *Emergency Research.* Federal regulators recently carved out an exception to the norm of disclosure and consent. FDA regulations now permit research experimentation on patients who have not consented, personally or through surrogates, in certain circumstances. Under the rule, an independent physician and an IRB must agree that the clinical trial concerns a life-threatening condition and that there is no proven, available treatment; that obtaining consent is not feasible; that the research cannot be carried out in another manner; and that the risks and benefits of the experimental procedure are reasonable under the circumstances. 21 C.F.R. §50.24.

The new regulations have been somewhat controversial because they explicitly abandon the Nuremberg Code's requirement of informed consent. See Nuremberg Code, available at ohsr.od.nih.gov/guidelines/nuremberg.html. Some commentators also maintain that these regulations allow research that has no therapeutic benefit for the immediate patient since they include patients who are near death with no hope of recovery. For commentaries on the new guidelines, see Richard S. Saver, Critical Care Research and Informed Consent, 75 N.C. L. Rev. 205 (1996); Jeremy Sugarman, Examining Provisions for Research Without Consent in the Emergency Setting, 37(1) Hasting Center Rep. 12 (Jan.-Feb. 2007); Symposium, In Case of Emergency: No Need for Consent, 27(1) Hastings Center Rep. 7-12 (1997).

Post-9/11, the FDA extended the emergency exception to informed consent to cover the "use of investigational in vitro diagnostic devices to identify chemical, biological, radiological, or nuclear agents without informed consent in some circumstances." Medical Devices; Exception from General Requirements for Informed Consent, 71 Fed. Reg. 32827, 32827 (2006). The new rule was issued without the usual notice and comment procedures. See also, Gail H. Javitt, Old Legacies and New Paradigms: Confusing "Research" and "Treatment" and Its Consequences in Responding to Emergent Health Threats, 8 J. Health Care L. & Pol'y 38 (2005).

10. *Inclusion of Women and Minorities.* The *Grimes* court focuses on the potential exploitation of the poor and members of minority groups. Commentators have also criticized the failure of medical research to include women and members of minority groups. The federal government responded in the NIH Revitalization Act of 1993, Pub. L. No. 103-43, 107 Stat. 122 (1993). See also NIH Policy and Guidelines Concerning the Inclusion of Women and Minorities as Subjects in Clinical Research (as amended October 2001), available along with other information at grants.nih.gov/grants/funding/women_min/women_min. htm; Allen L. Gifford, M.D., et al., Participation in Research and Access to Experimental Treatments by HIV-Infected Patients, 346 New Eng. J. Med. 1373 (2002); T.E. King, Jr., Racial Disparities in Clinical Trials, 346 New Eng. J. Med. 1400 (2002).

11. *"Biobanks," Informed Consent, and Privacy.* Privacy concerns pervade medical research. How will medical researchers be able to identify potentially appropriate medical research subjects without having access to medical records? How confidential are the records of medical research projects? These issues are growing increasingly complex, in part due to large-scale research involving medical records, biological samples, and genetic testing. As one example, researchers in the U.K. are moving forward with plans to collect genetic and lifestyle "data from half a million middle-aged Britons over the next decade." Gretchen Vogel, U.K.'s Mass Appeal for Disease Insights, 296 Science 824 (2002); and the program website, www.ukbiobank.ac.uk/. Privacy and commercialization rules for the database have not yet been finalized. For other examples, see Jack V. Tu et al., Impractability of Informed Consent in the Registry of the Canadian Stroke Network, 350 N. Eng. J. Med. 1414 (2004) and Julie R. Ingelfinger & Jeffrey M. Drazen, Registry Research and Medical Privacy, 350 N. Eng. J. Med. 1452 (2004). For academic commentaries on some of the key issues, see Ellen Wright Clayton, Informed Consent and Biobanks, 33 J. L. Med. & Ethics (2005); Russell Korobkin, Autonomy and Informed Consent in Nontherapeutic Biomedical Research, 54 UCLA L. Rev. 605 (2007) (focusing on stem cell research); and Mark A. Rothstein, The Role of IRBs in Research Involving Commercial Biobanks, 30 J. L. Med. & Ethics 105 (2002).

The HIPAA privacy rules discussed supra at pages 181-184 include provisions designed to ensure the privacy of information without creating insurmountable barriers to research. Critics nonetheless argued that the privacy rules would have unintended consequences for researchers. See, e.g., George J. Annas, Medical Privacy and Medical Research—Judging the New Federal Regulations, 346 New Eng. J. Med. 216 (2002); Jennifer Kulynynch & David Korn, The Effect of the New Federal Medical-Privacy Rules on Research, 346 New Eng. J. Med. 201 (2002).

12. *Research in Developing Countries.* It has become increasingly difficult to test drugs in Western countries because of strict regulations governing

safety, difficulties with compensation, and difficulty in recruiting a statistically meaningful number of study subjects. Many research-based companies are now outsourcing some of their trials to developing countries such as India. For a discussion involving testing in India, see Samiran Nundy & Chandra Gulhati, A New Colonialism? Conducting Clinical Trials in India, 352 N Eng. J. Med. 1633 (2005). What rules should apply to human subjects research conducted outside the United States by companies affiliated with U.S. companies or where the study results will be used to seek approval to market a drug in the United States? Informed consent issues are particularly salient in developing countries. See Roberto Rivera, Informed Consent: An International Researchers' Perspective, Am. J. Public Health 25 (2007) (recommendations regarding content and process for informed consent); Michael T. Krosin et al., Problems in Comprehension of Informed Consent in Rural and Peri-Urban Mali, West Africa, Clinical Trials 306 (2006).

13. *Resources and Commentaries.* HHS's Office for Human Research Protections maintains a Web site with links to key federal regulations and documents. www.hhs.gov/ohrp/. For influential criticisms of human subjects research, see the articles cited in *Grimes* and George J. Annas, Questing for Grails: Duplicity, Betrayal and Self-Deception in Research, 12 J. Contemp. Health L. & Pol'y 297 (1996); Jay Katz, Human Experimentation and Human Rights, 38 St. Louis U. L.J. 7 (1993). Important books on human subjects research include Baruch A. Brody, The Ethics of Biomedical Research: An International Perspective (1998); Claire Foster, The Ethics of Medical Research on Humans (2001); Jerry Menikoff and Edward P. Richards, What the Doctor Didn't Say: The Hidden Truth About Medical Research (2006).

4

Medical Malpractice

This chapter addresses those theories of physician and institutional liability that relate directly to the quality of care rendered, in short, classic medical malpractice actions. Other related types of liability arising from somewhat different theories of tort or contract are covered in Chapters 2 and 3, for instance, liability for refusing to accept patients, for releasing confidential medical information, or for failing to obtain informed consent. This medical malpractice chapter begins with a general overview of what we mean by medical mistakes or bad quality, and what other mechanisms besides tort liability exist for preventing or correcting bad quality. This is intended to prompt you to think about the proper aims of malpractice liability and how the tort system should function in the medical arena. We return to these themes at the end of the chapter with an examination of medical malpractice reform.

The core of the chapter develops the various components of the malpractice cause of action against physicians. It begins with the basic standard of care and how it is proved and then develops alternative theories of liability. Next, causation and affirmative defenses are surveyed, followed by a discussion of damages and settlement. The chapter then explores how these theories of liability apply to hospitals, and finally how hospital liability theories apply to managed care entities such as HMOs. Throughout, we try to achieve a useful mix of (1) explaining the basic elements of legal doctrine and its complexities, (2) outlining the pragmatics of litigating these types of cases, and (3) considering the implications for public policy.

Bibliography

There are several useful texts and treatises on medical malpractice, both from a practicing lawyer perspective and from a public policy perspective. The leading multi-volume treatise is D. Louisell & H. Williams, Medical Malpractice. A good source on trial techniques and medical issues is the multi-volume treatise,

Lee S. Goldsmith, Medical Malpractice: Guide to Medical Issues. Another useful resource is D. Danner, L. Varn & S. Mathias, Medical Malpractice: Checklists and Discovery. For a briefer text addressed to law students, see M. Boumil, et al., Medical Liability, Nutshell Series (2d ed. 2003). An excellent single-volume discussion by a law professor with extensive trial experience is Frank M. McClellan, Medical Malpractice: Law, Tactics, and Ethics (1994).

For historical and social accounts of the development and impact of medical malpractice law, see C. Chapman, Physicians, Law and Ethics (1984); Kenneth Allen DeVille, Medical Malpractice in Nineteenth-Century America (1990); Iain Hay, Money, Medicine, and Malpractice in American Society (1992); HEW, Report of the Secretary's Commission on Medical Malpractice (1973); Sylvia Law & Steven Polan, Pain and Profit: The Politics of Malpractice (1978); James C. Mohr, Doctors and the Law: Medical Jurisprudence in Nineteenth-Century America (1993); David Mechanic, Some Social Aspects of the Medical Malpractice Dilemma, 1975 Duke L.J. 1179; James C. Mohr, American Medical Malpractice Litigation in Historical Perspective, 283 JAMA 1731 (2000); E. Donald Shapiro, Medical Malpractice: History, Diagnosis, and Prognosis, 22 St. Louis U. L.J. 469 (1978); Theodore Silver, One Hundred Years of Harmful Error: The Historical Jurisprudence of Medical Malpractice, 1992 Wis. L. Rev. 1193; Catherine T. Struve, Doctors, The Adversary System, and Procedural Reform in Medical Liability Litigation, 72 Fordham L. Rev. 944 (2004).

A. MEDICAL MISTAKES AND QUALITY

1. The Nature and Extent of Medical Error

We begin with this inquiry: Why do medical mistakes occur, and what kinds of legal responses are appropriate? You should first read or review Chapter 1.B.4, which discusses the nature of medical decisionmaking in general. Then, consider the following accounts of why medical errors and injuries are so widespread.

■ MAKING MEDICAL ERRORS INTO "MEDICAL TREASURES"
David Blumenthal*
272 JAMA 1867 (1994)

Throughout most of this century, the public has granted physicians extraordinary autonomy and power in return for an implied promise that, among other things, physicians would guarantee the quality of care patients receive. Implicit in this social contract was the belief on both sides that physicians have the capability to practice error-free or nearly error-free medicine themselves and to ensure that the rest of the system functions just as well. This belief has

---

*M.D., Massachusetts General Hospital and Harvard Medical School.

served the interests of both parties to this contract. Physicians have enjoyed the resulting status, freedom, and material rewards. Patients have enjoyed the reassuring fantasy that when they are ill, they can expect their physicians to make the health care system perform flawlessly.

Comfortable as this arrangement has been, it is proving dysfunctional. Physicians are encouraged to hold themselves to unattainable standards, to deny evidence of error, and thus to overlook opportunities for improving themselves and the health care system as a whole. When inevitable errors occur, patients feel betrayed and enraged. These feelings fuel the malpractice crisis that is itself a major deterrent to the openness required for quality improvement.

The paradox of modern quality improvement is that only by admitting and forgiving error can its rate be minimized. For error reduction to occur, physicians must become more comfortable with their fallibility, and patients must become more accepting of their own vulnerability.

■ ERROR IN MEDICINE*
Lucian L. Leape**
272 JAMA 1851 (1994)

For years, medical and nursing students have been taught Florence Nightingale's dictum—first, do no harm. Yet evidence from a number of sources, reported over several decades, indicates that a substantial number of patients suffer treatment-caused injuries while in the hospital.

In 1964 Schimmel[3] reported that 20 percent of patients admitted to a university hospital medical service suffered iatrogenic injury [i.e., injury caused by treatment] and that 20 percent of those injuries were serious or fatal. Steel et al.[4] found that 36 percent of patients admitted to a university medical service in a teaching hospital suffered an iatrogenic event, of which 25 percent were serious or life threatening. More than half of the injuries were related to use of medication. In 1991 Bedell et al.[5] reported the results of an analysis of cardiac arrests at a teaching hospital. They found that 64 percent were preventable. Again, inappropriate use of drugs was the leading cause of the cardiac arrests. Also in 1991, the Harvard Medical Practice Study reported the results of a population-based study of iatrogenic injury in patients hospitalized in New York State in 1984.[6] Nearly 4 percent of patients suffered an injury that prolonged their hospital stay or resulted in measurable disability. For New York State, this equaled 98,609 patients in 1984. Nearly 14 percent of these injuries were fatal. If these rates are typical of the United States, then [nearly 100,000] people die each year

---

*Copyright © 1994, American Medical Association.
**M.D., Harvard School of Public Health.

[3] Schimmel EM. The hazards of hospitalization. Ann Intern Med. 1964; 60:100-110.

[4] Steel K, Gertman PM, Crescenzi C, et al. Iatrogenic illness on a general medical service at a university hospital. N Eng. J Med. 1981; 304:638-642.

[5] Bedell SE, Deitz DC, Leeman D, Delbanco TL. Incidence and characteristics of preventable iatrogenic cardiac arrests. JAMA 1991; 265:2815-2820.

[6] Brennan TA, Leape LL, Laird N, et al. Incidence of adverse events and negligence in hospitalized patients: results of the Harvard Medical Practice Study I. N Eng. J Med. 1991; 324:370-376.

partly as a result of iatrogenic injury, the equivalent of three jumbo-jet crashes every two days.

When the causes are investigated, it is found that most iatrogenic injuries are due to errors and are, therefore, potentially preventable. For example, in the Harvard Medical Practice Study, 69 percent of injuries were due to errors (the balance was unavoidable). . . . [I]njuries are but the "tip of the iceberg" of the problem of errors, since most errors do not result in patient injury. . . . When errors have been specifically looked for, however, the rates reported have been distressingly high. Autopsy studies have shown high rates (35 percent to 40 percent) of missed diagnoses causing death. One study of errors in a medical intensive care unit revealed an average of 1.7 errors per day per patient, of which 29 percent had the potential for serious or fatal injury. . . .

Given the complex nature of medical practice and the multitude of interventions that each patient receives, a high error rate is perhaps not surprising. The patients in the intensive care unit study, for example, were the recipients of an average of 178 "activities" per day. The 1.7 errors per day thus indicate that hospital personnel were functioning at a 99 percent level of proficiency. However, a 1 percent failure rate is substantially higher than is tolerated in industry, particularly in hazardous fields such as aviation and nuclear power. As W. E. Deming points out, even 99.9 percent may not be good enough: "If we had to live with 99.9 percent, we would have: 2 unsafe plane landings per day at O'Hare[,] 16,000 pieces of lost mail every hour, 32,000 bank checks deducted from the wrong bank account every hour."

WHY IS THE ERROR RATE IN THE PRACTICE OF MEDICINE SO HIGH?

Physicians, nurses, and pharmacists are trained to be careful and to function at a high level of proficiency. Indeed, they probably are among the most careful professionals in our society. It is curious, therefore, that high error rates have not stimulated more concern and efforts at error prevention. . . . The reasons are to be found in the culture of medical practice.

Physicians are socialized in medical school and residency to strive for error-free practice. There is a powerful emphasis on perfection, both in diagnosis and treatment. In everyday hospital practice, the message is equally clear: Mistakes are unacceptable. Physicians are expected to function without error, an expectation that physicians translate into the need to be infallible. One result is that physicians, not unlike test pilots, come to view an error as a failure of character—you weren't careful enough, you didn't try hard enough. This kind of thinking lies behind a common reaction by physicians: "How can there be an error without negligence?"

. . . It has been suggested that this need to be infallible creates a strong pressure to intellectual dishonesty, to cover up mistakes rather than to admit them. The organization of medical practice, particularly in the hospital, perpetuates these norms. Errors are rarely admitted or discussed among physicians in private practice. Physicians typically feel, not without reason, that admission of error will lead to censure or increased surveillance or, worse, that their colleagues will regard them as incompetent or careless. Far better to conceal a mistake or, if that is impossible, to try to shift the blame to another, even the patient.

Yet physicians are emotionally devastated by serious mistakes that harm or kill patients. Almost every physician who cares for patients has had that experience, usually more than once. The emotional impact is often profound, typically a mixture of fear, guilt, anger, embarrassment, and humiliation. . . .

Thus, although the individual may learn from a mistake and change practice patterns accordingly, the adjustment often takes place in a vacuum. Lessons learned are shared privately, if at all, and external objective evaluation of what went wrong often does not occur. As Hilfiker[19] points out, "We see the horror of our own mistakes, yet we are given no permission to deal with their enormous emotional impact. . . . The medical profession simply has no place for its mistakes." . . .

The paradox is that although the standard of medical practice is perfection — error-free patient care — all physicians recognize that mistakes are inevitable. Most would like to examine their mistakes and learn from them. From an emotional standpoint, they need the support and understanding of their colleagues and patients when they make mistakes. Yet, they are denied both insight and support by misguided concepts of infallibility and by fear: fear of embarrassment by colleagues, fear of patient reaction, and fear of litigation. . . .

LESSONS FROM PSYCHOLOGICAL AND HUMAN FACTORS RESEARCH

. . . Most errors result from aberrations in mental functioning. Thus, to understand why errors occur we must first understand normal cognition. Although many theories have been espoused, and experts disagree, a unitary framework has been proposed by Reason[26] that captures the main themes of cognitive theory and is consistent with empirical observation. It goes as follows. . . . Skill-based errors are called "slips." These are unconscious glitches in automatic activity. Slips are errors of action. Rule-based and knowledge-based errors, by contrast, are errors of conscious thought and are termed "mistakes." The mechanisms of error vary with the level.

SLIPS

Skill-based activity, is automatic. A slip occurs when there is a break in the routine while attention is diverted. The actor possesses the requisite routines; errors occur because of a lack of a timely attentional check. In brief, slips are monitoring failures. They are unintended acts. . . .

A variety of factors can divert attentional control and make slips more likely. Physiological factors include fatigue, sleep loss, alcohol, drugs, and illness. Psychological factors include other activity ("busyness"), as well as emotional states such as boredom, frustration, fear, anxiety, or anger. All these factors lead to preoccupations that divert attention. Psychological factors, though considered "internal" or endogenous, may also be caused by a host of external factors, such as overwork, interpersonal relations, and many other forms of stress. Environmental factors, such as noise, heat, visual stimuli, motion, and other physical phenomena, also can cause distractions that divert attention and lead to slips.

---

[19] Hilfiker D. Facing our mistakes. N Eng. J Med. 1984; 310.118-122.
[26] Reason J. Human Error. Cambridge, Mass: Cambridge University Press; 1992.

MISTAKES

Rule-based errors usually occur during problem solving when a wrong rule is chosen—either because of a misperception of the situation and, thus, the application of a wrong rule or because of misapplication of a rule, usually one that is strong (frequently used), that seems to fit adequately. Errors result from misapplied expertise.

Knowledge-based errors are much more complex. The problem solver confronts a novel situation for which he or she possesses no preprogrammed solutions. Errors arise because of lack of knowledge or misinterpretation of the problem. Pattern matching is preferred to calculation, but sometimes we match the wrong patterns. Certain habits of thought have been identified that alter pattern matching or calculation and lead to mistakes. These processes are incompletely understood and are seldom recognized by the actor. . . . The complex nature of cognition, the vagaries of the physical world, and the inevitable shortages of information and schemata ensure that normal humans make multiple errors every day. . . .

■ A COMPLEX SORROW: REFLECTIONS ON CANCER AND AN ABBREVIATED LIFE*
Marianne A. Paget

I am a sociologist and I specialize in the study of mistakes. I was at Northwestern for the year as a postdoctoral fellow in law and social science. My fellowship involved a new direction of research: examining how lawyers talk about medical errors. For some time I had been examining how physicians talk about mistakes. In The Unity of Mistakes: A Phenomenological Interpretation of Medical Work (1988) . . . I argued that clinical medicine is an error-ridden activity. I mean by error-ridden activity that mistakes are an intrinsic feature of medical work, that they cannot be avoided. I do not mean that physicians are at fault in making mistakes, though they, sometimes, are at fault. I mean that their work is intrinsically experimental, uncertain, and prone to error. . . .

I planned to locate a law firm that specialized in medical and legal disputes about malpractice where I could do field work focusing on negligence as a discourse about personal injury: how cases are processed, how expert testimony is acquired, and how settlements of claims are negotiated and resolved. . . . How error is reasoned about in legal disputes and how it is articulated in medical circles are vastly different topics and yet I hope to reveal both as forms of discourse about personal misfortune in patient care. . . .

It was while attending the first trial late in December 1987 that I began to experience back pain. . . . I had what I thought was a back injury that was taking a long time to heal. In January, I saw a physician at the student health service and was told that I was having muscle spasms, presumably from an injured muscle deep in my mid-back. Over the next few months the pain worsened and a regimen of Ibuprofen did not do much good. I had increasing difficulty using my right arm

---

*Copyright © 1993, Temple University Press. Reprinted by permission.

for driving and for carrying packages or books. I returned to the student health center several times because my condition did not improve. (My health insurance plan was connected with the university's student health service.) In April, while in Florida visiting my mother, I saw another physician who told me, once again, that I was having muscle spasms and pain from an injured muscle in my back. Thus, I had a diagnosis, but—as I was to discover too late—the wrong one. In late May, I entered physical therapy and my condition improved greatly, though the back pain was never fully resolved.

Eventually, I learned that errors in my diagnosis had jeopardized my life. . . . I was told that [I had] incurable [cancer]. Friends packed my household and I flew home to Brookline, Massachusetts, to begin treatment at the Dana-Farber Cancer Institute. I struggled with the shock of the diagnosis and with the irony of my situation. I felt very vulnerable.

It was not just that mistakes were made, though they were. It was that so many mistakes were made. My Northwestern University physician did not order a chest X-ray in the course of investigating the source of my back pain. The Florida physician, who did order one, misread it as normal. He did not notice the presence of an abnormality in my chest X-ray. Furthermore, he failed to send the X-ray to a radiologist for review. His errors were crucial. Had he seen the abnormality, or had a radiologist seen it, I would have been able to undergo surgery, which would have enhanced the probability of my survival, at least for a time. Both the physician at Northwestern University and I relied on the Florida physician's reading of the X-ray. We continued to assume that the problem was a muscle injury. Soft-issue injuries take a long time to heal, sometimes longer than broken bones. I entered physical therapy. Almost four months passed before another X-ray revealed the tumor. By that time, I had several tumors in my liver and other nodules in both lungs.

In a word, my physicians were negligent. I had just begun research on negligence; now I was an example of it. . . .

Although they cause harm, most mistakes in medicine are not negligent mistakes. Because they are not negligent, they are not compensated. They fall, literally, outside the purview of tort law. Just as troubling, in political contexts, medical mistakes are transfigured as insurance claims. They are debated not as injuries to patients requiring compensation, but as signs of litigiousness or avarice among plaintiffs and their lawyers. A crisis of injury in an error-ridden activity thus becomes an insurance crisis, a crisis in covering claims.

Mistakes are not abstract events or numbers, but lived phenomena everyone experiences and must reckon with. A mistake is an incorrect effect of an act, a wrong result. . . . We use the result to discern the wrongness of what was achieved. Taking the wrong path illustrates this. . . . In fact, the archaic meanings of mistake and error refer to taking the wrong path (*Mistaka*) or going astray and wandering about (*Errare*). . . .

Knowledge that medicine is full of error is not widespread. The reasons for this are complicated. Physicians do not talk freely about errors in their work. They are commonly reticent or silent about them. When they do talk, they frequently prefer technical terms, terms that mask their experience of error. In much the same way, they also use technical terms to mask their entire subjectivity. This is a typical feature of masculine and scientific culture. Too, the idea of endemic error radically undermines their claim to expertise. Rather, it throws the claim of expertise under new light. Physicians are "expert" in a work that proceeds by trial and error. . . . This is not to say that physicians always make mistakes. Rather I mean that error is an intrinsic problem of the diagnostic and therapeutic process.

The meaning of these events to me is that they have converged in a crisis with a life-threatening disease, which I am struggling to overcome. I am brought to an encounter with my death through these events, a series of mistakes at many levels. It is not that I am a victim of error or even of chance. There is no simple perpetrator here.

I am the subject of error. I embody it. Even my body has erred. Cancer is above all a mistake of the body. A cell goes awry in replication, not just once, but several times. It produces a mutation. This mutation reproduces itself again and again. No one seems to know how to stop the unregulated cell growth of mutating cells, least of all me. It is best if they can be cut away; if not, then killed. That is the strategy of scientific medicine.

Strangely, my knowledge of error has helped me deal with the errors in my care. Had I not known about the prevalence of error in medicine I would not have been able to process what has happened to me without bitterness. . . .

I have examined the first errant X-ray of my chest and many, many X-rays and CAT scans since then. I have talked with friends. I have spoken at length with attorneys both in Illinois and in Florida about my care. In March 1989, a lawyer filed a notice of negligence for me against the Florida physician. In due course the physician was informed of his mistake and shown the chest X-ray. Both he and I were deposed. His insurance company offered to settle out of court. I agreed. I did not file suit in Illinois, though I believe my physician at Northwestern University was negligent. The suit would have been more complicated and difficult to argue from a legal and clinical point of view. More important to me, the physician at Northwestern University recognized his mistakes. At least, I think he did. He knew that he missed the diagnosis because he did not order a chest X-ray until August. He knew that the long delay compromised my life.

Error, however, has not been the focus of my concern this last year. Rather cancer has been. And it is cancer that I have fought. . . . Now I write about my life and my work, and my work and my life, and my writing distracts me from the immediacy of my death. My work still excites me. There is so much more to do and say.

[Shortly after she wrote this, Marianne Paget died.]

Notes: Medical Mistakes

1. *The Extent of Medical Error.* A ground-breaking study of 6,712 medical records reported that, over a broad range of situations, patients in the United States receive only about 55 percent of the care recommended by various quality guidelines. Elizabeth A. McGlynn et al., The Quality of Health Care Delivered to Adults in the United States, 348 New Eng. J. Med. 2635 (2003). The classic polemic against the medical establishment is Ivan Illich, Limits to Medicine: Medical Nemesis: The Expropriation of Health 35 (1977) ("The pain, dysfunction, disability, and anguish resulting from technical medical intervention . . .

make the impact of medicine one of the most rapidly spreading epidemics of our time.").

Are you surprised or shocked by the 100,000 annual deaths caused by medical mistakes that the Harvard researchers extrapolated from their study in New York state (discussed in the Leape article)? In this influential study, the researchers evaluated 30,000 hospital medical records in New York state to determine how frequently medical treatment causes injury, what proportion of those injuries are due to negligence, and how many of those negligent injuries are compensated by the tort system. Judgments about causation, negligence, and the extent of injury were made by expert physician reviewers. Paul Weiler et al., A Measure of Malpractice (1993). Similar studies were conducted in California in 1974, and in Utah and Colorado in the late 1990s, producing remarkably similar findings. See generally Tom Baker, The Medical Malpractice Myth (2005); Michelle M. Mello & Troyen A. Brennan, Deterrence of Medical Errors: Theory and Evidence for Malpractice Reform, 80 Tex. L. Rev. 1595 (2002). These findings received widespread publicity with the release of a seminal report, Institute of Medicine, To Err Is Human: Building a Safer Health System (2000). This report calls for renewed efforts to redesign medical care systems to prevent many common mistakes, and it calls for reporting systems that would collect and disseminate better information about where and how medical mistakes are occurring.

The Harvard researchers further concluded that almost half of the 100,000 projected deaths from medical error are attributable to negligence, that is, departures from the standard of care. These figures compare with fewer than 50,000 people killed in auto accidents each year and 15,000 killed by firearms. Realize, though, that most people who die as the result of medical treatment do not die in the prime of life; many are old or feeble patients whose prospects for long-term survival are dim at best. For additional critique of these findings, see Rodney A. Hayward & Timothy P. Hofer, Estimating Hospital Deaths Due to Medical Errors: Preventability Is in the Eye of the Reviewer, 286 JAMA 415 (2001); Clement J. McDonald et al., Deaths Due to Medical Errors Are Exaggerated in Institute of Medicine Report, 284 JAMA 93 (2000).

Professor Mark Grady reasons that medical mistakes are this common because medical science has progressed so rapidly and is capable of much more than it once was. "New technology can enlarge people's opportunities to forget to use precaution and thereby be negligent." Why Are People Negligent? Technology, Nondurable Precautions, and the Medical Malpractice Explosion, 82 Nw. U. L. Rev. 293, 295 (1988). Renowned philosophers Samuel Gorovitz and Alasdair MacIntyre also argue that a high error rate is inevitable in medicine because of the human condition and the limits of technology. Toward a Theory of Fallibility, Hastings Center Rep., Dec. 1975, at 13. See also Peter Jacobson, Medical Liability and the Culture of Technology, in Medical Malpractice and the U.S. Health Care System (W. Sage & R. Kersh, eds., 2006). Are these views consistent with commonly held attitudes and expectations about modern medicine as conveyed by mass media? Could there be some therapeutic or social benefit to the blind faith that people sometimes place in their doctors? See Chapter 1.B.3. Viewed in this light, is it good to counter mass delusion by debunking the myth of infallibility?

2. *Bibliography*. Additional discussions of medical error and measuring and improving quality can be found at Symposium, 22(2) Health Affairs (March 2003); Symposium, 46 Perspectives in Biology and Medicine 1 (Winter 2003); Rosemary Gibson & Janardan Prasad Singh, Wall of Silence: The Untold Story of Medical Mistakes That Kill and Injure Millions of Americans (Lifeline Press, 2003); Robert M. Wachter & Kaveh G. Shojania, Internal Bleeding: The Truth Behind America's Terrifying Epidemic of Medical Mistakes (Rugged Land, 2004); Virginia A. Sharpe & Alan I. Faden, Medical Harm: Historical, Conceptual and Ethical Dimensions of Iatrogenic Illness (1998); Symposium, Patient Injury, Medical Errors, Liability and Reform, 29 J.L. Med. & Ethics 248 (2001); Symposium, 76 Milbank Q. 515 (1998).

3. *Conceptual Distinctions.* Roughly a third of malpractice claims are for diagnostic errors (especially failure to diagnose cancer), a third are for surgical errors (improper technique, slip of knife, foreign objects left inside); and a third are for improper medical treatment (e.g., drug reaction, anesthesia error, birth injury). Regardless of the type of medical treatment involved, consider, as you read the cases in the remainder of this chapter, how you would classify the various mistakes that led to injury. Are they "slips" or judgment errors? Are judgment errors due to misperception of the problem, choice of the wrong rule of action, or misapplication of the rule? Are errors the responsibility of any one actor, or do they result in flaws in the overall *system* for coordinating and delivering care? For more on the latter distinction, see Institute of Medicine, supra, and a series of articles exploring the nature of medical error, running in the Annals of Internal Medicine 2002-2003. Renowned medical sociologist Elliot Friedson introduces another distinction in Doctoring Together (1975):

> "Normal," excusable mistakes are those that every physician could conceive of making because of lack of information, the uncertainty of medical knowledge, the limitation of available techniques, and the uniqueness of the case. Many physicians would not even call these "mistakes"; in the interviews some called them "so-called mistakes." Such normal mistakes are less mistakes than they are unavoidable events; they are not so much committed by the doctor as they are suffered or risked. They do not reflect on the physician's competence so much as on his luck. Thus, one should not judge or criticize a colleague's apparent mistakes because "there but for the grace of God go I."
>
> In contrast to normal mistakes are deviant mistakes. Essentially, deviant mistakes seemed to be those that are thought to be due to a practitioner's negligence, ignorance, or ineptitude, reflecting upon his lack of basic or reasonable competence, ethicality, conscientiousness, and judgment. They consist in failures to follow the widely agreed-on rules of good practice. These are the mistakes that are frequently called "blatant" or "gross," "serious" being an adjective more often used to delineate the consequence of a mistake rather than its analytic character.

Timothy Stolzfus Jost, in the article that comes next, introduces two additional relevant distinctions:

> A patient may receive a medical procedure that is technically appropriate but . . . [still] suffer a variety of affronts to dignity from health care professionals [such as

failure to explain what is happening]. . . . A doctor may be unnecessarily rude or abrupt with a patient, or show contempt for the value of a patient's time. . . . These violations of social values and norms . . . seldom result in litigation or regulatory action, but frequently result in patient dissatisfaction. . . .

Finally, medical errors must be distinguished from medical failures. Some medical failures are not errors in the sense that anyone is culpable for their occurrence. They are simply due to unforeseeable reactions of a particular patient to treatment, unavoidable failure of equipment, the current limits of medical knowledge, or the ultimately intractable complexity of the human body. Even though such failures should in most instances not result in either tort or regulatory sanctions, an effective quality assurance system can discover them, and identify their causes, and perhaps assure they do not happen again.

4. *The Patient's Perspective.* Why do patients, even thoughtful and sensitive ones like Marianne Paget, seek to blame doctors for their mistakes? Popular opinion sometimes thinks that malpractice plaintiffs are just trying to capitalize on their misfortune in order to hit the jackpot by suing a rich or well-insured doctor, or that plaintiffs are seduced into this attitude by personal injury lawyers looking for a big contingency fee. Certainly, there is some element of truth in this account, but to a large extent many patients also feel genuinely angry and wronged by how they were treated. In one law office (the one that represented the plaintiff in the first case below), 56 percent of inquiries about malpractice over a ten-year period were prompted by the doctor's referring unpaid bills to a collection agency, and 60 percent of potential clients were told by a nurse that malpractice had occurred. J. Reagan McLaurin et al., Pitfalls for the Practitioner: A Claimant's View of Medical Malpractice, Carolina Health Serv. Res. 97 (Summer 1994). A similar study in five states found that 53 percent of patients who contacted a law firm had poor relationships with their doctors. L. Huycke & M. Huycke, Characteristics of Potential Plaintiffs in Malpractice Litigation, 120 Ann. Intern. Med. 792 (1994). A review of deposition transcripts found that, in 70 percent of the cases, the patients complained of one or more of the following behaviors by the doctor: devaluing patients' views, deserting the patient, and delivering information poorly. See Wendy Levinson, Physician-Patient Communication: A Key to Malpractice Prevention, 272 JAMA 1619 (1994). See also Frank Sloan et al., Suing for Medical Malpractice ch. 4 (1993); Wendy Levinson et al., Physician-Patient Communication: The Relationship with Malpractice Claims, 277 JAMA 553 (1997); Debra Roter, The Patient-Physician Relationship and Its Implications for Malpractice Litigation, 9 J. Health Care L. & Policy 304 (2006).

Patients also sometimes sue simply to find out more about what went wrong and why. See Barry Werth, Damages: One Family's Legal Struggles in the World of Medicine (1998).

5. *Physicians' Attitudes Toward Making Mistakes.* Marianne Paget's dramatic and moving account of her imminent death is an example of a growing genre of academic and popular writing in the form of personal narrative. Equally compelling are doctors' accounts of their guilt, defensiveness, and self-doubt that result from recognizing the tragic consequences of their errors. Many examples of these confessional narratives are contained in Paget's earlier work, cited in her main excerpt. For other compelling examples, see the moving description by

Dr. Hilfiker (cited in n.19 of the Leape article) of his horror upon discovering that he had mistakenly killed his patient's fetus which he erroneously thought had been expelled through a miscarriage; Atul Gawande, When Doctors Make Mistakes, New Yorker, Feb. 1, 1999, at 40; Atul Gawande, Complications: A Surgeon's Notes on an Imperfect Science (2002); and the collection of articles in 20 Health Aff. 241 (2001) and 21(4) Health Aff. 232 (2002). A classic study of how medical professionals respond to error is Charles Bosk, Forgive and Remember: Managing Medical Failure (2d ed. 2003).

6. *Telling Patients and Apologizing.* Should physicians be required, as an aspect of their fiduciary duty to patients, to inform patients when a bad outcome is due to a medical mistake? This question is receiving considerable attention. The private accreditation body in charge of hospitals (the JCAHO, Joint Commission on the Accreditation of Healthcare Organizations) has instituted a "sentinel events" reporting policy that requires hospitals to make physicians inform patients or their families when unexpected death or serious injury is caused by medical care rather than by the natural course of disease. See Symposium, 35 J. Health L. 179 (2002). A few states require the same. Wm. Sage et al., Bridging the Relational-Regulatory Gap: A Pragmatic Information Policy for Patient Safety and Medical Malpractice, 59 Vand. L. Rev. 1263 (2006).

Medical and health policy literature is focusing on how best to conduct these difficult conversations and whether they increase litigation risk. K. M. Mazor et al., Communicating with Patients About Medical Errors: A Review of the Literature, 164 Arch. Intern. Med. 1690 (2003); Thomas H. Gallagher et al., Patients' and Physicians' Attitudes Regarding the Disclosure of Medial Errors, 289 JAMA 1001 (2003); K. M. Mazor et al., Health Plan Members' Views About Disclosure of Medical Errors, 140 Ann. Intern. Med. 409 (2004); Carol B. Liebman & Chris Stern Hyman, Medical Error Disclosure, Mediation Skills, and Malpractice Litigation, 23(4) Health Aff. 23 (Aug. 2004); David M. Studdert et al., Disclosure of Medical Injury to Patients: An Improbable Risk Management Strategy, 26(1) Health Aff. 215 (Jan. 2007); Symposium, 166 Arch. Intern. Med. 1585 (2006).

When doctors reveal medical errors to patients, should they also apologize, either from a genuine feeling of remorse, or as a strategic way to head off medical malpractice litigation?

> Doctors' apologies for medical mistakes may not be a cure-all for litigation, but explaining unforeseen outcomes and making early settlement offers have proven effective, say lawyers who have participated in the process in the last decade. The concept is called "full disclosure/early offer," and it's spreading. The U.S. Department of Veterans Affairs' Veterans Health Administration — as well as a number of hospital systems and insurers across the nation — are among the entities that have adopted variations of the policy. . . . Plaintiffs' and defense attorneys agree that the program — often referred to as Sorry Works! from The Sorry Works! Coalition, . . . — is a sound strategy miscast in the public perception as a touchy-feely ritual. . . . [H]ealth care providers willing to admit when they have made an error and quickly get on top of it cut down on the anger that leads to litigation. . . .
>
> Michael A. Stidham, whose Jackson, Ky., practice includes representing Department of Veterans Affairs (V.A.) patients, has settled three cases with the

Veterans Affairs Medical Center in Lexington, Ky.—two on the same morning—and lost a bench trial in a medical malpractice case that involved a suicide. Stidham said that he likes the system and thinks that its wider application could help to reduce docket backlogs. In contrast, a case against a local hospital can take three to four years to get to trial. "The only thing I really find lacking in it at this point is that I don't believe they tell the prospective plaintiffs that they have the right to discuss their offers with an attorney. A lot of men and women don't understand why they're receiving these offers," he said. Stidham noted that "I didn't always get everything I wanted, but I didn't leave with a bad taste in my mouth, and left with a satisfied client, which is the most important thing."

Ginny M. Hamm, the special assistant U.S. attorney assigned to the V.A. medical center in Lexington who worked with the former hospital chief of staff, Dr. Steve S. Kraman, to introduce a centerwide disclosure program in 1987, said that a full and lengthy explanation always precedes an offer. Since Hamm did her first disclosure case in 1989, the "golden rule" has been to tell veterans or their families that they should seek counsel when the hospital meets with them to disclose what went wrong, she said. Kraman, as chief of staff, would speak to the veteran and his family on behalf of the entire medical center, offering an apology and explaining the error, then "hand off to me for the settlement," she said. Hamm added that if the V.A. determined that no mistake was made, it would hold a "closure" meeting explaining its finding to the veteran. Kraman, who now serves on the board of The Sorry Works! Coalition, said that he was aware of only two cases in which angry patients sued for damages. "The vast majority of people respond in kind. If treated honestly, they don't even want money. They want to see that some good comes out of a bad situation," Kraman said. Peter Geier, Emerging Med-Mal Strategy: "I'm Sorry," National L. J., July 24, 2006.

See also Jonathan Todres, Toward Healing and Restoration for All: Reframing Medical Malpractice Reform, 39 Conn. L. Rev. 667 (2006); Erin Ann O'Hara, Apology and Thick Trust: What Spouse Abusers and Negligent Doctors Might Have in Common, 79 Chi.-Kent L. Rev. 1055 (2004); Lee Taft, Apology and Medical Mistake: Opportunity or Foil?, 14 Ann. Health L. 55 (2005); Douglas N. Frenkel & Carol B. Liebman, Words That Heal, 140 Ann. Intern. Med. 482 (2004); K. M. Mazor et al., Health Plan Members' Views on Forgiving Medical Errors, 11 Am. J. Manag. Care 49 (2005).

7. *Physicians' Attitudes Toward Being Sued.* In contrast with their private regret over poor medical outcomes, most doctors view a malpractice suit as an unjustified affront to their professional integrity and reputation. According to one explanation:

Physicians typically invest a great deal of emotion in the malpractice issue, usually to a degree that is out of proportion to the actual risk. It is hard to understand why this is the case at times, but . . . [the] explanation lies in the adversarial process. Physicians believe, in most cases rightfully so, that their devotion to patients runs deep. It draws them out of the commercial world and into a dyad of trust and intimacy. Thus it is particularly shocking for physicians when they are brought crashing back into market liberalism through the vehicle of a lawsuit. It is felt as a betrayal and can be an extremely stressful experience for the physician-defendant. The blame usually does not fall on the patient (perhaps paternalistically, the physician cannot blame him or her) but rather on the lawyer. The charge of negligence is felt as an unwarranted criminal accusation, and the doctor immediately becomes the victim. In this way malpractice litigation excites the basest emotions. Troyen A. Brennan et al., Liability, Patient Safety, and Defensive Medicine, in Medical Malpractice and the U.S. Health Care System 93, 109-110 (W. Sage & R. Kersh, eds. 2006).

Here is one example of how a physician reacted to being sued:

I was angry and incredulous. Three months before the surgery [performed by someone else, which caused the injury,] I had examined the patient and written two sentences in the record: That was my entire participation in the case. . . . As the trial approached, the psychological stress became devastating. I had to continue seeing patients, but my thoughts were troubling: Who will sue next? Am I missing something that will come back to haunt me? And, though I'd done nothing wrong, could I somehow be as incompetent as the plaintiff's attorneys imply? . . . I worried that the stigma of accusation would cause patients and peers to see me as less competent and caring. . . .

The trial began . . . five years after the alleged malpractice. The plaintiff's attorney immediately tried to make me look selfish, uncaring and inept. And here — in sharp contrast to my office — I had no control of the situation. I knew the correct answers. I knew that my medical treatment had been perfectly appropriate. But my answers were often limited to "yes" or "no." Denied fuller explanation, I could readily be hanged by my own testimony. . . .

[Although I was eventually dropped from the suit], it's still hard not to feel stigmatized. The lawyers advised me to forget it, but it's not that simple. Every year I have to fill out forms from my malpractice insurer, hospital staffs and state licensing boards. I'm asked whether I've ever been convicted of a felony and whether a malpractice claim has ever been brought against me. So it's OK to have been accused of murder — but not of malpractice. A more serious problem is the effect on my attitude toward patients. The lawyers would have me believe that the experience might make me a better doctor, or at least a more careful one. But I had not been careless. A litigious patient, egged on by a greedy lawyer, had simply cast his net as wide as possible, and I had been snared. Confronted by the same medical situation again — or a hundred times over — I would have done no differently.

But I am more cautious. I know how easy it is for patients to initiate malpractice suits — and how difficult it is for physicians to extricate themselves from them. So I'm extremely apprehensive about small problems that develop and that might encourage a patient to become litigious. And I constantly feel the fear that motivates defensive medicine. As I order yet another neuro-imaging study or send a patient for confirming opinions whenever he or she expresses the slightest doubt about my management, I regret the expenditure of precious health care dollars, but I have to protect myself and my livelihood. Elliott M. Perlman, M. D., Well-managed Case Gets Caught in Malpractice Fervor, Am. Med. News, Feb. 21, 1994. (Reprinted with permission from Dr. Perlman, who is an ophthalmologist in solo practice and on the faculty at Brown University Medical School.)

Another doctor graphically depicts his feeling of violation after a string of suits in quick succession: "From being a virgin for 20 years, all of a sudden I was gang raped." N. Hupert et al., Processing the Tort Deterrent Signal: A Qualitative Study, 43 Soc. Sci. & Med. 1 (1996). See also H. C. Snyder, Jury of My Peers: A Surgeon's Encounter with the Malpractice Crisis (1991); F. Patrick Hubbard, The

Physician's Point of View Concerning Medical Malpractice, 23 Ga. L. Rev. 295 (1989). Does this type of response cause you concern about whether malpractice law is having its intended social effect? How constructive are physicians' responses to this deterrent signal likely to be? See page 375 for a discussion of the meaning and extent of the "defensive medicine" caused by this liability threat.

2. Measuring the Malpractice System

■ THE MEDICAL MALPRACTICE MYTH
Tom Baker*

Medical malpractice premiums are skyrocketing. "Closed" signs are sprouting on health clinic doors. Doctors are leaving the field of medicine, and those who remain are practicing in fear and silence. Pregnant women cannot find obstretricians. Billions of dollars are wasted on defensive medicine. And angry doctors are marching on state capitols across the country. All this is because medical malpractice litigation is exploding. Egged on by greedy lawyers, plaintiffs sue at the drop of a hat. Juries award eye-popping sums to undeserving claimants, leaving doctors, hospitals, and their insurance companies no choice but to pay huge ransoms . . .

This is the medical malpractice myth. . . . None of this bears even a passing resemblance to reality. In fact, the research is so clearly to the contrary that the most interesting question is why the research has not changed people's minds. . . . Built on a foundation of urban legend mixed with the occasional true story, supported by selective references to academic studies, and repeated so often that even the mythmakers forget the exaggeration, half truth, and outright misinformation employed in the service of their greater good, the medical malpractice myth has filled doctors, patients, legislators, and voters with the kind of fear that short circuits critical thinking.

This fear has inspired legislative action on a nationwide scale three times in my lifetime: [the mid-1970s, the mid-1980s, and the early 2000s]. . . . This time around we have a lot more information. First, we know from [various] studies that the real problem is too much medical malpractice, not too much litigation. . . . The real costs of medical malpractice are the lost lives, extra medical expenses, time out of work, and pain and suffering of tens of thousands of people every year, the vast majority of whom do not sue. . . . "[U]ndeserving" people sometimes bring medical malpractice claims because they do not know that the claims lack merit and because they cannot find out what happened to them (or their loved ones) without making a claim. Most undeserving claims disappear before a trial; most trials end in a verdict for the doctor; doctors almost never pay claims out of their own pockets; and hospitals and insurance companies refuse to pay claims

---

*© 2005, University of Chicago Press. Tom Baker is a law professor at the University of Connecticut.

unless there is a good evidence of malpractice. If a hospital or insurance company does settle a questionable claim to avoid a huge risk, there is a very large discount. This means that big payments to undeserving claimants are the very rare exception, not the rule. . . .

This is a book with a mission. My goal is reframing the public discussion about medical malpractice lawsuits . . . [so that] the people who know a lot about medicine and the people who know a lot about law can start to talk *to* each other, rather than *at* each other, about the role that law can play in improving the quality of health care.

Notes: Facts and Figures

1. *The Epidemiology of Malpractice Suits.* To appreciate the concern that doctors have about being sued in the modern legal climate, consider that, prior to 1960, only one in seven doctors had ever been sued in their entire career. Today, claims are filed against about one in seven doctors *each year*. This explains why malpractice law is often the focal point for discussion of tort reform in state and federal legislatures, and why tort reform is one of the AMA's highest legislative priorities, appearing to rank above other social concerns such as universal access to health care.

Although most doctors complain about the threat of malpractice suits, they are not all equally affected. Malpractice claims are not spread uniformly. Some specialties (surgery, anesthesiology, obstetrics, and emergency medicine) produce claims much more frequently than others and some doctors within the same specialty are sued more often than others. In one study of malpractice insurance claims in Florida from 1974-1983, physicians averaged almost one claim per year, but 60 percent of doctors suffered no claims at all, and only 13 percent had any *paid* claims, even though Florida is one of the more litigious states. Physicians who had any claims in the first six years of this study were more than twice as likely to have one or more claims in the next three years. Randall R. Bovbjerg & Kenneth Petronis, The Relationship Between Physicians' Malpractice Claims History and Later Claims, 272 JAMA 1421 (1994).

2. *Plaintiffs' Lawyers.* As Prof. Baker summarizes, and as his book thoroughly documents, a flurry of empirical research over the past decade allows us to address the contentious debate over malpractice litigation with something more than anecdotal opinion. For instance, the claim that too many frivolous suits are filed is belied by the fact that most experienced malpractice lawyers are very selective in the cases they agree to take, due to the costs of litigation and the uncertainty of prevailing. In one study of six firms, 502 potential plaintiffs called over a ten-day period. Of these, 85 (17 percent) were selected for expert review of the medical records. Sixty-two percent of these were rejected, usually for insufficient damages, and only one-quarter for lack of negligence. For callers who were rejected without medical review, the overwhelming reason (73 percent) was insufficient damages. L. Huycke & M. Huycke, Characteristics of Potential Plaintiffs in Malpractice Litigation, 120 Ann. Intern. Med. 792 (1994). See also Kenneth DeVille, Act First

and Look Up the Law Afterward? Medical Malpractice and the Ethics of Defensive Medicine, 19 Theoretical Med. & Bioethics 569 (1998) (an excellent overview, both for doctors and lawyers, of the factors that influence patients' decisions to consult a lawyer, lawyers' decisions to bring a case, the chances of success, and the likely recovery); L. Laska, Medical Malpractice Cases Not to File, 20 Mem. St. U. L. Rev. 27 (1989). Naturally, less established malpractice attorneys may decide not to be this selective. See generally Catherine T. Harris et al., Who Are Those Guys? An Empirical Examination of Medical Malpractice Plaintiffs' Attorneys, 58 S.M.U. L. Rev. 225 (2005); Stephen Daniels & Joanne Martin, Plaintiff's Lawyers, Specialization, and Medical Malpractice, 59 Vand. L. Rev. 1051 (2006).

3. *Jury Bias.* It appears that physicians' concerns about juries being biased in favor of injured patients are exaggerated. For the most part, these research findings are much more supportive of juries than is popular opinion. When malpractice complaints go to trial, plaintiffs win only 20 to 30 percent of the time. This compares with an overall success rate of about 50 percent for plaintiffs in general civil litigation. Interviews with jurors in malpractice cases also confirm that, generally speaking, they enter the case sympathetic to doctors and suspicious of plaintiffs' motives to "make a fast buck." Neil Vidmar, Medical Malpractice and the American Jury (1995). For other empirical studies and reviews, see William M. Sage & Rogan Kersh, Medical Malpractice and the U.S. Health Care System (2006); Frank Sloan & Lindsey M. Chepke, Ill-Suited? Medical Malpractice at a Crossroads (2008); David A. Hyman & Charles Silver, Medical Malpractice Litigation and Tort Reform: It's the Incentives Stupid, 59 Vand. L. Rev. 1085 (2006); Symposium, 4 J. Empirical Leg. Stud. 1 (2007).

Although doctors win most of the time, how accurate these verdicts are is another question. Accuracy, of course, is in the eye of the beholder, since there is no agreement on what the proper "gold standard" should be for evaluating jury verdicts. The best that researchers can do is to ask expert neutral physicians whether the medical records reveal any substandard care causing injury. When they do so, researchers find a statistically significant, but far from perfect, correlation between the expert reviewer's opinion and the jury's verdict in the same case. For instance, one study compared how cases were resolved by juries with how the physician-run insurer had evaluated the case before trial for purposes of settlement negotiations. It found that plaintiffs won 42 percent of the cases that the insurer's consultants considered "indefensible," but plaintiffs won only 21 percent of those considered "defensible." This study also found that wins and losses were not influenced by the severity of injury, indicating that juries were not swayed purely by sympathy for the plaintiff. The amount of damages did vary with the strength of the liability case, even after controlling for the severity of the injury. Therefore, the expected value of a malpractice claim (i.e., the expected award times the chances of winning) was twenty-five times larger for claims that reviewers judged to be meritorious than for ones they judged to be without merit. This gives contingent fee lawyers a strong incentive to weed out weaker or "frivolous" claims. Mark I. Taragin et al., The Influence of Standard of Care and Severity of Injury on the Resolution of Medical Malpractice Claims, 117 Ann. Intern. Med. 780 (1992). Other studies show that, when plaintiffs win, damages are appropriately correlated with the patients' age and severity of injury.

In a thorough review of the evidence, Prof. Peters concludes that juries, on balance, reach defensible results and are not biased against physicians; if anything, juries are biased in doctors' favor. Philip G. Peters, The Role of the Jury in Modern Malpractice Law, 87 Iowa L. Rev. 911 (2002); Philip G. Peters, Doctors and Juries, 105 Mich. L. Rev. 1453 (2007) (multiple studies are "startlingly consistent," that "the probability of a plaintiff's verdict grows as the evidence of negligence improves"). Compare Jeffrey O'Connell & Christopher Pohl, How Reliable Is Medical Malpractice Law? A Review of "Medical Malpractice and the American Jury," 12 J. L. & Health 359 (1998) (insightful review of both Neil Vidmar's research of jury verdicts and the Harvard study findings, concluding that malpractice law is not well designed to produce accurate and fair results, and advocating instead a no-fault compensation system), with David A. Hyman, Medical Malpractice and the Tort System: What Do We Know and What (If Anything) Should We Do about It?, 80 Tex. L. Rev. 1639 (2002) (criticizing malpractice system but also expressing skepticism about no-fault compensation).

Finding a statistical association between jury results and expert opinion means only that jury verdicts as a whole are not entirely random or unpredictable. Results in individual cases are still highly erratic. Also, as the numbers from the study by Taragin et al. reflect, depending on how one conceives of the correct "gold standard," juries produce a large number of both false positives (incorrect findings of negligence) and false negatives (incorrect findings of no liability), perhaps more of the latter than the former. The materials in section 4.D.4 outline alternatives for liability determination other than the jury trial that rely more on expert opinion. Even if these alternatives were to produce greater accuracy, what other values would they sacrifice?

Another measure of the accuracy and rationality of the malpractice system is lawyers' behavior in settling cases. As discussed in section 4.E, many more cases settle than go to trial. Lawyers take their clues for when and how much to settle by observing how juries behave. If juries don't reach accurate results or if their behavior is unpredictable, then settlement decisions are not likely to be accurate. One study, which used independent physician specialists to evaluate medical records in 51 cases, found that malpractice insurers were just as likely to agree to payment through settlement (about half the time) when there was a negligent injury as when there was not. The only significant predictor of agreement to pay was the degree of injury, not negligence. Troyen Brennan, Colin Sox & Helen Burstin, Relation Between Negligent Adverse Events and the Outcomes of Medical-Malpractice Litigation, 335 New Eng. J. Med. 1963 (1996). For a critique of these findings, see Tom Baker, Reconsidering the Harvard Medical Practice Study Conclusions About the Validity of Medical Malpractice Claims, 33 J. L. Med. & Ethics 501 (2005). Another study found that malpractice claims involving verifiable errors are much more likely to result in a payment to the patient, and that such payments are substantially higher than in claims without medical errors that are settled. David M. Studdert et al., Claims, Errors and Compensation Payments in Medical Malpractice Litigation, 354 New Eng. J. Med. 2024 (2006).

4. *Piecing It All Together*. Based on the data and concepts discussed in these notes, Randall Bovbjerg has created the following diagram, adapted from an earlier version by Don Harper Mills (who ran the California study). The diagram is conceptual, not to scale, but it provides some rough scope for the issues addressed throughout this chapter.

Relationship between Injuries & Claims

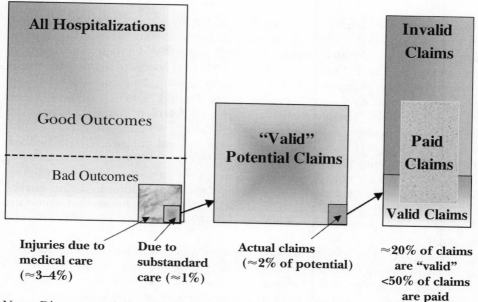

Note: Diagram scale is only approximate.

In any medical encounter, there is a considerable chance of a disappointing outcome. However, most of these poor results are the unavoidable consequence of the disease itself and the inherent limits of medical science. Of all hospital admissions, only about 4 percent involve an injury caused by medical treatment. Of these, only about one-fourth (1 percent of the total) are the result of substandard care. Only about 2 percent of negligent injuries result in claims being filed with insurers. In part, this is because the great majority of these injuries are temporary or minor. Surprisingly, however, most claims are for injuries not caused by negligence. Fewer than half of all claims result in payment, usually through settlement.

5. *Looking Ahead*. The next reading considers the full range of possible legal responses that are available for medical mistakes and other deficiencies in the quality of health care delivery. As you read it, consider which responses are appropriate for which types of mistakes, and how malpractice suits compare with other types of legal oversight.

3. Approaches to Improving Quality of Care

■ THE NECESSARY AND PROPER ROLE OF REGULATION TO ASSURE THE QUALITY OF HEALTH CARE*
Timothy Stolzfus Jost**
25 Hous. L. Rev. 525 (1988); 22 U.C. Davis L. Rev. 593 (1989); 37 Ariz. L. Rev. 825 (1995)

Assuring the quality of the care provided by medical professionals and institutions has been a concern of the law from ancient times. The Code of Hammurabi mandated that a doctor who negligently killed a patient or destroyed a patient's sight should have his hand cut off. Medical licensure statutes, providing for licensure examinations and professional discipline, date from the thirteenth century in Europe and were pervasive in the United States by the end of the nineteenth century. The alternative approach of deterrence and punishment of medical error through malpractice litigation also has venerable roots. English malpractice cases date from the fourteenth century, and American cases date from the eighteenth century.

Concern for the quality of medical care has recently taken on a new urgency, however, evidenced by a rash of federal legislation attempting to assure quality. The driving force behind this heightened concern is a belief that emerging changes in the structure of the health care industry could have a negative effect on the quality of medical care. . . .

These recent developments have impelled a lively debate as to what needs to be done by whom to assure quality of care and prevent medical error. No consensus has yet emerged. One position is that the forces that have traditionally been relied on to assure quality of care, professional ethics and socialization, have been and remain adequate to the job. Another is that the market forces recently unleashed are not only capable of controlling health care costs, but also of assuring health care quality. A third position is that self-regulation, through accreditation, certification, and hospital medical staff privileges can assure quality. The continued option of medical malpractice litigation offers a fourth alternative for quality assurance. This article will evaluate each of these alternatives and find them wanting, individually and collectively. Each has an important role to play in assuring the quality of health care, but ultimately each alone, and all together, are inadequate. A fifth quality control alternative, government intervention through regulation, must finally be explored. Regulation, this article will contend, is necessary to fill significant gaps left by other methods of quality control and to assure that these other mechanisms operate properly to assure quality and prevent medical error. . . .

---

*This excerpt is a combination of three articles, the second one entitled Regulatory Approaches to Problems in the Quality of Medical Care: Diagnosis and Prescription (© 1989 by the Regents of the University of California), and the third one entitled Oversight of the Quality of Medical Care: Regulation, Management, or the Market? They are reprinted with permission. Headings, footnote numbering, and to some extent the structure of the argument have been altered from the original.

**Law professor at Washington & Lee University.

II. THE MEANING OF QUALITY AND ERROR

A consideration of strategies for quality assurance should begin with an examination of the meaning of quality and error. Donabedian, the leading theorist of health care quality, . . . categorizes [quality] evaluation mechanisms in his famous typology as concerned with structure, process, or outcome.[2] A structural evaluation (e.g., a licensure examination) focuses on underlying capacity to deliver quality care: How much does the doctor know; how well is the hospital equipped? . . . [S]tructural aspects of care are the easiest to define and to evaluate; thus, many strategies rely, at least in part, on structural evaluation.

Process evaluation studies the process through which care is delivered. It considers, for example, whether a drug was properly prescribed in the appropriate dosage given the patient's symptoms. Process is more difficult to evaluate than structure. Process evaluation is usually based on professional consensus as to appropriate procedures for a given problem. It forms the basis for many peer review programs. It has been criticized as overemphasizing the technical nature of care and contributing to health care cost inflation through this emphasis. Moreover, process norms are model treatments for model cases. It is difficult to adapt them to address the wide variations found in patients and their conditions.

Finally, outcome analysis considers the results of care: Did the patient get better; did the condition improve? Comparing hospital mortality and morbidity statistics for treatment of a particular condition is a form of outcome analysis. Outcome analysis is the most difficult form of quality evaluation because the duration, timing, or extent of outcomes of optimal care are often hard to specify. Data on the outcomes of care delivered by professionals or institutions cannot be compared usefully unless adjustments are made for variations in case mix and severity of conditions. It is often difficult to relate a specific outcome to a particular medical intervention, and outcomes are often clear only when it is too late to affect practice. Yet outcome analysis looks at the ends of medical care rather than the means, and is thus ultimately most telling. The medical malpractice system has always begun its inquiry with a bad outcome, though it ultimately relies on process analysis. . . .

[G]rowing evidence indicates that a significant proportion of medical malpractice actions are filed against a relatively small number of professionals. While several reasons for this trend may exist, one plausible explanation is that a small number of deficient professionals cause many patient injuries. . . . Undoubtedly, a substantial proportion of medical injury [also] occurs from the occasional failure of otherwise competent professionals. . . . Such mistakes do not necessarily evidence more fundamental deficiencies, and [society] should handle these problems differently than the problems caused by impaired or incompetent physicians. . . .

---

[2] Donabedian, Criteria and Standards for Quality Assessment and Monitoring, 12 Quality Rev. Bull. 99 (1986); Donabedian, Commentary on Some Studies on the Quality of Care, Health Care Fin. Ref., 1987 Supp., at 75, 76-77; 1 A. Donabedian, Explorations in Quality Assessment and Monitoring: The Definition of Quality and Approaches to Its Assessment 4-6 (1980).

III. Strategies for Assuring Quality and Preventing Error

A. PROFESSIONAL SELF-REGULATION

The first line of defense for assuring the quality of health care is professional self-regulation. Professional self-regulation takes a number of forms, which are sufficiently distinct to deserve separate treatment. First, professionals are educated and socialized to assure the quality of their own work. Second, professionals informally review the quality of the work of their colleagues. Third, professionals and institutions sponsor and administer certification and accreditation programs aimed at assuring the quality of their peers. Finally, professionals practicing within institutions police the quality of their associates through medical staff privileges and quality assurance programs. . . .

In practice, medical socialization often proves inadequate to limit medical error and assure quality. When professionals make mistakes, they often react not by acknowledging the error and trying to correct it, but rather by "normalizing" the mistake or shunning responsibility for it. . . . Physicians are reluctant to engage in self-criticism, except when they criticize themselves in the presence of supportive colleagues to gain sympathy and reassurance.[4] . . . Physicians resist any more formalized system of evaluation of their work. Medical judgments are considered to be idiosyncratic and beyond review; scrutiny of these judgments shows lack of trust and acceptance of the maturity of the professional. Formalized systems of review, such as morbidity and mortality review committees, are systematically subverted to the use of excusing rather than correcting physician error. . . .

Professional certification and institutional accreditation programs represent another, more formal, form of professional self-regulation. Examples of such programs include physician specialty board certification, certification of various allied medical professionals, and the JCAHO [Joint Commission on the Accreditation of Healthcare Organizations. This organization is a private accreditation group for hospitals and nursing homes. Its standards dominate the industry because most facilities consider Joint Commission accreditation essential in order to be financially viable.] . . . The primary function of certification and accreditation programs is to provide information. These programs cannot keep a professional from practicing or an institution from providing health care. . . . Presumably, a certification program will produce information that is primarily of value to the constituency that sponsors the program. . . . Most certification programs are sponsored by sellers of services. For example, the specialty boards are sponsored by specialists, the JCAHO by doctors and hospitals. . . . Certification programs can emerge as a form of brand name or trademark identification . . . to designate professionals who are highly or specially qualified, allowing buyers to distinguish these professionals from others who are not so designated. . . . Certification programs may also emerge, however, that are detrimental to the efficient operation of markets [by restricting competition from noncertified providers]. . . .

---

[4] See C. Bosk, Forgive and Remember, Managing Medical Failure, 138-39 (1979) (describing the ritual of "putting on the hairshirt," whereby the erring physician confesses his errors to other physicians, who in turn extend understanding and forgiveness).

[E]ven if certification program[s] serve essentially efficient purposes, . . . [they usually] serve only to exclude the worst providers; they do not identify the best. [For instance, the vast majority (75-80 percent) of new doctors seek board certification and a similar percentage of hospitals have JCAHO accreditation.] . . . Because certification and accreditation programs are not primarily concerned with identifying high quality providers for consumers, they serve that function rather poorly. Most certification and accreditation bodies rely on structural evaluation tools which for reasons set out above, are often not very reliable indicators of quality. Most specialty certification boards focus on processing initial entrants and do little to assure the continued competence of those already certified. They lack disciplinary mechanisms to remove providers who have ceased to be competent. (The JCAHO, for example, seldom disaccredits hospitals.) . . .

The final form of professional self-regulation is internal institutional self-regulation: staff privilege and quality assurance programs. . . . Under JCAHO accreditation requirements (and state law in some states) physicians must normally be admitted to the medical staff of a hospital before they can admit patients. . . . Most physicians have staff privileges, often in several hospitals. Most hospitals, again in response to the mandate of JCAHO requirements and state law, also have quality assurance programs that review the work of professionals practicing within the hospital. . . . [U]nlike other forms of peer review, the medical staff privileges system has a direct coercive sanction to influence behavior: the denial or revocation of the right of access to facilities essential for an effective medical practice. . . .

Like other quality assurance systems, however, the medical staff privilege system also is subject to serious limitations. . . . [P]hysicians face incentives to be too lax in their judgments, particularly in dealing with physicians already on staff. It is never a comfortable task to sit in judgment of one's peers with whom one works on a day to day basis. A physician in this position must always deal with the temptation to give the benefit of the doubt and gloss over a colleague's errors. It may also in some instances be in the economic self-interest of physicians making medical staff privilege decisions to overlook the misdeeds of colleagues who are the source of business through referrals or service orders. . . .

[A final form of professional self-regulation is medical licensing. Although licensing is done by the state, not the profession, licensing boards are staffed by physicians, and many of the standards are set or administered by the profession.] Before a person may be licensed as a physician, for example, he or she must complete an educational program leading to a Medical Doctor or Doctor of Osteopathy degree, complete a period of postgraduate clinical training of from one to three years (depending on the state), pass an examination, and satisfy a screening for "character." These requirements provide some assurance of capacity to render competent professional judgment, though the assurance is not absolute. . . .

Another task of regulation is to deal with practicing professionals that cease to be competent. . . . In recent years licensure boards have attempted to exercise greater oversight over the ongoing competence of medical practitioners through their disciplinary function. The boards' influence has been modest. . . . Perhaps the most important factor limiting the effectiveness of medical boards in addressing incompetence is the fact that most licensure boards are still composed predominantly of physicians. Physicians are reluctant to criticize each other for technical and judgment errors. Unless a physician has violated professional norms as well as technical norms, it is difficult for many physicians to find it within themselves to support disciplinary action. . . . The primary concern of professional discipline has historically not been quality, or even competence, but rather "professionalism." Since professionalism has often been interpreted to mean not competing against fellow professionals, this fact has supported the arguments of those who believe that the main goal and effect of licensure has been cartelization of professional services. . . . It is necessary, therefore, to look beyond [professional self-regulation] to other forms of quality control. . . .

B. THE MARKET AS A QUALITY CONTROL MECHANISM

Recent scholarship on health care quality regulation has argued cogently that the market can play an important role in assuring health care quality. . . . Professionals and institutions that deliver services of unacceptable quality in a properly functioning market will face declining demand for their services and decreasing revenues. They will thus improve the quality of their services to recapture the consumer market. If the market works properly, therefore, no regulatory intervention is necessary to alter provider behavior.

This scenario depends, however, on . . . the ability of consumers to make useful judgments about the quality of medical care through their own search and experience. . . . Those who believe that the market is up to the task of assuring quality in health care stress the agency role that primary care physicians play in referring and ordering services for patients. They argue that even though patients themselves may not be able to identify high quality providers, once they choose a primary care physician, that physician can assure the provision of high quality goods and services for subsequent care. . . . Research examining physician referral patterns offers little support for this belief. . . . Though physicians may claim that their primary concern in referring patients to specialists is quality of care, in fact, studies tend to find that referring behavior is less influenced by evaluations of technical competence than it is by factors such as affability of the consultant, patient preferences, previous use of the consultant by the referring physician, personal familiarity with the consultant, reciprocal referrals from the consultant, and eschewal of patient "stealing" by consultants. . . .

Prescribing and admitting practices are also undoubtedly influenced by considerations other than quality evaluation. Physicians prescribing a particular drug are often responding more to the fawning solicitations of pharmaceutical company detail men or to the demands of their patients than to their own experience with the pharmaceutical. A doctor may admit a patient to a particular hospital because it is the only hospital that will give him staff privileges, or because it is most convenient to his office, rather than because it is the hospital most suited to the patient's needs. A doctor may also refrain from referring a patient to another physician more qualified than himself, preferring to keep the patient's business. Whatever the doctor's motives may be for a particular referral or lack of referral, the patient is, for all the reasons already given, seldom in a position independently to evaluate that judgment, or even its results. . . . Because consumers lack reliable sources of information, the market cannot be counted on to assure quality. . . .

D. REGULATORY APPROACHES TO QUALITY ASSESSMENT

Once quality problems are identified, a variety of regulatory approaches and methods are available to address them. At one end of the spectrum, programs could focus on auditing performance and providing feedback. To the extent that practitioners or institutions are unaware of problems in their care delivery process, merely noting those problems may suffice to bring improvement. . . . At the other end of the spectrum, a variety of sanctions exist to restrain professionals who exhibit severe problems. The traditional medical licensure board sanctions of suspension or revocation temporarily or permanently remove the physician from practice. They are certainly appropriate for professionals whose impairment or incompetence interferes with their practice and for those engaged in criminal or unethical conduct. . . .

Sanctions can also serve a deterrent function. The single most important assurance of quality medicine is the professional's desire to provide good medical care based on an indeterminate mix of professional ethics, personal self-esteem, concern for reputation, and fear of sanctions that may result from a medical error. . . . Fear of license revocation might suffice to keep the physician inclined to defraud or to sexually abuse his patients from acting. This fear may even force the substance abuser into treatment. Obviously, however, some physicians have such serious impairments that they will not respond to deterrence, and the incompetent physician may not know how to respond.

Deterrence is also one of the primary purposes of the medical malpractice system. Most agree that medical malpractice litigation is not a terribly effective system of compensation. It undercompensates many victims of medical error, overcompensates others, and imposes wholly unreasonable administrative costs. On the other hand, it does have a deterrent effect of undetermined extent. Moreover, it is arguable that the medical malpractice system's deterrent effect is greatest in dealing with the problem that is most intractable to other regulatory approaches — the occasional mistake.

Because medical malpractice liability insurance is by and large not experience-rated, the threat of litigation probably has little deterrent effect on the truly incompetent or seriously impaired physician (though such a physician may have reason to fear the disciplinary system). A competent doctor, on the other hand, realistically has little fear of license revocation but is not immune from malpractice litigation if a momentary inadvertence has disastrous consequences. Therefore, to the extent that such errors can be prevented, the potential for malpractice liability is the primary legal stimulus for prevention.

While this result is the greatest benefit of the medical malpractice system, it is also its greatest weakness. Much of the criticism of the malpractice system comes from the fact that competent physicians face malpractice suits for aberrational errors. Thus, the Damoclean threat of malpractice litigation results in an undetermined but substantial amount of unnecessary medical treatment. . . .

Notes: Quality Measurement and Control

1. *Overview.* The purpose of this reading is to put in broader context the role that malpractice law plays in the deterrence and punishment of medical error and

in the improvement of medical quality. To sharpen your focus, review the types of bad medical outcomes identified earlier, the dimensions of quality surveyed by Jost, and the various social and legal responses available, noting which responses are addressed to which types and dimensions of poor quality. Based on the resulting patterns and gaps, how would you articulate the strongest case for the role of tort law? What types of medical mistakes should it be most concerned with? Which types should it ignore?

2. *Prosecuting Doctors.* Professor Jost fails to mention a final source of legal oversight — criminal law. In several highly publicized cases, physicians have been found guilty of manslaughter or other criminal charges for making blatant errors or ignoring obvious signs of trouble. See, e.g., Einaugler v. New York Supreme Court, 109 F.3d 836 (2d Cir. 1997) (criminal charges for mistaking a dialysis catheter for a feeding tube in a nursing home patient and then delaying transfer to a hospital after the mistake was discovered). P. Grunsven, Criminal Prosecution of Health Care Providers for Clinical Mistakes and Fatal Errors, 29 J. Health & Hosp. L. 107 (1996); See generally John Humbach, Criminal Prosecution for HMO Treatment Denial, 11 Health Matrix (Winter 2001).

3. *Donabedian's Categories.* To sharpen your understanding of the structure/process/outcome categories developed by Donabedian, consider which category best describes the way that each of the following measures ensures the quality of motor vehicle driver safety: (1) requiring drivers to pass a written exam; (2) requiring an on-road test; (3) vehicle inspection laws that check brake lights, windshield wipers, etc.; (4) enforcing speed limits; (5) increasing insurance premiums when drivers are involved in accidents.

4. *Outcomes Measures, Surgical Scorecards, and the Market for Quality.* As Professor Jost reports (in the second of his articles), both government regulation and industry self-regulation have taken a turn toward assessing quality through outcomes measures:

> [I]nstitutional survey methodology has dramatically improved in the recent past. Traditionally, institutional licensure and accreditation inspections have focused almost exclusively on the structural characteristics of institutions: their physical plant, administrative protocols, and staff qualifications. They have largely ignored the processes through which care is delivered in the institution or the quality of the outcomes with that care. This is beginning to change. The JCAHO, for example, has announced its intention to implement an inspection system that would be much more attentive to defects in the quality of the care delivery process and to patient outcomes. The DHHS has recently instituted a nursing home survey system that involves resident interviews and direct observation of resident care, administration of medications, and feeding of residents.

The third of Professor Jost's articles, which is excerpted in Chapter 1.B.5, reports that similar initiatives can be seen in the managed care industry. Through its accreditation organization, the National Committee for Quality Assurance (NCQA), it is promoting the development and use of quality "report cards" that allow consumers to compare the performance of HMOs and other health plans. The current version, known as HEDIS (for Health Plan and Employer Data and Information Set), relies on measures such as consumer satisfaction, rates of childhood immunization and cancer screening, and management of asthma and diabetes. Similarly, the Leapfrog Group, a coalition formed by business organizations, has generated interest in using market forces to promote quality by encouraging larger employers and health plans to contract only with providers that perform well on standardized quality benchmarks. See Robert S. Galvin, The Business Case for Quality, 20 Health Aff. 57 (2001). These efforts are geared more toward the information needs of employers as purchasers of insurance than to the needs of individual patients choosing a doctor or hospital.

Much more controversial are governmental efforts to rank hospitals and perhaps also physicians according to how well their patients do. The Center for Medicare and Medicaid Services (CMS), which oversees Medicare and Medicaid, for a time released hospital mortality statistics based on the percentage of Medicare patients who die. Although these statistics were adjusted to reflect the expected death rate due to the patients' diagnoses, hospitals complained bitterly that the adjustment factors were far too crude to accurately reflect variations in the severity of illness among individual patients who have the same diagnosis. As a consequence of the uproar, CMS ceased publishing these statistics. Now, it encourages hospitals and physicians to report a variety of quality measures focused on process steps in caring for heart attacks, pneumonia, and surgery patients. See www.hospitalcompare.hhs.gov/.

Efforts in New York state and Pennsylvania have been more successful, however. There, regulators have released "surgical scorecards" that report the risk-adjusted death rates from heart surgery, not only at individual hospitals, but also for specific doctors. These statistics tell whether more or fewer patients die than expected, given the severity of the condition. In New York, the release of these scorecards was followed by a 41 percent drop in risk-adjusted mortality from cardiac surgery, although this may be due in part to doctors and hospitals manipulating the reporting system. See J. Green & N. Winfeld, Report Cards on Cardiac Surgeons, 332 New Eng. J. Med. 1229 (1995); Note, Grading the Report Card, Yale J. Reg. 207 (1995). So far, however, studies have found a persistent failure of consumers to use comparative quality information in selecting physicians, hospitals, or health insurers. See Michelle M. Mello & Troyen A. Brennan, Deterrence of Medical Errors: Theory and Evidence for Malpractice Reform, 80 Tex. L. Rev. 1595 (2002). See generally Kristin Madison, Regulating Health Care Quality in an Information Age, 40 U.C. Davis L. Rev. (2007).

See Chapter 1.B.5 for additional discussion and sources about these developments. At this point, consider what remedies a physician might have if he can show that he is losing business because of a negative government report card that he claims is wrong or misleading due to insufficient measurement of the true health status of his patients. He claims that his score card is worse than average because, owing to his preeminent skill and reputation, he attracts the most difficult cases.

5. *A Look Ahead*. Hospitals that vigorously monitor doctors through their medical staff review processes face the threat of suit by doctors who are refused admitting privileges and, as a result, lose patients. The chilling effect of this legal threat on hospitals' quality assurance activities is substantial enough that Congress included a qualified immunity from these suits in the Health Care Quality Improvement Act of 1986, discussed later in this chapter. This concern has also

resulted in states implementing peer review confidentiality statutes that limit access to information generated by these hospital review processes. The impact of these statutes on malpractice actions is addressed further below at page 360. Another body of law that relates to this overview is addressed in Chapter 2.C.1., which discusses in more detail the state licensing process mentioned in the Jost article.

6. *Total Quality Management.* Central to any comprehensive discussion of health care quality is the newly emerging concept of "continuous quality improvement" (CQI), also known as "total quality management" (TQM). This is a managerial concept imported from manufacturing industries. It owes its popularity to W. E. Deming and Joseph M. Juran, management gurus whose ideas were first implemented by Japanese companies and are considered an important reason why they so quickly surpassed American quality standards in consumer electronics and automobile manufacturing. In health care, CQI signals a paradigm shift away from identifying isolated mistakes and deterring malefactors, to improving the quality of all outcomes through systems improvements. CQI assumes that professionals generally are diligent and well motivated and so only need better information and support in order to do a better job. Its philosophy is captured in the title of the first reading in this chapter, Making Medical Errors into "Medical Treasures," since it views mistakes as opportunities to learn, not occasions for blame and punishment. CQI attempts to target the entire range of medical outcomes, not simply to eliminate the "bad apples," and it sees errors as resulting more from system flaws than from individual misfeasance. Institute of Medicine, Crossing the Quality Chasm: A New Health System for the Twenty-first Century (2001); Stephen R. Latham, System Responsibility: Three Readings of the IOM Report on Medical Error, 27 Am. J.L. & Med. 145 (2001); 335 New Eng. J. Med., issues 12-15 (1996); Symposium, 16 Health Aff. No. 3 (May 1997); Symposium, 12 Widener L. Rev. 1 (2005).

Troyen Brennan, another advocate of quality regulation, has teamed up with Donald Berwick, a proponent of quality improvement, to write New Rules: Regulation, Markets, and the Quality of American Health Care (1996), which argues that the entire legal regime is antithetical to the philosophy of quality improvement. Can you imagine how that might be the case? For a contrary argument, see David A. Hyman & Charles Silver, The Poor State of Health Care Quality in the U.S.: Is Malpractice Liability Part of the Problem or Part of the Solution?, 90 Corn. L. Rev. 893 (2005).

B. PHYSICIAN LIABILITY

1. The Custom-Based Standard of Care

■ McCOURT v. ABERNATHY
457 S.E.2d 603 (S.C. 1995)

SHAW, Acting Associate Justice.

[The following facts are quoted from Wendy McCourt's medical record: "This patient is a 23-year-old white female who was admitted to the hospital with shortness of breath and chest wall pain. The patient states about five days prior to admission, she was working with some horses doing castrations. While trying to hold a horse, the horse suddenly bolted and hyperextended her left shoulder. . . . The patient also relates that about two days prior to the horse incident, she pricked her finger with a pin. She continued working around manure and other agents in the barns with the horses. She had developed a slight redness around the pin prick over the fat pad of the left second finger."]

[Doctors Abernathy and Clyde are board certified family practitioners who practice together in Anderson, South Carolina.] . . . There is evidence Wendy was seen by Dr. Abernathy in his office at the time [of the horse incident] and was treated for a pulled muscle. [Three or four days later,] on Sunday, March 13, her condition worsened and Wendy went to the Anderson Memorial Hospital emergency room. She was experiencing greater pain and had difficulty breathing. Dr. Clyde examined Wendy at that time and treated her for a pulled chest muscle. There is evidence Dr. Clyde treated the puncture wound to Wendy's finger at that time.[2] She was given prescriptions for Motrin and Co-Tylenol. She returned to her home.

The following day, March 14, Wendy's condition became significantly worse and she again sought treatment at the emergency room. She was examined by an emergency room physician who ran some blood tests. This physician indicated an immediate need to admit Wendy to the hospital. He telephoned Dr. Abernathy and was given permission to admit Wendy. At 6:30 that evening, Dr. Abernathy examined Wendy and observed the injured finger, for which he prescribed Keflex, an oral antibiotic.

At 9:00 the following morning, both Dr. Abernathy and Dr. Clyde saw Wendy while making rounds at the hospital. By that time, Wendy's condition had worsened yet more and the doctors consulted Dr. Kovaz, an internist. Although appellants requested a consult from Dr. Kovaz, they did not express any urgency in his seeing her. After examining Wendy, Dr. Kovaz immediately moved her to the intensive care unit with a diagnosis of sepsis, a bacterial infection. Although treatment with intravenous antibiotics was begun at that time, her condition continued to deteriorate. Over the next four days, her skin began to slough off, her eyes filled with blood, her feet turned black, she bled from her nose, mouth and pores, and she became bloated beyond recognition. On March 19, 1988, Wendy McCourt died from beta strep septicemia with multiple organ system failure secondary to the sepsis.*

Respondent presented expert testimony from Dr. Neal Craine and Dr. Kenneth DeHart. Dr. Craine stated Wendy's illness was caused by "an unfortunate circumstance where transient bacteria in the bloodstream landed in an area already traumatized by the injury with the horse." He testified, assuming, as the "Death Summary" indicates, Dr. Abernathy saw Wendy on the ninth, she

---

[2] Steven McCourt testified Dr. Clyde pointed out the puncture wound on Wendy's finger which Dr. Clyde proceeded to clean and dress. He stated the finger was red and swollen to almost twice the normal size, and was having some sort of discharge. He further testified the wound was very noticeable and Wendy indicated it was a result of a pin prick that occurred a couple of days earlier.

*[In the popular press, beta strep is known as the "flesh-eating" bacteria. Septicemia is an extremely serious condition in which an infection invades the bloodstream and spreads throughout the body, much like a localized cancer can metastasize. — EDS.]

had a puncture wound to the finger and it was known she was working around horses, he should have put her on preventive antibiotics on that day. He stated it would also have been below the standard of care for Dr. Clyde to have observed an infected finger on the thirteenth and not treat her with antibiotics nor order laboratory tests. He stated he felt Wendy had a 100 percent chance of survival on the thirteenth had she been started on antibiotics at that time. Based on the test results received on the afternoon of the fourteenth, he stated that a doctor should know the patient was seriously ill and should have suspected sepsis. He concluded Wendy's life could have been saved if antibiotics had been started on the ninth, which would have prevented or treated an early infection of the finger. He also stated, more likely than not, Wendy could have been saved on the thirteenth by treatment with antibiotics as well as on the fourteenth with aggressive antibiotic therapy. He stated it was also below the standard of care to wait until the fifteenth to call in a specialist.

Dr. DeHart likewise testified [that] ... failure to treat [the infected finger] prophylactically fell below the standard of care. ... As to Dr. Abernathy's treatment on the fourteenth, he testified it was "profoundly below the standard of care," not because he missed the diagnosis, but because he failed to order aggressive observation and failed to request consultation intervention.

Ths matter was tried to a jury and on January 7, 1993 the jury returned the following verdicts for appellant: [$700,000 in actual damages and $1,000,000 in punitive damages against Dr. Abernathy, and $350,000 in actual damages and $500,000 in punitive damages against Dr. Clyde.] TOTAL VERDICTS: $2,550,000. . . .

Appellants first contend the trial judge erred in failing to charge several jury instructions relating to mistake in diagnosis or error in judgment in a medical malpractice cause of action.[4] . . . [T]he appellants assert all of the charges stand for the proposition that a physician is not liable for a mistake in diagnosis or error in judgment if he acts within the appropriate standard of care. . . . We disagree. . . . [T]he requested charges may have a tendency to confuse the jury. Some of the charges imply to the jury that an error in judgment is actionable only if made in bad faith. Such an instruction would impose an unrealistic burden on the plaintiff to prove the doctor's judgment was rendered with less than good faith.

. . . [T]he trial judge gave the following relevant charges:

> . . . The mere fact that the plaintiff's expert may use a different approach is not considered a deviation from the recognized standard of medical care. Nor is the standard violated because the expert disagrees with a defendant as to what is the best or better approach in treating a patient. Medicine is an inexact science, and generally qualified physicians may differ as to what constitutes a preferable

---

[4] Oral request #1: When a physician exercises ordinary care and skill in keeping within recognized and proven methods, he is not liable for the result of a bona fide mistake of judgment. There is no responsibility unless it is negligent, as I have defined that to you, so as to be inconsistent with that degree of skill which is the duty of every physician practicing in his specialty to possess and use. . . . Request #13: Ladies and Gentlemen, when a physician exercises ordinary care and skill in keeping within recognized and proven methods, he is not liable for the result of a mere mistake of judgment or for a bad result which does not occur because of any negligence on his part. There is no responsibility for error of judgment or for a bad result unless it is so negligent as to be inconsistent with that degree of skill which it is the duty of every practitioner practicing in his specialty to possess.

course of treatment. Such differences due to preference . . . do not amount to malpractice.

I further charge you that the degree of skill and care that a physician must use in diagnosing a condition is that which would be exercised by competent practitioners in the defendant doctor's field of medicine. In South Carolina the question of whether a physician, in making a diagnosis deviated from the applicable standard of care either by not employing a particular procedure or by not ordering a particular test is to be determined by what an ordinary careful and prudent physician would have done under the same or similar circumstances. . . .

Negligence may not be inferred from a bad result. Our law says that a physician is not an insurer of health, and a physician is not required to guarantee results. He undertakes only to meet the standard of skill possessed generally by others practicing in his field under similar circumstances.

Even if we were to assume the appellants' requested charges were the current and correct law of the state, we find the instructions [given] as a whole clearly intimate that a mere mistake in diagnosis or error in judgment alone is insufficient to support a finding of malpractice. Accordingly, we find no error.

Appellants next contend the trial judge erred in denying their motions for new trial . . . on the basis of the excessiveness of the punitive damages awards. They contend the damages are excessive and, because there was no evidence of conduct rising to the level of recklessness, the verdict was the result of passion and prejudice. We disagree.

In order for a plaintiff to recover punitive damages, there must be evidence the defendant's conduct was wilful, wanton, or in reckless disregard of the plaintiff's rights. A conscious failure to exercise due care constitutes wilfulness. . . .

We find the record before us contains evidence that both Dr. Abernathy and Dr. Clyde consciously failed to exercise due care in treating Wendy. This evidence includes, but is not limited to: (1) failure to properly diagnose and treat Wendy within the standard of care on three separate occasions; (2) failure to order timely diagnostic tests in light of continual complaints and no improvement of Wendy's condition; (3) failure to appreciate the seriousness of Wendy's deteriorating condition in the face of highly abnormal blood work; (4) failure to aggressively monitor Wendy's deteriorating condition; and (5) failure to promptly seek the immediate aid of a specialist once the seriousness of Wendy's condition became apparent. While the evidence indicates a more severe degree of culpability on the part of Dr. Abernathy than Dr. Clyde, the record contains sufficient evidence of conduct on the part of both doctors to support the awards of punitive damages. The jury's determination of damages is entitled to substantial deference. We find no abuse of the trial judge's discretion in this respect. . . . Affirmed.

■ LOCKE v. PACHTMAN
521 N.W.2d 786 (Mich. 1994)

MALLETT, Justice.

In this medical malpractice action, the trial judge granted defendants' motion for a directed verdict at the close of the plaintiff's proofs. The court of appeals affirmed, finding that plaintiff had failed to make a prima facie showing of the standard of care related to defendants' allegedly negligent conduct. We affirm.

I

On August 5, 1981, plaintiff Shirley Locke underwent a vaginal hysterectomy with entocele and rectocele repair at the University of Michigan Hospital.[1] The procedure was performed by defendant, Dr. Judith Pachtman, then a fourth-year resident in gynecology. Codefendant, Dr. James Roberts, was the attending physician and was present for most of the surgery.[2]

Dr. Pachtman testified that she performed the first two procedures, the hysterectomy and entocele repair, without complication, although the entocele repair took longer than expected. Following the entocele repair, Dr. Roberts left the room to attend another operation that had been previously scheduled.

Dr. Pachtman then began the rectocele repair. Upon Dr. Pachtman's initial insertion into the levator ani muscle, the needle she was using broke. One-half to two-thirds of the needle, a length of about 1.5 cm, broke off and lodged somewhere within that muscle. Dr. Pachtman searched unsuccessfully for the broken portion of the needle for 15 to 20 minutes. At that time, Dr. Roberts returned and joined Dr. Pachtman in searching for the needle fragment.

Drs. Pachtman and Roberts utilized a silver probe to X-ray the affected area, in an attempt to locate the broken portion of the needle. After ascertaining the approximate location of the fragment, they decided to close the old incision and to continue their search through a new incision. After unsuccessfully searching for the needle for another 45 minutes to one hour, they abandoned the search and closed the second incision. Both doctors indicated that they felt it was in the plaintiff's best interest to terminate the surgery at that point, even though they had failed to locate the needle fragment.

Plaintiff testified that after the surgery Dr. Pachtman informed her of the needle breakage and stated that the needle was entrenched in the muscle and therefore could remain there without causing her any problems. However, after experiencing considerable pain and discomfort, plaintiff consulted with another physician, Dr. Frances Couch. Dr. Couch advised removing the needle fragment, and, subsequently, she performed the surgical procedure, successfully locating and removing the broken portion of the needle.

Plaintiff filed suit against Drs. Pachtman and Roberts, alleging negligence on various grounds, including the use of a needle that they knew or should have known was too small and failing to locate and remove the needle fragment. Plaintiff claimed that she suffers from severe pain, disfigurement, and limitation

---

[1] As explained at trial, an entocele is an out-pouching or hernia of the peritoneal cavity where the bowel protrudes into the area between the vagina and the rectum. A rectocele is a hernial protrusion of the rectum through the posterior vaginal wall.

[2] At trial, Dr. Roberts explained that he was the senior medical officer involved in the procedure. However, he also stated that, as attending physician, his role was to act as assistant and consultant to Dr. Pachtman, who actually performed the surgery. Dr. Pachtman essentially agreed with Dr. Roberts' characterization of his role in the procedure, but asserted nevertheless that, as attending physician, Dr. Roberts had "ultimate responsibility" for the surgery.

of body movement and functions, as well as experiencing mental and emotional distress. Plaintiff's husband, Danny Locke, filed a derivative claim.

In testimony presented at trial, plaintiff's expert witness, Dr. Couch, was unable to identify any negligent conduct on the part of either Dr. Pachtman or Dr. Roberts. Dr. Couch also stated that she could not give an opinion regarding the adequacy of the needle size, because she had never viewed the needle intact. She explained that she could not identify the size of the needle without viewing the needle in its entirety.

When questioned generally regarding the cause of needle breakage and its relation to the standard of care, Dr. Couch made two separate statements. At one point Dr. Couch stated that the standard of care did not relate to needle breakage at all, but rather to how one dealt with it, suggesting that needle breakage was simply one of the risks of surgery. Later, without relating this point to a standard of care, she noted that a surgeon's "incorrect technique" often causes a needle to break. When asked to describe what she meant by incorrect technique, Dr. Couch described instances in which a surgeon fails to manipulate the needle correctly, such as by inserting it at the wrong angle or applying too much force. Dr. Couch also testified that she had previously had a needle break while performing surgery.

In addition to Dr. Couch's expert testimony, plaintiff introduced evidence regarding a number of statements allegedly made by Dr. Pachtman following the surgery. Plaintiff's brother, Reverend Gary Heniser, testified that, while he was at the hospital visiting his sister, Dr. Pachtman told him, "['I] knew the needle was too small when I used it.'" Coplaintiff Danny Locke testified that Dr. Pachtman had also spoken to him about the surgery: "[S]he told me that it was her fault, that she used the wrong needle, and she was sorry." Finally, Shirley Locke testified that Dr. Pachtman had told her: "I knew that needle was too small when the new scrub nurse handed it to me. It wasn't her fault because she was new, but I chose to use it anyway and it's my fault and I am really sorry. . . ."

Both Dr. Pachtman and Dr. Roberts testified at trial. Neither acknowledged any negligent behavior in the choice of needle, the needle breakage, or their subsequent search for the needle fragment.

At the close of plaintiff's proofs, the trial court granted defendants' motion for directed verdict on the ground that plaintiff had failed to make a prima facie showing regarding the standard of care. Plaintiff's motion for a new trial was denied, and, in a divided opinion, the court of appeals affirmed. . . .

II

Proof of a medical malpractice claim requires the demonstration of the following four factors: (1) the applicable standard of care, (2) breach of that standard of care by the defendant, (3) injury, and (4) proximate causation between the alleged breach and the injury.[6] To survive a motion for directed verdict, the plaintiff must make a prima facie showing regarding each of the above elements.

---

[6] [Michigan statutes state:]

In an action alleging malpractice the plaintiff shall have the burden of proving that in light of the state of the art existing at the time of the alleged malpractice: (a) The defendant, if a

Plaintiff argues that the lower courts erred in finding that she had failed to demonstrate the standard of care applicable to defendants' conduct. Plaintiff contends that expert testimony was sufficient to establish this point, and, further, that the standard of care and breach of that standard were inferable under the doctrine of res ipsa loquitur and because the alleged negligence was within the common understanding of the jury.

We agree with the lower courts' determination that no prima facie showing was made, and therefore we affirm the directed verdict entered for the defendants.

A

. . . Plaintiff argues first that the standard of care attributable to Dr. Pachtman was established by way of expert testimony. This court has long recognized the importance of expert testimony in establishing a medical malpractice claim, and the need to educate the jury and the court regarding matters not within their common purview. As we have previously explained:

> In a case involving professional service the ordinary layman is not equipped by common knowledge and experience to judge of the skill and competence of that service and determine whether it squares with the standard of such professional practice in the community. For that, the aid of expert testimony from those learned in the profession involved is required.

While we have recognized exceptions to this requirement, the benefit of expert testimony, particularly in demonstrating the applicable standard of care, cannot be overstated.

In this case, plaintiff contends that the standard of care applicable to Dr. Pachtman was established by Dr. Couch's expert testimony. For this point, plaintiff relies on Dr. Couch's statement that needle breakage often occurs because of the surgeon's "incorrect technique." Plaintiff asserts that this testimony, coupled with Dr. Pachtman's admissions regarding use of a needle she knew to be too small, were sufficient to establish the standard of care and breach of that standard.

Dr. Couch's testimony with regard to the standard of care associated with needle breakage was rather confused. At one point she suggested that needle breakage was merely one of the risks of surgery, and that needle breakage did not ordinarily signal a violation of the standard of care. . . . Dr. Couch later testified that needle breakage may be attributable to a surgeon's "incorrect technique":

---

general practitioner, failed to provide the plaintiff the recognized standard of acceptable professional practice in the community in which the defendant practices or in a similar community, and that as a proximate result of the defendant failing to provide that standard, the plaintiff suffered an injury. (b) The defendant, if a specialist, failed to provide the recognized standard of care within that specialty as reasonably applied in light of the facilities available in the community or other facilities reasonably available under the circumstances, and as a proximate result of the defendant failing to provide that standard, the plaintiff suffered an injury.

Q. From your experience and your training can the manner in which a surgeon utilizes a needle cause it to break?

A. I would say most of the time that's the case. It's a matter of incorrect technique.

Q. Could you discuss that?

A. Well, a needle is curved. If you forget the needle is curved and you push against the curve instead of with the curve the needle will break. If you try to put a needle through an instrument it doesn't go through steel. If it's not positioned correctly in a tissue and you're trying to draw it through against a clamp it will break. . . . Generally that's most of the reason why they break. You are putting force against where it wasn't made to be put against.

As the lower courts found, it is indeed questionable whether Dr. Couch's latter testimony on this point was sufficient to establish a standard of care with regard to "incorrect technique." Dr. Couch, while presenting one way in which needles break, never went so far as to relate that discussion to a standard of care. In effect, she never explained what a reasonably prudent surgeon would do, in keeping with the standards of professional practice, that might not have been done by Dr. Pachtman. Accordingly, the jury would have had no standard against which to measure Dr. Pachtman's conduct. This factor, coupled with the conflicting nature of Dr. Couch's testimony, leads us to believe that the standard of care was not sufficiently established. . . .

B

Plaintiff next argues that the statements allegedly made by Dr. Pachtman were themselves sufficient to establish the standard of care and breach of that standard. Plaintiff contends that her case is governed by this court's decision in Orozco v. Henry Ford Hosp., 408 Mich. 248, 290 N.W.2d 363 (1980). . . . Plaintiff's reliance upon *Orozco* is misplaced. In *Orozco*, the plaintiff testified that during his hernial surgery he heard one of the surgeons say, "Oops, I cut in the wrong place." Following the surgery, one of his testicles atrophied. At trial, an expert witness testified that this injury was likely due to an impairment of the blood supply to the testicles during the surgery.

At the close of Orozco's proofs, the trial court granted the defendants' motion for a directed verdict, and the court of appeals affirmed, finding that the plaintiff had failed to make a prima facie showing of the applicable standard of care.[9] This court reversed the court of appeals by per curiam opinion. The court found that expert testimony was not necessary because jury members would be able to determine, from their own common knowledge, whether the defendants' actions violated the applicable standard of care. As the court explained:

Here Orozco offered the fact of the injury, a medical explanation of how that injury likely occurred, and an admission by the surgeon that he cut in the wrong place. Paraphrasing *Lince*, "[t]he question is whether the action of defendants

---

[9] In reaching this conclusion, the court of appeals relied on Lince v. Monson. In *Lince*, this court held that expert testimony was required in order for the jury to determine whether the defendants violated the standard of care when they mistakenly sutured the plaintiff's ureter in responding to excsssive bleeding. 363 Mich. at 142, 108 N.W.2d 845.

conformed to standards of good practice in the community. Common knowledge and the experience of ordinary laymen do ... equip them to give the answer in a case such as this" when an expert testifies that the likely cause of injury was an impairment of the blood supply to the testicles in the course of the operation and the plaintiff testifies that the surgeon said, "Oops, I cut in the wrong place."

... This decision was in line with previous case law holding that expert testimony is not normally required where the defendant mistakenly treated or did injury to a portion of the body that was free of disease and not designated for treatment. Sullivan v. Russell, 417 Mich. 398, 408, 338 N.W.2d 181 (1983) (no expert testimony was necessary where a dentist mistakenly ground three of the plaintiff's teeth not intended for treatment); Higdon v. Carlebach, 348 Mich. 363, 374, 83 N.W.2d 296 (1957) (expert testimony was not required where a dentist, using a rotating disk to separate two of the plaintiff's teeth, mistakenly cut into her tongue).

Turning to the present case, we hold that the lower courts correctly concluded that Dr. Pachtman's statements were insufficient to make a prima facie showing. While the statements may have indicated Dr. Pachtman's belief that she made a mistake or acted in error, a jury could not reasonably infer from those statements alone that Dr. Pachtman's actions did not conform to the standard of professional practice for the community as a whole.

Unlike the situation presented in *Orozco*, the standard of care associated with needle choice and needle breakage is not accessible to the jury absent expert guidance. Plaintiff has provided no guidance with regard to what options were available to Dr. Pachtman and which of them she should have chosen. In short, there was no testimony regarding what a reasonably prudent surgeon would have done in Dr. Pachtman's situation. We agree with the court of appeals determination that the jury should not be left to speculate in this regard. It is precisely to avoid such speculation that expert testimony is ordinarily required. ...

E

Plaintiff asserts liability against Dr. Roberts on grounds ... [of] negligent supervision. However, ... plaintiff's negligent supervision claim is also not supported by the record. There was uncontroverted testimony, including testimony from plaintiff's own expert, to the fact that it was not unusual for an attending physician at University of Michigan Hospital to leave a resident alone during portions of a procedure. There was no testimony suggesting that such action was violative of a standard of care, nor do we find that point inferable by the jury. Therefore this claim is also without merit. ...

CAVANAGH, C.J., and RILEY, BRICKLEY, BOYLE and ROBERT P. GRIFFIN, JJ., concur.

LEVIN, Justice (dissenting). ...

The question presented is whether Pachtman's statements—in effect admitting error but not in lawyer jargon such as "standard medical practice in this community"—are prima facie evidence of the standard of care and breach. ...

The majority concludes that Pachtman's statements may have expressed her belief that she violated her personal standard of care, and her personal standard of care may have been higher than the prevailing standard of care among physicians in the community. . . . It is no more probable, however, that the statements concerned her personal standard of care than that they concerned the generally applicable standard of care. The statements refer neither to a personal nor a general standard of care. The statements can reasonably be read either way, and a jury should decide the meaning of Pachtman's statements.[10] . . . This is not a case in which a physician merely expressed general dissatisfaction with her overall performance or merely expressed regret.

Cases from other jurisdictions indicate that statements like Pachtman's — that confess error with reasonable specificity — are prima facie evidence of the standard of care and breach.

In Greenwood v. Harris, 362 P.2d 85, 87-88 (Okla. 1961), the plaintiff alleged that the physician erroneously diagnosed her pregnancy as a tumor, and then performed unnecessary surgery that left the plaintiff with an unsightly and painful scar. The plaintiff's only evidence concerning the standard of care was the physician's statements to the plaintiff and her husband that he "should have made more tests," and that he "wasn't satisfied with the lab report [and] should have had the tests run again, . . . should have made some other tests." The Oklahoma Supreme Court held that those statements alone were prima facie evidence of the standard of care and breach. The court said: We can interpret these statements in no other way than as an admission that a faulty diagnosis had been made due to the failure of the defendant to use and apply the customary and usual degree of skill exercised by physicians in the community. . . .

In Sheffield v. Runner, 163 Cal. App. 2d 48, 328 P.2d 828 (1958), a physician's statement that he should have put the patient in a hospital was held to be prima facie evidence of the standard of care and breach. In Wickoff v. James, 159 Cal. App. 2d 664, 324 P.2d 661 (1958), a physician's statement that he "sure messed up" was held to be prima facie evidence of the standard of care and breach. In Robertson v. LaCroix, 534 P.2d 17, 19 (Okla. App., 1975), a physician's statement that he "just made a mistake and got over too far" during surgery was held to be prima facie evidence of the standard of care and breach. . . .

Other state supreme courts have found that the standard of care was not established by statements that fail to explain with relative precision what the physician should have done. . . . In Maxwell v. Women's Clinic, 102 Idaho 53, 54, 625 P.2d 407 (1981), the plaintiff claimed that the defendant physician negligently performed a tubal ligation. The plaintiff's only evidence regarding the standard of care was the physician's statement that he "obviously messed up." The Idaho Supreme Court held that summary judgment against the plaintiff was properly granted because the plaintiff did not present sufficient evidence of breach of the standard of care.[4] In both *Maxwell* and [*Cobbs*], the physicians'

---

[10] In Wooten v. Curry, 50 Tenn. App. 549, 552, 554, 362 S.W.2d 820 (1961), as distinguished from the instant case, the physician, under the law of Tennessee, was subject to liability for malpractice if his conduct fell below his personal standard of care. . . . [See also Burton v. Brooklyn Doctor's Hospital, 452 N.Y.S.2d 875 (1982) (modifying treatment to conduct a medical experiment violates duty to exercise physicians' best judgment, even though treatment rendered was within existing standard of care).]

[4] In Cobbs v. Grant, 8 Cal. 3d 229, 238, 104 Cal. Rptr. 505, 502 P.2d 1 (1972), the physician's statement that he "blamed himself for [the plaintiff] being back in there [the hospital]" was held not to be prima facie evidence of the standard of care and breach.

statements did not explain relatively precisely — as did Pachtman's — how they
had erred.

I conclude, consistent with precedent from other jurisdictions, that
Pachtman's statement satisfied Locke's burden of presenting prima facie evidence
of the standard of care and breach.

■ THE ROLE OF THE JURY IN MODERN MALPRACTICE LAW
Philip G. Peters, Jr.*
87 Iowa L. Rev. 909 (2002)

A. TRADITIONAL DEFERENCE TO MEDICAL CUSTOMS

For more than a century, courts have given physicians the power to set their own
standard of care. This delegation of standard-setting authority to private parties
dramatically distinguished malpractice actions from other negligence litigation. . . .
In most negligence actions, the defendant's compliance with industry customs is
simply one factor for the jury to consider. . . . Since the late nineteenth century, courts
have treated physicians quite differently. Medical customs are not merely admissible;
they define the physician's legal standard of care.[2] In the words of Dean Prosser, the
custom-based standard of care "gives the medical profession . . . the privilege, which
is usually emphatically denied to other groups, of setting their own legal standards of
conduct, merely by adopting their own practices."

By deferring conclusively to medical customs, the courts materially changed the
function that the jury would perform in malpractice actions. In an ordinary
negligence action, the jury must consider all of the evidence adduced and then
determine whether the defendant has behaved reasonably under the circumstances.
To do so, the jury must make important judgments about the value of life and
personal safety and about the proper level of safety precautions. In a malpractice
action, by contrast, the jury does not make these value judgments. Instead, they have
been delegated to the medical profession. The jury's job is merely to determine
whether the defendant has complied with the norms set by the industry.

B. THE RECENT RETREAT FROM A CUSTOM-BASED STANDARD

Gradually, quietly and relentlessly, state courts are abandoning the custom-
based standard of care.[3] Thus far, a dozen states have expressly refused to equate

---

*Ruth L. Hulston, Professor of Law, University of Missouri-Columbia. Reprinted with
permission.
[2] See, e.g., James A. Henderson, Jr. & John A. Siliciano, Universal Health Care and the
Continued Reliance on Custom in Determining Medical Malpractice, 79 Cornell L. Rev. 1382, 1384
(1994) (stating custom is rule in medical malpractice); Alan H. McCoid, The Care Required of Medical
Practitioners, 12 Vand. L. Rev. 549, 560, 605-06 (1959) (same); Clarence Morris, Custom and
Negligence, 42 Colum. L. Rev. 1147, 1158 (1942) (stating custom normally should define standard of
care); Theodore Silver, One Hundred Years of Harmful Error: The Historical Jurisprudence of
Medical Malpractice, 1992 Wis. L. Rev. 1193, 1212 (stating custom determines standard of care).
[3] This migration away from the custom-based standard of care is described at much greater
length in Philip G. Peters, Jr., The Quiet Demise of Deference to Custom: Malpractice Law at the
Millennium, 57 Wash. & Lee L. Rev. 163, 166-68 (2000).

reasonable care with customary practices. . . . These states now use a "reasonable physician" test. Another nine states, although not explicitly addressing the role of custom, have also endorsed the "reasonable physician" test. In these states, . . . the jury decides whether the physician behaved reasonably, not whether she complied with custom. Although experts still battle in the courtroom, they argue about what physicians *should* do, not what physicians *ordinarily* do.

In addition to the states that have moved to a reasonability standard, several other states have case law that is too ambiguous or inconsistent to classify confidently. As a consequence, the fraction of states that unambiguously endorse the custom-based standard of care has fallen from a clear majority to a shrinking plurality.

Finally, courts in states that purportedly endorse the custom-based standard often allow plaintiffs more latitude than the law on the books would imply. Plaintiffs in these states commonly reach a jury even when their experts have stated only that the defendant's conduct is not "acceptable" or "appropriate" or fails to meet the "standard of care." The experts in these cases have not been required to testify that the defendant deviated from customary practice. . . .

Whatever the explanation, it is clear today that courts defer less to physicians than they once did and are less willing to erect special rules for health care providers. For example, physicians are no longer exempt from the antitrust laws. In many states, physicians no longer enjoy the protection from corporate competition once provided by the corporate practice prohibitions. In tort law, physicians have lost the protection of the strict locality rule and are also required to obtain informed consent. In addition, courts appear to be retreating from some of the special "no duty" rules that once typified medical malpractice law, such as the rule that pharmacists have no duty to warn patients about incompatible prescriptions and the rule that "on call" doctors have no duty to emergency patients until they establish a physician-patient relationship. Abandonment of the custom-based standard of care is consistent with this trend away from special rules for health care providers. The weakening of support for the custom-based standard of care is also consistent with the gradual movement of twentieth century tort law away from special duties tailored for specific social contexts and toward a general obligation of reasonable care. . . .

D. IMPLICATIONS

Whether de jure or de facto, the shift away from the customary standard and to a reasonable physician standard takes the task of standard-setting away from the profession and assigns it to the jury. The centrality of this doctrinal shift cannot be overstated. The delegation of standard-setting authority to the professions is unique in tort law. It is the foundation upon which the field of medical malpractice law has been built. Under the custom-based standard of care, . . . the jury determines what the customary practice *is*. It does not decide what the custom *ought* to be. The law assigns the normative judgment to the medical profession. . . . Under the jury-applied reasonable physician standard, by contrast, the *jury* determines what a reasonable physician would have done under similar circumstances, not the profession. Medical customs, to the extent that they exist, are admissible, but they are not binding on the jury. . . . The crucial unanswered question is whether jurors can handle that task responsibly. . . .

[E.] CONFIDENCE IN MEDICAL CUSTOMS

Scholars and courts have articulated two quite distinct rationales for trusting clinical practices. The first is faith in the professionalism of physicians. The second is faith in the power of the market to make medical practices efficient. In the real world, however, medical practices live up to neither ideal. Historically, both courts and scholars have trusted physicians to put the welfare of patients above all other interests. . . .

Regrettably, much of this confidence in physician norms is misplaced. Recent research demonstrates that physicians, like the rest of us, are driven not only by science and fidelity to patient interests, but also by habit, self-interest and other competing considerations. . . . As a result, medical customs have a veneer of scientific validity that is too often undeserved. . . . Medicine has also undergone a recent structural transformation. . . . Insurers are using a variety of strategies to make physicians more cost-conscious. . . .

Under these circumstances, it seems reasonable to revisit the assumption that medical customs are uniquely reliable. The unwavering faith that the law once placed in physicians was probably naive from the outset and predictably has weakened in a more realistic and cynical age. . . .

[Moreover, the] argument in favor of a custom-based standard of care turns on [a] fundamental assumption . . . that medical customs will be readily ascertainable. . . . In reality, however, medical practices rarely provide [a] stable, ascertainable benchmark. . . . In the past few decades, medical researchers have learned that clinical practices vary dramatically and inexplicably. A number of studies, starting with the classic work of John Wennberg,[4] have demonstrated that physician practices vary widely, even within narrow geographic limits. . . . [A] Medicare study found that procedure rates varied by more than three hundred percent for more than one-half of the procedures studied.

In addition to the geographic variation that permeates clinical medicine, the highly differentiated nature of medical problems is also a barrier to the formation of medical customs. Patients vary in ways that resist standardization. This variation in patients is matched by a similar variety in possible therapeutic responses, each with its own mix of benefits, risks and costs. At the same time, physicians vary in their preferences and in their knowledge of the medical literature. Finally, the movement of many employers away from fee-for-service health plans and toward managed care plans has produced significant differences among health plans in their resources and their cost-containment philosophies. Under these circumstances, there will rarely be a "custom" that provides a clear rule of decision. . . .

There is an additional erroneous assumption underlying the idea that a custom-based standard will provide a more ascertainable and predictable standard. In truth, few trial experts can be expected to have an accurate sense of what most physicians are doing. As David Eddy notes, "[I]t is a major research task to figure out what practitioners in a community are doing."[5] As a consequence, experts who are asked questions about the standard of care are

---

[4] See, e.g., John Wennberg, Dealing with Medical Malpractice Variations: A Proposal for Action, Health Aff., Summer 1984, at 6, 7.

[5] David M. Eddy, The Use of Evidence and Cost Effectiveness by the Courts: How Can It Help Improve Health Care?, 26 J. Health, Pol., Pol'y & L. 387, 396 (2001).

unlikely to have a reliable understanding of customary norms across the nation or even in similar communities. Instead, their testimony is more likely to be a barometer of their own practices. . . .

H. SUMMARY OF POTENTIAL ADVANTAGES OF JURY STANDARD-SETTING

Abandonment of the custom-based standard of care in favor of a reasonable physician standard offers several potential advantages. Most importantly, the reasonable physician standard assigns the task of legal standard-setting to representatives of the community, rather than to the regulated industry. Jury decisionmaking is more likely to incorporate community values. Moreover, the flexibility of the reasonable physician standard provides more protection for innovators and less shelter for those adhering to antiquated customs. Furthermore, the reasonable physician standard is a more honest way to accomplish these goals than bending the custom-based standard to cure its shortcomings. The reasonable physician standard of care also gives the health care industry an incentive to engage the community in a dialogue about health care resources. At the same time, it allows the courts to supervise the influence of the managed care industry on clinical practices.

Notes: The Custom-Based Standard of Care

1. *Overview.* These readings introduce a number of complexities and nuances in the basic malpractice standard of care: the error-in-judgment rule, the standard of care for residents and specialists, the availability of punitive damages, the liability of consulting and attending physicians, admissions of error, and sensitivity to resource constraints. These detailed issues are taken up later in this chapter. The main focus of these notes is this more general inquiry: How does malpractice law define which bad results are compensated and which are not? On this point, in what respects are *McCourt* and *Locke* in agreement? In what respects do they disagree? If each of their respective facts and procedural histories were presented to the other court, would you expect a similar result?

2. *Verbal Formulations.* Courts constantly tinker with the precise verbal formulation of the basic standard of care that should be instructed to the jury and uttered by the expert witnesses. This creates havoc for the imprecise lawyer or judge. Illustrative is McCarty v. Mladineo, 636 So. 2d 377 (Miss. 1994), where the court reversed a verdict in favor of the defendant physician, holding that it was error to instruct that the standard is that of a "minimally competent physician." Instead, the court ruled that the jury should be instructed in terms of the "reasonably prudent, minimally competent" physician.

An error in the opposite direction occurred in the trial in Smith v. Menet, 530 N.E.2d 277 (Ill. App. Ct. 1988). There, the plaintiff's lawyer had his favorable verdict reversed because, in questioning his expert witness, he asked whether the defendant's conduct "fell within the standard of *good* medical care." Because the only negative testimony was in response to this defective question, the court ruled there was insufficient evidence to sustain the verdict, explaining, "when good is interpreted to mean better than average, it contradicts the applicable standard," even though in prior cases the same court had used phrases such as "the reasonable skill which a physician in good standing would use."

Deposition testimony Dr. Abernathy gave in the *McCourt* case indicates that he was on academic probation for a time while a student at the University of South Carolina Medical School. Are "below average" doctors automatically liable for their mistakes, or are we to suppose that, as in Garrison Keillor's Lake Wobegon, most doctors are at or above average? The focus on "average" skill and judgment should not mislead one into thinking that any sort of numerical dividing line or litmus test exists. See Hood v. Phillips, 554 S.W.2d 160, 165 (Tex. 1977) (rejecting an instruction to the jury that creates the impression that "the standard for malpractice is to be determined by a poll of the medical profession").

Similarly, it has been observed that the custom-based standard is not strictly determined by actual practice. Instead, it is one that inquires whether existing practices are "accepted" within the profession. Professor Joseph King explains that the distinction between accepted and actual practice is the focus of much of this linguistic debate. Joseph King, In Search of a Standard of Care for the Medical Profession: The "Accepted Practice" Formula, 28 Vand. L. Rev. 1213 (1975). By way of analogy, consider whether, if the automobile driving standard of care were determined by custom, should someone who speeds up through a yellow light be found negligent? Many, or even a majority, of drivers in some communities may actually do this, but we all know they are not supposed to. For additional discussion, see generally Page Keeton, Medical Negligence: The Standard of Care, 10 Tex. Tech. L. Rev. 351 (1979); 18 A.L.R.4th 603 (1982); Leonard J. Nelson, Helling v. Carey Revisited: Physician Liability in Age of Managed Care, 25 Seattle U. L. Rev. 775 (2002); Ben A. Rich, Medical Custom and Medical Ethics: Rethinking the Standard of Care, 14 Cambridge Q. Healthcare Ethics 27 (2005); and the sources cited in n.2 of the Peters article.

3. *Supervising Physicians.* As *Locke* indicates, supervising physicians are liable under a standard of care for reasonable supervision. Other cases explore the extent of liability when a physician is consulted on an informal basis. Consider, for instance, a doctor discussing a difficult case with her colleagues in the physicians' lounge, or in a passing conversation in the hallway. These cases frequently turn on whether any doctor-patient relationship was ever established, for, as explained in Chapter 2.B.1, no professional duty of care attaches unless such a relationship was formed.

4. *Is Medical Consensus Real or Imagined?* What do you think about Prof. Peters's argument that the law often imagines a professional consensus that in fact does not exist. Here are the similar views of a practicing physician:

> To be quite candid, I have no idea what the standard of care really is, and my point is that neither does anyone else. . . . The implementation of the term in the judicial setting . . . disregards in large part the intangible and interpersonal patient variables that so often affect the medical outcome. . . . In fact, there is no standard of care. The medical body of knowledge contains both fact and opinion. Each case must be assessed on its individual merits, including intangible factors and only from a prospective viewpoint. Robert P. Nirschl, Delving into the Myth of "Standard of Care," Am. Med. News, Dec. 16, 1988, at 24.

If law really is this disconnected from reality, what difficulties and dangers does this create? Consider the issue from both the plaintiff's and the defendant's perspectives.

Suppose the "snowflake" attitude in the previous quote (every patient is unique) is correct. Does this mean that the custom-based standard is entirely a figment of the judicial imagination? Even if custom is not nearly so unitary and precise as we might sometimes imagine, does this negate the fact that, for any set of clinical facts, however unique, there are decisions or actions that virtually no doctor would find acceptable? In other words, do these sentiments do anything more than establish that, in many cases, the actual standard of care is very broad and allows for major differences of opinion?

Assuming the latter is correct, how do we make sure that expert witnesses are honestly testifying to a breach of (or compliance with) the standard of care and not merely expressing a strong personal preference or opinion? See Travers v. District of Columbia, 672 A.2d 566 (D.C. 1996) (holding that the expert testimony established only personal preference or opinion, not prevailing custom). More than this, even experts' personal opinions may overstate what they themselves do in actual practice. Several studies have shown that most doctors are actually less thorough, prompt, or accurate than experts have claimed they are in particular lawsuits. Wm. Meadow & Cass Sunstein, Statistics, Not Experts, 51 Duke L.J. 629 (2001). These authors conclude, therefore, that proof of custom should be even more rigorous, using statistical or survey evidence rather than expert opinion. See also Tim Cramm et al., Ascertaining Customary Care in Malpractice Cases: Asking Those Who Know, 37 Wake Forest L. Rev. 699 (2002). However, others agree with Prof. Peters that the persistent failure of actual practice to measure up to accepted medical standards reinforces the case for a reasonable physician standard for liability. Richard Lempert, Following the Man on the Clapham Omnibus: Social Science Evidence in Malpractice Litigation, 37 Wake Forest L. Rev. 903 (2002). See generally Symposium, Empirical Approaches to Proving the Standard of Care in Medical Malpractice Cases, 37 Wake Forest L. Rev. 663 (2002) (thorough discussion of the problem, with multiple critiques and proposals for reform); Bryan A. Liang, Medical Malpractice: Do Physicians Have Knowledge of Legal Standards and Assess Cases as Juries Do?, 3 U. Chi. L. Sch. Roundtable 59, 90 (1996).

Keep these problems in mind as we consider the locality rule, respectable minority rule, and evidentiary rules introduced in later readings.

5. *Punitive Damages.* Do you think Drs. Abernathy and Clyde in the *McCourt* case deserved to be hit with punitive damages? In many states, public policy forbids liability insurance from covering punitives because this would dilute the intended impact on the defendant, so punitives have to be paid from the doctors' own personal assets. Would this change your opinion?

Punitive damages are still rare in medical malpractice cases, owing to the complexity of medical judgment, the good motives of virtually all doctors, and the high regard in which most juries hold doctors in general. However, there is a noted trend toward more punitive damage awards against doctors—in large cities, they are now awarded in over 10 percent of malpractice cases that reach a verdict. In recent years, a number of states have set limits on the amount of punitives relative to compensatory damages (for instance, no more than three times compensatory damages).

Regardless of your opinion about the *McCourt* case, it contains (according to allegations in the plaintiffs' brief) several inflammatory elements that are frequently seen in cases that receive punitives: failure to treat aggressively a seriously ill patient; failure to admit promptly and candidly to the seriousness of the mistake; and suggestions that the medical records might have been altered after the fact. In a rare decision, one court reduced from $5 million to $2 million a punitive award against a nursing home for the death of a patient, finding that there was no evidence of recklessness, and that the amount was ten times the compensatory damage and several times the defendant's net worth. Stogsdill v. Healthmark Partners, 377 F.3d 827 (8th Cir. 2004). See generally Frank M. McClellan, Medical Malpractice: Law, Tactics, and Ethics ch. 8 (1994); M. Rustad & T. Koenig, Reconceptualizing Punitive Damages in Medical Malpractice: Targeting Amoral Corporations, Not "Moral Monsters," 47 Rutgers L. Rev. 975 (1995); Robert Shaw, Punitive Damages in Medical Malpractice: An Economic Evaluation. 81 N.C. L. Rev. 2371 (2003).

The potential for punitive damages may be vastly heightened as juries increasingly begin to learn of the financial incentives that HMOs and other forms of constrained insurance create for doctors to minimize treatment costs. Some of these incentives cause a personal conflict of interest because doctors are paid in a fashion that directly rewards economizing efforts. As noted at page 330 few cases squarely confront whether this is permissible. There is no doubt, however, that plaintiffs will be eager to get this type of inflammatory evidence before the jury. In Muse v. Charter Hospital, 452 S.E.2d 589 (N.C. Ct. App. 1995), the jury awarded $6 million in punitives (subsequently reduced for technical reasons) against a psychiatric hospital that was found to have discharged a suicidal patient because his insurance ran out. In the most notorious instance to date, Fox v. Health Net, a California jury awarded $77 million in punitive damages in a breach of contract action against an HMO that had refused to pay for an innovative cancer treatment, which the surviving family claimed resulted in the patient's death. The verdict was reportedly affected by the fact that the HMO's medical director was paid in a fashion that rewarded him in proportion to the number of claims he turned down. If a method of physician payment is otherwise legal and consistent with public policy, should plaintiffs be allowed to introduce at trial the form of payment for the sole purpose of suggesting an economic motivation? So far, most courts have ruled this type of evidence to be irrelevant to the issue of negligence and potentially inflammatory. Shea v. Esensten, 622 N.W.2d 130 (Minn. Ct. App. 2001). To the contrary, however, Neade v. Portes, 739 N.E.2d 496 (Ill. 2000), ruled that evidence of economic motivation is admissible in a medical malpractice case. See generally Paul R. Sugarman & Valerie A. Yarasbus, Admissibility of Managed Care Financial Incentives in Medical Malpractice Cases, 34 Tort & Ins. L.J. 735 (1999). See page 240 for further discussion.

2. Variations in the Standard of Care

The black-letter law is simple to utter, but more difficult to implement. Physicians are judged by the standard of care that is established by prevailing practice and professional consensus. But seldom can one find a monolithic, clearly defined "right way" of doing things that almost all doctors agree to. Medical practice is highly variable and judgmental. This leads us to consider which variations in practice or opinion can legitimately be used to adjust the standard of care in a given case, and which cannot. The following materials explore variations that are structured around (1) schools of thought and training, (2) practice location and specialization, and (3) source of payment.

■ JONES v. CHIDESTER
610 A.2d 964 (Pa. 1992)

PAPADAKOS, Justice.

We granted review in this case in order to reexamine our test for the defense of the so-called two schools doctrine in a medical malpractice case arising in the context of a jury instruction. The necessity of our reexamination arises from the vacillation of the Superior Court and our court in applying the appropriate standard.

A medical practitioner has an absolute defense to a claim of negligence when it is determined that the prescribed treatment or procedure has been approved by one group of medical experts even though an alternate school of thought recommends another approach, or it is agreed among experts that alternative treatments and practices are acceptable. The doctrine is applicable only where there is more than one method of accepted treatment or procedure. In specific terms, however, we are called upon in this case to decide once again whether a school of thought qualifies as such when it is advocated by a "considerable number" of medical experts or when it commands acceptance by "respect[ed], reputable and reasonable" practitioners. The former test calls for a quantitative analysis, while the latter is premised on qualitative grounds.

The facts indicate that in November, 1979, Appellant, Billy Jones, underwent orthopedic surgery on his leg performed by Dr. John H. Chidester. In order to create a bloodless field for the surgery, the surgeon employed a tourniquet which was elevated and released at various intervals. Because of subsequent problems with the leg, the patient was referred to a neurosurgeon who determined that Jones had suffered nerve injury to the leg. Additional examinations by other doctors confirmed that the nerve injury had resulted in a condition known as "drop foot."

At trial in June, 1988, Jones complained, inter alia, that his nerve injury was the result of Dr. Chidester's use of the tourniquet. Both sides presented testimony by medical experts supporting their positions. Unsurprisingly, Dr. Chidester's experts told the court and jury that his technique was acceptable medically in this particular case, and the plaintiffs' experts insisted that it constituted unacceptable practice. At the close of the evidence, the court gave the following instruction to the jury:

> . . . Ladies and gentlemen, I instruct you upon this additional principle of law known as the two schools of thought doctrine. This principle provides that it is improper for a jury to be required to decide which of two schools of thought as to proper procedure should have been followed in this case, when both schools have their respective and respected advocates and followers in the medical profession. . . . Thus, under the two schools of thought doctrine, a physician in

the position of Dr. Chidester will not be held liable to a plaintiff merely for exercising his judgment in applying the course of treatment supported by a reputable and respected body of medical experts, even if another body of medical experts' opinion would favor a different course of treatment. . . .

The jury returned a verdict in favor of Dr. Chidester. . . . On appeal, Jones argues that under Pennsylvania law, the test for the doctrine is "considerable number" rather than "reputable and respected" as the court had charged the jury.

We note at the outset of our analysis that there appears to be confusion and contradiction in the use of these standards — a confusion apparent even between the trial court's charge to the jury ("reputable and respected") and its subsequent opinion denying the post-trial motion ("considerable number"). . . . The initial modern case in this jurisdiction on the subject of the two schools of thought doctrine was Remley v. Plummer, 79 Pa. Superior Ct. 117 (1922). Relevant portions of that opinion are as follows:

> The question actually passed upon by the jury was not whether the defendants, in their handling of the case, had been guilty of negligence in not following a well-recognized and established mode of treatment, but rather, which of two methods, both having their respective advocates and followers of respectable authority, was the safer and better from a surgical standpoint. . . . Where competent medical authority is divided, a physician will not be held responsible if in the exercise of his judgment he followed the course of treatment advocated by a considerable number of his professional brethren in good standing in his community. . . .
>
> Thus practitioners of a reputable school of medicine are not to be harassed by litigation and mulcted in damages because the course of treatment prescribed by that school differs from that adopted by another school: (citations omitted) . . . As we said in Patten v. Wiggin, "The jury are not to judge by determining which school, in their judgment, is the best." "If the treatment is in accordance with a recognized system of surgery, it is not for the court or jury to undertake to determine whether that system is best, nor to decide questions of surgical science on which surgeons differ among themselves:" . . . The testimony clearly showed a difference of medical opinion expressed by physicians and surgeons of unquestioned standing and reputation, and the defendants were not negligent for having adopted the view held by the majority of their brethren who testified.

. . . Other jurisdictions also appear to waffle between the two standards. . . . In Borja v. Phoenix General Hospital, Inc., 727 P.2d 355 (Az. 1986), the court [held] that the doctrine requires only support by a "respectable minority." California has defined its standard as one where "a physician chooses one of alternative accepted methods of treatment, with which other physicians agree." Meier v. Ross General Hospital, 445 P.2d 519 (Cal. 1968). Florida has adopted the "respectable minority" test in Schwab v. Tolley, 345 So. 2d 747 (Fla. App. 1977), while Arkansas accepts the doctrine when any alternative "recognized method" is employed by the physician. Rickett v. Hayes, 511 S.W.2d 187 (Ark. 1974). . . .

It is incumbent upon us to settle this confusion. The "two schools of thought doctrine" provides a complete defense to malpractice. It is therefore insufficient to show that there exists a "small minority" of physicians who agree with the defendant's questioned practice. Thus, the Superior Court's "reputable and respected by reasonable medical experts" test is improper. Rather, there must be a considerable number of physicians, recognized and respected in their field, sufficient to create another "school of thought." . . . A school of thought should be adopted not only by "reputable and respected physicians" in order to insure quality but also by a "considerable number" of medical practitioners for the purpose of meeting general acceptance even if it does not rise to the level of a majority. . . .

In recognizing this doctrine, we do not attempt to place a numerical certainty on what constitutes a "considerable number." The burden of proving that there are two schools of thought falls to the defendant. The burden, however, should not prove burdensome. The proper use of expert witnesses should supply the answers. Once the expert states the factual reasons to support his claim that there is a considerable number of professionals who agree with the treatment employed by the defendant, there is sufficient evidence to warrant an instruction to the jury on the two "schools of thought." It then becomes a question for the jury to determine whether they believe that there are two legitimate schools of thought such that the defendant should be insulated from liability.

Reversed and remanded for a new trial consistent with this opinion.

McDermott, Justice, concurring.
. . . [W]hether it [is] best to chill or heat, use medicines, intervene with scalpel or await nature, or approach from back, front, top or bottom to reach the site of ill, are questions over which doctors disagree. One group of doctors of skill and competence may withhold the scalpel, another group of equal competence may believe in quick response. When each group has its advocates, and each has its arguable reasons, a doctor of either cannot be faulted if he properly administers the one to his knowledge and experience seems the better, so long as that group is comprised of a sufficient number of reputable and respected members.

Thus, an isolated expert cannot argue it was his own belief that a procedure was inappropriate, because then this belief would be elevated, against experience and knowledge, to a separate level, though a considerable portion of the world of medicine be against it.

I join in the opinion of the majority.

Zappala, Justice, concurring.
While I join in the opinion, I vehemently disagree with the majority that the existence of two schools of medical thought may ever be a question of fact to be submitted to a jury. . . . It is the responsibility of the trial judge to determine in the first instance whether there are two schools of medical thought so that competent medical authority as to a course of treatment is divided. It is a question of law for the trial judge. It is not a question of fact. In all other respects, I agree with the majority's analysis of the two schools of medical thought doctrine.

■ CHAPEL v. ALLISON
785 P.2d 204 (Mont. 1990)

Sheehy, Justice.
. . . Lawrence A. Chapel was injured when he was kicked by a horse on February 18, 1983. He was taken to the emergency room at Livingston Memorial

Hospital where he was treated by Dr. James G. Allison [for a severe leg fracture]. . . . He applied a long leg cast extending from Chapel's mid-thigh down to and including his foot. . . . The cast was removed May 2, 1983. Chapel's leg exhibited a varus deformity (bow-leggedness) which required surgery, a procedure called an "osteotomy," to straighten the bowed leg. . . .

Chapel had been a patient of Dr. Allison's for nearly 20 years, the doctor treating ailments from common illnesses up to and including sprains, fractures, and an initial treatment for a ruptured disc. Chapel's injury was of the kind which would fall within the area of practice of an orthopedic surgeon. It would also fall within the area of practice of a properly qualified general practitioner. . . . Dr. Allison claimed during the litigation that he possessed the requisite degree of knowledge for treating Chapel because of his 24 years of practice in which he had treated 1,000 fractures, 50 of which involved the tibia and 15 of which involved the tibial plateau, and one instance of the same injury, but without the wound overlying the fracture site.

The expert testimony produced by the plaintiff Chapel came from an orthopedic surgeon from Denman, Massachusetts, Dr. Stephen Sand, board-certified in the specialty of orthopedic surgery. His testimony was as follows:

Q. Based upon what you have learned by reviewing all of the documents that we mentioned, have you been able to form a reasonable judgment on what the standards of care are in the Livingston-Bozeman area in Montana for the care and treatment of an injury such as was sustained by Mr. Chapel by a general practitioner? . . .

A. My opinion, based on the review of the information that you have stated, and my contact with a general practitioner in the area, is that a general practitioner would not, under ordinary circumstances, handle this type of case or injury.

. . . At the close of Chapel's case in chief, . . . the court granted Dr. Allison's motion for a directed verdict. . . . The district court said that proof of the competency of Dr. Sand to testify in the matter was "very shaky"; that the plaintiff did not call Dr. Kurtz, a Bozeman doctor, upon whom Dr. Sand had relied for information as to the area of practice for a general practitioner; that Dr. Allison had testified that in his opinion Chapel was bow-legged before the accident and despite the leg injury and disc surgery the same year, that Chapel was able to go elk hunting in the mountains for a two-week period; that the other doctors whose testimony appeared in the case have all in effect said that there was no fault. . . .

During pretrial procedures before the district court, the plaintiff made a motion in limine that the "same locality rule" (infra) was not applicable in this case. The court denied the motion, saying:

The court specifically determines that the rule applicable in this case is that Dr. Allison will be held to the standard of care in February 1983 of a licensed general practitioner, who is not board certified, in the same or similar communities within Montana. Provided, however, experts from elsewhere and in other specialties will be considered competent to testify if they are medically qualified and if they are in fact familiar with the standards for a general practitioner in Livingston or similar communities in Montana at the time in question. . . .

Formerly, the standard of care required of a physician or surgeon in treating a patient was to exercise as reasonable care and skill which "is usually exercised by physicians or surgeons of good standing of the same system or school of practice in the community in which he resides, having due regard to the condition of medical or surgical science at that time." The "same locality rule" restricted the geographical area from which the degree of care exercised by a physician or surgeon could be determined to the community in which the doctor resided.

In Tallbull v. Whitney, 564 P.2d 162 (Mont. 1977), this court examined the "same locality rule" and determined that the foundation for it no longer existed. The reasons given were that the accessibility of medical literature, the frequency and availability of national, regional and state medical meetings, advances of communication of medical knowledge, transportation advances, and the opportunity for rural community doctors to gain medical knowledge in the same manner as doctors in more populous regions in the state, all made the "same locality rule" outdated. In *Tallbull*, this court expanded the rule saying:

> For the foregoing reasons, we hold that Montana's "locality rule" imposes on a physician undertaking the care of a patient the legal duty of possessing and exercising that reasonable and ordinary degree of learning, skill and care possessed and exercised by physicians of good standing of the same school of practice in the same or similar locality in Montana. A similar locality in Montana within the meaning of this rule is a locality of similar geographical location, size and character in a medical context.

The *Tallbull* rule was modified insofar as it applied to an orthopedic surgeon in Aasheim v. Humberger, 695 P.2d 824 (Mont. 1985). There, this court recognized that the defendant was a nationally board-certified orthopedic surgeon and had received comparable training and passed the same national board certification tests as all other board-certified orthopedic specialists in the nation. On that basis, this Court held that when a defendant in a medical negligence action was a board-certified specialist, his skill and learning would be measured by "the skill and learning possessed by other doctors in good standing, practicing in the same specialty and who hold the same national board certification." Thenceforth, board certified specialists in Montana would be subject to a national standard of care.

In Glover v. Ballhagen, 756 P.2d 1166 (Mont. 1988), . . . the doctor was a board-certified family practitioner. In *Glover*, we concluded that: ". . . the standard of care to which a board certified family practitioner will be held is that skill and learning possessed by other doctors in good standing, practicing with the same national board certification." . . .

Not answered in the foregoing cases, and raised as an issue in this case, is whether a non-board-certified general practitioner, practicing in a Montana community, who treats a patient for an injury of a kind which would fall within an area of practice of an orthopedic surgeon should be held to the degree of care, knowledge and skill of the specialist. . . . Because of the broad implications to the medical community and to injured patients lurking in whatever decision we made on this issue, we ordered rebriefing and oral argument on the issue and invited briefs from amici curiae. Here are the arguments marshalled by each side:

Counsel for Chapel maintains that in an age of increasing specialization, a doctor in general practice is under a legal duty, in diagnosing or treating a patient, to seek consultation with or refer a patient to a specialist when the doctor knows or should know in the exercise of reasonable care that the services of a specialist are indicated. Chapel further argues that if there is another mode of treatment that is likely to be more successful for which the physician does not have the facilities or the training to administer, but which is available from specialists, it is the doctor's duty to so advise the patient, and failure to apprise the patient of these facts would constitute a breach of that duty. . . .

Dr. Allison contends that restricting the degree of care to the same or similar communities in Montana is proper because he confronts illnesses and injuries in serving his community whereas practitioners in a larger city devote much of their practice to initial diagnoses with referral to a specialist for anything beyond routine care. Dr. Allison also contends that it would be impracticable to require a general practitioner to be held to the standard of care of whatever area of expertise in which his treatment might fall, including an orthopedic surgeon, a dermatologist, a neurologist, an obstetrician, an internist, and so on.

An amicus brief filed by the Montana Trial Lawyers Association . . . contend[s] that there is a trend away from the locality rule in most states which apply a national standard of care, typically defined as "a physician is under a duty to use that degree of care and skill which is expected of a reasonable competent practitioner in the same class to which it belongs, acting in the same or similar circumstances." Trial Lawyers contend that the phrase "the same or similar circumstances" allows the trier of fact to take into account and to weigh local conditions when the standard is applied, so as to reflect the same "general facilities, services, and options" which were available to the treating doctor. . . .

An amicus brief was received from the Montana Hospital Association. Essentially, this brief points out the rather dire prospects faced by rural hospitals in Montana. It states that all of Montana's 64 hospitals were only marginally profitable for the past five years but that rural hospitals experienced increasing financial losses. The losses are occurring primarily because of reduced utilization of rural hospitals. Some of the reductions are due to public policies and issues undertaken at both the federal and state levels with cutbacks in federal and state Medicare and Medicaid programs. The importance of a rural doctor to a rural hospital is emphasized in the brief and the hospitals contend that the similar locality rule is needed in rural areas to keep physicians there providing essential health services and utilizing local rural hospital services. . . .

The brief of the Montana Medical Association recognizes the implications of the problem and seems to be seeking a middle ground for its resolution. Thus, with regard to general practitioners, its brief recommends that we continue to adopt the "same or similar locality" standard, without geographical limitations for general practitioners but allow the "national" specialist standard to be applied to any physician who holds himself or herself out as a specialist. . . . The brief suggests that the elimination of the Montana boundary restriction on the locality rule is warranted. . . . It points out that if the "same or similar locality" rule for general practitioners is any locality similar in the United States, sound policy reasons support such a change, including . . . the increased availability of expert witnesses, the lack of which would be some justification for alterations in the law. The brief contends for a balance to be struck between the right of a negligently injured patient to receive compensation through the availability of expert testimony and the right of a doctor to due process and a fair hearing, by insuring that those experts who do testify possess solid practical experience in the type of practice at issue.

On balance, the position asserted by the Montana Medical Association as to the standard of care applicable in cases of this type, with slight modification, appears suitable for adoption by us. . . . [W]e abandon the "locality" rule which is limited to Montana communities. . . . The geographical restriction of the state boundary is too narrow in view of the necessity of expert testimony; yet, as the Association contends, the national standard should not exclude local considerations which face rural general practitioners. Accordingly, we hold that a non-board-certified general practitioner is held to the standard of care of a "reasonably competent general practitioner acting in the same or similar community in the United States in the same or similar circumstances." See Shilkret v. Annapolis Emergency Hospital Association, 349 A.2d 245 (Md. 1975). "Similar circumstances" permits consideration by the trier of fact of legitimate local factors affecting the ordinary standard of care including the knowledge and experience of the general practitioner, commensurate with the skill of other competent physicians of similar training and experience, with respect to the type of illness or injury he confronts and the resources, facilities and options available to him at the time. . . . This opinion applies only to general practitioners, and does not affect board-certified specialists or board-certified general or family practitioners. . . .

Reversed and remanded for further proceedings in accordance with this opinion.

Notes: Variations in the Standard of Care — Location, Schools of Thought, Experiments, and Specialization

1. *The Respectable Minority Rule.* Reaching a different result from that in *Jones* on the quantitative versus qualitative standard is Hood v. Phillips, 554 S.W.2d 160 (Tex. 1977). For a detailed review, see Note, 44 J. Urb. Contemp. L. 211 (1993).

Intertwined with the "respectable minority" or "two schools of thought" doctrine is the "error in judgment" concept discussed in the *McCourt* case (page 300), since it conveys the same notion of absence of negligence when doctors make an educated choice among two or more reasonable paths. For a while, courts were shying away from the "error in judgment" language, however, because it seems to convey to the jury that doctors are liable only if they act in bad faith, but now the error-in-judgment instruction appears to be making a small comeback. See Hal Arkes & Cindy Schipani, Medical Malpractice v. The Business Judgment Rule: Differences in Hindsight Bias, 73 Or. L. Rev. 586 (1994) (arguing that doctors should be given discretion similar to business managers to make mistakes as long as they act in good faith); Jeffrey O'Connell & Andrew S. Boutros,

Treating Medical Malpractice Claims Under a Variant of the Business Judgment Rule, 77 Notre Dame L. Rev. 373 (2002) (same); Charles Caldwell & Evan Seamone, Excusable Neglect in Malpractice Suits Against Radiologists, 16 Ann. Health L. 43 (2007) (similar); Joseph H. King, Reconciling the Exercise of Judgment and the Objective Standard of Care in Medical Malpractice, 52 Okla. L. Rev. 49 (1999).

2. *Medical Experiments.* Does the "considerable number" formulation allow sufficient room for medical experimentation? Requiring that a sizeable number of doctors follow a practice means that the first few to innovate do so at their own risk. Is strict liability an appropriate standard for medical experimentation? Early decisions generally held "yes," but most modern courts say "no," holding that doctors are bound by a standard of reasonable experimentation. Brook v. St. John's Hickey Memorial Hospital, 380 N.E.2d 72 (Ind. 1978) (no liability for hitting a nerve while injecting needle in the leg instead of the arm; "therapeutic innovation has long been recognized as permissible; . . . even where there is an established mode of treatment, the physician may be permitted to innovate somewhat if he can establish that, in his best judgment, this was for the benefit of his patient"); Hood v. Phillips, 554 S.W.2d 160 (Tex. 1977) ("physicians should be allowed to experiment in order that medical science can provide greater benefits for humankind"; jury should have been allowed to decide based on expert testimony that controversial surgery was unreasonable and discredited). In order for this justification to hold, however, the innovation must be done for therapeutic reasons, not purely for research curiosity. This usually means the deviation from standard therapy is fairly minor or existing treatment is wholly inadequate. As a German authority explains:

> [T]hree different types of procedure must be distinguished: (i) *Therapeutic treatment*, whereby the patient is treated with [one of the] normal and approved (or orthodox) procedures; (ii) *Therapeutic experiments*, whereby the patient is treated with new methods and techniques for primarily (though not exclusively) therapeutic purposes. This is also known as therapeutic research or "innovative therapy"; (iii) *Research experiments*, whereby persons, either patients or test subjects, are treated with new methods and drugs for purely scientific purposes. Dieter Giesen, Civil Liability of Physicians for New Methods of Treatment and Experimentation: A Comparative Examination, 3 Med. L. Rev. 22 (1995).

See also Nancy King, Experimental Treatment: Oxymoron or Aspiration?, 25(4) Hastings Center Rep. 6 (July 1995).

Liability for experimental deviations from customary practice is more often avoided by resorting to informed consent law. Because modern experiments are usually accompanied by careful disclosure of the risks and procedures, in most instances the patient has been informed of the therapy's experimental status and has consented to the increased risks. In order for this consent to be effective, is it sufficient to disclose simply (1) the risks of the experimental therapy (which, by definition, are not well known), (2) the fact that this is an experiment, or also (3) the comparative risks and benefits of the alternative, standard procedure? In practice, only (1) and (2) are usually done. Nevertheless, the consent is usually sufficient to avoid liability, unless of course the procedure itself was improperly performed. See Slater v. Optical Radiation Corp., 961 F.2d 1330 (7th Cir. 1992) (experiment okay if patient is informed of risks); Karp v. Cooley, 493 F.2d 408 (5th Cir. 1974) (first patient to receive an artificial heart expressly consented to all aspects of operation); Fiorentino v. Wenger, 280 N.Y.S.2d 373 (N.Y. 1967) (doctor liable where he failed to disclose he was the only one in the country who performed a discredited operation).

Even if doctors and hospitals are not legally obligated to compensate fully informed patients who are injured in medical experiments, should they do so voluntarily, as a matter of public policy, considering the sacrifice the patient has made for the benefit of science? Many hospitals and drug companies agree to pick up at least the costs of treatment for injuries in experiments they conduct or fund. For additional discussion of these various questions, see Chapter 3.C.5; President's Commission, Compensating for Research Injuries (1982); Comment, 78 Wash. L. Rev. 229 (2003); Anna Mastroianni, Liability, Regulation and Policy in Surgical Innovation, 16 Health Matrix 351 (2006).

3. *Unorthodox Medicine.* Less frequently litigated is whether the "schools of thought" doctrine protects doctors who practice completely unorthodox or unscientific medicine, such as homeopathy, naturopathy, or even faith healing. If the practitioner is not a licensed M.D., then presumably only the standards of that group apply. If a physician incorporates alternative theories, or uses them exclusively, then a tougher issue is presented. In the leading, and virtually the only, case — one involving a cancer patient who died after her doctor treated her with nutritional therapy — the court held that "we see no reason why a patient should not be allowed to make an informed decision to go outside currently approved medical methods in search of an unconventional treatment." Schneider v. Revici, 817 F.2d 987 (2d Cir. 1987). In that case, the doctor had carefully documented a consent form that advised the patient to seek conventional treatment as well, and the jury rejected the claim that the doctor had fraudulently misrepresented the prospects of success for the treatment. In a licensing case not involving malpractice, however, the court held that a doctor who uses homeopathic medicines prepared from "moss, the night shade plant, and various other . . . substances" can be disciplined for engaging in unprofessional conduct, even though his patients were fully informed and there was no evidence that he posed a risk of harm to anyone. In re Guess, 393 S.E.2d 833 (N.C. 1990). See also Brown v. Shyne, 151 N.E. 197 (N.Y. 1926) (chiropractor who practices medicine will be held to the standard of a physician). See generally Michael H. Cohen, Complementary and Alternative Medicine: Legal Boundaries and Regulatory Perspectives (1998); J. Brad Kallmyer, A Chimera in Every Sense: Standard of Care for Physicians Practicing Complementary and Alternative Medicine, 2 Ind. Health L. Rev. 225 (2005).

4. *Legal Effect of Schools-of-Thought Rules.* In conventional cases, more important than how exactly the "two schools" or "error in judgment" rules are phrased is their legal effect. Do you agree with the majority or with Justice Zappala's concurrence in *Jones*? Also, do you agree that the defendant should bear the burden of proof; in other words, is this doctrine an affirmative defense, or must the plaintiff negate the existence of alternative schools as part of his prima facie case? If the defendant bears the burden and the doctrine merely results in instructing the jury, how does one avoid the concern expressed in Justice

McDermott's concurrence in *Jones* that an "isolated expert" should not be allowed to elevate his mere personal belief to a binding standard of care?

A minority of courts give the doctrine greater force by using it to direct a verdict where the conflicting expert testimony merely shows a "difference of opinion" and not that the defendant was beyond the bounds of any respectable practice. See, e.g., Chumbler v. McClure, 505 F.2d 489 (6th Cir. 1974) (directed verdict for defendant is proper despite conflict in testimony and the fact the Dr. McClure was the only doctor in town who followed the disputed practice; "the test for . . . community standards is not to be determined solely by a plebiscite"); Baldor v. Rogers, 81 So. 2d 658 (Fla. 1954) (plaintiff verdict reversed) ("The testimony of numbers of physicians who took the witness stand is in hopeless conflict about the wisdom of using the method employed by the appellant. . . . [B]ecause of the divergence of views, . . . the testimony lacks much as a basis for a verdict"), rev'd on reh'g, 81 So. 2d 661 (upholding verdict on the basis of lack of informed consent); Laughridge v. Moss, 294 S.E.2d 672 (Ga. Ct. App. 1982) (directed verdict for defendant).

Even if this harder stance is taken, however, it is still relatively simple for the plaintiff's expert to create a jury issue on the question of "respectability." Consider which of the following is sufficient to get the case in front of the jury:

1. "I would never do it that way."
2. "No one I know of does it that way."
3. "In my opinion, no respectable doctor should do it that way; some may do so, but that's not considered good medical practice."

How difficult do you suppose it is for an expert who starts at the first position to move to the third?

5. *Locality Rules.* A classic statement of the reasons for the old "strict" locality rule can be found in Small v. Howard, 128 Mass. 131, 136 (1880) ("It is a matter of common knowledge that a physician in a small country village . . . [is] but seldom called upon as a surgeon to perform difficult operations. He would have but few opportunities of observation and practice in that line such as public hospitals or large cities would afford."). Have these conditions really changed that much? Another reason the strict locality rule has been overturned is that the "conspiracy of silence" among medical professionals made it extremely difficult for a plaintiff to find a qualified expert witness, even in cases of egregious negligence. The seminal decision on liberalizing the locality rule is Pederson v. Dumouchel, 431 P.2d 973 (Wash. 1967) ("The fact that several careless practitioners might settle in the same place cannot affect the standard of [care]. . . . Negligence cannot be excused on the ground that others in the same locality practice the same kind of negligence. No degree of antiquity can give sanction to usage bad in itself."). For historical discussion of the locality rule, see T. Silver, One Hundred Years of Harmful Error: The Historical Jurisprudence of Medical Malpractice, 1992 Wis. L. Rev. 1193 (arguing that locality originally was just a relevant factor but mistakenly was converted into an absolute rule); Jon Walz, The Rise and Gradual Fall of the Locality Rule in Medical Malpractice Litigation, 18 DePaul L. Rev. 408 (1969).

Chapel indicates that the differences among the modern locality rules may be more in appearance than in substance. A national standard tends to be "lowered" (or, more properly, varied) by its inclusion of a "similar circumstances" qualifier, while a local standard tends to be "raised" (or universalized) when applied to board-certified specialists. The meaning and significance of board certification is explained further below. Of the following three factors, which do you think is *most* relevant in defining "similarity" of location or circumstances: (1) population density; (2) medical facilities (consider similar towns with and without a teaching hospital); or (3) socioeconomics, such as portion of population without insurance or on Medicaid? See generally, Annots., 18 A.L.R.4th 603 (1982); 99 A.L.R.3d 1133 (1980).

It may be possible to raise even the strict locality standard to a national level with testimony in the particular case that local doctors follow the national practice. Idaho is one of the few states to retain the strict locality standard, where it is codified by statute. Plaintiff's efforts to circumvent it by attempting to qualify national experts have resulted in about a dozen state supreme court decisions clarifying when national standards apply. At first, it appeared the court had adopted the Montana rule that board certification automatically invokes a national standard, but it later retreated to holding that this depends on the testimony in each case. See Grimes v. Green, 746 P.2d 978 (Idaho 1987). See also Henning v. Thomas, 366 S.E.2d 109 (Va. 1988) (expert from another part of the country allowed to testify to a state-wide standard of care for orthopedic surgeons by asserting that uniform national standards apply in all states).

As these cases indicate, the primary significance of the locality dimension of the standard of care is not the influence these words have when instructed to the jury, but instead is on who is qualified to testify on both sides of the case. Issues of witness qualification are discussed below. It suffices for now to observe that, in most jurisdictions today, experts need not actually practice in the specialty or locational category that defines the standard of care, they need only demonstrate some acquaintance with the relevant standard of care. This liberalization in expert qualification may be just as or more important in practical effect than how the standard of care is defined in theory.

6. *The Specialization Dimension of the Standard of Care.* In addition to geography and schools of practice, the custom-based standard is adjusted according to the physician's specialization. Thus, a surgeon or obstetrician is held to a higher standard than is a general practitioner who performs the same procedure. Specialty practice is usually designated by "board certification," meaning that the physician has passed special training and testing requirements set by one of the two dozen American Boards of Medical Specialties. Observe how the *Chapel* court deals with the question of board certified family practitioners. Do you agree, considering that family practice is one of the classic forms of general practice?

What about subspecialties? Rather than just general surgery, suppose a physician is regarded as a specialist in cardiac surgery, or pediatric cardiac surgery, or in a particular heart valve replacement for children. How does one square the notion that the standard is elevated for specialists with the rule that the standard should not be elevated simply because the defendant is more highly skilled or experienced than average? In resolving this dilemma, it may help to observe that one basis for elevating the standard of care to begin with—to that of a reasonably prudent physician as opposed to a reasonably prudent person—is that doctors hold themselves out as specially trained professionals. If this is key to the initial elevation, then how doctors hold themselves out as specialists and subspecialists may determine how many further gradations are possible. See, e.g., Aves v. Shah, 997 F.2d 762 (10th Cir. 1993) (general practitioner held to an obstetrics standard because she considered herself a specialist, and so did her patient).

Plaintiffs sometimes attempt to elevate a generalist standard by arguing that a doctor should be held to a specialist standard if she extends her practice to procedures or conditions that are not within the competence of an ordinary generalist, thereby becoming a de facto specialist. Although this does not usually succeed in just these terms, plaintiffs sometimes are able to conflate the generalist and specialist standards to some extent by arguing, as in *Chapel*, that, although a generalist might have rendered treatment as well as could be expected, he failed to recognize his own limitations and call in a specialist when one was needed.

Locke v. Pachtman, in the prior set of cases, raises the additional complication of what standard applies to a doctor-in-training. Licensure of M.D.s occurs only after they complete four years of medical school and pass a series of standardized exams. They then go through a period of apprenticeship, partially or wholly in a hospital setting, in which they are known as "residents" (the older term is "interns"). Those who seek board certification go through much longer residencies. Even though residents have just received their M.D.s and practice only under supervision, most courts, as in *Locke,* hold them to at least a normal standard of care for general practitioners, reasoning that, if they aren't ready to practice as full-fledged doctors, they should not be represented as such to patients. Many courts go further and hold them to an elevated standard, somewhere between generalists and specialists, since they are usually in specialty training at highly sophisticated teaching and research hospitals. See Justin Ward, Medical Residents: Should They Be Held to a Different Standard of Care?, 22 J. Leg. Med. 283 (2001). See, e.g., Jistarri v. Nappi, 549 A.2d 210 (Pa. Super. Ct. 1988) (orthopedic resident held to an intermediate standard of care). Prof. King argues that, following informed consent principles, residents who disclose their status as trainees should be held to a trainee standard, whereas those who don't should be held to a fully practicing specialist standard. Joseph H. King, The Standard of Care for Residents and Other Medical School Graduates in Training, 55 Am. U. L. Rev. 683-751 (2006). See also Phelps v. Physicians Ins. Co. of Wis., Inc., 698 N.W.2d 643 (Wis. 2005) (holding first-year obstetrics resident to standard of care of other such residents).

Problem: What Is the Standard of Care?

Imagine a law school grading regime in which your final grade could be docked from one to five points each time you failed to answer correctly a question posed to you in class, but only if you had failed to meet the prevailing "standard of care" in preparation for the class. (In other words, you are penalized only if you are at "fault" for not knowing, with fault defined as not preparing.) Write a statement of what you view as the prevailing standard of care in your school for class preparation. What is the highest standard to which you might be held? Are there "accepted" alternative or "minority" standards? Does the standard vary according to 1L vs. 2L vs. 3L, or for first vs. second semester 1Ls, or according to full-time vs. night students? Should the prevailing standard differ in top-ten national schools as opposed to non-ABA-accredited schools?

In an evidentiary hearing, who should be allowed to testify about such a standard: only current students at the same school; students at another school; anyone who has graduated from law school within ten years; faculty; administrators?

Would such a regime cause you to prepare excessively, i.e., more than you needed to in order to do well on the exam?

Note: The Impact of Economic Constraints

Health law scholars have debated the important question of whether existing standards of medical practice embodied in the law will conflict with the increasingly prevalent economic constraints that are meant to alter existing medical practices.[1] Consider, for instance, an HMO or Medicaid physician who declines to order a test because of its expense, feeling that other diagnostic information is sufficient. If other physicians who practice under generous, fee-for-service reimbursement would usually order the test, is the HMO physician automatically liable in any case where he misses the correct diagnosis, or can he raise the economic constraints that exist in an HMO setting as a defense to the prevailing standard of care? Surprisingly, considering the number of patients treated in economically constrained environments, questions like this have not been squarely confronted by the courts. Partly, this is because HMOs and their physicians have been sued for malpractice less than might be expected, and when claims are filed, they are frequently resolved through arbitration. The absence of case law on this question is also due to the fact that, when HMOs are sued, defense counsel are highly reluctant to raise resource constraints as an excuse for fear that this admits too much (second-rate medicine) and that plaintiffs might turn this argument against them by inflaming the jury to impose punitive damages, as discussed at page 316.

Indeed, in a series of lawsuits, *plaintiffs'* lawyers have argued that an HMO physician's decision to withhold treatment, such as a Pap smear or biopsy to detect cancer, was inappropriately influenced by how the doctor was paid. The common law is still undeveloped because most of these cases have been settled or dismissed for procedural reasons prior to trial. In the few reported decisions, one court ruled that it was proper to exclude evidence that profit motivation might have

---

[1] In 1975, Randall Bovbjerg wrote the definitive analytical work on the application of malpractice doctrine to HMOs, The Medical Malpractice Standard of Care: HMOs and Customary Practice, 1975 Duke L.J. 1375. In 1981, the Texas Law Review published a lengthy debate among James Blumstein, Rand Rosenblatt, and Peter Schuck about precisely this issue. Symposium, 59 Tex. L. Rev. 1345 (1981). More recently, see E. Haavi Morreim, Holding Health Care Accountable (2001); Mark A. Hall, The Malpractice Standard Under Health Care Cost Containment, 17 Law, Med. & Health Care 347 (1989); Maxwell J. Mehlman, The Patient-Physician Relationship in an Era of Scarce Resources: Is There a Duty to Treat?, 25 Conn. L. Rev. 349 (1993); Laura Athens Mellas, Adapting the Judicial Approach to Medical Malpractice Claims Against Physicians to Reflect Medicare Cost Containment Measures, 62 Colo. L. Rev. 287 (1991); John A. Siliciano, Wealth, Equity, and the Unitary Medical Malpractice Standard, 77 Va. L. Rev. 439 (1991); Note, 103 Yale L.J. 1297 (1994).

caused an HMO physician to fail to hospitalize a patient with labor complications, observing that such evidence "was only marginally relevant [to malpractice] and potentially very prejudicial." Madsen v. Park Nicollet Medical Center, 419 N.W.2d 511, 515 (Minn. Ct. App. 1988), rev'd on other grounds, 431 N.W.2d 855 (Minn. 1988). See also Pulvers v. Kaiser Foundation Health Plan, 160 Cal. Rptr. 392, 394 (Cal. Ct. App. 1979) (HMO incentive plan not contrary to public policy). However, Neade v. Portes, 739 N.E.2d 496 (Ill. 2000), ruled that evidence of economic motivation is admissible in a medical malpractice case. Is it possible to reconcile these conflicting decisions by observing that, where negligent treatment exists, a financial inducement can be found to be a contributing factor, but, standing alone, it does not constitute an independent tort? Would the second point hold true, however, if the financial inducement is not known to the patient? The discussion at page 240 addresses whether an informed consent cause of action exists for failure to disclose payment methods that create a conflict of interest.

This slim case law on plaintiffs' use of financial incentives in suits against HMOs and their doctors still does not address whether HMO physicians can invoke economic constraints as a defense. The one case that comes closest to being on point is Wickline v. State, 239 Cal. Rptr. 810 (Cal. Ct. App. 1986), which is reprinted at page 483. It found that no malpractice occurred when a Medicaid patient lost her leg as the result of being released from the hospital in four days rather than the eight days her doctors requested. The treating physicians blamed the state Medicaid program because it refused to pay for any more than four days. The court's rejection of liability says very little about the legal standard of care, however, since the patient chose not to sue her doctors, only Medicaid. She relied on her doctors as her expert witnesses against the state, and they naturally were not willing to testify that they gave her substandard medicine. Therefore, the key issue was not litigated. This case does illustrate, however, that there is often a wide range in acceptable standards of practice from the minimum to the optimal — here, from four to eight days — so that there may be plenty of room to accommodate economically constrained practice patterns within existing standards of care, especially under the "respectable minority rule."

If lawyers were to seek special legal protection for HMO and Medicaid doctors, they might also do so through the similar locality rule, by arguing that physicians who practice under unconstrained, fee-for-service insurance are not from sufficiently similar situations to give relevant testimony. How would you evaluate such an argument based on the cases above? In Moss v. Miller, 625 N.E.2d 1044 (Ill. App. Ct. 1993), the court reversed a defense verdict against a prisoner who alleged negligent failure to refer him to a specialist. The fatal flaw in the trial was simply the inclusion of an ordinary similar locality standard in the jury instructions. The court was concerned that the jury would be misled, in light of counsel's arguments that prisons are a distinct locality. The court held:

> [T]hose practicing the medical arts in the penitentiary are held to the same standard of care as [other doctors]. To hold otherwise would be to abandon reason and common sense. . . . [W]e recognize constraints necessarily exist in correctional institutions which may well have a negative effect on the ability to delivery medical services. . . . However, those types of constraints, while interfering with

proper medical care, do not lessen the standards required of the medical arts practitioner.

Consider, also, whether physicians should be held to a lesser standard when treating indigent patients for free, a topic that is discussed in several of the articles cited in footnote 1 above. Are these questions easier if patients are thought to have a choice over the matter? Consider, for instance, whether subscribers to an HMO plan should be allowed to contractually specify a lower but acceptable standard of care than that which prevails elsewhere in their community, so that their health insurance will be more affordable. That topic is discussed further at page 381.

Because these important questions remain largely unresolved, we must use the conceptual tools in existing malpractice law to anticipate how courts might analyze them when they are squarely confronted. Doing so also serves as a good review of the prior discussion. The following problem provides a concrete situation on which to focus your thoughts. After you have worked through the problem, you might want to consult the more general analysis that one of the editors of this book has written, which is excerpted on the Web site for this book, www.health-law.org.

Problem: Economic Malpractice

You are legal counsel to Metropolis Inner City Hospital (MICH), a public facility that is bound by statute to treat all patients regardless of their ability to pay. Naturally, the hospital is chronically strapped for funds. Controversy is fast developing within the medical staff over the use of high osmolar contrast media (HOCM) versus low osmolar contrast media (LOCM) in diagnostic imaging procedures, such as angiography. This is an invasive procedure to visualize the blockage in blood vessels by injecting a substance that shows up under X-ray (the "contrast media"). The substance's "osmolarity" affects its safety, with lower being better. Toxic effects are usually temporary (pain, nausea, altered kidney or nervous functions), but some are permanent, and some deaths have been documented. Although HOCMs are approved as safe and effective by the FDA, they have osmolarities of up to seven times that of blood plasma and consequently produce undesirable effects in some patients. Concerns over the toxicity of HOCMs led to the development of LOCMs, the first of which became commercially available ten years ago. Although all adverse reactions can be reduced by using LOCMs instead of HOCMs, HOCMs are usually well tolerated and affected patients respond quickly to treatment. Fortunately, fatal adverse reactions appear to be very infrequent. However, on a purely medical basis, with no cost considerations taken into account, there is no scientific reason to use anything other than LOCMs owing to the significant reduction in the prevalence of all degrees of adverse reactions.

The higher incidence of adverse reactions to HOCMs can be reduced by identifying patients at highest risk, such as those with asthma, allergies, renal or cardiac impairment, diabetes, etc. The American College of Radiology issued a set of guidelines for use of HOCMs vs. LOCMs based on various risk factors. However, risk stratification schemes cannot identify all persons who will react adversely to HOCMs. There is still a statistical benefit that can be realized by giving LOCM to patients who are placed in a low-risk category.

Both HOCMs and LOCMs produce images of similar quality. LOCMs, however, are about ten to twenty times higher cost per dose than HOCMs ($20 vs. $200-$400). Although the higher cost may not be viewed as outrageous per procedure, if all procedures at MICH were to use LOCMs, costs would total over $500,000 a year.

Five years ago, about 9 percent nationally of radiological exams requiring contrast media were done with LOCMs. By this year, this number had climbed to 70 percent. Previously, MICH has used LOCMs only for high-risk patients. Physicians at MICH have expressed liability concerns about the continued use of HOCMs for any patients. Despite adherence to risk stratification procedures, the very availability of LOCMs concerns them. LOCM manufacturers have helped to fuel these concerns by telling the radiologists that the use of any contrast agent other than LOCMs could constitute malpractice.

How would you advise the hospital on the physicians' demands to eliminate all use of HOCMs? See Jacobson & Rosenquist, The Introduction of Low-Osmolar Contrast Agents in Radiology, 260 JAMA 1586 (1988).

3. Qualification and Examination of Medical Experts

This section surveys a variety of common evidentiary and discovery issues encountered in malpractice litigation—primarily, how litigants in medical malpractice cases prove or dispute the standard of care.

■ THOMPSON v. CARTER
518 So. 2d 609 (Miss. 1987)

PRATHER, Justice, for the court:
At issue in this appeal . . . [is] the admissibility of a nonphysician's expert testimony on the issue of a physician's standard of care with respect to the use and administration of pharmaceutical drugs.

In this medical malpractice action, Lynette Inez Thompson contended she developed Stevens Johnson Syndrome as a result of Dr. Robert Carter's negligent prescribing of the drug Bactrim. From a directed verdict in the circuit court of Harrison County, Thompson appeals, assigning as error . . . [the court's refusal] to admit the testimony of Michael P. Hughes, a pharmacologist and toxicologist, on the issues of liability and causation. . . .

Mr. Hughes testified that he had received a bachelor's degree from Millsaps College with major in chemistry and minor in biology and a master's degree in both Pharmacology and Toxicology. In the process of obtaining his degrees, he had taken five or six courses in Pharmacology and between eight and ten courses in Toxicology. After completing his graduate degree programs, Mr. Hughes became coordinator of the Regional Poison Control Center for the entire State of Mississippi. As coordinator for the Poison Control Center, which is located at the University of Mississippi Medical Center, Mr. Hughes was often consulted by physicians for suggested treatment of poisoning victims and other types of adverse reactions to various compounds or drugs. Mr. Hughes further testified he was on the teaching staff at the University of Mississippi Medical School and taught Pharmacology and Toxicology to both dental and medical students. Additionally Hughes had taken training to render emergency medical care as an "emergency medical technician."

Mr. Hughes testified that by virtue of his education and work experience, he was familiar with the drug Bactrim and its indications as well as its contraindications. Likewise, he was familiar with Stevens Johnson Syndrome and its causes.

The trial court found that Hughes was qualified to testify as an expert witness as to causation in the field of Pharmacology and Toxicology, but was not qualified to testify concerning the standard of care to which physicians are required to conform with respect to the use and administration of drugs. . . .

Appellant had no other expert witness to testify concerning causation or standard of care with respect to use and administration of drugs. A proffer of Mr. Hughes' testimony was offered which, if admitted, would have made a prima facie case. After the proffer, the trial court granted Carter's motion for directed verdict on the grounds that Thompson failed to establish the standard of care by an expert possessing a medical degree. . . .

The issue . . . is whether an expert witness, called to establish the standard of care in pharmaceutical litigation for physicians, must possess a medical degree. This court holds that he does not. What is necessary is that the witness possess medical knowledge, however obtained.

Generally, if scientific, technical, or other specialized knowledge will assist the trier of fact to understand the evidence or to determine a fact in issue, an expert witness may testify thereto in opinion form or otherwise. A witness may qualify as an expert based on his knowledge, skill, experience, training, education, or a combination thereof. Qualification as an expert does not necessarily rest upon the educational or professional degree a witness possesses. Simply put, before one may testify as an expert, that person must be shown to know a great deal regarding the subject of his testimony. As a pharmacologist/toxicologist, Hughes was an expert in the area in which his testimony was offered.

Other jurisdictions have held likewise. In Cornfeldt v. Tongen, 262 N.W.2d 684 (Minn. 1977), a chief nurse anesthetist was not allowed to provide expert testimony relative to the use of anesthesia because he was not licensed to practice medicine. The Minnesota Supreme Court held the nurse was competent to testify notwithstanding the lack of a medical degree if he otherwise had sufficient scientific and practical experience about the matter to which he would have testified. . . .

The instant record reflects that Michael P. Hughes, who taught medical students and advised and counseled physicians as to drug use and administration, through his skill, knowledge, training, and education, knew the standard of care to which physicians adhered when prescribing Bactrim. Therefore, this court holds that he was qualified to deliver expert testimony, notwithstanding his lack of a medical degree, on the issue of a physician's standard of care in the use and administration of this drug.

This is not to say that every pharmacologist or toxicologist is qualified to testify as an expert to establish the physicians' standard of care. Only if the witness possesses scientific, technical or specialized knowledge on a particular topic will he qualify as an expert on that topic. This witness qualified as an expert and should have been permitted to testify as to a physician's standard of care in issue here. . . .

[Four justices dissented.]

■ **TROWER v. JONES**
520 N.E.2d 297 (Ill. 1988)

CUNNINGHAM, Justice.

[Dr. Jones misdiagnosed plaintiff's abdominal pains as gastroenteritis, an inflammation of the bowel. When her symptoms failed to improve, another doctor diagnosed plaintiff as having pelvic inflammatory disease (p.i.d.), an infection of the fallopian tubes that can cause sterility. Plaintiff's left fallopian tube and ovary were removed, after which her symptoms subsided. Since her illness, she has been unable to conceive. Plaintiff brought a medical malpractice action against Dr. Jones.]

. . . Plaintiffs called Dr. James K. Martins as their expert witness. His testimony during direct examination included a discussion of his education, his experience as a physician, and other credentials. He also explained how he became involved in this case. He stated that he was a "fellow" of the American Board of Medical Legal Consultants (Board) and that the Board had asked him to review the case. He described the Board as "a group of medical legal consultants that attempt to determine whether lack of standard of care, injuries, or malpractice has occurred in a variety of cases." He explained that when the Board sends him a medical file to review, the file comes with a check, the amount of which depends upon how voluminous the file is.

On cross-examination, Dr. Martins acknowledged that the Board is a for-profit organization and that its purpose is to review cases involving suspected malpractice and to furnish expert testimony. Dr. Martins further acknowledged that most of the Board's cases are obtained through attorneys. He further stated that 80 percent of his professional time is devoted to work for the Board. He stated that since 1983, when he began working for the Board, he had reviewed over 700 cases for the Board, had given depositions in approximately 60 of those cases and had given expert trial testimony in approximately 30 of those cases. He acknowledged that these trials had encompassed over a dozen states throughout the country, and had involved matters as diverse as alleged inadequate neurological examination, osteomyelitis (an infection in bone), septicemia following a cortisone injection, and alleged failure to diagnose a brain tumor. Over objection, he was asked the following question regarding the approximately 30 trials in which he has given expert testimony: "All of these cases have been for plaintiffs, or that is people suing doctors?" Dr. Martins responded, "Of the majority, yes." . . .

Many years ago this court indicated . . . that it was error (though harmless) to permit a plaintiff (injured in a collision with a train) to ask a defendant's expert medical witness how many times he had testified on behalf of the various streetcar lines of Chicago. Several early decisions of this court also arguably indicate that an expert should not be questioned regarding compensation received for testifying in cases unrelated to the parties or their attorneys. . . .

Since these cited Illinois cases were decided many years ago, both the difficulty and paramount importance of thorough, comprehensive cross-examination of experts have increased markedly. Cross-examination has been made more difficult in part by the increased latitude given experts when rendering their opinions. For example, . . . experts can now render opinions without prior disclosure of the underlying facts or data upon which those opinions are based. Further, experts can now render opinions based upon certain inadmissible evidence (if such evidence is reasonably relied upon by experts in the field in forming opinions upon the subject). Although we view this expansion as prudent, we do recognize the added burden which these changes place upon a party during cross-examination in attempting to discredit his opponent's expert, and we also recognize that these changes heighten the importance of such cross-examination. Adding to the importance of effective cross-examination is the proliferation of expert "locator" services which, as a practical matter, can help the litigants of either side of most any case find an expert who will help advocate the desired position. As this case helps illustrate, many experts today spend so much of their time testifying throughout the country that they might be deemed not only experts in their field but also experts in the art of being a persuasive witness and in the art of handling cross-examination. As was stated in Kemeny v. Skorch, 159 N.E.2d 489 (Ill. App. 1959), little has the nonlitigating public (including the jury) realized "the true rhetorical masterpieces that came from the lips of medical experts."

The combined effect of both the greater latitude given expert witnesses during direct examination and the expertise of many expert witnesses as expert witnesses is aptly set forth by Professor Michael H. Graham as follows:

> In combating testimony of the expert witness, opposing counsel must rely upon his skill in probing at weaknesses in the basis and reasoning of the witness whether or not disclosed upon direct, without letting the witness reinforce his direct testimony in the process. He must do this with an expert witness more familiar with the subject matter. Of course, counsel also has available the use of learned treatises to assist him in fencing with the witness. Unfortunately fencing with the witness is the impression the cross-examination of an expert witness often leaves with the jury, an impression trial counsel would prefer to avoid. The difficulty in conducting a successful destructive cross-examination is compounded by the growing number of experts whose livelihood is dependent in large part upon the litigation process. Such experts with their vast amount of litigation experience become exceptionally proficient in the art of expert witness advocacy. Graham, Impeaching the Professional Expert Witness by Showing of Financial Interest, 53 Ind. L.J. 35, 40 (1977).

We have long recognized that the principal safeguard against errant expert testimony is the opportunity of opposing counsel to cross-examine, which includes the opportunity to probe bias, partisanship or financial interest. . . . We believe that the questions regarding Dr. Martins' income which are at issue here were permissible. . . . [W]e reach our decision based on an appreciation of the fact that the financial advantage which accrues to an expert witness in a particular case can extend beyond the remuneration he receives for testifying in that case. A favorable verdict may well help him establish a "track record" which, to a professional witness, can be all-important in determining not only the frequency with which he is asked to testify but also the price which he can demand for such testimony. We find pertinent the following commentary from a recent annotation:

> That an expert in a particular field may be in effect a "professional witness" in lawsuits, rather than being more or less exclusively a practitioner whose employment in a lawsuit as a witness is merely incidental to his or her profession, is a matter which is likely to bear on the credibility of that expert, since a significant portion of the expert's livelihood may thus depend on his or her desirability as a favorable and convincing witness, thus possibly leading to a temptation for the witness to color findings and testimony to suit the needs of the proponent party, rather than to evaluate and present the subject matter of the testimony with complete impartiality. 39 A.L.R.4th 742, 746 (1985).

We thus find that it was proper to inquire how much Dr. Martins was earning annually from services relating to rendering expert testimony, and we find no impropriety in inquiring into such income for the two years immediately preceding trial. . . . We also find that the circuit court properly permitted counsel to inquire, on cross-examination, as to the frequency with which Dr. Martins testifies for plaintiffs. . . . Obviously, the fact that a physician testifies only for one category does not necessarily mean that his testimony is not credible. For example, a physician may adopt a policy of testifying only on behalf of other physicians in order to avoid the resentment among his colleagues which could arise from testifying on behalf of individuals suing physicians. This would not mean that he testifies on behalf of doctors who he believes were actually negligent, but only that (for personal reasons) he prefers not to testify for plaintiffs regardless of the merits of their case. . . . There is no sufficient reason why this information cannot be weighed and evaluated by the jury along with all of the other evidence pertaining to the credibility of an expert witness. . . .

Notes: Qualification and Impeachment of Experts

1. *The Practice Dimension*. Observe that the requirements for qualifying an expert to testify on the standard of care are distinct from those for testifying about causation or extent of injuries. The former is our primary focus here. On the latter, see sections D.1 and E.

As the omitted dissent in Thompson v. Carter reveals, the American courts are split on the issue of the competency of nonphysicians to testify on the standards of patient care required of medical practitioners. In general accord with *Thompson*, see Pratt v. Stein, 444 A.2d 674 (Pa. Super. Ct. 1982) (pharmacologist permitted to testify on proper use of drugs); Marshall v. Medical Assoc. of Rhode Island, 677 A.2d 425 (R.I. 1996) (pediatrician permitted to testify about emergency physician's treatment of animal bite wound). An example of the more restrictive viewpoint is found in Bell v. Hart, 516 So. 2d 562 (Ala. 1987), which, in a similar case, refused to admit expert opinions from a pharmacist and a toxicologist. See also Boehm v. Mayo Clinic Rochester, 690 N.W.2d 721 (Minn. 2005) (nurse practitioner lacked sufficient training or practical experience to testify about the standard of care for restraining the head movement of a patient after surgery by a thoracic surgeon). Similar objections can be lodged against physicians as well. See, e.g., Williams v. Wadsworth, 503 N.W.2d 120 (Minn. 1993) (cardiologist who had not performed lymphangiogram in ten years could not testify against endocrinologist); Chase v. Mary Hitchcock Memorial Hospital, 668 A.2d 50 (N.H. 1995) (general practitioner who did not usually handle premature deliveries could not testify against obstetrician). However, most courts do not require physician experts to practice in precisely the same specialty as the defendant. It is also curious to observe how courts react when physicians are called to testify against nonphysicians. Again, decisions are split. Paris v. Kreitz, 331 S.E.2d 234 (N.C. Ct. App. 1985) (physician may testify against nurse, but not against physician's assistant); Sullivan v. Edward Hospital, 806 N.E.2d 645 (Ill. 2004) (physician may not testify about the standard of care for nurses in restraining a patient from falling out of bed); McMillan v. Durant, 439 S.E.2d 829 (S.C. 1993) (neurosurgeon who teaches in nursing courses can testify against nurses). See generally Note, Competency of Medical Expert Witnesses: Standards and Qualifications, 24 Creighton L. Rev. 1359 (1991).

2. *The Geographic Dimension.* Another dimension of an expert's qualification in addition to specialty and licensure is geographic location of practice. Where the jurisdiction follows a local or state-wide standard of care, is it necessary for the expert to actually live and practice in that location? Generally, no; courts allow experts to assert knowledge of local practices through professional contacts in addition to actual practice. In Idaho, this has been elevated to a high art form in about a half dozen state Supreme Court cases that clarify precisely what extent of local inquiry will suffice for properly educating an out-of-area expert. See Rhodenhouse v. Stutts, 868 P.2d 1224 (Idaho 1994) (expert's bare statement in affidavit that he is familiar with local practice does not suffice; must show he talked with a local specialist; not sufficient merely to review medical records and depositions of other doctors); Gubler v. Boe, 815 P.2d 1034 (Idaho 1991) (plaintiff must show that the local doctors his expert consulted were practicing in the same town the year the treatment was rendered). Another technique for qualifying out-of-state experts is for them to assert that national standards apply equally in every location. See, e.g., Henning v. Thomas, 366 S.E.2d 109 (Va. 1988). But see Falcon v. Cheung, 848 P.2d 1050 (Mont. 1993) (university physician may not testify to rural standard of care if he has never practiced in that setting).

3. *Impeaching Hired Guns.* Trower v. Jones adopts the prevailing modern approach to impeaching experts as "hired guns." See also Wilson v. Stilwell, 309 N.W.2d 898 (Mich. 1981); Henning v. Thomas, supra. Older cases sometimes frequently disallowed this type of impeachment as irrelevant or prejudicial. Some modern courts still tend to restrict insinuations of an "opinion for sale" to clarify the status of "professional experts." For instance, one court ordered a new trial where plaintiff's counsel unfairly characterized the hospital's expert as a " 'hired' gun who peddles his expertise randomly" and where plaintiff's counsel introduced extensive evidence about all of the defense expert's various sources of income, including fees from patient care and from consulting unrelated to malpractice

litigation. The court reasoned that "there must be, and is, a point beyond which inquiry is/will be held to be prejudicial, too intrusive and only serving to divert the case into collateral matters." Mohn v. Hahnemann Medical College, 515 A.2d 920-923 (Pa. Super. Ct. 1986). For a survey of legal and regulatory actions that can be taken to reprimand or control medical experts, see Gary N. McAbee, Improper Expert Medical Testimony: Existing and Proposed Mechanisms of Oversight, 19 J. Leg. Med. 257 (1998); Fred L. Cohen, The Expert Medical Witness in Legal Perspective, 25 J. Leg. Med. 185 (2004). See also Austin v. American Ass'n of Neurological Surgeons, 253 F.3d 967 (7th Cir. 2001) (expert witness had no right to challenge his suspension from a professional medical association for giving "irresponsible" testimony). For a general analysis and critique, with proposals for reform, see Jody Menon, Adversarial Medical and Scientific Testimony and Lay Jurors, 21 Am. J.L. & Med. 282 (1995).

4. *Statutory Reforms.* A number of states have cracked down on the perceived abuses of hired-gun, out-of-state, and inexperienced experts by enacting statutes that set more demanding qualifications. Common examples include requiring the expert (1) to reside in or near the state; (2) to have been in active practice in recent years (which excludes full-time teachers and researchers as well as "consultants"); (3) to practice in the same or overlapping specialty, or to have performed the same type of procedure, in recent years; and/or (4) to be licensed in the same professional category. These statutes often contain "escape valves" that give trial courts limited discretionary authority to waive these requirements for just cause. See Johnson v. Price, 743 So. 2d 436 (Ala. 1999) (refusing to allow a board-certified general surgeon to testify against an osteopath with certification from the American Osteopathic Board of Surgery, relating to a surgical mistake); Rodgers v. Adams, 657 So. 2d 838 (Ala. 1995) (dental specialist was "similarly situated" to general dentist because he had trained in general dentistry before specializing); Miranda v. National Emergency Servs., Inc., 41 Cal. Rptr. 2d 593 (Ct. App. 1995) ("on call" emergency physician not sufficiently qualified to meet statutory requirements for testifying against full-time emergency physician); Sutphin v. Platt, 720 S.W.2d 455 (Tenn. 1986) (upholding constitutionality of residency rule because escape clause avoided hardship).

■ DAUBERT v. MERRELL DOW PHARMACEUTICALS, INC.
509 U.S. 579 (1993)

Justice BLACKMUN delivered the opinion of the Court.

In this case we are called upon to determine the standard for admitting expert scientific testimony in a federal trial.

Petitioners Jason Daubert and Eric Schuller are minor children born with serious birth defects. They and their parents sued respondent in California state court, alleging that the birth defects had been caused by the mothers' ingestion of Bendectin, a prescription anti-nausea drug marketed by respondent. Respondent removed the suits to federal court on diversity grounds.

After extensive discovery, respondent moved for summary judgment, contending that Bendectin does not cause birth defects in humans and that petitioners would be unable to come forward with any admissible evidence that it does. In support of its motion, respondent submitted an affidavit of Steven H. Lamm, physician and epidemiologist, who is a well-credentialed expert on the risks from exposure to various chemical substances. Doctor Lamm stated that he had reviewed all the literature on Bendectin and human birth defects — more than 30 published studies involving over 130,000 patients. No study had found Bendectin to be a human teratogen (i.e., a substance capable of causing malformations in fetuses). On the basis of this review, Doctor Lamm concluded that maternal use of Bendectin during the first trimester of pregnancy has not been shown to be a risk factor for human birth defects.

Petitioners did not (and do not) contest this characterization of the published record regarding Bendectin. Instead, they responded to respondent's motion with the testimony of eight experts of their own, each of whom also possessed impressive credentials. These experts had concluded that Bendectin can cause birth defects. Their conclusions were based upon "in vitro" (test tube) and "in vivo" (live) animal studies that found a link between Bendectin and malformations; pharmacological studies of the chemical structure of Bendectin that purported to show similarities between the structure of the drug and that of other substances known to cause birth defects; and the "reanalysis" of previously published epidemiological (human statistical) studies.

The District Court granted respondent's motion for summary judgment. The court stated that scientific evidence is admissible only if the principle upon which it is based is "sufficiently established to have general acceptance in the field to which it belongs." The court concluded that petitioners' evidence did not meet this standard. Given the vast body of epidemiological data concerning Bendectin, the court held, expert opinion which is not based on epidemiological evidence is not admissible to establish causation. Thus, the animal-cell studies, live-animal studies, and chemical-structure analyses on which petitioners had relied could not raise by themselves a reasonably disputable jury issue regarding causation. Petitioners' epidemiological analyses, based as they were on recalculations of data in previously published studies that had found no causal link between the drug and birth defects, were ruled to be inadmissible because they had not been published or subjected to peer review.

The United States Court of Appeals for the Ninth Circuit affirmed. Citing Frye v. United States, 54 App.D.C. 46, 47, 293 F. 1013, 1014 (1923), the court stated that expert opinion based on a scientific technique is inadmissible unless the technique is "generally accepted" as reliable in the relevant scientific community. . . . The court emphasized that other Courts of Appeals considering the risks of Bendectin had refused to admit reanalyses of epidemiological studies that had been neither published nor subjected to peer review. . . .

In the 70 years since its formulation in the *Frye* case, the "general acceptance" test has been the dominant standard for determining the admissibility of novel scientific evidence at trial. Although under increasing attack of late, the rule continues to be followed by a majority of courts, including the Ninth Circuit.

The *Frye* test has its origin in a short and citation-free 1923 decision concerning the admissibility of evidence derived from a systolic blood pressure deception test, a crude precursor to the polygraph machine. In what has become a famous (perhaps infamous) passage, the then Court of Appeals for the District of Columbia described the device and its operation and declared:

Just when a scientific principle or discovery crosses the line between the experimental and demonstrable stages is difficult to define. Somewhere in this twilight zone the evidential force of the principle must be recognized, and while courts will go a long way in admitting expert testimony deduced from a well-recognized scientific principle or discovery, the thing from which the deduction is made must be sufficiently established to have gained general acceptance in the particular field in which it belongs. Because the deception test had "not yet gained such standing and scientific recognition among physiological and psychological authorities as would justify the courts in admitting expert testimony deduced from the discovery, development, and experiments thus far made," evidence of its results was ruled inadmissible.

The merits of the *Frye* test have been much debated, and scholarship on its proper scope and application is legion. See, e.g., Green, Expert Witnesses and Sufficiency of Evidence in Toxic Substances Litigation: The Legacy of Agent Orange and Bendectin Litigation, 86 Nw.U.L.Rev. 643 (1992) (hereinafter Green); Black, A Unified Theory of Scientific Evidence, 56 Ford.L.Rev. 595 (1988); Imwinkelried, The "Bases" of Expert Testimony: The Syllogistic Structure of Scientific Testimony, 67 N.C.L.Rev. 1 (1988); Gianelli, The Admissibility of Novel Scientific Evidence: Frye v. United States, A Half-Century Later, 80 Colum. L.Rev. 1197 (1980). Petitioners' primary attack, however, is not on the content but on the continuing authority of the rule. They contend that the *Frye* test was superseded by the adoption of the Federal Rules of Evidence. We agree. . . . Rule 702, governing expert testimony, provides:

> If scientific, technical, or other specialized knowledge will assist the trier of fact to understand the evidence or to determine a fact in issue, a witness qualified as an expert by knowledge, skill, experience, training, or education, may testify thereto in the form of an opinion or otherwise. Nothing in the text of this Rule establishes "general acceptance" as an absolute prerequisite to admissibility. . . . [A] rigid "general acceptance" requirement would be at odds with the "liberal thrust" of the Federal Rules and their "general approach of relaxing the traditional barriers to 'opinion' testimony." Beech Aircraft Corp. v. Rainey, 488 U.S., at 169, 109 S.Ct., at 450 (citing Rules 701 to 705). . . .

That the *Frye* test was displaced by the Rules of Evidence does not mean, however, that the Rules themselves place no limits on the admissibility of purportedly scientific evidence. . . . The adjective "scientific" implies a grounding in the methods and procedures of science. Similarly, the word "knowledge" connotes more than subjective belief or unsupported speculation. . . . Of course, it would be unreasonable to conclude that the subject of scientific testimony must be "known" to a certainty; arguably, there are no certainties in science. But, in order to qualify as "scientific knowledge," an inference or assertion must be derived by the scientific method. . . .

Rule 702 further requires that the evidence or testimony "assist the trier of fact to understand the evidence or to determine a fact in issue." This condition goes primarily to relevance. . . . See United States v. Downing, 753 F.2d 1224, 1242 (CA3 1985) ("An additional consideration under Rule 702—and another aspect of relevancy—is whether expert testimony proffered in the case is sufficiently tied to the facts of the case that it will aid the jury in resolving a factual dispute"). This consideration has been aptly described by Judge Becker as one of "fit." "Fit" is not always obvious, and scientific validity for one purpose is not necessarily scientific validity for other, unrelated purposes. . . .

That these requirements are embodied in Rule 702 is not surprising. Unlike an ordinary witness, see Rule 701, an expert is permitted wide latitude to offer opinions, including those that are not based on first-hand knowledge or observation. Presumably, this relaxation of the usual requirement of first-hand knowledge — a rule which represents "a 'most pervasive manifestation' of the common law insistence upon 'the most reliable sources of information,'" Advisory Committee's Notes on Fed.Rule Evid. 602 — is premised on an assumption that the expert's opinion will have a reliable basis in the knowledge and experience of his discipline.

Faced with a proffer of expert scientific testimony, then, the trial judge must determine at the outset whether the expert is proposing to testify to (1) scientific knowledge that (2) will assist the trier of fact to understand or determine a fact in issue. This entails a preliminary assessment of whether the reasoning or methodology underlying the testimony is scientifically valid and of whether that reasoning or methodology properly can be applied to the facts in issue. We are confident that federal judges possess the capacity to undertake this review. Many factors will bear on the inquiry, and we do not presume to set out a definitive checklist or test. But some general observations are appropriate.

Ordinarily, a key question to be answered in determining whether a theory or technique is scientific knowledge that will assist the trier of fact will be whether it can be (and has been) tested. . . . K. Popper, Conjectures and Refutations: The Growth of Scientific Knowledge 37 (5th ed. 1989) ("[T]he criterion of the scientific status of a theory is its falsifiability, or refutability, or testability").

Another pertinent consideration is whether the theory or technique has been subjected to peer review and publication. Publication (which is but one element of peer review) is not a sine qua non of admissibility; it does not necessarily correlate with reliability, and in some instances well-grounded but innovative theories will not have been published. Some propositions, moreover, are too particular, too new, or of too limited interest to be published. But submission to the scrutiny of the scientific community is a component of "good science," in part because it increases the likelihood that substantive flaws in methodology will be detected. The fact of publication (or lack thereof) in a peer-reviewed journal thus will be a relevant, though not dispositive, consideration in assessing the scientific validity of a particular technique or methodology on which an opinion is premised.

Additionally, in the case of a particular scientific technique, the court ordinarily should consider the known or potential rate of error, see, e.g., United States v. Smith, 869 F.2d 348 (7th Cir. 1989) (surveying studies of the error rate of spectrographic voice identification technique), and the existence and mainte-nance of standards controlling the technique's operation.

Finally, "general acceptance" can yet have a bearing on the inquiry. . . . Widespread acceptance can be an important factor in ruling particular evidence admissible, and a known technique that has been able to attract only minimal support within the community may properly be viewed with skepticism.

The inquiry envisioned by Rule 702 is, we emphasize, a flexible one. Its overarching subject is the scientific validity — and thus the evidentiary relevance and reliability — of the principles that underlie a proposed submission. The focus, of course, must be solely on principles and methodology, not on the conclusions that they generate.

Throughout, a judge assessing a proffer of expert scientific testimony under Rule 702 should also be mindful of other applicable rules. Rule 703 provides that expert opinions based on otherwise inadmissible hearsay are to be admitted only if the facts or data are "of a type reasonably relied upon by experts in the particular field in forming opinions or inferences upon the subject." Rule 706 allows the court at its discretion to procure the assistance of an expert of its own choosing. Finally, Rule 403 permits the exclusion of relevant evidence "if its probative value is substantially outweighed by the danger of unfair prejudice, confusion of the issues, or misleading the jury. . . ." Judge Weinstein has explained: "Expert evidence can be both powerful and quite misleading because of the difficulty in evaluating it. Because of this risk, the judge in weighing possible prejudice against probative force under Rule 403 of the present rules exercises more control over experts than over lay witnesses." Weinstein, 138 F.R.D., at 632.

. . . Vigorous cross-examination, presentation of contrary evidence, and careful instruction on the burden of proof are the traditional and appropriate means of attacking shaky but admissible evidence. See Rock v. Arkansas, 483 U.S. 44, 61, 107 S.Ct. 2704, 2714, 97 L.Ed.2d 37 (1987). Additionally, in the event the trial court concludes that the scintilla of evidence presented supporting a position is insufficient to allow a reasonable juror to conclude that the position more likely than not is true, the court remains free to direct a judgment, and likewise to grant summary judgment. Cf., e.g., Turpin v. Merrell Dow Pharmaceuticals, Inc., 959 F.2d 1349 (CA6) (holding that scientific evidence that provided foundation for expert testimony [about Bendectin], viewed in the light most favorable to plaintiffs, was not sufficient to allow a jury to find it more probable than not that defendant caused plaintiff's injury). These conventional devices, rather than wholesale exclusion under an uncompromising "general acceptance" test, are the appropriate safeguards where the basis of scientific testimony meets the standards of Rule 702. . . .

Accordingly, the judgment of the Court of Appeals is vacated and the case is remanded for further proceedings consistent with this opinion.

Notes: Forensic Medicine and Epidemiological Evidence

1. *Forensic Science.* Earlier editions of this casebook devoted hundreds of pages to issues of medical proof in civil and criminal litigation generally. Medical and similar scientific expertise is critical in areas as diverse as criminal law, paternity disputes, and competency hearings. Lawyers in these cases draw from countless scientific disciplines and specific techniques such as autopsies, genetics and DNA fingerprinting, polygraphs, and hypnosis-induced memory. See generally, D.H. Kaye, Science in Evidence (1997); David Faigman et al., Modern Scientific Evidence (1997); David Faigman et al., Science in the Law: Forensic

Science Issues (2002); Federal Judicial Center, Reference Manual on Scientific Evidence (1994); Forensic Science (G. Davies ed. 2d ed. 1986). Earlier in the twentieth century, issues like these dominated the field of law and medicine, which was then known as "medical jurisprudence." See James C. Mohr, Doctors and the Law: Medical Jurisprudence in Nineteenth-Century America (1993). Today, these topics are covered in more depth in specialized courses on advanced evidence law, or on law and science more generally.

2. *The relevance of* Daubert. The relevance of *Daubert*, a products liability case against a drug manufacturer, to medical malpractice cases against doctors may not be readily apparent. This case appears in these materials for two main reasons: (1) law and medicine has strong historical roots in the field of forensic science; and (2) epidemiological and statistical evidence of the sort at issue in *Daubert* is increasingly important in medical and other litigation. *Daubert* has generated extensive debate over the range of experts and topics of testimony to which it applies. Rule 702 allows expert testimony on an unlimited range of technical or specialized topics; scientific knowledge is only one subset. For a time, courts and commentators thought *Daubert* might be limited to only scientific theories or techniques. However, in Kumho Tire Co. v. Carmichael, 526 U.S. 137 (1999), the Court clarified that *Daubert* also applies to "technical or other specialized knowledge," and so it sustained a trial court's decision to exclude as unreliable the proffered testimony of an expert on tire failure, in a case claiming that a manufacturing defect caused a tire to blow out. Similarly, it seems clear that *Daubert* factors can be used to evaluate economic testimony going to damages calculations in medical malpractice cases (that is, the extent and measure of injuries) and medical expertise on causation issues (whether the injuries resulted from the physician's error or would have happened anyway). See Note, Navigating Uncertainty: Gatekeeping in the Absence of Hard Science, 113 Harv. L. Rev. 1467 (2000). See generally, D.H. Kaye, The Dynamics of *Daubert*: Methodology, Conclusions, and Fit in Statistical and Econometric Studies, 87 Va. L. Rev. 1934 (2001). Consider, for instance, that in the Bendectin controversy, plaintiffs had one physician, Dr. Palmer, who was willing to state unequivocally that the drug caused the plaintiff's defects. He stated:

> It is my opinion . . . that [animal in vivo and in vitro studies, and epidemiological and other human data] shows that Bendectin and specifically its component, doxylamine succinate, has teratogenic properties. . . . I have also examined the medical records pertaining to Brandy Turpin and it is my opinion . . . that Bendectin did cause the limb defects from which she suffers.

Nevertheless, the 9th Circuit in *Daubert* agreed with the 6th Circuit in *Turpin* (which the Supreme Court cites favorably) in concluding that this failed to create a jury issue: "This testimony is [no]thing more than a personal belief or opinion. . . . Dr. Palmer does not testify on the basis of the collective view of his scientific discipline, nor does he take issue with his peers and explain the grounds for his differences. Indeed, no understandable scientific basis is stated. Personal opinion, not science, is testifying here." 959 F.2d 1349.

As discussed earlier, however, just this type of qualitative opinion testimony is exactly what malpractice litigants almost always rely on. More rigorous quantitative proof is seldom available because the medical mistake at issue is rarely common and widespread enough to be subjected to the large epidemiological studies that the courts favor in suits against pharmaceutical companies. Presumably, more is demanded in the drug cases because better evidence is available. Is this a correct application of *Daubert*, or should scientific evidence that is admissible in any case be admitted in every case (assuming it is equally relevant to a fact in issue)? Is weak scientific evidence "prejudicial" just because a jury might use it to reject stronger evidence? See generally Jerome P. Kassierer & Joe S. Cecil, Inconsistency in Evidentiary Standards for Medical Testimony, 288 New Eng. J. Med. 1392 (2002).

Much more controversial is whether *Daubert* might be used to block expert testimony on the medical standard of care. Although this requires a certain type of scientific or technical expertise, it relates to standards of professional practice and clinical judgment, not the use of a scientific method to arrive at conclusions about facts in the case. See, e.g., Reese v. Stroh, 907 P.2d 282 (Wash. 1995).

3. *Junk Science. Daubert* was decided after several years of controversy over whether judges were allowing too much "junk science" to prevail in court. The accusation is frequently made that a paid expert can always be found to testify on both sides of any proposition. See, e.g., Peter W. Huber, Galileo's Revenge: Junk Science in the Courtroom (1991). The Bendectin drug is often cited as a leading example of how the unjustified threat of liability can cause a beneficial medical product to be pulled from the market even though virtually the entire scientific community believes it is safe.

One way to conceive of the difference between *Frye* and *Daubert* is that *Frye* deferred to collective opinion of the scientific community, whereas *Daubert* asks judges themselves to determine what constitutes "good science," employing factors such as those mentioned in the opinion. Are judges up to this task? How does this compare with how the medical standard of care is determined?

Some commentators, harshly critical of the way the adversarial system distorts scientific truth, call for more sweeping reforms. One possibility is greater use of neutral, court-appointed experts or special masters, which is standard practice in Europe and was long ago the norm in the United States. In the United States, this practice is still allowed by the federal rules but is infrequently done. Another potential reform is to create specialized tribunals (often called "science courts") composed of adjudicators who themselves possess scientific expertise. For an introduction to these proposals, see James Martin, The Proposed "Science Court," 75 Mich. L. Rev. 1058 (1977); Samuel Gross, Expert Evidence, 1991 Wis. L. Rev. 1113 (1991); Symposium, Expert Evidence, 16 Law & Human Behav. 253-379 (1992); K. Kreiling, Managing Expert Evidence: An Overview, 36 Jurimetrics J. 121 (1996); Margaret Farrell, Coping with Scientific Evidence: The Use of Special Masters, 43 Emory L. J. 927 (1994).

4. Daubert's *Impact*. Initially, it was thought that *Daubert* made it easier for "junk science" to be introduced than was the case under the *Frye* rule. Increasingly, it appears, however, that *Daubert* may have had just the opposite effect. Bert Black, Francisco J. Ayala, and Carol Saffran-Brinks, Science and the Law in the Wake of *Daubert*: A New Search for Scientific Knowledge, 72 Tex. L. Rev. 715, 722 (1994). On remand, the 9th Circuit reaffirmed its prior opinion. It reasoned: (1) the plaintiffs' experts had developed their positions specifically in response to litigation and therefore deserved heightened skepticism; (2) no

independent scientists agreed with them; and (3) the evidence flunked *Daubert*'s "fit" test because it showed at most only an increased risk, not actual causation of birth defects for any of these particular plaintiffs. Daubert v. Merrell Dow Pharmaceuticals, 43 F.3d 1311. Does this violate the Supreme Court's command not to confuse the underlying methods with the scientists' conclusions? In a subsequent decision, the Court affirmed a trial judge's decision to exclude opinion testimony from established scientists based on animal studies and epidemiological evidence that the plaintiff's lung cancer was caused by his exposure to PCBs. The Court held that it was not an abuse of discretion for the judge to conclude that "there [was] simply too great an analytical gap between the data and the opinion proffered." General Electric Co. v. Joiner, 118 S. Ct. 512 (1997). For other courts that excluded apparently conventional scientific evidence applying the *Daubert* standards, see Chikovsky v. Ortho Pharmaceutical Corp., 832 F.Supp. 341 (S.D. Fla. 1993) (obstetrician not allowed to testify that Retin-A causes birth defects); Wade-Greaux v. Whitehall Lab., 874 F.Supp. 1441 (D.V.I. 1994) (animal studies not sufficient to show nasal decongestant caused birth defects).

5. *State Law.* Recognize that *Daubert* states only federal law. Prior to *Daubert*, the majority of states adhered to the *Frye* rule, and following *Daubert*, of the handful that have reconsidered the issue, almost half have reaffirmed *Frye*. Joseph R. Meaney, From *Frye* to *Daubert*: Is a Pattern Unfolding?, 35 Jurimetrics 191 (1995) ("*Frye* supporters can send get well cards, but the funeral has been postponed."). For general commentary and critique on *Daubert* and the state of the law, see Symposium, Translating Science into Law: Lessons from Doctors, Judges, and Lawyers about the Use of Medical Evidence in the Courtroom, 36 New Eng. L. Rev. 573 (2002); Symposium, Scientific Evidence after the Death of *Frye*, 15 Cardozo L. Rev. 1745 (1994); Lee Loevinger, Science as Evidence, 35 Jurimetrics J. 153 (1995); Developments, Confronting the New Challenges of Scientific Evidence, 108 Harv. L. Rev. 14881 (1995); P. Giannelli & E. Imwinkelried, Scientific Evidence (1986). For discussion prior to *Daubert*, see the sources cited in the opinion.

6. *Epidemiological Evidence.* Focusing on the kind of epidemiological evidence that prevailed in the Bendectin case, consider situations where that evidence favors the plaintiff. How strong a statistical association must be shown before causation is actually proven? If the study is well designed, it will control for "confounding factors" that might offer an innocent explanation for the observed harm. A good study also uses an observation technique that attempts to sample objectively a random or representative selection from the population at large. Even when these criteria for sound methodology are met, a difficulty arises from using probability figures for a large number of cases to decide what happened in the particular case under litigation. A pressing example of this dilemma comes from the current litigation over silicone breast implants. The largest study to date (400,000 respondents and 10,000 patients), conducted at Harvard, shows a 24 percent increased risk of "connective tissue disease," amounting to 1 in 3000 women each year attributable to the implants. The authors interpreted this study as ruling out any "large hazard," but plaintiffs' attorneys hailed it as confirming their previously-discredited allegations. Numerous other physicians are willing to testify that they are convinced that implants cause these illnesses because their patients often improve markedly when the implants are removed. N.Y. Times,

Feb. 28, 1996, at A14. Is this the type of evidence that should go to the jury? On remand, the 9th Circuit in *Daubert* agreed with a number of other courts that, under a civil standard (preponderance of the evidence), plaintiffs must show an increased risk of at least 200 percent in order to create a jury issue on causation, because only then can it be said with scientific certainty that the hazardous agent "more likely than not" caused the injury compared with all other possible causes. In medical malpractice cases, many of these difficulties over statistical uncertainty are avoided using the "loss of chance" theory, which allows partial recovery even when causation is less likely than not. Also, contrast the different levels of proof necessary to justify regulation as opposed to compensation in tort. Even a slight and uncertain elevated risk may be sufficient to ban or regulate a carcinogen, environmental hazard, or medical drug. See generally Lucian Leape, Quantitative Risk Assessment in Regulation of Environmental Carcinogens, 4 Harv. Envtl. L. Rev. 86 (1980); Public Citizen v. Young, 831 F.2d 1108 (1987).

For additional commentary on these and other aspects of statistical proof and jury competence, see The Evolving Role of Statistical Assessments as Evidence in the Courts (Feinberg ed. 1989); Stephen E. Feinberg et al., Understanding and Evaluating Statistical Evidence in Litigation, 36 Jurimetrics J. 27 (1995); Daniel Shaviro, Statistical-Probability Evidence and the Appearance of Justice, 103 Harv. L. Rev. 530 (1989); Craig R. Callen, Adjudication and the Appearance of Statistical Evidence, 65 Tul. L. Rev. 457 (1991); Symposium, Decision and Inference in Litigation, 13 Cardozo L. Rev. 253-1079 (1991); M. Dore, A Commentary on the Use of Epidemiological Evidence in Demonstrating Cause-in-Fact, 7 Harv. Envtl. L. Rev. 429 (1983); Bert Black & David Lilienfeld, Epidemiological Proof in Toxic Tort Litigation, 52 Ford L. Rev. 732 (1984); T. Brennan, Causal Chains and Statistical Links: The Role of Scientific Uncertainty in Hazardous Substance Litigation, 73 Cornell L. Rev. 469 (1988); Harold Ginzburg, Use and Misuse of Epidemiological Data in the Courtroom: Defining the Limits of Inferential and Particularistic Evidence in Mass Tort Litigation, 12 Am. J.L. & Med. 423 (1986); Steve Gold, Causation in Toxic Torts: Burdens of Proof, Standards of Persuasion, and Statistical Evidence, 96 Yale L.J. 376 (1986); Scott Brewer, Scientific Expert Testimony and Intellectual Due Process, 107 Yale L. J. 1535 (1998); Lars Noah, Sanctifying Scientific Peer Review: Publication as a Proxy for Regulatory Decisionmaking, 59 U. Pitt. L. Rev. 677 (1998).

■ TRIAL TACTICS AND METHODS*
Robert E. Keeton**
1973

Plaintiff Peter Park alleges that Defendant David Dell, an anesthesiologist, negligently injected liquid anaesthesia into tissues of plaintiff's arm rather than into the vein, causing damage to nerves and producing disability. At trial, a professor of neurology, who did not treat plaintiff and does not have personal

---

*Adapted from materials developed by the Instructors in Trial Practice at Harvard Law School. Reprinted with permission.

**Formerly Professor at Harvard Law School and subsequently a trial court judge.

knowledge of the relevant medical history, is called as an expert witness for the plaintiff. [The following demonstrates how] hypothetical questions [might] be framed as to the cause of plaintiff's disability and as to whether the defendant's conduct failed to measure up to professional standards:

Doctor, as the basis for my next question, please assume the following as facts:

(1) Peter Park, on January 6, 19X3, went to the Dental Clinic of Ames Memorial Hospital for an operation to be conducted by Dr. John Rogers, an oral surgeon, the operation having been scheduled to treat a serious infection of Peter Park's gums, which had been diagnosed by Dr. Rogers as advanced gingivitis;

(2) Defendant, Dr. David Dell, was the attending anesthesiologist at that operation;

(3) Defendant, Dr. Dell, began to anesthetize Peter Park for the operation by an injection of a liquid anesthesia, called Brevitol, into Peter Park's left arm;

(4) The first injection produced no effect of drowsiness; also, immediately after that injection, Peter Park complained of severe pain in the arm and requested that the proposed operation not be done and that he be released;

(5) Defendant, Dr. David Dell, with the assistance of others, restrained Peter Park forcefully, and, without checking again to be sure the needle was properly seated, so as to cause the injection to go into the vein where it was supposed to go, Dr. Dell injected additional liquid anaesthesia, called Brevitol, into plaintiff's left arm;

(6) After the second injection of Brevitol failed to produce the intended effect, Dr. Dell and others again restrained Peter Park forcibly, and Dr. Dell administered gas as an anaesthetic;

(7) Dr. Rogers, the oral surgeon, then proceeded with the operation;

(8) Peter Park remained at the Dental Clinic after the operation for about four hours, and during that time continued to complain of pain in his left arm and of what he described to attendants as a crawling sensation in the fingers of his left hand and in his left arm; . . .

(9) The pain gradually went away during the next few days, but Peter Park was, and is, still not able to straighten into the full open position the third and fourth fingers of his left hand;

(10) In February, 19X3, Peter Park came to you, on the recommendation of a friend, and his condition was as you found it to be and as you have described it in your testimony today in this court, including sensory and motor deprivation in the left arm, centering in the region of the third and fourth fingers, and damage to the ulnar and median nerves.

Doctor, given these assumptions and findings, have you an opinion, with reasonable certainty, as to the cause of the condition of Peter Park's arm?

Yes, I do.

What is that opinion?

Brevitol injected into his arm missed the vein and entered the tissues, causing nerve damage.

Doctor, given the same set of assumptions and findings, have you an opinion, with reasonable certainty, as to whether the attending anesthesiologist, Dr. Dell, acted in accordance with the professional standards of medical practice among anesthesiologists in this and similar communities while attending Peter Park on January 6, 19X3?

I do.

What is that opinion?

He did not.

Please explain in what way Dr. Dell did not act in accordance with these professional standards.

He missed the vein with the needle, shot a batch of Brevitol into the tissues of the arm, and failed to check the placement of the needle before injecting a second batch, after the first failed to have its expected effect.

■ McCOURT v. ABERNATHY
457 S.E.2d 603 (S.C. 1995)

[The following is part of the examination of one of the plaintiff's experts in the case excerpted at page 300, taken from the trial court record. The expert is a physician practicing emergency medicine in South Carolina.]

Q. Did you have an opportunity to go over the medical records thoroughly?

A. I have.

Q. Did you have an opportunity to read the deposition of Steve McCourt?

A. I have.

Q. Did you have an opportunity to read the deposition of Dr. David Potts?

A. Yes.

Q. Would you tell the jury, please, what your opinions are in regards to the treatment that Mrs. McCourt received on March the 9th, if you have any opinions in that regard?

A. The opinion I form is based on the information that has been given to me; in part the death summary, and in part the comments that have been made today. But I feel that indeed if an infectious finger was presented on the 9th, if indeed the individual was evaluated on the 9th, I feel that it falls below the standard of care not to have treated that prophylactically.

Q. All right. Tell us what the standard of care, meaning the proper practice, for March the 9th would have been if done correctly.

A. . . . I would view this as a dirty wound . . . or contaminated. There are a number of guidelines promulgated in part by the American College of Surgeons and others that would suggest that individuals who are showing signs of infection, which could be localized tenderness or pain, with a contaminated wound, would benefit from prophylactic antibiotics.

■ STANG-STARR v. BYINGTON
532 N.W.2d 26 (Neb. 1995)

CAPORALE, Justice. . . .

Pursuant to verdict, the district court dismissed this action wherein [] Teri Stang-Starr claims she was damaged by the negligent failure of [] Dr. Robert T. Byington to properly diagnose and treat abnormalities in her cervix. [Over a period of eight months, Byington obtained three Pap smears. The first showed moderate cellular abnormalities. The second report incorrectly stated no malignant cells were present. The lab made a mistake and should have said the sample was unsatisfactory and therefore the evaluation was inconclusive. The third Pap smear, followed by a biopsy, found stage IV cervical cancer. The defense disputed whether a correct diagnosis would have made a difference, arguing that it was not possible for moderate abnormalities to progress to full-scale cancer so quickly. The jury found in favor of the defendant doctor.] Stang-Starr . . . here asserts that the district court erred by refusing to permit her to question her medical experts regarding medical texts and treatises upon which they relied in their testimony. . . .

During the trial, Stang-Starr called two physicians to testify on her behalf as expert witnesses: Dr. Manford Oliphant and Dr. William Woodard. . . . Based on his knowledge and information obtained from textbooks, medical literature, and personal experience, Oliphant formed an opinion, to a reasonable medical probability, as to the standard of care required of a board-certified obstetrician in May 1986 in Lincoln or similar communities. He then testified that he had read a particular technical bulletin issued by the [American College of Obstetrics] as a predicate to formulating some of the opinions on dysplasia to which he had testified. When Stang-Starr offered that bulletin into evidence, Byington successfully interposed a hearsay objection.

Stang-Starr then made an offer of proof of the bulletin and of material found in more than 12 textbooks concerning gynecology and colposcopy. She proposed that Oliphant would identify the text as authority in the field, identify the text as a basis of opinion, and identify and read specific passages of the material upon which Oliphant relied in testifying. The district court sustained Byington's hearsay objections to the offers.

Woodard then took the stand and testified that in forming his opinion, he had reviewed five or six textbooks, other specifically named textbooks, 15 to 18 journal articles, and the college bulletin identified earlier. In making an offer of proof, Stang-Starr represented that were Woodard allowed to respond to questions about those medical authorities, he would describe the textbooks by title, author, and date of publication, but would not attempt to quote from the actual text. Byington's hearsay objection to the offer was sustained. . . .

On cross-examination, Woodard testified generally as to what the medical literature suggested. When asked on cross-examination whether he had experienced a patient's cancer to progress from normal to invasive within nine months, he replied that the "literature suggests that the original Pap smear was improper or was one of those false negatives, from 15 to 40 percent, and that the cancer doesn't go that rapidly." . . .

On redirect examination, Woodard was asked whether in his opinion there existed in May 1986 diagnostic chaos as to how a gynecologist should have responded to moderate dysplasia in Pap smears. Woodard responded that there was no confusion as to what to do about dysplasia from a gynecologist's standpoint. When asked what the basis for his statement was, Woodard began to reply about the technical bulletin referred to earlier. Byington objected on the basis of hearsay and lack of foundation. Stang-Starr then withdrew the question, and the redirect examination continued with the following questions and answers: . . .

Q. Okay. Let me hand you, Dr. Woodard, a copy—first of all, will you verify what's been marked as . . . the . . . technical bulletin . . . and refer you to page 3 under "Evaluation of Abnormalities." . . .

Q. Do those two paragraphs address the approach to an abnormal Pap smear when the report comes back?

A. Yes, they do.

Q. Would you please give us your interpretation of those two paragraphs from that . . . bulletin? . . .

The objection was sustained. . . .

When offered to prove the truth of matters asserted in them, learned writings, such as treatises, books, and articles regarding specialized areas of knowledge, are clearly hearsay. 2 McCormick on Evidence §321 (John W. Strong 4th ed. 1992). There was no exception for learned treatises at common law, and medical textbooks and professional articles are not admissible to prove the substantive facts stated therein. . . . We have permitted the use of standard medical texts and other authorities for the purpose of impeaching, contradicting, or discrediting a witness through cross-examination. . . . We have not, however, permitted the use of such materials as independent evidence of the opinions and theories advanced by the parties. As explained in Van Skike v. Potter, 73 N.W. 295, 299 (Neb. 1887):

> [E]ven if they are regarded as authoritative, [medical texts] cannot be read to the jury as independent evidence of the opinions and theories therein expressed or advocated. One objection to such testimony is that it is not delivered under oath; a second objection is that the opposite party is thereby deprived of the benefit of a cross-examination; and a third and perhaps a more important reason for rejecting such testimony is that the science of medicine is not an exact science. There are different schools of medicine, the members of which entertain widely different views, and it frequently happens that medical practitioners belonging to the same school will disagree as to the cause of a particular disease, or as to the nature of an ailment with which a patient is afflicted, even if they do not differ as to the mode of treatment. Besides, medical theories, unlike the truths of exact science, are subject to frequent modification and change, even if they are not altogether abandoned. For these reasons it is very generally held that when, in a judicial proceeding, it becomes necessary to invoke the aid of medical experts it is safer to rely on the testimony of competent witnesses who are produced, sworn, and subjected to a cross-examination, than to permit medical books or pamphlets to be read to the jury.

. . . While it is likely that the practice of medicine is more of a science today than it was almost a century ago when we decided *Van Skike*, the fact remains that the *Van Skike* reasoning continues to be sound. We are thus not persuaded that we should abandon our longstanding rule in this regard.

Nor does the fact that the out-of-court statements contained in the authorities were offered in the guise of forming the bases for the testifying experts' opinions alchemically transmute them from inadmissible hearsay into admissible nonhearsay. When Stang-Starr attempted to elicit testimony from her witness concerning what a particular authority has reported about an issue, she was attempting to use her witness to recite the opinion of each authority cited instead of eliciting her witness' expert opinion derived from the witness' own knowledge and experience. The witness was merely seeking to act as a conduit for inadmissible hearsay. The recitation of a passage by a nontestifying authority, even if such is in conformity with the opinion of the testifying expert, is hearsay.

As observed in United States v. Williams, 431 F.2d 1168, 1172 (5th Cir.1970):

> If the witness has gone to only one hearsay source and seeks merely to summarize the content of that source, then he is acting as a summary witness, not an expert. . . . When, however, the witness has gone to many sources—although some or all be hearsay in nature—and rather than introducing mere summaries of each source he uses them all, along with his own professional experience, to arrive at his opinion, that opinion is regarded as evidence in its own right and not as an attempt to introduce hearsay in disguise.

. . . Accordingly, the district court did not err in sustaining Byington's objections to the proffered evidence or the offers of proof made in regard to the evidence. . . .

Notes: Examination of Experts; Introduction of Treatises and Guidelines

1. *Hypothetical Questions.* The rigors of evidence rules governing the questioning of expert witnesses have been considerably loosened over the past generation. The excerpt from Robert Keeton's 1973 book displays the older form in which (1) each factual underpinning for the expert's opinion was explicitly stated hypothetically prior to eliciting the expert's opinion, and (2) each hypothetical foundation point had to be independently proved in evidence. This hypothetical question approach produced a horribly complex chain of thought for the jury to absorb and, for lawyers, meant agonizing decisions about strategy and heightened chances for error. The lawyer's task was to decide whether to state as part of the hypothetical basis for an expert's opinion facts in dispute or based on evidence that might not be admitted. If the jury were to find that one of the subsidiary assumptions was false, or the court were to exclude the source of evidence for that point, then it could easily be argued that the expert's entire testimony was worthless.

The modern approach, embodied in Federal Rules of Evidence 701, 702, 703 and 705, and followed now in most states, is demonstrated in the testimony taken from the *McCourt* case. Both aspects of the older approach stated above are now rejected. Instead, experts' opinions may be based on information that is not in evidence if it is the type of information experts in that field normally rely on in forming opinions. These foundation points do not have to be disclosed before giving an opinion. All of these matters are left to cross-examination by the opposing lawyer. Still, do you think some of the older technique might be valuable in direct examination? Selective restatement of the foundational points, either prior to or following the expert's statement of opinion, could help to reinforce strengths in the case and how well reasoned the opinion is. For additional discussion, see Ronald Carlson, Policing the Basis of Modern Expert Testimony, 39 Vand. L. Rev. 577 (1986); Michael Graham, Expert Witness Testimony and the Federal Rules of Evidence: Insuring Adequate Assurance of Trustworthiness, 1986 U. Ill. L. Rev. 43; Monroe Inker, A Practical Guide to Using Expert Testimony Under the Federal Rules of Evidence, 31 Prac. Law. 21 (1985); Faust Rossi, Modern Evidence and the Expert Witness, 12 Litig. 18 (1985).

2. *Learned Treatises.* Modern practice has also loosened somewhat with respect to the use of learned treatises. The emerging approach, adopted in Federal Rules of Evidence 803(18), is to allow testimony, either in direct or cross-examination, from learned treatises, guidelines, or other similar authoritative sources that the expert acknowledges are reliable. The court may also take judicial notice of their reliability. However, these statements may not be received as exhibits but only read into evidence. Naturally, the states vary in the extent to which they have adopted this liberalization. They also vary considerably in the extent to which, under the older practice, these authorities could be used in cross-examination. Some states require the expert to admit he relied on the authority; others require only that he acknowledge the general authoritativeness of the treatise or other written source. See Annot., 38 A.L.R.2d 77 (1958 & Supp.).

3. *Practice Guidelines.* One type of documentary evidence that has unique status in medical malpractice actions is the "package inserts" for prescription drugs (compiled in the Physicians' Desk Reference (PDR)), which contain FDA-required warnings and instructions for use. As noted at page 404 and as discussed in an omitted portion of Thompson v. Carter supra, these written guidelines are directly admissible as independent evidence on the standard of care under the hearsay exception for tabulations, lists, and directories generally relied on by persons in particular occupations. Fed. R. Evid. 803(17). Some courts treat package inserts as especially authoritative by declaring that they are prima facie proof of the standard of care, subject to rebuttal that physicians commonly depart from the instructions in particular situations.

Observe in *Stang-Starr* that it is much more difficult to introduce other officially promulgated statements of medical standards adopted by professional societies such as the AMA and the various certification boards for medical specialties. These "practice guidelines" are also being issued in greater numbers by government research agencies such as the National Institute of Health (NIH), which convene experts in the field to deliberate on an area of medical practice and issue a consensus statement advising physicians of the best approach to particular clinical situations. Should explicit statements of consensus standards of care from these authoritative national sources be subjected to the same hearsay hurdles as medical treatises and scholarly articles written by only one or a few individuals? Even under the modern treatment of medical authorities illustrated in the McCourt v. Abernathy testimony, courts often rule that practice guidelines can only be referred to and recited by testifying experts, not introduced directly as independent proof. Many commentators, however, argue that if the source is sufficiently authoritative, and the guidelines sufficiently relevant, they should not only be admitted as independent evidence of the standard of care, they should be taken as conclusive, or at least presumptive, proof of the standard of care. For various analyses of existing law and proposals for change, see generally Troyen

Brennan, Practice Guidelines and Malpractice Litigation: Collision or Cohesion?, 16 J. Health Pol. Pol'y & L. 67 (1991); Jodi Finder, The Future of Practice Guidelines: Should they Constitute Conclusive Evidence of the Standard of Care?, 10 Health Matrix 67 (2000); R. E. Leahy, Rational Health Policy and the Legal Standard of Care: A Call for Judicial Deference to Medical Practice Guidelines, 77 Cal. L. Rev. 1483 (1989); J. Rosser Matthews, Practice Guidelines and Tort Reform: The Legal System Confronts the Technocratic Wish, 24 J. Health Pol. Pol'y & L. (1999); Michelle Mello, Of Swords and Shields: The Use of Clinical Practice Guidelines in Medical Malpractice Litigation, 149 U. Pa. L. Rev. 645 (2000); Note, 61 Wash. & Lee L. Rev. 479 (2004); Arnold J. Rosoff, The Role of Clinical Practice Guidelines in Health Care Reform, 5 Health Matrix 369 (1995); John C. West, The Legal Implications of Medical Practice Guidelines, 27 J. Health & Hosp. L. 97 (1994).

Practice guidelines are usually used offensively by plaintiffs against doctors who deviate from them, but they can also be used defensively by doctors to justify their treatment decisions. A. Hyams et al., Medical Practice Guidelines in Malpractice Litigation: An Early Retrospective, 21 J. Health Pol. Pol'y & L. 295 (1996). Thousands of these detailed practice guidelines currently exist and their numbers are rapidly proliferating as a consequence of the perceived need to bring greater rationality and standardization to medical practice. Guidelines issued by government agencies and professional societies are used not only to advise physicians of proper practice, but increasingly are being adapted by public and private insurers as a basis for conducting utilization review activities that determine what treatments are paid for by health insurance. These newer guidelines are geared toward determining when treatment is unnecessary, and therefore are more relevant to defending than to prosecuting a malpractice claim. Some states have viewed these guidelines as a possible way to blunt the impact of defensive medicine — the tendency of physicians to perform unnecessary procedures out of a fear of liability. Maine was the first state to declare by statute that certain officially promulgated guidelines are directly admissible and create an "affirmative defense," but Maine does not allow plaintiffs to use these designated guidelines unless they are put in issue by the defense. Is this differential weight justifiable? Consider the argument in Mark A. Hall, The Defensive Effect of Medical Practice Policies in Malpractice Litigation, 54 L. & Contemp. Probs. 119 (Spring 1991):

> This difference in the [offensive vs. defensive] posture of the [case] is critical because of the possibility that two schools of practice might prevail. With this possibility in mind, it makes eminent sense to hold that it is not conclusive for a plaintiff to establish that the defendant violated *one* established standard. However, the opposite holds for a defendant who complies with at least one established professional guideline: Because it is not necessary for a doctor to show that unanimous professional consensus supports his conduct, a defense is sufficiently established if the doctor shows only that she complied with *at least* one respectable body of opinion.

Observe also that most guidelines purport to state optimal, not minimally acceptable, practice. Does this mean, though, that guidelines should be inadmissible by plaintiffs or only receive lesser weight?

If authoritative medical practice guidelines were to be given special weight in more states, then one must consider which organizations have authoritative stature. Are guidelines issued by a national association or government agency relevant under a similar locality standard in a rural setting? May guidelines adopted by insurers (including HMOs) be considered? In many hospitals and HMOs, efforts are being made to develop treatment protocols that are based on specific scientific evidence from actual patients at the facility rather than being based on broad professional opinion. This movement toward evidence-based, institution-specific guidelines is seen as desirable for three reasons: (1) decentralized efforts will generate many more guidelines, (2) these guidelines are likely to be more useful because they are more clinically specific, and (3) physicians who participate in their development are more likely to comply with them. What objections do you imagine, however, from the plaintiff's lawyer when a physician attempts to defend himself with the institution's own guideline?

4. *Physician Report Cards.* Another emerging source of evidence that is likely to be controversial comes from "report cards" and "physician profiles" that some states are beginning to keep on individual doctors. These reports contain statistics on the number of good and bad outcomes for particular types of high-profile treatment such as cardiac bypass surgery. These statistics are not unlike the kind of information hospital peer review committees traditionally compile on infection rates, blood loss, tissue analysis, and other technical aspects of surgery, but those sources of information are cloaked in the peer review privilege discussed at page 360, which keeps them confidential. The newer report cards are discoverable, but are they admissible? One commentator predicts not, based on irrelevance. Courts are cautious about admitting evidence of previous similar wrongdoing because of the potential for undue prejudice and the reluctance to greatly expand the scope of litigation. This type of evidence is generally limited to instances involving the very same mistake. See Paul D. Rheingold, The Admissibility of Evidence in Malpractice Cases: The Performance Records of Practitioners, 58 Brook. L. Rev. 75 (1992). See generally Symposium, 58 Brook. L. Rev. 85 (1992); Aaron S. Kesselheim et al., Will Physician-Level Measures of Clinical Performance Be Used in Medical Malpractice Litigation?, 295 JAMA 1831 (2006).

5. *Empirical Evidence of Medical Custom.* With so many available and emerging sources of empirical evidence regarding medical custom, one must wonder why courts have not been more demanding regarding the foundation for experts who testify about medical custom. Courts traditionally have allowed experts to testify based on their general experience and opinion rather than requiring them to show they have actually studied in or researched in a scientific or methodical fashion how physicians usually behave in similar circumstances. Perhaps this is a holdover from a century ago when, under a local standard of care, nothing more could be expected. However, as noted above, at page 326, this often results in testimony that is demonstrably inaccurate. Accordingly, several scholars have advocated either allowing or encouraging experts to conduct surveys of physicians, or to analyze databases reflecting actual physician practices, in order to support their expert opinions. Could this help to overcome difficulties that plaintiffs face in finding qualified experts? Might this be *required* as a basic element of the scientific validity of experts' assertions about professional practice, under Daubert v. Merrell Dow Pharmaceuticals, Inc., 509 U.S. 579 (1993)? For a

thorough analysis of these proposals and their many problems, see Symposium, Empirical Approaches to Proving the Standard of Care in Medical Malpractice Cases, 37 Wake Forest L. Rev. 663 (2002).

Problem: Practice Guidelines

Jane Austere is a 62-year-old female with a history of severe diabetes and high blood pressure. She lives in a small town in a rural county of a state that follows the national standard of care for specialists. Following surgery on her left knee performed under general anesthesia at the local public hospital, she was suddenly unable to speak normally. This is consistent with brain damage caused by decreased oxygen to the brain, among other possible causes. Jane brings a medical malpractice action against her anesthesiologist.

Several national organizations have issued guidelines for monitoring ventilation (breathing) during surgery. Two years before Jane's operation, the anesthesiology department at the hospital studied all these guidelines and adopted the following as its view of the best compromise among all their various nuances:

> Every patient receiving general anesthesia shall have the adequacy of ventilation evaluated regularly and frequently. Quantitative monitoring of the CO_2 content and the volume of expired gas is encouraged, but not required. . . . These guidelines are not intended to displace the physician's discretion to conform treatment to the particular clinical circumstances of the individual patient. Jane's anesthesiologist admits that he did not perform quantitative measures of CO_2 and volume of exhaled air because he considers visual observation of breathing to be sufficient in all cases. Jane's expert testifies that she could have suffered decreased oxygen because her breathing slowed or paused for a minute or two. In his opinion, quantitative measures are advisable for a patient in Jane's condition. The hospital had recently purchased new equipment that can make these measures continuously and much less obtrusively than was the case before.

The defense lawyer tries to introduce this hospital guideline as evidence of the standard of care. What objections are likely, and what response would you make? If the guidelines were admitted, what instruction should the judge give to the jury, assuming this jurisdiction follows a national standard of care?

■ DUQUETTE v. SUPERIOR COURT
778 P.2d 634 (Ariz. App. 1989)

CONTRERAS, Judge.
In this special action, we consider the issue of whether defense counsel in a medical malpractice action may engage in *ex parte* communications with the plaintiff's treating physicians without having obtained plaintiff's consent. . . .

[One-year old Eric Lamberty] was diagnosed as having a dermoid tumor in and around his spinal column. The tumor required surgery. . . . Following the surgery, the Lambertys filed a civil action against Dr. Duquette alleging that he committed medical malpractice by failing to: (1) treat Eric properly during his birth hospitalization, and (2) diagnose the tumor in a timely fashion. Scottsdale Memorial Hospital was also a named defendant under an agency theory of liability.

In the summer of 1987, defense attorneys for petitioners conducted *ex parte* interviews of approximately thirteen of plaintiff's treating physicians without the express consent of plaintiff, his parents, or his counsel. . . . [P]laintiffs filed a motion to bar testimony and to disqualify counsel. . . . Petitioners seek special action review of that portion of Judge Moroney's order barring plaintiff's treating physicians from testifying as expert witnesses unless first offered as witnesses by plaintiffs. . . .

[P]etitioners first contend that the *ex parte* communications between plaintiff's treating physicians and defense attorneys were not improper because the physician-patient privilege had been waived. . . . The Arizona statute precludes a physician from being examined about any communications made by the patient concerning his condition or any knowledge of the condition obtained through personal examination of the patient without the consent of the patient. . . . [P]etitioners contend that the real parties in interest waived the privilege when they: 1) placed Eric's medical condition in issue by filing suit, and 2) claimed Eric's medical expenses as damages in their civil complaint. . . .

[T]he Arizona Supreme Court [has] stated that when a plaintiff "places a particular medical condition at issue by means of a claim or affirmative defense, . . . then the privilege will be deemed waived with respect to that particular medical condition." In accordance with [this ruling], we conclude that Eric's parents have waived the physician-patient privilege by placing their son's medical condition at issue through initiation of litigation.

This waiver is not absolute however, and we believe petitioners' reliance on implied waiver in support of the propriety of *ex parte* communications is misplaced. In this regard, we agree with those cases which conclude that even where the physician-patient privilege has been impliedly waived, the holder of the privilege waives only his right to object to discovery of pertinent medical information which is sought through the formal methods of discovery authorized by the applicable Rules of Civil Procedure. . . .

Those courts which have taken the view that a defendant's counsel may interview the plaintiff's treating physicians *ex parte* have identified a number of factors and policies for allowing such informal methods of discovery. These include decreased litigation costs, the potential to eliminate non-essential witnesses, early evaluation and settlement of claims, the ease of scheduling interviews as opposed to depositions, and greater spontaneity and candor in the interview than in the deposition. Annot., 50 A.L.R. 4th 714.

Those courts which have taken an opposite view and have held that the defendant's counsel is limited to the formal methods of discovery listed within the Rules of Civil Procedure have based their decisions on varying propositions. Among the reasons relied upon in refusing to grant permission for informal *ex parte* interviews are the broad privacy interest underlying the physician-patient relationship, the potential tort liability of physicians for breach or invasion of privacy, the potential that defense counsel may seek to improperly influence plaintiff's treating physicians or may discourage the physician from testifying, the duty of loyalty from the physician to the patient, and the view that discovery rules determine the extent of the physician-patient privilege. Id. . . .

We note, . . . that a ban on *ex parte* communications does not preclude defense attorneys from contacting plaintiff's treating physicians. Rather, such a ruling merely limits the methods of contact available to the defense attorney to those methods authorized by our Rules of Civil Procedure. . . .

[W]e believe that the unique nature of the physician-patient relationship justifies a ban on *ex parte* communications. We recognize that such a ban allows the plaintiff to engage in *ex parte* communications with his physician witnesses while it prohibits the defendant from gaining equal access. However, this inequality of access to the physician witnesses does not preclude the defendant from availing himself of the full panoply of discovery devices. . . . [W]e do not believe that such practical concerns as cost efficiency and ease of scheduling are of paramount concern to a proper resolution of the issue. . . . We believe the public has a widespread belief that information given to a physician in confidence will not be disclosed to third parties absent legal compulsion, and we further believe that the public has a right to have this expectation realized. See Petrillo v. Syntex Laboratories, Inc., 499 N.E.2d 952, 959-62 (1986). We agree with the Petrillo court when, in limiting physician disclosure to court authorized methods of discovery, it stated:

> Discussion of the patient's confidences under any other circumstances, such as the *ex parte* conference, could be inconsistent with the duties of a fiduciary for the physician would, in effect, engage in conduct which may be contrary to a fiduciary's obligation of good faith and, in addition, may be potentially harmful to the interests of the patient which are unrelated and irrelevant to the mental or physical condition placed at issue in the lawsuit. . . .

A second set of considerations supporting a prohibition on *ex parte* communications involves the pressure brought to bear on the physician. . . . Although the physician is free to reject such a request and thereby force the defense attorney to utilize formal methods of discovery, we believe that this option does not acceptably reduce the pressure on the physician. . . . [A] substantial number of physicians are insured by a single "doctor owned" insurer. Realistically, this factor could have an impact on the physician's decision. In other words, the physician witness might feel compelled to participate in the *ex parte* interview because the insurer defending the medical malpractice defendant may also insure the physician witness.

An additional factor that must be taken into consideration is that a physician who allows himself to be interviewed *ex parte* embarks, perhaps unknowingly, on a course which may involve a breach of professional ethics and potential liability. First, participation in an *ex parte* interview may constitute a breach of the physician's professional code of ethics. . . . Thus, the physician's voluntary participation in the *ex parte* interview may subject him or her to professional discipline as well as potential tort liability. . . .

An additional consideration supporting a ban on *ex parte* interviews involves the practical difficulty in determining the scope of the waiver of the physician-patient privilege. The scope of the waiver is often in dispute, and absent court participation in the discovery process, resolution of that dispute is left to the defense attorney and the physician witness. We believe that this scenario places both the defense attorney and the physician in an untenable position. As the Iowa Supreme Court stated in Roosevelt Hotel Ltd. Partnership v. Sweeney, 394 N.W.2d 353, 357 (1986):

Placing the burden of determining relevancy on an attorney, who does not know the nature of the confidential disclosure about to be elicited, is risky. Asking the physician, untrained in the law, to assume this burden is a greater gamble and is unfair to the physician. We believe this determination is better made in a setting in which counsel for each party is present and the court is available to settle disputes. . . . Accordingly, we hold that defense counsel in a medical malpractice action may not engage in non-consensual *ex parte* communications with plaintiff's treating physicians.

We now consider the sanction imposed by the trial court. . . . Prior to today's decision, the law on this issue in the State of Arizona was unsettled. . . . Given this situation, we believe that it was an abuse of discretion for the trial court to summarily impose the sanction of preclusion of testimony. . . .

Remanded.

Notes: Discovery and Confidentiality

1. *Medical Records.* Investigation of a potential malpractice claim by a plaintiff's lawyer starts with obtaining and reviewing his client's own medical records. The initial review may be conducted inside the law firm by someone such as a nurse paralegal who has some medical training, but thorough investigation usually entails sending the record out for expert review prior to initiating suit. Hospital medical records are too large, complex, and various to adequately summarize in the context of this book. An illustration of the types of documents and sorts of information one might find in a typical hospital chart can be found on the Web site for this book, www.health-law.org, which contains excerpts from the trial record in McCourt v. Abernathy, page 300. Take a look at these samples. On first inspection, they may be hard to digest, but see if you can read them in a way that tells a story. The usual components of a medical story are: (1) history and symptoms; (2) exam, testing, and diagnosis; (3) treatment; and (4) outcome. Following that structure, see if you can identify in these records how Wendy first presented her symptoms, what additional symptoms her physicians observed, what tests they performed and why, where the diagnosis went wrong, and what the resulting effect was on her treatment.

2. *Spoliation of Evidence.* Medical malpractice cases frequently contain allegations that medical records have been altered to cover up mistakes. If true, this obviously creates problems for the defense, which is then subject to various damaging presumptions or waivers of defenses, if not penalties for outright fraud and deceit. See generally, Comment, Spoliation of Evidence and Medical Malpractice, 14 Pace L. Rev. 235 (1994).

3. *Waiver of Confidentiality.* Although a malpractice plaintiff waives her right to confidentiality in the medical records and treatment relationship at issue in the litigation, that waiver does not extend to any treatment the plaintiff might have

ever received, even by the same doctor. Courts tailor the waiver to fit the allegations of the complaint in order to avoid deterring suit by unnecessarily forcing a plaintiff to expose all embarrassing or private aspects of her medical past. See, e.g., R.K. v. Ramirez, 887 S.W.2d 836 (Tex. 1994).

4. *Ex Parte Interviews*. In *Duquette*, the court declined to impose a penalty the first time the prohibition on *ex parte* interviews was announced in the state. Other courts, however, have barred defendants from using physician witnesses who were improperly contacted. Additional penalties might include a tort action against the interviewed physician for breach of confidence, or a disciplinary action against the lawyer.

The waiver of the physician-patient privilege, and the corresponding prohibition of informal discovery, apply equally to any civil action, such as automobile accidents or products liability, in which the plaintiff's medical condition is placed at issue. As should be obvious, the prohibition against contacting the plaintiff's doctor informally applies only to non-party physicians. A defendant doctor can talk all he wants with his own lawyer. Acosta v. Richter, 671 So.2d 149 (Fla. 1996). The issue is cloudier, however, if the defendant and non-party doctors practice together in the same partnership, or if they both work at the same hospital that is named in the suit. Testin v. Dryer Medical Clinic, 605 N.E.2d 1070 (Ill. App. 1992) applied the ban on *ex parte* interviews to a plaintiff's subsequent treating physician who was director of the clinic in which the defending physician worked. Ritter v. Rush Presbyterian-St. Luke's Med. Ctr., 532 N.E.2d 327 (Ill. App. 1988) applied the ban to a hospital lawyer's communication with other treating physicians in the same hospital but observed in dictum that this prohibition should not be carried so far as to "effectively prevent [a] hospital from defending itself by barring communication with [a] physician for whose conduct the hospital is allegedly liable." What strategy does this suggest for a plaintiff's lawyer in deciding whether to name a hospital as a defendant? In deciding how many physicians to name as defendants? What may a hospital lawyer safely investigate when the plaintiff's precise allegations and theories of liability are unknown? According to Keith Emmons, an Illinois lawyer, "the best present option would appear to be the early identification of all potentially liable practitioners and entities and the appointment of separate defense counsel for [each one] even before they become named defendants." Each lawyer can interview her own client, and nothing in the *ex parte* rule appears to prevent the lawyers from talking among themselves, or does it?

For recent cases pro and con on the *ex parte* rule, see Brandt v. Pelican, 856 S.W.2d 658 (Mo. 1993) (allowing informal interviews); Domako v. Rowe, 475 N.W.2d 30 (Mich. 1991) (same); Samms v. District Court, Fourth Judicial District of the State of Colorado, 908 P.2d 520 (Colo. 1996) (same, but only if opposing attorney is given notice and chance to attend informal interview); Heller v. Mutual Ins. Co., 32 Cal. Rptr.2d 200 (Cal. 1994) (refusing to impose civil damages against doctor who gave *ex parte* information); Burger v. Lutheran Gen. Hosp., 759 N.E.2d 533 (Ill. 2001) (upholding statute that allowed ex parte communications between hospital and physician's lawyers); Crist v. Moffatt, 389 S.E.2d 41 (N.C. 1990) (prohibiting *ex parte* contact); Kitzmiller v. Henning, 437 S.E.2d 452 (W.Va. 1993) (same); Scott v. Flynt, 704 So. 2d 998 (Miss. 1996) (same). For commentary and analysis, see Elliot B. Oppenheim, Physicians as Experts Against

Their Own Patients? What Happened to the Privilege?, 63 Def. Couns. J. 254 (1996); W. McVisk, A More Balanced Approach to *Ex Parte* Interviews by Treating Physicians, 20 Loy. U. Chi. L.J. 819 (1989); P. Corboy, *Ex Parte* Contacts Between Plaintiff's Physicians and Defense Attorneys: Protecting the Patient-Litigant's Right to a Fair Trial, 21 Loy. U. Chi. L.J. 1001 (1990); Note, The Permissibility of *Ex Parte* Communications Between Plaintiff's Treating Physicians and Defense Counsel, 59 Mo. L. Rev. 441 (1994); Annot., 50 A.L.R.4th 714 (1986).

5. *Peer Review Confidentiality.* Other sources of confidentiality and evidentiary privilege protect the defendant in a malpractice action. The primary sources are: (1) peer review confidentiality statutes; (2) the attorney-client communication privilege; and (3) the lawyer's work product privilege. We will discuss only the first of these, and only briefly. See the Web site for this book, www.health-law.org, for additional information.

Peer review confidentiality attaches by statute in most states to various standing hospital committees that investigate the competence of individual practitioners and the quality of care rendered within the institution. In order to ensure candor and vigorous participation in these activities, state statutes protect from discovery any records generated by these committees. A few decisions have recognized a common-law privilege protecting self-evaluation or self-improvement efforts even in the absence of such statutes. The peer review confidentiality statutes produce a steady stream of litigation over precisely which committees and records they cover. See generally Lisa M. Nijm, Pitfalls of Peer Review, 24 J. Legal Med. 541 (December 2003); Gail Friend et al., Identifying and Protecting the Peer Review and Medical Committee Privilege, 49 Baylor L. Rev. 607 (1997); S. Scheutzow & S. Gillis, Confidentiality and Privilege of Peer Review Information: More Imagined than Real, 7 J.L. & Health 169 (1992) (containing extensive analysis of individual states); Annots., 60 A.L.R.4th 1273 (1988); 81 A.L.R.3d 944 (1977).

One major area of dispute concerns "incident reports" and investigations conducted by hospital risk management departments. Compare Gregory v. Heritage Hosp., 594 N.W.2d 455 (Mich. 1999) (incident reports are privileged) with Columbia/HCA Healthcare Corp. v. Eighth Judicial District Court, 936 P.2d 844 (Nev. 1997) (incident reports are discoverable). The hospital might also seek to protect these reports as attorney work product, or to protect the communications they report under the attorney-client privilege. These claims are not always successful, for reasons summarized on the Web site. See, e.g., Samaritan Foundation v. Goodfarb, 862 P.2d 870 (Ariz. 1993) (hospital lawyers who interviewed nurse witnesses were not acting as lawyers for the nurses, only for the hospital).

Out of concern that state law too narrowly protects the ability of health care institutions to investigate, correct, and report medical safety issues, Congress adopted a discovery privilege and liability protection in 2005. The Patient Safety and Quality Improvement Act protects from discovery any reports of medical errors made by health care providers to certified "patient safety organizations," such as the JCAHO. However, any such records must be maintained only for patient safety evaluation purposes, and not for patient care or billing purposes. The goal is to encourage efforts to improve medical quality in arenas outside the traditional peer review process, for instance, by sharing information among different facilities or with private accreditation organizations. See Symposium, 35 J. Health L. 179 (2002). Attacking the view that liability exposure deters error reporting or quality improvement, see David A. Hyman & Charles M. Silver, The Poor State of Health Care Quality in the U.S.: Is Malpractice Liability Part of the Problem or Part of the Solution?, 90 Cornell L. Rev. 893 (2005).

6. *The Costs of Litigation.* The complexity of medical malpractice cases, and the costs of medical expertise, mean that these are expensive cases to litigate, often costing at least $50,000 in out-of-pocket expenses. Overall, less than half of medical malpractice premiums collected end up in the pockets of injured patients.

C. ALTERNATIVE THEORIES OF LIABILITY

Observing the difficulties that plaintiffs often have in qualifying expert witnesses and proving a breach of the standard of care, it is understandable that their lawyers are eager to find theories of liability that do not rely on the custom-based standard of care, or at least that do not require the use of expert testimony. The following readings survey several such theories, beginning with more conventional ones and concluding with no-fault and strict liability.

1. Res Ipsa and Negligence Per Se

■ LOCKE v. PACHTMAN
521 N.W.2d 786 (Mich. 1994)

[The facts are stated in the main excerpt at page 303. Briefly, a long, flexible needle broke off while Dr. Pachtman was performing surgery. After searching, she could not find it, and so a second operation was required to remove it. The court held there was insufficient expert testimony from the plaintiff for the case to go to the jury.]

Plaintiff next argues that even if expert testimony was insufficient, her case against Dr. Pachtman should have proceeded to the jury on the theory of res ipsa loquitur. Specifically, plaintiff contends, under this doctrine, a prima facie case was made, with regard to both the needle breakage and the fact that defendant terminated the surgery without having recovered the needle. The lower courts rejected these arguments, as do we. . . .

The following four factors a[re] necessary to a res ipsa loquitur claim:

(1) the event must be of a kind which ordinarily does not occur in the absence of someone's negligence;

(2) it must be caused by an agency or instrumentality within the exclusive control of the defendant;

(3) it must not have been due to any voluntary action or contribution on the part of the plaintiff . . .

(4) [e]vidence of the true explanation of the event must be more readily accessible to the defendant than to the plaintiff.

In the medical malpractice context, the crucial element, and that most difficult to establish, will often be the first factor, i.e., that the event is of a kind that does not ordinarily occur in the absence of negligence. A bad result will not itself be sufficient to satisfy that condition. . . . This does not mean that a bad result cannot be presented by plaintiffs as part of their evidence of negligence, but, rather, that, standing alone, it is not adequate to create an issue for the jury. Something more is required, be it the common knowledge that the injury does not ordinarily occur without negligence or expert testimony to that effect. . . . Neither standard was met here. . . . Even plaintiff's own expert acknowledged at one point that needle breakage is one of the risks of surgery, suggesting that faulty equipment might be a cause of breakage. . . .

Plaintiff relies on this court's holding in LeFaive v. Asselin, 262 Mich. 443, 247 N.W. 911 (1933). In *LeFaive*, the court held that a jury could determine, without the aid of expert testimony, that the defendant's action in inadvertently leaving a needle within the plaintiff's incision violated the applicable standard of care. Plaintiff's analogy to *LeFaive* is inapposite. In *LeFaive*, the act of leaving the needle within the incision was one of carelessness, from which negligence may easily be discerned. However, a far different situation is presented where a needle breaks off, and the surgeon, despite attempts to locate the fragment, is unable to. One could not reasonably conclude, on the basis of common knowledge, that such an event does not ordinarily occur in the absence of negligence. . . .

Notes: Res Ipsa Loquitur and Negligence Per Se

1. *Other Examples. Locke* is an example of one of several typical, recurring situations in which courts will sometimes allow the case to go to the jury without expert testimony on deviation from customary practice. Other typical scenarios involve: leaving other foreign objects behind after surgery, such as clamps and sponges; injury to a part of the body that was not involved in the operation; and removal of the wrong organ or appendage. These cases are argued and decided under several doctrinal categories that overlap with res ipsa loquitur: "negligence per se"; the "common knowledge rule"; and "obvious negligence." As noted in Flowers v. Torrance Memorial Hospital Medical Center, 35 Cal. Rptr. 2d 685 (Cal. 1994), the gist of all these doctrines is captured in Bob Dylan's *Subterranean Homesick Blues* (Columbia Records 1965): "[Y]ou don't need a weatherman to know which way the wind blows." In the words of a Tennessee court, however, the medical negligence must be "as plain as a fly floating in a bowl of buttermilk." German v. Nichopoulos, 577 S.W.2d 197 (Tenn. Ct. App. 1978).

These various doctrinal categories are not all identical, however, and they are often applied somewhat differently in medical malpractice cases than they are in conventional tort cases. The "common knowledge" rule allows the jury to make simple factual findings from its own experience and knowledge base. It allows some facts to be found even though there are gaps in the supporting evidence, but it usually does not allow a finding of negligence without any expert testimony at all. Res ipsa loquitur is a stronger rule because it does allow this result, in proper circumstances. Negligence per se is stronger still; it can result in the judge directing a verdict of negligence as a matter of law. Note that this use of negligence per se differs from the standard application, which finds negligence as a matter of law only when a statute is violated; here, no statutory violation is required. Negligence per se in malpractice cases tends to be restricted, however, to certain extreme factual situations, such as incorrect sponge counts or amputating the wrong leg, in which negligence is so obvious as to be beyond dispute. See, e.g., Guilbeau v. St. Paul Fire and Marine Insurance Co., 325 So. 2d 395 (La. Ct. App. 1976) ("the general rule . . . is that a surgeon's failure to remove a sponge or pad before closing an incision may be regarded as negligence per se" justifying a directed verdict for plaintiff). For a case-by-case comparison among these rules, see Annot., 49 A.L.R.4th 63 (1986).

Notice how these three doctrines, without meaning to do so, tend to shift the focus from what physicians ordinarily do in similar cases, to what the jury thinks was reasonable in the particular case. Therefore, these doctrines do not simply overcome a gap in the evidence; they tend to alter the substantive standard of liability.

2. *Doctrinal Variations.* Res ipsa loquitur potentially applies to any type of medical mistake, as long as the elements of the rule are met. Because some of these elements are matters that are not usually in the common knowledge of jurors, however, plaintiffs frequently need expert testimony to establish them, as illustrated in *Locke*. Res ipsa loquitur in such cases allows the jury to fill in by inference the gaps that remain in expert testimony rather than displacing expert testimony entirely.

For a contrasting view that takes a more expansive approach than *Locke* to the availability of res ipsa loquitur and the "common knowledge rule," see Jones v. Harrisburg Polyclinic Hospital, 437 A.2d 1134 (Pa. 1981) (res ipsa applies whenever there is a "fund of common knowledge" from which to draw lay inferences), and an excellent student note on the case, 21 Duq. L. Rev. 547 (1983). Compare generally De Leon Lopez v. Corporacion Insular de Seguros, 931 F.2d 116 (1st Cir. 1991) (expert not needed where hospital switched babies born at same time), and Seavers v. Methodist Medical Center, 9 S.W.3d 86 (Tenn. 1999) (where patient suffered nerve damage in arm while being restrained in a hospital bed, res ipsa applies even when the issue is not within "the fund of common knowledge" but requires expert testimony to establish its elements), and Toppino v. Herhahn, 673 P.2d 1297 (N.M. 1983) (it is common knowledge that reconstructive breast surgery should result in breast of same size and shape as the other one), *with* Miller v. Jacoby, 33 P.3d 68 (Wash. 2001) (res ipsa applies to failure to fully remove a surgical drain but not to negligence in inserting the drain), and Sisson v. Elkins, 801 P.2d 722 (Okla. 1990) (res ipsa does not apply to surgeon who cut the wrong blood vessel, despite testimony he was negligent), and Bearfield v. Hauch, 595 A.2d 1320 (Pa. Super. Ct. 1991) (severing nerve during gallbladder surgery does not raise inference of negligence absent expert testimony to that effect, because usual results from this surgery are not within "fund of common knowledge").

Is the first element of res ipsa satisfied by the mere fact that, statistically speaking, a harmful effect rarely occurs if the procedure is performed properly? See Clark v. Gibbons, 426 P.2d 525 (Cal. 1967) (the rarity of the problem alone is not enough, but coupled with actual evidence of possible negligent acts this does suffice to support a jury verdict; operation had to be terminated prematurely because anesthesia wore off too early).

The factor requiring exclusive control is often not applied literally in medical malpractice actions, under the reasoning that it is unduly demanding considering that the team approach to treatment often means that no single defendant is exclusively responsible and the plaintiff is often not in a position to observe who performs which tasks. The classic case is Ybarra v. Spangard, 208 P.2d 445 (Cal. Ct. App. 1949), which allowed res ipsa to be instructed where a patient suffered a shoulder injury while under anesthesia for an appendectomy. The court observed that it should be the defendants' burden to come forward with evidence about who among those present in the operating room was and was not responsible for the injury. For a review of the application of these rules in cases of multiple medical defendants, see Annot., 67 A.L.R.4th 544 (1989).

3. *Legal Effect.* Locke v. Pachtman focuses on the conditions required for applying the res ipsa doctrine. Also at issue in these cases are the legal effects of the doctrine when it does apply. In *Locke*, the doctrine would have resulted in presenting the case to the jury. Other courts go further and use the doctrine to instruct the jury to find liability against at least one of the defendants, although this is much more controversial. See, e.g., Anderson v. Somberg, 338 A.2d 1 (N.J. 1975) (adopting this approach in a case similar to *Locke*, over a heated dissent accusing the majority of forcing the jury to act without "any semblance of rationality, . . . as the whimsy of the moment dictates, . . . no more a rational process than were trial by ordeal or trial by combat"). But see Salgo v. Leland Stanford Jr. University Board of Trustees, 317 P.2d 170 (Cal. 1957) (improper to direct verdict for plaintiff where factual dispute existed over whether needle injection hit the spinal cord and where experts disagreed over whether such a mistake would constitute negligence). An intermediate approach, followed by a substantial minority of states, is to create some type of rebuttable presumption or shift in the burden of proof when the elements of res ipsa are met.

4. *Legal Trend.* In earlier years, many legal commentators urged that res ipsa loquitur and similar liberalizing rules were necessary to aid plaintiffs with legitimate claims who were confronted with "the conspiracy of silence" on the part of physicians refusing to appear as expert witnesses. See, e.g., *Salgo*, supra. In more recent times, now that it is much easier to find qualified experts, the attitudes of commentators in both legal and medical journals have all but completely reversed. These rules are now often described as unfair to defendant physicians. Many of the statutory reforms adopted in the mid-1970s and mid-1980s include modifications of the res ipsa loquitur doctrine in medical malpractice litigation. See references and discussion in section G. A particularly outspoken expression of the modern view is found in Priest v. Lindig, 583 P.2d 173, 175 n.7 (Alaska 1976), where the court asserted that the legislative history of the Alaska statute abolishing res ipsa loquitur in medical malpractice cases was intended to counteract "the *intolerable* rule of law resulting in astronomically high malpractice insurance rates" (emphasis added). For commentary on these rules, see K. Albin, Res Ipsa Loquitur and Expert Opinion Evidence in Medical Malpractice Cases, 82 Va. L. Rev. 325 (1996).

2. Ordinary Negligence

It is one thing to argue that medical custom is common knowledge or can be presumed from the outrageousness of the doctor's behavior. It is another thing altogether to argue that liability should be imposed regardless of medical custom or contrary to known medical custom. That is the result in the following decision, which is the most infamous of all medical malpractice cases.

■ HELLING v. CAREY
519 P.2d 981 (Wash. 1974)

HUNTER, Associate Justice.

This case arises from a malpractice action instituted by the plaintiff (petitioner), Barbara Helling.

The plaintiff suffers from primary open angle glaucoma. Primary open angle glaucoma is essentially a condition of the eye in which there is an interference in the ease with which the nourishing fluids can flow out of the eye. Such a condition results in pressure gradually rising above the normal level to such an extent that damage is produced to the optic nerve and its fibers with resultant loss in vision. The first loss usually occurs in the periphery of the field of vision. The disease usually has few symptoms and, in the absence of a pressure test, is often undetected until the damage has become extensive and irreversible.

The defendants (respondents), Dr. Thomas F. Carey and Dr. Robert C. Laughlin, are partners who practice the medical specialty of ophthalmology. Ophthalmology involves the diagnosis and treatment of defects and diseases of the eye.

The plaintiff first consulted the defendants for myopia, nearsightedness, in 1959. At that time she was fitted with contact lenses. She next consulted the defendants in September, 1963, concerning irritation caused by the contact lenses. Additional consultations occurred in October, 1963; February, 1967; September, 1967; October, 1967; May, 1968; July, 1968; August, 1968; September, 1968; and October, 1968. Until the October 1968 consultation, the defendants considered the plaintiff's visual problems to be related solely to complications associated with her contact lenses. On that occasion, the defendant, Dr. Carey, tested the plaintiff's eye pressure and field of vision for the first time. This test indicated that the plaintiff had glaucoma. The plaintiff, who was then 32 years of age, had essentially lost her peripheral vision and her central vision was reduced to approximately 5 degrees vertical by 10 degrees horizontal.

Thereafter, in August of 1969, after consulting other physicians, the plaintiff filed a complaint against the defendants alleging, among other things, that she sustained severe and permanent damage to her eyes as a proximate result of the defendants' negligence. During trial, the testimony of the medical experts for both the plaintiff and the defendants established that the standards of the profession for that specialty in the same or similar circumstances do not require routine pressure tests for glaucoma upon patients under 40 years of age. The reason the pressure test for glaucoma is not given as a regular practice to patients under the age of 40 is that the disease rarely occurs in this age group. Testimony indicated, however, that the standards of the profession do require pressure tests if the patient's complaints and symptoms reveal to the physician that glaucoma should be suspected.

The trial court entered judgment for the defendants following a defense verdict. . . .

We find this to be a unique case. The testimony of the medical experts is undisputed concerning the standards of the profession for the specialty of ophthalmology. It is not a question in this case of the defendants having any greater special ability, knowledge and information than other ophthalmologists which would require the defendants to comply with a higher duty of care than that "degree of care and skill which is expected of the average practitioner in the class to which he belongs, acting in the same or similar circumstances." Pederson v. Dumouchel, 72 Wash. 2d 73, 79, 431 P.2d 973 (1967). The issue is whether the defendants' compliance with the standard of the profession of ophthalmology, which does not require the giving of a routine pressure test to persons under 40 years of age, should insulate them from liability under the facts in this case where the plaintiff has lost a substantial amount of her vision due to the failure of the defendants to timely give the pressure test to the plaintiff.

The defendants argue that the standard of the profession, which does not require the giving of a routine pressure test to persons under the age of 40, is adequate to insulate the defendants from liability for negligence because the risk of glaucoma is so rare in this age group. The testimony of the defendant, Dr. Carey, however, is revealing as follows:

Q: Now, when was it, actually, the first time any complaint was made to you by her of any field or visual field problem?

A: Really, the first time that she really complained of a visual field problem was the August 30th date. [1968.]

Q: And how soon before the diagnosis was that?

A: That was 30 days. We made it on October 1st.

Q: And in your opinion, how long, as you nor have I the whole history and analysis and the diagnosis, how long had she had this glaucoma?

A: I would think she probably had it ten years or longer.

Q: Now, Doctor, there's been some reference to the matter of taking pressure checks of persons over 40. What is the incidence of glaucoma, the statistics, with persons under 40?

A: In the instance of glaucoma under the age of 40, is less than 100 to one percent. The younger you get, the less the incidence. It is thought to be in the neighborhood of one in 25,000 people or less.

Q: How about the incidence of glaucoma in people over 40?

A: Incidence of glaucoma over 40 gets into the 2 to 3 percent category, and hence, that's where there is this great big difference and that's why the standards around the world has been to check pressures from 40 on.

The incidence of glaucoma in one out of 25,000 persons under the age of 40 may appear quite minimal. However, that one person, the plaintiff in this instance, is entitled to the same protection, as afforded persons over 40, essential for timely detection of the evidence of glaucoma where it can be arrested to avoid the grave and devastating result of this disease. The test is a simple pressure test, relatively inexpensive. There is no judgment factor involved, and there is no doubt that by giving the test the evidence of glaucoma can be detected. The giving of the test is harmless if the physical condition of the eye permits. The testimony indicates that although the condition of the plaintiff's eyes might have at times prevented the defendants from administering the pressure test, there is an absence of evidence in the record that the test could not have been timely given.

Justice Holmes stated in Texas & Pac. Ry. v. Behymer, 189 U.S. 468, 470, 23 S. Ct. 622, 623, 47 L. Ed. 905 (1903): "What usually is done may be evidence of what ought to be done, but what ought to be done is fixed by a standard of reasonable prudence, whether it usually is complied with or not." In The T. J. Hooper, 60 F.2d 737, on page 740 (2d Cir. 1932), Justice Hand stated: "(I)n most cases reasonable prudence is in fact common prudence; but strictly it is never its measure; a whole calling may have unduly lagged in the adoption of new and available devices. It never may set its own tests, however persuasive be its usages. *Courts must in the end say what is required; there are precautions so imperative that even their universal disregard will not excuse their omission.*" (Italics ours.)

Under the facts of this case reasonable prudence required the timely giving of the pressure test to this plaintiff. The precaution of giving this test to detect the incidence of glaucoma to patients under 40 years of age is so imperative that irrespective of its disregard by the standards of the opthalmology profession, it is the duty of the courts to say what is required to protect patients under 40 from the damaging results of glaucoma.

We therefore hold, as a matter of law, that the reasonable standard that should have been followed under the undisputed facts of this case was the timely giving of this simple, harmless pressure test to this plaintiff and that, in failing to do so, the defendants were negligent, which proximately resulted in the blindness sustained by the plaintiff for which the defendants are liable.

There are no disputed facts to submit to the jury on the issue of the defendants' liability. Hence, a discussion of the plaintiff's proposed instructions would be inconsequential in view of our disposition of the case.

The judgment of the trial court and the decision of the court of appeals is reversed, and the case is remanded for a new trial on the issue of damages only.

■ MEDICAL UNCERTAINTY, DIAGNOSTIC TESTING, AND LEGAL LIABILITY*
Eric E. Fortess & Marshall B. Kapp**
13 Law, Med. & Health Care 213 (1985)

Health care cost considerations exert increasing influence today over clinical decisionmaking. One way to help contain costs while maintaining the quality of health care may be to increase among both physicians and patients an

*Reprinted with the permission of the American Society of Law, Medicine & Ethics.

**When this article was written, Dr. Fortess was an associate professor of health administration and the director of the Health Administration Concentration at Suffolk University School of Management in Boston, Massachusetts. Mr. Kapp was associate professor of legal medicine in the Department of Medicine in Society at Wright State University School of Medicine in Dayton, Ohio.

acknowledgment of, and tolerance for, a reasonable degree of medical uncertainty. By medical uncertainty we mean here those clinical situations in which, based on available data, absolute scientific proof regarding some aspect of a patient's health status cannot be obtained. . . .

For a variety of reasons, physicians are generally reluctant to acknowledge openly the existence and role of uncertainty in medical care.[2] Traditional medical training does not go deeply into the theory, mathematics, and management of uncertainty. Moreover, physicians tend to insist on maintaining professional control and dominance, to believe in the potential therapeutic efficacy of both the patients' and the professionals' unquestioning confidence in a treatment, and to perceive that many patients will not accept a physician who claims not to be omniscient. . . . The main impetus for physicians' overuse of diagnostic and therapeutic modalities is their intellectual desire to know as much as possible about the facts of each case, whether or not any of the additional data generated will materially affect the course of treatment or the ultimate outcome. Other factors are the Western philosophy that action is superior to inaction and the "technological imperative" perspective that whatever technology can do should be done.[4] . . .

A physician comfortable with his or her own uncertainty[6] can usually convince the patient to accept incomplete or indefinite answers and explanations. This acceptance implies a change in emphasis from a Mechanistic Paradigm to a . . . Probabilistic Paradigm. This conceptual framework recognizes that absolute certainty is neither obtainable, identifiable, nor always desirable. . . . Put simply, past a certain point, the chance of achieving a small gain in certainty is not worth the costs — in any respect — of the effort. . . .

Most physicians appreciate the logic of diagnostic and therapeutic restraint in the face of inescapable medical uncertainty. Yet many argue that such restraint could result in patient-initiated medical malpractice suits predicated on provision of less than maximal care. To protect themselves, they resort to "defensive medicine," one cause of rising health care costs. "Defensive medicine" is an ambiguous, often carelessly used term for which Hershey has supplied the most useful working definition: "Poor practice (a deviation from what the physician believes is sound practice and which is generally so regarded) induced by a threat of liability."[14] A 1983 American Medical Association study claims that 40 percent of the AMA's members prescribe additional tests and 27 percent provide additional treatment at least in part because of the perceived threat of litigation. . . .

Most importantly, our public policymakers assume that uncontrolled health care costs are indeed due partially to a medical malpractice system that engenders defensive medicine. This perception has led to the introduction in Congress of bills that would substantially alter the medical malpractice system in an attempt to control one aspect of federal health care costs.

In spite of the furor over defensive medicine, cost-effective medical practice and the prudent management of legal risks can co-exist. An examination of

---

[2] H. Bursztajn et al., Medical Choices, Medical Chances (Delacorte Press, New York, 1981).
[4] See V. Fuchs, Who Shall Live? Health, Economics and Social Change (Basic Books, New York, 1974).
[6] See J. Katz, The Silent World of Doctor and Patient (Free Press, New York, 1984), 165-206.
[14] N. Hershey, The Defensive Practice of Medicine: Myth or Reality, Milbank Memorial Fund Quarterly 50(1):69, 72 (January 1972).

malpractice jurisprudence supports this thesis and refutes many widespread but incorrect perceptions. . . . By expressly recognizing that the same clinical problem can be approached in a range of different but equally acceptable ways (based either on the physician's philosophical convictions or on recognition of the limited state of medical knowledge), the legal system in essence respects and condones medical uncertainty and embraces the Probabilistic Paradigm. . . .

Contrary to popular medical belief, the mere existence of a particular diagnostic or treatment technology does *not* automatically create a legal imperative to use that technology indiscriminately. . . . The case most often cited to prove that rampant judicial intervention has wreaked havoc with medical standard-setting and necessitated the defensive practice of medicine is Helling v. Carey. . . . The medical profession reacted to the *Helling* decision with somber predictions that the quality of medical practice would fall and the cost of health care would rise, due to the overuse and misuse of diagnostic testing. It was argued that money, time, and other resources would be diverted from real needs and that patients would be unnecessarily exposed to iatrogenic risks. These predictions have in large measure gone unfulfilled. Whatever surge in defensive medicine and costs can be traced directly to *Helling* is attributable to a misperception, rather than to an accurate appraisal of the current status of the law and its requirements.

Basically, the *Helling* case, for all its attendant publicity, simply represents a legal anomaly. With the exception of the 1979 *Gates v. Jensen* case[1] in which the same Washington Supreme Court ignored a legislative attempt to return to the professional standard and instead ratified the *Helling* approach, the *Helling* precedent has not been applied in any reported malpractice lawsuit in any jurisdiction. . . .

[Nevertheless], *Helling*, as almost the sole example of direct legal intervention in setting the stringency of a medical standard, bears closer scrutiny. . . . We propose the following method of analysis, based on the mathematics of diagnostic testing, as a model . . . that may be applied to other tests to demonstrate that cost-effective medicine is also legally defensible. . . .

[Glaucoma] is diagnosed with one or more of three tests: tonometry, to measure intraocular pressure; perimetry, to evaluate the patient's field of vision; and funduscopy of the optic disc to detect "cupping" of the head of the optic nerve. In screening for glaucoma, ophthalmologists customarily use a tonometric test first. Tonometry usually involves light contact of the pressure-measuring instrument, the tonometer, on the anesthetized eye. If a pressure greater than 22 millimeters of mercury is found, the other tests may then be used to confirm or reject a diagnosis of glaucoma. Diagnosis is complicated by the fact that some people can have glaucoma without high intraocular pressure, while others can have high pressure (ocular hypertension) without developing glaucoma. . . . If glaucoma is diagnosed, treatment may include drugs to lower intraocular pressure, laser therapy, or surgery.

The diagnostic tests for glaucoma are thus not perfect, and actual disease states do not correspond totally with test results. Two major types of diagnostic error can occur: false negative test results with diseased patients and false positive test results with disease-free individuals. The ability of a test to correctly identify people with a

---

[1] 595 P.2d 919 (Wash. 1979).

disease is called its *sensitivity,* and its ability to correctly identify people without disease is its *specificity.* A test with few false negative results is highly sensitive, while one with few false positives is very specific. [Screening tests, like the tonometry pressure test used to detect possible glaucoma, are usually designed to err on the side of false positives, considering that false negatives—missing an actual case—are worse than falsely suspecting a number of healthy cases. In addition, even a low false positive *rate,* that is, very good test specificity, will produce a high *number* of false positives if the underlying incidence of the disease is very low, because lots of people have to be tested in order to ferret out the few true positives.] . . .

How do the probabilities of diagnostic testing relate to the *Helling* case? . . . Let us consider a hypothetical population of 25,000 individuals under age forty, of whom one has glaucoma. . . . Applying the estimates representing the best test performance, sensitivity of 70 percent and specificity of [95] percent, to our hypothetical population produces 1,250 false positive results. . . . If one is a true positive and 1,250 are false positives, then we can calculate that [the probability of truly having glaucoma when there is a positive test result is about 0.0008.] . . . Repeating the test, or performing the other two tests—perimetry and funduscopy, each with its own imperfect sensitivity and specificity—will shrink the pool of [false positives] but may never separate the one diseased person from the others. [Therefore, all may need to be treated. In addition, we must consider, even the one true positive may not be detected because of the rate of false negatives. Finally, when detected, treatment for the one true positive may not be safe and effective.] . . .

We have seen that in our hypothetical population, tonometry will probably produce [1,251] positive test results, of which only one truly identifies a person with glaucoma. Several disturbing issues arise. . . . What does the physician do with these patients, over 99.99 percent of whom don't have glaucoma? Does the physician have a duty to inform every patient of the possibility of glaucoma, causing great anxiety in many? Must the physician carefully monitor the thousands of patients identified as being at "increased risk" for glaucoma? What are the costs to society of mislabeling many people as "at risk" and then following and retesting them, perhaps for years? . . .

In retrospect, the *Helling* plaintiff should have been tested on the basis of her complaints and symptoms, despite her youth. But what would constitute good practice in one specific and unusual medical situation should not in itself be sufficient reason to institute a broad policy to test [all] young people for glaucoma.

■ ONE HUNDRED YEARS OF HARMFUL ERROR: THE HISTORICAL JURISPRUDENCE OF MEDICAL MALPRACTICE*
Theodore Silver**
1992 Wis. L. Rev. 1193

A medical malpractice action is identical in all vital respects to any and every suit sounding in negligence. That simple truth, however, has been lost in a maze

*Reprinted by permission of the Wisconsin Law Review.
**Professor of Law and M.D., Touro College Jacob D. Fuchsberg Law Center.

of judicial mistakes one century in the making. . . . Courts do not frequently offer a rationale for the professional custom rule. A few have suggested that medicine is too complex and the human body too temperamental to allow that a doctor be held to the simple standard of reasonableness. . . . Such explanations might at first seem sensible, but sensible they surely are not. First, medicine is no more complex than scores of other professional undertakings. . . . Organ transplantation is glamorous, but surely it is no more complicated or unpredictable in outcome than taming wild animals, designing a nation-wide marketing plan, or evaluating a new corporate security. All these pursuits are prey to the unknown and unknowable, and all demand expertise of a high order. With regard to medicine, complexity and uncertainty provides no greater reason for fashioning a standard of care after custom than they would in any other professional endeavor. . . .

Negligence is nothing more nor less than a failure to do what a reasonable person would under the prevailing circumstance. From a more refined perspective it is a failure to assess reasonably the costs and benefits associated with a given course of conduct, and thus to decide on its advisability. Justice Learned Hand . . . reduced the matter to quasi-mathematical terms, creating the famed Hand calculus: "Possibly it serves to bring this notion into relief to state in algebraic terms: if the probability be called P; the injury, L; and the burden, B; liability depends upon whether B is less than L multiplied by P: i.e., whether $B < PL$."[69]

The complexity of any technical field, medicine included, may well disable a lay juror who seeks independently to assess the relative risks and benefits attending a given course of conduct. That, however, only means that the juror needs advice from experts (genuine experts) who can identify the risks and benefits at issue. Thus informed, there is no reason that a juror cannot and should not pass on the appropriateness of anyone's conduct, including a physician's.

Without expert assistance a lay juror cannot determine whether it is negligent to discharge a particular cardiac patient from the hospital without prescribing anticoagulants. Yet, to make the determination, the juror requires only that an expert explain how the omission affects the matter of risks and benefits. An expert might explain that, according to standard medical wisdom, anticoagulants present a variety of risks and adverse effects, and, to the extent competent information allows, he might provide estimates of such risks in quantitative terms. . . . Armed with this knowledge, the jury would be competent to determine, as it does in any other negligence suit, whether the defendant physician had acted with reasonable care. . . .

Notes: Ordinary Negligence and the "Hand Formula"; Defensive Medicine

1. *Helling* met with an immediate storm of criticism in the legal and medical literature and upset the insurance industry even more, causing many insurers to

---

[69] Conway v. O'Brien, 111 F.2d 611 (2nd Cir. 1940).

feel that the deluge of expanded legal liability had reached revolutionary levels of social and political policy. This decision, along with the concurrence printed below, was credited with contributing to the withdrawal in the mid-1970s of many insurers from the medical malpractice market and the resulting "crisis" in medical malpractice, discussed in section G.

Is *Helling* really all that revolutionary? Can it be justified, for instance, using the res ipsa loquitur and negligence per se rules articulated in the previous notes, or is it simply an example, noted above at page 311, of courts rejecting a medical custom standard of liability in favor of a reasonable physician standard? See, e.g., United Blood Services v. Quintana, 827 P.2d 509 (Colo. 1992) (plaintiff is entitled to show that blood bank's methods for screening for AIDS virus, which were standard at the time, were not sufficiently protective because blood banks had failed to quickly adopt new safer methods). There is an obvious difference, however, between allowing a plaintiff to reach the jury without an expert on a contested question of fact and conceding that all medical opinion is opposed to the plaintiff's position. There is also an obvious difference between allowing the case to go to the jury and finding negligence as a matter of law. Did the defendant have a fair chance to present the data described in the Fortess and Kapp article? Do you think this information would have mattered to the *Helling* court? Prof. Peters explains that "in one respect, the *Helling* decision was and remains genuinely aberrant. No other court has endorsed the Washington Supreme Court's decision to take the issue of medical negligence away from the jury and to rule, without the benefit of expert testimony, that a customary practice is negligent as a matter of law. This aspect of *Helling* was deeply flawed and has justly contributed to its reputation as a rogue case. However, *Helling*'s rejection of customary norms was not aberrant. Not only has *Helling*'s rejection of customary standards survived in Washington with the eventual blessing of the legislature, but many other courts have reached the same conclusion. Although few of these courts have expressly relied on *Helling*, perhaps because of its notoriety, many have agreed with its rejection of customary standards." Philip G. Peters, The Quiet Demise of Deference to Custom: Malpractice Law at The Millennium, 57 Wash. & Lee L. Rev. 163, 171 (2000).

Immediately following *Helling*, the Washington legislature attempted to explicitly overrule it by a statute, but the state supreme court interpreted the statute as being consistent with its decision in *Helling*, since the statute refers to the skill and care "possessed" by physicians rather than "practiced" by them. Gates v. Jensen, 595 P.2d 919 (Wash. 1979). A subsequent decision clarifies, however, that "absent exceptional circumstances such as were present in *Helling*, expert testimony will be necessary to show whether or not a particular practice is reasonably prudent" and to clarify what skill and knowledge Washington physicians actually possess. Harris v. Groth, 663 P.2d 113 (Wash. 1983). The net effect, then, is to adopt the same "reasonable physician" standard that exists in many other states.

2. *The Technological Imperative.* It is often said that medicine in general, and doctors in particular, operate under a "technological imperative," which compels the use of all available technology, regardless of the economic, and sometimes even the medical, costs. This imperative is reinforced by the threat of liability, because doctors who want to obtain and use a new piece of equipment or new

surgical technique that others are using can always point to the liability concerns of being the last one on the block to innovate. For instance, in Washington v. Washington Hospital Center, 579 A.2d 177 (D.C. 1990), a brain-damaged patient won $4.5 million because the hospital failed to acquire a newer, better machine for monitoring oxygen levels during surgery. The monitor was in use in some, perhaps many, other hospitals, but not in all, and the plaintiff's expert equivocated on whether the new monitor was required by the standard of care at the time of the injury. However, there was evidence that the hospital's chief anesthesiologist, prior to the accident, had asked the hospital to purchase the new monitor, citing as support the potential legal threat of not complying with the emerging national standard of care.

When the technology in question is diagnostic, it produces information relevant to additional courses of treatment. This information often leads to a "clinical cascade," in which further testing is required to confirm or reject the initial test, and then to various paths of treatment. Along the way, other potential or actual problems are often uncovered or created, which precipitate additional testing or treatment. Thus, early intervention and additional information in medicine often spawns greater, not lesser, costs. For instance, one study found that women undergoing annual mammograms have a 50 percent chance of receiving a false positive result over the course of 10 years, and a 19 percent chance of undergoing an unnecessary biopsy. One HMO spent $33 to evaluate false positive results for every $100 spent on breast cancer screening. J. G. Elmore et al., Ten-Year Risk of False Positive Screening Mammograms and Clinical Breast Examinations, 338 New Eng. J. Med. 1089 (1998). An accompanying editorial argues that these results do not justify refusing to do routine mammograms for women under age 50, but they do support informing younger women of these odds and giving them the opportunity to decline. But see H. Gilbert Welch, Informed Choice in Cancer Screening, 285 JAMA 2776 (2001) (observing the practical difficulties in resolving these issues simply by presenting the choice to patients). For discussion of these issues as they relate to electronic fetal monitoring during childbirth, see Note, 51 Stan. L. Rev. 807 (1999). See generally Elliot Fisher & Gilbert Welch, Avoiding the Unintended Consequences of Growth in Medical Care: How Might More Be Worse?, 281 JAMA 46 (1999); H. Gilbert Welch, Questions About the Value of Early Intervention, 22 New Eng. J. Med. 1472 (1996); Richard A. Deyo, Cascade Effects of Medical Technology, 23 Ann. Rev. Pub. Health 23 (2002).

Given the financial and professional impetus for doing all that is possible in medicine, why do you suppose eye doctors in 1974 had restrained themselves from routinely testing all patients for glaucoma? How likely is this collective restraint to be exercised after *Helling*? Is this kind of collective restraint — selective use of new technology — good or bad for society? Who should make these decisions: doctors, patients, courts, or regulators?

A questionnaire administered several years after *Helling* revealed that it had not affected ophthalmology practice as much as had been expected. Doctors reported that they often performed the glaucoma test on patients under 40, but this was true both within and outside Washington state, and both before and after the court's decision. It appears that the testimony given in the case, that routine testing for younger patients was never done, was simply wrong. Jerry Wiley, The

Impact of Judicial Decision on Professional Conduct: An Empirical Study, 55 S. Cal. L. Rev. 345 (1982). In 2005, the U.S. Preventive Services Task Force reviewed all available evidence and concluded that there was "insufficient evidence to recommend for or against screening adults for glaucoma." Due to "uncertainty of the magnitude of benefit from early treatment and given the known harms of screening and early treatment," the task force "could not determine the balance between the benefits and harms of screening for glaucoma."

What does this suggest about the accuracy and utility of using tort law to evaluate and regulate medical practice? For additional discussion of the empirical issues in *Helling*, see Bovin et al., Cost-Effectiveness of Screening for Primary Open Angle Glaucoma, 3 J. Med. Screening 154 (1996); Comment, Rational Health Policy and the Legal Standard of Care: A Call for Judicial Deference to Medical Practice Guidelines, 77 Cal. L. Rev. 1483 (1989); Schwartz & Komesar, Damages and Deterrence: An Economic View of Medical Malpractice, 298 New Eng. J. Med. 1282 (1978).

3. *The Hand Formula.* Consider how the Hand formula might actually come out in the *Helling* case, using the numbers in Fortess and Kapp and additional reasonable assumptions. Start with the value for L, which represents the injury. What do you think reasonable compensation would be for the partial loss of vision Helling suffered (tunnel vision, but still functional eyesight)—$100,000, $250,000, $500,000 or more? What are the possible values for the other factors? Starting with B, the burden of injury prevention, assume 25,000 people are screened at a cost of $10 each. How much should be added to B for the unnecessary treatment and anxiety caused by false positives—$100 per person? $200? $500? Next, what value should be used for P, the probability of loss prevention? Realize that screening all 25,000 does not guarantee detecting the one bad case, and if it is detected, it is not always possible to treat it effectively. Suppose detection and treatment are only 70 percent effective. Suppose they are only 50 percent effective. What would the value of the loss have to be in order to balance out these costs and probabilities? See Wm. Schwartz & Neil Komesar, Doctors, Damages and Deterrence, 298 New Eng. J. Med. 1282 (1978).

4. *Defensive Medicine.* Despite all the controversy, some type of pressure testing has in fact become routine in all eye exams. Perhaps the costs are lower than supposed or the sensitivity and specificity have been improved. Or perhaps this is an example of the phenomenon described as "defensive medicine." This phrase is often used by doctors in a highly pejorative way to accuse the legal system of fostering unnecessary or harmful medical practice adopted solely to avoid liability and not for patient welfare. On the other hand, defensive medicine might be characterized as a perfectly appropriate result of the deterrent effect of liability, which encourages safer practices and more vigilance against error. In the middle ground, defensive medicine might be defined as medical practices adopted for liability reasons that are marginally or potentially beneficial but that, on balance, are wasteful. One must try to be clear in this debate about which understanding of the term is meant.

One place to start is to ask why the worst form of defensive medicine would ever occur. Since nonbeneficial medical procedures impose medical risks from side effects and cost more money, why don't these counter pressures force doctors to resist the legal pressures? One answer is that, under fee-for-service reimbursement, the economic costs of extra procedures are borne by insurance and contribute to doctors' revenues. Observe that liability concerns conceivably could also manifest themselves through lengthier counseling with patients (to acquire greater insight into their lifestyle habits and past medical history) or through more library research (to learn more about difficult, borderline cases)—much as we see in law firms that are paid by the hour—but this is not the sort of behavior complained of. Instead, it is said that physicians manifest defensive concerns by increasing the number of tests and procedures—no surprise since they are paid on a fee-for-service basis. Given this, is defensive medicine likely to abate, or at least assume a different form, as payment shifts to a different form? See Daniel Kessler & Mark McClellan, Malpractice Law and Health Care Reform: Optimal Liability Policy in an Era of Managed Care, 84 J. Pub. Econ. 175 (2002) (finding that managed care restrictions and liability reforms have similar and reinforcing effects in reducing defensive practices, which suggests that both payment incentives and liability pressures contribute to excess medical costs).

Another reason doctors may minimize or ignore the medical risks created by nonbeneficial defensive medicine is that these risks may be less likely to result in large damage verdicts. A single omitted diagnosis concentrates the harms of omission in a single case. A mild side effect spreads the harms of commission over a large number of cases, none of which is likely to result in suit. Also, side effects from unnecessary procedures may be more difficult to prove. Consider, for instance, that while too many X-rays may cause an increased risk of cancer, it is almost impossible to detect the specific origin of any particular case of cancer. Occasionally, however, one does see a successful suit for the harmful effects of unnecessary treatment, especially surgery. E.g., Riser v. American Med. Int'l, 620 So. 2d 372 (La. Ct. App. 1993) (liability for unnecessary arteriogram that caused patient to die from a stroke).

5. *The Extent of Defensive Medicine.* How precisely to define defensive medicine and the extent to which it contributes to the total costs of health care are still matters very much in debate. See generally U.S. Office of Technology Assessment, Defensive Medicine (1994). Based on estimates of tens of billions of dollars, the AMA and other interest groups continue to press for sweeping federal relief from state malpractice laws as one means to lower health care costs, but others sharply criticize the methodology behind the estimates. For additional discussion of defensive medicine and physicians' perceptions of the legal system, see page 287; Tom Baker, The Medical Malpractice Myth (2005); Troyen A. Brennan et al., Liability, Patient Safety, and Defensive Medicine, in Medical Malpractice and the U.S. Health Care System 93, 109-110 (W. Sage & R. Kersh, eds. 2006); David Studdert et al., Defensive Medicine Among High-Risk Specialist Physicians, 293 JAMA 2609 (2005); Kenneth DeVille, Act First and Look up the Law Afterward? Medical Malpractice and the Ethics of Defensive Medicine, 19 Theoretical Med. 569 (1998); D. Kessler & M. McClennan, Do Doctors Practice Defensive Medicine?, Q.J. Econ., May 1996, at 353; Note, The Medical Malpractice Threat: A Study of Defensive Medicine, 1971 Duke L.J. 939; Symposium, 21 J. Health Pol. Pol'y L. 185 (1996).

6. *Negative Defensive Medicine.* Perhaps the most serious harm of defensive medicine, however, is when it operates in the opposite direction, to discourage

doctors from doing certain procedures. This is known as "negative" defensive medicine. Because the malpractice liability threat is especially high for labor and delivery, many general practitioners have stopped delivering babies, some obstetricians refuse to take certain high risk cases or restrict their practice to gynecology, and others refuse to accept Medicaid patients for whom the reimbursement is too low to compensate for the liability risk. This aggravates the serious shortage of physicians in rural areas and creates barriers to care for other disadvantaged population groups who are more prone to premature births or to being on Medicaid.

A large and prominent medical group in San Diego adopted a policy of transferring patients and all their family members if they filed a malpractice claim. In one case, the court ruled that this could constitute illegal abandonment, interference with the doctor-patient relationship, and breach of fiduciary duties if the transfer hampered access to care or lacked sufficient notice and opportunity to find a new physician. Scripps Clinic v. Superior Court, 108 Cal.App.4th 917, 134 Cal.Rptr.2d 101 (Cal.App. 2003). In Williams v. St. Joseph Hospital, 629 F.2d 448 (7th Cir. 1980), the court found that this could constitute an antitrust violation.

Problem: To Test or Not to Test

Older women are at higher risk of giving birth to children with certain congenital defects such as Down's syndrome. Amniocentesis, the test for these defects, itself poses risks of causing a miscarriage. The universal, accepted practice for pregnant women without a family history of defects is to use amniocentesis routinely only for women age 35 or over. The logic is that, under 35, the statistical risk of miscarriage is greater than the chance of detecting serious birth defects. Also, amniocentesis can have false positives, which can result in erroneously aborting a healthy fetus.

How would you evaluate the age-35 rule-of-thumb under *Helling*? Under the Hand formula? Under informed consent law? Consider this both from the situation of a younger woman who is not tested who delivers a baby with Down's syndrome, and an older woman who is tested, resulting in the miscarriage of a healthy fetus.

3. Breach of Contract

■ SULLIVAN v. O'CONNOR
296 N.E.2d 183 (Mass. 1973)

KAPLAN, Justice.

The plaintiff patient secured a jury verdict of $13,500 against the defendant surgeon for breach of contract in respect to an operation upon the plaintiff's nose. . . . The declaration was in two counts. In the first count, the plaintiff alleged that she, as patient, entered into a contract with the defendant, a surgeon, wherein the defendant promised to perform plastic surgery on her nose and thereby to enhance her beauty and improve her appearance; that he performed the surgery but failed to achieve the promised result; rather the result of the surgery was to disfigure and deform her nose, to cause her pain in body and mind, and to subject her to other damage and expense. The second count, based on the same transaction, was in the conventional form for malpractice, charging that the defendant had been guilty of negligence in performing the surgery. . . . The jury returned a verdict for the plaintiff on the contract count, and for the defendant on the negligence count. The judge then instructed the jury on the issue of damages.

As background to the instructions and the parties' exceptions, we mention certain facts as the jury could find them. The plaintiff was a professional entertainer, and this was known to the defendant. The agreement was as alleged in the declaration. More particularly, judging from exhibits, the plaintiff's nose had been straight, but long and prominent; the defendant undertook by two operations to reduce its prominence and somewhat to shorten it, thus making it more pleasing in relation to the plaintiff's other features. Actually the plaintiff was obliged to undergo three operations, and her appearance was worsened. Her nose now had a concave line to about the midpoint, at which it became bulbous; viewed frontally, the nose from bridge to midpoint was flattened and broadened, and the two sides of the tip had lost symmetry. This configuration evidently could not be improved by further surgery. The plaintiff did not demonstrate, however, that her change of appearance had resulted in loss of employment. Payments by the plaintiff covering the defendant's fee and hospital expenses were stipulated at $622.65. . . .

By his exceptions the defendant contends that the judge erred in allowing the jury to take into account anything but the plaintiff's out-of-pocket expenses (presumably at the stipulated amount). The defendant excepted to the judge's refusal of his request for a general charge to that effect, and, more specifically, to the judge's refusal of a charge that the plaintiff could not recover for pain and suffering connected with the third operation or for impairment of the plaintiff's appearance and associated mental distress. . . . We conclude that the defendant's exceptions should be overruled.

It has been suggested on occasion that agreements between patients and physicians by which the physician undertakes to effect a cure or to bring about a given result should be declared unenforceable on grounds of public policy. But there are many decisions recognizing and enforcing such contracts, see annotation, 43 A.L.R.3d 1221, and the law of Massachusetts has treated them as valid, although we have had no decision meeting head on the contention that they should be denied legal sanction. These causes of action are, however, considered a little suspect, and thus we find courts straining sometimes to read the pleadings as sounding only in tort for negligence, and not in contract for breach of promise, despite sedulous efforts by the pleaders to pursue the latter theory.

It is not hard to see why the courts should be unenthusiastic or skeptical about the contract theory. Considering the uncertainties of medical science and the variations in the physical and psychological conditions of individual patients, doctors can seldom in good faith promise specific results. Therefore it is unlikely that physicians of even average integrity will in fact make such promises. Statements of opinion by the physician with some optimistic coloring are a different thing, and may indeed have therapeutic value. But patients may transform such statements into firm promises in their own minds, especially when they have been disappointed in the event, and testify in that sense to sympathetic juries.[2] If actions for breach of promise can be readily maintained, doctors, so it is said, will be frightened into practising "defensive medicine." On the other hand, if these actions were outlawed, leaving only the possibility of suits for malpractice, there is fear that the public might be exposed to the enticements of charlatans, and confidence in the profession might ultimately be shaken. See Miller, The Contractual Liability of Physicians and Surgeons, 1953 Wash. L.Q. 413, 416-423. The law has taken the middle of the road position of allowing actions based on alleged contract, but insisting on clear proof. Instructions to the jury may well stress this requirement and point to tests of truth, such as the complexity or difficulty of an operation as bearing on the probability that a given result was promised. See annotation, 43 A.L.R.3d 1225, 1225-1227.

If an action on the basis of contract is allowed, we have next the question of the measure of damages to be applied where liability is found. Some cases have taken the simple view that the promise by the physician is to be treated like an ordinary commercial promise. . . . Thus in Hawkins v. McGee, 84 N.H. 114, 146 A. 641, the defendant doctor was taken to have promised the plaintiff to convert his damaged hand by means of an operation into a good or perfect hand, but the doctor so operated as to damage the hand still further. The court, following the usual expectancy formula, would have asked the jury to estimate and award to the plaintiff the difference between the value of a good or perfect hand, as promised, and the value of the hand after the operation. . . . Other cases, including a number in New York, without distinctly repudiating the *Hawkins* type of analysis, have indicated that a different and generally more lenient measure of damages is to be applied. . . .

The factors, already mentioned, which have made the cause of action somewhat suspect, also suggest moderation as to the breadth of the recovery that should be permitted. Where, as in the case at bar and in a number of the reported cases, the doctor has been absolved of negligence by the trier, an expectancy measure may be thought harsh. We should recall here that the fee paid by the patient to the doctor for the alleged promise would usually be quite disproportionate to the putative expectancy recovery. To attempt, moreover, to put a value on the condition that would or might have resulted, had the treatment succeeded as promised, may sometimes put an exceptional strain on the imagination of the factfinder. . . .

The question of recovery on a reliance basis for pain and suffering or mental distress requires further attention. We find expressions in the decisions that pain and suffering (or the like) are simply not compensable in actions for breach of contract. The defendant seemingly espouses this proposition in the present case. True, if the buyer under a contract for the purchase of a lot of merchandise, in suing for the seller's breach, should claim damages for mental anguish caused by his disappointment in the transaction, he would not succeed; he would be told, perhaps, that the asserted psychological injury was not fairly foreseeable by the defendant as a probable consequence of the breach of such a business contract.

---

[2] Judicial skepticism about whether a promise was in fact made derives also from the possibility that the truth has been tortured to give the plaintiff the advantage of the longer period of limitations sometimes available for actions on contract as distinguished from those in tort or for malpractice.

See Restatement: Contracts, §341, and comment *a*. But there is no general rule barring such items of damage in actions for breach of contract. It is all a question of the subject matter and background of the contract, and when the contract calls for an operation on the person of the plaintiff, psychological as well as physical injury may be expected to figure somewhere in the recovery, depending on the particular circumstances. . . .

In the light of the foregoing discussion, all the defendant's exceptions fail: The plaintiff was not confined to the recovery of her out-of-pocket expenditures; she was entitled to recover also for the worsening of her condition, and for the pain and suffering and mental distress involved in the third operation. . . .

Notes: Liability Based on Contract or Fraud

1. *Strategic Choice of Theories.* The application of a contractual theory of liability in medical malpractice is rare, and, as illustrated in *Sullivan*, the courts usually impose a very high standard for proving a contractual breach. Nevertheless, plaintiffs persist for four reasons: raising the standard of care and avoiding the need to produce expert medical testimony; seeking a longer statute of limitations; avoiding restrictions imposed by medical malpractice reform statutes; and avoiding doctrines of sovereign or charitable immunity. Even where a contract action exists, the second and third strategies do not always work. Courts tend to impose the tort-law requirements when an action sounds in medical malpractice, regardless of the precise legal theory, and many statutory reforms define "medical malpractice actions" to include both tort and contract theories.

2. *Promises, Imagined and Real.* The *Sullivan* case involves an allegation of contractual guarantee of a particular result in plastic surgery. Another common situation involves a woman who conceives a child following a sterilization procedure. See generally Annot., 43 A.L.R.3d 1221 (1972 & Supp.). Courts express hostility to these and other contract theories in a variety of ways. In addition to raising the standard of proof to clear and convincing evidence and lowering damages to a reliance rather than an expectation measure, some courts also require the plaintiff to show separate consideration for the promise of a cure, apart from the doctor's normal fee for performing the procedure, or they require the guarantee to be in writing. See, e.g., Herrera v. Roessing, 533 P.2d 60 (Colo. 1975). Other states have achieved the same policy by statute. But see Burns v. Wannemaker, 343 S.E.2d 27 (S.C. 1986) (no separate consideration required for dentist's breach of express warranty with respect to fitting dentures).

What type of communication is sufficient to meet a clear and convincing proof standard? *Compare* Ferlito v. Cecola, 419 So. 2d 102 (La. Ct. App. 1982) (dentist's promise to "make your teeth real pretty" does not create a promise of complete satisfaction with respect to repairing crooked and discolored teeth), and Anglin v. Kleeman, 665 A.2d 747 (N.H. 1995) (alleged statements that surgery would make knee stronger and enable patient to resume football were opinions and not promises), *with* Doerr v. Villate, 220 N.E.2d 767 (1966) (assurance that sterilization will prevent pregnancy sufficient to support contract cause of action). As a practical matter, most surgeons avoid these disputes by including in the signed informed consent form a statement that specifically denies any guarantee of results and asserts only that the surgeon will use his professional skills in the accepted manner. After signing such a document, can the patient claim not to have understood its plain language? Is such a document similar to a release or covenant not to sue, which generally are not enforced? See Chapters 2.B.2 and 4.D.4.

3. *Advertising.* HMOs and other forms of managed care insurance create an arena in which contractual theories may have much greater prominence. Garden variety contract claims naturally arise when HMO subscribers complain that deliberate decisions to refuse treatment breached the promise of covered services contained in their insurance contract. Where the complaint sounds more in classic malpractice due to poorly performed treatment, mistaken diagnoses, or the like, contract theory might be based on advertising or promotional statements. Explicit image building efforts with the public at large were once a rarity in medicine, but now there is a glut of ads in newspapers, on billboards, and over the airwaves touting the quality of various medical institutions such as hospitals or HMOs. Even if these and similar assertions cannot be taken as warranting specific results from particular procedures, they can be argued to heighten the ordinary standard of care. Consider, for instance, an HMO that advertises "total health care" or that it has "over 1000 of the best doctors" in the region. See Allan S. Brett, The Case Against Persuasive Advertising by HMOs, 326 New Eng. J. Med. 1353 (1992). As George Anders explains,

> HMOs don't present themselves as the medical equivalent of a tawdry motel chain or a discount clothing store in a rundown part of town, blithely selling an inferior product in the name of having the cheapest possible price. Managed-care companies promise to uphold standards through their cost cutting, simply by targeting wasteful practices. Health Against Wealth: HMOs and the Breakdown of Medical Trust 59 (1996).

Should the same concerns expressed in *Sullivan* about allowing doctors to give "therapeutic assurances" cause courts to take a protective view of quality assurances issued by medical institutions? Giordano v. Ramirez, 503 So. 2d 947 (Fla. Dist. Ct. App. 1987), held that a health care plan that promised a "high standard of competence, care, and concern for the welfare and needs of subscribers" did not undertake a higher than normal standard of care. Accord, Pulvers v. Kaiser Foundation Health Plan, 160 Cal. Rptr. 392 (Cal. Ct. App. 1980). However, in Dunn v. Praiss, 656 A.2d 413 (N.J. 1995), the court accepted for purposes of argument that a contractual theory might be maintained based on language in an HMO's description of benefits that "Plan members receive health care from a large number of well-qualified, highly trained physicians." Nevertheless, the court dismissed the claim on technical grounds for failure to raise it in time. See also McClellan v. Health Maintenance Organization of Pennsylvania, 604 A.2d 1053 (Pa. Super. Ct. 1992) (allowing patient to plead HMO breached contract by misrepresenting that physicians were qualified and would make appropriate referrals). See generally Comment, Contractual Theories of Recovery in the HMO Provider-Subscriber Relationship, 36 Buff. L. Rev. 119 (1987).

4. *Abandonment and Switching Doctors.* Contractual theories also arise frequently in the form of allegations that physicians "abandoned" a patient by totally neglecting the patient or by failing to give the required attention.

Abandonment claims may sound in negligence, but they also can be said to be grounded in the contractual obligation to attend the patient properly and continuously until care for the particular illness is no longer needed. In this respect, the physician has failed to provide the personal professional services demanded under the contract of medical care. See Chapter 2.B.3. Employing a somewhat different theory, Maryland's high court ruled that a breach of contract action can be stated, based on informed consent principles, against a doctor who allows a training physician to perform part of an operation, where the patient alleges that the more experienced doctor expressly stated he would do the operation. Dingle v. Belin, 749 A.2d 157 (Md. 2000).

5. *Fraud.* Closely related to the contract and guarantee situations represented by *Sullivan* are situations where a physician is accused of fraudulent statements or intentional misrepresentation of the results that can be expected from treatment. Most of these cases involve unethical practices and criminal activities by charlatans who are not licensed physicians or are persons who have had medical licenses revoked in the past for improper practices. There are many alleged "doctors" who offer unorthodox treatment for weight loss, baldness, cancer, or other conditions where afflicted patients are especially susceptible to false hopes for cure. The most well-known action in this field was the prosecution of a chiropractor "faith healer" for murder in the case of a young child with cancer in her eye. The prosecutor obtained a conviction for first-degree murder under a felony-murder theory that characterized the chiropractor's false promises as "grand theft." The California Supreme Court reversed, asserting that grand theft is not the type of felony that usually creates personal danger to human life and so could not support the felony-murder rule. People v. Phillips, 414 P.2d 353 (Cal. 1966). The case did not end at this point, however. The prosecutor persisted and in a second jury trial the chiropractor was convicted of second-degree murder. On appeal, the intermediate appellate court upheld the conviction on grounds that the defendant maliciously caused the child's death by fraudulently discouraging the parents from seeking proper treatment. People v. Phillips, 270 Cal. App. 2d 381, 75 Cal. Rptr. 720 (Cal. Ct. App. 1969). For a review of the background of the case see W. Curran, Law-Medicine Notes—Program in Medicolegal Relations 161-164 (1989).

Some cases do not involve frankly criminal conduct but rather overzealous assurances to patients before or after treatment, or both. In order to sustain liability for fraud, however, the plaintiff would be required to prove that statements of fact, not opinion, were knowingly false. Practitioners can often claim they have an honest belief based on a few documented "miraculous" cures. See, e.g, Schneider v. Revici, excerpted at page 421.

6. *Implied Warranties.* Contractual theories based on express statements should be distinguished from those based on implied warranties. Implied warranties that arise automatically from the sale of consumer products do not generally attach to professional services. Where products are involved in medical care, they are usually considered by the courts as incidental to medical services and therefore as not giving rise to implied warranties or other forms of products liability on the part of doctors or hospitals. Products liability theories may, however, be stated against manufacturers of medical drugs and devices. For additional discussion, see section C.6.

4. Vicarious Liability

■ FRANKLIN v. GUPTA

567 A.2d 524 (Md. App. 1990)

WILNER, Judge.

. . . Appellant, an unfortunate soul with a host of physical and emotional problems, also developed carpal tunnel syndrome — a condition that causes pain in the wrist and muscle weakness in the hand. He consulted Dr. Shanker L. Gupta, a general surgeon, who recommended surgical treatment for that condition.

. . . Dr. Herbert S. T. Lee, an anesthesiologist, and Gary J. Sergott, a certified registered nurse anesthetist, were assigned by the hospital to administer and monitor the anesthesia. Unfortunately, Dr. Lee was also scheduled to administer and monitor anesthesia to another patient in another operating room at the hospital at the same time. Dr. Lee chose to tend to the other patient, and so the actual administration and monitoring of the anesthesia to appellant fell to Nurse Sergott. As we shall see, things did not go as planned. The anesthesia administered by Nurse Sergott was not only not effective, but appellant suffered certain physical and emotional trauma from it, and the surgery was eventually cancelled.

As a result of this experience, appellant filed a claim with the Health Claims Arbitration Office against Dr. Gupta, Dr. Lee, Nurse Sergott, and the hospital. After an evidentiary hearing, the arbitration panel found no liability on the part of any of the defendants and entered an award in their favor. Appellant rejected the award and filed suit in the Circuit Court for Baltimore City.

After a de novo trial, the jury agreed with the arbitration panel that there was no liability on the part of Dr. Gupta, but it concluded that the other defendants were culpable. It returned a verdict in favor of Dr. Gupta but against Dr. Lee, Nurse Sergott, and the hospital in the amount of $375,000. . . . [The trial court granted the three losing defendants' motions for a new trial or, in the alternative, remittitur of all but $50,000, citing the failure of appellant to show convincing evidence that the treatment rendered caused most of his injuries. Plaintiff appealed.]

I. UNDERLYING FACTS

We mean no disrespect when we say that appellant was not a picture of health when he presented himself at the hospital on July 16, 1981 — the day before his scheduled surgery. He had a history of syncope (temporary blackouts), asthma, emphysema, bronchitis, hyperthyroidism, chronic depression, and a nervous condition. He was also excessively — "morbidly" — obese; five feet, five inches tall, he weighed 295 pounds. He was permanently and totally disabled from employment and subsisted from Social Security disability benefits.

Dr. Lee, as we indicated, was designated by the hospital as the anesthesiologist for appellant's surgery, along with Nurse Sergott. Dr. Lee visited appellant on the afternoon of the 16th for an "anesthesia evaluation." Because of the patient's asthma, obesity, and hyperthyroidism, Dr. Lee recognized that appellant was a "high risk patient for anesthesia"; he therefore decided against a general anesthesia and opted instead for an axillary or brachial block.[1] He did not, however, . . . discuss the case in any way with Nurse Sergott. . . . Nurse Sergott independently decided to use a brachial block; he decided, by himself, which drug to use for that purpose; and he also decided, by himself, what analgesic to use and how it was to be administered. . . .

At some point shortly after administering the third dose of [local anesthesia], Nurse Sergott noticed that the block was "patchy" — i.e., "[t]he media flesh was not completely blocked on his hand." He wanted to give appellant another block, but Dr. Gupta insisted that he put appellant to sleep. Believing that general anesthesia was inappropriate and that, "being a surgeon, [Dr. Gupta] is not aware of anesthesia," Nurse Sergott decided to consult Dr. Lee who, . . . then busy with another patient under anesthesia and unable to leave, agreed that appellant should be given another brachial block and not put to sleep.

. . . While Nurse Sergott was conferring with Dr. Lee, appellant's breathing became shallow. Indeed, according to the medical record, he became cyanotic — i.e., his skin turned blue because of lack of oxygen in the body. He then became bradycardic (slow heartbeat) and had a period of asystole (his heart stopped beating entirely). . . . Appellant was promptly intubated and given Atropine and cardiopulmonary resuscitation, and his heartbeat returned to normal. At that point, Dr. Lee appeared and instructed Dr. Gupta to cancel the surgery.

Appellant remained in the hospital until his discharge on July 21, 1981. He never did have the surgery on his wrist. [He alleged that the delay caused by the nurse anesthesist's indecision and inability to properly anesthetize him aggravated his underlying medical conditions and caused permanent injury. . . .]

IV. JURY INSTRUCTIONS

. . . At the close of the evidence, appellant submitted . . . Proposed Instruction No. 11, captioned "Responsibility and Liability of Surgeon — the Captain of the Ship Doctrine." The relevant part of it is as follows:

> While Mr. Franklin was being prepared to undergo surgery, Dr. Gupta, the surgeon, is ordinarily regarded in law as having the exclusive responsibility and control over the case. . . . [H]e can thus be held responsible for any acts of negligence committed during the operation by any nurse anesthetist or assisting physician who is under his direction, no matter whether or not such assistant is an employee of Church Home Hospital. For the purposes of the surgery, nurse Sergott and the other members of the operating room staff are referred to as "borrowed servants" for whose acts the surgeon and the employer (the Church Home Hospital) must be responsible. . . .

The court declined to give . . . instructions . . . about any vicarious liability on the part of Dr. Gupta for the acts or omissions of Dr. Lee or Nurse Sergott. Instead, it told the jury, in relevant part that . . . "Dr. Gupta is to be judged in his capacity as a surgeon. Dr. Lee is to be judged in his capacity as an anesthesiologist;

---

[1] An axillary or brachial block is designed to anesthetize the entire arm, but nothing more.

and Mr. Sergott is to be judged in his capacity as a certified, registered nurse anesthetist. . . ."

[No] expert witness asserted any direct negligence on the part of Dr. Gupta. Nor did . . . any expert witness assert, as a matter of standard medical or hospital practice, that Dr. Gupta, as the surgeon employed to operate on appellant's wrist, had the expertise, the duty, or the right to supervise or control the method of anesthesia, the agents used to achieve the anesthesia, the dosages of those agents, the preoperative examination and evaluation of appellant by Lee and/or Sergott, the extent of communication and collaboration between them, or the precise manner in which Sergott conducted himself in the holding area and in the operating room.[5] There was no evidence that Dr. Gupta actually exercised, or attempted to exercise, any such supervision or control. Proposed Instruction No. 11, then, was not based on any factual predicate but on an assumed principle of law.

The principle underpinning the instruction has become popularly—and sometimes erroneously or misleadingly—called the "captain of the ship" doctrine. As explained in Thomas v. Raleigh General Hosp., 358 S.E.2d 222, 224 (W. Va. 1987): "Under this doctrine, a surgeon is likened to the captain of a ship, in that it is his duty to control everything going on in the operating room. Thus, liability is imposed by virtue of the surgeon's status and without any showing of actual control by the surgeon." As pointed out by Price, The Sinking of the "Captain of the Ship," 10 J. Legal Med. 323 (1989), this "Captain of the Ship" doctrine is but one of several theories of vicarious liability on the part of hospitals and surgeons for acts of negligence committed in the operating room. It is helpful, in examining the doctrine, to consider its context, its purpose, its scope, and how the courts have dealt with it.

A hospital, like any "master" or employer, is liable under agency principles for the negligence of its servants or employees. That would include nurses, physicians, and other medical and nonmedical personnel employed by it. Until fairly recently, however, in Maryland and in many states, this vicarious liability under agency law was of little assistance to plaintiffs injured by malpractice because of the eleemosynary (or governmental) immunity enjoyed by most hospitals. See Annotation, 25 A.L.R.2d 29 (1952).

Whether for that reason or whether because hospitals in earlier days were regarded less as comprehensive health care providers in their own right than as "innkeeper[s], providing a facility for patients to be treated by their privately retained physicians" (Price, supra, 10 J. Legal Med. at 340), courts began to impose liability on the surgeon for what went on in the operating room. The first theory employed was the traditional "borrowed servant" doctrine now expressed in Restatement (Second) of Agency §227.[6] The notion was that the surgeon acted as a special employer who borrowed nurses and other attendants from their general employer—the hospital—and thus became liable for their negligence. See, in general, Annotation, 12 A.L.R.3d 1017 (1967). Liability under that

---

[5] Dr. Gupta . . . conceded only that it was part of his duty to see that the patient is properly anesthetized before beginning to operate.

[6] "A servant directed or permitted by his master to perform services for another may become the servant of such other in performing the services. He may become the other's servant as to some acts and not as to others."

doctrine, of course, requires a showing that the surgeon actually controlled or had a right to control the details of the servant's conduct.

In McConnell v. Williams, 361 Pa. 355, 65 A.2d 243 (1949), the Pennsylvania Court essentially applied that doctrine, but in doing so it likened the surgeon to the captain of a ship. Unfortunately, that simile came to receive more attention than the actual holding in the case. The defendant was an obstetrician employed to attend the plaintiff during her pregnancy. The delivery, by cesarian section, was a difficult one. When the baby was removed from the womb, the defendant handed her to an intern to tie the cord and administer silver nitrate to the eyes. The intern performed the latter task negligently; he put too much solution in the eyes and failed to irrigate, thereby causing severe damage to the child's eyes. The intern was a hospital employee but had been designated by the obstetrician to assist. The action against the obstetrician was based solely on a theory of vicarious liability for the intern's negligence. At the time the case reached the Pennsylvania Supreme Court, the hospital enjoyed charitable immunity and therefore could not be made to answer for the intern's negligence.

Unlike most cases, the obstetrician acknowledged in his testimony that his liability "was to continue until the baby was turned over to the family doctor" and that "he had complete control of the operating room and of every person within it while the operation was in progress." It was in that light that the court, after reciting the general law relating to borrowed servants, including the requirement of control, made the statement that

> it can readily be understood that in the course of an operation in the operating room of a hospital, and until the surgeon leaves that room at the conclusion of the operation . . . he is in the same complete charge of those who are present and assisting him as is the captain of a ship over all on board, and that such supreme control is indeed essential in view of the high degree of protection to which an anaesthetized, unconscious patient is entitled. . . . [I]f operating surgeons were not to be held liable for the negligent performance of the duties of those then working under them, the law would fail in large measure to afford a means of redress for preventable injuries sustained during the course of such operations.

McConnell is sometimes credited with having spawned a new "separate and independent concept of agency" in hospital settings. Price, supra, 10 J. Legal Med. at 331. That may be giving *McConnell* too much credit. . . . [T]he *McConnell* court made clear that the issue of control by the surgeon was one of fact, not of law. In its concluding paragraph, it said that "[i]t is for the jury to determine whether the relationship between defendant and the interne, at the time the child's eyes were injured, was that of master and servant." 65 A.2d at 48.

Some courts that seemingly have made surgeons strictly liable for the negligence of others in the operating room, or that have used the expression "captain of the ship," have in reality done nothing more than apply res ipsa loquitur or a doctrine of negligence per se to the physician. Most of these cases involved the leaving of sponges or other foreign substances in the body, and the court adopted the view that, in such circumstances, negligence on the part of the surgeon can be inferred from the mere happening of the event. The surgeon's negligence, in other words, was direct, not vicarious. References in these cases to the "captain of the ship" are usually in the context of rejecting as a defense to such inferred negligence that the surgeon relied on an erroneous sponge count by the nurse.

In summary, a careful analysis of the cases cited as "captain of the ship" cases generally reveals that the court has applied traditional agency concepts and that, where the surgeon has been held liable, the liability has either been direct (even if inferred) or based on evidence that the negligent actors were, in fact, under his direct supervision and control. As in *McConnell*, the rhetoric often tends to obscure the factual underpinning of the holding.[7]

To the extent that the doctrine is regarded as an expansion of the traditional borrowed servant rule, most courts have either expressly rejected it or have declared it inapplicable when the negligent actor is an anesthesiologist or nurse anesthetist. Two theories have been advanced for the rejection or limitation. The first was well expressed in Thomas v. Raleigh General Hosp., supra, 358 S.E.2d 222, 225:

> We reject the captain of the ship doctrine. The trend toward specialization in medicine has created situations where surgeons do not always have the right to control all personnel within the operating room. . . . An assignment of liability based on a theory of actual control more realistically reflects the actual relationship which exists in a modern operating room.[8]

. . . Compare Baird v. Sickler, 69 Ohio St. 2d 652, 433 N.E.2d 593 (1982) (surgeon could be liable for the negligent conduct of a nurse anesthetist where the evidence showed that the surgeon "exercised and possessed" the right to control the nurse's actions and actually "participated in the administering of the anesthetic.").

The second theory, applied by some courts, is that, with the curtailment or abolition of the hospital's charitable or governmental immunity, by statute or

---

[7] The Texas Court in Sparger v. Worley Hospital, Inc., 547 S.W.2d 582, 584 (Tex. 1977), put its judicial finger on the problem:

Similes sometimes help to explain a factual situation, but in legal wiring, phrases have a way of being canonized and of growing until they can stand and walk independently of the usual general rules. Mr. Justice Frankfurter once wrote concerning such phrase-making in judicial opinions: "The phrase . . . is an excellent illustration of the extent to which uncritical use of words bedevils the law. A phrase begins life as a literary expression; its felicity leads to its lazy repetition; and repetition soon establishes it as a legal formula, undiscriminatingly used to express different and sometimes contradictory ideas." Tiller v. Atlantic Coast Line R. Co., 318 U.S. 54, 68, 63 S. Ct. 444, 452, 87 L. Ed. 610 (1943). The result in the use of captain of the ship is that a surgeon or physician may be held liable, not as others upon the basis of the general rule of borrowed servant, but as captain of the ship.

[8] May v. Broun, 261 Or. 28, 492 P.2d 776, 781 (1972), also espoused the first theory, pointing out at 781:

Changes have also been occurring in the confines of operating rooms. Surgeons are operating more and more in a highly mechanized environment wholly created by hospitals. Much highly technical equipment, now considered necesssary, is furnished by the hospital and operated by personnel which the hospital hires and trains. As a result, in most instances, a surgeon cannot actually have direct supervision or control over such equipment and the persons who operate it even when he is present, if he is going to give the concentration and attention to the surgery which his patient has the right to expect.

judicial decision, an expanded liability on the part of the surgeon is no longer necessary. . . .

Maryland ventured into these waters only once — 76 years ago. In Hunner v. Stevenson, supra, 122 Md. 40, 89 A. 418, . . . [the plaintiff] sued the doctor, not for anything he did or didn't do directly, but on the theory that, as the surgeon, he was responsible for the negligence of other hospital personnel in the post-operative treatment and dressing of the wound. The court said as to that issue: . . . "It would be unreasonable to expect such a one as the record shows the appellant to be — performing operations in five different hospitals in Baltimore, and in one at Frederick, in addition to his other practice — to continue to dress the wounds and have personal charge of the after-treatment in all cases until the patient is discharged from the hospital."

. . . From our analysis of how other courts have dealt with the issue at hand, we reject any "captain of the ship" theory of liability. . . . The correct doctrine to apply is the traditional "borrowed servant" rule. Where the evidence suffices to support a finding that the surgeon in fact had or exercised the right to control the details of another person's work or conduct in the operating room and the other elements of the rule are satisfied, the trier of fact may find that the surgeon was the "special employer" and is therefore liable for the negligence of the borrowed servant.

That was not the case here, however. As we indicated, there was no evidence that Dr. Gupta in any way supervised or controlled, attempted to supervise or control, or had the right or power to supervise or control, the conduct and decisions of Dr. Lee or Nurse Sergott. Proposed Instruction No. 11 was therefore properly rejected. . . .

Notes: Physicians' Vicarious Liability; "Captain of the Ship"

1. *The* Franklin *Case.* Acknowledging that Dr. Gupta did not actually determine which anesthesia to use and how to administer it, are you convinced beyond any reasonable dispute that he lacked the *right* and *power* to do so? It was agreed that he could at least halt the operation if he was not satisfied. What about Dr. Lee, the anesthesiologist? Was he any more responsible, in actuality or in theory, for what the nurse did wrong? As it turns out, he and the nurse were found liable, along with the hospital (albeit, for only $50,000). How strong is the "captain of the ship" case against Dr. Lee? See generally Nancy King, The Physician as Captain of the Ship: A Critical Appraisal (1988).

2. *The Effect on Hospital Liability.* Captain of the ship and borrowed servant are not only theories of liability against doctors, they are also theories of defense asserted by hospitals. Where a surgeon controls a negligent nurse, hospitals assert that they are not vicariously liable even though they are the nurse's employer because they lent their "servant" to the physician. See Krane v. St. Anthony Hospital System, 738 P.2d 75 (Colo. Ct. App. 1987). However, most courts hold the hospital jointly liable unless the doctor instructs the nurse to do an act that is not within the general scope of duty. Restatement (Second) of Agency §227.

The erosion of hospitals' charitable immunity and the rise of complex, technologically dependent team treatment are discussed further in section F.1. Are there any other theories of liability that you think should be affected by these developments? Some in the academic and public policy community contend that hospitals should be *exclusively* liable for all negligent medical care rendered on their premises, without regard to the physician's specialty or relationship with the hospital, thus absolving individual physicians from any liability, even for their own mistakes. See pages 474.

3. *Professional Corporations.* Physicians' vicarious liability is not restricted to the borrowed servant rule. It can also arise by virtue of being an employer of or partner with the medical professional who makes a negligent mistake. In the partnership setting, doctors are not individually liable for negligence committed by their colleagues unless they are involved in the treatment. The partnership as an entity however, is, liable, and doctors who are general partners have unlimited individual liability for making good the partnership's debts, so the liability exposure effectively exists in general partnerships. See Annot., 85 A.L.R.2d 889 (1962 & Supp.). This is one reason doctors seek to organize as professional corporations, which combine the tax advantages of a partnership with the liability protections of a corporate form. However, many state professional corporations statutes protect physicians only from contractual or business obligations, not tort obligations, or have been interpreted in this fashion by restrictive court decisions. Thus, physicians continue to be jointly and severally liable for the professional torts of member physicians. See, e.g., Pediatric Neurosurgery v. Russell, 44 P.3d 1063 (Colo. 2002).

More recently, states have enacted "limited liability corporation" statutes that make it even easier to combine the tax benefits of partnerships with the liability protections of the corporate form. These have proven to be wildly popular. Although they retain the same constraints on the ability to avoid professional liability, some of these statutes adopt the innovation that physicians are vicariously liable only if they supervise the physician at fault.

Moreover, these liability rules affect only the obligation to patients. They can always be altered internally by indemnification agreements among partnering physicians or with their corporate entities.

5. Strict Liability

■ HELLING v. CAREY
519 P.2d 981 (Wash. 1974)

[The facts and majority opinion are excerpted at page 365. The following is the concurring opinion by Justice Utter, in which two other justices concurred.]

I concur in the result reached by the majority. I believe a greater duty of care could be imposed on the defendants than was established by their profession. The duty could be imposed when a disease, such as glaucoma, can be detected by a simple, well-known harmless test whose results are definitive and the disease can be successfully arrested by early detection, but where the effects of the disease are irreversible if undetected over a substantial period of time.

The difficulty with this approach is that we as judges, by using a negligence analysis, seem to be imposing a stigma of moral blame upon the doctors who, in this case, used all the precautions commonly prescribed by their profession in diagnosis and treatment. Lacking their training in this highly sophisticated profession, it seems illogical for this court to say they failed to exercise a reasonable standard of care. It seems to me we are, in reality, imposing liability, because, in choosing between an innocent plaintiff and a doctor, who acted reasonably according to his specialty but who could have prevented the full effects of this disease by administering a simple, harmless test and treatment, the plaintiff should not have to bear the risk of loss. As such, imposition of liability approaches that of strict liability.

Strict liability or liability without fault is not new to the law. Historically, it predates our concepts of fault or moral responsibility as a basis of the remedy. Wigmore, Responsibility for Tortious Acts: Its History, 7 Harv. L. Rev. 315, 383, 441 (1894). As noted in W. Prosser, The Law of Torts §74 (3d ed. 1964):

> There are many situations in which a careful person is held liable for an entirely reasonable mistake. . . . In some cases the defendant may be held liable, although he is not only charged with no moral wrongdoing, but has not even departed in any way from a reasonable standard of intent or care. . . . There is "a strong and growing tendency, where there is blame on neither side, to ask, in view of the exigencies of social justice, who can best bear the loss and hence to shift the loss by creating liability where there has been no fault." (Footnote omitted.)

Tort law has continually been in a state of flux. It is

> not always neat and orderly. But this is not to say it is illogical. Its central logic is the logic that moves from premises — its objectives — that are only partly consistent, to conclusions — its rules — that serve each objective as well as may be while serving others too. It is the logic of maximizing service and minimizing disservice to multiple objectives. Keeton, Is There a Place for Negligence in Modern Tort Law?, 53 Va. L. Rev. 886, 897 (1967).

When types of problems rather than numbers of cases are examined, strict liability is applied more often than negligence as a principle which determines liability. Peck, Negligence and Liability Without Fault in Tort Law, 46 Wash. L. Rev. 225, 239 (1971). There are many similarities in this case to other cases of strict liability. Problems of proof have been a common feature in situations where strict liability is applied. Where events are not matters of common experience, a juror's ability to comprehend whether reasonable care has been followed diminishes. There are few areas as difficult for jurors to intelligently comprehend as the intricate questions of proof and standards in medical malpractice cases.

In applying strict liability there are many situations where it is imposed for conduct which can be defined with sufficient precision to insure that application of a strict liability principle will not produce miscarriages of justice in a substantial number of cases. If the activity involved is one which can be defined with sufficient precision, that definition can serve as an accounting unit to which the costs of the activity may be allocated with some certainty and precision. With this possible, strict liability serves a compensatory function in situations where the defendant is, through the use of insurance, the financially more responsible person. Peck, Negligence and Liability Without Fault in Tort Law, supra, at 240, 241.

If the standard of a reasonably prudent specialist is, in fact, inadequate to offer reasonable protection to the plaintiff, then liability can be imposed without fault. . . . Where [glaucoma] can be detected by a simple, well-known harmless test, where the results of the test are definitive, where the disease can be successfully arrested by early detection and where its effects are irreversible if undetected over a substantial period of time, liability should be imposed upon defendants even though they did not violate the standard existing within the profession of ophthalmology. . . .

Notes: Designing a No-Fault Liability System

1. *Overview.* No jurisdiction has come close to embracing Justice Utter's reasoning as a basis for individual liability of physicians. Indeed, as the next case discloses, there has been a move to restrict the application of strict liability in the medical arena even where it normally applies — to products liability for defective drugs and medical equipment. See, e.g., Newmark v. Gimbel's Inc., 258 A.2d 697 (N.J. 1969) ("the nature of [medical] services, the utility of and the need for them, involving as they do, the health and even survival of many people, are so important to the general welfare as to outweigh in the policy scale any need for the imposition on dentists and doctors of the rules of strict liability in tort").

In contrast with strict liability of individual defendants, however, is the related notion of no-fault compensation programs administered by the government. Even though strict liability has not found many adherents in the context of traditional tort suits against doctors, it has attracted considerable attention as the basis for an administrative compensation system for medical injuries. These no-fault liability proposals resemble the workers' compensation schemes that replaced negligence suits against employers in the first half of the twentieth century. The basic structure is to define a range of compensable events, establish a schedule of economic and noneconomic damages, and create an administrative system for filing claims and resolving factual disputes and questions of interpretation. See generally Paul C. Weiler, Medical Malpractice on Trial (1991); P. Weiler, The Case for No-Fault Medical Liability, 52 Md. L. Rev. 908 (1993). Each of these components offers potential advantages over current tort law, but also presents sources of controversy and difficulties in design and implementation, as explored in the following notes.

2. *Defining Compensable Events.* As the *Helling* concurrence argues, defining compensable events in terms of negative medical outcomes, without regard to fault or the standard of care, has the advantages of greater simplicity, the reduction of pejorative accusations against well-meaning professionals, and the increased social justice of covering seriously injured patients regardless of the behavior that caused the injury. Proponents of no-fault argue that traditional malpractice liability does a poor job of deterrence because doctors perceive lawsuits as largely random and uncontrollable events, medical malpractice insurance is widespread and not experience-rated, and deterrent signals create

unnecessary and costly "defensive medicine." See generally Michelle M. Mello & Troyen A. Brennan, Deterrence of Medical Errors: Theory and Evidence for Malpractice Reform, 80 Tex. L. Rev. 1595 (2002). The hope is that a well-crafted no-fault system could correct some or all of these deficiencies.

The difficulty with designing a no-fault compensable system, however, is defining exactly which events trigger compensation. *Helling* may present compelling facts, but in many medical encounters causation is complex and not all failures to achieve perfect results are avoidable. Subjecting these questions to litigation would prove costly, but they are essential to defining the scope of strict liability. Moreover, it is difficult to define which bad results are avoidable or unexpected without allowing concepts of fault to creep back in, since a less-than-perfect outcome is compensable only if "correct" medical procedures would have avoided it. Consider, for instance, how you would determine which of various versions of the following events is subject to no-fault compensation: misdiagnosis; adverse drug reactions; and post-surgical infections. Can you make such a determination without suggesting the doctors did something wrong? Can you do so without alluding to what most other doctors do in the same situation?

One way to circumvent these difficulties is simply to list for each major category of treatment or illness which outcomes are considered abnormal enough to warrant compensation as a medical injury. Naturally, this would be a large, complex undertaking. One version of this approach is contained in the work of Laurence Tancredi and colleagues, who have proposed a set of "Accelerated Compensation Events" (ACEs) for obstetrics. See R. Bovbjerg, L. Tancredi, & D. Gaylin, Obstetrics and Malpractice: Evidence on the Performance of a Selective No-Fault System, 265 JAMA 2836 (1991); C. Havighurst & L. Tancredi, Medical Adversity Insurance: A No-Fault Approach to Medical Malpractice and Quality Assurance, 51 Milbank Mem. Fund Q. 125 (1973). More recently, the architects of the New York and Utah studies of medical malpractice have drawn on these empirical findings to present a fresh case for non-fault compensation for all medical injuries, with a focus on institutional or enterprise liability, in order to encourage a more systemic approach to the improvement of medical quality. See David Studdert & Troyen Brennan, No-Fault Compensation for Medical Injuries: The Prospect for Error Prevention, 286 JAMA 217 (2001); David Studdert, Toward a Workable Model of Non-Fault Compensation for Medical Injury in the United States, 27 Am. J.L. & Med. 225 (2001); Mello & Brennan, supra. See generally Larry Palmer, Patient Safety, Risk Reduction, and the Law, 36 Hous. L. Rev. 1609 (1999); Edward P. Richards & Thomas R. McLean, Administrative Compensation for Medical Malpractice Injuries: Reconciling the Brave New World of Patient Safety and the Torts System, 49 St.L.U. L.J. 73 (2004); Frank Sloan & Lindsey M. Chepke, Ill-Suited? Medical Malpractice at a Crossroads (2008).

3. *Costs and Administrative Efficiency.* The other two components of proposals for no-fault compensation attempt to make damages more predictable and dispute resolution speedier and less costly. These advantages are articulated further in sections D.4 and G. Of particular note is the fact that, under the conventional tort system, less than 50 percent of malpractice insurance premiums end up in the pockets of injured patients. The hope is that savings in administrative and legal costs and the somewhat lower awards from a no-fault system will largely offset the increase in the number of claims that are filed, so that

the total costs of the system remain the same but it covers more people and operates more fairly. These virtues alone are substantial enough that in the 1980s the AMA proposed a *fault-based* administrative compensation system. There is the potential, however, that as the system becomes less costly and more accessible, the number of claims will skyrocket, since research has shown that the number of patients who now sue is a tiny fraction (1 to 2 percent) of the total number who are injured by medical care. Accordingly, the AMA has stopped promoting its administrative reform proposal. However, the idea has been taken up by others, in the form of resolving malpractice disputes through administrative hearings or specialized "health courts." See Symposium, J. Health Care L. & Policy 217 (2006); Catherine Struve, Doctors, the Adversary System, and Procedural Reform in Medical Liability Litigation, 72 Fordham L. Rev. 943 (2004); Eleanor D. Kinney, Administrative Law Approaches to Medical Malpractice Reform, 49 St. L.U. L.J. 45 (2004); Michelle Mello et al., "Health Courts" and Accountability for Patient Safety, 84 Milbank Q. 459 (2006).

The other drawback to no-fault schemes is their costs and how they are distributed. Even with administrative efficiencies, full compensation for all medical injuries will be much more expensive in total than the present system because so many injuries now are entirely uncompensated. To keep a no-fault system affordable, proponents usually set tight caps on total recoverable damages. As discussed in section E, this resolution of the funding dilemma in essence shifts compensation from the most severely to the least severely injured victims of medical error.

4. *Childbirth and Vaccine Injuries.* The closest real-world tests of these ideas that has occurred in this country are the limited no-fault schemes enacted in Florida and Virginia to cover designated injuries from child birth — the arena that produces the greatest liability exposure. Both programs cover only severe, permanent brain damage. Other injuries in obstetrics such as death, birth defects, and nonneurological physical injury are left to the regular tort system. Because of this limited scope, very few claims have been filed (only three a year in Virginia) or paid (only 12 a year in Florida). See Randall R. Bovbjerg & Frank A. Sloan, No Fault for Medical Injury: Theory and Evidence, 67 Univ. Cin. L. Rev. 53 (1998); David M. Studdert et al., The Jury Is Still In: Florida's Birth-Related Neurological Injury Compensation Plan after a Decade, 25 J. Health Pol. Pol'y & L. 499 (June 2000); Symposium, 60(2) L. & Contemp. Probs. (Spring 1997). Compensation for these cases is focused primarily on the unreimbursed costs of medical care; compensation for lost earnings and for pain and suffering are severely limited. Based on these restrictions, Professor Mehlman argues that these statutes are vulnerable to challenge under the Americans with Disabilities Act. See M. Mehlman, Bad "Bad Baby" Bills, 20 Am. J.L. & Med. 129 (1994).

The federal government has also established limited no-fault compensation schemes, covering side effects from certain common vaccinations. See pages 402 and 516. More encompassing administrative no-fault systems for all medical injuries have been adopted in Sweden, Finland, and New Zealand (the latter as part of a compensation system for all accidental injuries). See Patricia Danzon, The Swedish Patient Compensation System, 15 J. Leg. Med. 199 (1994); Walter Gelhorn, Medical Malpractice Litigation (U.S.) — Medical Mishap Compensation

(N.Z.), 73 Cornell L. Rev. 170 (1988); Symposium, 59 L. Contemp. Probs. (Fall 1996).

5. *Neo-No Fault.* A final variation is no fault by voluntary agreement, also known as "neo-no fault." Jeffrey O'Connell is the architect of this idea, in Neo-No Fault Remedies for Medical Injuries: Coordinated Statutory and Contractual Alternatives, 45 J. Law & Contemp. Probs. 125 (1986). See also Jeffrey O'Connell & Evan Stephenson, Binding Statutory Early Offers by Defendants, Not Plaintiffs, in Personal Injury Suits, 54 Depaul L. Rev. 233 (2005); J. Hersch, et al, An Empirical Assessment of Early Offer Reform for Medical Malpractice, 36 J. Leg. Stud. — (2007). The gist is that if doctors or hospitals promptly volunteer to cover the uncompensated economic consequences of a medical injury, then patients would be precluded from suing in tort for noneconomic damages (or, in other versions, they would be taxed various costs if they then sued and failed to recover more than the offer). If you had as a client the doctors in the *Locke* case (page 303), would you advise making this type of voluntary offer of payment?

6. Products Liability

These materials focus on the professional liability of those who deliver health care services: doctors, hospitals, and HMOs. Also important in the medical arena is the institutional liability of those who manufacture and sell medical drugs and equipment. Length constraints do not allow an in-depth treatment of these additional sources of liability, so we provide only a survey of products liability. Rather than attempt to master all the twists and turns of medical products liability, read this case and the following notes with these more general questions in mind: Why is strict liability justified here but not for medical services? Should special limitations be placed on strict liability out of concern for holding down medical costs or ensuring access to care? And, where liability exists, how is it shared among the responsible parties (manufacturer, hospital, and physician)?

■ BROWN v. SUPERIOR COURT
751 P.2d 470 (Cal. 1988)

Mosk, Justice.

In current litigation several significant issues have arisen relating to the liability of manufacturers of prescription drugs for injuries caused by their products. Our first and broadest inquiry is whether such a manufacturer may be held strictly liable for a product that is defective in design. The remaining questions relate to the scope of liability of producers of diethylstilbestrol (DES). . . .

A number of plaintiffs filed actions in the San Francisco Superior Court against numerous drug manufacturers which allegedly produced DES, a substance plaintiffs claimed was used by their mothers to prevent miscarriage. They alleged that the drug was defective and they were injured in utero when their mothers ingested it. . . .

A typical complaint in the complex litigation names 170 or more drug companies as defendants. It is alleged that they manufactured DES from the same formula, and that the drug was unsafe for use in preventing miscarriage and resulted in severe injury to plaintiff. Defendants knew that the drug contained a cancer-causing substance, yet they failed to warn users or their physicians of these dangerous characteristics. Plaintiff seeks to hold defendants liable on theories of strict liability, breach of express and implied warranty, fraud, and negligence. In the event plaintiff is unable to identify the manufacturer of the specific brand of DES that caused her injuries, she seeks to hold liable "those defendant manufacturers who manufactured a substantial share of the appropriate market for said drug." . . .

I. STRICT LIABILITY

. . . Strict liability differs from negligence in that it eliminates the necessity for the injured party to prove that the manufacturer of the product which caused injury was negligent. It focusses not on the conduct of the manufacturer but on the product itself, and holds the manufacturer liable if the product was defective. In 1965, . . . the Restatement Second of Torts published section 402A, which set forth the strict liability doctrine [for product liability].[9] . . .

[There are] three types of product defects. First, there may be a flaw in the manufacturing process, resulting in a product that differs from the manufacturer's intended result. The archetypal example of such a defect [is] a Coca Cola bottle that explode[s]. . . . Second, there are products which are "perfectly" manufactured but are unsafe because of the absence of a safety device, i.e., a defect in design. . . . Plaintiff asserts this test should be applied in the present case because DES contained a design defect. The third type of defect . . . is a product that is dangerous because it lacks adequate warnings or instructions. According to plaintiff, defendants here failed to warn of the dangers inherent in the use of DES. . . .

[T]he American Law Institute, in considering whether to adopt a rule of strict liability, pondered whether the manufacturer of a prescription drug should be subject to the doctrine. During a rather confusing discussion of a draft of what was to become section 402A, a member of the institute proposed that drugs should be exempted from strict liability on the ground that it would be "against the public interest" to apply the doctrine to such products because of "the very serious tendency to stifle medical research and testing." Dean Prosser, who was the reporter for the Restatement Second of Torts, responded that the problem was a real one, . . . [but it] could be dealt with in the comments to the section. . . . At the next meeting of the institute in 1962, section 402A was approved together with comment *k* thereto.

---

[9] Section 402A provides:

(1) One who sells any product in a defective condition unreasonably dangerous to the user or consumer or to his property is subject to liability for physical harm thereby caused to the ultimate user or consumer, or to his property, if (a) the seller is engaged in the business of selling such a product, and (b) it is expected to and does reach the user or consumer without substantial change in the condition in which it is sold.

(2) The rule stated in Subsection (1) applies although (a) the seller has exercised all possible care in the preparation and sale of the product, and (b) the user or consumer has not bought the product from or entered into any contractual relation with the seller.

The comment provides that the producer of a properly manufactured prescription drug may be held liable for injuries caused by the product only if it was not accompanied by a warning of dangers that the manufacturer knew or should have known about. It declares:

> *k.* Unavoidably unsafe products. There are some products which, in the present state of human knowledge, are quite incapable of being made safe for their intended and ordinary use. These are especially common in the field of drugs. An outstanding example is the vaccine for the Pasteur treatment of rabies, which not uncommonly leads to very serious and damaging consequences when it is injected. Since the disease itself invariably leads to a dreadful death, both the marketing and use of the vaccine are fully justified, notwithstanding the unavoidable high degree of risk which they involve. Such a product, properly prepared, and accompanied by proper directions and warning, is not defective, nor is it unreasonably dangerous. The same is true of many other drugs, vaccines, and the like, many of which for this very reason cannot legally be sold except to physicians, or under the prescription of a physician. It is also true in particular of many new or experimental drugs as to which, because of lack of time and opportunity for sufficient medical experience, there can be no assurance of safety, or perhaps even of purity of ingredients, but such experience as there is justifies the marketing and use of the drug notwithstanding a medically recognizable risk. The seller of such products, again with the qualification that they are properly prepared and marketed, and proper warning is given, where the situation calls for it, is not to be held to strict liability for unfortunate consequences attending their use, merely because he has undertaken to supply the public with an apparently useful and desirable product, attended with a known but apparently reasonable risk.

Comment *k* has been analyzed and criticized by numerous commentators. While there is some disagreement as to its scope and meaning, there is a general consensus that, although it purports to explain the strict liability doctrine, in fact the principle it states is based on negligence. That is, comment *k* would impose liability on a drug manufacturer only if it failed to warn of a defect of which it either knew or should have known. This concept focuses not on a deficiency in the product — the hallmark of strict liability — but on the fault of the producer in failing to warn of dangers inherent in the use of its product that were either known or knowable — an idea which "rings of negligence."[4]

Comment *k* has been adopted in the overwhelming majority of jurisdictions that have considered the matter. . . . We are aware of only one decision that has applied the doctrine of strict liability to prescription drugs. (Brochu v. Ortho Pharmaceutical Corp., 642 F.2d 652 (1st Cir.1981).[6] Most cases have embraced

---

[4] The test stated in comment *k* is to be distinguished from strict liability for failure to warn. Although both concepts identify failure to warn as the basis of liability, comment *k* imposes liability only if the manufacturer knew or should have known of the defect at the time the product was sold or distributed. Under strict liability, the reason why the warning was not issued is irrelevant, and the manufacturer is liable even if it neither knew nor could have known of the defect about which the warning was required. . . . [Most jurisdictions adopt the negligence approach to failure to warn. See cases collected in Annot., 33 A.L.R.4th 368 (1984).]

[6] In *Brochu*, the plaintiff had taken an oral contraceptive which contained 100 milligrams of estrogen as well as other ingredients. According to the evidence at trial, estrogen posed a serious risk of harm to her, and the defendant manufactured another contraceptive pill containing only 50 milligrams of estrogen which was equally effective.

the rule of comment *k* without detailed analysis of its language. A few, notably Kearl v. Lederle Laboratories, 218 Cal. Rptr. 453 (Cal. App. 1985), have conditioned application of the exemption stated therein on a finding that the drug involved is in fact "unavoidably dangerous," reasoning that the comment was intended to exempt only such drugs from strict liability. And in Collins v. Eli Lilly Co. 342 N.W.2d 37 (Wis. 1984), it was held that comment *k* was applicable only if the drug in question was placed on the market without adequate testing because of exigent circumstances.

We appear, then, to have three distinct choices: (1) to hold that the manufacturer of a prescription drug is strictly liable for a defect in its product because it was defectively designed, . . . or because of a failure to warn of its dangerous propensities even though such dangers were neither known nor scientifically knowable at the time of distribution;[8] (2) to determine that liability attaches only if a manufacturer fails to warn of dangerous propensities of which it was or should have been aware, in conformity with comment *k*; or (3) to decide, like *Kearl* . . . that strict liability for design defects should apply to prescription drugs unless the particular drug which caused the injury is found to be "unavoidably dangerous." We shall conclude that, . . . because of the public interest in the development, availability, and reasonable price of drugs, the appropriate test for determining responsibility is the test stated in comment *k*; for these same reasons of policy, we disapprove the holding of *Kearl*. . . .

1. DESIGN DEFECT

. . . While the "ordinary consumer" may have a reasonable expectation that a product such as a machine he purchases will operate safely when used as intended, a patient's expectations regarding the effects of such a drug are those related to him by his physician, to whom the manufacturer directs the warnings regarding the drug's properties.[9] The manufacturer cannot be held liable if it has provided appropriate warnings and the doctor fails in his duty to transmit these warnings to the patient or if the patient relies on inaccurate information from others regarding side effects of the drug.

The second test, which calls for the balancing of risks and benefits, is inapposite to prescription drugs, according to defendants, because it contemplates that a safer alternative design is feasible. While the defective equipment in . . . cases involving mechanical devices might be "redesigned" by the addition of safety devices, [defendants contend] there is no possibility for an alternative design for a drug like DES, which is a scientific constant compounded in accordance with a required formula.

. . . [W]e seriously doubt the claim that a drug like DES cannot be "redesigned" to make it safer. For example, plaintiff might be able to demonstrate at trial that a particular component of DES rendered it unsafe as a miscarriage preventative and that removal of that component would not have affected the

---

[8] We agree with the suggestion of a commentator that a manufacturers' knowledge should be measured at the time a drug is distributed because it is at this point that the manufacturer relinquishes control of the product. Wade, On the Effect in Product Liability of Knowledge Unavailable Prior to Marketing, 58 N.Y.U. L. Rev. 734 (1983).

[9] It is well established that a manufacturer fulfills its duty to warn if it provides adequate warning to the physician. See, e.g., Davis v. Wyeth Laboratories, Inc., 399 F.2d 121 (9th Cir. 1968).

efficacy of the drug. Even if the resulting product, without the damaging component, would bear a name other than DES, it would do no violence to semantics to view it as a "redesign" of DES. Or plaintiff might be able to prove that other, less harmful drugs were available to prevent miscarriage. . . .

But there is an important distinction between prescription drugs and other products. . . . In [ordinary] cases, the product is used to make work easier or to provide pleasure, while in the former it may be necessary to alleviate pain and suffering or to sustain life. Moreover, unlike other important medical products (wheelchairs, for example), harm to some users from prescription drugs is unavoidable. Because of these distinctions, the broader public interest in the availability of drugs at an affordable price must be considered in deciding the appropriate standard of liability for injuries resulting from their use. . . .

If drug manufacturers were subject to strict liability, they might be reluctant to undertake research programs to develop some pharmaceuticals that would prove beneficial or to distribute others that are available to be marketed, because of the fear of large adverse monetary judgments. Further, the additional expense of insuring against such liability — assuming insurance would be available — and of research programs to reveal possible dangers not detectable by available scientific methods could place the cost of medication beyond the reach of those who need it most.

Dean Prosser summed up the justification for exempting prescription drugs from strict liability as follows:

> The argument that industries producing potentially dangerous products should make good the harm, distribute it by liability insurance, and add the cost to the price of the product, encounters reason for pause, when we consider that two of the greatest medical boons to the human race, penicillin and cortisone, both have their dangerous side effects, and that drug companies might well have been deterred from producing and selling them.

. . . Defendants cite a host of examples of products which have greatly increased in price or have been withdrawn or withheld from the market because of the fear that their producers would be held liable for large judgments. For example, according to defendant E.R. Squibb & Sons, Inc., Bendectin, the only antinauseant drug available for pregnant women, was withdrawn from sale in 1983 because the cost of insurance almost equalled the entire income from sale of the drug. Before it was withdrawn, the price of Benedictin increased by over 300 percent. Drug manufacturers refused to supply a newly discovered vaccine for influenza on the ground that mass inoculation would subject them to enormous liability. The government therefore assumed the risk of lawsuits resulting from injuries caused by the vaccine. Franklin & Mais, Tort Law and Mass Immunization Programs, 65 Cal. L. Rev. 754 (1977); Feldman v. Lederle Laboratories, 460 A.2d 203 (N.J. Super. 1983). One producer of diphtheria-tetanus-pertussis vaccine withdrew from the market, giving as its reason "extreme liability exposure, cost of litigation and the difficulty of continuing to obtain adequate insurance." There are only two manufacturers of the vaccine remaining in the market, and the cost of each dose rose a hundredfold from 11 cents in 1982 to $11.40 in 1986, $8 of which was for an insurance reserve. The price increase roughly paralleled an increase in the number of lawsuits from one in 1978 to 219 in 1985. . . .

There is no doubt that, from the public's standpoint, these are unfortunate consequences. And they occurred even though almost all jurisdictions follow the negligence standard of comment k. It is not unreasonable to conclude in these circumstances that the imposition of a harsher test for liability would not further the public interest in the development and availability of these important products. . . .

3. THE *KEARL* TEST

One further question remains in this aspect of the case. Comment k, as we have seen, provides that the maker of an "unavoidably unsafe" product is not liable for injuries resulting from its use if the product is "properly prepared, and accompanied by proper directions and warning." With the few exceptions noted above, the courts which have adopted comment k have viewed all prescription drugs as coming within its scope.

Kearl suggested that not all drugs are "unavoidably dangerous" so as to merit the protection of the negligence standard of comment k, and it devised a test to separate those which meet that description from those which do not. It held that the question whether a drug should be exempt from strict liability as "unavoidably dangerous" presents a mixed question of law and fact which should be decided on the basis of evidence to be taken by the trial judge out of the presence of the jury. The judge should determine, after hearing the evidence,

> (1) whether, when distributed, the product was intended to confer an exceptionally important benefit that made its availability highly desirable; (2) whether the then-existing risk posed by the product was both "substantial" and "unavoidable"; and (3) whether the interest in availability (again measured as of the time of distribution) outweighs the interest in promoting enhanced accountability through strict liability design defect review. . . .

We acknowledge that there is some appeal in the basic premise of *Kearl*. It seems unjust to grant the same protection from liability to those who gave us thalidomide as to the producers of penicillin. If some method could be devised to confine the benefit of the comment k negligence standard to those drugs that have proved useful to mankind while denying the privilege to those that are clearly harmful, it would deserve serious consideration. But we know of no means by which this can be accomplished without substantially impairing the public interest in the development and marketing of new drugs, because the harm to this interest arises in the very process of attempting to make the distinction.

Under the "mini-trial" directed by *Kearl*, a drug manufacturer has no assurance that a product he places on the market will be measured by the liability standard of comment k. . . . [A] trial court could decide, perhaps many years later, that in fact another product which was available on the market would have accomplished the same result. Further, the question of the superiority of one drug over another would have to be decided not in the abstract but in reference to the plaintiff, since the advantages of a drug cannot be isolated from the condition of a particular patient. Thus, in one case the drug that injured the plaintiff might be the better choice, while this would not be true as to another user.

An additional matter that militates against adoption of the *Kearl* approach is that, as the court of appeal observed, different trial judges might reach different conclusions as to whether the same drug should be measured by strict liability principles, because the determination in each case depends on the evidence as well as the subjective determination of the judge regarding such matters as what constitutes an "exceptionally important benefit" of a drug. We do not see how a reviewing court could harmonize these differing conclusions without ignoring the fundamental rule that a trial court's decision on the facts must be upheld if it is based on substantial evidence. . . .

In conclusion, and in accord with almost all our sister states that have considered the issue, we hold that a manufacturer is not strictly liable for injuries caused by a prescription drug so long as the drug was properly prepared and accompanied by warnings of its dangerous propensities that were either known or reasonably scientifically knowable at the time of distribution.[12] . . .

Notes: Products Liability for Defective Drugs and Medical Devices

1. *Other Cases.* The DES drug is only one example of the massive litigation that ensues when it is discovered that a widely used drug or medical device has a previously unknown potential harm. Other notable examples include Vioxx (arthritis treatment), silicone breast implants, childhood and adult vaccines, Bendectin (a pregnancy antinausea drug), Dalkon Shield (an intrauterine contraceptive device), and the birth control pill. Some manufacturers, such as Dow-Corning in the breast implant cases, have declared bankruptcy when faced with billions of dollars in liability claims. See generally Michael D. Green, Bendectin and Birth Defects: The Challenges of Mass Toxic Substances Litigation (1996); Marcia Angell, Evaluating the Health Risks of Breast Implants: The Interplay of Medical Science, the Law, and Public Opinion, 334 New Eng. J. Med. 1513 (1996); Marcia Angell, Science on Trial: The Clash of Medical Evidence and the Law in the Breast Implant Case (1996); Jonathan Van O'Steen, The FDA Defense: Vioxx and the Argument Against Federal Preemption of State Claims for Injuries Resulting from Defective Drugs, 48 Ariz. L. Rev. 67 (2006).

2. *Medical Devices.* The only example comment *k* cites of unavoidably unsafe products are medical drugs, but its rationale might also apply to medical devices such as pacemakers and various artificial implants. Is there any basis on which to distinguish these two categories of medical products? Most courts conclude "no," and so refuse to apply strict liability to medical devices as well. See Tansy v. Dacomed Corp., 890 P.2d 881 (Okla. 1994) (penile implant that failed due to overuse); Annot., 70 A.L.R.4th 16 (1989). Should the same be true for medical

---

[12] Our conclusion does not mean, of course, that drug manufacturers are free of all liability for defective drugs. They are subject to liability for manufacturing defects, as well as under general principles of negligence, and for failure to warn of known or reasonably knowable side effects. It should also be noted that the consumers of prescription drugs are afforded greater protection against defects than consumers of other products, since the drug industry is closely regulated by the Food and Drug Administration, which actively controls the testing and manufacture of drugs and the method by which they are marketed, including the contents of warning labels.

devices available to consumers in stores, such as thermometers, heating pads, and crutches? Are tampons "medical devices"? What about condoms? Where do each of these lie on the line drawn by the *Brown* court between products "used to make work easier or to provide pleasure" versus those "necessary to alleviate pain and suffering" or prevent illness? See O'Gilvie v. International Playtex Inc., 821 F.2d 1438 (10th Cir. 1987) (applying ordinary strict liability to toxic shock syndrome allegedly caused by tampons); Artiglio v. Superior Court, 27 Cal. Rptr. 2d 589 (Ct. App. 1994) (comment *k* covers breast implants despite their use for cosmetic purposes); Hufft v. Horowitz, 5 Cal. Rptr. 2d 377 (Ct. App. 1992) (distinguishing implanted medical devices that, like drugs, are available only from physicians and go inside the body, from ordinary commercial medical products such as wheelchairs).

3. *The* Kearl *Rule.* Do you agree with the *Brown* decision or with the rejected *Kearl* decision on the following question: When comment *k* potentially applies, should the court be allowed to consider whether the particular product was in fact unavoidably unsafe, that is, whether a safer feasible design was actually unavailable? A number of other courts have answered "yes," requiring manufacturers to make this showing in each case before invoking the comment *k* defense. See, e.g., Freeman v. Hoffman-LaRoche, Inc., 618 N.W.2d 827 (Neb. 2000) (comment *k* does not give blanket immunity for acne medicine; "unavoidably unsafe" depends on case-by-case factual analysis). For a while, this appeared to be the majority position. More recently, the American Law Institute's Restatement (Third) of the Law of Torts: Products Liability (1998) leans heavily in favor of the *Brown* rule. Section 6 elevates the concerns expressed in comment *k* to the status of a special exception for drugs and medical devices, which declares that a medical product is subject to design defect liability only if "the foreseeable risks of harm are sufficiently great in relation to the foreseeable therapeutic benefits such that health care providers . . . would not prescribe the drug or medical device to *any* class of patients" (emphasis added). The comments explain: "[A]s long as a given drug or device provides net benefits for some category of patients, it should be available to that group, albeit with adequate warnings and instructions supplied to learned intermediaries." Granted, but does this explain why manufacturers should not have to account for failing to use an even safer or more beneficial design? See generally George W. Conk, Is There a Design Defect in the Restatement (Third) of Torts: Products Liability?, 109 Yale L.J. 1087 (2000); James A. Henderson & Aaron D. Twerski, Drug Designs Are Different, 111 Yale L.J. 151 (2001); Symposium, 30 Seton Hall L. Rev. 202 (1999).

4. *Hospital and Physician Liability. Brown's* holding of no strict liability applies only to design and warning defects. When drugs and medical devices suffer from manufacturing defects, strict products liability clearly applies, but only to manufacturers and distributors, not to hospitals or doctors, so long as the product is not altered by the provider. Consider, for instance, the needle that broke during surgery in the Locke v. Pachtman case (page 303). If the needle had broken due to a manufacturing flaw, as opposed to misuse, the hospital and doctor would not have been responsible, even though they were in the chain of distribution. The reason is that, in this context, the needle is seen as merely a supply that is incidental to the sale of a service, and therefore the doctor, not the patient, is the end user. Magrine v. Krasnico, 97 N.J. 228 (1967) (dentist not responsible for

broken needle); note, The Physician as Consumer, 79 Nw. U. L. Rev. 460 (1984); Annot., 100 A.L.R.3d 1205 (1980). The same reasoning does not apply as strongly when considering other medical supplies such as pacemakers and neck braces that are more clearly sold by hospitals as individual products. Most courts, however, find that hospitals generally are not covered by products liability law for defects in their supplies or equipment that are used directly for patient care. See, e.g., Cafazzo v. Central Medical Health Service, Inc., 668 A.2d 521 (Pa. 1995) (neither doctor nor hospital strictly liable for defective prosthesis implanted in patient's jaw). Naturally, hospitals can be held liable for failing to reasonably inspect and maintain equipment and medical devices.

5. *Blood Shield Statutes.* The one instance where manufacturers and distributors of medical supplies have avoided strict liability even for *manufacturing* defects is contaminated blood transfusions. Despite careful screening, a certain portion of donated or purchased blood is contaminated with impurities such as hepatitis or AIDS viruses. For a while, courts wrestled with whether blood banks or hospitals that sell defective blood are selling a product or instead only performing a service. See Brody v. Overlook Hospital, 332 A.2d 596 (N.J. 1975) (blood banks not subject to strict liability; reversing contrary decision by lower court). To resolve the legal uncertainty produced by these inconsistent holdings, virtually all states have enacted "blood shield" statutes declaring that blood products are not subject to strict products liability. These statutes often apply as well to human organs and tissues used for transplants. Annot., 75 A.L.R. 5th 229 (2000); Annot., 24 A.L.R. 4th 508 (1982); Comment, 2 Ind. Health L. Rev. 295 (2005).

Several courts have ruled that these statutes do not cover companies that manufacture drugs from blood products, such as the "clotting factor" that pharmaceutical companies produce to keep hemophiliacs from bleeding. See In re Rhone-Poulenc Rorer, Inc., 51 F.3d 1293 (7th Cir. 1995). Because this manufacturing process requires combining blood from many different donors in order to distill a single batch of clotting factor, virtually all severe hemophiliacs — some 10,000 in all — were infected with the AIDS virus during the early 1980s before adequate screening tests were available. The manufacturers agreed to settle a class action suit for roughly $100,000 for each person infected. See Conk, supra, 109 Yale L.J. 1087 (2000).

6. *Computerized Medicine.* The computerization of medicine creates novel opportunities for design defect and related theories of products liability. Physicians and nurses increasingly are using software programs that prescribe or recommend diagnostic and treatment decisions, for instance, by analyzing lists of symptoms and assigning probabilities to alternative diagnoses. If these computer algorithms are found to contain an error, perhaps the designer, seller, or hospital purchaser can be found liable. Related issues arise from medical information or advice given on Web sites that are proliferating rapidly. For discussion and analysis, see B. H. Lamkin, Medical Expert Systems and Publisher Liability: A Cross-Contextual Analysis, 43 Emory L.J. 731 (1994); M. Metzger, Legal Implications of Computer-Aided Medical Diagnosis, 9 J. Leg. Med. 313 (1988); Nicolas P. Terry, Cyber-Malpractice: Legal Exposure for Cybermedicine, 25 Am. J.L. Med. 327 (1999).

7. *Vaccine Liability.* As the *Brown* court observes, liability risks have caused massive cost increases and outright unavailability for certain drugs even though

manufacturers, for the most part, have been subject only to negligence-type liability, not strict liability. Do the negative social consequences of negligence liability warrant even more sweeping legal protections? Some have speculated that if a vaccine for AIDS is developed, no company would want to market it due to liability risks. As the *Brown* court briefly notes, similar concerns prompted Congress to enact the National Childhood Vaccine Injury Act of 1986, 42 U.S.C. §300aa-10, which implements a compensation fund for children claiming injuries from common immunizations. This fund employs a no-fault scheme similar to those described at page 392, as a voluntary alternative to suit for damages under state tort law. The fund provides full compensation for economic losses without a showing of fault, but limits pain and suffering damages to $250,000. If the plaintiff opts for suit under state tort law, the statute declares that compliance with FDA warning and labeling requirements creates a presumption of adequacy. See Shalala v. Whitecotton, 514 U.S. 268 (1995); Derry Ridgway, No-Fault Vaccine Insurance: Lessons from the National Vaccine Injury Compensation Fund, 24 J. Health Pol. Pol'y & L. 59 (1999); Lainie Rutkow et al. Balancing Consumer and Industry Interests in Public Health: The National Vaccine Injury Compensation Program and Its Influence During the Last Two Decades, 111 Penn St. L. Rev. 681 (2007); Annot., 129 A.L.R. Fed. 1 (1996).

8. *Federal Preemption.* Displacement of state tort law might also result from FDA regulation. The FDA imposes extensive testing requirements for safety and effectiveness before prescription drugs and potentially dangerous medical devices can be marketed. After approval, the FDA also extensively regulates the labeling instructions and warnings that manufacturers must give doctors. Is there any basis in public policy for holding manufacturers liable for design defects or warning deficiencies that the FDA finds acceptable? Consider the discussion in Chapter 2. C.3. of the FDA approval process, which notes that the FDA relies primarily on information supplied by and tests commissioned by the pharmaceutical manufacturers themselves, rather than the FDA conducting its own investigations. See Note, 103 Harv. L. Rev. 773 (1990).

FDA regulation might absolve manufacturers of liability in one of two ways. First, regulatory compliance might act as a substantive defense to liability under state tort law by demonstrating actual reasonableness or nondefectiveness. Second, federal law might be found to preempt state tort liability. The response to these two arguments differs between drugs and devices. For both drugs and devices, state courts usually allow regulatory compliance only as evidence, but not as conclusive proof, of reasonable care. A few states by statute declare that regulatory compliance creates a rebuttable presumption of nonliability or protects manufacturers from punitive damages. See Garcia v. Wyeth-Ayerst Lab., 385 F.3d 961 (6th Cir. 2004); Note, 84 N.C.L. Rev. 737 (2006).

As for federal preemption, the "overwhelming majority of courts" have found no federal preemption for prescription drugs because the federal statute overrides state law only where "there is a direct and positive conflict." Abbott v. American Cyanamid Co., 844 F.2d 1108 (4th Cir. 1988). Such a conflict might be found with respect to warnings of risk if the FDA labeling requirements were exclusive, that is, if the FDA were to preclude any additional warnings than those it imposes. See Feldman v. Lederle Labs, 561 A.2d 288 (N.J. 1989) (state law preempted where FDA explicitly forbade any change in labeling without its approval); cf. Cipollone v. Liggett Group, 505 U.S. 504 (1992) (cigarette package labeling requirements preempt state law failure-to-warn suits). Prohibiting additional warning is plausible under the view that excessive warnings can confuse doctors and patients and lead to suboptimal use of the drug. In the FDA's view, its labeling requirements are optimal, not minimal, and it is desirable to employ uniform standards about which risks are serious enough to warn against, so that alternative drugs can be accurately compared; otherwise, a doctor might prescribe a more dangerous drug just because its competitor went overboard in warning against theoretical but unsubstantiated risks. However, the FDA remains unclear in most instances about whether it actively prohibits manufacturers from adding additional warnings. Also, the FDA has flip-flopped over time on what effects its labeling rules have, most recently arguing that they do preempt state tort law. 71 Fed. Reg. 3934 (2006); Catherine Sharkey, Preemption by Preamble, 56 DePaul L. Rev. 227 (2007). Given this uncertainty, manufacturers are reluctant to depart from the FDA script, even though some courts continue to assume they are free to do so.

For medical devices, the preemptive effect of federal regulation for medical devices is even cloudier. The Food, Drug and Cosmetics Act appears to expressly preempt state law in §360k(a), which declares that states may not imposed any "requirement which is different from or in addition to" those imposed by the FDA. Based on this, a number of circuit courts found products liability actions preempted, but others did not. The Supreme Court ruled 5-4 that no preemption occurs for medical devices that receive only cursory FDA review. Medtronic Inc. v. Lohr, 518 U.S. 470 (1996). The precise reasoning is obscure due to fractured voting, but preemption is still possible where the very design defect attacked by a plaintiff was specifically approved by the FDA. E.g., Martin v. Medtronic, Inc., 254 F.3d 573 (5th Cir. 2001) (FDA approval for pacemaker preempts tort liability for design defect). Also, claims that device manufacturers were not honest with the FDA in obtaining approval are preempted. Buckman Co. v. Plaintiffs' Legal Committee, 531 U.S. 341 (2001).

See generally Mary J. Davis, Discovering the Boundaries: Federal Preemption of Prescription Drug Labeling Product Liability Actions, SSRN 903757 (2006); Wm. Dreier, Liability for Drug Advertising, Warnings, and Frauds. 58 Rutgers L. Rev. 615 (2006); Richard Ausness, Should the Courts Defer to the FDA's New Interpretation of the Medical Device Amendments?, 80 Tul. L. Rev. 727 (2006); Note, Cardozo L. Rev. 38 (2005); Annot., 98 A.L.R. Fed. 124 (1990).

9. *Learned Intermediaries and Direct-to-Consumer Advertising.* The *Brown* court adopts a negligence standard for failing to warn of the risks of medical drugs. As the court observes in n.9, for prescription drugs this warning generally needs to be given only to doctors, not to patients. Under tort law's "learned intermediary" rule, it is up to physicians to determine how these warnings should be incorporated into their treatment decisions and which warnings should be passed along to patients. Reyes v. Wyeth Labs, 498 F.2d 1264 (5th Cir. 1974). The learned intermediary rule does not apply to "over-the-counter" drugs purchased directly by consumers, however, and several courts have held it does not apply to mass immunization vaccines or to prescription drugs that are commonly available

just for the asking, without any particular medical problem. The classic instance of the latter is the birth control pill. In these situations, manufacturers can be sued for failures to warn consumers directly. See Davis v. Wyeth Labs, 399 F.2d 121 (9th Cir. 1968) (polio); MacDonald v. Ortho Pharmaceutical Corp., 475 N.E.2d 65 (Mass. 1985) (birth control pills). Increasingly, drug companies are advertising directly to the public a wide range of pharmaceuticals for common maladies, encouraging people to ask their doctor to prescribe drugs for seasonal allergies, baldness, and heartburn, for instance. This is partly in response to restrictions imposed by managed care insurers. Symposium, 346 New Eng. J. Med. 523 (2002). One influential court has held, with respect to birth control implants, that advertising directly to consumers precludes application of the learned intermediary rule. Perez v. Wyeth Laboratories, 734 A.2d 1245 (N.J. 1999). See generally Richard C. Ausness, Will More Aggressive Marketing Practices Lead to Greater Tort Liability for Prescription Drug Manufacturers?, 37 Wake Forest L. Rev. 97 (2002); Jack Karns, Direct Advertising of Prescription Drugs: The Duty to Warn and the Learned Intermediary Rule, 3 DePaul J. Health Care L. 273 (2000); Lars Noah, Advertising Prescription Drugs to Consumers: Assessing the Regulatory and Liability Issues, 32 Ga. L. Rev. 141 (1997); Nancy Plant, The Learned Intermediary Doctrine: Some new Medicine for an Old Ailment, 81 Iowa L. Rev. 1007 (1996); Note, 51 Stan. L. Rev. 1343 (1999).

10. *Package Inserts and "Off-Label" Use.* Where the learned intermediary rule applies, patients can still sue drug manufacturers for inadequate warnings to their physicians, and naturally patients can also sue their physicians who ignore drug risks or fail to warn them personally. These suits against physicians are brought as standard negligent practice or breach of informed consent actions, however. In such actions, the FDA's required warning to physicians, known as the "package insert," becomes one possible source of evidence against the physician. The instructions on package inserts do not strictly bind physicians; FDA law allows them to use approved drugs in any fashion they want, even if the particular use is not approved (so-called off-label use). This is particularly common, for instance, in cancer treatment and, to a lesser extent, AIDS treatment. Nevertheless, as discussed above at page 352, most courts have held that plaintiffs may introduce package inserts directly into evidence on the standard of care as an exception to the hearsay rule, and a few have held that package inserts create a rebuttable, prima facie case for liability when the defendant doctor deviates from the instructions, shifting the burden of proof to the doctor to show that the departure was accepted practice. See Salgo v. Leland Stanford Jr. University, 317 P.2d 170 (Cal. Ct. App. 1957) (package insert admissible but not conclusive of standard of care); Spensieri v. Lasky, 94 N.Y.2d 231 (1999) (same); Garvey v. O'Donoghue, 530 A.2d 1141 (D.C. App. 1987) (package insert is prima facie evidence of standard of care); Note, 51 Stan. L. Rev. 1343 (1999). If physicians intentionally and nonnegligently use a drug for purposes other than those approved by the FDA, or in a manner that contradicts the manufacturer's warnings, does this absolve the manufacturer from products liability? See K. Stoffelmayr, Products Liability and "Off-label" Uses of Prescription Drugs, 63 U. Chi. L. Rev. 275 (1996) (finding that the cases split into five different lines, from no liability, to liability if off-label use is widespread, to full liability).

11. *"Detail Men."* *Brown* focuses on holding manufacturers responsible for risks knowable *at the time of sale* (the court's n.8). The FDA requires pharmaceutical manufacturers to continue monitoring adverse reactions to their products even after approval, and to change or intensify warnings if different or greater risks materialize. As described in Sterling Drug, Inc. v. Yarrow, 408 F.2d 978 (8th Cir. 1969), this information is collected and these after-market warnings are distributed through pharmaceutical "detail men" who permeate hospitals and doctors' offices trying to encourage doctors to use their products. The court upheld a jury verdict finding a manufacturer liable for failing to use this means of communication where, one year prior to the plaintiff's starting treatment with the drug, medical publications began to report an association between the drug and certain serious side effects:

> Appellant usually communicates its product information to physicians prescribing its products: (1) by "detail men," who are specially trained field representatives engaged in selling and promoting the use of its products by personal calls in which oral presentations are made and literature and samples delivered, (2) by listings of drugs in an annually published advertising medium known as Physicians' Desk Reference, (3) by "product cards" which are mailed and distributed by detail men to physicians and are available at medical conventions and hospital exhibits, and (4) by special letters mailed to physicians. . . . Nevertheless, the detail men who made regular personal calls on prescribing physicians and customers were never, in the relevant period, instructed to invite attention of the physicians and customers to the reported dangers. . . . The warnings of side effects . . . were limited to the product cards, the Physicians' Desk Reference and to the "Dear Doctor" letter dated February 1963 . . . [that were sent] to all [248,000] physicians and hospital personnel in the United States. . . .
>
> The direct and circumstantial evidence amply supports a finding that . . . Dr. Olson (and other general practitioners) receive so much literature on drugs that it is impossible to read all of it; that Dr. Olson relied on detail men, medical conventions, medical journals and conversations with other doctors for information on drugs he was prescribing; that Dr. Olson was inundated with literature and product cards of various manufacturers; that a change in literature and an additional letter were insufficient to present new information to Dr. Olson; that detail men visit physicians at frequent intervals and could give an effective warning which would affirmatively notify the doctor of the dangerous side effects of chloroquine phosphate on the retina. These findings of fact were not clearly erroneous. . . .
>
> This does not mean that every physician in the United States must have been given an immediate warning by a personal messenger. But it does mean that the trial court was justified in finding that it was unreasonable to fail to instruct the detail men, at least, to warn the physicians on whom they regularly called of the dangers of which appellant had learned, or in the exercise of reasonable care should have known. . . . [Moreover], the "Dear Doctor" letter could have been reasonably found to be lacking in emphasis, timeliness and attention inviting qualities. A reasoning mind could find that appellant's warning actions were unduly delayed, reluctant and lacking in a sense of urgency.

Drug company "detail men" can also be a source of liability when they minimize the significance of official warnings in their eagerness to sell their product. See, e.g., Incollingo v. Ewing, 282 A.2d 206 (Pa. 1971) (official warning ineffective where detail men emphasized antibiotic's effectiveness and wide acceptance while downplaying known side effects). For additional discussion, see the incredible saga of the fifteen year litigation (two trials and three state supreme court decisions) in Feldman v. Lederle Labs, 625 A.2d 1066 (N.J. 1993), concerning the failure to warn that a common antibiotic can cause teeth to turn gray. See generally James Britain, Product Honesty is the Best Policy: A Comparison of Doctors' and Manufacturers' Duty to Disclose Drug Risks, 79 Nw. U. L. Rev. 342 (1984).

Review Questions: Products Liability

Under the majority rule, what is the potential liability of the manufacturer (Mfg.) and the physician (Dr.) or hospital in each of the following situations? What attitudes of public policy support liability or nonliability in each situation?

1. Dr. implants a pacemaker. Before doing so, he fails to ascertain that it is operational. It turns out to be a dud.
2. With FDA approval, Mfg. markets a new, powerful chemotherapy drug for kidney cancer. The package insert warns that it is not intended for use in any other cancer. Dr. decides to use the drug for pancreatic cancer, which, using standard treatment, currently has extremely dim prognosis (10 percent chance of survival). The drug's toxic effects kill the cancer patient. Dr. obtains only generic, routine informed consent ("We'll be treating you with various chemical agents that have a significant risk of toxic side effects, including death"), but does not say anything about using a new drug intended for a different purpose.
3. Korkafine is a widely used and recommended over-the-counter drug for hayfever type allergies. Mfg. widely advertises it both to the public under the brand name Snuffle, and also directly to physicians, since many people consult physicians about their allergies. After five years on the market, it was discovered that, when korkafine is taken in conjunction with okra (a southern vegetable), a bizarre chemical reaction occasionally happens that causes mild hair loss. After some deliberation, the FDA allows the drug to remain on the market as long as Mfg. adds the okra warning to others on the package and in any written promotional materials. Three years later, suit is brought against Mfg. by a rapidly balding Southerner who, with his Dr.'s knowledge, decided to use Snuffle every spring and fall during pollen season.

D. CAUSATION AND AFFIRMATIVE DEFENSES

Having surveyed numerous theories that can be used to establish a physician's breach of duty, we now turn to other elements of the basic medical malpractice cause of action: causation, affirmative defenses, and damages.

1. *Causation*

■ HERSKOVITS v. GROUP HEALTH COOPERATIVE
OF PUGET SOUND
664 P.2d 474 (Wash. 1983)

DORE, Justice.

... The personal representative of Leslie Herskovits' estate initiated this survivorship action against Group Health Cooperative of Puget Sound (Group Health), alleging failure to make an early diagnosis of her husband's lung cancer. Group Health moved for summary judgment for dismissal on the basis that Herskovits probably would have died from lung cancer even if the diagnosis had been made earlier, which the trial court granted.

The complaint alleged that Herskovits came to Group Health Hospital in 1974 with complaints of pain and coughing. ... Plaintiff contends that Herskovits was treated thereafter only with cough medicine. ... In the early spring of 1975, Mr. and Mrs. Herskovits went south in the hope that the warm weather would help. Upon his return to the Seattle area with no improvement in his health, Herskovits visited Dr. Jonathan Ostrow on a private basis for another medical opinion. Within three weeks, Dr. Ostrow's evaluation and direction to Group Health led to the diagnosis of cancer. In July of 1975, Herskovits' lung was removed, but no radiation or chemotherapy treatments were instituted. Herskovits died 20 months later, on March 22, 1977, at the age of 60.

At hearing on the motion for summary judgment, plaintiff was unable to produce expert testimony that the delay in diagnosis "probably" or "more likely than not" caused her husband's death. ... Dr. Ostrow testified that if the tumor was a "stage 1" tumor in December 1974, Herskovits' chance of a five-year survival would have been 39 percent. In June 1975, his chances of survival were 25 percent assuming the tumor had progressed to "stage 2". Thus, the delay in diagnosis may have reduced the chance of a five-year survival by 14 percent. ... It is Group Health's contention that plaintiff must prove that Herskovits "probably" would have survived had the defendant not been allegedly negligent; that is, the plaintiff must prove there was at least a 51 percent chance of survival. ...

This court has held that a person who negligently renders aid and consequently increases the risk of harm to those he is trying to assist is liable for any physical damages he causes. Restatement (Second) of Torts §323. ... This court heretofore has not faced the issue of whether, under §323(a), proof that the defendant's conduct increased the risk of death by decreasing the chances of survival is sufficient to take the issue of proximate cause to the jury. Some courts in other jurisdictions have allowed the proximate cause issue to go to the jury on this type of proof. These courts emphasized the fact that defendants' conduct deprived the decedents of a "significant" chance to survive or recover, rather than requiring proof that with absolute certainty the defendants' conduct caused the physical injury. The underlying reason is that it is not for the wrongdoer, who put the possibility of recovery beyond realization, to say afterward that the result was inevitable.

Other jurisdictions have rejected this approach, generally holding that unless the plaintiff is able to show that it was more likely than not that the harm was caused by the defendant's negligence, proof of a decreased chance of survival is not enough to take the proximate cause question to the jury. These courts have concluded that the defendant should not be liable where the decedent more than likely would have died anyway. . . .

III

We are persuaded by the reasoning of the Pennsylvania Supreme Court in *Hamil v. Bashline*, 392 A.2d 1280 (Pa. 1978). While *Hamil* involved an original survival chance of greater than 50 percent, we find the rationale used by the *Hamil* court to apply equally to cases such as the present one, where the original survival chance is less than 50 percent. The plaintiff's decedent was suffering from severe chest pains. His wife transported him to the hospital where he was negligently treated in the emergency unit. The wife, because of the lack of help, took her husband to a private physician's office, where he died. In an action brought under the wrongful death and survivorship statutes, the main medical witness testified that if the hospital had employed proper treatment, the decedent would have had a substantial chance of surviving the attack. The medical expert expressed his opinion in terms of a 75 percent chance of survival. . . .

The *Hamil* court distinguished the facts of that case from the general tort case in which a plaintiff alleges that a defendant's act or omission set in motion a force which resulted in harm. In the typical tort case, the "but for" test, requiring proof that damages or death probably would not have occurred "but for" the negligent conduct of the defendant, is appropriate. In *Hamil* and the instant case, however, the defendant's act or omission failed in a duty to protect against harm from another source. Thus, as the *Hamil* court noted, the factfinder is put in the position of having to consider not only what did occur, but also what might have occurred. "Such cases by their very nature elude the degree of certainty one would prefer and upon which the law normally insists before a person may be held liable." . . . The *Hamil* court held that once a plaintiff has demonstrated that the defendant's acts or omissions have increased the risk of harm to another, such evidence furnishes a basis for the jury to make a determination as to whether such increased risk was in turn a substantial factor in bringing about the resultant harm.

. . . The following quotation from *Hicks v. United States*, 368 F.2d 626, 632 (4th Cir. 1966), is frequently cited in cases adopting loss of a chance because it succinctly defines the doctrine:

> Rarely is it possible to demonstrate to an absolute certainty what would have happened in circumstances that the wrongdoer did not allow to come to pass. The law does not in the existing circumstances require the plaintiff to show to a certainty that the patient would have lived had she been hospitalized and operated on promptly. . . .

The recent case of *James v. United States*, 483 F. Supp. 581 (N.D. Cal. 1980), concerned the failure to diagnose and promptly treat a lung tumor. The court concluded that the plaintiff sustained its burden of proof even without statistical evidence, stating:

As a proximate result of defendant's negligence, James was deprived of the opportunity to receive early treatment and the chance of realizing any resulting gain in his life expectancy and physical and mental comfort. *No matter how small that chance may have been* — and its magnitude cannot be ascertained — no one can say that the chance of prolonging one's life or decreasing suffering is valueless.

. . . We hold that medical testimony of a reduction of chance of survival from 39 percent to 25 percent is sufficient evidence to allow the proximate cause issue to go to the jury. . . . To decide otherwise would be a blanket release from liability for doctors and hospitals any time there was less than a 50 percent chance of survival, regardless of how flagrant the negligence. . . . We reverse the trial court and reinstate the cause of action.

PEARSON, Justice (concurring).

. . . In medical malpractice cases such as the one before us, cause in fact must usually be established by expert medical testimony, and must be established beyond the balance of probabilities. In a case such as this, medical testimony must be relied upon to establish the causal relationship between the liability-producing situation and the claimed physical disability resulting therefrom. The evidence will be deemed insufficient to support the jury's verdict, if it can be said that considering the whole of the medical testimony the jury must resort to speculation or conjecture in determining such causal relationship. In many recent decisions of this court we have held that such determination is deemed based on speculation and conjecture if the medical testimony does not go beyond the expression of an opinion that the physical disability "might have" or "possibly did" result from the hypothesized cause. To remove the issue from the realm of speculation, the medical testimony must at least be sufficiently definite to establish that the act complained of "probably" or "more likely than not" caused the subsequent disability.

The issue before the court, quite simply, is whether Dr. Ostrow's testimony satisfies th[is] standard. . . . In order to make this determination, we must first define the "subsequent disability" suffered by Mr. Herskovits. Therein lies the crux of this case. . . .

If the injury is determined to be the death of Mr. Herskovits, then under the established principles of proximate cause plaintiff has failed to make a prima facie case. Dr. Ostrow was unable to state that probably, or more likely than not, Mr. Herskovits' death was caused by defendant's negligence. On the contrary, it is clear from Dr. Ostrow's testimony that Mr. Herskovits would have probably died from cancer even with the exercise of reasonable care by defendant. . . .

If, on the other hand, we view the injury to be the reduction of Mr. Herskovits' chance of survival, our analysis might well be different. Dr. Ostrow testified that the failure to diagnose cancer in December 1974 probably caused a substantial reduction in Mr. Herskovits' chance of survival. The . . . standard of proof is therefore met.

I note here that two other problems are created by the latter analysis. First, we have never before considered whether the loss or reduction of a chance of survival is a compensable injury. And second, this analysis raises the issue of whether an action for reduction of the chance of survival can be brought under the wrongful death statute. Confronted with these problems, . . . I turn to consider how other jurisdictions have dealt with similar cases. . . .

Having concluded this somewhat detailed survey of the cases cited by plaintiff, what conclusions can we draw? First, the critical element in each of the cases is that the defendant's negligence either deprived a decedent of a chance of surviving a potentially fatal condition or reduced that chance. To summarize, in Hicks v. United States the decedent was deprived of a probability of survival; in Jeanes v. Milner the decedent's chance of survival was reduced from 35 percent to 24 percent; in O'Brien v. Stover, the decedent's 30 percent chance of survival was reduced by an indeterminate amount; in McBride v. United States the decedent was deprived of the probability of survival; in Kallenberg v. Beth Israel Hospital the decedent was deprived of a 20 percent to 40 percent chance of survival; in Hamil v. Bashline the decedent was deprived of a 75 percent chance of survival; and in James v. United States the decedent was deprived of an indeterminate chance of survival, no matter how small.

The three cases where the chance of survival was greater than 50 percent (*Hicks*, *McBride*, and *Hamil*) are unexceptional in that they focus on the death of the decedent as the injury, and they require proximate cause to be shown beyond the balance of probabilities. Such a result is consistent with existing principles in this state, and with cases from other jurisdictions cited by defendant. The remaining four cases allowed recovery despite the plaintiffs' failure to prove a probability of survival. . . . I am convinced that these cases reflect a trend to the most rational, least arbitrary, rule by which to regulate cases of this kind. I am persuaded to this conclusion not so much by the reasoning of these cases themselves, but by the thoughtful discussion of a recent commentator. King, Causation, Valuation, and Chance in Personal Injury Torts Involving Preexisting Conditions and Future Consequences, 90 Yale L.J. 1353 (1981).

King's basic thesis is explained in the following passage, which is particularly pertinent to the case before us:

> . . . A plaintiff ordinarily should be required to prove by the applicable standard of proof that the defendant caused the loss in question. What caused a loss, however, should be a separate question from what the nature and extent of the loss are. This distinction seems to have eluded the courts, with the result that lost chances in many respects are compensated either as certainties or not at all. . . . A more rational approach, however, would allow recovery for the loss of the chance of cure even though the chance was not better than even. The probability of long-term survival would be reflected in the amount of damages awarded for the loss of the chance. . . .

Under the all or nothing approach, typified by Cooper v. Sisters of Charity of Cincinnati, Inc., 27 Ohio St. 2d 242, 272 N.E.2d 97 (1971), a plaintiff who establishes that but for the defendant's negligence the decedent had a 51 percent chance of survival may maintain an action for that death. The defendant will be liable for all damages arising from the death, even though there was a 49 percent chance it would have occurred despite his negligence. On the other hand, a plaintiff who establishes that but for the defendant's negligence the decedent had a 49 percent chance of survival recovers nothing. . . .

These reasons persuade me that the best resolution of the issue before us is to recognize the loss of a less than even chance as an actionable injury. Therefore, I would hold that plaintiff has established a prima facie issue of proximate cause by producing testimony that defendant probably caused a substantial reduction in Mr. Herskovits' chance of survival.

The decedent's personal action for loss of this chance will survive to his personal representatives. The family of the decedent should also be allowed to maintain an action for the lost chance of recovery by the decedent. I would interpret the wrongful death statute to apply to cases of this type. Under this interpretation, a person will "cause" the death of another person whenever he causes a substantial reduction in that person's chance of survival.

Finally, it is necessary to consider the amount of damages recoverable in the event that a loss of a chance of recovery is established. Once again, King's discussion provides a useful illustration of the principles which should be applied:

> To illustrate, consider a patient who suffers a heart attack and dies as a result. Assume that the defendant-physician negligently misdiagnosed the patient's condition, but that the patient would have had only a 40 percent chance of survival even with a timely diagnosis and proper care. Regardless of whether it could be said that the defendant caused the decedent's death, he caused the loss of a chance, and that chance-interest should be completely redressed in its own right. Under the proposed rule, the plaintiff's compensation for the loss of the victim's chance of surviving the heart attack would be 40 percent of the compensable value of the victim's life had he survived (including what his earning capacity would otherwise have been in the years following death). The value placed on the patient's life would reflect such factors as his age, health, and earning potential, including the fact that he had suffered the heart attack and the assumption that he had survived it. The 40 percent computation would be applied to that base figure. . . .

BRACHTENBACH, Justice (dissenting).

. . . Malpractice suits represent a class of controversies where extreme caution should be exercised in relaxing causation requirements. The physician serves a vital function in our society, a function which requires the assumption of a duty to the patient. Yet, his profession affords him only an inexact and often experimental science by which to discharge his duty. Moreover, the tendency to place blame on a physician who fails to find a cure is great. Thus policy considerations do not, on balance, weigh in favor of abandoning the well established requirements of proximate cause.[13]

. . . Usually the substantial factor test has been applied only in situations where there are two causes, either of which could have caused the event alone, and it cannot be determined which was the actual cause. For example, A and B both start separate fires which combine to burn C's house. Either fire alone would have caused the same result, but C cannot prove that "but-for" the negligence of either

---

[13] There is also a difference between the standard of proof for proximate cause to show liability and the standard of proof to show the amount of damages after liability is established. Courts are willing to relax proof requirements on the issue of damages, once liability is shown. Therefore, statistical data may be of greater value at the damage stage, especially with regard to future damages that are necessarily subject to some uncertainties and contingencies.

A or B the house would not have burned. Therefore, to prevent both A and B being relieved of liability, the "but-for" test is abandoned, and the question becomes whether the conduct of A or B was a substantial factor in causing the fire that injured C. Under this test, either A or B could be held liable for the damage. Except in situations where there are coequal causes, however, defendant's act cannot be a substantial factor when the event would have occurred without it. . . .

Thus, I would not resolve the instant case simply by focusing on the 14 percent differentiation in the chance to survive five years for the different stages of cancer. Instead, I would accept this as an admissible fact, but not as proof of proximate cause. To meet the proximate cause burden, the record would need to reveal other facts about the patient that tended to show that he would have been a member of the 14 percent group whose chance of five years' survival could be increased by early diagnosis. . . .

Other statistics admitted into evidence also tend to show the inconclusiveness of the statistics relied on by the majority. One study showed the two-year survival rate for this type of cancer to be 46.6 percent for stage one and 39.8 percent for stage two. Mr. Herskovits lived for 20 months after surgery, which was 26 months after defendant allegedly should have discovered the cancer. Therefore, regardless of the stage of the cancer at the time Mr. Herskovits was examined by defendant, it cannot be concluded that he survived significantly less than the average survival time. Hence, it is pure speculation to suppose that the doctor's negligence "caused" Mr. Herskovits to die sooner than he would have otherwise. . . .

Cases alleging misdiagnosis of cancer are increasing in number, perhaps because of the increased awareness of the importance of early detection. These cases, however, illustrate no more than an inconsistency among courts in their treatment of the problems of proof. See Annot., Malpractice in Connection with Diagnosis of Cancer, 79 A.L.R.3d 915 (1977). Perhaps as medical science becomes more knowledgeable about this disease and more sophisticated in its detection and treatment of it, the balance may tip in favor of imposing liability on doctors who negligently fail to promptly diagnose the disease. But, until a formula is found that will protect doctors against liability imposed through speculation as well as afford truly aggrieved plaintiffs their just compensation, I cannot favor the wholesale abandonment of the principle of proximate cause. For these reasons, I dissent.

Notes: Causation and Loss of Chance

1. Unlike conventional personal injury litigation where the victim first encounters the defendant in a generally healthy condition, malpractice plaintiffs usually start out sick. Moreover, the injury is more often failure to improve rather than a more garden-variety bodily injury. These factors, coupled with the complexities of human biology, result in causation issues demanding as much or more of a lawyer's time and attention as do issues regarding standard of care.

2. *The Traditional Test.* Under the traditional "more likely than not test," plaintiffs sometimes lose on summary judgment or have their verdicts overturned because the expert testimony is expressed in terms of "reasonable possibility"

rather than "probability." A few courts have gone further, however, and required expert testimony of a "reasonable medical certainty." See, e.g., Steineke v. Share Health Plan of Nebraska, 518 N.W.2d 904 (Neb. 1994). One court insisted:

> The issue is not merely one of semantics. There is a logical reason for the rule [requiring "reasonable medical certainty"]. For a factfinder to award damages for a particular condition to a plaintiff, he must find as a fact that the condition was legally caused by the defendant's conduct. Here, the only evidence offered was that it was "probably caused," and that is not enough. Perhaps in the world of medicine nothing is absolutely certain. Nevertheless, doctors must make decisions in their own profession every day based on their own expert opinions. Physicians must understand that it is the intent of our law that if the plaintiff's medical expert cannot form an opinion with sufficient certainty so as to make a medical judgment, there is nothing on the record with which a jury can make a decision with sufficient certainty so as to make a legal judgment. McMahon v. Young, 276 A.2d 534 (Pa. 1971).

See generally Jeff Lewin, The Genesis and Evolution of Legal Uncertainty about "Reasonable Medical Certainty," 57 Md. L. Rev. 380 (1998).

3. *The Concurrence.* Oddly, Justice Pearson's concurring opinion is actually the plurality opinion since it garnered four votes, in contrast with the two votes for Justice Dore. The dissent had three. What is the difference between Justice Pearson's and Justice Dore's conception of the loss-of-chance theory? Does this conceptual debate make any practical difference in the fact patterns that are actionable, the case's procedural posture, or the measure of damages? The concurrence specifies the measure of damages rather clearly (or does it)? How should damages be measured under the main opinion?

Most courts agree that full damages should not be awarded under a loss-of-chance theory, but rather should be discounted by the portion of chance that was lost. What is the correct portion in *Herskovits*, however: 39 percent, 25 percent or 14 percent? Many courts might reason that he lost all, not just a portion, of his preexisting 39 percent since he in fact died. Even if this is not correct in theory, in practice it is rare to have testimony about the precise chance of survival that results *after* the mistake (i.e., in this case, the 25 percent). Absent this testimony, do damages become too speculative to award? Note the comment in n.13 of the dissent. For thoughtful analysis generally, see Lars Noah, An Inventory of Mathematical Blunders in Applying the Loss-of-a-Chance Doctrine, 70 Mo. L. Rev. (2005).

Why should damages be discounted only if the chance of survival was less than 50 percent? Isn't full damages at 51 percent but half damages at 49 percent just as arbitrary as the causation/no-causation line the plurality complains of? Despite this concern, there has been no movement to reduce full damages under ordinary but-for causation.

4. *Wrongful Death Actions.* Another complication, noted by the concurrence, is whether the loss-of-chance theory applies under wrongful death statutes, in contrast with the patient's own survival action. Consider, again, whether it matters which theory of loss-of-chance one adopts, the majority or concurrence. These statutes vary in their precise wording and the precise theory of damages, so predictably courts reach different results. For a contrasting view, see Kramer v. Lewisville Memorial Hospital, 858 S.W.2d 397 (Tex. 1993).

5. *Causation vs. Breach of Duty.* Observe that loss of chance is not, strictly speaking, a theory of liability. It is a theory of causation or injury. Breach of duty must still be positively demonstrated under the normal "more likely than not" standard. Thus, testimony that if a procedure or test had been done the patient's chances would have improved does not suffice to establish that the treatment is required by the standard of care.

6. *Fear of Death or Disease.* Following the argument in the *Herskovits* concurrence, can a loss-of-chance theory be applied even if the loss has not yet occurred? Most courts have not yet taken loss of chance this far. In Fabio v. Bellomo, 504 N.W.2d 758 (Minn. 1993), the court held that a delayed diagnosis of cancer was not actionable where chemotherapy successfully brought the cancer into remission, even though the patient might prove that the delay shortened her life expectancy by increasing the odds that cancer would recur. The obstacle in such actions is that the loss complained of—shortened life—has not yet happened, but query whether there has not been some loss of the "chance interest" described in the *Herskovits* concurrence.

Where there is some actual, present medical injury, plaintiffs may recover for the possibility that the harms may get worse in the future. For instance, Fein v. Permanente Medical Group, excerpted at page 436, allowed recovery for the economic costs from a shortened life expectancy and increased risk of disease caused by the misdiagnosis of a heart attack that left the patient in a weakened condition. As observed in n.1 of the *Herskovits* dissent, these elements of damage do not require any unique theory of liability since actual injury is already established and the only issue is its full extent. Also, where there is present injury, it may be possible to recover as an element of damages the emotional distress over worrying about future death or disease.

It may be possible to avoid showing present injury if the only damages being sought are economic, for the costs of monitoring future health problems caused by increased risk of disease. See, e.g., Sutton v. St. Jude Med. S.C., 419 F.3d 568 (6th Cir. 2005) (recognizing a right to recover for increased risk of future harm when a possibly defective implanted medical device required medical monitoring). These "medical monitoring" theories have been tested in a number of lawsuits, usually involving toxic exposures rather than medical errors. Victor E. Schwartz et al., Medical Monitoring: Should Tort Law Say Yes?, 34 Wake Forest L. Rev. 1057 (1999); Symposium, 88 Va. L. Rev. 1921 (2002); Comment, 32 Wm. Mitchell L. Rev. 1095 (2006).

Recovery is not as readily available, however, where the *only* injury is *emotional*. In such cases, another body of precedent addresses whether tort actions can be maintained for negligent infliction of a purely emotional injury. Traditionally this was not actionable except in specialized cases such as the mishandling of a corpse. In recent decades, however, courts have liberalized this theory of action, but in a highly complex and contradictory fashion that is impossible to summarize here. See J. Mark Appleberry, Negligent Infliction of Emotional Distress: A Focus on Relationships, 21 Am. J.L. & Med. (1995); Andrew R. Klein, Fear of Disease and the Puzzle of Futures Cases in Tort, 35 U.C. Davis L. Rev. 965 (2002); Scott Marrs, Mind Over Body: Trends Regarding the Physical Injury Requirement in Negligent Infliction of Emotional Distress and "Fear of Disease" Cases, 28 Tort & Insur. L.J. 1 (1992). In general, courts require that the distress be especially severe and that some special relationship or characteristic exists that limits the range of potential claimants. In the medical context, the doctor-patient relationship and the act of medical treatment can easily satisfy the special relationship requirement. The severe distress element has been found to be satisfied in two notable medical situations: fear of cancer and fear of AIDS. A few cases have ruled that doctors or institutions can be sued when their negligence reasonably causes patients to fear they have a dread disease, even if the evidence fails to establish that negligence worsened their prospects. Roes v. FHP, Inc., 985 P.2d 661 (Haw. 1999); Ferrara v. Galluchia, 5 N.Y.2d 16 (1958); Note, 1997 U. Ill. L. Rev. 639; 50 A.L.R.4th 12 (1986).

Fear of AIDS exposure has produced considerable litigation. The typical scenario involves a patient who discovers after surgery that her doctor carried the AIDS virus (HIV) and the patient then suffers a period of great distress until receiving a series of conclusive negative HIV tests. Courts are divided on whether these claims are actionable (usually stated as informed consent actions), with disputes centering on whether the fear is reasonable in light of the extent of actual exposure during treatment. Another version of AIDS phobia involves a false positive HIV test result such that, for a period of time, the patient falsely thinks he has AIDS. With certain limitations, courts have allowed these versions of negligent infliction of distress actions as well. See Chizmar v. Mackie, 896 P.2d 196 (Alaska 1995) (actionable despite no physical injury); R.J. v. Humana of Florida, 652 So. 2d 360 (Fla. 1995) (actionable if some physical harm can be shown from unnecessary treatment).

7. *Other States.* Most jurisdictions to consider the issue have accepted some form of the loss-of-chance doctrine. For a particularly thorough review of decisions and theories, see Delaney v. Cade, 873 P.2d 175 (Kan. 1994). One loss-of-chance case allowed this theory to go to the jury even though the deceased patient had only a 10 percent chance of survival, at best. Wendland v. Sparks, 574 N.W.2d 327 (Iowa 1998). For an example of a contrary decision, see Williams v. Spring Hill Memorial Hospital, 646 So. 2d 1373 (Ala. 1994). A compromise position is to allow recovery for an increased risk of harm, but only if there is "reasonable medical certainty" that defendant's negligence caused the increased risk. Holton v. Memorial Hospital, 679 N.E.2d 1202 (Ill. 1997). A full collection of decisions is contained in Annot., 54 A.L.R.4th 10 (1987). For recent commentary, see Todd Aagaard, Note, Identifying and Valuing the Injury in Lost Chance Cases, 96 Mich. L. Rev. 1335 (1998); David A. Fischer, Tort Recovery for Loss of a Chance, 36 Wake Forest L. Rev. 60 (2001); Margaret Berger & Aaron D. Twerski, Uncertainty and Informed Choice, 104 Mich. L. Rev. 258 (2005).

Problem: Loss of a Chance

Group Health, the *Herskovits* defendant, is an HMO. HMOs attempt to reduce costs of medical care by eliminating marginal tests, where the potential "yield" of the tests in accurate findings of disease is low compared to the unit cost of the diagnostic testing. If these cost containment policy decisions render some "missed diagnoses" statistically inevitable, should the health care provider be liable under the "lost chance" doctrine? Consider, for instance, Pap smears, which detect cervical cancer. Suppose the HMO were to calculate that testing every second year rather than every year would save $5 million for its population of 50,000 women patients and, statistically, would increase the number of untreatable cases from ten to eleven per year and decrease the treatable cases from ten to nine per year. That is, assume that, in this population, the HMO can expect 20 cases of cervical cancer a year. With testing every year, ten could be detected in time and successfully treated, but with testing every two years, only nine could be. Can any woman covered by the HMO who then has untreatable cervical cancer sue under a loss of chance theory? Assume that, once incurable cervical cancer is found, there is no way after the fact to be sure whether it is one of the cases that could have been successfully detected and treated.

2. Statutes of Limitations

■ CUNNINGHAM v. HUFFMAN
609 N.E.2d 321 (Ill. 1993)

HEIPLE, Justice.
. . . On March 1, 1977, Dr. Merrill Huffman, a physician specializing in obstetrics and gynecology and a member of the Carle Clinic Association (Carle), inserted an intrauterine device (IUD) into plaintiff, Lynn Cunningham. Subsequently, plaintiff began complaining of cramping, an unusually heavy and lengthy menstrual period, and mid-cycle spotting. Then, on April 8, 1980, after Huffman's probing failed to disclose the presence of the 1977 IUD, he inserted another.

Plaintiff continued to experience medical problems. On March 12, 1981, Huffman performed [a] tubal ligation. At that time he also removed an IUD. Despite this procedure, there was no change in her condition. Plaintiff last saw Huffman on December 14, 1983.

On June 19, 1986, plaintiff again sought care for her condition at Carle, but this time from . . . Dr. Melinda Dabrowski, the only doctor with an opening at the time. Plaintiff's complaints to Dabrowski also concerned menstrual cycle abnormalities. Dabrowski's care of plaintiff continued into August 1988.

On November 25, 1988, Dr. James Yambert attended to plaintiff in Carle's emergency room for abdominal pain. At that time, an X-ray photograph revealed a foreign object in plaintiff's pelvic region consistent with an IUD. Yambert then referred plaintiff to Powell, the OB-GYN doctor on call at the time. Powell ordered an ultrasound vaginal probe which failed to disclose the presence of the IUD. Powell did not review the X-ray taken earlier that day. Powell understood the plaintiff's problem to be menstrual cycle abnormalities. On December 19, 1988, plaintiff underwent surgery wherein a physician not associated with Carle Clinic removed an IUD.

On March 21, 1989, plaintiff brought a . . . medical malpractice lawsuit against defendants Huffman . . . and Carle [Clinic]. . . . The circuit court of Champaign County dismissed . . . plaintiff's complaint with prejudice, finding that plaintiff was time-barred. . . .

Section 13-212 of the Code provides, in relevant part, that "in no event shall such action be brought more than four years after the date on which occurred the act or omission or occurrence alleged in such action to have been the cause of such injury or death." Relying on the decisions of several other jurisdictions, plaintiff argued that the continuous course of treatment doctrine tolled the running of the statute of repose until the end of the patient/physician relationship, so long as there has been continuous treatment — whether negligent or not — for a condition occasioned by a prior negligent act. See Metzger v. Kalke (Wyo. 1985), 709 P.2d 414; see also Comstock v. Collier (Colo. 1987), 737 P.2d 845, 849 (and cases cited). . . .

Count V . . . averred that a continuous course of treatment was involved because a tubal ligation is a prevention of pregnancy and, if not properly performed, the woman may still become pregnant. . . . Plaintiff further alleged that the insertion of one of the IUDs in a manner that caused it to be imbedded in the uterus constituted a continuing negligent act which endured until its presence was revealed to plaintiff on November 25, 1988, or until it was removed on December 19, 1988. The trial court denied plaintiff's motions.

On appeal, the appellate court affirmed the dismissal . . . as to Huffman, but held that the trial court erred in dismissing those same counts, as to Carle [Clinic], without leave to amend. . . . The appellate court stated that in medical malpractice actions, the statute of repose is triggered only on the last day of treatment, and if the treatment is for the same condition, there is no requirement that the negligence be continuous throughout the treatment. Carle now appeals to this court and asks us to determine whether the continuous course of treatment doctrine applies to a multispecialty health care institution. . . .

Subject to the fraudulent concealment exception provided in §13-215 of the Code, the legislature has clearly stated that no "action be brought more than four years after the date on which occurred the act or omission or occurrence alleged in such action to have been the cause of such injury." Confronted with the clear, unambiguous language of the statute, we cannot adopt the continuous course of treatment doctrine as formulated by the appellate court.

We find it significant that the General Assembly has amended §13-212 numerous times but has never expressly provided for any exception to the statute of repose except for cases of fraudulent concealment. Had the General Assembly intended the continuous course of treatment doctrine to be the law of this state, it could have specifically provided so, as the legislative bodies in New York and Texas have done. . . . Given the attention paid to the so-called medical malpractice crisis in recent years, it is fair to assume that the Illinois General Assembly was aware of such developments and purposefully declined to act. We are not alone in our interpretation today. The courts in Delaware, Kansas and Maryland have also come to the same conclusion when confronted with statutes similar to ours. Although we are cognizant of several jurisdictions which have adopted the doctrine without legislative initiative, we decline to follow suit.

Notwithstanding our rejection of the continuous course of treatment doctrine, the Illinois statutory scheme does not necessarily preclude the cause of action asserted by plaintiff. Critical to the plaintiff's claim is the construction of the word *occurrence* in §13-212. Plaintiff argues that, correctly construed, "occurrence" may include a continuing *negligent* course of treatment for a specific condition. We agree. . . .

In construing the meaning of the phrase *the act or omission or occurrence*, we find it improbable that the General Assembly intended the word *occurrence* to be limited to a single event. Had it so intended, it could have simply stated that the statute begins to run on the happening of the "specific act" or "specific omission." Further, to so narrowly construe this phrase could lead to absurd and unjust results. For example, if the word *occurrence* were interpreted to mean a single isolated event, patients who discovered that they were gravely injured due to negligent or unnecessary exposure to X-ray radiation or administration of medication over a span of years might be able to recover little, if any, in the way of damages. This would be so because a single dosage of radiation or medicine might be harmless, whereas treatment over time might be either disabling or even fatal. . . . Surely, the law could not contemplate such an unjust result.

    . . . [We hold] that a plaintiff is not barred by the statute of repose if she can demonstrate that there was an ongoing course of continuous negligent medical treatment. . . . We point out that once treatment by the negligent physician is discontinued, the statute of repose begins to run, regardless of whether or not the patient is aware of the negligence at termination of treatment. This is so because the statute of repose is triggered by the "act or omission or occurrence" causing an injury, rather than by the patient's discovery of the injury as is the case with a statute of limitations. Although such a statutory scheme may result in harsh consequences, such as when a cause of action is barred even before its discovery, . . . our legislature enacted this four-year outer limit on malpractice liability specifically to curtail the "long tail" exposure to medical malpractice claims brought about by the advent of the discovery rule. Thus, the statute of repose must be triggered once treatment terminates.

    We also emphasize that there must be a continuous course of *negligent* treatment as opposed to a mere continuous course of treatment. In our reading of the statute, the word *occurrence*, like the words *act* and *omission*, necessarily only encompasses the continuum where the physician was negligent. . . . If the physician's treatments subsequent to discovery and disclosure cannot be deemed negligent, the statute of repose begins to run at the time of the physician's discovery and disclosure rather than at termination of treatment. . . . If the physician should purposely conceal the discovery of the negligence, however, neither the statute of limitations nor the statute of repose would be triggered. In the cases of nondisclosure, the fraudulent concealment provision in §13-215 of the Code affords the patient five years after discovery of the cause of action to commence the suit.

    We now turn to the issue of whether the tort of continuing negligent treatment applies to a multispecialty clinic when several doctors negligently treat a patient for a specific problem over a finite time span. We find that to the extent a party brings an action against the clinic as an entity in and of itself, rather than on a theory of vicarious liability, plaintiff can state a cause of action against a multispecialty clinic.

    In this case, plaintiff sought care from Carle Clinic as an entity. Although it appears plaintiff had a right of preference as to the physician she wanted to see, the ultimate assignment decision was Carle's. It was merely fortuitous that plaintiff was treated by more than one of Carle's physicians. . . . It would be inequitable to allow Carle to escape liability merely because it had the ability to assign different doctors to plaintiff over a period of time. . . .

Accordingly, the judgment of the appellate court is affirmed but its rationale is rejected. [That is, the complaint is dismissed against Dr. Huffman, but may proceed against the Clinic.] . . .

[Chief Justice Miller, dissented, arguing that plaintiff failed to state any grounds for holding the clinic independently liable, apart from its vicarious liability for the mistakes of its individual physicians.]

Notes: Statutes of Limitations

1. *Tolling Rules. Cunningham* introduces three distinct but related doctrines that potentially toll the statute of limitations in medical malpractice cases: continuing treatment; fraudulent concealment; and the "discovery rule." The case focuses on the first of these. The second tolls the statute if the physician knows about the injury but does not tell the patient. The third applies where neither the patient nor the doctor are aware of the mistake, such as when a surgeon leaves a foreign object inside the body. An extreme example of the discovery rule is found in Heinrich v. Sweet, 44 F. Supp. 2d 408 (D. Mass. 1999), where a patient's family was awarded $8 million for death caused 40 years earlier by unsuccessful, experimental radiation treatment for an inoperable brain tumor. The court ruled that the statute was tolled because the family did not realize until 1995 that the experimental therapy had been given or that the patient had died from the radiation treatment instead of from the tumor. See generally Annots., 70 A.L.R.3d 7 (1976); 50 A.L.R.4th 250 (1986).

2. *Statutory Changes.* In recent decades, most states have modified their statutes of limitations in response to the perceived "crisis" in medical malpractice litigation, discussed in section 4.G. Typical is a baseline limitations period of one to two years, which is subject to some degree of tolling, and an outer limitations period of three to five years, known as a "statute of repose." Even though the continuing treatment rule and the discovery rule were thought to be the main target of these reforms, in some jurisdictions the courts have found ways to keep these rules alive, at least in some fashion. See, e.g., New v. Armour Pharmaceutical Co., 58 F.3d 445 (9th Cir. 1995) (mere discovery by a hemophiliac that he received a blood product tainted by the AIDS virus was not enough to start the statute running; statute was tolled until he first experienced serious symptoms); Booth v. Wiley, 839 N.E.2d 1168 (Ind. 2005) (statute is tolled until eye patient learns that doctor's negligence rather than preexisting condition was the cause of problems following surgery); compare Damiano v. McDaniel, 689 So. 2d 1059 (Fla. 1997) (refusing to create a hardship exception to the statute of repose for AIDS cases); Rudenauer v. Zafiropoulos, 837 N.E.2d 278 (Mass. 2005) (statute of repose is absolute, even though patient's death from cancer did not occur until ten years after the failure to diagnose). Where the statute itself provides for some form of a discovery rule, it is much less likely the courts will feel inclined to enforce one on their own. For instance, in Jones v. McDonald, 631 So. 2d 869 (Ala. 1993), the court ruled that the continuing treatment rule does not apply where the statute itself preserves the discovery rule. There, however, the statute allowed only six months after discovery to file. Would any length of time do? The court in Garcia v.

La Farge, 893 P.2d 428 (N.M. 1995), held that due process requires giving plaintiffs a minimum reasonable time to sue after discovery of negligence. There, the statute of repose happened to expire 85 days after discovery of the doctor's misdiagnosis, which the court held was not sufficient.

3. *Constitutional Challenges.* Malpractice reform statutes have been subject to facial constitutional challenges as well. Several states have struck down shortened statutes of limitations in their entirety, usually on grounds of equal protection, because they target only one type of tort action — medical malpractice. Some of these decisions find an absence of rational basis for this selective restriction, while others justify fundamental-interest heightened scrutiny based on an "open courts" constitutional provision that guarantees the right to sue for personal injury. See, e.g., Kenyon v. Hammer, 688 P.2d 961 (Ariz. 1984) (shorter limitations period for medical malpractice than for other tort cases violates equal protection); Martin v. Richey, 711 N.E.2d 1273 (Ind. 1999) (a two-year period does not give a reasonable opportunity to sue for a patient who claimed that her physician negligently failed to diagnose breast cancer that she did not discover until three years later). Contra Choroszy v. Tso, 647 A.2d 803 (Maine 1994) (statute constitutional, despite failure to discover misdiagnosis; rational basis test applies, despite "open courts" provision); Jennings v. Burgess, 917 S.W.2d 790 (Tex. 1996) (statute valid if it does not produce unreasonable result in the particular case). For discussion of the Indiana case, see Symposium, Indiana's Medical Malpractice Reform, 31 Ind. L. Rev. 1043 (1998). See generally section G of this chapter.

4. *The* Cunningham *Decision.* Where the continuing treatment rule applies, there are two versions, as noted in *Cunningham.* The conventional version applies even to a single act of negligence. It holds that the statute does not start to run until treatment for the same condition has been completed. The rationale is well stated in Watkins v. Fromm, 488 N.Y.S.2d 768 (App. Div. 1985):

> It would be absurd to require a wronged patient to interrupt corrective efforts by serving a summons on the physician or hospital superintendent. . . . [T]he trust and confidence that marks the physician-patient relationship puts the patient at a disadvantage to question the doctor's techniques and gives the patient the right to rely upon the doctor's professional skill without the necessity of interrupting a continuing course of treatment by instituting suit. The exception not only provides the patient with the opportunity to seek corrective treatment from the doctor, but also gives the physician a reasonable chance to identify and correct errors made at an earlier stage of treatment.

The second version, adopted in *Cunningham,* applies only where there is continuing negligence. Here, the rationale for the doctrine is more formal: it is to operationalize the statutory definition of what event triggers the statute running. Strictly speaking, then, this second version is not a tolling doctrine.

Observe the two distinct arguments Ms. Cunningham made for finding that treatment had continued. One was that a tubal ligation continues throughout the years of potential fertility. The continuity of treatment is usually broken, however, when treatment ceases for the condition that was mistreated. See, e.g., Konstantikis v. Kassipidis, 602 N.Y.S.2d 67 (App. Div. 1993) (no continuing treatment occurred for surgery that accidentally caused infertility where subsequent treatment of infertility addressed other problems). Where the mistake is failure to diagnose, does the negligence continue until the doctor makes the correct diagnosis? Fabio v. Bellomo, 504 N.W.2d 758 (Minn. 1993) (no, for failure to diagnose lump as breast cancer, even though patient saw her doctor 60 times over four years and misdiagnosis was repeated several times); Sander v. Geib, Elseton, Frost P.A., 506 N.W.2d 107 (S.D. 1993) (yes, where incorrect reading of a Pap smear was repeated and subsequent visits were for general gynecological exams); Chambers v. Conaway, 883 S.W.2d 156 (Tex. 1993) (yes, under similar facts, even past the point where misdiagnosis was repeated). See generally K. Safavi, Multispecialty Group Practice Liability and the Continuous Course of Treatment Doctrine, 27 J. Health & Hosp. L. 72 (1994).

Cunningham is unusual because the subsequent negligence was not committed by the same doctor. Carle Clinic is a very large, multi-site, medical group, similar to the Mayo Clinic. Many of its patients have insurance through HMOs. As more people receive their treatment from large, managed care networks, this ruling takes on more significance. Consider, though, how significant and close in time the subsequent negligence must be in order to continue the tolling. In Watkins v. Fromm, supra, the court held that continued treatment by a medical group tolled the statute against two doctors even though the two doctors left the group more than three years before it concluded its treatment of the patient. In *Cunningham*, suppose that Dr. Dabrowski (the second doctor) was not negligent. Then, the only subsequent act of negligence would have been Dr. Powell's, some five years after plaintiff last saw Dr. Huffman. Did his slip-up contribute in any way to the plaintiff's injuries?

3. Affirmative Defenses

All of the standard affirmative defenses available in other tort actions can be used in medical malpractice cases. The following decision reviews a number of these, as well as other strands of doctrine from earlier in the chapter. Focus your attention on the aspects of the case that concern release from liability, contributory negligence or comparative fault, and assumption of risk.

■ SCHNEIDER v. REVICI
817 F.2d 987 (2d Cir. 1987)

MINER, Circuit Judge.

Emanuel Revici, M.D. and the Institute of Applied Biology, Inc. (the "Institute") appeal from a judgment . . . arising from Dr. Revici's treatment of plaintiff Edith Schneider's breast cancer with unconventional, noninvasive cancer therapy, after she had been advised by numerous doctors to undergo a biopsy and had refused to do so. Edith Schneider and her husband asserted . . . : (1) fraud, premised on Dr. Revici's alleged promise to cure Mrs. Schneider of breast cancer; and (2) medical malpractice. . . . After the district judge refused to charge the jury on the affirmative defense of express assumption of risk, the jury . . . awarded

Edith Schneider and her husband $1,000,000.00 and $50,000.00 respectively. Because the jury found that Mrs. Schneider was equally responsible, through her own culpable conduct, for the damages she suffered, the awards were halved to $500,000.00 and $25,000.00, pursuant to New York's comparative negligence statute.

On appeal, Dr. Revici and the Institute challenge the district court's refusal to charge with respect to an alleged covenant not to sue and express assumption of risk as affirmative defenses, either of which would serve as a total bar to recovery. Appellants also contend that numerous evidentiary rulings were erroneous. . . .

I. BACKGROUND

In October 1981, Dr. Cocoziello discovered a lump in appellee Edith Schneider's right breast during her annual gynecological checkup. . . . Mrs. Schneider was examined by Dr. Abessi and Dr. Volke, who both separately advised her to undergo a biopsy and possibly a partial mastectomy, depending upon the analysis of the biopsied tissue. She refused.

In November 1981, Mrs. Schneider consulted with Dr. Emanuel Revici, . . . a physician and researcher who treats cancer patients with "non-toxic," noninvasive methods that have not been adopted by the medical community. Mrs. Schneider had learned of Dr. Revici and his novel cancer therapy from a radio program. After Mrs. Schneider signed a detailed consent form,[1] Dr. Revici diagnosed cancer of the right breast and began treatment with selenium [a nonmetallic element used in electronic devices] and dietary restrictions. . . . After 14 months of treatment, the tumor had increased in size, and cancer had spread to her lymph system and left breast. Mrs. Schneider finally underwent a bilateral mastectomy at Memorial Sloan-Kettering Hospital in January 1983, followed by 16 months of conventional chemotherapy. . . .

A. EVIDENTIARY RULINGS

. . . The trial court excluded records of patients successfully treated by Dr. Revici on the grounds that the issue in medical malpractice is not whether a particular treatment is effective but whether that treatment is a deviation from accepted medical practice in the community. The trial court's statement of the law of medical malpractice is correct. However, evidence as to the effectiveness of Dr. Revici's treatment method was relevant to show that he did not make a false representation with intent to defraud. Any error in excluding the patient records

---

[1] Mrs. Schneider signed a consent form that reads as follows:

. . . I fully understand that some of the treatment procedures and medications are still investigatory awaiting further research and submission for F.D.A. approval. . . . I am aware that the practice of medicine is not an exact science and I acknowledge that no guaranties have been made to me as to the results of the treatment procedures and medications. . . . I therefore release Dr. Emanuel Revici from all liabilities to me, including all claims and complaints by me or by other members of my family. I am here because I wish to try the Revici methods and preparations for disease control. . . .

Dr. Revici testified that Mrs. Schneider had told him that she had not seen other doctors and had not yet had a mammogram. He testified that because of this, he explained the consent form to her in great detail. . . .

was clearly harmless, however, in light of the jury's finding that Dr. Revici was not liable on the claim of common law fraud. Dr. Revici's sole liability was founded on medical malpractice, which is amply supported by the record, and the evidence of the effectiveness of his treatment was not relevant to that issue. . . .

Defendants' expert witness, Gerhard Schrauzer, had testified about the nutritional value of selenium — testimony directed at negating the fraud claim against Dr. Revici. To rebut that testimony, plaintiffs called Victor Herbert, M.D., who authored two books concerning health and nutrition fads. . . . Appellants object to the trial court's failure to strike his testimony in the following exchange:

Q: Could you tell us whether Dr. Emanuel Revici is recognized by the National Council Against Health Fraud and in what manner? [Objection]
A: We recognize him as a quack, we recognize his treatment as snake oil. We consider him, in quotes, one of the cruelest killers in the United States.

. . . The labels applied to Dr. Revici by Dr. Herbert should not have been countenanced by the district judge. Dr. Herbert was entitled to furnish his opinion on the efficacy of Dr. Revici's treatment and on the consequences likely to befall patients who accepted it in lieu of traditional treatment. These views could have been forcefully expressed without the incendiary labels "quack" and "one of the cruelest killers." However, viewing the testimony in the context of the emphatic opinions that were properly expressed, we do not believe the failure to strike the use of inflammatory characterizations warrants reversal. The labels, though improper, added but slight impact to the force of Dr. Herbert's testimony.

We have considered the other evidentiary arguments of appellants and find them to be without merit.

B. COVENANT NOT TO SUE

New York law recognizes the efficacy of a covenant not to sue in the context of medical treatment:

> Specifically, where a patient voluntarily agrees to undergo an experimental and inherently dangerous surgical procedure, the parties may covenant to exempt the physician from liability for those injuries which are found to be the consequences of the non-negligent, proper performance of the procedure. . . . That is to say, that an experimental procedure which, because of its inherent dangers, may ordinarily be in and of itself a departure from customary and accepted practice (and thus possibly actionable as malpractice) even if performed in a non-negligent manner, may be rendered unactionable by a covenant not to sue.

Colton v. New York Hospital, 414 N.Y.S.2d 866, 876 (Sup. Ct. 1979), and cases there cited. However, New York requires that "a covenant not to sue . . . must be strictly construed against the party asserting it. Moreover, its wording must be 'clear and unequivocal.'" The form signed by Mrs. Schneider lacks the precision required by New York law.

In the first place, the form was not labeled a covenant or agreement not to sue but was instead captioned "CONSENT FOR MEDICAL CARE." . . . Second, the one paragraph of the consent form that bears on legal liability is not "clear and unequivocal." . . . To "release . . . from all liabilities" can plausibly be understood only to relinquish claims currently existing, rather than to promise not to sue in the future on claims that may subsequently arise. . . .

The district judge did not err in declining to submit the covenant not to sue issue to the jury.

C. ASSUMPTION OF RISK

. . . In 1975, New York adopted a comparative negligence statute eliminating contributory negligence as a total bar to recovery. Prior to adoption of the statute a plaintiff was required to be free of any negligence contributing in the slightest degree to his injury, in order to recover. The plaintiff's own negligence was viewed as an intervening cause, between the defendant's negligent act and the plaintiff's injury, which prevented any recovery. Dowd v. New York, Ontario & W. Ry. Co., 63 N.E. 541 (N.Y. 1902). See generally Arbegast v. Board of Educ., 480 N. E.2d 365, 368 (N.Y. 1985).

The doctrine of assumption of risk was a defense to an action for the recovery of damages for personal injuries, prior to the adoption of the comparative negligence statute. . . . While assumption of risk, like contributory negligence, barred recovery, it was predicated on a theory of contract rather than on a theory of culpable conduct: the plaintiff's agreement, either express or implied, to absolve the defendant from responsibility. "Express" assumption of risk resulted from an advance agreement that the defendant need not use reasonable care for the plaintiff's benefit. "Implied" assumption of risk, on the other hand, was founded on plaintiff's unreasonable and voluntary consent to the risk of harm from defendant's conduct with full understanding of the possible harm. Restatement (Second) of Torts §496B, 496E.

In 1975, New York's Civil Practice Law and Rules were amended by the addition of a pure comparative negligence statute. . . . In accord with the plain language of the statute . . . commentators assumed that under the new comparative negligence statute assumption of risk was no longer a total bar to recovery, but simply diminished the amount of damages recoverable. . . . [However,] [i]n 1985, the Court of Appeals of New York . . . held that express assumption of risk would provide a complete defense, while implied assumption of risk was subsumed by [the comparative negligence statute]: "[The statute] requires diminishment of damages in the case of an implied assumption of risk but, except as public policy proscribes an agreement limiting liability, does not foreclose a complete defense that by express consent of the injured party no duty exists and, therefore, no recovery may be had." Arbegast, 480 N.E.2d at 371. . . .

In the case before us, appellees contend that it is against public policy for one expressly to assume the risk of medical malpractice and thereby dissolve the physician's duty to treat a patient according to medical community standards. . . . [W]e see no reason why a patient should not be allowed to make an informed decision to go outside currently approved medical methods in search of an unconventional treatment. While a patient should be encouraged to exercise care for his own safety, we believe that an informed decision to avoid surgery and conventional chemotherapy is within the patient's right "to determine what shall be done with his own body," Schloendorff v. Society of the New York Hospital, 105 N.E. 92 (N.Y. 1914) (Cardozo, J.). . . .

While we do not determine, in the case before us, whether Mrs. Schneider expressly assumed the risk of Dr. Revici's treatment, we hold that there existed sufficient evidence — in the language of the Consent for Medical Care form that she signed, and in testimony relating to specific consent informed by her awareness of the risk of refusing conventional treatment to undergo the Revici method — to allow the jury to consider express assumption of risk as an affirmative defense that would totally bar recovery. It was therefore error for the district court to deny the defendants' request for a jury charge on the issue, and we reverse and remand for that reason.

Notes: Affirmative Defenses

1. Schneider v. Revici introduces a complex thicket of doctrines that overlap to a large extent but that are also conceptually distinct: (1) the standard of care for experimental care or "alternative" practitioners; (2) informed consent (the discussion of which is omitted in this excerpt); (3) release from liability, or waiver of the right to sue; (4) contributory negligence or comparative fault; and (5) assumption of risk. (1) and (2) are explored elsewhere because they go to basic elements in the cause of action. See Chapters 3.C and 4.B.2. In addition, the fraud action mentioned in the decision is explored at page 381, and the evidentiary point is addressed in section B.3.

The focus here is on the affirmative defenses stated in (3), (4), and (5). Observe the extent of both overlap and independence among these. Even though the release was not effective, the court still found the consent form could establish assumption of risk. And even though there was no instruction on assumption of risk, the jury found 50 percent comparative fault. For a contrasting decision from over a century ago, see Nelson v. Harrington, 40 N.W. 228 (Wis. 1888) (patient not contributorily negligent in seeking care from "clairvoyant physician" even though he knew in advance what the treatment was; "the proposition that one holding himself out as a medical practitioner, . . . because he resorts to some peculiar method . . . [is] exonerated from all liability for unskillfulness on his part, no matter how serious the consequences may be, cannot be entertained" and is contrary to public policy).

2. *Waiver of Liability.* Generally speaking, releases of liability or waivers of the right to sue for medical negligence, signed at the time of treatment, are unenforceable as contrary to public policy, even if they are correctly worded. The seminal decision is Tunkl v. Regents, discussed in the next case and excerpted at page 123. See Annot., 6 A.L.R.3d 704 (1966 & Supp.). *Revici* is consistent with this law because it holds only that a release of liability prior to a claim arising is potentially valid only to the extent that it specifies *nonnegligent* performance of nonstandard care. Releases are also commonly obtained and enforced when patients leave the hospital against medical advice ("AMA").

Releases from liability or covenants not to sue for negligent care are also valid if signed *after* the harm occurs and the claim arises. This is how parties settle a dispute. A critical aspect of legal practice is to correctly distinguish between the two forms—release vs. covenant—because of the effect on the liability of joint tortfeasors. Many malpractice actions are brought against more than one defendant—several doctors or a hospital as well as the doctors. Plaintiffs often agree to settle with one or more of the less culpable or less-well-insured parties while keeping the others on the hook. At common law, a release from liability of one joint tortfeasor had the automatic effect of releasing all the others, even if the release stated to the contrary, because it was seen as extinguishing a single, indivisible cause of action; covenants not to sue do not have this effect, however. This rule has been reversed in most states, but releases are still dangerous in some states. See, e.g., Gilbert v. Sycamore Municipal Hospital, 622 N.E.2d 788 (Ill. 1993) (settlement with doctor extinguishes vicarious liability of hospital even though settling parties expressly reserved the right to sue hospital).

3. *Contributory Fault and Mitigation of Damages. Revici* addresses comparative fault and contributory negligence only in passing, but this was obviously a large part of the case since it resulted in halving the jury verdict. Presumably, this finding was based on Ms. Schneider's foolishness in believing Dr. Revici's claims and ignoring advice to seek conventional treatment at the same time.[1] What other actions might constitute contributory fault, either during, before, or following treatment? Notice in n.1 that Ms. Schneider misled Dr. Revici about her medical history. See also Fall v. White, 449 N.E.2d 628 (Ind. Ct. App. 1983) (patient contributed to his own death by heart attack when he failed to reveal to the doctor that he was experiencing chest pains); Annot., 33 A.L.R.4th 790 (1984). Consider also that, where a doctor is given an inaccurate or incomplete medical history, this may also negate any primary finding of negligence on the doctor's part.

In other cases, courts have found contributory fault where the patient blatantly ignored doctors' orders or failed to return for follow-up visits, as instructed. See Harlow v. Chin, 545 N.E.2d 602 (Mass. 1989) (13 percent fault found where patient failed to contact doctor when pain got much worse); Gruidl v. Schell, 519 N.E.2d 963 (Ill. App. Ct. 1988) (patient 40 percent negligent in failing to report that lump in neck grew larger). But see Tobia v. Cooper Hospital University Medical Center, 643 A.2d 1 (N.J. 1994) (doctors' duty of care includes protecting patients from harming themselves, in a case where an 85-year-old fell off a stretcher trying to go to the bathroom unattended); Durphy v. Kaiser Foundation Health Plan, 698 A.2d 459 (D.C. 1997) (patient's failure to follow instructions, resulting in foot amputation, does not bar recovery for prior act of negligence by doctor). See generally Annot., 84 A.L.R.5th 619 (2000). Patient negligence that occurs *after* the doctor's can also go to mitigation of damages rather than mitigation of fault. See George Washington University v. Waas, 648 A.2d 178 (D.C. 1994) (patient's failure to follow instructions and cooperate with

---

[1] Subsequent studies have shown, however, that selenium in fact inhibits several types of cancer. In one study, it cut cancer deaths in half. The benefit was so dramatic, the researchers felt compelled to halt the placebo wing of the study. Graham Colditz, Selenium and Cancer Prevention: Promising Results Indicate Further Trials Required, 276 JAMA 1984 (1996).

follow-up treatment mitigates damages from failure to diagnose cancer but does not bar recovery).

Can patients be found at fault for their behavior *leading up to* their medical condition? In general, no. Doctors take their patients as they find them. See Mercer v. Vanderbilt Univ., 134 S.E.3d 121 (Tenn. 2004) (no contributory fault by patient who suffered brain damage from a negligent medical mistake during treatment for a car accident caused by the patient's own alcohol consumption); Jensen v. Archbishop Bergan Mercy Hospital, 459 N.W.2d 178 (Neb. 1990) (no contributory negligence even though patient's failure to lose weight may have caused the pulmonary embolism that was negligently treated). But see Cobo v. Raba, 495 S.E.2d 362 (N.C. 1998) (a patient who was also a doctor could be found contributorily negligent for engaging in repeated unprotected homosexual intercourse with prostitutes and for delays in seeking treatment once he became HIV-infected). Similarly, in the context of mitigation of damages, patients do not have to submit to risky surgery or medication to correct a negligent injury, even if medically advised. See, e.g., Robins v. Katz, 391 N.W.2d 495 (Mich. Ct. App. 1986) (patient could refuse second foot surgery to correct mistakes made the first time). But see Corlett v. Caserta, 562 N.E.2d 257 (Ill. App. Ct. 1990) (Jehovah's Witness who refused blood transfusion to correct gastric bleeding following colon surgery must "bear a proportionate share of tort liability").

4. *Good Samaritans.* Another affirmative defense of unique importance to medical malpractice is the "Good Samaritan" immunity statutes enacted in all states. These laws are intended to encourage doctors to come to the aid of injured strangers ("Is there a doctor in the house?") by reducing the standard of care to gross negligence or recklessness when they respond to an emergency or render first aid. Usually, one thinks of these accident scenes occurring on the highway or in public places, but because the wording of these statutes varies, it is sometimes possible to argue they apply in hospital settings or in doctors' offices. See Annot., 68 A.L.R.4th 294 (1989). The case for this interpretation is stronger if the physician who claims immunity is a true volunteer, that is, not the patient's usual doctor and not assigned to emergency care. In a few states, these statutes apply to ordinary medical care only when physicians treat indigent patients for free, but they cover all types of treatment, not just emergencies. Comment, Statutory Immunity for Volunteer Physicians, 1 Widener L. Symp. J. 425 (1996); Paul A. Hattis, Overcoming Barriers to Physician Volunteerism, 2004 U. Ill. L. Rev. 167.

These statutes first arose during the 1960s after a flurry of press reports discussing the legal vulnerability of doctors who aid accident or heart attack victims on the scene. In fact, there were no recorded malpractice suits against doctors in such situations. William J. Curran, The Not-so-Good Samaritan Laws, 270 New Eng. J. Med. 1003 (1964). See S. Levmore, Waiting for Rescue: An Essay on the Evolution and Incentive Structure of the Law of Affirmative Obligations, 72 Va. L. Rev. 879 (1986).

5. *Hospital Immunity.* Other sources of potential immunity have more relevance for hospitals than for physicians and so are discussed later in this chapter. These include charitable immunity for nonprofit facilities, and governmental immunity for state and municipal facilities. In most states, these immunities have disappeared or have been greatly scaled back.

4. Arbitration and Waiver of Liability

The next case concerns arbitration. It is important in its own right, since various forms of alternative dispute resolution are increasingly being used for medical care. But it has broader importance as well. It explains the legal framework in which contractual agreements might be used to alter the core standard of care or to waive malpractice liability entirely. The key question is how far this precedent might extend in those directions.

■ MADDEN v. KAISER FOUNDATION HOSPITAL
552 P.2d 1178 (Cal. 1976)

TOBRINER, Justice.

Defendants appeal from an order denying enforcement of an arbitration provision in a medical services contract entered into between the Board of Administration of the State Employees Retirement System (hereafter board) and defendant Kaiser Foundation Health Plan. Plaintiff, a state employee who enrolled under the Kaiser plan, contends that she is not bound by the provision for arbitration. The instant appeal presents the issue whether an agent or representative, contracting for medical services on behalf of a group of employees, has implied authority to agree to arbitration of malpractice claims of enrolled employees arising under the contract. . . .

When plaintiff first enrolled under the Kaiser plan in 1965, it did not contain an arbitration provision. On April 1, 1971, however, the Kaiser Foundation Health Plan, anticipating the inclusion of an arbitration provision, mailed to all subscribers a brochure which, in describing the terms and benefits of the plan, stated that claims involving professional liability and personal injury must be submitted to arbitration. Shortly thereafter, on May 28, 1971, the Kaiser Foundation Health Plan and the board amended their contract in several respects and included a provision for binding arbitration of "any claim arising from the violation of a legal duty incident to this Agreement."[2]

On August 1, 1971, plaintiff underwent a hysterectomy at the Kaiser Hospital in Los Angeles. During the surgery, her bladder was perforated; blood transfusions were required; plaintiff thereafter contracted serum hepatitis.

Plaintiff filed a malpractice complaint against Kaiser and the blood banks. Kaiser moved to stay the action and compel arbitration. Opposing this motion, plaintiff filed a declaration stating that because of absence from work by reason of illness she had not received the April 1971 brochure, that she was not aware of the execution of the arbitration agreement in May of 1971, and thus had no knowledge that the Kaiser plan, at the time of her operation, required arbitration of malpractice claims. By order of April 22, 1974, the trial court denied the

---

[2] The arbitration agreement stated that it was retroactive to April 1, 1971, the date of the Kaiser brochure advising subscribers of the arbitration clause. Since plaintiff's claim arose after May 28, 1971, we need not consider whether the agreement can be retroactively effective to require arbitration of claims arising before it was finally approved.

motion to stay the action and compel arbitration. Kaiser appeals from that order.

2. *The board, as agent for the employees, had implied authority to provide for arbitration of malpractice claims.*

Government Code §§22774, 22790 and 22793 authorize the board to negotiate contracts for group medical plans for state employees. In negotiating such agreements and amendments the board acts as the agent or representative of the employees. . . .

We shall explain that although the courts in the past regarded arbitration as an unusual and suspect procedure, they now recognize it as an accepted method of settlement of disputes. Since Civil Code §2319 grants an agent the authority to do whatever is "proper and usual" to carry out his agency, the board enjoyed an implied authority to agree to arbitration of malpractice claims of enrolled employees. . . .

In Crofoot v. Blair Holding Corp., 260 P.2d 156, 170 (Cal. App. 1953), Justice Peters summarized the evolution of legal attitudes toward arbitration.

> Arbitration has had a long and troubled history. The early common law courts did not favor arbitration, and greatly limited the powers of arbitrators. But in recent times a great change in attitude and policy has taken place. Arbitrations are now usually covered by statutory law, as they are in California. Such statutes evidence a strong public policy in favor of arbitrations, which policy has frequently been approved and enforced by the courts.

Subsequent decisions confirm the self-evident fact that arbitration has become an accepted and favored method of resolving disputes, praised by the courts as an expeditious and economical method of relieving overburdened civil calendars.

The transformation of legislative and judicial attitudes toward arbitration has encouraged a dramatic development in the use of this procedure. A 1952 study estimated that "aside from personal injury cases and cases in which the government is a party, more than 70 percent of the total civil litigation is decided through arbitration rather than by the courts" (Mentschikoff, The Significance of Arbitration — a Preliminary Inquiry (1952) 17 Law & Contemp. Prob. 698). In the following decades arbitration further expanded its role to encompass in certain circumstances disputes requiring evaluation of personal injury claims: California and many other states now require arbitration of uninsured motorist claims, and proposals for no-fault automobile insurance frequently provide for arbitration. . . .

The matter becomes even clearer if we narrow our focus to arbitration of disputes arising under group contracts. In collective bargaining agreements, which, like the present contract, are negotiated by elected representatives on behalf of a group of employees, arbitration has become a customary means of resolving disputes. . . .

Finally, we observe the growing interest in and use of arbitration to cope with the increasing volume of medical malpractice claims. Henderson, Contractual Problems in the Enforcement of Agreements to Arbitrate Medical Malpractice, 58 Va. L. Rev. 947, 956 (1972). . . .

We therefore conclude that an agent or other fiduciary who contracts for medical treatment on behalf of his beneficiary retains the authority to enter into an agreement providing for arbitration of claims for medical malpractice.[11]

3. *The principles that govern contracts of adhesion do not bar enforcement of the arbitration amendment.*

. . . Contending that the Kaiser contract is one of adhesion, plaintiff argues that the courts should refuse to enforce its arbitration clause on the ground that the clause is inconspicuous, unexpected, and disrupts the members' reasonable expectation that a malpractice claim will be adjudicated by trial by jury. We explain our reason for concluding that the principles governing adhesion contracts do not cover the present case. . . .

In the characteristic adhesion contract case, the stronger party drafts the contract, and the weaker has no opportunity, either personally or through an agent, to negotiate concerning its terms. The Kaiser plan, on the other hand, represents the product of negotiation between two parties, Kaiser and the board, possessing parity of bargaining strength. Although plaintiff did not engage in the personal negotiation of the contract's terms, she and other public employees benefitted from representation by a board, composed in part of persons elected by the affected employees, which exerted its bargaining strength to secure medical protection for employees on more favorable terms than any employee could individually obtain.

In many cases of adhesion contracts, the weaker party lacks not only the opportunity to bargain but also any realistic opportunity to look elsewhere for a more favorable contract; he must either adhere to the standardized agreement or forego the needed service. Plaintiff, on the other hand, enjoyed the opportunity to select from among several medical plans negotiated and offered by the board, some of which did not include arbitration provisions, or to contract individually for medical care. . . .

To support her contract of adhesion argument, plaintiff points to Tunkl v. Regents of University of California, 383 P.2d 441 (Cal. 1963); that decision, however, serves instead to illuminate by contrast the nonoppressive character of the contract in the present case. In *Tunkl*, defendant hospital presented to all incoming patients a document entitled "Conditions of Admission," which provided that the patient release the hospital from liability for negligent or wrongful acts. We observed that the "would-be patient is in no position to reject the proffered agreement, to bargain with the hospital, or in lieu of agreement to

---

[11] Amicus suggests that we should fashion a new rule to the effect that no arbitration provision in a group insurance policy will bind the beneficiary absent proof of the beneficiary's actual knowledge of that provision. In the present case, Kaiser provided plaintiff with a brochure describing the Kaiser plan, including the arbitration provision. Apart from plaintiff's own testimony, neither the board nor Kaiser have any way of proving whether or not plaintiff read all or part of that brochure. The orderly administration of the plan would be impossible if it were to depend on such proof. Amicus acknowledges as much; it does not maintain that no provision of the Kaiser plan can be enforced against a beneficiary who enrolls without actual knowledge of that provision; it would, instead provide only that arbitration provisions cannot be enforced without actual knowledge. But Amicus' proposal for a special rule which discriminates against enforcement of arbitration clauses would be viable only if arbitration were an extraordinary procedure, and one especially disadvantageous for the beneficiary — propositions which we have rejected in . . . cases cited in this opinion.

find another hospital." Thus, the patient had no realistic choice but to assent to a standardized agreement under which he waived his right to recover for negligently inflicted injuries.

As we have explained, plaintiff, in contrast to *Tunkl*, benefitted from the board's assertion of equal power on her behalf, enjoyed the opportunity to choose from among alternative medical plans, and waived no substantive right. We conclude that *Tunkl* is not controlling in the instant setting; the principles of adhesion contracts, as elucidated and applied in *Tunkl* and the other cases we have cited, do not bar enforcement of terms of a negotiated contract which neither limit the liability of the stronger party nor bear oppressively upon the weaker. Accordingly, such principles do not bar enforcement of the arbitration amendment against plaintiff Madden.

4. *Enforcement of the arbitration provision does not violate constitutional or statutory protections of the right to trial by jury.* . . .

Plaintiff further contends that the arbitration provision in the Kaiser contract fails because it does not expressly waive the parties' constitutional right to jury trail. But to predicate the legality of a consensual arbitration agreement upon the parties' express waiver of jury trial would be as artificial as it would be disastrous.

When parties agree to submit their disputes to arbitration they select a forum that is alternative to, and independent of, the judicial — a forum in which, as they well know, disputes are not resolved by juries. Hence there are literally thousands of commercial and labor contracts that provide for arbitration but do not contain express waivers of jury trial. Courts have regularly enforced such agreements; in [one case], for example, we unanimously affirmed an order compelling an employer to submit a contract dispute to arbitration, although the arbitration provision did not expressly waive the employer's right to trial by jury. Relying on this consistent pattern of judicial decision, contracting parties, such as Kaiser and the board in the case at bar, continue to draft arbitration provisions without express mention of any right to jury trial. Before today no one has so much as imagined that such agreements are consequently invalid; to destroy their viability upon an extreme hypothesis that they fail expressly to negative jury trials would be to frustrate the parties' interests and destroy the sanctity of their mutual promises. . . .

We conclude that the trial court erred in denying Kaiser's motion to compel arbitration and in refusing to stay the action against Kaiser. . . .

Mosk, Justice (dissenting).

I dissent. . . .

It must be emphasized that the plaintiff enrolled in the Kaiser plan in 1965, at a time when the master contract between Kaiser and the Board of Administrators of the State Employees Retirement System contained no arbitration clause and apparently none was contemplated. . . . Six years after plaintiff's original enrollment in the plan, without her knowledge or consent, the board purporting to act on her behalf agreed with Kaiser to amend the master contract to provide that plaintiff's claims must be submitted to arbitration. . . . Had the original master contract executed by the board and Kaiser provided for arbitration, plaintiff might have been bound thereby when she signed a written enrollment in the program. But six years after enrollment by plaintiff an amendment providing for abdication of fundamental rights can be effective only if plaintiff consents thereto in writing. This is manifest when the two rights purportedly abandoned by the board on behalf of plaintiff are as fundamental as recourse to the courts of the state and trial by jury. . . .

Notes: Alternative Dispute Resolution; Contractually Set Standards of Care

1. *Pros and Cons of Arbitration.* Professor Thomas Metzloff explains:

> Arbitration in and of itself does not radically change how a dispute is litigated apart from the identity of the decisionmaker. Discovery may be somewhat limited and the hearing itself is hopefully shorter. But beyond such tinkering, the use of an arbitration format does not usually alter many of the procedural elements that malpractice defenders find objectionable. . . . Significantly, arbitration does not change the basic tort theory of liability. Thomas B. Metzloff, The Unrealized Potential of Malpractice Arbitration, 31 Wake Forest L. Rev. 203, 215 (1996).

Where arbitration differs is in the formality of the proceedings and the length of the hearing. Based on the experience at Kaiser, when cases are arbitrated they are resolved in about half the time and the hearings often last only one or two days. However, arbitration can also be more expensive because the parties have to split the costs of the arbitrators, in contrast with the judicial system which is essentially free. Arbitration also tends to produce different results than litigation. Plaintiffs win about 50 percent more often than in jury trials; however, very large recoveries are rare. Conventional wisdom is that arbitration more often produces "compromise verdicts," although Metzloff's experience is to the contrary.

Professor Metzloff explains that, "in the simplistic nature of the tort reform debates, patient advocates are against [arbitration] because doctors are for it; arbitration has become a prisoner of war." Accordingly, arbitration of medical malpractice disputes is rare, except in the HMO context. Even then, it is still the exception. To understand why, consider whether, on balance, arbitration really is pro-plaintiff or pro-defendant. Does it depend on the facts of the case? Consider small claims versus very large ones; cases where liability is hotly disputed; the parties' feelings about justice and vindication; and the interests of the lawyers on each side. If litigation truly were made speedier, less costly, and more predictable, would you expect an increase or decrease in the number of claims submitted? See generally Kathy L. Cerminara, Contextualizing ADR in Managed Care: A Proposal Aimed at Easing Tensions and Resolving Conflict, 33 Loyola U. Chi. L.J. 547 (2002); Rebecca Cerny, Arbitration or Litigation: Efficacy and Fairness in Resolving Medical Malpractice Disputes, 27 J. Health & Hosp. L. 193 (1994); Bryan Liang, Understanding and Applying Alternative Dispute Resolution Methods in Modern Medical Conflicts, 19 J. Leg. Med. 397 (1998); Symposium: Medical Malpractice Dispute Resolution, 28 Cap. U. L. Rev. 249 (2000); Symposium, 60 L. Contemp. Probs. (Winter 1997); Annot., 24 A.L. R.5th 1 (1994).

2. *Mediation.* In contrast with the *Madden* setting, agreements to arbitrate made after a claim arises are not controversial; this is a standard form of alternative dispute resolution. Also of growing significance are voluntary agreements to mediate malpractice disputes. In mediation, the parties go through a structured process designed to sharpen their understanding of the other side's perspective and to search for common ground. The process is entirely nonbinding, but some courts are beginning to mandate that parties pursue mediation before litigating. Catherine S. Meschievitz, Mediation and Medical Malpractice: Problems with Definition and Implementation, Law & Contemp. Probs., Winter 1991, at 195; Thomas B. Metzloff, Alternative Dispute Resolution Strategies in Medical Malpractice, 9 Alaska L. Rev. 429 (1992). In contrast with voluntary binding arbitration and voluntary nonbinding mediation are mandatory nonbinding screening panels. As discussed in section G, many states require malpractice parties to submit their disputes to panels composed of doctors and lawyers that render advisory opinions on the merits, with the hope of encouraging settlement or early dismissal. This has proven to be a failure. Can you see why?

3. *Varying the* Madden *Facts.* Is it crucial to the holding in *Madden* that the plaintiff had several insurance options available, not all of which required arbitration? What about an employee who is offered only a single HMO insurance policy at work? Many state statutes encouraging malpractice arbitration allow these agreements to be revoked retroactively within one to three months of signing. Does this provide the element of choice required to avoid adhesion contract characterization? What if revocation is allowed only prospectively, i.e., for disputes that have not yet arisen or treatment not yet rendered?

4. *Other Rulings.* For a decision that disagrees with *Madden,* see Canon v. Lane, 867 P.2d 1235 (Okla. 1993) (contrary to public policy for employer to bind HMO subscribers to agreement to arbitrate all future disputes). More controversial than the *Madden* setting are agreements to arbitrate signed at the point of treatment, that is, upon admission to the hospital or when arriving at the doctor's office. Typically, the patient is given no obvious choice (although in fact the provider may provide treatment anyway if the patient refuses to sign). In different versions of this context, courts have been more inclined to follow *Tunkl* and find unconscionability. See, e.g., Broemmer v. Abortion Services of Phoenix, 840 P.2d 1013 (Ariz. 1993) (arbitration agreement signed at abortion clinic invalid as an adhesion contract, even though stated in bold letters at the top of the form, because it did not specifically mention waiver of the right to a jury trial, and "plaintiff was under a great deal of stress" and "was not experienced in commercial matters"); Sosa v. Paulos, 924 P.2d 357 (Utah 1996) (unconscionable where given to patient when she was already in surgical gown, even though she had right to revoke within 14 days). But see Pietrelli v. Peacock, 16 Cal. Rptr. 2d 688 (Cal. Ct. App. 1993) (mother's agreement to arbitrate disputes with physician binds child even though child was not yet born at time of contract); Buraczynski v. Eyring, 919 S.W.2d 314 (Tenn. 1996) (agreement to arbitrate signed prior to treatment is not unconscionable where patient is given a choice and has thirty days to revoke); Vicksburg Partners v. Stephens, 911 So.2d 507 (Miss. 2005) (arbitration agreement with nursing home is not unconscionable despite being an adhesion term in the standard agreement).

In one decision, the court struck down an arbitration agreement as applied, ruling that Kaiser fraudulently ran its arbitration process to strategically gain an unfair advantage on the panel and to create needless delay so that the plaintiff would die before the decision, resulting in lower damages. Engalla v. The Permanente Medical Group, 938 P.2d 903 (Cal. 1997). See also Sosa v. Paulos, supra (agreement unconscionable where losing claimant is required to pay all the arbitration costs, but requiring all the arbitrators to be physicians is not per se unconscionable).

5. *Altering Tort Law by Contract.* The *Tunkl* decision discussed in *Madden* is excerpted at page 123. It states the general law that providers cannot enforce waivers of malpractice liability. In contrast with total waivers, however, are agreements to alter the prevailing legal standards. If parties can agree to arbitrate, can they also agree to change the substantive rules that determine liability during arbitration, assuming that other elements of unconscionability are avoided (adequate notice and some element of choice)? Clark Havighurst is the leading advocate of contractually determined standards of care. He proposes the following language to be included in HMO-type health insurance contracts:

> Because the costs of unlimited legal rights (and their enforcement) must ultimately be borne by you and other plan subscribers, you agree that, in any legal action brought by you against a Plan Provider for injury suffered in the course of your treatment, you will be entitled to recover damages only if such injury was caused by gross negligence on the part of the Provider. Gross negligence is distinguishable from ordinary negligence and is characterized by willful neglect of your personal well-being or reckless disregard for the consequences of some act or omission. Health Care Choices: Private Contracts as Instruments of Health Reform 296 (1995). See also Richard A. Epstein, Medical Malpractice: The Case for Contract, 1 Am. Bar Found. Res. J. 87 (1976); Symposium, Law & Contemp. Probs., Spring 1986.

Professor Maxwell Mehlman is the leading opponent of these agreements, arguing that principles of fiduciary contracting prohibit them. M. Mehlman, Fiduciary Contracting: Limitations on Bargaining Between Patients and Health Care Providers, 51 U. Pitt. L. Rev. 365 (1990). See also Chapter 2.B.2; Jennifer Arlen, Private Contractual Alternatives to Malpractice Liability, in Medical Malpractice and the U.S. Health Care System (W. Sage & R. Kersh, eds., 2006).

Would the assumption of risk doctrine applied in Schneider v. Revici, page 421, validate these types of agreement? What else might be determined by contract? Consider: the statute of limitations; the allowable elements of recoverable damages; who is entitled to testify as an expert; and anything else from the long list of legal reforms discussed in section G. Even if these are not contrary to public policy, is it plausible to assume that ordinary consumers will focus their attention on this many discrete elements of their insurance policies or hospital admission forms? Even if these are noticed by consumers, can it be said they have meaningful choice if they lack the opportunity to bargain over each component of the package? In theory, the private market could offer a differentially priced checklist of legal options, but in practice this is never done. Why not? See generally Mark A. Hall, Making Medical Spending Decisions ch. 7 (1997).

6. *Consumer-Directed Health Care.* As discussed at page 67, health insurers and employers are turning more to types of coverage that place more responsibility on patients to pay for treatment themselves out of pocket. If a patient refuses treatment his physician recommends due to expense, what defenses might protect the physician if he or she continues to treat the patient with less effective care (assuming that the less expensive treatment does not work or causes harm)? For preliminary discussions, see Haavi Morreim, High-Deductible Health Plans: New Twists on Old Challenges from Tort and Contract, 59 Vand. L. Rev. 1207 (2006); Mark A. Hall, Paying for What You Get, and Getting What You Pay For, 69 Law & Contemp. Prob. 159 (Autumn 2006).

5. *Informed Consent Law*

Informed consent law is covered in Chapter 3. This body of law is usually not thought of as a defense to malpractice liability; rather, it is an alternative theory of liability. Nevertheless, we mention informed consent law here because its principles have important similarities to various defenses, and because the complex relationship between informed consent liability and ordinary malpractice liability cannot be fully understood until this point. See generally Jerry Menikoff, Demanded Medical Care, 30 Ariz. St. L.J. 1091 (1998).

Earlier, we saw that a number of alternative theories of physician liability potentially avoid the need for expert testimony about the standard of care. Informed consent liability is another such alternative theory, and it is the one that is most frequently tried. Typically, plaintiffs' lawyers allege breach of informed consent along with breach of the standard of care. Liability rarely is found to rest exclusively on this allegation, however, separate from ordinary malpractice. This is because informed consent liability is distinct from negligence liability only within a limited range of circumstances. This can be illustrated by distributing physicians' competency in responding to any given condition across a range of treatment options, as follows:

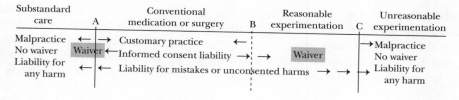

Ordinary malpractice liability exists for harms that result from doing less than or more than what most reasonable physicians would do (to the left of A and the right of C), or for making a mistake while giving conventional treatment (between A and C). Ordinary malpractice liability does not exist for unavoidable side effects that result from conventional treatment done competently. Informed consent liability, in contrast, might apply across this full range of treatment options. Where it overlaps with ordinary malpractice, however, it is mostly redundant. Deviations from customary practice are negligent, regardless of the presence or absence of consent. We have just seen that the prevailing standard of care generally speaking cannot be waived.

For the most part, then, informed consent law has unique effect only where treatment decisions comply with customary practice. The main exceptions to this generalization are for treatments at the two borders between customary and nonstandard care. At the right-hand border, B, which leads into experimental treatment, physicians who are purposefully more aggressive than is customary can avoid malpractice liability if they obtain informed consent for experiments that are considered reasonable innovations. At point C, however, experiments become too radical to permit consent.

Informed consent law also operates at the left-hand border with customary care, to help resolve ambiguous cases in what in fact is a large gray zone rather than a bright line. For instance, where there are competing schools of thought or alternative courses of acceptable treatment, informed consent can play a strong defensive role for a physician who follows an unorthodox approach or one subscribed to by only a minority of physicians. An example is found above in Schneider v. Revici. Finally, informed consent can be used defensively by physicians to disclaim any promise of a guaranteed result, thereby foreclosing possible contract liability as discussed in section C.3.

We return now to the middle zone, where informed consent operates separately from ordinary malpractice. Informed consent liability attaches to unavoidable side effects from competent treatment if the harms were not sufficiently disclosed to the patient. The key question is what standard of disclosure applies? This is discussed at length in Chapter 3, as part of the law that defines the structure of the physician-patient relationship. There, we learn that informed consent law has four different doctrinal foundations: battery law; custom-based negligence; patient-centered negligence; and fiduciary law. Only one of these three—custom-based negligence—determines disclosure obligations according to what other doctors commonly disclose to their patients, thereby requiring expert testimony just like regular medical malpractice. The other theories can be established through patient testimony and common knowledge. But the custom-based version of informed consent liability prevails in many, perhaps most, states. Moreover, in all states informed consent liability is difficult to demonstrate because, in order for causation to be established, it must be shown that the patient would have opted to decline treatment that is generally acceptable. Also, the jury must conclude that the alternative treatment would not have caused a worse outcome due to its own risks of failure or side effects.

E. DAMAGES AND SETTLEMENT

■ FEIN v. PERMANENTE MEDICAL GROUP
695 P.2d 665 (Cal. 1985)

KAUS, Justice.

In this medical malpractice action, both parties appeal from a judgment awarding plaintiff about $1 million in damages. Defendant claims that the trial court committed reversible error . . . in failing to order that the bulk of plaintiff's award be paid periodically rather than in a lump sum. Plaintiff . . . maintains that the trial court, in fixing damages, should not have applied two provisions of the Medical Injury Compensation Reform Act of 1975 (MICRA): Civil Code §3333.2, which limits noneconomic damages in medical malpractice cases to $250,000, and Civil Code §3333.1, which modifies the traditional "collateral source" rule in such litigation. Plaintiff's claims are based on a constitutional challenge similar to the challenges to other provisions of MICRA that we recently addressed and rejected in Roa v. Lodi Medical Group, Inc., 695 P.2d 164 (Cal. 1985) [upholding the following limits on lawyers' contingency fees in medical malpractice cases: 40 percent of the first $50,000, 33 percent of the next $50,000, 25 percent of the next $100,000, and 10 percent of any amounts above $200,000]. We conclude that the judgment should be affirmed in all respects.

I

On Saturday, February 21, 1976, plaintiff Lawrence Fein, a 34-year-old attorney, . . . felt a brief pain in his chest as he was riding his bicycle to work. [The pain returned several times and worsened over the next few days. He saw two doctors and a nurse pracitioner with the defendant, which is affiliated with Kaiser-Permanente, but each time the pain was treated as a muscle spasm. It turned out to be a heart attack.] . . .

Following a period of hospitalization and medical treatment without surgery, plaintiff returned to his job on a part-time basis in October 1976, and resumed full-time work in September 1977. By the time of trial, he had been permitted to return to virtually all of his prior recreational activities—e.g., jogging, swimming, bicycling and skiing.

In February 1977, plaintiff filed the present action, alleging that his heart condition should have been diagnosed earlier and that treatment should have been given either to prevent the heart attack or, at least, to lessen its residual effects. The case went to judgment only against Permanente. . . .

At trial, Dr. Harold Swan, . . . testified to the damage caused by the attack. He stated that as a result of the attack a large portion of plaintiff's heart muscle had died, reducing plaintiff's future life expectancy by about one-half, to about 16 or 17 years. Although Dr. Swan acknowledged that some of plaintiff's other coronary arteries also suffer from disease, he felt that if plaintiff had been properly treated his future life expectancy would be decreased by only 10 to 15 percent, rather than half. . . .

The jury awarded $24,733 for wages lost by plaintiff to the time of trial, $63,000 for future medical expenses, and $700,000 for wages lost in the future as a result of the reduction in plaintiff's life expectancy.[1] Finally, the jury awarded $500,000 for "noneconomic damages," to compensate for pain, suffering, inconvenience, physical impairment and other intangible damages sustained by plaintiff from the time of the injury until his death. . . .

---

[1] Plaintiff did not claim that the heart attack would reduce his earning capacity during his lifetime.

The trial court . . . reduced the noneconomic damages to $250,000, reduced the award for past lost wages to $5,430—deducting $19,303 that plaintiff had already received in disability payments as compensation for such lost wages—and ordered defendant to pay the first $63,000 of any future medical expenses not covered by medical insurance provided by plaintiff's employer, as such expenses were incurred. At the same time, the court declined to order that the award for future lost wages or noneconomic damages be paid periodically pursuant to Code of Civil Procedure §667.7, determining that the statute was not "mandatory" and that "under the unique facts and circumstances of this case" a periodic payment award of such damages would "defeat[ ] rather than promote[ ]" the purpose of §667.7. [The following excerpt focusses on how these various components of damages were calculated. The excerpt at page 508 addresses whether the statutory limits are constitutional.] . . .

V

Defendant . . . argues that the trial court erred in permitting the jury to award damages for the loss of earnings attributable to plaintiff's so-called lost years, i.e., the period of time by which his life expectancy was diminished as a result of defendant's negligence. We believe that this was clearly a proper element of plaintiff's damages. . . . [R]ecovery of such damages is consistent with the general rule permitting an award based on the loss of future earnings a plaintiff is likely to suffer because of inability to work for as long a period of time in the future as he could have done had he not sustained the accident.[10] . . .

Defendant alternatively argues that the jury should have been instructed to deduct from plaintiff's prospective gross earnings of the lost years, the "saved" cost of necessities that plaintiff would not incur during that period. Although there is some authority to support the notion that damages for the lost years should be assessed on the basis of plaintiff's "net" loss, we need not decide that issue in this case because defendant neither requested such an instruction at trial nor presented any evidence of anticipated cost savings that would have supported such an instruction. . . .

After the jury returned its verdict, defendant requested the trial court to enter a judgment—pursuant to §667.7 of the Code of Civil Procedure—providing for the periodic payment of future damages, rather than a lump-sum award. . . . The statute provides that "[i]n any [medical malpractice action], a

---

[10] The comments in the Restatement 2d Torts §924 state:

d. Loss or impairment of earning capacity for the future. The extent of future harm to the earning capacity of the injured person is measured by the difference, viewed as of the time of trial, between the value of the plaintiff's services as they will be in view of the harm and as they would have been had there been no harm. This difference is the resultant derived from reducing to present value the anticipated losses of earnings during the expected working period that the plaintiff would have had during the remainder of his prospective life, but for the defendant's act. Accordingly, the trier of fact must ascertain, as nearly as can be done in advance, the difference between the earnings that the plaintiff would or could have received during his life expectancy but for the harm and the earnings that he will probably be able to receive during the period of his life expectancy as now determined. . . .

superior court shall, at the request of either party, enter a judgment ordering that money damages or its equivalent for future damages of the judgment creditor be paid in whole or in part by periodic payments rather than by a lump-sum payment if the award equals or exceeds fifty thousand dollars ($50,000) in future damages."[11] . . .

Nonetheless, for several reasons relating to the specific facts of this case, we conclude that the trial court judgment should not be reversed on this ground. To begin with, although the court formally rejected defendant's motion for a periodic payment order, its judgment did provide for the periodic payment of the damages which the jury awarded for plaintiff's future medical expenses, directing the defendant to pay such expenses "as [they] are incurred up to the amount of $63,000."

Second, with respect to the award of noneconomic damages, . . . the jury was not instructed to designate the portion of the noneconomic damage award that was attributable to future damages, and it did not do so. Instead, it returned an undifferentiated special verdict awarding noneconomic damages of $500,000. Because of defendant's failure to raise the periodic payment issue earlier, plaintiff was deprived of the opportunity to seek a special verdict designating the amount of "future noneconomic damage." . . .

Third and finally, there is the question of the $700,000 award for lost future earnings. Although in general lost future earnings are a type of future damage particularly suitable to a periodic payment judgment, this case presents a somewhat unusual situation because the damages awarded are solely attributable to the earnings of plaintiff's lost years. If the trial court had ordered such damages paid periodically over the time period when the loss was expected to be incurred, the damages would have been paid in their entirety after plaintiff's expected death, and thus — if the life expectancy predictions were accurate — plaintiff would not have received any of this element of damages. . . .

Thus, in sum, we conclude that none of the defendant's contentions call for a reversal of the judgment.

---

[11] Section 667.7 provides in relevant part:

As a condition to authorizing periodic payments of future damages, the court shall require the judgment debtor who is not adequately insured to post security adequate to assure full payment of such damages awarded by the judgment. . . . Such payments shall only be subject to modification in the event of the death of the judgment creditor. . . . However, money damages awarded for loss of future earnings shall not be reduced or payments terminated by reason of the death of the judgment creditor, but shall be paid to persons to whom the judgment creditor owed a duty of support, as provided by law, immediately prior to his death. . . . By authorizing periodic payment judgments, it is the further intent of the legislature that the courts will utilize such judgments to provide compensation sufficient to meet the needs of an injured plaintiff and those persons who are dependent on the plaintiff for whatever period is necessary while eliminating the potential windfall from a lump-sum recovery which was intended to provide for the care of an injured plaintiff over an extended period who then dies shortly after the judgment is paid, leaving the balance of the judgment award to persons and purposes for which it was not intended. It is also the intent of the legislature that all elements of the periodic payment program be specified with certainty in the judgment ordering such payments and that the judgment not be subject to modification at some future time which might alter the specifications of the original judgment.

VII

We now turn to plaintiff's contentions.

As noted, although the jury by special verdict set plaintiff's noneconomic damages at $500,000, the trial court reduced that amount to $250,000 pursuant to Civil Code §3333.2. Plaintiff challenges this ruling, contending that §3333.2 is unconstitutional on a number of grounds. In many respects, plaintiff's argument tracks the constitutional objections to other provisions of MICRA that we have recently rejected in *Roa*. . . . [This portion of the opinion is excerpted at page 508.]

For similar reasons, plaintiff's constitutional challenge to Civil Code §3333.1—which modifies this state's common law "collateral source" rule—is also without merit. Under the traditional collateral source rule, a jury, in calculating a plaintiff's damages in a tort action, does not take into consideration benefits—such as medical insurance or disability payments—which the plaintiff has received from sources other than the defendant—i.e., "collateral sources"— to cover losses resulting from the injury. Under §3333.1, subdivision (a), a medical malpractice defendant is permitted to introduce evidence of such collateral source benefits received by or payable to the plaintiff; when a defendant chooses to introduce such evidence, the plaintiff may introduce evidence of the amounts he has paid—in insurance premiums, for example—to secure the benefits. Although §3333.1, subdivision (a)—as ultimately adopted—does not specify how the jury should use such evidence, the legislature apparently assumed that in most cases the jury would set plaintiff's damages at a lower level because of its awareness of plaintiff's "net" collateral source benefits. . . .

In addition, §3333.1, subdivision (b) provides that whenever such collateral source evidence is introduced, the source of those benefits is precluded from obtaining subrogation either from the plaintiff or from the medical malpractice defendant. As far as the malpractice plaintiff is concerned, subdivision (b) assures that he will suffer no "double deduction" from his tort recovery as a result of his receipt of collateral source benefits; because the jury that has learned of his benefits may reduce his tort award by virtue of such benefits, the legislature eliminated any right the collateral source may have had to obtain repayment of those benefits from the plaintiff. . . .

[T]he legislature clearly did not act irrationally in choosing to modify the collateral source rule as one means of lowering the costs of malpractice litigation. In analyzing the collateral source rule more than a decade ago, we acknowledged that most legal commentators had severely criticized the rule for affording a plaintiff a "double recovery" for "losses" he had not in reality sustained, and we noted that many jurisdictions had either restricted or repealed it. . . .

The judgment is affirmed.

■ ROBERTS v. STEVENS CLINIC HOSPITAL
345 S.E.2d 791 (W. Va. 1986)

NEELY, Justice.

In this appeal we decide whether we should sustain a McDowell County Circuit Court $10,000,000 jury award [for compensatory damages] in favor of the parents and two siblings of Michael Joseph Roberts, a 2 1/2-year-old child who died as the result of medical malpractice. [A surgeon punctured his bowel trying to correct a problem that was causing severe diarrhea. He died from the resulting infection.] . . .

Kenneth and Joyce Roberts are a young couple who . . . gave birth to Michael Joseph Roberts. . . . Michael was the darling of the whole family. He was both an intelligent and happy little boy who was particularly close to his mother. The jury had before it substantial evidence that since Michael's death Joyce has been overwhelmed by grief and that the Roberts' family is no longer a happy household. . . . Joyce spent many nights crying and writing poems to Michael, and there was evidence that she continues to suffer from chronic diarrhea and vomiting. . . .

At trial the plaintiff introduced into evidence a professionally prepared, twenty minute, videotape that combined "home movie" video recordings of Michael taken by a neighbor with a series of still, colored, photographs of Michael and the family. The audio background for this video presentation consisted of tape recordings of the child's voice as well as Joyce's voice singing and talking to the child. It is the defendant's contention that this film was a "theatrical" presentation that artistically highlighted certain aspects of Michael's life and Joyce's relationship to Michael in an inaccurate way.

We have reviewed the tape in its entirety and we find nothing inflammatory or prejudicial about it. . . . The purpose of the videotape was to demonstrate that Michael was a healthy, intelligent, enthusiastic, and well loved child. So as a preliminary matter, the videotape was relevant. In our review of the tape, we find no artistic highlighting that emphasizes some scenes or photographs more than others, and we find no merit in the defendant's assertion that because the mother's voice went on several seconds after the screen turned black, an unduly sentimental atmosphere was evoked that would have prejudiced the jury.

This court has not previously addressed the admissibility of videotape "Day-in-the-Life" films. . . . We are not unmindful of the potential dangers inherent in such presentations. As one court has explained: Almost always an edited tape necessarily raises issues as to every sequence portrayed of whether the event shown is fairly representative of fact, after the editing process, and whether it is unduly prejudicial because of the manner of presentation. Bolstridge v. Central Maine Power Co., 621 F. Supp. 1202 (D.C. Me. 1985) (plaintiff's "Day-in-the-Life" videotape excluded when open court testimony could demonstrate similar evidence, and admission of videotape would create risk of distracting jury and unfairly prejudicing defendant). . . . But, we shall not reverse a trial court's decision in these matters unless the record shows a clear abuse of discretion. . . .

We now come to the most serious problem in this case, namely the closing argument of plaintiff's counsel. In a nutshell, the reason that we are compelled to reduce the jury's award from $10,000,000 to $3,000,000 is that plaintiff's counsel implied, in his closing argument, that the duty of the jury was to place a value on Michael's life. No objection along those lines, however, was made during the closing argument, and for that reason we are undisposed to reverse the entire trial because, technically, the error was waived.[5] . . .

---

[5] . . . In the roughly seven seconds available to counsel to make the strategic decision whether to object, it probably dawned on counsel that an objection and "curative" instruction would serve only to reinforce plaintiff's counsel's point.

[Plaintiff's counsel] argued that if a $10,000,000 race horse had been killed through the negligence of a veterinary hospital, the measure of damages would be exactly $10,000,000. At another point in the argument counsel asked what would have happened if someone had approached Michael's parents with an envelope containing ten, $1,000,000 winning lottery tickets and asked the parents if they would trade Michael's life for the tickets. Finally, counsel made reference to the American space program where billions of dollars are spent to avoid the loss of a single life. Representative excerpts from counsel's closing argument are as follows:

> ... Now if Michael were a race horse and the Stevens Clinic Hospital operated a veterinarian hospital and a race horse named Michael died as a result of the negligence of a veterinary doctor, you wouldn't have any trouble in returning a verdict for millions of dollars because you know that that's what race horses are worth. You tell me, you tell the family, are horses entitled to better care than children? And are children less valuable than horses? ...

Our wrongful death statute specifically sets forth the losses for which damages can be recovered.[8] Obviously, if the measure of damages were the value of a human life then, arguably, no jury verdict could be excessive. The death of a family member, particularly a child, involves inconsolable grief for which no amount of money can compensate.... We believe that our conclusion in this regard is grounded in sound public policy, which we now proceed to discuss.[9] ...

[B]ecause less than 6 percent of all serious lawsuits are tried, the most important thing that courts do is to cast a shadow of legal rules within which litigants can craft their own custom-made settlements.... Without the occasional jury award that is at least ten times greater than what the parties would have settled for immediately after the tragedy, there would be no incentive on the part of clients to temper the ... anti-settlement proclivities of their lawyers by urging quick payment of just claims. ...

Ideally, in a case such as the one before us where the negligence of the defendants is palpable, some just compensation for Michael's death would have been forthcoming within 30 days. Yet Michael died in July, 1982 and it is now April, 1986 without the Roberts' having received any compensation whatsoever for Michael's loss.

---

[8] W. Va. Code §55-7-6 [1982] provides:

> The verdict of the jury shall include, but may not be limited to, damages for the following: (A) Sorrow, mental anguish, and solace which may include society, companionship, comfort, guidance, kindly offices and advice of the decedent; (B) compensation for reasonably expected loss of (i) income of the decedent, and (ii) services, protection, care and assistance provided by the decedent; (C) expenses for the care, treatment and hospitalization of the decedent incident to the injury resulting in death; and (D) reasonable funeral expenses. ...

[9] While the plaintiffs furnished us with a number of cases where jury verdicts of this magnitude have been approved, the plaintiffs in those cases had suffered severe personal injuries that necessitated enormous future medical care costs and also loss of earning capacity. These elements are absent in this case.

When the defendants moved for leave to file an appeal in this court, the court asked the parties to describe the settlement negotiations that preceded the trial. Such information is generally inadmissible and incompetent to show liability or set the measure of damages. But we believe that settlement discussions have some bearing on the necessarily subjective criteria that appellate courts use to determine a proper remittitur, because such a determination affects future settlement negotiations. . . .

About two months before trial plaintiff's counsel made a written offer to both defendants to settle for $5,000,000, which was approximately half of the total available insurance coverage of $10,250,000. No response was received from the defendants until the Friday afternoon before the Monday morning trial date! At that time defendant Magnus offered $100,000 and the offer was rejected. The next day the offer was increased to $125,000, and after one week of trial, when most of the plaintiff's evidence was in, and both defendants had reason to expect a substantial verdict, defendant Magnus increased the offer to $220,000.

In light of the statistically demonstrable fact that settlement rather than litigation is the true cynosure of the whole judicial process, in this case, then, we not only ask ourselves how much money the Roberts family should receive to compensate them for the losses enumerated under the Wrongful Death Statute; we also ask ourselves what jury award in a case of this type will establish the proper climate for out-of-court settlements. . . . Accordingly, . . . the case is remanded to the circuit court with directions to enter a remittitur of $7,000,000 and enter judgment on the verdict for $3,000,000 or, in the alternative, at the option of the plaintiff, to award a new trial.

Reversed and remanded with directions.

McHUGH, Justice and McGRAW, Justice dissented, [arguing that there was no basis for remittitur. Brief excerpts from their opinions follow]:

The $10,000,000 verdict in this case would be divided among four individuals. . . . [A]ccording to Jury Verdict Research, Inc., the average verdict in the year 1985 in medical malpractice cases in this country exceed[ed] $1,000,000. . . .

It must also be remembered that the verdict here was for permanent damages. Damages in a wrongful death case for nonpecuniary losses, such as mental anguish (unlike damages for pecuniary losses), should not be reduced to present value. The jury is not to determine its award for solatium in a wrongful death case by determining a lump sum amount which, when invested, will result in an annual amount which is at once fair and just. Whether an award for solatium is excessive is not properly determined by calculating its annual yield. . . .

[The defendants' insurance policy had an upper limit of $10,250,000.] The insurance companies coldly asserted that this case was simply not "worth" $10,000,000 and maintained that reduction to a more "reasonable" figure was appropriate. So, with incredible candor, the majority admits that its members put their heads together and came up with a figure of $3,000,000. In other words, the majority anticipates that the defendants could combine to commit acts of malpractice resulting in over three times the amount of harm to a single individual than the amount of harm to Michael Roberts and his family. I readily concede my inability to imagine a set of circumstances over three times more tragic than the circumstances presented in this case.

Notes: Damages; Wrongful Life Cases

1. *Hedonic Damages.* Damages for loss of enjoyment of life are sometimes referred to as "hedonic damages." See generally R. Palfin & B. Danninger, Hedonic Damages: Proving Damages for Lost Enjoyment of Living (1990); Eric A. Posner & Cass R. Sunstein, Dollars and Death, 72 U. Chi. L. Rev. 537 (2005). One must distinguish carefully among versions of hedonic damages in order to make an accurate statement of the law. The situation in which they are the most readily recoverable is as an element of pain and suffering, where an injury has left the plaintiff alive and aware but disabled. The situation in which they are least recoverable is where the plaintiff is killed or left comatose. The inability to experience the loss of life's pleasures usually means that they cannot be claimed as a form of pain and suffering. But a few courts disagree. For a thorough review of the law with majority and dissenting views, see generally McDougald v. Garber, 536 N.E.2d 372 (N.Y. 1989). See also Annot., 34 A.L.R.4th 293 (1984). *Fein* presents a third situation, where a plaintiff is fully abled in the present, but is likely to die early. Here, it is possible to receive some form of compensation for lost enjoyment of life by characterizing the damages as distress and anguish in the present over realizing that one's life is shortened. The traditional view, however, is that no recovery is allowed for the value of life itself, under the view that it is impossible or unseemly to place a value on life.

Measurable *economic* damages, however, do pertain to a shortened life. Review *Fein* to clarify the difference between economic damages during life and as a result of a shortened life. Which set of economic damages raises the possibility of a "necessities-of-living" offset? Which set relies on diminished earning capacity?

Other exceptions to the general rule that loss of life is not compensated arise by virtue of wrongful death statutes. Review the version of this statute in the *Roberts* case and the components of damages that were recognized and rejected there. You will observe that these statutes do not directly overturn the general rule. How, then, do they justify noneconomic damages in cases of instantaneous death?

2. *Wrongful Life and Wrongful Birth.* "Wrongful life" and "wrongful birth" cases are where these concepts are put to their greatest test in medical malpractice litigation. In contrast to wrongful death actions that ask what is the value of a *lost* life, wrongful life and birth actions ask what are the damages for a life *brought into being* that *should not* have been. There are two typical scenarios. First, if a doctor fails to identify or avoid a birth defect, a claim can result for the expenses and anguish of living life with a severe handicap. Second, if a sterilization procedure fails, an action can result for the expenses of raising a normal, healthy child, as well as for any harms attendant to pregnancy and childbirth.[1] The first scenario presents the greatest conceptual difficulties.

The first difficulty is causation. Usually, the only way to avoid a birth defect once it is detected is by aborting. Of course, there is always the question whether the parents would have made this decision, but there is the more fundamental

---

[1] A third scenario, which entails wrongfully maintaining an existing life by refusing to disconnect life support, is presented in Anderson v. St. Francis-St. George Hospital, 671 N.E.2d 225 (Ohio 1996).

realization that the only way *this* child could have avoided the severe defect is to not be born at all. Therefore, one must measure damages by comparing the two states of severe disability with nonexistence.

At first, these causation and damages difficulties were insurmountable for the courts. Shortly after abortions became commonplace, however, courts began to allow limited forms of these actions. See William J. Curran, Genetic Counseling and Wrongful Life, 68 Am. J. Pub. Health 501 (1978). They distinguished between "wrongful life" actions, which are the child's own claims for the suffering and expenses of being alive, and "wrongful birth" actions, which are the parents' claims for having to raise a handicapped child. Most courts allow only the latter — the parents' claim — and even then limit the damages to mostly economic ones, such as the "extraordinary" costs of intensive care and treatment. (Query why not the "ordinary" costs as well?) Emotional distress damages are not recoverable in a number of states because it is thought that the emotional benefits of having a child at all outweigh the emotional harms of the severe handicap. Again, it is usually not factually possible to make a claim for failure to have a healthy child. Nevertheless, a number of other states allow juries to weigh the competing benefits and burdens of having the child at all and award damages for a net emotional loss.

A very few states also allow the handicapped child to maintain his own action, but the damages are similarly constrained to the economic costs of managing life as a disabled adult. The leading case is Turpin v. Sortini, 643 P.2d 954 (Cal. 1982). This is no different, however, from allowing the parents to recover the costs of care for the child's *entire* lifetime rather than for only the years of dependency. A very few courts have rejected both causes of action entirely. See, e.g., Atlanta Obstetrics & Gynecology Group v. Abelson, 398 S.E.2d 557 (Ga. 1990). Also, several state legislatures, motivated by antiabortion sentiments, have restricted or abolished these causes of action. Note, Wrongful Birth Actions: The Case Against Legislative Curtailment, 100 Harv. L. Rev. 2017 (1987) (arguing these statutes are unconstitutional).

In "wrongful conception" cases (i.e., those involving failed sterilizations), courts usually allow only the medical expenses of birth but not the economic costs of raising a normal, healthy child. Although child-rearing costs clearly result from the failed sterilization, as a matter of social policy most courts are not willing to allow a jury to find that children, on balance, are a burden. Other courts, however, allow recovery of both the economic and the emotional costs of having an unexpected child, subject to the jury's views on the value of offsetting benefits. One court went so far as to allow recovery of child-rearing costs with no offset, under the view that emotional benefits are usually offset only against emotional, not economic, burdens. Marchiniak v. Lundborg, 450 N.W.2d 243 (Wis. 1990).

There are a host of cases, and almost as many law review articles, on this topic. For a sampling of the latter, see, e.g., Alexander M. Capron, Tort Liability in Genetic Counseling, 79 Colum. L. Rev. 618 (1979); Michael B. Laudor, In Defense of Wrongful Life: Bringing Political Theory to the Defense of a Tort, 62 Fordham L. Rev. 1675 (1994); Philip G. Peters, Rethinking Wrongful Life: Bridging the Boundary Between Tort and Family Law, 67 Tul. L. Rev. 397 (1992); Mark Strasser, Misconceptions and Wrongful Births: A Call for a Principled Jurisprudence, 31 Ariz. St. L.J. 161 (1999); Deanna A. Pollard, Wrongful Analysis in Wrongful Life Jurisprudence, 55 Ala. L. Rev. 327 (2004); Wendy F. Hensel, The Disabling Impact of Wrongful Life and Wrongful Birth Actions, 40 Harv. C.R.-C.L. L. Rev. 141 (2005). For a feminist critique, arguing that courts have judged these issues by male norms, see Shelley A. Ryan, Wrongful Birth: False Representations of Women's Reproductive Lives, 78 Minn. L. Rev. 857 (1994). See generally Annot., 74 A.L.R.4th 798 (1989).

The potential for wrongful life litigation is greatly increasing with the explosion in genetic tests, not only for congenital defects but also for "normal" diseases later in life such as cancer. Far-reaching genetic mapping projects currently under way are likely to increase exponentially our current ability to detect predisposition to genetic conditions.

3. *The Size of Awards.* Most years, medical malpractice cases regularly produce some of the highest verdicts in the country, in the range of $20 million to $50 million or more. Usually, these involve severely damaged newborns. But, focusing on these extreme cases gives a false impression of what typical damages awards are in medical malpractice cases. Even a more systematic reading of reported decisions can give a false impression since only the rare claim reaches appellate review and review is more likely when the actual or potential damages award is high. Substantial empirical research sheds considerable light on the experience in more typical malpractice claims.

When claims are filed, about 40 percent result in payment, most by settlement. Fewer than 10 percent of malpractice claims are tried, and only about 20 to 30 percent of these produce plaintiff verdicts. Most jury verdicts are well below $1 million. A study of verdicts from large cities in 2001 found that the median award was $77,000 for temporary injuries, $412,000 for permanent injuries, and $837,000 for death; no plaintiff with a temporary injury received a jury verdict exceeding $1 million. David A. Hyman & Charles Silver, Medical Malpractice Litigation and Tort Reform: It's the Incentives Stupid, 59 Vand. L. Rev. 1085, 1105 (2006).

Considering both jury verdicts and claims settled outside of litigation, the median payout in Florida in 2003 was $150,000 (mean of $300,000), with the median for temporary injuries ranging from $17,000 to $59,000, depending on the extent of injury. Only 6 percent of paid claims were for $1 million or more. Neil Vidmar et al., Uncovering the "Invisible" Profile of Medical Malpractice Litigation, 54 DePaul L. Rev. 315 (2005). Nationally, paid claims in 2003 averaged $263,000, with the highest 10 percent averaging $1.2 million. Amitabh Chandra et al., The Growth of Physician Medical Malpractice Payments, *W5 Health Aff. 240 (2005).* Although settlement amounts have increased substantially over time, the increase in recent years has been roughly proportionate to increases in the population and in the costs of medical care. Id.; Bernard Black et al., Stability, Not Crisis: Medical Malpractice Claim Outcomes in Texas, 2 J. Empirical Legal Stud. 207 (2005). Settlements rarely are for amounts greater than the limits of physicians' liability insurance, so physicians almost never have to use personal assets to pay claims. Kathryn Zeiler et al., Physicians' Insurance Limits and Malpractice Payments, 36 J. Leg. Stud. In press (2007).

Considering that fewer than half of malpractice claims receive any payment, and that these are expensive cases to litigate, injured patients have difficulty finding a lawyer willing to take their case when their potential damages are less than $50,000. See Hyman & Silver, supra, 59 Vand. L. Rev. at 1118.

For additional data see David M. Studdert et al., Claims, Errors and Compensation Payments in Medical Malpractice Litigation, 354 New Eng. J. Med. 2024 (2006); U.S Dept. of Justice, Medical Malpractice Insurance Claims in Seven States (2007).

4. *Settlements.* Additional research indicates that, when cases go to trial, the variation in jury awards *in the aggregate* is broadly consistent with the severity of injury, although for a given category of injury, *individual* jury awards are highly erratic, varying by a factor of ten or more. Randall R. Bovbjerg et al., Valuing Life and Limb in Tort: Scheduling "Pain and Suffering," 83 Nw. U. L. Rev. 908 (1989). See Symposium, 54 L. & Contemp. Probs. 1 (Winter 1991). This unpredictability makes it difficult to settle cases, even where liability is relatively clear. Also, doctors are often reluctant to settle because of the negative publicity and their desire for personal vindication. Accordingly, medical malpractice cases are twice as likely to go to trial as are other personal injury suits. Michael Saks, Do We Really Know Anything About the Behavior of the Tort Litigation System — And Why Not?, 140 U. Pa. L. Rev. 1147, 1128 (1992).

Nevertheless, most malpractice awards are obtained through settlement. Settlement amounts are influenced by the reputation and experience of the particular lawyers and expert witnesses representing plaintiffs, with lawyers receiving significantly more if their track record in front of juries shows they are able to land sizeable verdicts. See Catherine T. Harris et al., Placing "Standard of Care" in Context: The Impact of Witness Potential and Attorney Reputation in Medical Malpractice Litigation, 3 J. Empirical Leg. Stud. 467 (2006). Also, settlement amounts tend to correlate with the strength of a case, although the degree of injury has more influence than with the degree of fault. Philip Peters, What We Know About Malpractice Settlements, 92 Iowa L. Rev. 1783 (2007). On the other hand, settlement tends to suppress the average amount of the award. In a study from Florida, only about a fifth of paid claimants recovered more than their economic loss, and most recovered less, on account of the discounting that occurs in settlement negotiations. The average pretrial settlement paid about half of economic losses. Even those who won at trial recovered on average only 22 percent more than economic losses. Frank Sloan et al., Suing for Medical Malpractice (1993). Again, this is due in part to settlement. Plaintiffs often settle even after receiving favorable jury verdicts, since a posttrial settlement avoids the cost and delay of an appeal. The vast majority of $1 million-plus verdicts are settled for somewhat less. Neil Vidmar et al., Million Dollar Medical Malpractice Cases in Florida: Post-Verdict and Pre-Suit Settlements, 59 Vand. L. Rev. 1343 (2006); David Hyman, et al., Do Defendants Pay What Juries Award?, 4 J. Empirical Leg. Stud. 3 (2007). An insurer is likely to insist on appealing only if it is confident in the merits or if it sees the case as a good opportunity to set a favorable precedent for future cases. Review the facts in McCourt v. Abernathy at page 300. As defense counsel, what would you have settled the case for after trial?

5. *Dropping a Claim.* As just noted, over half of malpractice claims filed are closed (resolved) without payment, some by court dismissal, but many because the insurer refuses to pay and the plaintiff simply drops the claim. How can a lawyer

ethically drop a case, though, once she learns it is not possible to settle? Generally, there are two options: (1) have an agreement (preferably written) with the client that the case is being taken on for purposes of settlement only; (2) seek the judge's permission to withdraw. The latter is necessary only if suit has been filed. Many judges will be reluctant to grant this permission if diligent investigation before suit would have disclosed the case's weaknesses.

6. *Scheduled Damages.* One notable proposal to make jury awards more predictable is to create a schedule of pain and suffering damages according to a matrix of the following factors: whether the injury is temporary or permanent; life expectancy; and whether the injury is minor, significant, major, or grave. These scheduled damages could then either be mandated, given to the jury as advisory guidelines, or used by the judge to police excessively large or small verdicts. Moreover, the scheduled amounts could be based on a collection of actual prior jury verdicts rather than on legislative or administrative assessments. See Bovbjerg et al., supra.

7. *The Collateral Source Rule.* It may seem difficult on the surface to justify the traditional collateral source rule that allows plaintiffs double recovery of their medical bills or lost income, but in theory this is sensible because most third-party health and disability insurers have a contractual right of subrogation that allows them to be reimbursed for their payments from the tort award. In practice, however, such subrogation claims are rare, owing to the difficulty in allocating lump sum tort awards or settlements among various damages components. Moreover, many states have statutes that limit or preclude the ability of insurers to enforce these contractual provisions.

A more practical justification for not offsetting collateral source recoveries is the need to provide plaintiffs a source for paying their attorneys' fees. This is also a practical justification for unlimited pain and suffering awards. This perhaps best explains why physicians push so strongly for malpractice reform statutes that limit these elements of damage, since they go a long way toward removing lawyers' economic motivation for taking the case in the first place. Note that the *Roa* case decided the same day as *Fein* upheld California's statutory limits on the size of contingency fees.

Recall from page 283 the research that indicates many injured patients sue because they are worried primarily about the costs of medical treatment or in response to hospitals' or doctors' attempts to collect on their overdue bills. How does this information bear on this debate? Would you advise hospitals and doctors to voluntarily pick up the costs of extended treatment for injured patients without admitting liability?

Exercise: "A Day in the Life"

Interview someone you know who suffers from a physical or mental infirmity, or someone who lives with such a person. Write a script for a demonstrative exhibit (video, charts, still photographs, etc.) that details a day or week in the life of this individual. Explain your strategic decisions regarding what to highlight or dramatize and what to leave out or avoid, in order to maximize the exhibit's emotional impact without having it excluded altogether.

Exercise: Damages Settlement

Conduct a settlement negotiation with one of your classmates in the following hypothetical:[1]

> Joe Jenks is paralyzed from the waist down as a result of negligently performed surgery on his back. At the time of the surgery he was 30 years of age and employed as a forklift operator for Wheeling Manufacturing Co. He graduated from high school at age 18, spent two years in the army (receiving an honorable discharge), and immediately after discharge went to work for Wheeling. Before the surgery he was in good health, except for chronic back pain that plagued him for six months after he fell while playing basketball. He earned $30,000 as a forklift operator in the year before the accident. In addition, that same year he earned $20,000 moonlighting as a security guard on evenings and weekends. He has never been married and lives alone. He was a below-average student in high school, graduating at the bottom of his class. He was, however, a well-liked and ambitious young man who had a strong aptitude for mechanics. His paralysis is permanent.

Take the lawyer's position on one side or the other in a suit against the orthopedic surgeon. Make up and stick to the client facts you need that aren't given. Assume that investigating and trying the case will cost the plaintiff's lawyer $50,000 in out-of-pocket expenses and will cost the doctor's insurer $150,000 in legal fees and expenses. Assume further that your jurisdiction has no damages cap, but does have a collateral source offset statute and a periodic payout statute. Engage in negotiations attempting to reach a definite settlement. If successful, then reveal to the other side the actual "bottom line" or "top dollar" you would have been willing to agree to. If you haven't reached a settlement after half an hour, then determine how far apart you are by stating your final best offers.

■ BLEDAY v. OUM GROUP
645 A.2d 1358 (Pa. Super. Ct. 1994)

HUDOCK, Judge.

. . . Appellants secured malpractice insurance through Insurers for the period of February, 1988, through February, 1989. The policy obtained by Appellants contained the following [provision]:

> The company shall have the right and duty to defend any suit against the insured seeking damages because of such injury even if any of the allegations of the suit are groundless, false or fraudulent. The company may make such investigation and settlement of any claim or suit as it deems expedient.

Within the time period covered by said policy, Tracey Worchesky (Worchesky) instituted an action against Appellants. The nature of her claim was that she had to seek corrective surgery from another podiatrist because she

---

[1] This is taken from Frank M. McClellan, Medical Malpractice: Law, Tactics, and Ethics (1994).

never properly recovered from surgery performed by Dr. Bleday. . . . [O]ver the objection of Appellants, Insurers settled Worchesky's claim for $10,000.[1] Insurers stated that the settlement was a result of a business decision which was made to "avoid the cost of litigation and the uncertainties of a jury trial."

. . . Appellants filed a complaint against Insurers and Adjusters . . . alleg[ing] that Insurers breached their duty of good faith to Appellants by settling Worchesky's claim without their consent. . . . With respect to damages, Appellants assert that they will be subjected to increased insurance premiums, loss of earnings, and harm to reputation since Dr. Bleday's name will be placed on the National Physician Data Bank, a list of doctors who have been involved in malpractice actions. . . . The trial court granted the [defendants' motion to dismiss]. . . . Appellants assert that Insurers, despite the policy language "deems expedient," have the duty to act in good faith in the handling of its claims. . . .

After a thorough review of case law from other jurisdictions, we conclude that, although judicial deference must be given to the decision of an insurance company to settle a claim within the policy limits, a claim for bad faith may, in limited circumstances, be asserted against the insurance company notwithstanding a "deems expedient" provision. A "deems expedient" provision in an insurance contract cannot be interpreted to convey to an insurance company an absolute right to settle a claim within the policy limits if such settlement was contrary to the intent and expectation of the parties. However, after a thorough review of the complaint filed by Appellants, we find that Appellants did not sufficiently plead a cause of action in bad faith against Insurers, and, thus, the trial court properly granted Insurers' preliminary objections.

Several jurisdictions hold that a "deems expedient" provision in an insurance contract conveys to an insurer an absolute right to settle the claims of the insured within the insurance policy limits. . . . In Feliberty v. Damon, 527 N.E.2d 261 (N.Y. 1988), a medical malpractice panel found that the appellant committed malpractice and was liable in the amount of $743,000. Before judgment was entered and without his consent, the appellant's insurer settled the claim for $700,000, an amount within the policy limits. The appellant sought compensatory and punitive damages from the insurer, asserting that his reputation was damaged as a result of the settlement. The New York court, in granting the insurer's motion to dismiss the complaint, held that the insurance company had an absolute right to settle under the language of the policy. . . .

In Shuster v. South Broward Hospital, 591 So.2d 174 (Fla. 1992), . . . the court opined:

> The language of the ["deems expedient"] provision is clear and the insured was put on notice that the agreement granted the insurer the exclusive authority to control settlement and to be guided by its own self-interest when settling the claim for amounts within the policy limits. The obvious intent behind placing the provision in the agreement was to grant the insurer the authority to decide whether to settle or defend the claim based on its own self-interest, and this authority includes settling for the nuisance value of the claim. Therefore, we

---

[1] As one of the grounds for objecting to the settlement, Appellants assert that Worchesky, at no time, submitted an expert report to support her claim of injury. The only expert report was secured by [Insurers], and it stated that Dr. Bleday was not negligent.

interpret the provision as granting the insurer the discretion to settle cases for amounts within the policy limits, regardless of whether the claim is frivolous or not. . . .

However, the court further stressed that every contract that is entered into requires the good faith performance of its provisions, and, thus, the "deems expedient" provision is not absolute. . . .

Based on the facts in the case herein, we find that Appellants have not sufficiently pled a cause of action in bad faith. . . . We believe, as the Supreme Court of Florida did in *Shuster*, that something more is required to maintain a cause of action for bad faith when a claim is settled within the policy limits. However, we leave for another day to define what circumstances constitute bad faith; it is enough to say that they are not present in the instant case. . . .

■ REGULATORY SYSTEM IN SHAMBLES; NEGLIGENT DOCTORS STAY ON JOB
Bruce Butterfield & Gerard O'Neill
*Boston Globe, Oct. 2, 1994**

A nine-month investigation of malpractice by the Boston Globe Spotlight Team examined more than 1,000 court cases of scores of doctors across the state who have been sued repeatedly over the last ten years—some more than ten times. Yet nearly all continue to practice virtually unregulated and unpenalized. . . . Records of the most-sued doctors reveal a malpractice trail of anguish and suffering across the state: children maimed for life; babies dead from botched deliveries; women dying needlessly of breast and cervical cancers; patients left paraplegic, incontinent or crippled. . . . In case after case, the story is the same. Doctors at the center of the malpractice problem are frequently sued, but never admit wrongdoing regardless of the severity of the case.

And there is nobody willing to force them: not fellow doctors, not medical insurers, and not even the courts where settlements are almost always subject to secrecy agreements. . . . Deficient doctors in Massachusetts rarely lose their licenses. They never lose malpractice insurance. When they get in trouble in one hospital, they are often passed to another. The result is a medical monitoring system turned on its head. . . .

Take the case of Dr. Grahshyam P. Massand—currently practicing at Somerville Hospital. Massand has been sued 10 times since 1985, been subject to hospital restrictions on his work, lost privileges at one hospital, and moved to another. . . . If patients should have been able to find out about any problem doctor, it should have been about Massand. His record was well known by medical, regulatory and insurance officials alike. But in many cases, the slow-footed Board of Registration in Medicine doesn't even know who the repeatedly sued doctors are. Insurers know, but shroud nearly everything they do—and everything they

---

*This is the first of a five-part series of articles. The last two paragraphs of this excerpt are from another article in the same series, Brian C. Mooney, Doctors with Dubious Records Start Fresh in Other States, Boston Globe, Oct. 5, 1994.

fail to do — in confidentiality. The agency that insures two-thirds of all doctors is the quasi-public Massachusetts Professional Insurance Association, established in the mid-1970s and dominated by doctors and hospital executives who sit on its board of directors. Despite its public mission, it is protective and secretive to its core. . . . Its executives say they process the paper and pay the bills, but don't get involved with discipline. "I mean, it's not our job," says Tracy Gehan Leu, spokeswoman for the agency.

The real job of disciplining bad doctors is left to the Board of Registration in Medicine. But the board's efforts on the malpractice front have all but collapsed. Massand is one of only a handful of repeatedly sued doctors who have been formally charged by the board. Still, after a decade marked by disastrous cases, he continues to hang onto his license.

Far more common are doctors like Sherman Stein — untouched by the board despite frequent and severe malpractice complaints. . . . Stein was sued for negligence, and his insurers settled in a secret agreement in 1992. By then, Stein had left a trail of lawsuits and patients claiming they were injured or maimed by him. But he was no longer around — he had moved on to become head of neurosurgery at Cooper Hospital in Camden, N.J., with an ostensibly spotless record. In all, Stein has had 11 malpractice suits filed against him since 1985, and a twelfth filed only months before that — one of the worst records of any doctor in the state. At least six of those suits resulted in secret settlements to avoid trial. . . .

Judges as well as lawyers routinely sidestep a 1986 state law banning confidential settlements, which occur in about one third of all medical malpractice suits. . . . [I]n the overwhelming majority of cases in which plaintiffs are paid, the settlement is masked by a bland order "stipulating dismissal" of the complaint and a patient's promise not to talk about it under a threat of forfeiture. . . . In many cases, the record is a sham: Judgment is recorded for the doctor even though the insurer paid a substantial sum to the plaintiff. . . .

These clamps on the flow of information to the public outrage activists in the small but growing health consumer movement. "This is ultimately a question of the right to know," said U.S. Rep. Ron Wyden (D.-Or.), principal sponsor of the bill that created the national data bank and cosponsor of a pending bill that would open up some of its information to the public. . . . Wyden's bill, opposed by the AMA, would disclose information about physicians and others who have had medical privileges restricted or had two or more payouts in malpractice suits.

Notes: Settlement; National Practitioner Data Bank; Insurance

1. *Bleday* reflects the prevailing law that insurers with "deems expedient" language control the decision to settle. Other courts have ruled, however, that as soon as the defendant's lawyer determines that the insurer and the doctor are at odds on settlement, the lawyer has a conflict of interest and therefore a duty to notify the doctor and give him a chance to obtain other counsel. Even if the doctor cannot block the insurer's decision, he might want to release the insurer from further involvement and bear the costs of defending himself. Breach of this duty to disclose could result in an action for legal malpractice. Rogers v. Robson,

Masters, Ryan, Brumund & Belon, 407 N.E.2d 47 (Ill. 1980). The physician-owned malpractice insurers that exist in many states are more sympathetic to allowing physicians to control the decision to go to trial than are independent, "commercial" insurers. In many states, insurance is available with language that requires the doctor's consent to settle, but in other states, insurers prohibit such clauses because they deter settlement. Interestingly, where such clauses exist, they increase the cost of insurance by 1 to 3 percent, which physicians are often willing to pay so they can have more control over whether they will be reported to the National Practitioner Data Bank (NPDB). For an exploration of the psychology of settlement in this context, see Ralph Peeples et al., 41 J. Health & Soc. Behav. 333 (2000). See generally Scott Thomas, An Insurer's Right to Settle Versus its Duty to Defend Nonmeritorious Medical Malpractice Claims, 16 J. Leg. Med. 545 (1995).

When doctors want to settle, they have more legal leverage because insurers can be held liable for exposing doctors to uninsured damages beyond their policy limits. See generally Kent D. Syverud, The Duty to Settle, 76 Va. L. Rev. 1113 (1990); Annot., 18 A.L.R.5th 474 (1995).

In Florida, physicians successfully sponsored a ballot initiative in 2004 to cap lawyers' contingency fees in medical malpractice cases in order to deter suits. But lawyers got the upper hand with a competing measure, also approved by voters, that automatically revokes the medical license of any physician who has three malpractice judgments against him. It is predicted that this mandatory "three strikes" law will put pressure on physicians to quickly settle suits against them, in order to avoid any strikes, and therefore will increase the number of suits.

2. *Secrecy.* As the Boston Globe article reflects, some doctors very much want to settle malpractice suits to avoid attracting attention. Even though the NPDB was implemented in 1989 to require disclosure of all payments in claims against doctors, defense lawyers are often able to avoid these laws by (1) stipulating that payment will come from an institutional defendant such as a hospital or medical clinic rather than the doctor; (2) stipulating that the doctor is not at fault; and (3) presenting an uncontested motion to seal the court records for cause. Query whether it is ethically permissible for a plaintiff's lawyer to participate in such a stipulation or motion that neither she nor her client actually believes.

Public outrage following the Boston Globe's investigative reporting led to a 1996 law in Massachusetts requiring the medical licensing board to collect and provide on request information about each complaint against a doctor in which any payment is made to the plaintiff. California requires that this information be made available to the public through the Internet. See Matthew E. Brown, Redefining the Physician Selection Process and Rewriting Medical Malpractice Settlement Disclosure Webpages, 31 Am. J.L. & Med. 479 (2005). Many commentators view these mandatory reporting requirements as an obstacle to settlement. E.g., Wm. Sage et al., Bridging the Relational-Regulatory Gap: A Pragmatic Information Policy for Patient Safety and Medical Malpractice, 59 Vand. L. Rev. 1263 (2006). At present, the NPDB requires settlements of *any* size to be reported, even those of "nuisance value." Unlike the Massachusetts system, however, the NPDB does not allow public access to this information. Instead, the information is collected only for use by state licensing boards or by medical institutions when they review physicians' competence for licensing or credentialing purposes. Litigants have access only in cases that allege a hospital was negligent in allowing a doctor to use its facilities.

3. *Malpractice Insurance.* One might think that physicians who are repeatedly sued would be put out of business because they could no longer afford their malpractice insurance, much like high-risk automobile drivers. Malpractice insurance, however, is not generally "experience-rated," that is, premiums usually are not set according to each doctor's track record. Instead, premiums are usually adjusted only for the doctor's location and practice specialty. Premiums can vary by as much as five-fold based on location and ten-fold based on specialty. See Frank Sloan et al., Insuring Medical Malpractice (1991); William M. Sage, Medical Malpractice Insurance and the Emperor's Clothes, 54 DePaul L. Rev. 463 (2005). For the most part, the lack of a rating system for physicians individually is in keeping with empirical evidence that malpractice claims, on average, are largely unpredictable events. In one study, doctors who were sued in a six-year baseline period had only a 3 percent chance of being sued in a subsequent three-year period. Randall R. Bovbjerg & Kenneth R. Petronis, The Relationship between Physicians' Malpractice Claims History and Later Claims, 272 JAMA 1421 (1994). Of course, this does not excuse the failure of physician-owned insurers to do something about the few doctors who are sued and lose repeatedly. Additional discussion about the structure of the medical malpractice insurance market is in section G.

F. INSTITUTIONAL LIABILITY

While most doctors are well insured, some are not; and even those who are do not always make the most attractive targets for suit. Moreover, many medical errors do not result from physicians' mistakes. Therefore, plaintiffs are sometimes eager to hold the institutions in which physicians practice responsible for bad medical outcomes. There are two prominent institutions: hospitals and insurers, especially HMOs. These targets of suit entail both unique theories of liability and unique defenses against liability, which the follow sections explore.

You will learn shortly that two distinct theories of liability have emerged: vicarious and direct. In the former, the institution is held strictly liable for acts of negligence by member physicians, based on the physician's relationship with the institution. Observe how this branch of liability takes shape according to differences in how types of physicians are connected with hospitals. Direct liability, the second branch, depends on showing some wrongdoing by the institution's management with respect to physician competence and patient care. Here, the issue is what responsibility is it realistic to assign to lay managers with respect to clinical matters? Overarching this development of legal doctrine is an evolution in judicial and public attitudes about the role that institutions play in the delivery of health care. This change has occurred both with respect to hospital liability and in the migration of liability from hospitals to HMOs. To set these materials in their historical context, then, we begin with a now outmoded, but still seminal decision.

1. Hospital Liability

■ SCHLOENDORFF v. SOCIETY OF NEW YORK HOSPITAL
105 N.E. 92 (N.Y. 1914)

CARDOZO, J.

In the year 1771, by royal charter of George III, the Society of the New York Hospital was organized for the care and healing of the sick. During the century and more which has since passed, it has devoted itself to that high task. It has no capital stock; it does not distribute profits; and its physicians and surgeons, both the visiting and the resident staff, serve it without pay. Those who seek it in search of health are charged nothing if they are needy, either for board or for treatment. The well-to-do are required by its by-laws to pay $7 a week for board, an amount insufficient to cover the per capita cost of maintenance. Whatever income is thus received is added to the income derived from the hospital's foundation, and helps to make it possible for the work to go on. The purpose is not profit, but charity. . . .

To this hospital the plaintiff came in January, 1908. She was suffering from some disorder of the stomach. She asked the superintendent or one of his assistants what the charge would be, and was told that it would be $7 a week. She became an inmate of the hospital, and after some weeks of treatment, the house physician, Dr. Bartlett, discovered a lump, which proved to be a fibroid tumor. He consulted the visiting physician, Dr. Stimson, who advised an operation. The plaintiff's testimony is that the character of the lump could not, so the physicians informed her, be determined without an ether examination. She consented to such an examination, but notified Dr. Bartlett, as she says, that there must be no operation. She was taken at night from the medical to the surgical ward and prepared for an operation by a nurse. On the following day ether was administered, and, while she was unconscious, a tumor was removed. Her testimony is that this was done without her consent or knowledge. She is contradicted both by Dr. Stimson and by Dr. Bartlett, as well as by many of the attendant nurses. For the purpose of this appeal, however, since a verdict was directed in favor of the defendant, her narrative, even if improbable, must be taken as true. Following the operation, and, according to the testimony of her witnesses, because of it, gangrene developed in her left arm, some of her fingers had to be amputated, and her sufferings were intense. She now seeks to charge the hospital with liability for the wrong.

Certain principles of law governing the rights and duties of hospitals, when maintained as charitable institutions have, after much discussion, become no longer doubtful. It is the settled rule that such a hospital is not liable for the negligence of its physicians and nurses in the treatment of patients. Hillyer v. St. Bartholomew's Hospital, [1909] 2 K.B. 820. This exemption has been placed upon two grounds. The first is that of implied waiver. It is said that one who accepts the benefit of a charity enters into a relation which exempts one's benefactor from liability for the negligence of his servants in administering the charity. The hospital remains exempt, though the patient makes some payment to help defray the cost of board. Such a payment is regarded as a contribution to the income of the hospital, to be devoted, like its other funds to the maintenance of the charity. The second ground of the exemption is the relation subsisting between a hospital and the physicians who serve it. It is said that this relation is not one of master and servant, but that the physician occupies the position, so to speak, of an independent contractor, following a separate calling, liable, of course, for his own wrongs to the patient whom he undertakes to serve, but involving the hospital in no liability, if due care has been taken in his selection. On one or the other, and often on both of these grounds, a hospital has been held immune from liability to patients for the malpractice of its physicians. The reasons that have led to the adoption of this rule are, of course, inapplicable where the wrong is committed by a servant of the hospital and the sufferer is not a patient. It is therefore also a settled rule that a hospital is liable to strangers — i.e., to persons other than patients — for the torts of its employees committed within the line of their employment.

In the case at hand, the wrong complained of is not merely negligence. It is trespass. Every human being of adult years and sound mind has a right to determine what shall be done with his own body; and a surgeon who performs an operation without his patient's consent commits an assault, for which he is liable in damages. This is true, except in cases of emergency where the patient is unconscious, and where it is necessary to operate before consent can be obtained. The fact that the wrong complained of here is trespass, rather than negligence, distinguishes this case from most of the cases that have preceded it. . . . [The plaintiff] had never waived the right to recover damages for any wrong resulting from this operation, for she had forbidden the operation. In this situation, the true ground for the defendant's exemption from liability is that the relation between a hospital and its physicians is not that of master and servant. The hospital does not undertake to act through them, but merely to procure them to act upon their own responsibility. . . .

The wrong was not that of the hospital; it was that of physicians, who were not the defendant's servants, but were pursuing an independent calling, a profession sanctioned by a solemn oath, and safeguarded by stringent penalties. If, in serving their patient, they violated her commands, the responsibility is not the defendant's; it is theirs. There is no distinction in that respect between the visiting and the resident physicians. Whether the hospital undertakes to procure a physician from afar, or to have one on the spot, its liability remains the same. . . .

It is true, I think, of nurses, as of physicians, that, in treating a patient, they are not acting as the servants of the hospital. The superintendent is a servant of the hospital; the assistant superintendents, the orderlies, and the other members of the administrative staff are servants of the hospital. But nurses are employed to carry out the orders of the physicians, to whose authority they are subject. The hospital undertakes to procure for the patient the services of a nurse. It does not undertake, through the agency of nurses, to render those services itself. The reported cases make no distinction in that respect between the position of a nurse and that of a physician and none is justified in principle. If there are duties performed by nurses foreign to their duties in carrying out the physician's orders, and having relation to the administrative conduct of the hospital, the fact is not established by this record, nor was it in the discharge of such duties that the defendant's nurses were then serving. The acts of preparation immediately preceding the operation are necessary to its successful performance, and are really part of the operation itself. They are not different in that respect from the administration of the ether. Whatever the nurse does in those preliminary stages is done, not as the servant of the hospital, but in the course of the treatment of the patient, as the delegate of the surgeon to whose orders she is subject. The hospital is not chargeable with her knowledge that the operation is improper any more than with the surgeon's.

If, however, it could be assumed that a nurse is a servant of the hospital, . . . [w]as she to infer from the plaintiff's words that a distinguished surgeon intended to mutilate the plaintiff's body in defiance of the plaintiff's orders? Was it her duty, as a result of this talk, to report to the superintendent of the hospital that the ward was about to be utilized for the commission of an assault? I think that no such interpretation of the facts would have suggested itself to any reasonable mind. The preparation for an ether examination is to some extent the same as for an operation. The hour was midnight, and the plaintiff was nervous and excited. . . . There may be cases where a patient ought not to be advised of a contemplated operation until shortly before the appointed hour. To discuss such a subject at midnight might cause needless and even harmful agitation. About such matters a nurse is not qualified to judge. She is drilled to habits of strict obedience. She is accustomed to rely unquestioningly upon the judgment of her superiors. No woman occupying such a position would reasonably infer from the plaintiff's words that it was the purpose of the surgeons to operate whether the plaintiff forbade it or not. I conclude, therefore, that the plaintiff's statements to the nurse on the night before the operation are insufficient to charge the hospital with notice of a contemplated wrong. . . .

The conclusion, therefore, follows that the trial judge did not err in his direction of a verdict. A ruling would, indeed, be an unfortunate one that might constrain charitable institutions, as a measure of self-protection, to limit their activities. A hospital opens its doors without discrimination to all who seek its aid. It gathers in its wards a company of skilled physicians and trained nurses, and places their services at the call of the afflicted, without scrutiny of the character or the worth of those who appeal to it, looking at nothing and caring for nothing beyond the fact of their affliction. In this beneficent work, it does not subject itself to liability for damages, though the ministers of healing whom it has selected have proved unfaithful to their trust.

Notes: Hospital Liability; Charitable and Governmental Immunity

1. Schloendorff. For a fascinating account of the history of this famous case, see Paul Lombardo, Phantom Tumors and Hysterical Women: Revising Our View of the *Schloendorff* Case, 33 J. L. Med. Ethics 791 (2005). He reveals that the unconsented operation was a hysterectomy.

Is Justice Cardozo's rejection of hospital liability as absolute as it first appears? What about the qualification, "if due care has been taken in [the doctor's] selection"? What if the court were more demanding about the nurse's duty to speak up? Compare these potential theories of liability with those introduced in the modern landmark case of Darling v. Charleston Community Hospital, excerpted at page 467.

2. *Charitable Immunity.* The rule of charitable immunity was subjected to an increasing number of exceptions — distinguishing between paying and nonpaying patients, patients and strangers, and administrative versus professional acts — until it eventually crumbled. The leading decision is President of Georgetown College v. Hughes, 130 F.2d 810 (D.C. Cir. 1942), which observed that charitable hospitals could simply purchase insurance to protect themselves from economic catastrophe. The gist of this changed attitude is best captured in a colorful dissent by the renowned Pennsylvania Justice Musmanno in Michael v. Hahnemann Medical College and Hospital of Philadelphia, 172 A.2d 769 (Pa. 1961):

> Hospitals then were little better than hovels in which the indigent were gathered for the primitive cures available. The wealthy and the well-to-do were cared for in their homes. The hospital or infirmary was more often than not part of the village parish. Charity in the biblical sense prevailed. And if it happened that some poor mortal was scalded by a sister of mercy, who exhausted from long hours of vigil and toil, accidentally spilled a ladle of hot soup on a hand extended for nourishment, there was no thought of lawsuits against the philanthropists who made the meager refuge possible. But if, following such a mishap, litigation should have been initiated in the courts, it is not difficult to understand why judges would be reluctant to honor such a complaint, convinced on the basis of humanity, that an enterprise utterly devoid of worldly gain should be exempt from liability. A successful lawsuit against such a feeble structure might well have demolished it and have thus paralyzed the only helping hand in the world of unconcern for the rag-clothed sick and the crutchless disabled.
>
> The situation today is quite different. Charitable enterprises are not housed in ramshackly wooden structures. They are not mere storm shelters to succor the traveler and temporarily refuge those stricken in a common disaster. Hospitals today, to a large extent, are mighty edifices, in stone, glass and marble. They maintain large staffs, they use the best equipment that science can devise, they utilize the most modern methods of helping themselves to the noblest purpose of man, that of helping one's stricken brother. But they do all this on a business basis, and properly so. . . . And if the hospital is a business for the purpose of collecting money, it must be a business for the purpose of meeting its obligations. . . .

Despite this shift in attitude, a number of states retain a version of charitable immunity in statutes that limit the amount of recovery against nonprofit hospitals or charities generally to anywhere from $10,000 to $500,000. See Keene v. Brigham & Women's Hospital, 439 Mass. 223 (2003); Note, The Quality of Mercy: "Charitable Torts" and their Continuing Immunity, 100 Harv. L. Rev. 1382 (1987); Annot., 25 A.L.R. 4th 517 (1983).

3. *Governmental Immunity.* Public hospitals might also claim governmental immunity under the common law concept that "the king can do no wrong." See, e.g., Withers v. University of Kentucky, 939 S.W.2d 340 (Ky. 1997) (university hospital is a "state agency" immune from suit). Most states, however, have abrogated governmental immunity to some degree by statute, as has the federal government. This abrogation is often limited, though, to "ministerial" or "proprietary" functions, thus preserving many of the same arcane distinctions that arose under charitable immunity and the *Schloendorff* rule. See, e.g., Moser v. Heistand, 681 A.2d 1322 (Pa. 1996) (immunity exists only for suits based simply on physician error, not for suits based on failures in administration that result in

physician error). See generally John Akula, Sovereign Immunity and Health Care: Can Government Be Trusted?, 19(6) Health Aff. 152 (Dec. 2000). Substantial immunity is still common in many states for psychiatric hospitals, and full immunity is still preserved for injuries suffered during the course of active military duty. See Feres v. United States, 340 U.S. 135 (1950). In sharp contrast, Veterans Administration (VA) hospitals are subject by statute to a form of strict liability, without regard to negligence. See Brown v. Gardner, 115 S. Ct. 552 (1994).

4. *Subsequent Developments in Vicarious Liability.* The refusal to apply ordinary principles of respondeat superior even to employed nurses gave way in later decades to a rule that held the hospital responsible for "administrative" errors, in contrast with errors in medical judgment. What resulted was a string of arcane distinctions and inconsistent decisions concerning such routine medical acts as administering medication, giving injections, and applying casts. For instance, giving a blood transfusion to the wrong patient was considered "administrative," whereas giving the wrong blood to the right patient was labeled an error of medical judgment. See generally Bing v. Thunig, 143 N.E.2d 3 (N.Y. 1957). As will be seen in the next case, these cracks in hospitals' liability armor eventually led to the outright reversal of *Schloendorff* by *Bing*. The modern issue, then, becomes how does standard respondeat superior apply to physicians who are not, strictly speaking, employees.

On the modern status of hospital liability generally, see James Smith, Hospital Liability; Mary Bertolet & Lee Goldsmith, Hospital Liability: Law and Practice; Aspen Hospital Law Manual.

■ADAMSKI v. TACOMA GENERAL HOSPITAL
579 P.2d 970 (Wash. Ct. App. 1978)

REED, Acting Chief Judge.
. . . On January 9, 1974, plaintiff injured his finger while playing basketball. According to plaintiff the bone had broken and was protruding from a gash on the palmar surface of the finger. Plaintiff, aided by a friend, forced the bone back into position, applied a crude splint, covered the wound with a makeshift bandage and continued the game. Later that evening he presented himself for treatment at the emergency room of Tacoma General. . . . [T]he physician in charge, Dr. Tsoi . . . irrigated, debrided and cleansed the wound with saline solution and the cut was closed completely with nylon sutures and bandaged. [Because Dr. Tsoi did not realize the bone had been exposed, he did not sufficiently treat the wound for a deep infection. After plaintiff contacted a series of nurses and other doctors, the wound was reopened and cleaned three days later at another hospital, and the finger eventually healed properly.] . . .

Plaintiff brought this action for damages against Dr. Tsoi, Tacoma Emergency Care Physicians, Inc., P.S. (TECP), a group of physicians who had contracted with Tacoma General, and Tacoma General, alleging as to the latter that (1) Dr. Tsoi was negligent in his diagnosis and treatment, (2) Dr. Tsoi was acting as the Hospital's agent, and (3) the Hospital's nurse-employees were negligent.

Tacoma General moved for summary judgment in its favor, asserting it could not be held liable for Dr. Tsoi's negligence upon the theory of respondeat superior because the doctor was not acting as its agent (employee-servant). Tacoma General argued the doctor was an independent contractor over whose actions it neither had nor exercised any right of control. . . .

According to the [] supporting documents, on January 1, 1973 the Hospital contracted with TECP, a group of five licensed physicians, among them Dr. Tsoi, to furnish emergency room physicians on a 24-hour basis. The contract specifically classifies the emergency room doctors as "independent contractors" and not "agents or employees" of the Hospital. The agreement further provided inter alia that (1) Tacoma General alone is to bill patients for the fees of the physicians, who agree to charge going rates; (2) the Hospital undertakes to collect from the patient, by suit if necessary; (3) Tacoma General guarantees TECP $10,000 per month; (4) after certain deductions TECP is to be credited with 85 percent of all doctor fees collected, less the $10,000 guaranty; the Hospital retains 15 percent for its collection services; (5) the emergency room doctors must be members of Tacoma General's staff and may not carry on a private practice in Pierce County, although they are not prohibited from (a) providing emergency room service to other hospitals, (b) assisting private physicians with surgery upon request, (c) teaching medical subjects and (d) providing medical laboratory consulting services; (6) emergency room physicians are precluded from utilizing the emergency room as a "source of private practice"; (7) if TECP desires to furnish a physician other than one of the five named in the contract, Tacoma General's Board must first consent; (8) Tacoma General and TECP will each procure and maintain "professional liability, negligence, errors and omissions, and public liability" policies with limits of $1 million.

On this record, the trial court concluded that Dr. Tsoi was an independent contractor and not an employee of the Hospital, and thus refused to hold the Hospital liable on a respondeat superior theory. . . .

We have found no Washington cases addressing the problems inherent in the application of the doctrine of respondeat superior to the hospital-physician relationship. Tacoma General argues that the ordinary rules of agency must be applied and that if this is done, Dr. Tsoi must be held to be an independent contractor for whose negligent acts the Hospital is not responsible. . . . Tacoma General points out that nowhere in its contract with TECP does it reserve the right to exercise any control over the actual medical treatment rendered to its emergency room patients. Rather, Tacoma General argues, the only contract requirement is that the doctors must be members of Tacoma General's staff and conform to the usual and accepted professional and ethical standards of conduct.

The experience of the courts has been that application of hornbook rules of agency to the hospital-physician relationship usually leads to unrealistic and unsatisfactory results, at least from the standpoint of the injured patient. Consequently, we have seen a substantial body of special law emerging in this area; the result has been an expansion of hospital liability for negligent medical acts committed on its premises.

For many years the majority of courts followed the rule espoused by Tacoma General and held that physicians, because of their skill and training in a highly technical field, were not subject to control by hospital lay boards and thus could not be servants or employees in the sense required by the doctrine of respondeat superior. Rather, physicians were classified as independent contractors with the result that the hospitals in which they labored could not be held vicariously liable for their medical mistakes. . . . The rationale of *Schloendorff* was followed in many jurisdictions until the decision in Bing v. Thunig, 143 N.E.2d 3 (N.Y. 1957). In a masterful opinion by Judge Fuld, the New York court rejected Cardozo's "professional skill" theory of immunity as being out of step with the times. In essence, the *Bing* court reasoned that other highly skilled professionals were not being excluded from application of the rule of respondeat superior and no valid reason existed for excluding medical practitioners per se. Judge Fuld stressed that hospitals had become more than just a place for physicians to bring their patients for treatment; that, in fact, the hospital itself renders care and treatment through its facilities and employees. In holding the hospital responsible for the negligence of its nurses, Judge Fuld stated:

> The conception that the hospital does not undertake to treat the patient, does not undertake to act through its doctors and nurses, but undertakes instead simply to procure them to act upon their own responsibility, no longer reflects the fact. Present-day hospitals, as their manner of operation plainly demonstrates, do far more than furnish facilities for treatment. They regularly employ on a salary basis a large staff of physicians, nurses and internes, as well as administrative and manual workers, and they charge patients for medical care and treatment, collecting for such services, if necessary, by legal action. Certainly, the person who avails himself of "hospital facilities" expects that the hospital will attempt to cure him, not that its nurses or other employees will act on their own responsibility.

Once again the majority of courts chose to follow the New York court's lead and embraced the *Bing* concept that, in certain cases the doctrine of respondeat superior may serve to render a hospital liable for the negligent acts of the medical personnel who deliver its service to its patients. Since *Bing*, the principal difficulty encountered by the courts has been in determining in which cases to apply the rule of vicarious liability. Application of the traditional right of control test has not solved the problem because the governing body of a hospital never actually exercises, nor can it exercise, much control over a physician's medical decisions and his actual treatment of patients, even when he is clearly an employee of the hospital, such as an intern or resident.

Even before *Schloendorff* and *Bing*, however, the California court, in Brown v. La Societe Francaise de Bienfaisance Mutuelle, 138 Cal. 475, 71 P. 516 (1903) applied the doctrine of respondeat superior to the hospital-physician relationship because (1) the patient in the case sought treatment primarily from the hospital, and (2) the hospital paid the doctor a salary. It is on the basis of the "Brown formula" that many courts now regularly hold hospitals liable for the negligence of their interns and resident physicians.

Conversely, where the patient contacts his personal physician and is by him admitted to a hospital for treatment, and the doctor looks directly to the patient for his fees, the courts uniformly treat the physician as an independent contractor. Such a holding results in a refusal to impose vicarious liability upon the hospital for the physician's medical mistakes even though they may occur on hospital premises.

The *Brown* formula does not, however, cover all the possible variations of the hospital-doctor-patient relationship; the most troublesome situation has been that where the patient, not having contacted his personal physician, presents himself at the hospital for treatment and is there provided with or referred to a physician, usually a specialist, who is neither an intern, resident or other salaried employee of the hospital. The courts generally look to all of the facts and circumstances to determine if the hospital and doctor enjoy such a "significant relationship" that the rule of respondeat superior ought to apply.[1] . . . In such cases, it should make no difference that the physician is compensated on some basis other than salary or that he bills his patient directly. These are artificial distinctions, the efficacy of which has long since disappeared and to the perpetuation of which we do not subscribe.

An example of the more enlightened approach is found in . . . Beeck v. Tucson General Hospital, 18 Ariz. App. 165, 500 P.2d 1153 (1972). [There] a summary judgment in favor of the hospital was reversed, the appellate court finding the relationship between the hospital and the physician in charge of its radiology department was that of employer-employee. Even though the doctor and his partner contracted to staff the department and were compensated by a percentage of revenues rather than by salary, the court found a significant relationship between hospital and doctor and applied the doctrine of respondeat superior. In support of its holding, the Arizona court noted the following pertinent facts: (1) the hospital billed for the radiologist's services; (2) the doctors received no other compensation; (3) the doctors agreed generally not to engage in private practice; (4) the doctors were solely responsible for operation of the department; (5) the doctors provided their own insurance coverage; (6) the doctors were to comply with the policies, rules and regulations of the hospital and the American Osteopathic Association; (7) the contract term was five years, terminable upon 120 days' written notice; (8) the hospital owned all the equipment and office supplies and provided the supporting technicians; (9) the patient had no choice in selecting a radiologist, the hospital having made that choice for her. The court noted that . . . the doctor was employed for an extended period of time; and he performed a service which was "an inherent function of the hospital, a function without which the hospital could not properly achieve its purpose." Finally, the fact that Mrs. Beeck had signed a document acknowledging that all those performing services for her, including the radiologist, were independent contractors, and not employees or agents of the hospital, gave the Arizona court little pause: "Unless the radiologist were actually an independent contractor the clause reciting him to be so is of no effect." . . .

In Schagrin v. Wilmington Medical Center, Inc., 304 A.2d 61 (Del. S. Ct. 1973) . . . [the] court appears to fasten on a nondelegable duty to the public which was assumed by the hospital when it, although not required by law to do so, elected to staff and maintain emergency room services as part of its total hospital enterprise.[5]

---

[1] The term "significant relationship" is suggested in Cunningham, The Hospital-Physician Relationship: Hospital Responsibility for Malpractice of Physicians, 50 Wash. L. Rev. 385 (1975), wherein the author opines that the courts, without saying so, appear to be working toward an "enterprise tort," with the inquiry being addressed solely to whether the tort occurred within the scope of the "hospital enterprise" which is defined as "any service, medical or otherwise, the hospital purports to provide the patient."

[5] . . . [T]he Washington State Board of Health has adopted rules and regulations . . . [that] require a licensed hospital to provide emergency care services in accordance with the community's needs and the hospital's capabilities. . . . One requirement is that there must be a physician

Turning to the case before us it can readily be seen that . . . Dr. Tsoi was performing "an inherent function of the hospital, a function without which the hospital could not properly achieve its purpose," Beeck v. Tucson General Hospital, i.e., he was an integral part of the total hospital function or enterprise. Clearly, when one considers all the facts and circumstances of the relationship between Tacoma General and its emergency room physicians, a substantial and genuine issue arises as to whether that relationship is that of principal and agent. It was error to resolve this issue by summary judgment.

Moreover, where a physician is found not to be the actual agent of the hospital, the latter may still be held responsible for his departures from good medical practice under the so-called holding out or ostensible agent theory. Restatement (Second) Agency §267, p.578 (1958) sets forth the rule as follows: "One who represents that another is his servant or other agent and thereby causes a third person justifiably to rely upon the care or skill of such apparent agent is subject to liability to the third person for harm caused by the lack of care or skill of the one appearing to be a servant or other agent as if he were such." . . .

In Howard v. Park, 37 Mich. App. 496, 195 N.W.2d 39 (1972), the defendant clinic referred a little girl patient to an independent doctor for removal of a leg cast using a "vibrating wheel." The patient sustained severe cuts and sought damages from the clinic. The *Howard* court found the clinic liable on ostensible agency grounds. The court noted that (1) treatment took place in the clinic; (2) the clinic chose the physician; and (3) the clinic billed on its stationery for the physician's charges. The court refused to adopt a requirement that the patient must inquire as to the treating doctor's status in order to entertain a reasonable belief he was the hospital's employee. . . .

Tacoma General argues, however, that there can be no "ostensible agency" or agency by estoppel as it is sometimes called, in the absence of proof of an "affirmative misrepresentation" of Dr. Tsoi's status. . . . On the contrary, a "holding out" or representation may arise when the hospital acts or omits to act in some way which leads the patient to a reasonable belief he is being treated by the hospital by one of its employees.

In the instant case, a jury could find that Tacoma General held itself out as providing emergency care services to the public. A jury could find that plaintiff reasonably believed Dr. Tsoi was employed by the Hospital to deliver that emergency room service. It appears plaintiff was not advised to the contrary and, in fact, he believed he was being treated by the Hospital's agent; in addition, the written instructions provided him after surgery could reasonably be interpreted as an invitation to return for further treatment if plaintiff could not contact his personal physician. The form bearing this instruction also carried the title "Tacoma General Hospital Emergency Care." Clearly, when the facts before the trial court and the fair inferences therefrom are viewed in a light most favorable to plaintiff, a jury could find that the emergency room personnel were "held out" as

---

responsible for the services, whose functions and responsibilities are subject to the medical direction of the hospital. It could thus be argued that Washington state has imposed upon hospitals a duty to provide emergency care services to the public and that they cannot shift the responsibility by contract. This concept was neither developed nor argued at either the trial court level nor in this court on appeal.

employees of the Hospital. It was error, therefore, not to submit this issue to the jury. . . .

For this and the other reasons we have outlined, summary judgment was an inappropriate method of disposing of plaintiff's claims.

Notes: Hospital Vicarious Liability

1. *Hospital Control.* Is it consistent with the prohibition of the corporate practice of medicine to hold a hospital responsible for the professional mistakes of its agent-physicians? The corporate practice of medicine doctrine holds that it is illegal for corporations to subject physicians to the control of lay management because this would constitute the unlicensed practice of medicine. If respondeat superior liability is premised on the principal's control of an agent's actions, how can it coexist with this prohibition of corporate control of physicians? One court, agreeing with this logic, surprisingly held that a health center cannot, as a matter of law, be held responsible for a physician's negligence. Daly v. Aspen Center for Women's Health, 134 P.3d 450 (Colo.App. 2005). Another decision, issued with respect to an HMO, found it necessary to declare the corporate practice of medicine doctrine "totally abolished" in order to hold the HMO vicariously liable for an employed physician's mistake. Sloan v. Metropolitan Health Council of Indianapolis, 516 N.E.2d 1104 (Ind. Ct. App. 1987). The court also reasoned, consistent with other decisions, that respondeat superior does not require actual control but merely a finding that the negligent acts occurred within the course and scope of employment. Otherwise, hospitals could not be held responsible for employed nurses, or airlines for employed pilots. Perhaps based on this thinking, other courts have not found it necessary to abolish the corporate practice of medicine doctrine in order to hold hospitals liable for physicians' errors. See, e.g., McDonald v. Hampton Training School for Nurses, 486 S.E.2d 299 (Va. 1997) (vicarious liability attaches even though hospital does not control actual medical judgment); Dias v. Brigham Medical Associates, Inc., 438 Mass. 317 (2002) (same, for a medical group).

2. *"Captain of the Ship."* One hospital defense against vicarious liability that still remains is the "captain of the ship" or borrowed servant doctrine discussed at page 387. The effect of this doctrine is not only to hold physicians (usually surgeons) responsible for subordinate doctors and nurses, but sometimes also to relieve the hospital from vicarious responsibility. This occurs when a hospital employee's negligent acts are directed or supervised by a physician who is not an agent of the hospital; then, the independent physician can be found to have temporarily "borrowed" the hospital's employee. Courts usually find that the hospital and the physician in charge share the employee and therefore share liability. See, e.g., Tonsic v. Wagner, 329 A.2d 497 (Pa. 1974). However, courts sometimes hold the doctor solely liable if he instructs the nurse to do an act that contravenes hospital policy. See, e.g., Hoffman v. Wells, 397 S.E.2d 696 (Ga. 1990). See also Restatement (Second) of Agency §227.

3. *Indemnification Agreements.* The principles of vicarious liability introduced here apply to other medical institutions than just hospitals. Materials below explore for instance how vicarious liability applies to HMOs. Earlier, it was

observed that physician practice groups or clinics can be held liable as an entity for the negligence of one of their members. It is possible in all of these circumstances, however, to reallocate liability among the parties through the use of indemnification agreements. These agreements do not alter the rights of the injured patient, but they do affect which of several joint tortfeasors can seek contribution or indemnification from the others. Negotiating these indemnification agreements is a major aspect of contract drafting, especially in managed care settings.

4. *Adamski* introduces three concepts of vicarious liability: actual agency (which includes simple employment); ostensible agency; and nondelegable duty (also known as enterprise liability). The third of these is discussed below and at page 391. The first two tend to blend together based on the facts and circumstances of the arrangement. Which facts and circumstances mentioned in *Adamski* and the cases it cites are most relevant to actual agency? Which are most relevant to ostensible agency? How could an arrangement be structured to avoid the first characterization? What techniques would help to avoid the second characterization? Do you agree that the informed consent form is irrelevant to both characterizations? What about signs in the ER waiting room or physicians wearing identification badges?

5. *Facts and Circumstances.* In contrast with the facts-and-circumstances test applied in *Adamski*, most courts in recent years have held that emergency room physicians are subject to a jury finding of ostensible agency regardless of the specifics of the arrangement with the hospital. The courts' reasoning is reflected in the following cases: Gilbert v. Sycamore Municipal Hospital, 622 N.E.2d 788 (Ill. 1993) (hospital advertising itself as offering quality care contributes to the impression that doctors work for the hospital); Hardy v. Brantley, 471 So. 2d 358 (Miss. 1985) (emergency room patient is not in a position to inquire into the specifics of his doctor's contractual arrangements with the hospital); Simmons v. Tuomey Regional Medical Center, 533 S.E.2d 312 (S.C. 2000) (patient did not specifically choose any of the emergency room physicians that treated her). Where ostensible agency is applied outside the classic emergency room setting to hospital-based specialists such as radiologists and anesthesiologists, courts continue to be somewhat more open to argument both ways, depending on the facts and circumstances. Compare Milliron v. Francke, 793 P.2d 824 (Mont. 1990) (providing radiologist with office, equipment, personnel, and billing is not sufficient to establish agency relationship; in a rural setting, it is understood this is necessary to maintain adequate staffing); with Burless v. West Virginia Univ. Hospitals, 601 S.E.2d 85 (W. Va. 2004) (disclaimer in a consent form was not sufficient to inform patient giving birth that university physicians were not hospital employees); Sword v. NKC Hospitals, 714 N.E.2d 142 (Ind. 1999) (anesthesiologist could be found to be an apparent agent of a hospital that "aggressively marketed its services to the public . . . [as] 'the most technically sophisticated birthplace in the region'" and touted the "'full availability of a special anesthesiology team, experienced and dedicated exclusively to OB patients'"); York v. Rush-Presbyterian-St. Luke's Medical Center, 854 N.E.2d 635 (Ill. 2006) (same, based on twenty-eight page analysis of detailed testimony, even for a patient who himself was a surgeon and who picked most of his own doctors). See generally J. D. Ingram, Liability of Medical Institutions for the

Negligence of Independent Contractors Practicing on their Premises, 10 J. Contemp. Health L. & Pol'y 221 (1994).

6. *Office-Based Physicians.* Do you think the ostensible agency doctrine could apply to specialists who are not entirely hospital based, such as surgeons or consultants referred by a patient's primary care physician? So far, courts have not gone this far, but at least one has opened the possibility of holding hospitals vicariously liable even for physicians who maintain an office-based practice. In Kashishian v. Port, 481 N.W.2d 277 (Wis. 1991), the patient's personal physician admitted her to a teaching hospital for cardiac evaluation and called in a member of the medical school to perform a surgical procedure, which went awry. The court sent the case against the hospital back for trial, holding that "the plaintiff's contact with a private personal physician [is not] necessarily inconsistent with the hospital having held out specialists and/or consultants as its apparent agents. . . . [T]he doctrine of apparent authority is not limited to the emergency room context, [n]or is it limited to situations where a patient enters the hospital without a personal attending physician." At present, this is a distinctly minority position, but some courts appear willing to expand vicarious liability to any situation where "a patient seeks treatment from a hospital and not from a particular physician of the patient's choosing." Syracuse v. Diao, 707 N.Y.S.2d 570 (App. Div. 2000) (allowing case to go to trial where a patient simply called a specialized surgery center to request an appointment but did not ask for a particular physician).

7. *Reliance.* Ordinarily, the ostensible agency doctrine requires a showing that the injured party detrimentally relied on the representation of agency. If reliance is applied in a strict "but-for" causation fashion, it is impossible to show because few patients assert that they would have declined medical treatment at that institution if they had known the doctors were really independent contractors. Accordingly, a few courts have held that ostensible agency does not exist even in the classic emergency room situation. Albain v. Flower Hospital, 553 N.E.2d 1038 (Ohio 1990), overruled in Clark v. Southview Hospital & Family Health Center., 628 N.E.2d 46 (Ohio 1994). Most courts, however, have applied the reliance requirement in more psychological terms, holding that it is sufficient that the patient subjectively relied on the hospital to render the treatment and expected the doctors to be employees. See, e.g., *Clark*; *Sword*. Under this test, it is not necessary to show any alteration in the plaintiff's behavior on account of the hospital's holding out, only that the patient believed the hospital selected the physician. What justifies this liberalization of tort doctrine? In York v. Rush-Presbyterian-St. Luke's Medical Center, 854 N.E.2d 635 (Ill. 2006), the court explained, in finding apparent agency for an anesthesiologist, that "the relationship between a patient and health-care providers, both physicians and hospitals, presents a matrix of unique interactions that finds no ready parallel to other relationships," and so the "element of reliance . . . [on] a hospital involves unique circumstances that require unique rules."

8. *Enterprise Liability.* The enterprise liability concept referred to briefly in *Adamski* (see n.1) would hold hospitals automatically liable for all acts of negligence within their walls, regardless of the specifics of actual or apparent agency, that is, even if the doctor is conceded to be an obvious independent contractor. The rationale is one of nondelegable duty, namely, that the public policy supporting hospital responsibility is so strong that, as a matter of law, the

hospital may not avoid responsibility by delegating the function to an independent contractor. The classic example is an airline that attempts to shield itself from liability by retaining pilots as independent contractors.

So far, this nondelegable duty concept has been applied in only a few cases and only to emergency room care. The leading case is Jackson v. Power, 743 P.2d 1376 (Alaska 1987). Based on hospital licensing statutes and Joint Commission accreditation standards, the court observed that the hospital had assumed a duty to ensure adequate emergency room services. The court then concluded that a hospital "may not shield itself from liability by claiming that it is not responsible for the results of negligently performed health care when the law imposes a duty on the hospital to provide that health care. . . . We simply cannot fathom why liability should depend upon the technical employment status of the emergency room physician who treats the patient." Is this reasoning necessarily limited to emergency room care? To hospital-based physicians? So far, this is as far as courts have taken it. See Fletcher v. South Peninsula Hospital, 71 P.3d 833 (Alaska 2003) (refusing to extend the doctrine to surgeons). Other courts have refused to adopt the nondelegable duty doctrine at all. E.g., Baptist Memorial Hospital System v. Sampson, 969 S.W.2d 945 (Tex. 1998). One interesting decision, however, held that a hospital may have *voluntarily assumed* a nondelegable duty for all aspects of medical care in a birth injury case via the following language in its generic consent form: "I authorize [the] Hospital to furnish the necessary medical or surgical treatments, or procedures, . . . drugs and supplies as may be ordered by the attending physician(s) . . ." Pope v. Winter Park Healthcare Group, 939 So.2d 185 (Fla.App. 2006). Do you agree that this is all it takes for a hospital to assume responsibility for any physician's negligence?

9. *The Next Stage.* Falling between vicarious liability for some physicians and enterprise liability for all physicians is a position known as "direct institutional liability," in which hospitals are held liable even for acts of independent physicians, but only if the hospital management breached a duty of care owed directly to patients with respect to selecting or supervising the physician. That theory of liability is thought to have been introduced by the next case. See if you can discern in this case a major shift in liability, or instead whether its holding rests on a more conventional application of vicarious liability. To the extent it presages a new duty of hospitals, precisely what is the content of that duty?

■ DARLING v. CHARLESTON COMMUNITY MEMORIAL HOSPITAL
211 N.E.2d 253 (Ill. 1965), cert. denied, 383 U.S. 946 (1966)

SCHAEFER, Justice.

. . . On November 5, 1960, the plaintiff, who was 18 years old, broke his leg while playing in a college football game. He was taken to the emergency room at the defendant hospital where Dr. Alexander, who was on emergency call that day, treated him. Dr. Alexander, with the assistance of hospital personnel, applied traction and placed the leg in a plaster cast. A heat cradle was applied to dry the cast. Not long after the application of the cast plaintiff was in great pain and his toes, which protruded from the cast, became swollen and dark in color. They eventually became cold and insensitive. On the evening of November 6, Dr. Alexander "notched" the cast around the toes, and on the afternoon of the next day he cut the cast approximately three inches up from the foot. On November 8 he split the sides of the cast with a Stryker saw; in the course of cutting the cast the plaintiff's leg was cut on both sides. Blood and other seepage were observed by the nurses and others, and there was a stench in the room, which one witness said was the worst he had smelled since World War II. The plaintiff remained in Charleston Hospital until November 19, when he was transferred to Barnes Hospital in St. Louis and placed under the care of Dr. Fred Reynolds, head of orthopedic surgery at Washington University School of Medicine and Barnes Hospital. Dr. Reynolds found that the fractured leg contained a considerable amount of dead tissue which in his opinion resulted from interference with the circulation of blood in the limb caused by swelling or hemorrhaging of the leg against the construction of the cast. Dr. Reynolds performed several operations in a futile attempt to save the leg but ultimately it had to be amputated eight inches below the knee.

The evidence before the jury is set forth at length in the opinion of the Appellate Court and need not be stated in detail here. The plaintiff contends that it established that the defendant was negligent in permitting Dr. Alexander to do orthopedic work of the kind required in this case, and not requiring him to review his operative procedures to bring them up to date; in failing, through its medical staff, to exercise adequate supervision over the case, especially since Dr. Alexander had been placed on emergency duty by the hospital, and in not requiring consultation, particularly after complications had developed. Plaintiff contends also that in a case which developed as this one did, it was the duty of the nurses to watch the protruding toes constantly for changes of color, temperature and movement, and to check circulation every ten to twenty minutes, whereas the proof showed that these things were done only a few times a day. Plaintiff argues that it was the duty of the hospital staff to see that these procedures were followed, and that either the nurses were derelict in failing to report developments in the case to the hospital administrator, he was derelict in bringing them to the attention of the medical staff, or the staff was negligent in failing to take action. Defendant is a licensed and accredited hospital, and the plaintiff contends that the licensing regulations, accreditation standards, and its own bylaws define the hospital's duty, and that an infraction of them imposes liability for the resulting injury.

The defendant's position is stated in the following excerpts from its brief:

> It is a fundamental rule of law that only an individual properly educated and licensed, and not a corporation, may practice medicine. . . . Accordingly, a hospital is powerless under the law to forbid or command any act by a physician or surgeon in the practice of his profession. . . . A hospital is not an insurer of the patient's recovery, but only owes the patient the duty to exercise such reasonable care as his known condition requires and that degree of care, skill and diligence used by hospitals generally in that community. . . . Where the evidence shows that the hospital care was in accordance with standard practice obtaining in similar hospitals, and Plaintiff produces no evidence to the contrary, the jury cannot conclude that the opposite is true even if they disbelieve the hospital

witnesses. . . . A hospital is not liable for the torts of its nurse committed while the nurse was but executing the orders of the patient's physician, unless such order is so obviously negligent as to lead any reasonable person to anticipate that substantial injury would result to the patient from the execution of such order. . . . The extent of the duty of a hospital with respect to actual medical care of a professional nature such as is furnished by a physician is to use reasonable care in selecting medical doctors. When such care in the selection of the staff is accomplished, and nothing indicates that a physician so selected is incompetent or that such incompetence should have been discovered, more cannot be expected from the hospital administration.

The basic dispute, as posed by the parties, centers upon the duty that rested upon the defendant hospital. That dispute involves the effect to be given to . . . hospital regulations adopted by the State Department of Public Health under the Hospital Licensing Act, to the Standards for Hospital Accreditation of the American Hospital Association, and to the bylaws of the defendant. . . .

The conception that the hospital does not undertake to treat the patient, does not undertake to act through its doctors and nurses, but undertakes instead simply to procure them to act upon their own responsibility, no longer reflects the fact. Present-day hospitals, as their manner of operation plainly demonstrates, do far more than furnish facilities for treatment. They regularly employ on a salary basis a large staff of physicians, nurses and internes, as well as administrative and manual workers, and they charge patients for medical care and treatment, collecting for such services, if necessary, by legal action. Certainly, the person who avails himself of "hospital facilities" expects that the hospital will attempt to cure him, not that its nurses or other employes will act on their own responsibility. (Fuld, J., in Bing v. Thunig (1957), 2 N.Y.2d 656, 163 N.Y.S.2d 3, 11, 143 N.E.2d 3, 8.)

The Standards for Hospital Accreditation, the state licensing regulations and the defendant's bylaws demonstrate that the medical profession and other responsible authorities regard it as both desirable and feasible that a hospital assume certain responsibilities for the care of the patient.

We now turn to an application of these considerations to this case. . . . [W]e need not analyze all of the issues submitted to the jury. Two of them were that the defendant had negligently:

5. Failed to have a sufficient number of trained nurses for bedside care of all patients at all times capable of recognizing the progressive gangrenous condition of the plaintiff's right leg, and of bringing the same to the attention of the hospital administration and to the medical staff so that adequate consultation could have been secured and such conditions rectified; . . .

7. Failed to require consultation with or examination by members of the hospital surgical staff skilled in such treatment; or to review the treatment rendered to the plaintiff and to require consultants to be called in as needed.

We believe that the jury verdict [against the hospital] is supportable on either of these grounds. On the basis of the evidence before it the jury could reasonably have concluded that the nurses did not test for circulation in the leg as frequently as necessary, that skilled nurses would have promptly recognized the conditions that signalled a dangerous impairment of circulation in the plaintiff's leg, and would have known that the condition would become irreversible in a matter of hours. At that point it became the nurses' duty to inform the attending physician, and if he failed to act, to advise the hospital authorities so that appropriate action might be taken. As to consultation, there is no dispute that the hospital failed to review Dr. Alexander's work or require a consultation; the only issue is whether its failure to do so was negligence. On the evidence before it the jury could reasonably have found that it was. . . .

Judgment affirmed.

■ JOHNSON v. MISERICORDIA COMMUNITY HOSPITAL
301 N.W.2d 156 (Wis. 1981)

COFFEY, Justice.
. . . This action arose out of a surgical procedure performed at Misericordia by Dr. Salinsky on July 11, 1975, in which he unsuccessfully attempted to remove a pin fragment from Johnson's right hip. During the course of this surgery, the plaintiff's common femoral nerve and artery were damaged causing a permanent paralytic condition of his right thigh muscles with resultant atrophy and weakness and loss of function. . . .

[T]he jury found that Salinsky was negligent with respect to the medical care and treatment he afforded the plaintiff and attributed 20 percent of the causal negligence to him and 80 percent to the hospital. . . . [T]he only facts material to this review are those connected with Misericordia Hospital in appointing Dr. Salinsky to the medical staff with orthopedic privileges.

The record establishes that Misericordia was formerly . . . a nursing home known as Downtown Nursing Home, Inc. Subsequently, . . . all of the nursing home services were discontinued and the name "Misericordia Community Hospital" was adopted. The hospital known as Misericordia Community Hospital was not and has not been accredited by the Joint Commission on Accreditation of Hospitals. . . .

Dr. Salinsky applied for orthopedic privileges on the medical staff. In his application, Salinsky stated that . . . his privileges at other hospitals had never "been suspended, diminished, revoked, or not renewed." In another part of the application form, he failed to answer any of the questions pertaining to his malpractice insurance. . . .

Mrs. Jane Bekos, Misericordia's medical staff coordinator (appointed April of 1973), testifying from the hospital records, noted that Salinsky's appointment to the medical staff was recommended by the then hospital administrator, David A. Scott, Sr., on June 22, 1973. Salinsky's appointment and requested orthopedic privileges, according to the hospital records, were not marked approved until August 8, 1973. This approval of his appointment was endorsed by Salinsky himself. Such approval would, according to accepted medical administrative procedure, not be signed by the applicant but by the chief of the respective medical section. Additionally, the record establishes that Salinsky was elevated to the position of Chief of Staff shortly after he joined the medical staff. However, the court record and the hospital records are devoid of any information concerning the procedure utilized by the Misericordia authorities in approving either Salinsky's appointment to the staff with orthopedic privileges, or his elevation to the position of Chief of Staff.

Mrs. Bekos, testified that . . . she failed to contact any of the references in Salinsky's case. . . . Further, Mrs. Bekos stated that an examination of the Misericordia records reflected that at no time was an investigation made by anyone of any of the statements recited in his application. . . .

Dr. A. Howell, the hospital's medical director, stated that the hospital did not have a functioning credentials committee at this time, and therefore the executive committee . . . assume[d] the responsibility of evaluating and approving applications for medical staff privileges. . . . [T]he minutes of [the June 21st] meeting list Salinsky as an attending member of the defendant's medical staff at the meeting despite the fact that Salinsky's application for staff privileges had neither been recommended for approval, nor approved by the committee as of this date. . . .

At trial, the representatives of two Milwaukee hospitals, . . . gave testimony concerning the accepted procedure for evaluating applicants for medical staff privileges. Briefly, they stated that the hospital's governing body, i.e., the board of directors or board of trustees, has the ultimate responsibility in granting or denying staff privileges. However, the governing board delegates the responsibility of evaluating the professional qualifications of an applicant for clinical privileges to the medical staff. The credentials committee (or committee of the whole) conducts an investigation of the applying physician's or surgeon's education, training, health, ethics and experience through contacts with his peers in the specialty in which he is seeking privileges, as well as the references listed in his application to determine the veracity of his statements and to solicit comments dealing with the applicant's credentials. Once the credentials committee (or committee of the whole) has conducted their investigation and reviewed all of the information bearing on the applicant's qualifications, it relays its judgment to the governing body, which, as noted, has the final appointing authority.

The record demonstrates that had the executive committee of Misericordia, in the absence of a current credentials committee, adhered to the standard and accepted practice of investigating a medical staff applicant's qualifications and thus examined Salinsky's degree, postgraduate training, and contacted the hospitals referred to in his application, it would have found, contrary to his representations, that he had in fact experienced denial and restriction of his privileges, as well as never having been granted privileges at the very same hospitals he listed in his application. This information was readily available to Misericordia, and a review of Salinsky's associations with various Milwaukee orthopedic surgeons and hospital personnel would have revealed that they considered Salinsky's competence as an orthopedic surgeon suspect, and viewed it with a great deal of concern. . . .

[W]e hold that a hospital has a duty to exercise due care in the selection of its medical staff. . . . [O]ur holding is supported by the decisions of a number of courts from other jurisdictions. See . . . Annot., 51 A.L.R.3d 981 (1973). These cases hold that a hospital has a direct and independent responsibility to its patients, over and above that of the physicians and surgeons practicing therein, to take reasonable steps to (1) insure that its medical staff is qualified for the privileges granted and/or (2) to evaluate the care provided. . . .

The resolution of the issue of whether the hospital was negligent in granting Salinsky orthopedic surgical privileges and appointing him to its medical staff depends on whether Misericordia exercised that degree of care and skill as the average hospital exercises in selecting its medical staff. Applying this standard to the facts of this case, Johnson was only required to show that the defendant did not exercise reasonable care (that degree of care ordinarily exercised by the average hospital) to determine whether Salinsky was competent. . . . Therefore, the trial court's instruction that the hospital was required to exercise reasonable care in the granting of medical staff privileges and that reasonable care "meant that degree of care, skill and judgment usually exercised under like or similar circumstances by the average hospital," was proper.

Turning to the plaintiff's proof requirements, since the procedures ordinarily employed by hospitals in evaluating applications for staff privileges are not within the realm of the ordinary experience of mankind, we agree with the ruling of the appellate court that expert testimony was required to prove the same. . . .

There was credible evidence to the effect that a hospital, exercising ordinary care, would not have appointed Salinsky to its medical staff. Mr. Harden, administrator for Family Hospital, testified a hospital governing board with knowledge that an applicant for medical staff privileges had his orthopedic surgical privileges revoked at one hospital, on the recommendation of a panel of three orthopedic surgeons, and that his orthopedic privileges at another hospital were confined to simple operative procedures, would not, on the basis of this information, have granted him surgical privileges in that specialty. Dr. Sam Neeseman stated that a hospital's credentials committee, with knowledge of such events would not, in the exercise of ordinary care, have approved the applicant's request for orthopedic privileges. . . . Thus, the jury's finding of negligence on the part of Misericordia must be upheld as the testimony of Mr. Harden and Dr. Neeseman constituted credible evidence which reasonably supports this finding. . . .

[A]lthough [a hospital] must rely on the medical staff and in particular the credentials committee (or committee of the whole) to investigate and evaluate an applicant's qualifications for the requested privileges, . . . this delegation of the responsibility to investigate and evaluate the professional competence of applicants for clinical privileges does not relieve the governing body of its duty to appoint only qualified physicians and surgeons to its medical staff and periodically monitor and review their competency. . . . The facts of this case demonstrate that a hospital should, at a minimum, require completion of the application and verify the accuracy of the applicant's statements, especially in regard to his medical education, training and experience. Additionally, it should: (1) solicit information from the applicant's peers, including those not referenced in his application, who are knowledgeable about his education, training, experience, health, competence and ethical character; (2) determine if the applicant is currently licensed to practice in this state and if his licensure or registration has been or is currently being challenged; and (3) inquire whether the applicant has been involved in any adverse malpractice action and whether he has experienced a loss of medical organization membership or medical privileges or membership at any other hospital. The investigating committee must also evaluate the information gained through its inquiries and make a reasonable judgment as to the approval or denial of each application for staff privileges. The hospital will be charged with gaining and evaluating the knowledge that would have been acquired had it exercised ordinary care in investigating its medical staff applicants. . . . This is not to say that hospitals are insurers of the competence of their medical staff, for a hospital will not be negligent if it exercises the noted standard of care in selecting its staff.

Notes: Hospitals' Direct Liability; Risk Management Programs

1. *Direct vs. Vicarious Liability. Darling* is undoubtedly the most significant hospital liability case over the past 50 years. It is frequently referred to as a landmark decision in the field of hospital liability because it placed at least some degree of direct responsibility on the hospital for the maintenance of an acceptable standard of care of patients. Direct or "corporate" liability contrasts with vicarious liability in that it imposes on hospitals a duty of care owed directly to patients with respect to medical judgment. Conventional forms of direct liability entail primarily administrative, not medical, functions such as maintaining safe premises, sterile equipment, and adequate rules and regulations. *Darling* is recognized as extending direct corporate liability to substandard medical care rendered by independent doctors. Hospitals thus can be found liable for some act of negligence on their part with respect to patient care decisions made by independent doctors; vicarious liability, on the other hand, attaches regardless of the degree of hospital care but only when doctors are actual or apparent agents.

2. Darling's *Progeny.* Consider whether the *Darling* court actually intended to announce a new theory of liability. How else could the case have been reasoned, using principles from the previous case and notes? Commentators have observed that *Darling* achieved its status largely by virtue of the importance that academic commentators and subsequent decisions attached to it, and the vocal reaction of hospitals and physicians. The leading commentator was health law professor Arthur Southwick, in The Hospital's New Responsibility, 17 Clev.-Marshall L. Rev. 146 (1968); and The Hospital as an Institution—Expanding Responsibilities Change Its Relationship with the Staff Physician, 9 Cal. W. L. Rev. 429 (1973). For additional commentary, see T. Hardy, When Doctrines Collide: Corporate Negligence and Respondeat Superior When Hospital Employees Fail to Speak Up, 61 Tul. L. Rev. 85 (1986); Comment, The Emerging Trend of Corporate Liability: Courts' Uneven Treatment of Hospital Standards Leaves Hospitals Uncertain and Exposed, 47 Vand. L. Rev. 535 (1994). See generally Annot., 62 A. L.R.4th 692 (1988).

3. *Enterprise Liability and the Balance of Power.* What reaction to *Darling* would you expect from the medical profession and the hospital industry? Surprisingly, *Darling* was openly embraced by hospitals but vehemently attacked by physicians. It greatly influenced the standards of the Joint Commission and virtually became the official philosophy of the American Hospital Association. The AMA's reaction to the *Darling* decision was immediate and negative. In considering why this would be so, consider what *Darling* signals about the power relationship between hospitals and physicians. Would it be fair to impose hospital responsibility for

patient care without allowing hospital authority? In its comment on the case in 12 Citation 82 (1965), the AMA said, "The effect of this decision is unfortunate since it appears to place a hospital in a position where it must exercise control over the practice of medicine by physicians on its attending staff in order to avoid liability. This is apt to encourage control of the practice of medicine by persons who are not licensed physicians."

A similar reaction occurred in 1993 when the Clinton health care reform task force aired an idea for medical malpractice reform known as exclusive enterprise liability. As discussed at pages 495 and 523, exclusive enterprise liability would change existing law in two ways: (1) it would hold hospitals and HMOs vicariously liable for all negligent injuries caused by any member physician, regardless of status or contractual relationship with the institution; and (2) the institution would be solely liable, letting doctors entirely off the hook. Surprisingly, the hospital industry was interested in this idea but the AMA vehemently opposed it, causing the Clinton administration to quickly back away. Even though the AMA was clamoring for relief from medical malpractice, it viewed this proposal for abolishing physician liability as a Trojan Horse because of its implications for the relative power balance between doctors and medical institutions. See Frances Miller, Malpractice Liability and Physician Autonomy, 342 Lancet 973 (1993); Robert A. Berenson, Do Physicians Recognize Their Own Best Interests?, 13(2) Health Aff. 185 (1994).

Despite this hostility, some HMOs, most teaching hospitals, and virtually all government hospitals implement a de facto form of exclusive enterprise liability in which the institution pays for the physicians' malpractice insurance (usually as part of its own self-insured retention fund), defends all suits, and pays all judgments for claims arising from treatment at the institution. See generally Kenneth Abraham & Paul Weiler, Enterprise Liability and the Evolution of the American Health Care System, 108 Harv. L. Rev. 381 (1994); Frank Sloan & Lindsey M. Chepke, Ill-Suited? Medical Malpractice at a Crossroads (2008).

4. *Duty to Supervise and Nursing Negligence. Darling* and its progeny identify two forms of hospital negligence with respect to physicians: negligent selection and retention, and negligent supervision. The first of these, which is developed in Johnson v. Misericordia Community Hospital, is much less controversial. Observe that it was recognized in passing even in *Schloendorff*, supra. It entails reviewing physicians' competency and performance history before admission to the medical staff and periodically (typically every two years) thereafter.

The duty to supervise, in contrast, assumes *contemporaneous* supervision of daily treatment decisions *as they are made*. Several subsequent decisions have alluded to this duty of contemporaneous supervision, but few have squarely imposed it, distinct from the duty of care in selection and retention. Indeed, subsequent decisions in Illinois have expressly disavowed any such duty arising from *Darling*. See Pickle v. Curns, 435 N.E.2d 877 (Ill. App. Ct. 1982). Courts have reasoned that it would constitute bad medical practice and unlawful interference with the physician-patient relationship for lay administrators to actively review treatment decisions. See, e.g., Gafner v. Down East Community Hospital, 735 A.2d 969 (Me. 1999); Albain v. Flower Hospital, 553 N.E.2d 1038 (Ohio 1990).

Other courts, however, have rather explicitly imposed such a duty, at least in dictum. See, e.g., Thompson v. Nason Hospital, 591 A.2d 703 (Pa. 1991). Usually, these are cases of gross negligence in which the departure from medical standards is so blatant that it is possible to attribute to hospital administrators constructive knowledge of the error in progress. One route for attributing this knowledge is through nurses, under the logic that, at some point, nurses should object to or call to a superviser's attention treatment that is going extremely badly. Because nurses are hospital employees, this theory essentially holds hospitals vicariously liable for nurses' failure to speak up or intervene. See Strubhart v. Perry Memorial Hospital, 903 P.2d 263 (Okla. 1995); T. Hardy, supra, 61 Tul. L. Rev. 86 (1986) (the test under *Darling* should be "whether in a given situation a reasonable, prudent nurse would have spoken up about a physician's negligence"). Is this explanation consistent with the facts in *Darling*? Is it consistent with the practical realities of the doctor-nurse relationship? Recall Justice Cardozo's treatment of this very same theory of liability in *Schloendorff* supra.

5. *Risk Management.*

The newly created role in hospitals of "risk manager" marks the official recognition of a role that has become central to the way hospitals are run. Their role is clearly defined . . . "to avoid or minimize potential legal, and hence, financial loss for the health care provider." Although they may fulfill several different administrative functions, . . . I contend that current risk management practices in hospitals have risen to a pitch of near hysteria. They embody actions that are unprecedented in their intrusiveness into the doctor-patient relationship and are unethical in violating the rights of patients. . . . The typical responses of risk managers are wildly overactive. If people in ordinary life were to act in accordance with the minuscule probabilities on which risk management bases its decisions, we would all be in a constant state of paralysis. . . . Hospital administrators have refused to permit competent adult patients to reject burdensome treatment even when physicians concur with the patient's wish. It is not uncommon for administrators to request that a court order be obtained whenever there is a shred of doubt (which almost always exists) about what the law says. Where it was once physicians who overtreated patients because they believed it was their moral obligation to continue therapy, it is now hospital administrators and risk managers who more often insist on overtreatment out of fear of medical-legal liability. It is not a great exaggeration to view risk managers as enemies of patients. . . .

Who are these risk managers, and what is the origin of their role in the hospital? Some risk managers have law degrees, but most do not. Some are nurses who rose to the rank of supervisor and then moved into hospital administration, often after obtaining a master's degree. Others come from the ranks of hospital administrators, some with a degree in hospital or business administration. More rare are individuals with an advanced degree in a field such as sociology, and still others made their career in health planning or administration and were around long before the occupation of risk manager was invented. Large medical centers typically have an office of risk management in addition to in-house counsel. The staff of lawyers works together with risk management both in devising hospital policies that affect patients and in dealing with individual cases in which anyone suspects that there may be a risk of some sort.

The overall movement can be traced back to the late 1960s and early 1970s, when efforts were begun in industrial and other workplaces to reduce the costs of liability payments by underwriters and insurance companies. The trend widened, and in the 1980s risk management offices began to be established in hospitals . . .

to deal with concerns about possible liability arising out of incident reports in the hospital: a patient falling out of bed, a visitor slipping in a puddle of water in the corridor, an inadvertent injury to a patient in the course of treatment. . . . The original worries about legal liability have now expanded to encompass everything that might place the hospital in a bad light. Risk managers are now charged with the task of minimizing risks other than those of liability. They look out for the projected risks of bad publicity, the actions of a disgruntled employee, or the possible political ramifications of a medical decision or hospital policy. . . . Even when the patient has no family, and there is no one around who would sue the hospital, risk management is brought into the case. One of the peculiar features of this situation is the nearly automatic response by many physicians to call risk management whenever the slightest uncertainty is voiced about an ethical matter or vaguely perceived to have legal implications. . . . Ruth Macklin, Enemies of Patients (1993).

Does this account confirm the fears of the AMA about the consequences for physicians of exposing hospitals to liability?

Hospitals are now required to have risk management programs by Joint Commission accreditation standards, and, in a few states, by hospital licensing laws. Risk management programs are now common also in nursing homes and HMOs. On their structure and content generally, see American Society for Healthcare Risk Management, Risk Management Handbook for Health Care Facilities (1990); B. Youngberg, Essentials of Hospital Risk Management (1990).

6. *Informed Consent Liability.* One form of physician supervision for which courts have been especially reluctant to impose hospital liability is the duty to obtain informed consent. One might suppose that it easily falls within the hospital's administrative functions to ensure that patients have signed the proper paperwork before major operations are conducted, especially since nurses usually have a central role in obtaining informed consent. Most courts, however, hold that informed consent is solely the responsibility of the physician because the delicate considerations of what exactly to tell the patient and when are matters "particularly calling for the exercise of medical judgment." Valles v. Albert Einstein Medical Center, 805 A.2d 1232 (Pa. 2002) (no liability even for employed physician because "a medical facility cannot maintain control over this aspect of the physician-patient relationship"). For a critique, see Robert Gatter, The Mysterious Survival of the Policy Against Informed Consent Liability for Hospitals, 81 Notre Dame L. Rev. 1203 (2006); Note, 1 Ind. Health L. Rev. 253 (2004).

7. *Self-Imposed Standards.* The hospital licensing regulations, accreditation standards, and hospital bylaws referred to in the *Darling* opinion contained statements such as the following:

[Regulations]

The [hospital] board [of directors] shall be responsible for the maintenance of proper standards of professional work in the hospital and shall require that the medical staff function in conformity with reasonable standards of competency. . . .

[Accreditation Standards]

Maintaining high standards of medical care will depend upon the character of the [medical] staff and the effectiveness of its organization to carry out the following duties: 1. Selection of those recommended for staff appointments and hospital privileges. 2. Constant analysis and review of the clinical work done in the hospital. . . . It is the duty of the hospital [medical] staff through its chiefs of service and Executive Committee to see that members of the staff do not fail in the matter of calling consultants as needed.

[Medical Staff Bylaws]

The purpose of this organization shall be to insure that all patients admitted to the hospital or treated in the outpatient department receive the best possible care.

Another important aspect of the court's holding is that standards such as these, to which the hospital subscribed or was bound, can be introduced as evidence, but not conclusive proof, of the customary standard of administrative care that prevails in the hospital industry. See also the discussion at page 351 of practice guidelines and other written standards used to establish the medical standard of care against physicians. Is the effect of these standards to make a hospital strictly liable for any mistakes that doctors make? How would you revise these standards in order to perform their intended function in these various legal documents while at the same time moderating their liability effect?

8. *Hospital Custom.* Most courts hold hospitals to a national standard of care in selecting medical staff members. Would a similar locality standard be more appropriate? Consider the history and accreditation status of Misericordia Community Hospital, which was a very small hospital with relatively few medical staff. Under the national standard, are these factors relevant to the "like or similar circumstances" qualifier? See Note, Johnson v. Misericordia Community Hospital: Corporate Liability of Hospitals Arrives in Wisconsin, 1983 Wis. L. Rev. 453 (arguing that the *Misericordia* standards are too demanding for some hospitals). Observe, though, that the duty to fully investigate physicians' credentials is greatly eased now that hospitals can obtain records of past malpractice lawsuits and disciplinary actions by other hospitals from the National Practitioner Data Bank, described at page 453.

Hospital negligence cases are not as dependent on expert witnesses as are physician negligence cases, despite the *Johnson* court's holding on this point. Once the issue of physician negligence is established, issues of administrative care and proper oversight are subject to the "reasonable person" standard. Other courts sometimes hold that these issues are subject to commonsense understanding. If you were on a jury, would you consider a hospital negligent if it approved a physician who had been sued for malpractice three times in the past five years? If he had lost or settled two of the three suits for substantial amounts? Empirical studies show that physicians who have lost even small claims against them are more likely to pay on a malpractice claim in the near future, but these odds are increased only by 3 percent. See L. Smarr, Malpractice Claims: Does the Past Predict the Future?, 272 JAMA 1453 (1994).

9. *Medical Staff Committees.* Observe the brief discussion at the end of *Johnson* concerning the legal effect of the hospital's delegating the task of medical staff credentialing to members and committees of the medical staff. Recall that medical staff members are, generally speaking, not agents of the hospital. Therefore, could a hospital not claim in a typical case, where it merely follows the medical staff's recommendation, that it is not responsible for their sloppiness or poor judgment? Assume the hospital board has no way to know that the medical staff did a poor job or made a bad decision. This defense does not work for two reasons: (1) Although medical staff members are independent contractors in their medical status as practicing doctors, they are agents of the hospital in their administrative status while sitting on medical staff committees. Therefore, ordinary respondeat superior applies to their committee mistakes. (2) The duty to screen medical staff members is considered nondelegable. See Joiner v. Gonzales, 186 S.E.2d 307 (Ga. Ct. App. 1971).

Distributing liability in the opposite direction, would it be possible to hold medical staff members individually liable for doing a poor job in evaluating an applicant? Alternatively, could the medical staff be held liable as an entity? One court has answered "yes," holding that the medical staff can be sued as an unincorporated association, in which case, if one member were found negligent, all 141 could be held jointly and severally responsible. Corleto v. Shore Memorial Hospital, 350 A.2d 534 (N.J. Super. 1974). In practice, physicians are not individually exposed since hospitals usually assume responsibility for liability arising from medical staff review activities. See generally; W. Isele, The Hospital Medical Staff: Its Legal Rights and Responsibilities (1984); J. Horty & D. Mulholland, The Legal Status of the Hospital Medical Staff, 22 St. Louis U. L.J. 485 (1978).

10. *Puzzles to Ponder.* In *Johnson,* the jury found Dr. Salinsky negligent. Is this necessary to hold the hospital liable for its own negligence? If a hospital negligently admits a bad doctor to the medical staff, shouldn't it be liable for any injury the doctor causes, under the notion that the hospital's negligence is distinct from the doctor's? This question seems to never have been addressed directly by the courts. Uniformly, they find hospital negligence only where the doctor is also negligent. The best explanation for this limitation is one of proximate cause. A hospital's negligent screening of a physician is not sufficiently proximate to a patient's injury, even if it literally causes the injury, unless the injury results from the physician's own negligence as well.

Another doctrinal puzzle is whether hospitals who negligently credential a physician are liable to patients who are injured off premises in the doctor's private office. Although standard foreseeability and but-for causation tests would appear to be met, most courts hold that hospitals are liable only for injuries to hospital patients, even where the plaintiff can prove she relied on the hospital credentials in selecting the doctor. Again, the notion appears to be one of proximate cause, influenced by older notions of privity of contract. See Insinga v. LaBella, 543 So. 2d 209 (Fla. 1989) (no hospital liability for giving admitting privileges to a person masquerading as a physician, where injury occurred outside hospital); Pedroza v. Bryant, 677 P.2d 166 (Wash. 1984) (no hospital liability for negligence in prenatal care even though plaintiff had delivered her seven previous children at that hospital and she died at the hospital). But see Copithorne v. Framingham Union

Hospital, 520 N.E.2d 139 (Mass. 1988) (hospital duty extends to medical staff member who drugged and raped patient in her home). Should it make any difference if the doctor practices in a hospital-owned and leased medical office building right next door? What if the hospital owns an HMO which the doctor and patient belong to?

11. Other important sources of hospital liability are surveyed at Chapters 2.A and 3.B. Of particular importance is the federal Emergency Medical Treatment and Labor Act (EMTALA), which creates a form of strict liability for hospitals that refuse to treat patients who are in labor or in a serious emergency condition. Much of the litigation under EMTALA has addressed whether it essentially federalizes malpractice actions arising out of the emergency room (or potentially anywhere in the hospital). For the most part, courts have said "no," holding that the statute was intended to apply only to purposefully refusing standard care, not to errors in judgment or skill in carrying out treatment. See p. 127.

2. Managed Care Liability

We turn now to a new form of institution, one that combines medical delivery with medical financing. When confronted with HMOs' institutional liability, courts quickly applied the same structure of analysis that had developed for hospitals. Because HMOs differ in important respects from hospitals, however, the result of this analysis may not be the same. In the following materials, consider how different types of managed care entities and arrangements should be treated under the various theories and branches of no liability, vicarious liability, and direct liability.

■ BOYD v. ALBERT EINSTEIN MEDICAL CENTER
547 A.2d 1229 (Pa. Super. Ct. 1988)

OLSZEWSKI, Judge:

This is an appeal from the trial court's order granting summary judgment in favor of defendant/appellee, Health Maintenance Organization of Pennsylvania (hereinafter HMO). Appellant asserts that the trial court erred in granting the motion for summary judgment when there existed a question of material fact as to whether participating physicians are the ostensible agents of HMO. For the reasons stated below, we reverse the grant of summary judgment.

The facts, as averred by the parties in their pleadings and elicited through deposition testimony, reveal that at the time of her death, decedent and her husband were participants in the HMO. HMO is a medical insurance provider that offers an alternative to the traditional Blue Cross/Blue Shield insurance plan.[1] Decedent's husband became eligible for participation in a group plan provided by

---

[1] A Health Maintenance Organization is an organized system of health care which provides or arranges for a comprehensive array of basic and supplemental health care services. These services are provided on a prepaid basis to voluntarily enrolled members living within a prescribed geographic area. Responsibility for the delivery, quality and payment of health care falls to the managing organization—the HMO.

HMO through his employer. Upon electing to participate in this plan, decedent and her husband were provided with a directory and benefits brochure which listed the participating physicians. Restricted to selecting a physician from this list, decedent chose Doctor David Rosenthal and Doctor Perry Dornstein as her primary care physicians.

In June of 1982, decedent contacted Doctor David Rosenthal regarding a lump in her breast. Doctor Rosenthal ordered a mammogram to be performed which revealed a suspicious area in the breast. Doctor Rosenthal recommended that decedent undergo a biopsy and referred decedent to Doctor Erwin Cohen for that purpose. Doctor Cohen, a surgeon, is also a participating HMO physician. The referral to a specialist in this case was made in accordance with the terms and conditions of HMO's subscription agreement.[2]

On July 6, 1982, Doctor Cohen performed a biopsy of decedent's breast tissue at Albert Einstein Medical Center. During the procedure, Doctor Cohen perforated decedent's chest wall with the biopsy needle, causing decedent to sustain a left hemothorax. Decedent was hospitalized for treatment of the hemothorax at Albert Einstein Hospital for two days.

In the weeks following this incident decedent complained to her primary care physicians, Doctor David Rosenthal and Doctor Perry Dornstein, of pain in her chest wall, belching, hiccoughs, and fatigue. On August 19, 1982, decedent awoke with pain in the middle of her chest. Decedent's husband contacted her primary care physicians, Doctors Rosenthal and Dornstein, and was advised to take decedent to Albert Einstein Hospital where she would be examined by Doctor Rosenthal. Upon arrival at Albert Einstein emergency room, decedent related symptoms of chest wall pain, vomiting, stomach and back discomfort to Doctor Rosenthal. Doctor Rosenthal commenced an examination of decedent, diagnosed Tietze's syndrome,[3] and arranged for tests to be performed at his office where decedent underwent X-rays, EKG, and cardiac ioenzyme tests.[4] Decedent was then sent home and told to rest.[5]

During the course of that afternoon, decedent continued to experience chest pain, vomiting and belching. Decedent related the persistence and worsening of these symptoms by telephone to Doctors Rosenthal and Dornstein, who prescribed, without further examination, Talwin, a pain medication. At 5:30 that afternoon decedent was discovered dead in her bathroom by her husband, having expired as a result of a myocardial infarction.

---

[2] Doctor Rosenthal admitted in his deposition that HMO limited specifically the doctors to whom decedent could have been referred.

[3] Tietze's Syndrome is an inflammatory condition affecting the costochondral cartilage. It occurs more commonly in females, generally in the 30 to 50 range.

[4] HMO avers that decedent was returned to the doctor's office for testing because it was more comfortable and convenient for her. Appellant, however, asserts that the tests were performed in the doctor's office, rather than the hospital, in accordance with the requirements of HMO whose primary interest was in keeping the medical fees within the corporation.

[5] Appellant contends that Doctor Rosenthal acted negligently in ordering the tests to be performed in his office when decedent exhibited symptoms of cardiac distress. The safer practice, avers appellant, would have been to perform the tests at the hospital where the results would have been more quickly available. Appellant further contends that, despite Doctor Rosenthal's diagnosis of Tietze's Syndrome, the nature of the tests he ordered indicates that he was concerned about the possibility of a heart attack.

Appellant's complaint and new matter aver that HMO advertised that its physicians and medical care providers were competent, and that they had been evaluated for periods of up to six months prior to being selected to participate in the HMO program as a medical provider. The complaint further avers that decedent and appellant relied on these representations in choosing their primary care physicians. The complaint then avers that HMO was negligent in failing to

> qualify or oversee its physicians and hospital who acted as its agents, servants, or employees in providing medical care to the decedent nor did HMO of Pa. require its physicians, surgeons and hospitals to provide adequate evidence of skill, training and competence in medicine and it thereby failed to furnish the decedent with competent, qualified medical care as warranted.

Finally, appellant's new matter avers that HMO furnished to its subscribers documents which identify HMO as the care provider and state that HMO guarantees the quality of care.

Appellant's theory of recovery before the trial court was primarily one of vicarious liability under the ostensible agency theory. See Capan v. Divine Providence Hospital, 287 Pa. Super. 364, 430 A.2d 647 (1980). In granting defendant HMO's motion for summary judgment, the trial court found that plaintiff/appellant had failed to establish either of the two factors on which the theory of ostensible agency, as applied to hospitals in *Capan*, is based. On appeal, appellant contends that the evidence indicates that there exists a question of fact regarding whether HMO may be held liable under this theory. . . .

The group master contract provides that HMO "operates a comprehensive prepaid program of health care which provides health care services and benefits to Members in order to protect and promote their health, and preserve and enhance patient dignity." HMO was incorporated in 1975 under the laws of Pennsylvania and converted from a nonprofit to a for-profit corporation in 1981. HMO is based on the individual practice association model (hereinafter IPA), which means that HMO is comprised of participating primary physicians who are engaged in part in private practice in the HMO service area. Under the plan, IPA contracts with HMO to provide medical services to HMO members. IPA selects its primary and specialist physicians and enters into an agreement with them obligating the physician to perform health services for the subscribers of HMO.

The primary physician's role is defined as the "gatekeeper into the health care delivery system." "An HMO member must consult with his primary physician before going to a specialist and/or the hospital." If the primary physician deems it necessary, he arranges a consultation with an HMO participating specialist, which constitutes a second opinion. "Basically, with the primary physicians 'screening' the members' illnesses, excessive hospitalization and improper use of specialists can be reduced."

Member-patients use a physician directory and choose a conveniently located office of a participating primary physician. HMO members will only receive reimbursement from nonparticipating providers when the condition requiring treatment was of an immediate nature. Determinations of immediacy are made by the HMO quality assurance committee. In any event, persons desiring emergency nonprovider benefits must notify HMO or their primary physician of the emergency within 48 hours and must give written proof of the occurrence within ninety days after service is rendered. . . .

Primary physicians are paid through a mechanism termed "capitation." Capitation is an actuarially determined amount prepaid by HMO to the primary physician for each patient who has chosen his office. The dollar amount is based upon a predetermined rate per age group. The primary physicians are paid 80 percent of the capitation amount and the remaining 20 percent is pooled by IPA and goes back into a pooled risk-sharing fund as a reserve against specialty referral costs and hospital stays. Each primary care office has its own specialist fund and hospital fund established by allocating a predetermined amount each month for each member who has chosen that primary care office. The surplus from the specialist fund is returned to the primary care office. The hospital fund, however, is governed by a hospital risk/incentive-sharing scheme which anticipates a number of inpatient days per members per year. If the actual hospital utilization is less than anticipated, the HMO and IPA each receive 50 percent of the savings. IPA must place the savings in the Special IPA risk-sharing account and must use the funds to offset losses resulting from unanticipated physician costs. If utilization is greater than anticipated, IPA is responsible for 50 percent of the loss up to the amount of uncommitted funds in the Special IPA risk sharing account. . . .

HMO asserts that because the theory of ostensible agency has been applied in Pennsylvania only to the relationship between hospitals and independent contractor physicians, the theory is not appropriate in the instant situation. We emphasize, however, that when this court introduced the concept of ostensible agency to this Commonwealth in *Capan*, supra, we based that decision in large part upon "the changing role of the hospital in society [which] creates a likelihood that patients will look to the institution" for care. Because the role of health care providers has changed in recent years, the *Capan* rationale for applying the theory of ostensible agency to hospitals is certainly applicable in the instant situation. . . .

We find that the facts indicate an issue of material fact as to whether the participating physicians were the ostensible agents of HMO. HMO covenanted that it would "[provide] health care services and benefits to Members in order to protect and promote their health. . . ." "HMOPA operates on a direct service rather than an indemnity basis." Appellant paid his doctor's fee to HMO, not to the physician of his choice. Then, appellant selected his primary care physicians from the list provided by HMO. Regardless of who recommended appellant's decedent to choose her primary care physician, the fact remains that HMO provides a limited list from which a member must choose a primary physician. Moreover, those primary physicians are screened by HMO and must comply with a list of regulations in order to honor their contract with HMO.

Further, as mandated by HMO, appellant's decedent could not see a specialist without the primary physician's referral. As HMO declares, the primary physician is the "gatekeeper into the health care delivery system." "An HMO member must consult with his primary physician before going to a specialist and/or the hospital." Moreover, appellant's decedent had no choice as to which specialist to see. In our opinion, because appellant's decedent was required to follow the mandates of HMO and did not directly seek the attention of the specialist, there is an inference that appellant looked to the institution for care and not solely to the physicians; conversely, that appellant's decedent submitted herself to the care of the participating physicians in response to an invitation from HMO. See comment (a), Restatement (Second) Agency §267. . . .

We conclude, therefore, that the trial court erred when it granted HMO's motion for summary judgment on the ground that the participating physicians were not the ostensible agents of HMO. . . .

McEwen, Judge, concurring.

I concur in the result reached by the majority since the author, after a very careful analysis of the issues presented in this appeal, reaches the quite basic principle that issues of material fact may not be resolved by summary judgment.

I write only because it appears to me that the learned trial court improperly resolved by summary judgment the basic factual issue of whether the literature, in which HMO "guaranteed" and "assured" the quality of care provided to its subscribers, had been distributed to appellant or to other subscribers of HMO.

It might also be mentioned that while the court was understandably uncertain as to the theories upon which plaintiff was proceeding,[1] it appears that the amended complaint of plaintiff does contain factual averments supporting a breach of warranty claim.

■ WICKLINE v. STATE
239 Cal. Rptr. 810 (Cal. Ct. App. 1986)

Rowen, Associate Justice.

[Lois Wickline, who was treated under California's Medicaid program (known as "Medi-Cal"), sued the State, but not her physician, for negligently causing her premature discharge from the hospital, resulting in complications that eventually necessitated amputation of her right leg. Wickline alleged that her premature discharge was the fault of Medi-Cal's erroneous withholding of its authorization for her continued hospitalization.] This is an appeal from a judgment for plaintiff entered after a trial by jury. For the reasons discussed below, we reverse the judgment.

Principally, this matter concerns itself with the legal responsibility that a third party payor, in this case, the State of California, has for harm caused to a patient when a cost containment program is applied in a manner which is alleged to have affected the implementation of the treating physician's medical judgment. . . .

I

Responding to concerns about the escalating cost of health care, public and private payors have in recent years experimented with a variety of cost containment

---

[1] The trial court noted in its opinion that

the gravamen of plaintiff's complaint is that HMO of PA guaranteed or warranted the quality of care provided. . . . Plaintiff's theory of recovery . . . is not entirely clear. A reading of the complaint suggests Plaintiff is proceeding upon grounds of corporate liability. However, in his answer to the motion of HMO of PA for summary judgment, plaintiff contends HMO of PA is vicariously liable through ostensible agency.

mechanisms. We deal here with one of those programs: The prospective utilization review process.

At the outset, this court recognizes that this case appears to be the first attempt to tie a health care payor into the medical malpractice causation chain and that it, therefore, deals with issues of profound importance to the health care community and to the general public. For those reasons we have permitted the filing of amicus curiae briefs in support of each of the respective parties in the matter to assure that due consideration is given to the broader issues raised before this court by this case. . . .

Early cost containment programs utilized the retrospective utilization review process. In that system the third party payor reviewed the patient's chart after the fact to determine whether the treatment provided was medically necessary. If, in the judgment of the utilization reviewer, it was not, the health care provider's claim for payment was denied.

In the cost containment program in issue in this case, prospective utilization review, authority for the rendering of health care services must be obtained before medical care is rendered. Its purpose is to promote the well recognized public interest in controlling health care costs by reducing unnecessary services while still intending to assure that appropriate medical and hospital services are provided to the patient in need. However, such a cost containment strategy creates new and added pressures on the quality assurance portion of the utilization review mechanism. The stakes, the risks at issue, are much higher when a prospective cost containment review process is utilized than when a retrospective review process is used.

A mistaken conclusion about medical necessity following retrospective review will result in the wrongful withholding of payment. An erroneous decision in a prospective review process, on the other hand, in practical consequences, results in the withholding of necessary care, potentially leading to a patient's permanent disability or death.

II

Though somewhat in dispute, the facts in this case are not particularly complicated. In 1976, Wickline a married woman in her mid-40's, with a limited education, was being treated by Dr. Stanley Z. Daniels (Dr. Daniels), a physician engaged in a general family practice, for problems associated with her back and legs. Failing to respond to the physical therapy type of treatment he prescribed, Dr. Daniels had Wickline admitted to Van Nuys Community Hospital (Van Nuys or Hospital) in October 1976 and brought in another physician, Dr. Gerald E. Polonsky (Dr. Polonsky), a specialist in peripheral vascular surgery, to do a consultation examination. Peripheral vascular surgery concerns itself with surgery on any vessel of the body, exclusive of the heart.

Dr. Polonsky examined plaintiff and diagnosed her condition as arteriosclerosis obliterans with occlusion of the abdominal aorta, more generally referred to as Leriche's Syndrome. . . .

According to Dr. Polonsky, the only treatment for Leriche's Syndrome is surgical. In Wickline's case her disease was so far advanced that Dr. Polonsky concluded that it was necessary to remove a part of the plaintiff's artery and insert a synthetic (Teflon) graft in its place.

After agreeing to the operation, Wickline was discharged home to await approval of her doctor's diagnosis and authorization from Medi-Cal for the recommended surgical procedure and attendant acute care hospitalization. It is conceded that at all times in issue in this case, the plaintiff was eligible for medical benefits under California's medical assistance program, the "Medi-Cal Act," which is more commonly referred to as Medi-Cal. (Welf. & Inst. Code, §§14000 et seq., 14000.4.)

As required, Dr. Daniels submitted a treatment authorization request to Medi-Cal, sometimes referred to as form "161," "MC-161" or "TAR." In response to Dr. Daniels' request, Medi-Cal authorized the surgical procedure and 10 days of hospitalization for that treatment.

On January 6, 1977, plaintiff was admitted to Van Nuys by Dr. Daniels. On January 7, 1977, Dr. Polonsky performed a surgical procedure in which a part of plaintiff's artery was removed and a synthetic artery was inserted to replace it. Dr. Polonsky characterized that procedure as "a very major surgery."

Later that same day Dr. Polonsky was notified that Wickline was experiencing circulatory problems in her right leg. He concluded that a clot had formed in the graft. As a result, Wickline was taken back into surgery, the incision in her right groin was reopened, the clot removed and the graft was resewn. Wickline's recovery subsequent to the two January 7th operations [was] characterized as "stormy." She had a lot of pain, some spasm in the vessels in the lower leg and she experienced hallucinating episodes. On January 12, 1977, Wickline was returned to the operating room where Dr. Polonsky performed a lumbar sympathectomy.

A lumbar sympathectomy is a major operation in which a section of the chain of nerves that lie on each side of the spinal column is removed. The procedure causes the blood vessels in the patient's lower extremity to become paralyzed in a wide open position and was done in an attempt to relieve the spasms which Wickline was experiencing in those vessels. Spasms stop the outflow of blood from the vessels causing the blood to back up into the graft. Failure to relieve such spasms can cause clotting.

Dr. Polonsky was assisted in all three surgeries by Dr. Leonard Kovner (Dr. Kovner), a board certified specialist in the field of general surgery and the chief of surgery at Van Nuys. Dr. Daniels was present for the initial graft surgery on January 7, 1977, and for the right lumbar sympathectomy operation on January 12, 1977.

Wickline was scheduled to be discharged on January 16, 1977, which would mean that she would actually leave the hospital sometime before 1 p.m. on January 17, 1977. On or about January 16, 1977, Dr. Polonsky concluded that "it was medically necessary" that plaintiff remain in the hospital for an additional eight days beyond her then scheduled discharge date. Drs. Kovner and Daniels concurred in Dr. Polonsky's opinion.

Dr. Polonsky cited many reasons for his feeling that it was medically necessary for plaintiff to remain in an acute care hospital for an additional eight days, such as the danger of infection and/or clotting. His principal reason, however, was that he felt that he was going to be able to save both of Wickline's legs and wanted her to remain in the hospital where he could observe her and be immediately available, along with the hospital staff, to treat her if an emergency should occur.

In order to secure an extension of Wickline's hospital stay, it was necessary to complete and present to Medi-Cal a form called "Request for Extension of Stay in Hospital," commonly referred to as an "MC-180" or "180." . . .

At Van Nuys, Patricia N. Spears (Spears), an employee of the hospital and a registered nurse, had the responsibility for completing 180 forms. In this case, as requested by Dr. Polonsky, Spears filled out Wickline's 180 form and then presented it to Dr. Daniels, as plaintiff's attending physician, to sign, which he did, in compliance with Dr. Polonsky's recommendation. All of the physicians who testified agreed that the 180 form prepared by Spears was complete, accurate and adequate for all purposes in issue in this matter.

Doris A. Futerman (Futerman), a registered nurse, was, at that time, employed by Medi-Cal as a Health Care Service Nurse, commonly referred to as an "on-site nurse." . . .

Futerman, after reviewing Wickline's 180 form, felt that she could not approve the requested eight-day extension of acute care hospitalization. While conceding that the information provided might justify some additional time beyond the scheduled discharge date, nothing in Wickline's case, in Futerman's opinion, would have warranted the entire eight additional days requested and, for those reasons, she telephoned the Medi-Cal Consultant. She reached Dr. William S. Glassman (Dr. Glassman), one of the Medi-Cal Consultants on duty at the time in Medi-Cal's Los Angeles office. The Medi-Cal Consultant selection occurred randomly. As was the practice, whichever Medi-Cal Consultant was available at the moment took the next call that came into the office. . . .

After speaking with Futerman on the telephone, Dr. Glassman rejected Wickline's treating physician's request for an eight-day hospital extension and, instead, authorized an additional four days of hospital stay beyond the originally scheduled discharge date. . . .

After review of Wickline's 180 form, Dr. Glassman testified that the factors that led him to authorize four days, rather than the requested eight days, was that there was no information about the patient's temperature which he, thereupon, assumed was normal; nothing was mentioned about the patient's diet, which he then presumed was not a problem; nor was there any information about Wickline's bowel function, which Dr. Glassman then presumed was functioning satisfactorily. Further, the fact that the 180 form noted that Wickline was able to ambulate with help and that whirlpool treatments were to begin that day caused Dr. Glassman to presume that the patient was progressing satisfactorily and was not seriously or critically ill. . . .

In essence, respondent argues, Dr. Glassman based his decision on signs and symptoms such as temperature, diet and bowel movements, which were basically irrelevant to the plaintiff's circulatory condition for which she was being treated and did not concern himself with those symptoms and signs which an ordinary prudent physician would consider to be pertinent with regard to the type of medical condition presented by Wickline.

Complying with the limited extension of time authorized by Medi-Cal, Wickline was discharged from Van Nuys on January 21, 1977. Drs. Polonsky and Daniels each wrote discharge orders. At the time of her discharge, each of plaintiff's three treating physicians were aware that the Medi-Cal Consultant had approved only four of the requested eight-day hospital stay extension. While all three doctors were aware that they could attempt to obtain a further extension of Wickline's hospital stay by telephoning the Medi-Cal Consultant to request such an extension, none of them did so. . . .

At trial, Dr. Polonsky testified that in the time that had passed since the first extension request had been communicated to Medi-Cal, on January 16th or 17th, and the time of her scheduled discharge on January 21, 1977, Wickline's condition had neither deteriorated nor become critical. In Dr. Polonsky's opinion no new symptom had presented itself and no additional factors had occurred since the original request was made to have formed the basis for a change in the Medi-Cal Consultant's attitude regarding Wickline's situation. In addition, he stated that at the time of Wickline's discharge it did not appear that her leg was in any danger.

Dr. Polonsky testified that at the time in issue he felt that Medi-Cal Consultants had the state's interest more in mind than the patient's welfare and that that belief influenced his decision not to request a second extension of Wickline's hospital stay. In addition, he felt that Medi-Cal had the power to tell him, as a treating doctor, when a patient must be discharged from the hospital. Therefore, while still of the subjective, noncommunicated, opinion that Wickline was seriously ill and that the danger to her was not over, Dr. Polonsky discharged her from the hospital on January 21, 1977. He testified that had Wickline's condition, in his medical judgment, been critical or in a deteriorating condition on January 21, he would have made some effort to keep her in the hospital beyond that day even if denied authority by Medi-Cal and even if he had to pay her hospital bill himself. . . .

All of the medical witnesses who testified at trial agreed that Dr. Polonsky was acting within the standards of practice of the medical community in discharging Wickline on January 21, 1977. . . .

Wickline testified that in the first few days after she arrived home she started feeling pain in her right leg and the leg started to lose color. In the next few days the pain got worse and the right leg took on a whitish, statue-like marble appearance. Wickline assumed she was experiencing normal recovery symptoms and did not communicate with any of her physicians. Finally, when "the pain got so great and the color started changing from looking like a statue to getting a grayish color," her husband called Dr. Kovner. It was Wickline's memory that this occurred about the third day after her discharge from the hospital and that Dr. Kovner advised Mr. Wickline to give extra pain medicine to the plaintiff.

Thereafter, gradually over the next few days, the plaintiff's leg "kept getting grayer and then it got bluish." The extra medication allegedly prescribed by Dr. Kovner over the telephone did not relieve the pain Wickline was experiencing. She testified that "by then the pain was just excruciating, where no pain medicine helped whatsoever." Finally, Wickline instructed her husband to call Dr. Kovner again and this time Dr. Kovner ordered plaintiff back into the hospital. Wickline returned to Van Nuys that same evening, January 30, 1977, nine days after her last discharge therefrom. . . .

Attempts to save Wickline's leg through the utilization of anticoagulants, antibiotics, strict bed rest, pain medication and warm water whirlpool baths to the lower extremity proved unsuccessful. On February 8, 1977, Dr. Polonsky amputated Wickline's leg below the knee because had he not done so "she would have died." The condition did not, however, heal after the first operation and on February 17, 1977, the doctors went back and amputated Wickline's leg above the knee. . . .

In Dr. Polonsky's opinion, to a reasonable medical certainty, had Wickline remained in the hospital for the eight additional days, as originally requested by him and her other treating doctors, she would not have suffered the loss of her leg. . . .

Dr. Polonsky testified that in his medical opinion, the Medi-Cal Consultant's rejection of the requested eight-day extension of acute care hospitalization and his authorization of a four-day extension in its place did not conform to the usual medical standards as they existed in 1977. He stated that, in accordance with those standards, a physician would not be permitted to make decisions regarding the care of a patient without either first seeing the patient, reviewing the patient's chart or discussing the patient's condition with her treating physician or physicians.

III

From the facts thus presented, appellant takes the position that it was not negligent as a matter of law. Appellant contends that the decision to discharge was made by each of the plaintiff's three doctors, was based upon the prevailing standards of practice, and was justified by her condition at the time of her discharge. It argues that Medi-Cal had no part in the plaintiff's hospital discharge and therefore was not liable even if the decision to do so was erroneously made by her doctors. . . .

As to the principal issue before this court, i.e., who bears responsibility for allowing a patient to be discharged from the hospital, her treating physicians or the health care payor, each side's medical expert witnesses agreed that, in accordance with the standards of medical practice as it existed in January 1977, it was for the patient's treating physician to decide the course of treatment that was medically necessary to treat the ailment. It was also that physician's responsibility to determine whether or not acute care hospitalization was required and for how long. Finally, it was agreed that the patient's physician is in a better position than the Medi-Cal Consultant to determine the number of days medically necessary for any required hospital care. The decision to discharge is, therefore, the responsibility of the patient's own treating doctor.

Dr. Kaufman testified that if, on January 21, the date of the plaintiff's discharge from Van Nuys, any one of her three treating doctors had decided that in his medical judgment it was necessary to keep Wickline in the hospital for a longer period of time, they, or any of them, should have filed another request for extension of stay in the hospital, that Medi-Cal would expect those physicians to make such a request if they felt it was indicated, and upon receipt of such a request further consideration of an additional extension of hospital time would have been given.

Title 22 of the California Administrative Code §51110, provided, in pertinent part, at the relevant time in issue here, that: "The determination of need for acute care shall be made in accordance with the usual standards of medical practice in the community."

The patient who requires treatment and who is harmed when care which should have been provided is not provided should recover for the injuries suffered from all those responsible for the deprivation of such care, including, when appropriate, health care payors. Third party payors of health care services can be held legally accountable when medically inappropriate decisions result from defects in the design or implementation of cost containment mechanisms as, for example, when appeals made on a patient's behalf for medical or hospital care are arbitrarily ignored or unreasonably disregarded or overridden. However, the physician who complies without protest with the limitations imposed by a third party payor, when his medical judgment dictates otherwise, cannot avoid his ultimate responsibility for his patient's care. He cannot point to the health care payor as the liability scapegoat when the consequences of his own determinative medical decisions go sour.

There is little doubt that Dr. Polonsky was intimidated by the Medi-Cal program but he was not paralyzed by Dr. Glassman's response nor rendered powerless to act appropriately if other action was required under the circumstances. If, in his medical judgment, it was in his patient's best interest that she remain in the acute care hospital setting for an additional four days beyond the extended time period originally authorized by Medi-Cal, Dr. Polansky should have made some effort to keep Wickline there. He himself acknowledged that responsibility to his patient. It was his medical judgment, however, that Wickline could be discharged when she was. All the plaintiff's treating physicians concurred and all the doctors who testified at trial, for either plaintiff or defendant, agreed that Dr. Polonsky's medical decision to discharge Wickline met the standard of care applicable at the time. Medi-Cal was not a party to that medical decision and therefore cannot be held to share in the harm resulting if such decision was negligently made.

In addition thereto, while Medi-Cal played a part in the scenario before us in that it was the resource for the funds to pay for the treatment sought, and its input regarding the nature and length of hospital care to be provided was of paramount importance, Medi-Cal did not override the medical judgment of Wickline's treating physicians at the time of her discharge. It was given no opportunity to do so. Therefore, there can be no viable cause of action against it for the consequences of that discharge decision. . . .

V

This court appreciates that what is at issue here is the effect of cost containment programs upon the professional judgment of physicians to prescribe hospital treatment for patients requiring the same. While we recognize, realistically, that cost consciousness has become a permanent feature of the health care system, it is essential that cost limitation programs not be permitted to corrupt medical judgment. We have concluded, from the facts in issue here, that in this case it did not.

For the reasons expressed herein, this court finds that appellant is not liable for respondent's injuries as a matter of law. That makes unnecessary any discussion of the other contentions of the parties.

Notes: Managed Care Liability

1. *The Components of Managed Care.* Managed care is a term that applies broadly to a wide variety of arrangements that restrict the generosity of traditional

health insurance. Managed care (1) restricts choice of physicians through networks and gatekeepers, (2) alters discrete treatment decisions through utilization review and prior authorization requirements, and (3) creates cost-constrained financial incentives through capitation payments and risk-sharing pools. Each of these components has distinct liability implications and can exist separately from the others. For instance, "managed indemnity" insurance does (2) but not (1) or (3), simply by adding utilization review to traditional insurance. Preferred provider organizations (PPOs) do (1) but not (3), and may do (2) but not necessarily. HMOs are the fullest embodiment of managed care because they incorporate all three components. In analyzing these cases and others that are likely to arise in the future, however, be sure to think individually about each of these components and observe how they might arise in a variety of different institutional forms. For general comprehensive commentary and analysis, see Haavi Morreim, Holding Health Care Accountable (2001); Jennifer Arlen & Wm. MacLeod, Malpractice Liability for Physicians and Managed Care Organizations, 78 NYU L. Rev. 1929 (2003); Gail Agrawal & Mark Hall, What If You *Could* Sue Your HMO? Managed Care Liability beyond the ERISA Shield, 47 St. Louis U. L.J. 235 (2003); B. Furrow, Managed Care Organizations and Patient Injury: Rethinking Liability, 31 Ga. L. Rev. 419 (1997); Clark Havighurst, Vicarious Liability: Relocating Responsibility for the Quality of Medical Care, 26 Am. J. L. Med. 7 (2000); Peter Jacobson & Neena Patil, Managed Care Litigation: Legal Doctrine at the Boundary of Tort and Contract, 57 Med. Care Res. & Rev. 440 (2000); Bryan A. Liang, Patient Injury Incentives in Law, 17 Yale L. & Pol'y Rev. 1 (1998); Gary T. Schwartz, Medical Malpractice, Tort, Contract and Managed Care, 1998 U. Ill. L. Rev. 885; Joanne B. Stern, Bad Faith Suits against HMOs: Finally, a Breakthrough, 20 Whittier L. Rev. 313 (1998).

2. *HMO Immunity.* In a few jurisdictions, HMOs are immune from suit for negligent treatment, in some states by statute and in one state formerly by court decision. Williams v. Good Health Plus, Inc., 743 S.W.2d 373 (Tex. Ct. App. 1987), resonates with hospital decisions early in the century by holding that an HMO logically cannot be held liable because the corporate practice of medicine doctrine prevents it from controlling physicians' treatment decisions. That decision has since been overturned by statute, however. Comment, 30 Tex. Tech. L. Rev. 1227 (1999). Economist Patricia Danzon is one who argues for HMO immunity under the theory that holding physicians individually liable is sufficient, unless the HMO agrees by contract to assume liability. Patricia M. Danzon, Tort Liability: A Minefield for Managed Care, 24 J. Leg. Stud. 491 (1997). See also Richard A. Epstein & Alan O. Sykes, The Assault on Managed Care: Vicarious Liability, Class Actions, and the Patient's Bill of Rights, 30 J. Leg. Stud. 625 (2002). Do you agree?

3. *Vicarious Liability.* There are two basic types of HMOs, with several permutations. The HMO type in *Boyd* was an Independent Practice Association (IPA), which is composed of a large contractual network of physicians who maintain practices in their own offices and see patients with many different types of insurance. For decisions similar to *Boyd*, see Schleier v. Kaiser Foundation Health Plan, 876 F.2d 174 (D.C. Cir. 1989); Villazon v. Prudential Health Care Plan, 843 So. 2d 842 (FL 2003). An agency relationship is much easier to establish with the other type of HMO, a staff or group model, in which a smaller number of

physicians work exclusively for a single HMO in a centralized clinic. What about a PPO (preferred provider organization) or POS (point of service) plan with an open network in which patients are encouraged to stay with the designated physicians but are free to go outside the network and select any doctor they want by paying a higher deductible or copayment? What about a closed network that is very large but has no gatekeeping restrictions, i.e., patients can see anyone they want when they want, but only within the network? See generally Comment, Managed Health Care: HMO Corporate Liability, Independent Contractors, and the Ostensible Agency Doctrine, 15 J. Corp. L. 535 (1990).

How might an IPA HMO alter its structure or operations to avoid the attribution of agency and vicarious liability? See Chase v. Independent Practice Ass'n, 583 N.E.2d 251 (Mass. App. Ct. 1991) (vicarious liability rejected where HMO contract stated the IPA only "arranged for" services but did not provide services directly); Jones v. U.S. Healthcare, 723 N.Y.S.2d 478 (App. Div. 2001) (an HMO "cannot be held vicariously liable for defendant doctors' and hospital's alleged malpractice in discharging plaintiff and her baby prematurely, where the . . . Group Master Contract, membership card and Member Handbook clearly state that doctors and hospitals participating in defendant's health care program are independent contractors"). But see Petrovich v. Share Health Plan, 719 N.E.2d 756 (Ill. 1999) (exculpatory language in insurance documents does not control if the patient didn't actually read or understand the documents). Because IPAs are now the dominant form of HMOs, and because HMO lawyers have widely adopted these techniques, the working assumption among both plaintiff's and defense lawyers is that HMOs generally cannot be held vicariously liable simply by virtue of forming a network and requiring gatekeeping. This is also confirmed in several of the state managed care liability statutes discussed on the next page. See Gail Agrawal & Mark Hall, What If You *Could* Sue Your HMO? Managed Care Liability beyond the ERISA Shield, 47 St. Louis U. L.J. 235 (2003).

4. *HMO Direct Liability.* The focus of *Boyd* is vicarious liability, but HMOs have also been held to the same type of direct corporate liability ushered in by Darling v. Charleston Community Memorial Hospital, page 467. Recall that for hospitals, direct corporate liability takes two basic forms: a duty of care in the selection of physicians, and a duty of care in the contemporaneous supervision of physicians. The former is readily applicable to HMOs as well. Several courts have held that they have the same obligation hospitals do to review the credentials and competency of physicians that they select for their network. See, e.g., McClellan v. Health Maintenance Organization, 604 A.2d 1053 (Pa. Super. Ct. 1992). HMOs are required under their own accreditation standards to engage in a hospital-like credentialing process, and increasingly they are required to do so by state regulation as well. Nevertheless, many managed care networks accept virtually "any willing provider," that is, anyone with a license who agrees to the network's payment terms. A "Dear Doctor" letter sent by one PPO to California physicians stated "Welcome to the PPO network. You are now part of a carefully selected panel of more than 300 hospitals and 21,000 physicians." Robert A. Berenson, Beyond Competition, 16 Health Aff., No. 2, at 171, 175 (1997). Some states require by statute that HMOs accept any qualified provider. Does either voluntary or mandatory nonselectivity undermine the basis for a duty of care in selection?

Recall that the second branch of *Darling* — the duty of contemporaneous supervision — is highly controversial with respect to hospitals and is accepted in only a very limited fashion in most jurisdictions because it doesn't make sense to require hospital administrators to actively intervene in medical treatment decisions. Is the case for an HMO's duty to supervise any stronger? Even if there is no such mandatory duty, however, consider whether HMOs have voluntarily assumed such a duty through their utilization review function. Is this not the essential point of *Wickline*, that when insurance companies choose to intervene in treatment decisions, they assume a duty of care in doing so? Accord Shannon v. McNulty, 718 A.2d 828 (Pa. Super. Ct. 1998) ("When . . . an insurer interjects itself into the rendering of medical decisions affecting a subscriber's care it must do so in a medically reasonable manner").

To remove any doubt about this issue, about a dozen states have adopted statutes that hold insurers liable for personal injuries caused by negligent or inappropriate administration of health insurance benefits. See Agrawal & Hall, supra; Note, 74 Temp. L. Rev. 507 (2001). There is considerable doubt, however, whether these statutes can legally apply to employer-provided health insurance, due to the federal preemption doctrine discussed in the following case. Controversy over adopting this liability principle as a matter of federal law has been a major stumbling block in Congress's deliberations over the managed care patient "bill of rights."

5. Wickline's *Holding*. The precise holding or nonholding of *Wickline* has been a source of considerable confusion, both in the courts and among lawyers and commentators. This confusion is due in part to the unusual tactical decision by the plaintiff's lawyer not to sue the treating physicians. As a result, the plaintiff was able to use the treating physicians as experts for her side, but the physicians were unwilling to indict themselves by testifying that the four-day stay fell below a minimally acceptable standard of care. Without such testimony, the court was forced to find no liability. Without any basis in the clinical evidence for finding anyone liable, much of what the court said about the competing responsibilities of physicians and insurers was rendered dictum.

Nevertheless, *Wickline* is still the seminal case on the issues it addresses. In trying to make sense of what the opinion means for future disputes, distinguish these two issues: (1) whether insurers are potentially on the liability hook for making bad coverage decisions and (2) whether physicians are off the liability hook when insurers are at fault. Realize it is possible to answer "yes" to (1) and no to (2); in other words, both can be held liable at the same time. Others sometimes interpret *Wickline* to mean, however, that the doctor's ultimate responsibility absolves the insurance company from blame. The most prominent instance of this reading of *Wickline* is a subsequent California decision, Wilson v. Blue Cross of Southern California, 271 Cal. Rptr. 876 (Cal. Ct. App. 1990). There, a psychiatric patient committed suicide after being released from the hospital when his private insurer stopped paying for his hospitalization benefits due to lack of medical necessity. The court found it necessary to distinguish and disapprove *Wickline* in order to allow the case to be tried against the insurer under a negligence theory. Is anything in *Wickline* opposed to such a holding? For a sampling of the extensive commentary on these two cases, see John Blum, An Analysis of Legal Liability in Health Care Utilization Review and Case Management, 26 Hous. L. Rev. 191

(1989); Comment, Health Care Utilization Review: Potential Exposures to Negligence Liability, 52 Ohio St. L.J. 1289 (1991).

Under *Wickline*, could insurer liability be imposed based not only on the substance of the utilization review decision, but also based on the process? What flaws were present in Medi-Cal's UR process? How feasible would it be to improve on that process?

If insurers can be found liable for negligent failures to approve necessary care, can they also be held accountable for negligent approvals of harmful care?

6. *Bringing Liability and Payment into Sync.* Does the potential liability under *Wickline* make sense from the physician's perspective? Physicians complain that it is unfair to hold them responsible for failing to provide treatment that insurance will not pay for. What realistic options did Mrs. Wickline's physicians have? How might the tort standard of medical appropriateness be brought more into sync with the insurance standard? One possibility is by referring to the law of abandonment, which is discussed in Chapter 2.B.3. There, we learn that physicians are able to terminate care in certain circumstances if they give proper notice and an opportunity to locate another physician. Whether lack of payment is a permissible reason to give this notice has not yet clearly been decided.

See also Chapter 4.B.2 for consideration of whether physicians practicing under managed care constraints should be held to a lower standard of care than under fee-for-service insurance.

7. *Few Cases but Big Verdicts.* One reason for the lack of clarity about the respective responsibilities of physicians and insurers is that there have been surprisingly few cases like *Wickline* and *Wilson* with decisions on the merits. This suggests that perhaps in practice insurers rarely deny coverage for care that is required by the minimal standard of medical practice. The paucity of suits may also be due to the preemption of state law by the federal ERISA statute, discussed in the next case. Others attribute the favorable malpractice record of staff model HMOs like Kaiser to their detailed programs of malpractice prevention and physician monitoring and to the availability of a grievance process for dissatisfied patients. William Curran & George Moseley, The Malpractice Experience of Health Maintenance Organizations, 70 Nw. U. L. Rev. 69 (1975). These characteristics typically do not exist, however, in the broad network model HMOs that currently prevail in the market. Further explanation for the small number of suits comes from a recent empirical study, which reports that plaintiffs' lawyers are reluctant to name health insurers in medical malpractice suits since this greatly complicates the litigation and is usually unnecessary given the fact that the treating physician is "on the hook" in any event (for reasons explained in *Wickline*). Also, plaintiffs' lawyers report seeing few or no cases where harm results from health insurers' refusing to pay for treatment that physicians request. Agrawal & Hall, supra.

Although there have been few successful cases against health insurers, when plaintiffs have succeeded, they sometimes win very large punitive damages awards, in the range of $50 million to $100 million. For instance, in Fox v. Health Net, a California jury awarded $77 million in punitive damages (plus $12 million compensatory) against an HMO that had refused to pay for an innovative cancer treatment, which the surviving family claimed resulted in the patient's death. This was eclipsed by the $120 million verdict in Goodrich v. Aetna U.S. Healthcare, $116 million of which were punitive damages. Like Fox, the Goodrich verdict was based on an HMO's reluctance to authorize expensive, state-of-the-art treatment for terminal cancer that it considered to be experimental. Similarly, an Ohio court awarded $30 million against a Blue Cross insurer for failing to pay for cancer treatment (Dardinger v. Athem, 2002 WL 31895279 (Oh. 2002)), and a Florida jury awarded $80 million against Humana for terminating coverage for a special therapy program for a child with cerebral palsy, although this verdict was subsequently set aside for improper instructions and evidence. Humana Health Ins. Co. v. Chipps, 802 So. 2d 492 (Fla. Dist. Ct. App. 2001).

Does this track record of very few successful verdicts, but some that are extremely large, create appropriate incentives for plaintiffs to sue? Is it likely to send appropriate deterrence signals to health insurers? Does the few number of suits suggest a need to remove barriers to suing health plans? Would a "floodgate" of litigation threaten the viability of the managed care industry or of its core cost-containment practices? For discussion from various perspectives, see the literature cited in note 1; David Studdert et al., Expanded Managed Care Liability: What Impact on Employer Coverage?, 18(6) Health Aff. 7 (Dec. 1999).

8. *Financial Incentives.* Another potential basis for direct liability against HMOs and managed care arrangements is the use of financial incentives to encourage physicians to economize. An insurer might avoid the entire issue of liability for second guessing medical judgment by paying doctors in a way that encourages them to economize in their own clinical decisionmaking. Using *Wickline's* notion of "defects in the design or implementation of cost containment mechanisms," is it possible nevertheless to argue that some financial incentives are too strong per se, or that in practice they caused a physician to err? Consider by analogy the suits in the 1990s against Domino's Pizza for pressuring its deliverers to drive too fast. As discussed in Chapter 4.B.1, financial incentives might also lead to claims for punitive damages in medical malpractice cases against physicians. Chapter 3.C.4 discusses whether incentives give rise to a claim for breach of fiduciary duty.

9. *Breach of Contract.* The *Boyd* concurrence suggests that HMO liability might also be based on a contractual or quasi-promissory theory, such as warranty or fraud. This possibility is explored in the notes following Sullivan v. O'Connor, at page 376. Is there a difference between the nature of the promises an HMO makes and those made by typical hospitals or doctors? Professor Brewbaker argues that, because HMOs, unlike hospitals, sell medical services, they undertake an implied warranty of quality which, as with doctors, promises nonnegligent care. Therefore, he argues that HMOs should be automatically liable for any negligent care delivered under their auspices, regardless of whether they fall under the theories of liability devised for hospitals. Wm. Brewbaker, Medical Malpractice and Managed Care Organizations: The Implied Warranty of Quality, 60 Contemp. Probs. 117 (Spring 1997).

10. *Employer Liability.* If insurers can be held liable for lack of care in selecting physicians and supervising treatment decisions, how about employers who construct their own managed care plans? Many large employers eliminate the "middle man" by contracting directly with hospitals and physicians on a self-insured basis. In doing so, an employer may either "rent a network," that is, contract with an existing network of providers, or it might form its own network. In either event, is it plausible to impose the same type of managed care liability on employers as on the insurers they have ousted? If such liability existed under state

law, it would likely be preempted for reasons addressed in the following case. For discussion, see Dana M. Muir, Fiduciary Status as an Employer's Shield: The Perversity of ERISA Fiduciary Law, 2 Univ. Pa. J. Lab. & Emp. L. 391 (2000).

11. *Exclusive Enterprise Liability*. The furthest extension of the concepts of enterprise liability developed for hospitals, HMOs, and other forms of managed care would be to hold a network of hospitals, doctors, and insurers exclusively liable at the highest institutional level for any medical mistake that occurs within any component part. If the health care delivery system were to move toward an "integrated delivery system" structure, commentators have speculated whether these networks should or will be the final point of liability focus. So far, most networks are only loosely formed contractual affiliations in which the parties (hospitals, doctors, and insurers) agree on a nonexclusive basis to market their services collectively to employers or other insurers. Does this entail sufficient integration, coordination, selection, and supervision to justify imposition of enterprise liability? Consider whether it is feasible for integrated delivery systems to influence the quality of care if these affiliations are nonexclusive, that is, if doctors and hospitals belong to several such networks? See generally K. Abraham & P. Weiler, Enterprise Medical Liability and the Choice of the Responsible Enterprise, 20 Am. J.L. & Med. 29 (1994); Clark C. Havighurst, Making Health Plans Accountable for the Quality of Care, 31 Ga. L. Rev. 587 (1997); Karen A. Jordan, Managed Competition and Limited Choice of Providers: Countering Negative Perceptions through a Responsibility to Select Quality Network Physicians, 27 Ariz. St. L.J. 875 (1995); William Sage, Enterprise Liability and the Emerging Managed Care Health Care System, 60(2) L. & Contemp. Probs. 159 (Spring 1997); Randall R. Bovbjerg & Robert Berenson, Enterprise Liability in the Twenty-First Century, in Medical Malpractice and the U.S. Health Care System (W. Sage & R. Kersh, eds., 2006).

12. *Class Action Suits*. In the late 1990s, a group of prominent plaintiffs' lawyers brought large class action suits against the major national HMOs under RICO, the federal white-collar crime statute, alleging that HMOs systematically misrepresent how generous they are in making coverage decisions, and fail to disclose utilization review restrictions and methods of physician payment. These claims were largely unsuccessful, for failure to show actual injury or to meet class action requirements. Maio v. Aetna, 221 F.3d 472 (3d Cir. 2000); In re Managed Care Litigation, 209 F.R.D. 678 (S.D. Fla. 2002). For analysis, see Kathy Cerminara, Taking a Closer Look at the Managed Care Class Actions, 11 Annals Health L. 1 (2002); Clark Havighurst, Consumers Versus Managed Care: The New Class Actions, 20(4) Health Aff. 2 (July 2001); David Studdert & Troyen Brennan, 342 New Eng. J. Med. 280 (2000). See generally Kathy Cerminara, The Class Action Suit as a Method of Patient Empowerment in the Managed Care Setting, 24 Am. J.L. Med. 7 (1998).

13. *Consumer-Driven Health Care*. As insurers recede from aggressive managed care, will these liability threats likewise recede, or will they be replaced with new theories of liability? According to one professor, consumer-driven health care opens up an entirely new arena of potential health plan liability in the form of failure to provide full or accurate information about health care options. Kristin Madison, ERISA and Liability for Provision of Medical Information, 84 N.C. L. Rev. 471-546 (2006).

Problem: Enterprise Liability

Mike Mulligan is administrator of Marcus Welby Hospital, a large facility in a metropolitan area. Mary Anne is the local lawyer. Mike has a plan to protect the hospital from the erosion of business that has resulted from managed care contracts taking more and more patients into the larger facilities nearby. Mulligan's plan is for the hospital to form its own managed care network. Mulligan would like to include as many of the local physicians as possible in the network. (Assume this is legal under antitrust law.) The network will then sell HMO type insurance to local residents. The revenue premiums will be split 50/50 between the hospital and the doctors, with the physician half going mostly to the primary care physicians. These primary care physicians will act as gatekeepers for hospitalization decisions, referrals to specialists in town, and referrals to larger hospitals for more complex care.

Mulligan consults Mary Anne about advice on the liability implications of this plan. The hospital has been named in a number of suits recently, and he is concerned at the formation stage about what new liability exposure the network will create and what steps are possible to manage or reduce that exposure. Taking the position of Mike Mulligan, how desirable would each of the following alternative ideas be from a business or practical perspective? Taking the position of Mary Anne, how desirable would each be from a legal perspective?

1. Automatically accept into the network any doctor with medical staff privileges at the hospital.
2. In contracting with doctors, insist on an indemnification clause that requires them to compensate the hospital for any paid claims that arise from the doctor's own fault.
3. Agree to purchase malpractice insurance for network physicians, defend any claims brought by patients, and pay for any resulting liability. Consider this option both for hospital-based care only and for all medical care.
4. Increase the size and authority of the risk management department, school them in the techniques of quality assurance and "total quality management," and impose a passel of practice guidelines that cover liability-sensitive areas of medicine.
5. Write insurance contracts so as to notify subscribers that network physicians are independent contractors. Post similar statements in doctors' waiting rooms, at hospital entrances, on hospital admission forms, and on informed consent forms. Review stationery, billing forms, and uniform dress to avoid creating the unintended impression of an agency relationship between the hospital and network physicians.
6. Have the risk management department and Mary Anne review all advertising and marketing materials to eliminate any statements that might create an expectation or image of receiving quality care.
7. Write insurance contracts so as to specifically promise an "adequate level of care, consistent with the coverage provided by this insurance and within the standards of care that prevail in other, similar locations in this state."

■AETNA HEALTH INC. v. DAVILA
543 U.S. 200 (2004)

Justice THOMAS delivered the opinion of the Court.

In these consolidated cases, two individuals sued their respective HMOs for alleged failures to exercise ordinary care in the handling of coverage decisions, in violation of a duty imposed by the Texas Health Care Liability Act (Texas Act). We granted certiorari to decide whether the individuals' causes of action are completely pre-empted by the . . . Employee Retirement Income Security Act of 1974 (ERISA) . . .

[Davila was covered by Aetna through his employer, and Calad was covered by CIGNA through her husband's employer.] Respondents both suffered injuries allegedly arising from Aetna's and CIGNA's decisions not to provide coverage for certain treatment and services recommended by respondents' treating physicians. Davila's treating physician prescribed Vioxx to remedy Davila's arthritis pain, but Aetna refused to pay for it. Davila did not appeal or contest this decision, nor did he purchase Vioxx with his own resources and seek reimbursement. Instead, Davila began taking Naprosyn, from which he allegedly suffered a severe reaction that required extensive treatment and hospitalization. [Editors' note: The Court fails to mention that Davila nearly died from bleeding ulcers and that, although Vioxx is much more expensive than Naprosyn, it has fewer side effects relating to bleeding ulcers.]

Calad underwent surgery, and although her treating physician recommended an extended hospital stay, a CIGNA discharge nurse determined that Calad did not meet the plan's criteria for a continued hospital stay. CIGNA consequently denied coverage for the extended hospital stay. Calad experienced postsurgery complications forcing her to return to the hospital. She alleges that these complications would not have occurred had CIGNA approved coverage for a longer hospital stay.

[In separate state-court suits,] respondents . . . argued that petitioners' refusal to cover the requested services violated their "duty to exercise ordinary care when making health care treatment decisions," and that these refusals "proximately caused" their injuries. Petitioners removed the cases to Federal District Courts, arguing that respondents' causes of action fit within the scope of, and were therefore completely pre-empted by, ERISA . . . The United States Court of Appeals for the Fifth Circuit consolidated their cases with several others raising similar issues. . . . After examining the causes of action available under [ERISA], the Court of Appeals determined that respondents' claims could possibly fall under . . . §502(a)(1)(B), which provides a cause of action for the recovery of wrongfully denied benefits. . . . [However, the court ruled that this case does not fall under ERISA because] respondents "are not seeking reimbursement for benefits denied them," but rather request "tort damages" arising from "an external, statutorily imposed duty of 'ordinary care.'" . . .

II

Congress enacted ERISA to "protect . . . the interests of participants in employee benefit plans and their beneficiaries" by setting out substantive regulatory requirements for employee benefit plans and to "provid[e] for appropriate remedies, sanctions, and ready access to the Federal courts." 29 U.S.C. §1001(b). The purpose of ERISA is to provide a uniform regulatory regime over employee benefit plans. To this end, ERISA includes expansive pre-emption provisions, see ERISA §514, which are intended to ensure that employee benefit plan regulation would be "exclusively a federal concern." ERISA's "comprehensive legislative scheme" includes "an integrated system of procedures for enforcement." . . . As the Court said in Pilot Life Ins. Co. v. Dedeaux, 481 U.S. 41 (1987):

> [T]he detailed provisions of §502(a) set forth a comprehensive civil enforcement scheme that represents a careful balancing of the need for prompt and fair claims settlement procedures against the public interest in encouraging the formation of employee benefit plans. The policy choices reflected in the inclusion of certain remedies and the exclusion of others under the federal scheme would be completely undermined if ERISA-plan participants and beneficiaries were free to obtain remedies under state law that Congress rejected in ERISA. The six carefully integrated civil enforcement provisions found in §502(a) of the statute as finally enacted . . . provide strong evidence that Congress did *not* intend to authorize other remedies that it simply forgot to incorporate expressly.

Therefore, any state-law cause of action that duplicates, supplements, or supplants the ERISA civil enforcement remedy conflicts with the clear congressional intent to make the ERISA remedy exclusive and is therefore pre-empted. . . . It follows that if an individual brings suit complaining of a denial of coverage for medical care, where the individual is entitled to such coverage only because of the terms of an ERISA-regulated employee benefit plan, and . . . if an individual, at some point in time, could have brought his claim under ERISA §502(a) . . . then the individual's cause of action is completely pre-empted by ERISA. . . .

III

The only action [Davila] complained of was Aetna's refusal to approve payment for Davila's Vioxx prescription. Further, the only relationship Aetna had with Davila was its partial administration of Davila's employer's benefit plan. Similarly . . . Calad contests only CIGNA's decision to refuse coverage for her hospital stay. . . . It is clear, then, that respondents complain only about denials of coverage promised under the terms of ERISA-regulated employee benefit plans. Upon the denial of benefits, respondents could have paid for the treatment themselves and then sought reimbursement through a §502(a)(1)(B) action, or sought a preliminary injunction. . . . [1]

Respondents contend, however, that the complained-of actions violate legal duties that arise independently of ERISA or the terms of the employee benefit plans at issue in these cases. Both respondents brought suit specifically under the Texas Act, alleging that petitioners "controlled, influenced, participated in and

---

[1] Respondents also argue that the benefit due under their ERISA-regulated employee benefit plans is simply the membership in the respective HMOs, not coverage for the particular medical treatments that are delineated in the plan documents. Respondents did not identify this possible argument in their brief in opposition to the petitions for certiorari, and we deem it waived.

made decisions which affected the quality of the diagnosis, care, and treatment provided" in a manner that violated "the duty of ordinary care." . . . The Texas Act does impose a duty on managed care entities to "exercise ordinary care when making health care treatment decisions," and makes them liable for damages proximately caused by failures to abide by that duty. However, if a managed care entity correctly concluded that, under the terms of the relevant plan, a particular treatment was not covered, the managed care entity's denial of coverage would not be a proximate cause of any injuries arising from the denial. Rather, the failure of the plan itself to cover the requested treatment would be the proximate cause.[2] More significantly, the Texas Act clearly states that "[it] . . . create[s] no obligation on the part of the health insurance . . . entity to provide to an insured or enrollee treatment which is not covered by the health care plan of the entity." Hence, . . . interpretation of the terms of respondents' benefit plans forms an essential part of their [state law] claim, and [state law] liability would exist here only because of petitioners' administration of ERISA-regulated benefit plans. Petitioners' potential liability under the Texas Act in these cases, then, derives entirely from the particular rights and obligations established by the benefit plans. . . . [R]espondents bring suit only to rectify a wrongful denial of benefits promised under ERISA-regulated plans, and do not attempt to remedy any violation of a legal duty independent of ERISA. . . .

[T]he Court of Appeals found significant that respondents "assert a tort claim for tort damages" rather than "a contract claim for contract damages," and that respondents "are not seeking reimbursement for benefits denied them." But, distinguishing between pre-empted and non-pre-empted claims based on the particular label affixed to them would "elevate form over substance and allow parties to evade" the pre-emptive scope of ERISA simply "by relabeling their contract claims as claims for tortious breach of contract." . . . In [previous Supreme Court cases finding pre-emption], the plaintiffs all brought state claims that were labeled either tort or tort-like. . . .

Respondents also argue—for the first time in their brief to this Court—that the Texas Act is a law that regulates insurance, and hence that ERISA §514(b)(2)(A) saves their causes of action from pre-emption.[3] This argument is unavailing. . . . ERISA §514(b)(2)(A) must be interpreted in light of the congressional intent to create an exclusive federal remedy in ERISA §502(a). Under ordinary principles of conflict pre-emption, then, even a state law that can arguably be characterized as "regulating insurance" will be pre-empted if it provides a separate vehicle to assert a claim for benefits outside of, or in addition to, ERISA's remedial scheme.

---

[2] To take a clear example, if the terms of the health care plan specifically exclude from coverage the cost of an appendectomy, then any injuries caused by the refusal to cover the appendectomy are properly attributed to the terms of the plan itself, not the managed care entity that applied those terms.

[3] ERISA §514(b)(2)(A) reads, as relevant: "[N]othing in this subchapter shall be construed to exempt or relieve any person from any law of any State which regulates insurance, banking, or securities."

IV

Respondents, their *amici,* and some Courts of Appeals have relied heavily upon Pegram v. Herdrich, 530 U.S. 211 (2000), in arguing that ERISA does not pre-empt or completely pre-empt state suits such as respondents'. . . . *Pegram* cannot be read so broadly. In *Pegram,* the plaintiff sued her physician-owned-and-operated HMO (which provided medical coverage through plaintiff's employer pursuant to an ERISA-regulated benefit plan) and her treating physician, both for medical malpractice and for a breach of an ERISA fiduciary duty. The plaintiff's treating physician was also the person charged with administering plaintiff's benefits; it was she who decided whether certain treatments were covered. We reasoned that the physician's "eligibility decision and the treatment decision were inextricably mixed." We concluded that "Congress did not intend [the defendant HMO] or any other HMO to be treated as a fiduciary to the extent that it makes mixed eligibility decisions acting through its physicians." . . .

[I]it was essential to *Pegram*'s conclusion that the decisions challenged there were truly "mixed eligibility and treatment decisions," i.e., medical necessity decisions made by the plaintiff's treating physician *qua* treating physician and *qua* benefits administrator. Put another way, the reasoning of *Pegram* "only make[s] sense where the underlying negligence also plausibly constitutes medical maltreatment by a party who can be deemed to be a treating physician or such a physician's employer." Cicio v. Does, 321 F.3d 83, 109 (C.A.2 2003) (Calabresi, J., dissenting in part). Here, however, petitioners are neither respondents' treating physicians nor the employers of respondents' treating physicians. Petitioners' coverage decisions, then, are pure eligibility decisions, and *Pegram* is not implicated. . . .

Justice GINSBURG, with whom Justice BREYER joins, concurring.

. . . [This] decision is consistent with our governing case law on ERISA's preemptive scope. I therefore join the Court's opinion. But, with greater enthusiasm . . . I also join "the rising judicial chorus urging that Congress and [this] Court revisit what is an unjust and increasingly tangled ERISA regime." DiFelice v. AETNA U.S. Healthcare, 346 F.3d 442, 453 (C.A.3 2003) (Becker, J., concurring). Because the Court has coupled an encompassing interpretation of ERISA's preemptive force with a cramped construction of the "equitable relief" allowable under §502(a)(3), a "regulatory vacuum" exists: "[V]irtually all state law remedies are preempted but very few federal substitutes are provided."

A series of the Court's decisions has yielded a host of situations in which persons adversely affected by ERISA-proscribed wrongdoing cannot gain make-whole relief [because] "there is a stark absence in [ERISA] itself and in its legislative history of any reference to an intention to authorize the recovery of extracontractual damages" for consequential injuries. . . . [F]resh consideration of the availability of consequential damages under §502(a)(3) is plainly in order. See 321 F.3d, at 106, 107 (Calabresi, J., dissenting in part) ("gaping wound" caused by the breadth of preemption and limited remedies under ERISA, as interpreted by this Court, will not be healed until the Court "start[s] over" or Congress "wipe[s] the slate clean"); *DiFelice,* 346 F.3d, at 467 ("The vital thing . . . is that either Congress or the Court act quickly, because the current situation is plainly untenable."); Langbein, What ERISA Means by "Equitable": The Supreme Court's Trail of Error in *Russell, Mertens,* and *Great-West*, 103 Colum. L. Rev. 1317, 1365 (2003). . . . The Government notes a potential amelioration. . . . [It] suggests that the Act, as currently written and interpreted, may "allo[w] at least some forms of 'make-whole' relief." . . . As the Court points out, respondents here declined the opportunity to amend their complaints to state claims for relief under §502(a). . . . But the Government's suggestion may indicate an effective remedy others similarly circumstanced might fruitfully pursue.

"Congress . . . intended ERISA to replicate the core principles of trust remedy law, including the make-whole standard of relief." *Langbein* 1319. I anticipate that Congress, or this Court, will one day so confirm.

Notes: ERISA Preemption

1. *Damages Under ERISA.* Under ERISA, patients who are wrongly denied health insurance benefits can recover compensation only for the costs of treatment, but not for consequential damages, pain and suffering, wrongful death, or punitive damages. Corcoran v. United Healthcare, Inc., 965 F.2d 1321 (5th Cir. 1992), dramatically illustrates the hardship caused by this restriction in available remedies. There, a woman miscarried late in her pregnancy due, she alleged, to the HMO's refusal to authorize hospitalization for pregnancy complications. The court limited her potential remedies under ERISA to an order for treatment or compensation for treatment costs. But, because the fetus had died, these remedies were meaningless. This restriction of damages is much more severe even than that imposed by ordinary contract law. See Sullivan v. O'Connor, page 376. Therefore, it is important to note the concurring Justices' argument in *Davila* that this limitation can and should be revisited. See Sarah Spisich, The Aftermath of *Davila:* Are Healthcare Enrollees Now in a Sinking Ship Without a Paddle?, 17(4) Health Lawyer 22 (Aug. 2005); Comment, 2006 BYU L. Rev. 1589 (2007).

The majority in *Davila* appears to think the outcome makes perfect sense according to congressional intent. Legislative history, however, reveals that Congress wrote ERISA primarily with pension benefits in mind, and long before managed care health insurance existed. Do you see why limiting damages to the costs of treatment might have made a lot more sense under traditional insurance? Assuming, as the concurrence argues, that ERISA's remedies no longer make sense for managed care insurance, whose responsibility is it to fix the problem: Congress's or the courts'? See Andrews-Clarke v. Travelers Ins. Co., 948 F. Supp. 49 (D. Mass. 1997) ("Although the [failure of the utilization reviewer to approve hospitalization for a deeply troubled alcoholic who later committed suicide] is extraordinarily troubling, even more disturbing to this Court is the failure of Congress to amend a statute that, due to the changing realities of the modern health care system, has gone conspicuously awry from its original intent. Does anyone care? Do you?"). In 2001, each chamber of Congress approved different versions of a "patients' bill of rights" that would have amended ERISA to allow tort damages against health insurers, but differences between the two bills were never reconciled.

2. *ERISA terminology* is obscure and confusing. Essentially, an ERISA "plan" exists any time an employer pays for health insurance. If the employer simply purchases health insurance, then technically there may be a distinction between the "plan" which is the decision to purchase, and the insurance, which is the contracted-for benefit. Would it be possible, using this distinction, to argue that ERISA preempts only suits against employers for failing to provide insurance, but not suits against insurers for failing to provide the benefits covered by the insurance? Observe how *Davila* avoids this issue in footnote 2 of the opinion, but a few lower courts have adopted this position. See, e.g., Washington Physicians Service Ass'n v. Gregoire, 147 F.3d 1039 (9th Cir. 1998) ("The mere fact that many [employers] choose to buy health insurance for their [employees] does not cause a regulation of health insurance automatically to 'relate to' any employee benefit plan — just as a decision to buy an apple a day for every employee, or to offer employees a gym membership, does not cause all state regulation of apples and gyms to 'relate to' employee benefit plans."). But see Hotz v. Blue Cross & Blue Shield of Massachusetts, 292 F.3d 57, 59-60 (1st Cir. 2002) ("Although the [employer plan/insurance plan] distinction is linguistically possible, it would mean that numerous past ERISA suits brought to secure payment for medical services from third-party providers under ERISA plans lacked a legal basis."). See generally, Russell Korobkin, The Failed Jurisprudence of Managed Care, and How to Fix It: Reinterpreting ERISA Preemption, 51 UCLA L. Rev. 457 (2003).

Regardless, ERISA preemption would still apply to situations where the employer self-insures, that is, pays for health care directly out of its own funds. In that case, ERISA clearly preempts state law liability against the employer. So far, courts have applied ERISA preemption equally to both purchased and self-funded health insurance, where tort and contract claims are concerned. This distinction is relevant, however, for purposes of preemption of state insurance regulation.

3. *Which Claims Are Preempted?* The end of the *Davila* opinion briefly alludes to ERISA's effect on more conventional medical malpractice claims that arise under managed care insurance. Lower court decisions clarify the following: ERISA clearly does not apply to a malpractice claim against only the treating physician for a medical mistake that is unaffected by health insurance. . . . Likewise, courts usually find no preemption if a plaintiff attempts to hold a health insurer vicariously liable for a treating physician's mistake. Pacificare of Oklahoma v. Burrage, 59 F.3d 151 (10th Cir. 1995); Rice v. Panchal, 65 F.3d 637 (7th Cir. 1995). This helps to explain *Davila's* reference to the fact that the plaintiffs' physicians in that case were not employees of the health plans.

The law is unsettled, however, when there is a medical treatment mistake and the plaintiff attempts to hold the insurer *directly* responsible because it selected bad physicians or influenced their treatment decisions. This is similar to the situation in Pegram v. Herdrich, 530 U.S. 211 (2000), which is discussed in *Davila*. There, the patient claimed that her doctor was influenced by profit distributions from the HMO and that this financial tie violates ERISA fiduciary standards. In the course of rejecting that claim under ERISA, the Court noted that the patient was free to pursue her claim in state court in the form of a medical malpractice suit. This strongly suggests that direct liability actions against HMOs for care provided by treating physicians are not preempted by ERISA, even after *Davila*.

In short, courts must distinguish between tort claims based on insurance coverage decisions, which are preempted, and medical malpractice liability, which is not preempted. In drawing this line, many lower courts have followed a rule of thumb that distinguishes between claims based on the *quantity* of care and those based on its *quality*. See, e.g., Dukes v. U.S. Healthcare, 57 F.3d 350 (3d Cir. 1995); Bauman v. U.S. Healthcare, Inc., 193 F.3d 151 (3d Cir. 1999). The *Davila* case makes no reference to this concept, however. Instead, it focuses on whether the insurer or the treating physician made the critical decision. Is that distinction likely to be sufficiently clear in most cases? What about situations where the treating physician is employed full time by an HMO, and the HMO instructs the physician that a particular treatment option is not approved, for instance, that women should not remain in the hospital longer than 48 hours following normal childbirth? That might be regarded as a quantity decision based on the insurance policy's medical appropriateness criteria, or it might be regarded as a form of direct HMO liability for interfering with physicians' ability to make good treatment decisions. Does *Davila* resolve which is the correct characterization?

One further complication: if it is possible to find an agency relationship between the HMO and the treating physician, should it matter that the HMO is not the physician's employer? Isn't the critical factor whether or not the physician agreed with, or acquiesced in, the HMO's decision? In *Davila*, the HMO refused to pay for treatments the physicians ordered, but, in many other cases, physicians may not order treatment they know the HMO won't pay for or that will cost the physician money under the HMO's payment incentives. Shouldn't patients be able to blame the HMO, at least in part, when this happens? In such cases, should *Davila* apply?

There is a large amount of academic literature discussing these issues, but most of it predates *Davila*. For subsequent analysis, see Aaron S. Kesselheim & Troyen A. Brennan, The Swinging Pendulum: The Supreme Court Reverses Course on ERISA and Managed Care, 5 Yale J. Health Pol'y L. & Ethics 451 (2005); Leonard A. Nelson, Aetna v. Davila: A Missed Opportunity, 31 Wm. Mitchell L. Rev. 843-896 (2005), Note, 84 Tex. L. Rev. 1347-1383 (2006).

4. *Medicare Preemption.* Preemption issues might also arise under Medicare, which has a restrictive set of remedies for beneficiaries. One important ruling held that Medicare's administrative review process does not preempt a state tort action against a private HMO that contracted to deliver Medicare services. McCall v. Pacificare of California, Inc., 21 P.3d 1189 (Cal. 2001).

G. MEDICAL MALPRACTICE REFORM

■ FEIN v. PERMANENTE MEDICAL GROUP
695 P.2d 665 (Cal. 1985)

Kaus, Justice.

In this medical malpractice action, both parties appeal from a judgment awarding plaintiff about $1 million in damages. . . . Plaintiff . . . maintains that the trial court, in fixing damages, should not have applied two provisions of the

Medical Injury Compensation Reform Act of 1975 (MICRA): Civil Code §3333.2, which limits noneconomic damages in medical malpractice cases to $250,000, and Civil Code §3333.1, which modifies the traditional "collateral source" rule in such litigation. Plaintiff's claims are based on a constitutional challenge similar to the challenges to other provisions of MICRA that we recently addressed and rejected in Roa v. Lodi Medical Group, Inc., 695 P.2d 164 (Cal. 1985) [upholding the following limits on lawyers' contingency fees in medical malpractice cases: 40 percent of the first $50,000, 33 percent of the next $50,000, 25 percent of the next $100,000, and 10 percent of any amounts above $200,000.]. We conclude that the judgment should be affirmed in all respects. . . .

[The facts are stated in the excerpt at page 436. On account of defendant's failure to diagnose Mr. Fein's heart condition,] the jury awarded $24,733 for wages lost by plaintiff to the time of trial, $63,000 for future medical expenses, and $700,000 for wages lost in the future as a result of the reduction in plaintiff's life expectancy.[1] Finally, the jury awarded $500,000 for "noneconomic damages," to compensate for pain, suffering, inconvenience, physical impairment and other intangible damages sustained by plaintiff from the time of the injury until his death. . . . The trial court . . . reduced the noneconomic damages to $250,000, reduced the award for past lost wages to $5,430 — deducting $19,303 that plaintiff had already received in disability payments as compensation for such lost wages — and ordered defendant to pay the first $63,000 of any future medical expenses not covered by medical insurance provided by plaintiff's employer, as such expenses were incurred. . . .

We begin with the claim that §3333.2 [limiting noneconomic damages to $250,000] denies due process because it limits the potential recovery of medical malpractice claimants without providing them an adequate quid pro quo. In rejecting a similar challenge to the periodic payment provision at issue in *American Bank*, we explained that

> [i]t is well established that a plaintiff has no vested property right in a particular measure of damages, and that the legislature possesses broad authority to modify the scope and nature of such damages. Since the demise of the substantive due process analysis of Lochner v. New York (1905) 198 U.S. 45, it has been clear that the constitutionality of measures affecting such economic rights under the due process clause does not depend on a judicial assessment of the justifications for the legislation or of the wisdom or fairness of the enactment. So long as the measure is rationally related to a legitimate state interest, policy determinations as to the need for, and the desirability of, the enactment are for the Legislature. 683 P.2d 670. . . .

[I]n enacting MICRA the legislature was acting in a situation in which it had found that the rising cost of medical malpractice insurance was posing serious problems for the health care system in California, threatening to curtail the availability of medical care in some parts of the state and creating the very real possibility that many doctors would practice without insurance, leaving patients

---

[1] Plaintiff did not claim that the heart attack would reduce his earnings capacity during his lifetime.

who might be injured by such doctors with the prospect of uncollectible judgments. In attempting to reduce the cost of medical malpractice insurance in MICRA, the legislature enacted a variety of provisions affecting doctors, insurance companies and malpractice plaintiffs. . . .

There is no denying, of course, that in some cases — like this one — §3333.2 will result in the recovery of a lower judgment than would have been obtained before the enactment of the statute. It is worth noting, however, that in seeking a means of lowering malpractice costs, the legislature placed no limits whatsoever on a plaintiff's right to recover for all of the economic, pecuniary damages — such as medical expenses or lost earnings — resulting from the injury, but instead confined the statutory limitations to the recovery of noneconomic damages, and — even then — permitted up to a $250,000 award for such damages. Thoughtful jurists and legal scholars have for some time raised serious questions as to the wisdom of awarding damages for pain and suffering in any negligence case, noting, inter alia, the inherent difficulties in placing a monetary value on such losses, the fact that money damages are at best only imperfect compensation for such intangible injuries and that such damages are generally passed on to, and borne by, innocent consumers. . . .

Faced with the prospect that, in the absence of some cost reduction, medical malpractice plaintiffs might as a realistic matter have difficulty collecting judgments for any of their damages — pecuniary as well as nonpecuniary — the legislature concluded that it was in the public interest to attempt to obtain some cost savings by limiting noneconomic damages. Although reasonable persons can certainly disagree as to the wisdom of this provision,[17] we cannot say that it is not rationally related to a legitimate state interest.[18]

A number of state courts have invalidated statutory provisions limiting damages in medical malpractice actions on a variety of theories (see, e.g., Wright v. Central Du Page Hospital Assn., 347 N.E.2d 736 (Ill. 1976); Carson v. Maurer,

---

[17] In its comprehensive report on the medical malpractice insurance crisis, the American Bar Association's Commission on Medical Professional Liability [explained] . . .

> [t]he arguments against limiting noneconomic loss are that medical malpractice should not be distinguished from other areas of professional malpractice or personal injury actions which have no ceiling on general damages, that general damages are as real to the plaintiff as economic loss, that a wrongdoer should pay for all the losses he has caused, including pain and suffering, and that the general damages portion of an award provides a fund out of which the plaintiff's attorney's fees can be deducted without leaving the plaintiff economically undercompensated.

[18] Indeed, even if due process principles required some "quid pro quo" to support the statute, it would be difficult to say that the preservation of a viable medical malpractice insurance industry in this state was not an adequate benefit for the detriment the legislation imposes on malpractice plaintiffs. As the United States Supreme Court observed in upholding the provisions of the Price-Anderson Act which placed a dollar limit on total liability that would be incurred by a defendant in the event of a nuclear accident: "'It should be emphasized . . . that it is collecting a judgment, not filing a lawsuit, that counts. . . . [A] defendant with theoretically "unlimited" liability may be unable to pay a judgment once obtained.'" (Duke Power Co. v. Carolina Env. Study Group 438 U.S. 59, 89-90 (1978).) Although we do not suggest that the legislature felt that §3333.2 alone — or for that matter any other single provision of MICRA — was essential to the survival of the medical malpractice insurance system, there is surely nothing in the due process clause which prevents a legislature from making a number of statutory changes which, in combination, provide the requisite benefit to justify the enactment.

424 A.2d 825, 836 (N.H. 1980)); others have upheld such limitations. (See, e.g., Johnson v. St. Vincent Hospital, Inc., 404 N.E.2d 585, 600-601 (Ind. 1980); Prendergast v. Nelson, 256 N.W.2d 657, 668-672 (Neb. 1977).) With only one exception, all of the invalidated statutes contained a ceiling which applied to both pecuniary and nonpecuniary damages, and several courts—in reaching their decisions—were apparently considerably influenced by the potential harshness of a limit that might prevent an injured person from even recovering the amount of his medical expenses[1]. . . . Accordingly, we conclude that §3333.2 does not violate due process.

Plaintiff alternatively contends that the section violates the equal protection clause, both because it impermissibly discriminates between medical malpractice victims and other tort victims, imposing its limits only in medical malpractice cases, and because it improperly discriminates within the class of medical malpractice victims, denying a "complete" recovery of damages only to those malpractice plaintiffs with noneconomic damages exceeding $250,000.

With respect to the first contention, it should be evident from what we have already said that the legislature limited the application of §3333.2 to medical malpractice cases because it was responding to an insurance "crisis" in that particular area and that the statute is rationally related to the legislative purpose. . . .

As for the claim that the statute violates equal protection because of its differential effect within the class of malpractice plaintiffs, the constitutional argument is equally unavailing. . . . Although plaintiff and a supporting amicus claim that the $250,000 limit on noneconomic damages is more invidious—from an equal protection perspective—than a complete abolition of such damages on the ground that the $250,000 limit falls more heavily on those with the most serious injuries, if that analysis were valid a complete abolition of damages would be equally vulnerable to an equal protection challenge, because abolition obviously imposes greater monetary losses on those plaintiffs who would have obtained larger damage awards than on those who would have recovered lesser amounts. Just as the complete elimination of a cause of action has never been viewed as invidiously discriminating within the class of victims who have lost the right to sue, the $250,000 limit—which applies to all malpractice victims—does not amount to an unconstitutional discrimination.

Nor can we agree with amicus' contention that the $250,000 limit is unconstitutional because the legislature could have realized its hoped-for cost savings by mandating a fixed-percentage reduction of all noneconomic damage awards. The choice between reasonable alternative methods for achieving a given objective is generally for the legislature, and there are a number of reasons why the legislature may have made the choice it did. . . . The legislature could reasonably have determined that an across-the-board limit would provide a more stable base on which to calculate insurance rates. Furthermore, as one amicus

---

[1] The one exception is Carson v. Mauer, supra, in which the New Hampshire court struck down a provision that imposed a limit only on noneconomic damages, a statute apparently modeled on §3333.2. As we noted in *Roa*, the *Carson* court—in invalidating a variety of provisions of its medical malpractice legislation—applied an "intermediate scrutiny" standard of review that is inconsistent with the standard applicable in this state.

suggests, the legislature may have felt that the fixed $250,000 limit would promote settlements by eliminating "the unknown possibility of phenomenal awards for pain and suffering that can make litigation worth the gamble." Finally, the legislature simply may have felt that it was fairer to malpractice plaintiffs in general to reduce only the very large noneconomic damage awards, rather than to diminish the more modest recoveries for pain and suffering and the like in the great bulk of cases. Each of these grounds provides a sufficient rationale for the $250,000 limit. . . .

The judgment is affirmed.

BIRD, Chief Justice, dissenting.

With today's decision, a majority of this court have upheld, in piecemeal fashion, statutory provisions that require victims of medical negligence to accept delayed payment of their judgments, that prohibit them from paying the market rate for legal representation, that deprive them of compensation for proven noneconomic damages greater than $250,000 and that divest them of the benefit of their own insurance policies. . . . [I]t is no longer possible to ignore the overall pattern of the MICRA scheme. In order to provide special relief to negligent healthcare providers and their insurers, MICRA arbitrarily singles out a few injured patients to be stripped of important and well-established protections against negligently inflicted harm. Crisis or no crisis, this court is duty bound to apply the constitutional guarantee against irrational and invidious legislative classifications. . . .

At first blush, $250,000 sounds like a considerable sum to allow for noneconomic damages. However, as amici California Hospital Association and California Medical Association candidly admit, most large recoveries come in cases involving permanent damage to infants or to young, previously healthy adults. Spread out over the expected lifetime of a young person, $250,000 shrinks to insignificance. Injured infants are prohibited from recovering more than three or four thousand dollars per year, no matter how excruciating their pain, how truncated their lifespans, or how grotesque their disfigurement. Even this small figure will gradually decline as inflation erodes the real value of the allowable compensation. . . .

There is no logically supportable reason why the most severely injured malpractice victims should be singled out to pay for special relief to medical tortfeasors and their insurers. The idea of preserving insurance by imposing huge sacrifices on a few victims is logically perverse. Insurance is a device for spreading risks and costs among large numbers of people so that no one person is crushed by misfortune. In a strange reversal of this principle, the statute concentrates the costs of the worst injuries on a few individuals.

The result is a fundamentally arbitrary classification. Under the statute, a person who suffers a severe injury — for example loss of limbs or eyesight — late in life may receive up to $250,000 for the resulting loss of enjoyment during his or her final years. An infant with identical injuries is limited to the same compensation for an entire lifetime of blindness or immobility. . . .

■ CRUSHED BY MY OWN REFORM
Frank Cornelius
N.Y. Times, Oct. 7, 1994

[This is an editorial from a lobbyist who encouraged the Indiana legislature to pass a $500,000 cap on damage awards in medical malpractice cases. He recounts how, during and after routine surgery, his physicians made a series of serious and crippling mistakes.] The cost of this cascading series of medical debacles is painful to tally: I am confined to a wheelchair and need a respirator to keep breathing. I have not been able to work. I have continuous physical pain in my legs and feet, prompting my doctor to hook me up to an apparatus that drips morphine. . . . My marriage is ending. . . . At the age of 49, I am told that I have less than two years to live. My medical expenses and lost wages, projected to retirement age if I should live that long, come to more than $5 million. . . .

The kicker, of course, is that I fought to enact the very law that limits my compensation. All my suffering might have been worthwhile, on some cosmic scale, if the law had accomplished its stated purpose. But it hasn't. Indiana's health care costs ranked 32d in per capita health care spending in 1990 — the same as in 1980. . . .

The prospect that these "reforms" will be enacted [by Congress] is frightening. Make no mistake, damage caps are arbitrary, wholly disregarding the nature of the injury and the pain experienced by the plaintiff. They . . . extend unwarranted special protection to the medical industry and remove the only effective deterrent to negligent medical care. . . . Medical negligence cannot be reduced simply by restricting consumers' legal rights. That will happen only when the medical industry begins to effectively police its own. I don't expect to live to see that day.

■ LEGISLATION ON MEDICAL MALPRACTICE: FURTHER DEVELOPMENTS AND A PRELIMINARY REPORT CARD*
Randall R. Bovbjerg**
22 U.C. Davis. L. Rev. 499 (1989)

. . . The story of malpractice insurance "crisis" is well-known. As recently as the late 1950s, only one doctor in seven had ever faced a claim in their entire professional lifetime, very large recoveries were exceedingly rare, and malpractice insurance premiums were priced accordingly.[7] Malpractice insurance first claimed

---

*Copyright © 1989 by the Regents of the University of California. Reprinted with permission. This is an edited version of an earlier draft of this article, which differs in minor respects from the published version. Also, the section on the 1990s comes from a separate publication by the same author entitled Medical Malpractice: Problems & Reforms (1995), published by the Urban Institute and the Intergovernmental Health Policy Project, with funding from the Robert Wood Johnson Foundation.

**Pronounced "Boh-berg," the author is Senior Research Associate, The Urban Institute, Washington, D.C.
[7] In 1962 the typical physician paid about half of one percent of gross income for coverage.

significant attention from policymakers in the late 1960s, as insurance and medical professionals became concerned about rising claims frequency and insurance rates.[8] Congressional hearings were held, and an executive study commission was convened. Policymakers first recognized a crisis in 1974 and 1975.

For unknown reasons, the frequency of malpractice claims, which had risen at a moderate rate through the sixties, turned sharply upward in the early 1970s. Moreover, in the early seventies insurers' investment earnings unexpectedly fell with the first oil crisis and the decline in the stock and bonds markets. Throughout, average jury awards and insurance claims payments were rising steadily, but premium increases lagged behind, followed by more wrenching [upward] adjustments later. The situation came to a head in 1974 and 1975. Especially in the leading states of New York and California, major insurers refused to continue writing coverage. Few other states faced such stark problems of availability, but by 1975 requests for very high premium increases were nearly universal.[16] The reaction of affected physicians was to seek regulatory relief from rate hikes as well as reform of the entire system of tort law and liability insurance. The mid-1970s saw a blossoming of such legislation across the states.

In the 1980s, however, problems reemerged. This time, the problem was more one of "affordability" than of availability. Availability of coverage had been bolstered by medical providers themselves. At least half of the market was underwritten for physicians by their own insurance companies, which are committed to maintaining coverage, unlike a commercial carrier.[19] In the 1980s, it was problems of nonmedical insureds that held center stage. Day care centers, liquor stores, city council members, indeed most ordinary seekers after liability insurance — all these people were finding coverage difficult and expensive to find, if it was available at all by 1984 and 1985. Lobbyists sought both state and federal reforms, numerous task forces were convened, and additional legislation ensued. So the 1980s crisis and responses differ from those of the 1970s. . . .

Both "malpractice" crises have been first and foremost crises of insurance, and most of the impetus for tort reform comes from problems in the insurance markets. Other motivations for reform come from perceived legal problems — not so much a crisis as a growing sense that tort law simply does not work "right," or achieve fairness, especially from the defendant's viewpoint.

Many reformers also worry about medical quality, though from different perspectives — either that quality is "too low" and hence contributes to the crisis or, alternatively, that crisis-induced fears of lawsuit change medical practice to the detriment of doctors and patients alike. What evidence supports these different views? . . .

---

[8] During the 1970s, malpractice premiums tripled, to some 1.8 percent of the typical physician's gross income.

[16] The leading national rating bureau recommended increases averaging 52 percent in 29 states for 1973, 92 percent in 32 states for 1974, and fully 197 percent in 48 states in the peak crisis year of 1975.

[19] Moreover, most sizable hospitals either self-insured or used "captive" insurers they controlled.

How bad have insurance problems been? This question is a highly relevant one for legislators and lawyers, for some courts have sought to judge the validity of tort reforms by whether the crisis was "bad enough" to justify curtailing plaintiffs' remedies.[22] The question is hard to answer, not only because data are less than comprehensive but also because a "crisis" is in the eye of the beholder. . . . Premiums for a constant dollar amount of coverage rose sharply in the 1970s and in the 1980s, but with a decline in "real," inflation-adjusted prices in between. [O]bstetrician-gynecologists paid three times as much for the same nominal dollar coverage in 1985 as in 1974.[25] . . .

Crisis is proclaimed when complaints are widespread or a vital activity seems threatened. Most recently, the apparent withdrawal of numerous obstetricians from the delivery of babies because of liability concerns has received the most attention. . . . However, general objections about how law handles malpractice claims, along with other personal injury cases, also underlie the push for reform. . . .

Complaints are legion, but three main objections predominate: First, too many lawsuits are encouraged. Leaving aside how many is too many, it is clear that a general "liberalization" of common law doctrines and processes has favored plaintiffs in recent decades. . . . Second, reformers argue that the system pays too much in many cases. Reports of occasional very large verdicts support the observation that damage awards can seem extravagant. . . . Third, judges and juries can make poor decisions on fault. All defendants complain that sympathy for plaintiffs can color results. Doctors particularly are concerned that lay jurors and judges do not appreciate when a bad outcome is simply unfortunate as opposed to the result of fault. This is of particular concern when the case is very old, and medical knowledge or the ability to treat a condition may have advanced in the interim. Some go so far as to characterize results as "haphazard" and the process a "game of chance" or "lottery."

Other complaints about the performance of the legal system concern plaintiffs as well as defendants, notably: The system costs too much and takes too long. Lawyers' fees are frequently deemed too costly, particularly on the plaintiff's side, where contingency fee arrangements can result in very large awards that seem disproportionate to the amount of effort involved. On the other hand, defense legal costs are also high, especially for complex cases like medical malpractice. Malpractice cases are not resolved quickly. Once filed, claims take an average of 25 months to close, but 16 percent take more than five years.

Most of these objections to legal-insurance practice apply to malpractice and other injuries alike. Some complaints simply reflect commonsense judgment, grounded more in anecdotes than in careful documentation and argument. In tort

---

[22] See, e.g., Jones v. State Bd. of Medicine, 97 Idaho 859, 555 P.2d 399 (1976) (remanded for determination of whether crisis existed); Boucher v. Sayeed, 459 A.2d 87, 91-92 (R.I. 1983) (stating that no crisis existed in 1981 to justify mandate for nonjudicial screening of malpractice claims).

[25] This is based on a 51 jurisdiction survey of price quotations for "mature" claims made coverage of $100,000 per occurrence and $300,000 per year. . . . This presentation fails to capture the reality that $100/300 coverage buys much less protection now than before. In fact, physicians buy considerably more coverage today than before the first crisis.

reform debates it is easy to be emotional and hard to be analytical, for key questions are whether claims or awards are "too high." Finally, one important complaint is seldom heard: that too few injured patients actually seek and receive payment. . . .

As one might expect, legislative enactments deal with the three areas of concern — insurance, law, and medicine. There is little attempt to address potentially more important social expectations that underlie behavior of claimants, who may or may not seek recovery, and jurors and judges, who may or may not grant it. . . .

The following section discusses the 1970s enactments. Section III below discusses the 1980s [and 1990s]. Each considers in turn reforms of insurance practice, regulation of medical quality, and legal rules and processes. Table 1 lists the major reforms.

II. THE 1970s

A. INSURANCE REFORMS[1]

Understandably, state legislatures reacted to the mid-1970s' crisis with numerous reforms meant to make malpractice insurance more available or more reasonably priced, especially for individual physicians, but for hospitals and other providers as well. Very often, legislatures mandated *Joint Underwriting Associations [JUAs]*. . . . The typical JUA is a state-overseen insurance pool in which all of the state's liability insurers are required to participate. . . . Unlike a conventional insurer, a JUA has special statutory guarantees of solvency that enable it to accept all or nearly all applicants for coverage (and hence to alleviate any crisis of availability). If losses exceed the premiums collected, JUAs can assess all participating insurers pro rata for the operating deficit, and can often also assess policyholders as well. . . .

Another important development was the appearance of a new "policy form" called "claims made" coverage, pioneered during the 1970s' crisis by the St. Paul Group, the leading commercial malpractice carrier. Traditional "occurrence" policies pay for any claim resulting from an occurrence in the policy year, no matter how long afterwards the claim may be brought. Such policies thus allow a "long tail" of hard-to-predict claims payments to continue for many years after premiums are collected, which means that insurers must accept considerable risk in rate making. In contrast, premiums collected from "claims made" policies, as the name implies, need cover only claims brought during the policy year. This means that [expected claims can be much more accurately forecasted], as the long tail is considerably shortened. . . .

---

[1] For additional discussion of the structure and reform of malpractice insurance, see Frank A. Sloan, Randall R. Bovbjerg & Penny B. Githens, Insuring Medical Malpractice (1991). — EDS.

Table 1
Categorizing the Major Legal Reforms of the 1970s and 1980s

A.   *Insurance reforms*
    1.   Joint Underwriting Associations (JUAs)
    2.   Limits on insurance cancellation
    3.   Mandates for liability coverage
    4.   Patient Compensation Funds (PCFs)
    5.   Reporting requirements

B.   *Reforms Aimed at Medical Quality*
    1.   Peer review requirements, protection from lawsuits
    2.   Powers of disciplinary boards increased
    3.   Reporting requirements, data compilation
    4.   Requirements for continuing medical education

C.   *Tort Reforms*
    Aimed at the number of lawsuits (insurance "frequency"):
    1.   Arbitration
    2.   Attorney fee controls
    3.   Certificate of merit
    4.   Costs awardable
    5.   Pretrial screening panels
    6.   Statues of limitations

    Aimed at size of recoveries ("severity"):
    1.   Ad damnums restricted
    2.   "Caps" on awards (noneconomic, total)
    3.   Collateral source offset (permissive, mandatory)
    4.   Joint & several liability changes
    5.   Periodic payments of damages ("structured" awards)
    6.   Punitive damage limits

    Aimed at plaintiffs' difficulty (or costs) of winning:
    1.   Expert witness requirements
    2.   Informed consent limits
    3.   Professional standard of care reasserted
    4.   Res ipsa loquitur restrictions
    5.   Statute of frauds for medical promises

    Aimed at functioning, cost of judicial process:
    1.   Mediation
    2.   Notice of intent to sue
    3.   Precalendar conference required
    4.   Preferred scheduling for malpractice cases . . .

C. TORT REFORMS

... To consider their genesis and likely effects, one can group [tort] reforms into five categories, according to apparent legislative intent in enacting the provisions, as in Table 1 above. ...

1. Reforms Addressing the Number of Lawsuits Brought

One of the 1970s reforms which addressed the number of lawsuits brought was *arbitration*. This method of resolution aims to substitute a less formal, less expensive, and more expeditious private process for the conventional courtroom procedures, thus easing access to dispute resolution. The major question here is whether a malpractice reform statute allows agreements to arbitrate *signed before* an injury occurs. Under the Uniform Arbitration Act or other state law, post-injury disputes that already exist as claims can normally be arbitrated or settled in any other mutually agreeable manner. Almost all states only permit voluntary arbitration; they do not positively encourage it.[101] Various provisions typically try to protect patients from unthinkingly signing away their right to a traditional trial.[102]

Attorney fee controls were very common enactments, since many medical observers blame excessive contingency fees for encouraging unwarranted lawsuits and depriving injured patients of a reasonable share of awards. Fee controls took two basic forms — regulation of awards in percentage terms[103] and by judicial review.

Two related reforms attempt to deter claimants from bringing frivolous lawsuits (presumably in hopes of coercing an early settlement). At least one state in the 1970s required plaintiffs' attorneys to provide *certificates of merit* that their suit is meritorious. ... *Pretrial screening panels* were very commonly enacted in the 1970s. Sometimes mislabeled "arbitration," such panels offer either a voluntary or a mandatory process for informally hearing a case prior to its coming to trial; the goal is to weed out frivolous cases and speed settlement of meritorious ones. But they have faced objections that they add delay,[109] extra cost, and merely another layer of discovery for plaintiffs in serious cases who expect to go to trial in any event.

Finally, almost all states changed *statutes of limitations*, which directly affect the number of suits likely to be filed. One change shortens the basic statute of limitations, either for medical malpractice cases or general civil cases. Many states codified a form of the "discovery rule" to limit the number of years that

---

[101] Michigan's statute uniquely mandates that malpractice insurers in turn require that their insured hospitals offer all their patients the option of arbitration. See Mich. Comp. Laws Ann. §500.3051-3062 (West 1983).

[102] These provisions include requirements about clear notice in arbitration agreement of waiver to jury trial, requirements that treatment may not be conditioned on a patient's agreement to arbitrate, and, most importantly, requirements that allow patients to repudiate the pre-injury agreement with 30 or 60 days after treatment.

[103] Most provisions created a sliding scale of maximum fees graduated by size of award. See, e.g., Cal. Bus. & Prof. Code §6146 (West Supp. 1989) (establishing fees of 40 percent of first $50,000, down to 10 percent over $200,000).

[109] Pennsylvania and Florida courts initially found panels constitutional, but later they found the panels as applied unconstitutional because of delays in application. See Aldana v. Holub, 381 So. 2d 231 (Fla. 1980); Mattos v. Thompson, 491 Pa. 385, 421 A.2d 190 (1980).

undiscovered medical malpractice lawsuits can toll the statute. States also sought to shorten the tolling period for minors in malpractice cases from the traditional 18 or 21 years of minority to some shorter period.

2. Reforms Addressing the Size of Recoveries.

Six types of statutes are important here: One is restricting the ability of claimants to list a specific (allegedly over-large) dollar amount sought in the ad damnum clauses of their initial complaint. Most states enacted such changes; their goal is twofold, first to limit the publicity obtainable by a malpractice claimant even before any evidence is presented, and second to limit a potential or an actual jury member's hearing about unsubstantiated general dollar amounts. . . .

Specific dollar *"caps" on awards* were probably the most significant reform in this area. They can be of two general sorts: First, many states have restricted an award's intangible, or noneconomic portion, namely that share not supported by specific amounts of medical bills, wage loss, and other costs. In general, these statutes have simply put a flat cap on the amount of noneconomic damages, ranging from $250,000 to $1 million.

The second type of cap is on total awards, that is, the entire amount that can be collected against one type of defendant or all defendants. The strongest version of this type of cap is the overall cap on all recoveries against medical practitioners by a claimant from an individual occurrence. The Indiana statute is the leading example; it restricts recovery from all medical defendants to $500,000. . . .

Many states' provisions for *collateral source offset* modified the common law rule that tort damages do not take into account other recoveries, such as life insurance, health insurance, or disability coverage. Mandatory offsets call for either the judge or the jury under the judge's instructions to subtract any payments from health insurance and the like from the liability award.[119] It is common for these requirements to allow plaintiffs to show that they paid or their employers paid for the coverages being offset, in which case they can be reimbursed for those payments. Permissive statutes, on the other hand, merely allow the jury to draw whatever inferences it will about the appropriate level of damages, given other sources of payment and any premiums paid for those other sources.[120] Government programs that have paid a claimant are often allowed subrogation rights, and life insurance is frequently excepted as a collateral source, perhaps because it is traditionally an individual rather than a collective purchase. . . .

Finally, "structured" awards have been mandated or permitted in many states. The idea here is to make *periodic payment of damages*, rather than the traditional "lump sum" payment. Structuring means that an insurance company or other payer of an indemnity purchase an annuity to pay a fixed periodic payment to a winning claimant. Thus market forces determine the appropriate

---

[119] E.g., Iowa Code Ann. §147.136 (West Supp. 1988) (held constitutional in Rudolph v. Iowa Methodist Medical Center, 293 N.W.2d 550 (Iowa 1980); N.H. Rev. Stat. Ann. §507-C:7I (1983) (held unconstitutional in Carson v. Maurer, 120 N.H. 925, 424 A.2d 825 (1980)).

[120] See, e.g., Ariz. Rev. Stat. Ann. §12-565 (1982 & Supp. 1988) (held constitutional in Eastin v. Broomfield, 116 Ariz. 576, 570 P.2d 744 (1977)); Kan. Stat. Ann. §60-471 (1986) (held unconstitutional in Wentling v. Medical Anesthesia Servs., 237 Kan. 503, 701 P.2d 939 (1985)).

discount rate, rather than the jury.[123] Another goal of periodic payments is the forthright paternalistic one of not allowing successful plaintiffs to fritter away their award and subsequently become wards of the state.

3. Reforms Addressing Likelihood of Winning

Many 1970s reforms shifted the relative burdens of litigation — and the likelihood the plaintiff will prevail — presumably in response to the earlier history of pro-plaintiff liberalization. Several types of enactment deserve mention. Many medical malpractice reform statutes in some fashion sought to cut back the judicially created doctrine of *informed consent* as a way of establishing liability. Many reform statutes have merely codified a relatively "liberal" version of judicial doctrine, or encouraged consent to be in writing. But most enactments attempted to cut back plaintiffs' ability to sue in various ways. Numerous enactments sought to reassert that malpractice is a matter of medical standards and expertise and to limit plaintiffs' ability to recover without traditional types of expert testimony. Provisions setting *requirements for expert witnesses* and reasserting the traditional *professional standard of care* for judging the negligence of medical providers are closely interrelated. . . .

Physician reformers were very concerned that jurors may "second guess" expert opinion, holding defendants to a higher standard, especially in sympathetic cases or where standards have advanced since the time of treatment. Accordingly, many statutes reaffirmed that the appropriate standard is what professionals do (rather than what laymen think they should do), often also reasserting a state or locality rule as well. The other side of this reform coin is a reassertion that the professional standard and its breach must be demonstrated through expert rather than lay testimony. Most expert witness requirements also attempt to limit the type of person who can qualify as an expert. In response to complaints that out-of-state, "professional" witnesses unfairly impugn in-state practitioners, states have limited the locality from which an expert can come and have set other requirements for experts' qualifications.

Similar restrictions on the doctrine of res ipsa loquitur were very frequently enacted in the mid-1970s. Res ipsa seems particularly unpopular with the medical profession, for it undercuts the need for expert testimony and seems at least on the surface to subject medical activities to lay standards. Many states thus sought to limit the use of the doctrine for malpractice cases in a number of ways: A few imposed a total ban. . . . A number sought to restrict its use in medical cases to particular circumstances.[138] . . .

---

[123] The jury also no longer needs to estimate the claimant's expected life, because the periodic award normally terminates with the payee's death. Occasionally, however, as in Florida, the balance of a lump sum that has not been paid out on a periodic basis is payable to the payee's estate.

[138] E.g., Nev. Rev. Stat. §41A.100 (1985) (restricting use unless foreign substance left in the body, explosion or fire during treatment, unintended burn, injury to body part not involved in treatment, procedure performed on wrong patient, organ, or limb, or other listed exceptions that may reestablish the rule); N.D. Cent. Code §26-40.1-07 (1978) (providing slightly shorter list such as foreign substance or surgery on wrong patient, organ, limb, or body part). This statute was held unconstitutional in Arneson v. Olson, 270 N.W.2d 125 (1978).

III. THE 1980s

Almost every 1980s state tort reform first surfaced in the previous decade; in the main, provisions simply spread to more states a decade later. . . . Although most 1980s reforms were those that had previously been enacted, two apparently novel ideas are worth noting. One notable development, thus far visible only in two states [Virginia and Florida], concerns severely deformed newborns. These laws seek to remove cases of severe neurological birth injuries from the tort-law-and-liability-insurance system into a purely social-insurance scheme. This is one version of a "no fault" approach, which trades an easier finding of responsibility for a far more structured approach to damages.[182]

A second development also seeks wholly to replace one part of the current liability system with a new approach. The National Childhood Vaccine Injury Act of 1986 authorized a "no fault" system to handle victims of vaccine-related accidents.[1] The Act calls for compensation to all who suffer adverse reactions in the course of vaccinations, but limits the amount of damages available. Vaccines pose a particular need to act, for public health calls for universal vaccination of certain kinds. Allowing patients or providers or both to decide not to undergo vaccination because of liability or personal fear would not be acceptable. The same rationale does not necessarily apply to all of tort reform. . . .

Three changes in the 1980s statutes deserve special emphasis: First is a *shift toward generic enactments*, away from malpractice-specific legislation. . . . The second change is that the federal government took a far more active stance in the 1980s than in prior years. . . . Traditionally, of course, insurance regulation, medical regulation, and the running of judicial systems and tort rules have all been left to states, although there seems ample justification for federal involvement in insurance, medical quality, and liability law. . . .

Third, state and federal lawmakers alike seem far more responsive in the 1980s to much more novel and far-reaching tort reforms. The *quasi-no-fault* concept is once again being taken seriously, at least partly because of the Virginia and Florida obstetrical statutes already mentioned. One approach is to delimit the scope of reform by covering only "designated compensable events";[197] another is to allow defendants to make plaintiffs "offers they cannot refuse" to settle for out-of-pocket economic losses without trial on liability. The American Medical Association has produced a proposal to replace the entire tort-based system of

---

[182] Passed in early 1987, The Virginia Birth-Related Neurological Injury Compensation Act, Va. Code Ann. §38.2-5000 to -5021 (Supp. 1988), substitutes a panel judgment for tort recovery. The statute automatically compensates any newborn deemed to have had "injury to the brain or spinal cord caused by the deprivation of oxygen or mechanical injury occurring in the course of labor, delivery or resuscitation in the immediate post-delivery period in a hospital which renders the infant permanently nonambulatory, aphasic, incontinent, and in need of assistance in all phases of daily living." Id. The provisions are clearly geared to one limited type of case that is very expensive under the current system. Payments under the new regime are to be financed by assessment of $5,000 per year on participating doctors who perform obstetrical services, a $250 assessment on all other licensed physicians, and $50 per infant delivered from hospitals. Id. Later that year, the Florida Birth-Related Neurological Injury Compensation Plan of 1987 similarly barred lawsuits against participating doctors for such injuries, referring such claims instead to a medical advisory panel.

[1] Title III of the Omnibus Health Act of 1986, Pub. L. No. 99-660, 100 Stat. 3743 (1986) (codified at 42 U.S.C. §300aa-1 to -33 (Supp. IV 1986).

[197] Tancredi, Designing a No-Fault Alternative, Law & Contemp Probs., Spring 1986, at 277, 277, 281-283.

litigation with an administrative tribunal modeled in many ways on the processes of the National Labor Relations Board. The proposal takes a worker's compensation-like approach but nonetheless retains a fault standard for determining liability, albeit with a slightly modified standard of care. Fault would be judged by national standards of "good practice," a slight advantage to claimants. The AMA holds that its system's simplicity, ease of access to a state-paid lawyer and a state administrative apparatus, and tightening of the standard of care would promote the filing of more valid claims, thus offsetting the "losses" of claimants' traditional rights to potentially larger recoveries. However, access to the courts would clearly be curtailed.

Private contracting has also received attention, although less in legislatures than in journals. The notion is to allow doctors and patients to "opt out" of the tort-and-insurance system for resolving medical misadventures, instead fashioning their own system through mutually satisfactory private agreements. The merits and demerits of such a system, both from practical and legal standpoints, have been well debated elsewhere. . . .

[Another proposal for reshaping liability rules is known as *exclusive enterprise liability.*] The focus of liability would be shifted from physicians to the hospitals or other enterprises within which they practice. . . . [As a result,] hospitals, group practices, clinics, HMOs, integrated health systems, health plans, or other entities would take more responsibility for avoiding and compensating injuries. . . . Originally promoted as a way for providers to arrange their own stable sources of liability coverage, [enterprise liability] reform is now touted as a vehicle for better quality control and perhaps also as a long-run platform for moving to no-fault. . . .

IV. THE 1990s AND THE FUTURE OF REFORM

After a legislative lull in the late 1980s through the early 1990s, interest in reform has picked up again. This time reform is not prompted by insurance crisis but rather by pressure from medical practitioners, concerns about potentially expensive defensive medicine, and a change in political climate — especially after the 1994 elections. Several states have enacted caps or other strong first-generation tort reforms in the mid-1990s, and federal legislation has come close to passage. Whether this marks the start of another reform era remains to be seen.

At the federal level, malpractice changes initially drew attention as an adjunct to health financing reform. . . . [There are] significant reasons for considering liability reform together with general changes in health financing and delivery. . . . [One] argument is that tort reform is needed to ease defensive medicine. Any savings could help offset the added costs of state or federal assistance for the uninsured or of budget cutting. This argument assumes that defensive overservice is substantial and that tort reform will curtail it. . . . These are substantial [and largely unproven] assumptions. . . .

[Another] rationale for considering tort reform in light of health reform is not much commented upon. This argument suggests that achieving the full social value of enhanced competition in health care requires better measurement and tracking of health outcomes, so that purchasers can shop for good value in health plans and medical care. Avoiding injury is an important element of maintaining quality. And many private and public efforts are attempting to improve monitoring of quality through health plan report cards or other data. In theory, insurers and self-insured employers should care about avoidable medical injury. . . . [U]nlike in lawsuits, health insurers can send systematic signals back to health care providers.

In practice, however, insurers and health plans have not taken such action. They seem preoccupied with larger competitive issues. . . . Thus, the greatest promise for improving injury prevention may reside in the development of a new, less legalistic system. If the system were less threatening to providers, perhaps health insurers could begin to use their emerging capabilities in efficient and meaningful ways to reduce malpractice occurrences and cost. In any event, both health reform bills and the emerging market reforms have failed to seize this opportunity to connect prevention of injury and monitoring of medical quality. . . .

V. ASSESSING THE REFORMS . . .

1. Tort Reforms Are Succeeding On Their Own Terms

Evidence of several kinds is accumulating that many tort reforms "work" as intended. What defines "success" for tort reforms? One can begin by reiterating that ever more state legislatures have enacted them. The record is certainly one of political success. This success seems to be continuing, as business and other groups continue to press for tort reforms.

Judicial success is also important, for invalidated reforms can have no effect. Here, reforms' record seems considerably better than their reputation.[204] Considerable publicity has gone to the judicial decisions invalidating the entire statutory reform schemes in New Hampshire and North Dakota,[205] and to the overturning of selected reforms, especially caps on awards. Less attention has gone to the thoroughgoing success of arguably the two most comprehensive sets of reform, those in California and Indiana.[206] In fact, most reforms in most states have survived — either by being upheld or from lack of challenge leading to reported decision. This general success of reforms in court is greatly underappreciated.

But do even these successfully passed and upheld reforms work as intended by reform advocates? Some legal scholarship has sought to address just what difference particular versions of reforms are apt to make. Legal scholarship can apply commonsense judgment about the strength of provisions and about how well proposed solutions match perceived problems. It can be noted, for example, that some apparent reforms actually codify common law rights rather than

---

[204] See generally Jenkins, "California's Medical Injury Compensation Reform Act: An Equal Protection Challenge," 52 So. Cal. L. Rev. 829 (1979); Redish, "Legislative Response to the Medical Malpractice Insurance Crisis: Constitutional Implications," 55 Tex. L. Rev. 759 (1977).

[205] Carson v. Maurer, 424 A.2d 825 (N.H. 1980); Arneson v. Olson, 270 N.W.2d 123, 131 (N.D., 1978).

[206] See, e.g., Fein v. Permanente Medical Group, 38 Cal. 3d 137, 695 P.2d 665, 211 Cal. Rptr. 368 (upholding limits on damages), *appeal dismissed*, 474 U.S. 892 (1985); Roa v. Lodi Medical Group, 37 Cal. 3d 920, 695 P.2d 164, 211 Cal. Rptr. 77 (1985) (upholding limits on attorney fees); Johnson v. St. Vincent Hosp., 273 Ind. 374, 404 N.E.2d 585 (1980) (upholding whole reform statute).

curtailing them significantly (though such enactments may forestall further pro-plaintiff liberalization), . . . and that reforms may address minor or even nonexistent problems. Given such formalistic analysis of the thoroughness of reform, it has been suggested that legislatures meant to effect very little change. This assessment seems unduly cynical. . . .

But the proof of the effectiveness pudding is in the eating. Most importantly, the growing body of empirical evidence about the effects of tort reforms is increasingly positive for the reformers. Researchers have assessed success according to the second main goal of reformers—not just ensuring the availability of liability coverage but also lowering premiums, at least relative to what these would have been without reform. . . .

The most credible assessments have come from independent empirical researchers who have statistically assessed the effect of tort reforms on claims frequency and severity and on insurance premiums.[219] After conducting several analyses over some years, Patricia Danzon concluded that a few reforms affected claims frequency and severity.[220] Specifically, she concluded that reductions in the statute of limitations reduce claims frequency, as do collateral source offsets; screening panels had no effect, and arbitration slightly increased claims. Claims severity is cut most by caps on awards (some 23 percent over some years), but it is also cut by collateral source offset and possibly by arbitration. Many reforms, however, either were not tested or showed no statistically significant effects. . . .

Thus, reforms on average are increasingly being shown to succeed on their own terms. However, the workings of reforms remain only partly illuminated. Just how do particular reforms achieve their savings? What features make some versions of a reform more consequential than others? Moreover, it is not yet documented that malpractice premiums have dropped to the extent that claims and awards have. Perhaps most importantly, no empirical assessment has yet been able to explain the ups and downs of malpractice claims: the crisis-associated rise and subsequent fall in claims frequency in both the 1970s and 1980s. Perhaps this development somehow reflects the tort reform climate created nationwide, almost independent of particular reforms enacted in individual states. The crisis-generated publicity about liability problems may have subtly altered the attitudes of claims adjusters, judges, and jurors about liability cases and thus discouraged plaintiffs and their attorneys from bringing some claims. If so, the effectiveness of tort reforms is even stronger than supposed, if less direct and possibly not sustainable over time.

On the other hand, changes in social attitudes could bring forth far more claims—for much more malpractice seems to exist than ever surfaces as claims. Considerable leeway thus seems to exist for claims frequency to change, both in reaction to tort reform (or common law development) and in response to underlying social trends not yet understood. Thus far, tort reforms have mainly tinkered with the basic tort-law-and-insurance system; it is unclear how much if at

---

[219] The researchers' technique is multivariate regression analysis, which essentially measures separately the impact of each specified tort reform, while holding constant other reforms and numerous background variables also thought to influence claims or premiums.

[220] Danzon, The Frequency and Severity of Medical Malpractice Claims: New Evidence, 49 Law and Contemp. Probs., Spring 1986, at 57; Danzon, The Frequency and Severity of Medical Malpractice Claims, 27 J.L. & Econ. 115 (1984).

all such laws can influence root causes like the extent of negligent injury, the willingness of injured parties to seek legal redress, and the underlying attitudes about tort compensation of potential and actual jurors. Absent other changes, one suspects claim trends will continue to rise in the longer run, after the one-time reductions achieved by some reforms. . . . In the long run, much depends on how the common law of tort continues to evolve. If past developments have brought us to the current state of affairs, future ones could move us back as well as forward. . . .

2. Judging Reforms On A Broader Basis

In the main, the case for tort reform has been built on the need to resolve insurance crises — curbing claims and awards so as to keep premiums affordable and doctors in their offices. Crisis and large jumps in prices make good reform politics — but bad legal strategy. . . . A better rationale is that the current tort-and-insurance system does not do what "we" want it to, regardless of crisis or noncrisis. In this larger sense, observing that tort reforms increasingly seem to "work" to cut claims and awards is really only the beginning of a full assessment of their desirability. The real issue is what . . . "we" want from this system. Do we want a liability system that mainly attempts to send appropriate signals to providers and individual risk-takers, or do we prefer a compensation system primarily concerned with the needy claimant? Do we want more or fewer claims brought? Do we think that liability assessments made in the current system by judges, juries, and claims settlers are accurate? . . . How much are we willing to pay for a system that must make difficult, sophisticated judgments about liability and damages? Do we want a more uniform, national system or continuing state-by-state variation? There is no social consensus on these issues, so a true assessment is not possible. The continuing social and political ferment surrounding liability law and insurance shows that this process is continuing.

Notes: Medical Malpractice Reform Statutes

1. *Deja Vu All Over Again.* With each edition of this casebook, it seems we are in the midst of, or just exiting from, yet another crisis in medical liability. As this book goes to press, we are seeing the waning of the latest widespread outcry about increasing malpractice insurance premiums and the impact on medical costs and access to care. In response, President Bush proposed a national set of reforms similar to those in California, but Congress failed to act. See U.S. Department of Health and Human Services, Confronting the New Health Care Crisis (July 2002). Also, several additional states have enacted damage caps in recent years. Prof. Bill Sage has aptly commented that "it is striking . . . that Congress is actively debating whether to adopt [a package of reforms] enacted in California in 1975, . . . [yet] the health care system has undergone revolutionary change since [then]. It is as if Rip van Winkle awoke from his twenty-year nap and went about his business equipped with antique weapons and dressed in yesteryear's fashions without the current townspeople thinking anything was amiss." William M. Sage, Unfinished Business: How Litigation Relates to Health Care Regulation, 28 J. Health Politics Policy & L. 387, 392 (2003). See generally Michelle Mello, David Studdert, & Troy

Brennan, The New Medical Malpractice Crisis, 348 New Eng. J. Med. 2281 (2003); Marc A. Rodwin et al., Malpractice Premiums and Physicians' Income: Perceptions of a Crisis Conflict with Empirical Evidence, 25(3) Health Aff. 750 (June 2006).

The purpose and constitutionality of the more prominent components of malpractice reform legislation are reviewed throughout the notes in this chapter. See sections B.3, C.1, C.5, D.2, and D.4. An excellent recent comprehensive analysis, with a focus on second-generation reforms and federal proposals, is Eleanor Kinney, Malpractice Reform in the 1990s: Past Disappointments, Future Success?, 20 J. Health Pol. Pol'y & L. 99 (1995). Various helpful symposia can be found in the 1986, 1991, and 1997 volumes of Law & Contemporary Problems, and in 36 St. Louis U. L.J. 817 (1992) and 6 J. Leg Med. 249 (1985). For additional description and analysis of reforms and their effects, see Frank Sloan & Lindsey M. Chepke, Ill-Suited? Medical Malpractice at a Crossroads (2008); Wm. Sage & Rogan Kersh, eds., Medical Malpractice and the U.S. Health Care System (2006); Symposium, 59 Vand. L. Rev. 1017 (2006); Symposium, 27 J. Leg. Med. 1 (2006); Symposium, 33 J. L. Med. & Ethics 414 (2005); Symposium, 5 Yale J. Health Policy, L. & Ethics 341 (2005); Symposium, 23(4) Health Affairs (Aug. 2004); Symposium, 54 Depaul L. Rev. 203 (2005); Symposium, 26 N. Ill. U. L. Rev. 439 (2006); David Studdert, Medical Malpractice, Michelle Mello & Troyen Brennan, 350 New Eng. J. Med. 283 (2004); Note, 56 Duke L.J. 611 (2006).

2. *Statutory Scope.* An important legal issue created by all malpractice reform statutes is precisely which actions they apply to and whether plaintiffs can state their claims in a manner that avoids these restrictions. These statutes typically are written to apply to professional negligence actions against practitioners of the healing arts. One route for avoiding them that appeared open for a while was the federal anti-dumping legislation discussed in Chapter 2.A. Some state limitations do not apply to actions under the federal statute. See Draper v. Chiapuzio, 9 F.3d 1391 (9th Cir. 1993). But courts have restricted the federal anti-dumping statute so that, for the most part, it does not apply to garden-variety malpractice complaints. Other avoidance techniques include framing the action with an alternative common law theory, such as breach of contract, fraud, or battery, or as institutional rather than professional negligence. See, e.g., Hutchinson v. Patel, 637 So. 2d 415 (La. 1994) (malpractice reform statute does not apply to duty-to-warn action against psychiatrist brought by the patient's wife since she was not his patient); Branch v. Willis-Knighton Med. Ctr, 636 So. 2d 211 (La. 1994) (statute does not apply to product liability action involving tainted blood). Courts also sometimes find that these statutes do not apply to nonphysicians. See, e.g., Rehm v. Lenz, 547 N.W. 2d 560 (S.D. 1996) (shorter statute of limitations does not apply to fraud and breach of contract action against marriage counselor alleged to have had sex with client). Another court found that a damages cap does not apply to a physician's professional corporation because the corporation is not a licensed professional, even though the doctor was a sole practitioner and the liability of his wholly owned corporation's was purely vicarious. Schwartz v. Brownlee, 482 S.E.2d 827 (Va. 1997). However, courts are sharply split on all of these issues. See generally Annots., 12 A.L.R.5th 1 (1993); 89 A.L.R.4th 887 (1992).

3. *Constitutional Challenges.* Damage caps have received the most constitutional scrutiny, with well over half the states having a supreme court decision on

point. The cases are split approximately evenly, with recent decisions tending to be hostile to malpractice and tort reform statutes. Virginia and Colorado broke with the pattern noted in *Fein* by sustaining a $1 million cap on *all* damages. Pulliam v. Coastal Emergency Services of Richmond, 509 S.E.2d 307 (Va. 1999); Garhart v. Columbia/Healthone, 95 P.3d 571 (CO 2004). See Annot., 26 A.L.R.5th 245 (1995); Carly Kelly & Michelle Mello, Are Medical Malpractice Damages Caps Unconstitutional?, 33 J. L. Med. Ethics 515 (2005); Elizabeth Stewart Poisson, Addressing the Impropriety of Statutory Caps on Pain and Suffering Awards in the Medical Liability System, 82 N.C. L. Rev. 759 (2004). For debate on the effectiveness of damage caps, see Catherine M. Sharkey, Unintended Consequences of Medical Malpractice Damages Caps, 80 N.Y.U. L. Rev. 391 (2005) (documenting that caps on noneconomic damages have led to higher economic awards); H.E. Frech et al., An Economic Assessment of Damage Caps in Medical Malpractice Litigation, 16 Health Matrix 693 (2006) (concluding that caps reduce costs and increase access); Leonard J. Nelson, et al., Damages Caps in Medical Malpractice Cases, 85 Milbank Q. 259 (2007) (reporting lack of clear evidence that caps have benefitted patients despite reducing malpractice costs).

Other reform elements generally fare better in the courts, but nevertheless encounter substantial opposition. The usual objections are either of the equal protection stripe contained in *Fein* or are based on a constitutional right to court access and to a jury trial. As Bovbjerg summarizes, in only a couple of states have courts rejected or accepted reform legislation in total. Usually, each provision must be litigated separately. See, e.g., Zeier v. Zimmer, 152 P.3d 861 (OK 2006) (striking down constitutionality of obtaining an expert affidavit prior to filing suit).

Historically, it has been possible to overcome these objections with a "quid pro quo" argument that the reform legislation replaces one legal remedy with another that is equally or more generous. It is on this basis that state workers' compensation laws were upheld in the early 1900s. Workers' compensation eliminates common law negligence actions against employers, but replaces them with a no-fault administered compensation scheme using scheduled damages. Observe how the *Fein* court dealt with the quid-pro-quo issue in n.18. Compare the AMA proposal summarized by Bovbjerg. Does it adequately meet this quid-pro-quo test?

Another maneuver to avoid constitutional objections is for the legislature to authorize parties to elect an alternative dispute resolution mechanism by contract. This is already common in the form of arbitration statutes. This could also be done for damages caps, limitations periods, and all the rest. Is there any constitutional barrier to the legislature authorizing the enforcement of contracts that courts would ordinarily find to be unconscionable adhesion contracts? In Florida, the state Supreme Court initially struck down a $450,000 cap on noneconomic damages (finding no quid pro quo existed), Smith v. Department of Insurance, 507 So. 2d 1080 (Fla. 1987), but then upheld the revised statute with an even lower limit of $350,000. University of Miami v. Echarte, 618 So. 2d 189 (Fla. 1993). The critical difference, according to the court, is that the new cap applied only if the plaintiff refused the defendant's request for binding arbitration. On the other hand, plaintiffs have little choice but to refuse, since accepting arbitration binds them to an even lower cap of $250,000 noneconomic damages.

4. *Public Policy Rhetoric vs. Evidence.* Consider the complaints against the legal system summarized by Bovbjerg. How accurate are they? Review the notes and materials in sections A and E. If a convincing case for malpractice reform cannot be made based on these arguments, how about one based simply on the need to contain overall health care spending? Malpractice insurance premiums total roughly $11 billion (hospitals and doctors combined, in 2003), but this is less than 1 percent of all health care spending. Of potentially greater significance are the "shadow" costs of malpractice litigation that occurs in the form of defensive medical practices. Doctors argue they cannot hold down the costs of treatment as long as they are exposed to the potential liability for omitting expensive but marginally beneficial care. Review the notes at page 375 to consider whether this is a compelling argument.

5. *Screening Panels.* The advisory screening panels Bovbjerg describes are usually composed of lawyers and doctors. Their purpose is to give litigants a more accurate view of the merits of their case in order to promote settlement. In most states, these panels' decisions are nonbinding, but in a few states screening panels have the power to dismiss "frivolous" cases that lack sufficient evidence to go to trial. See generally Jean A. Macchiaroli, Medical Malpractice Screening Panels: Proposed Model Legislation to Cure Judicial Ills, 58 Geo. Wash. L. Rev. 181 (1990). How helpful are the views of lawyers and doctors on the merits likely to be in predicting jury verdicts? In some states, plaintiffs' lawyers simply refuse to show up during the screening panel process, believing the information is not worth the time and effort and that any negative finding will not be that damaging even if it comes to the attention of the jury. A half-dozen states have abandoned screening panels and, as Bovbjerg notes, two others declared them unconstitutional based on evidence of their poor performance in practice. See Jona Goldschmidt, Where Have all the Panels Gone? A History of the Arizona Medical Liability Review Panel, 23 Ariz. St. L.J. 1013 (1992); Catherine Struve, Doctors, the Adversary System, and Procedural Reform in Medical Liability Litigation, 72 Fordham L. Rev. 943 (2004).

6. *Exclusive enterprise liability*, introduced at page 474, is the idea that best implements Bovbjerg's call for combining market and liability forces. If enterprise liability is focused on insurance plans such as integrated HMOs rather than just on hospitals, then the institution has both market and liability incentives to reduce medical error and improve the quality of care. See Kenneth S. Abraham & Paul C. Weiler, Enterprise Liability and the Evolution of the American Health Care System, 108 Harv. L. Rev. 381 (1994). Could this idea work if each physician affiliates nonexclusively with many competing HMOs and insurers, as is now common in many parts of the country? *Compare* William M. Sage, Kathleen E. Hastings & Robert A. Berenson, Enterprise Liability for Medical Malpractice and Health Care Quality, 20 Am. J.L. & Med. 1 (1994) (advocating insurance-based enterprise liability); *with* Kenneth S. Abraham & Paul C. Weiler, Enterprise Medical Liability and the Choice of the Responsible Enterprise, 20 Am. J.L. & Med. 29 (1994) (advocating delivery-based enterprise liability). See generally Randall R. Bovbjerg & Robert Berenson, Enterprise Liability in the Twenty-First Century, in Medical Malpractice and the U.S. Health Care System (W. Sage & R. Kersh, eds., 2006).

Even if exclusive enterprise liability is not officially enacted, it already exists in "virtual" form through private agreement. Some HMOs and many government and teaching hospitals purchase insurance for all their doctors and defend all lawsuits arising from treatment under their auspices. The HMO or hospital assuming full responsibility for all negligent medical care within the institution has the same effect as shifting liability entirely from the doctor. See W. Sage & J. Jorling, A World that Won't Stand Still: Enterprise Liability by Private Contract, 43 DePaul L. Rev. 1007 (1994). When Harvard's teaching hospitals implemented this scheme, the liability insurer began to monitor patterns of litigation and noticed recurring problems in anesthesia. The insurer asked the Harvard anesthesiologists to analyze the causes. Rather than blaming others or acting defensively, the group devised new techniques and equipment to lower the risk of mishap. As a result, anesthesia mortality dropped tenfold, and the Harvard anesthesia protocols have become standard across the country. See Abraham & Weiler, supra.

7. *What You See Depends on Where You Stand.* Considering Bovbjerg's closing comments, what perspectives do you think each of the following groups has on what are the fundamental social purposes of malpractice litigation and how well they are being achieved: (1) injured patients and their lawyers; (2) doctors; (3) patients who have not been injured (but some day may be), i.e., the general public. Try answering this question in terms of these three purposes: (1) compensating injured patients; (2) making wrongdoers pay for their harms; and (3) improving the quality of medicine. See generally Michael J. Saks, Daniel Strouse, & Nicholas Schweitzer, A Multiattribute Utility Analysis of Legal System Response to Medical Injuries, 54 DePaul L. Rev. 277 (2005); Roger B. Dworkin, The Process Paradigm: Rethinking Medical Malpractice, 41 Wake Forest L. Rev. 509 (2006).

Problem: Malpractice Reform Legislation

Look up the various components of the medical malpractice reform statute in your (or another) state in an annotated statute book. Categorize these components according to the chart on page 512 Which interest groups appear to have prevailed with the legislature — doctors, personal injury lawyers, or insurers? What has been the judicial reaction? When was the statute first enacted, and have there been subsequent amendments?

Glossary of Organizational Terms and Acronyms

In previous generations, it was necessary to learn a specialized vocabulary to study law and medicine. This is still true, but in the past that vocabulary was purely medical. Today, it includes many obscure organizational terms as well. This is a selected glossary of organizational terms and acronyms, adapted from Prospective Payment Assessment Commission, 1996 Report to Congress.

AFDC	Aid to Families with Dependent Children
AHA	American Hospital Association
AHRQ	Agency for Health Care Research and Quality
AMA	American Medical Association
CDHC	Consumer-Directed (or Driven) Health Care
CMS	Center for Medicare and Medicaid Services
COBRA	Consolidated Omnibus Budge Reconciliation Act of 1985
CON	Certificate of Need
DRG	Diagnosis-Related Group
DHHS	See HHS
ERISA	Employee Retirement Income Security Act of 1974
ESRD	End-Stage Renal Disease
FDA	Food and Drug Administration
HCFA	Health Care Financing Administration, now CMS
HHS	Health and Human Services, Department of
HIPAA	Health Insurance Portability and Accountability Act
HIV	Human Immunodeficiency Virus
HRA or HSA	Healthcare Reimbursement or Health Savings Account (see also MSA)

525

HMO   Health Maintenance Organization
IDS   Integrated Delivery System
IPA   Independent Practice Association
JCAHO   Joint Commission on Accreditation of Healthcare
               Organizations
MSA   Medical Savings Account
MSO   Management Services Organization
NCQA   National Committee for Quality Assurance
OBRA   Omnibus Budget Reconciliation Act
PHO   Physician-Hospital Organization
POS   Point of Service
PPO   Preferred Provider Organization
PPS   Prospective Payment System
PRO   Peer Review Organization
RBRVS   Resource-Based Relative Value Scale
SNF   Skilled Nursing Facility
SSI   Supplemental Security Income
TEFRA   Tax Equity and Fiscal Responsibility Act of 1982
UR/UM   Utilization Review, or Utilization Management

Community Rating—A method of determining an insurance premium structure that reflects expected utilization by the population as a whole, rather than by specific groups.

Consumer-Driven Health Care—An alternative to managed care, which seeks to activate patients to be cost-conscious consumers at the point of treatment, by requiring them to pay more out of pocket, and by providing better information about treatment options and costs.

Cost Shifting—Increasing revenues from some payers to offset uncompensated care losses and lower net payments from other payers.

Diagnosis-Related Groups (DRGs)—A system for determining case mix, used for payment under Medicare's PPS and by some other payers. The DRG system classifies patients into groups based on the principal diagnosis, type of surgical procedure, presence or absence of significant comorbidities or complications, and other relevant criteria. DRGs are intended to categorize patients into groups that are clinically meaningful and homogeneous with respect to resource use. Medicare's PPS currently uses 490 mutually exclusive DRGs, each of which is assigned a relative weight that compares its costlines to the average for all DRGs.

Fee-for-Service—A method of reimbursing health care providers in which payment is made for each unit of service rendered.

Health Maintenance Organization (HMO)—A managed care plan that integrates financing and delivery of a comprehensive set of health care services to an enrolled population. HMOs may contract with, directly employ, or own participating health care providers. Enrollees are usually required to choose from among these providers and in return have limited copayments. Providers may be paid through capitation, salary, per diem, or prenegotiated fee-for-service rates.

Health Savings Account (HSA)—A tax-sheltered account, similar to an IRA, and also known as a Healthcare Reimbursement Account (HRA) or Medical Savings Account (MSA), that is used to pay for medical expenses. It is coupled with high-deductible or "catastrophic" insurance, such that the HSA can pay for most ordinary expenses and insurance is used only for very expensive treatment.

Integrated Delivery System (IDS)—Any number of different arrangements among doctors, hospitals, other medical facilities, and insurers in which a full range of medical services is offered to employers, subscribers, or insurers. Includes conventional arrangements such as HMOs, as well as more innovative arrangements known as PHOs, PSNs, or MSOs, which are discussed in Chapter 10.

Managed Care—Any system of health service payment or delivery arrangements in which the health plan or provider attempts to control or coordinate health service use to contain health expenditures, improve quality, or both. Arrangements often involve a defined delivery system of providers having some form of contractual relationship with the plan.

Peer Review Organization (PRO)—An organization that contracts with HCFA to investigate the quality of health care furnished to Medicare beneficiaries and to educate beneficiaries and providers. PROs also conduct limited review of medical records and claims to evaluate the appropriateness of care provided.

Physician-Hospital Organization (PHO)—A joint venture or affliation among one or more hospitals and physicians or physician groups. The venture might encompass the full range of medical services, or only one or a few services.

Point-of-Service (POS)—A health plan allowing the enrollee to choose to receive a service from a participating or a nonparticipating provider, with different benefit levels associated with one or the other types of providers.

Preferred Provider Organization (PPO)—A health plan with a network of providers whose services are available to enrollees at lower cost than the services of nonnetwork providers. PPO enrollees may self-refer to any network provider at any time.

Prospective Payment—A method of paying health care providers in which rates are established in advance. Providers are paid these rates regardless of the costs they actually incur.

Prospective Payment System (PPS)—Medicare's acute care hospital payment method for inpatient care. Prospective per case payment rates are set at a level intended to cover operating costs for treating a typical inpatient in a given diagnosis-related group. Payments for each hospital are adjusted for differences in area wages, teaching activity, care to the poor, and other factors.

Relative Value Scale—An index that assigns weights to each medical service; the weights represent the relative amount to be paid for each service. The relative value scale used in the development of the Medicare Physician Fee Schedule consists of three cost components, physician work, practice expense, and malpractice expense.

Risk Adjustment—Increases or reductions in the amount of payment made to a health plan on behalf of a group of enrollees to compensate for health care expenditures that are expected to be higher or lower than average.

Uncompensated Care—Care rendered by hospitals or other providers without payment from the patient or a government-sponsored or private insurance program. It includes both charity care, which is provided without the expectation of payment, and bad debts, for which the provider has made an unsuccessful effort to collect payment due from the patient.

Utilization Review (UR)—A review of services delivered by a health care provider to evaluate the appropriateness, necessity, and quality of the prescribed services. The review can be performed on a prospective, concurrent, or retrospective basis.

Table of Cases

529

Index